Kaleidoscope

contemporary and classic readings in education 13th edition

KEVIN RYAN
Boston University

JAMES M. COOPER
University of Virginia

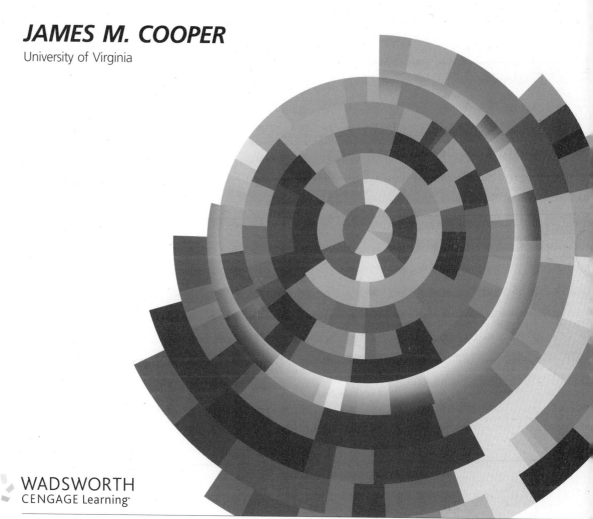

WADSWORTH
CENGAGE Learning

Australia • Brazil • Japan • Korea • Mexico • Singapore • Spain • United Kingdom • United States

WADSWORTH
CENGAGE Learning·

Kaleidoscope: Contemporary and Classic Readings in Education, 13th Edition
Kevin Ryan and James M. Cooper

Senior Publisher: Linda Ganster

Executive Editor: Mark Kerr

Developmental Editor: Kate Scheinman

Assistant Editor: Genevieve Allen

Editorial Assistant: Greta Lindquist

Senior Media Editor: Ashley Cronin

Marketing Manager: Kara Kindstrom

Marketing Coordinator: Klaira Markenzon

Marketing Communications Manager: Heather Baxley

Production Management and Composition: PreMediaGlobal

Manufacturing Planner: Rebecca Cross

Rights Acquisitions Specialist: Roberta Broyer

Text Researcher: Isabel Saraiva

Cover Designer: Norman Baugher

Cover Image: Courtesy of Jupiter Images

© 2013, 2010 Wadsworth, Cengage Learning

For product information and technology assistance, contact us at **Cengage Learning Customer & Sales Support, 1-800-354-9706.**

For permission to use material from this text or product, submit all requests online at **www.cengage.com/permissions.** Further permissions questions can be e-mailed to **permissionrequest@cengage.com.**

Library of Congress Control Number: 2011941647

ISBN-13: 978-1-111-83900-0

ISBN-10: 1-111-83900-X

Wadsworth
20 Davis Drive
Belmont, CA 94002-3098
USA

Cengage Learning is a leading provider of customized learning solutions with office locations around the globe, including Singapore, the United Kingdom, Australia, Mexico, Brazil, and Japan. Locate your local office at **www.cengage.com/global.**

Cengage Learning products are represented in Canada by Nelson Education, Ltd.

To learn more about Wadsworth, visit **www.cengage.com/wadsworth**

Purchase any of our products at your local college store or at our preferred online store **www.cengagebrain.com.**

Printed in the United States of America
1 2 3 4 5 6 7 15 14 13 12 11

CONTENTS

Contents

PREFACE

After we finished putting together this collection of educational articles, we went in search of a title. Our intention for the book was to offer educators an anthology rich in ways to conceive of teaching and learning. Our primary focus was on the quality of the individual entries, but we especially wanted to engage readers in a wide array of (often competing) points of view. As we struggled for a title, we remembered a favorite childhood toy: the kaleidoscope. This cylindrical instrument contains loose bits of colored glass between two flat plates and two mirrors. When the cylinder is shaken or rotated, it causes the bits of glass to be reflected in an endless variety of patterns. Somehow, the image of a kaleidoscope captured our goal for this book.

Our Endless Variety of Patterns

Kaleidoscope is intended for use either as a supplemental book of readings to accompany any "Introduction to Education," "Foundations of Education," or "Issues in Education" textbook, or as a core textbook itself.

The book's wide range of sources and writers—from classic writers like John Dewey and Carl Rogers to contemporary authors like Diane Ravitch, Elliot Eisner, Frederick Hess, Linda Darling-Hammond, and Alfie Kohn—makes it highly flexible and responsive to a broad variety of course needs. The text's mixture of topic areas includes students and teachers; schools and instruction; curriculum and standards; foundations, philosophy, and reform; educational technology; and diversity and social issues.

The material we have selected for *Kaleidoscope* is not technical and can be understood, we believe, by people without extensive professional backgrounds in education. The articles are relatively brief and originate from a variety of contributors, from classroom teachers, educational researchers, journalists, to educational reformers.

Some selections are summaries of research. Some are classic writings by noted educators. Some are descriptions of educational problems and proposed solutions. And, we hasten to add, we agree with the perspectives of some articles and do not agree with others. Our aim is to present a wide variety of philosophical and social science positions in order to reflect the varied voices heard in education today.

Endless Variety of Patterns: The Parts

Kaleidoscope is divided into eight parts. Part 1 concentrates on teachers, with articles ranging from personal reports by teachers to an article about what constitutes great teaching. Part 2 contains selections about students, dealing with topics from the changing nature of childhood in the United States to student cheating. Part 3 looks at schools, specifically the characteristics of good schools and ways to improve them. Part 4 examines curriculum issues and deals with the classic question: "What is most worth knowing?" Part 4 also continues to focus on what we believe is the major curricular issue facing today's educators: content standards and their accompanying high-stakes testing and assessment. The effects of the movement to increase students' academic achievement are reflected in a number of articles in other sections. Part 5 focuses on instruction and assessment, and includes selections on cooperative learning, classroom management, constructivist learning, differentiated instruction, and multiple intelligences. Part 6 contains articles on the foundations of education that discuss the historical, philosophical, psychological, and legal roots of contemporary education. Part 7 contains articles on contemporary educational reform efforts in the United States, focusing on several different avenues toward reform, including the No Child Left Behind Act. Finally, Part 8 focuses on various social issues affecting education in the United States today, with particular attention to ethnic and linguistic diversity as well as gender issues and special education inclusion efforts.

Special Learning Features of the Book

To facilitate understanding of the selections in this book, the thirteenth edition of *Kaleidoscope* includes a number of especially helpful features.

- Each of the eight major parts is introduced by a **part-opening overview** to place the readings into a broader context.
- A brief **biographical sketch of each author** appears at the beginning of each article. So, too, is a designation as to whether the article is a contemporary work or in our view an educational classic.
- We then introduce a **FOCUS Question** to guide the reader as to the most important point or issue to think about as he or she reads the article.
- This is followed by the specific, newly revised **InTASC standards** relating to the content of the article.
- **Key terms** are introduced at the beginning of each article, providing students valuable additions to their educational vocabularies and reminding them that a glossary of these terms is included at the end of the book. Students can test their knowledge of key terms with the interactive glossary flashcards on the companion website.
- The end of each reading features a **postnote**, which is our opportunity to address issues raised in the article.
- **Discussion questions**, following each Postnote, prompt readers to do some additional thinking about the major points made in the article.
- **Websites** point to further information on issues raised by the articles. **Video cases** offer opportunities to see subjects and issues raised by the articles worked by actual practicing teachers. Each video case is followed by questions, designed to help the reader focus on important aspects of the case.

- The **Glossary** of key terms at the end of the book is especially useful to those students taking their first course in education or those using this book as a primary text. A detailed subject index also appears at the end of the book.
- The **Correlating Table**, arranged alphabetically by topic, relates each *Kaleidoscope* selection to specific InTASC standards. We hope this chart will serve as a handy cross-reference for users of this book. This chart is printed on the inside covers of the text for easy reference.
- **Appendix, "Tips for Teaching: Educator's Resource Guide."** This handy multi-part special feature will assist your students in making classroom observations and participating in classroom discussions. Written in a student-centered fashion, it provides valuable information on issues related to classroom observation and data-gathering techniques. It also offers study tips both in the Appendix itself and by including relevant lists of websites for both students and educators.
- For this edition, go to CengageBrain.com and access the Education Media Library to view Cengage Learning's TeachSource **Video Cases**—four- to six-minute video clips filmed in actual classrooms and accompanied by teacher interviews, classroom "artifacts," and viewing questions—that bring the topics in this text to life. In addition, a companion website, also accessible via CengageBrain.com, offers glossary flashcards, links to relevant websites, an article review form, and other useful study tools and resources.

New Bits of Colored Glass: Features of the New Edition

We have completely revised and updated the thirteenth edition in response to extensive surveying of the market. As a result, you will see the following improvements.

1. We have added a new feature in response to the recent focus on professional standards for

all teachers. Recently, The Interstate Teacher Assessment and Support Consortium (**InTASC**) has developed a set of Model Core Teaching Standards. Where appropriate, the **InTASC Standards**, that relate to the content of an article, appears at the start of each article.

2. We have added *new* TeachSource **Video Cases**. Approximately half of the articles are now followed by recommended video cases from the Cengage Learning collection. These video cases bring the articles to life! They are opportunities to see subjects and issues raised by the articles worked by actual practicing teachers. We also provide several questions concerning each video case, helping the reader to focus on important aspects of the video case.

Acknowledgments

The book you have in your hands has our names on the cover. We are profoundly aware, however, that *Kaleidoscope: Contemporary and Classic Readings in Education* represents the creativity and hard work of many dedicated and highly skilled professionals. Among them are Mark Kerr, our highly supportive and responsive Executive Editor; our

equally supportive and ever-helpful Development Editor, Kate Scheinman; our Media Editor, Ashley Cronin; our Marketing Manager, Kara Kindstrom; Senior Project Manager, Divya Divakaran; and our Permissions Editor, Roberta Broyer. We feel fortunate to have worked with such quality team.

We are, also, grateful to a number of reviewers and survey respondents for their excellent recommendations and suggestions, most notably: Patricia Clanton, Southern Arkansas University; Diane Corrigan, Cleveland State University; Rosanne Dlugosz, Scottsdale Community College; Miriam Singer, Fairleigh Dickinson University; Tony Talbert, Baylor University; Mary Ware, SUNY Cortland; Alan Weber, Suffolk County Community College; Nelda Wellman, Northwestern State University; and Eleanor Wilson, University of Virginia.

In addition, we would like to offer a special note of thanks to the many users of this book who have been kind enough to share with us their impressions of it and their suggestions for how we might improve it in subsequent editions. We hope this tradition will continue as you send us your comments via the Cengage Learning website at **www.cengage.com/contact**.

Kevin Ryan and James M. Cooper

Teachers

Being a teacher today has special drawbacks. It is difficult to be a teacher in an age that mocks idealism. It is also difficult to be a teacher without the traditional authority and respect that once came with the title. Being a teacher in a time of permissive childrearing causes special strains, given that many students and some parents are filled with anti-authoritarian attitudes. It is punishing to work at an occupation that is not keeping up economically. It is painful to be part of a profession that is continually asked to solve deep social problems, do the essential job of educating children, and then is regularly criticized for its failings. A good case can be made for discouragement among teachers … even for self-pity.

This negativism, or at least acknowledgment of the negative, obscures the fact that teaching is one of the truly great professions. These passing conditions overlook the greatness that resides in the teacher's work. Current conditions are coming under increased scrutiny as the public and our leaders realize the need for a world-class teaching force. Change is coming.

Even amid the difficulties just cited, teachers are buoyed up by a deep conviction. While many adults struggle with the work-life question, "Am I engaged in significant work?" teachers have the luxury of always knowing that they are engaged in crucial, life-shaping work.

1

The Great Teacher Question: Beyond Competencies

Edward R. Ducharme

Edward R. Ducharme, a former teacher and teacher educator, is now a writer and consultant living in Brewster, Massachusetts.

"The Great Teacher Question: Beyond Competencies," by Edward R. Ducharme, *Journal of Human Behavior and Learning,* Vol. 7, No. 2, 1991. Reprinted by permission of the author.

FOCUS QUESTION

How can the teacher qualities mentioned by the author be learned?

InTASC

Standards 1, 2, 4, 6, and 9

KEY TERMS

- Aesthetic
- At-homeness
- Teacher competencies

I begin this essay by defining a great teacher as one who influences others in positive ways so that their lives are forever altered, and then asking a question I have asked groups many times. How many teachers fitting that description have you had in your lifetime? It is rare for anyone to claim more than five in a lifetime; the usual answer is one or two.

I ask this question of groups whose members have at least master's degrees, often doctorates. They have experienced anywhere from eighty to one hundred or more teachers in their lifetimes and usually describe no more than 2% of them as great. Those voting are among the ones who stayed in school considerably longer than most people do; one wonders how many great teachers those dropping out in the 9th or 10th grade experience in their lifetimes. My little experiment, repeated many times over the years, suggests that the number of great teachers is very limited. They should be cherished and treasured because they are so rare; we should do all that we can to develop more of them.

This paper is purely speculative; no data corrupt it; no references or citations burden it. It began as I sat with a colleague at a meeting in 1987 in Washington; we were listening to a speaker drone on about the competencies teachers need. I asked my friend: "How would you like to write a paper about qualities great teachers have that do not lend themselves to competency measurements?" The proposed shared writing exercise did not get much beyond our talking about it the next couple of times we saw each other, but I have continued to speculate on these qualities as I have read, taught, studied, talked with others, and relived my own learning experiences.

The remarks result from years of being with teachers, students, and schools; of three decades of being a teacher; of five decades of being a learner. There is no science in the remarks, no cool, objective look at teaching. These are personal reflections and observations to provoke, to get some of us thinking beyond numbers, test scores, attendance rates, and demographics, to reflect on the notion of the Great Teacher.

I am weary of competencies even though I recognize the need for specific indicators that teachers possess certain skills and knowledge. I believe, however, that good teacher preparation programs do more than a reasonable job on these and are doing better and better. Three conditions lead me to believe that most future graduates of teacher education programs will be competent. First, the overall quality of teacher candidates is improving; second, there is a great deal more known about helping to develop people to the point where they are competent; third, the level of the education professoriate has improved dramatically. Thus, I think that *most* preparation programs will be graduating competent teachers. We should begin to worry about what lies beyond competency.

My interests extend beyond competencies to qualities that I see from time to time as I visit classrooms. Few teachers possess even several of the qualities I will describe—no great teacher lacks all of them. In the remainder of this paper, I will name and describe the qualities and show what these qualities might look like in prospective teachers.

1. Penchant for and Skill in Relating One Thing with Another with Another and with Another

John Donne, the 17th century English poet and cleric, once wrote "The new science calls all into doubt." He was referring to the Copernican contention that the earth is not the center of the universe, that humankind may not be the cynosure of divine interest, countering beliefs that the old Ptolemaic system of earthcenteredness had fostered.

Donne saw relationships among things not readily apparent to many others. He recognized a new truth cancelled another belief, one that had affected attitudes and actions among his fellow Christians for a long time, and would have a dramatic effect. He knew that if something held eternally true were suddenly shown to be false, conclusively false, then other things would be questioned; nothing would be steadfast.

Many of us do not see the implications and relationships among seemingly unrelated events, people, places, works of art, scientific principles. Some great teachers have the ability to see these relationships and, equally important, help others see them. Donne saw them. His collected sermons evidence the intellectual force of great teachers.

I once took a course in which John Steinbeck's *The Sea of Cortez* and *The Grapes of Wrath* were among the readings. *The Sea of Cortez* is Steinbeck's ruminations on the vast complexity and interrelatedness of life under the water; *The Grapes of Wrath,* his ruminations on the complexities of life on land, on what happens when a natural disaster combines with human ineptness and lack of concern, one for the other. The professor used a word not much in vogue in those ancient days: ecology. He defined it as the "interrelatedness of all living things." He raised questions about the relationships of these issues to the problems of New York City and its schools, as we sat in class in Memorial Lounge at Teachers College, Columbia.

E. D. Hirsch, in *Cultural Literacy: What Every American Needs to Know,* has a series of provocative listings under each letter of the alphabet. His point is that in order to grasp the meanings of words on pages, readers must know things not part of the page. Hirsch's book contains pages of items. Under the letter C, he lists caste, cool one's heels, *Crime and Punishment,* coral reef, and czar. One would "know" such things by studying sociology, language, literature, biology, and history or, perhaps equally often, simply by living for a period of time and reading newspapers, watching movies, and so forth. Hirsch's point is that when one hears a sentence like "He runs his business as though he were the czar," one would think of autocratic, harsh rule, tyranny, Russia, lack of human rights. Some might think of how the word is sometimes spelled tsar and wonder why. Others might think of the song about the czar/tsar from *Fiddler on the Roof,* while a few would think the person incapable of pronouncing the word tsar. Hirsch has in mind one kind of "relating one field to another": that which occurs when one sees a known reference and makes the associative leap.

Edna St. Vincent Millay, in her poem on Euclid's geometry, also drew associations from seemingly unrelated things. She saw the design and texture in poetry related to the design and texture of a geometric theorem. The quality described here is the same quality that Donne and Steinbeck manifested: seeing the interrelatedness of things.

What does that quality look like in prospective teachers? Sometimes it is the person who sees the connections between sociological and educational themes; sometimes, the person who wants to introduce students to the variety of language by teaching them about snowflakes and the vast number of words Eskimos have for them; sometimes, the person who understands mathematics through music, in fact, it may be the person who says mathematics is a kind of music or that music is a kind of mathematics.

2. Lack of Fondness for Closure or, Put Another Way, Fondness for Questions over Answers

Many of us are constantly on the lookout for answers to questions. For example, we might give a great deal to know the answer to the two-part question: What makes a great teacher and how do we produce one? Of course, the answer to the first part of the question depends on who is answering it. For someone in need of specific guidance at some point in life, the great teacher may be the one pointing the way to a different kind of existence, the one making the individual feel strong. To another person, confident about life, the great teacher may be the one raising questions, challenging, making the person wonder about certitudes once held dearly.

I teach Leadership and the Creative Imagination, a course designed as a humanities experience for doctoral students in educational administration. In the course, students read twelve novels and plays, discuss them effectively, and write about them in ways related to the leadership theory literature, their own experience, and the works themselves.

In the fall semester of 1987, I had what has become a redundant experience. A student in the course stopped me in the hall after class one night in November. She said that she had taken the course because her advisor had said it would be a good experience for her. And, said she, she had truly enjoyed the early readings and the discussions. But now she found the readings troubling; they were causing her to question things she does, ways she relates to people, habits of thinking. She said that she was losing a sense of assuredness of what life was all about. The books, she said, just kept raising questions. "When do we get answers?" she asked.

We talked for a while, and I reminded her of a point I had made repeatedly during the first couple of classes: there are two kinds of books, answer books and question books. Writers of answer books raise provocative questions and then provide comfortable, assuring answers. Then there are the writers who raise the provocative issues—"Thou know'st 'tis common,—all that lives must die, passing through nature into eternity," (if you get the source of that, Hirsch will like you)—and then frustrate the reader looking for facile answers by showing that the realization in the statement prompts questions: Why must all that lives die? What does it mean to pass through nature into eternity? What or when is eternity? Are we supposed to know that all that lives must die?

The predisposition to raise questions is present in all of us to varying degrees. In young, prospective teachers, the predisposition takes on various shades and hues. They ask questions like: Why do some children learn more slowly than others? Tell me, why is that, whatever that may be, a better way to do it? But how do I know they learned it? In more mature prospective teachers coming back for a fifth year and certification, it might look different: Why is this more meaningful than that? Why should we teach this instead of that? Why does my experience teach me that this is wrong? What happens next? How do I know if this is right or wrong?

Persons with fondness for questions over answers recognize that most "answers" to complex questions are but tentative, that today's answers provoke tomorrow's uneasiness. As prospective teachers, they show a disrespect for finite answers to questions about human development, the limits of knowledge, the ways of knowing, the ways of doing. They itch to know even though they have begun to believe that they can never really know, that there is always another word to be said on every subject of consequence. Often, to answer-oriented teacher educators, these students are seen as hindrances instead of prospective great teachers. In truth, they stand the chance of provoking in their future students the quest to explore, to question, to imagine, to be comfortable with the discomfort of never "really knowing," of lifelong pursuit of knowledge.

3. Growing Knowledge, Understanding, and Commitment to Some Aspect of Human Endeavor; for Example, Science, Literature, Mathematics, or Blizzards

In the last several years, the point that teachers must know something before they can teach it has been made ad nauseam. We have admonitions from the Carnegie Forum to the Holmes Group to Secretary Bennett to the person on the street to all the teachers in the field who prepared with BS degrees in education all belaboring the obvious need for knowledge, albeit with a slightly different twist than the argument had the first twenty times around: teachers must have a bachelor's degree in an academic major before being admitted to a teacher preparation program.

But we all know that to know is not enough. Merely holding a bachelor of arts does not answer the question of the relationship between teacher and knowledge. What answers the question?

Teachers are rightfully and powerfully connected with knowledge when, even early in their learning careers, they begin to make metaphors to explain their existence, their issues and dilemmas, their joys and sorrows, from the knowledge they are acquiring. I speak not of that jaded notion of students being

excited by what they are learning. I get excited watching a baseball game, but it doesn't have much meaning for me the next day. I mean something including and transcending excitement. Great teachers are driven by the power, beauty, force, logic, illogic, color, vitality, relatedness, uniqueness of what they know and love. They make metaphors from it to explain the world; they are forever trying to understand the thing itself, always falling a bit short yet still urging others on. They are the teachers who make learners think what is being taught has value and meaning and may actually touch individual lives.

This quality shows itself in a variety of ways in prospective teachers. Often, it is hidden because that which captures the imagination and interest of a student may not be part of the course, may have no way of being known. I have never forgotten a young woman in a class I taught fifteen years ago. She was a freshman in one of those horrible introduction to education courses. For the last assignment, each student in the class had to teach something to the class. This young woman, who had spoken, but rarely and only when challenged during the semester, asked if the class might go to the student lounge when her turn came. I agreed; we went as a group. There was a piano in the room and she proceeded to play a piece by Chopin and explain to the class why it was an important piece of music. I suspected—and subsequent discussions with her bore out my thought—that this young woman saw the world through music, that she could explain almost anything better if she could use music as the metaphor, the carrier of her thoughts.

Most of us do not have students in our classes capable of playing a piece by Chopin, but we all have students who understand the world through a medium different from what the rest of the group may be using. Experience has taught many young people to hide this quality because it is not honored in classrooms.

4. A Sense of the Aesthetic

The development of the aesthetic domain in young people is critical to their growth and development; it is a fundamental right. The ability to grasp the beautiful makes us human; to deny that to young people is to deny their humanity. Great teachers often have an acutely developed sense of the aesthetic; they are unafraid to show their fondness for beauty in front of young people; they do so in such a manner as to make the young people themselves value beauty and their own perceptions of it.

For many young people, the world is a harsh and barren place, devoid of beauty. But in every generation, there are those who emerge spiritually changed from their schooling experiences, eager to face what is at times a hostile world. The changes are sometimes the result of a teacher with a sense of the aesthetic, one able to see beyond the everydayness and blandness of institutional life.

In a world stultified by the commercial definitions of beauty, individuals preparing to teach with this embryonic sense of the aesthetic are rare. Our own jadedness and mass-produced tastes make it difficult for us to recognize this quality in students. What does it look like? In its evolutionary phases, it might be an impulse to make the secondary methods classroom more attractive; it might be a choice of book covers; it might be in the selection of course materials for young people; it might be in the habits of an individual. I'm uncertain as to its many forms, but I am quite certain that when we see it we should treasure its existence and support its development.

5. Willingness to Assume Risks

There are teachers who say the right things, prescribe the right books, associate with the right people, but never take risks on behalf of others, beliefs, and ideas, never do more than verbalize. They are hollow shams.

The quality of risk-taking of great teachers is subtle, not necessarily that which puts people on picket lines, at the barricades, although it might be. The quality is critical to teacher modeling, for great teachers go beyond the statement of principles and ideas, beyond the endorsement of the importance of friendships, as they move students from the consideration of abstract principles to the actualization of deeds.

The 1960s and 1970s were filled with risk-taking teachers. While neither praising nor disparaging these obvious examples, I urge other instances for consideration inasmuch as the "opportunity" for collective risk-taking is a rare occurrence in the lives of most of us. While it was not easy to be a risk-taker then, it wasn't very lonely either. Other instances, some more prosaic, abound: teachers in certain parts of the country who persist in teaching evolution despite pressure to desist, teachers who assign controversial books despite adverse criticism, teachers who teach the Civil War and the Vietnam War without partisanship or chauvinism. These quiet acts of risk-taking occur daily in schools and universities; they instruct students of the importance of ideas joined with actions.

I recall my high school art teacher who took abuse from the principal because she demanded the right for her students to use the gymnasium to prepare for a dance. He rebuked and embarrassed her in front of the students for "daring to question [my] authority." His act prompted some of us to go to the superintendent to complain about him; we got the gym. But we also each had a private interview with the principal in which he shared his scorn and derision for us for having "gone over [my] head to the superintendent." We learned that acting on principles is sometimes risky, that we had to support a teacher who took risks for us, that actions have consequences, that a "good" act like defending a brave teacher can lead to punishment. But her risk-taking led us to risk-taking on behalf of another person and the resolution of a mild injustice.

Detecting this quality in the young is difficult. The young often appear cause-driven and it is hard to distinguish when students are merely following a popular, low-risk cause and when they are standing for something involving personal decisions and risk. We might see it in its evolutionary form in some quite simple instances. Many teacher educators suffer the indignity of seeing their ideas and principles distorted by the wisdom of the workplace, of having their students grow disenchanted with what they have been taught as they encounter the world of the school: "We'll knock that Ivory Tower stuff out of you here. This is the *real* world." Of course, we all know some of it should be knocked out, but much of it should remain. It is a rare student who during practical, internship, and early years of teaching remains steadfast to such principles as: all student answers, honestly given, merit serious consideration; or worksheets are rarely good instructional materials. It is risky for young pre-professionals and beginning professionals to dispute the wisdom of the workplace and maintain fidelity to earlier acquired principles. Perhaps in these seemingly small matters lies the quality to be writ large during the full career.

6. At-Homeness in the World

Great teachers live effectively in what often seems a perverse world. Acutely aware of life's unevenness, the disparities in the distribution of the world's goods, talents, and resources, they cry out for justice in their own special ways while continuing to live with a sense of equanimity and contribute to the world. They demonstrate that life is to be lived as fully as one can despite problems and issues. They show that one can be a sensitive human being caring about and doing things about the problems and issues, and, at the same time, live a life of personal fulfillment. They are not overwhelmed by the insolubility of things on the grand scale, for they are able to make sense of things on the personal level.

I once had a professor for a course in Victorian poetry. In addition to his academic accomplishments, the professor was a fine gardener, each year producing a beautifully crafted flower garden, filled with design and beauty.

We were reading "In Memoriam," the part in which Tennyson refers to nature, red in tooth and claw. All of a sudden, the professor talked about how, that morning, while eating his breakfast, he

had watched his cat stalk a robin, catch it, and devour part of it. He related the incident, of course, to the poem. (Clearly he had the quality alluded to earlier, the sense on inter-relatedness of things.) I am uncertain what I learned about "In Memoriam" that morning, but I know I learned that this man who earlier in the semester had pointed out the delicate beauty of some of Tennyson's lyrics had integrated death into his life while remaining sensitive to beauty, to love. It was partly through him that I began to see that the parts of life I did not like were not to be ignored nor to be paralyzed about. All this in the death of a bird? No, all this in a powerful teacher's reaction to the death of a bird in the midst of life.

And what does at-homeness in the world look like in prospective teachers? I am quite uncertain, very tentative about this one. Perhaps it shows itself in a combination of things like joy in life one day and despair over life the next as the young slowly come to grips with the enigmas of life, its vicissitudes and sorrows. The young are often studies in extremes as they make order of life, of their lives. As a consequence, one sees a few students with vast energy both to live life and to anguish over its difficulties. But one cannot arrive at the point of my professor with his lovely garden and dead robin simultaneously entertained in his head without a sense of the joyful and the tragic in life, without a constant attempt to deal with the wholeness that is life, without a sense of being at home in the world.

All prospective teachers have touches of each of these qualities which should be supported and nurtured so that their presence is ever more manifest in classrooms. But a few students have some of these qualities writ large. Buttressed by programs that guarantee competency in instructional skills, these individuals have the potential to become great teachers themselves, to be the teachers who take the students beyond knowledge acquisition and skill development to questioning, to wondering, to striving. We must, first, find these prospective teachers, help them grow and develop, treasure them, and give them to the young people of America, each one of whom deserves several great teachers during thirteen years of public schooling.

And what has all this to do with the preparation of teachers? Surely, preparing teachers to be competent in providing basic instruction to as many students as possible is enough of a major task. Clearly, the raising of reading scores, of math achievement levels, of writing skills, of thinking processes are significant accomplishments. Of course, all these things must be accomplished, and teacher preparation programs around the country are getting better and better at these matters.

But we must have more; we must have an increase in the presence of greatness in the schools, in the universities. Love for a teacher's kindness, gratitude for skills acquired, fondness for teachers—these are critically important. But equally important is the possibility that students will encounter greatness, greatness that transcends the everydayness of anyplace, that invites, cajoles, pushes, drags, drives, brings students into the possibilities that questions mean more than answers; that knowledge is interrelated; that there is joy to be had from beauty; that knowledge can affect people to the cores of their being; that ideas find their worth in actions; that life is full of potential in a sometimes perverse world.

POSTNOTE

Ducharme's article is provocative in its challenge to go beyond mere competence and instead reach for greatness in our teaching. The characteristics that he suggests embody greatness in teaching and are difficult to challenge because they ring true. They also are formidable if we want to become teachers who possess these characteristics.

In an effort to ensure that prospective teachers will be "safe to practice," many teacher educators focus their instruction on the knowledge and skills (competencies) new teachers will need to function effectively in classrooms. This article may be a "sight-raiser," a rare instance where the focus of teacher education is on what it will take to become a *great* teacher, not merely a *competent* one.

DISCUSSION QUESTIONS

1. Is a particular kind of teacher preparation needed to produce great, rather than just competent, teachers? Or does a prospective teacher need to earn competence before greatness can be achieved? Explain your answers.

2. Think of the great teachers you have had. Did they possess the characteristics Ducharme describes? Briefly discuss what made these teachers great.

3. Can you think of any other characteristics that great teachers possess that were not identified by Ducharme? If so, what are they?

RELATED WEBSITE RESOURCES AND VIDEO CASES

WEB RESOURCE:

The National Board of Professional Teaching Standards. Available at:

http://www.nbpts.org.

This organization has, for over two decades, led the fight both to define excellence in teaching and recognize excellent teachers.

▶❙❙ TEACHSOURCE VIDEO CASE

BECOMING A TEACHER: VOICES AND ADVICE FROM THE FIELD

Topics: Teaching as a Profession, Advice

What do practicing teachers say about their career choice? In this video, you'll hear voices from the field; novice teachers as well as long-time professionals reflect on why they became a teacher, the joys and challenges of the profession, and the many dimensions of being there for children to help them develop and learn. Throughout the segment, teachers offer their advice, culled from their own experiences, to new teachers just entering the profession. Go to the website for the Education Media Library at CengageBrain.com to watch the video clips, study the artifacts in the case, and reflect on the following questions.

1. What are the rewards of teaching cited by these teachers?

2. What is the essential ingredient to testing whether or not you should teach?

3. One of these new teachers suggests that you ought to "play the role" of teacher. Is this being authentic? Do you agree with this suggestion? Why or why not?

The Best Teachers I Have Known

Susan Allred

Susan Allred has spent 37 years in education, as both a teacher and administrator. Currently retired from public education, she now serves as an education consultant; susanallred@att.net.

"The Best Teachers I have Known," by Susan Allred, 2010, *Educational Leadership* 67(10), (online only). © 2010 by ASCD. Reprinted with permission. Learn more about ASCD at www.ascd.org.

FOCUS QUESTION

What characteristics do good teachers share in common?

InTASC
Standards 1, 2, 3, 5, and 10

One of the joys of retirement is having the time to reflect on our profession. Looking back over the 37 years I spent as an educator—20 of them as a teacher and 17 as an administrator—and reflecting on my own schooling as well, I think of the many highly effective teachers I've known. Spanning all grade levels, they engaged students in learning to the point of excitement and kindled the desire to keep on learning.

So what did these teachers have in common?

They Were Masters of Their Content

All of these teachers knew their subject matter. The questions they raised with students made it clear that it was OK not to know the details, but *not* OK not to pursue the answers. These teachers were enthusiastic about their subject matter, as though what was going on at that moment was the most important thing ever. They connected their content to everything they did.

One school had a science class for gifted and talented students. The science teacher lived and breathed science. One morning when I arrived at school—at 5:30 A.M., as was my habit—a car was already parked out in front. In it were a sleepy-eyed father and his twin daughters who were in 4th grade. As I walked toward the car, the girls were already bounding out the door. The father rolled down his window and said, "I hope it's all right for me to bring them. They said you'd be here, and they're sure the chicks in the lab hatched overnight. They couldn't wait to come. You know, they help the science teacher in the lab every morning."

Actually, I didn't know that they helped the science teacher, who didn't teach either of the children, but I did know that she shared her love of science with all the students in the school. By the time school started, every 4th grader had already been in to see the chicks.

They Were Insatiable Learners

Perhaps the most frustrated classroom teachers I have worked with or observed were those who thought that four years of undergraduate training should carry them through a 30-year career. These teachers feel oppressed by professional development of any kind. Their mantra is, "Just give me my kids, and let me teach."

The most effective teachers realize that the world and students have changed since they completed their undergraduate work, and they look for opportunities to address the gaps in their knowledge and ability. A middle school teacher learned about a local astronomical research laboratory and what it might offer students. The school curriculum didn't have a regular focus on astronomy, but a single trip helped this teacher realize that a world-class resource was in her backyard. Connections with the institute enabled students to watch and program the satellite dishes from their classroom computers. Students were then able to use the data collected on weather, planets, and stars in their daily science lessons. A teacher's enthusiasm for her own new learning enhanced her classroom.

In the final district in which I worked, we implemented the Baldrige Management System for Performance Excellence. This quality-based system, which requires constant review of data and information, created angst among many teachers. Professional development on the system met with mixed reviews.

But one day, a special education teacher called me into her room. She asked a kindergarten student to tell me about his "chart." "I was supposed to learn 50 words by Christmas," he said. Then he pointed to the October column on his bar graph and exclaimed, "See, I've learned 50 already. I get to learn more!" The teacher hadn't learned to use this system in her undergraduate work. Even though she was somewhat skeptical about whether it would work, she had learned it because she thought it might help her students. And it did.

They Had a Positive Outlook

Not earning enough money; having too many students, too many meetings, and too many levels of learners; trying to satisfy challenging expectations; and often feeling like the first line of defense against pandemics, child abuse, and student drug use—these are enough to get anybody down. But despite all these factors, effective teachers believe that today is the best day ever—and that tomorrow will be even better.

One compassionate 3rd grade teacher I knew vigorously lobbied to take into her class 12 students with special needs whom we were attempting to fully include in the regular student population. Late in September, I asked her to take on still another student—a little Finnish girl who didn't speak English. Three months later, the child was communicating well in the class. Just before Christmas break, the teacher left a note on my desk that read, "I just wanted to thank you for my class. You've apologized so often for the pressure it puts on me. But I love the students, and they are learning so very much. I would not have wanted it any other way."

They Were Team Members

Effective teachers know they cannot do the work alone. With so much information available these days, we need the best brains to work collaboratively to pull solutions together. It really does take a village.

But in high school, it's often more difficult to get this point across. The math department at the high school in which I was assistant principal was especially effective in this area. The department had aligned the curriculum both vertically and horizontally. A record-keeping system in the math office kept teachers current with what students knew and what they needed to know to move to the next level of math.

In the three years I held that position, not a single student was unsuccessful in math. If math teachers saw a new trend in student performance data that identified gaps in learning—for example, students not mastering polynomials—the department would revise the sequence or content of courses. Moreover, the advanced placement calculus teacher had a 100-percent pass rate (3 or better on the exam) for many years. That was possible because the department was committed to preparing the students through course sequencing, by ensuring mastery of skills before moving forward—providing tutoring, for example, and giving students extra time—and by frequently meeting with students, parents, and other teachers about students' achievement.

We had the same success in tech prep math, our applied mathematics program. Two teachers teamed up during their lunch and planning time to hold a special lab for students who struggled to pass the state exam. For many years, those teachers also had a 100-percent success rate.

They Created Communities for Success

The teachers I have described not only knew the achievement levels of their students, but also made sure that students knew where they were, where they needed to be, and how they would get there. Moreover, they created an environment in which students felt empowered and valuable and in which they learned to respectfully appreciate the differences in the room.

Through modeling and by clarifying expectations regarding conduct and engagement, these teachers promoted respectful interaction of students in their classrooms that was nothing short of democracy in action. Students could be at any level of learning ability or from any ethnic or religious group; students accepted one another with their body piercings, Goth clothing, dyed hair, or native dress. The focus was on learning.

These effective teachers did what all effective teachers do—they established clear and high expectations and gave students some choice in how they would learn. For example, rather than going over each homework item, one high school teacher had a process for students to report the items that gave them trouble—students wrote these down on a white board as they entered the room. Those were the items that the teacher reviewed. Students also had homework buddies so that if they had extra time, they could begin doing their homework together. Students suggested both strategies.

Another teacher had her students list on a strategy board the things that helped them learn particular concepts. A regular part of the day focused on "what works" and on "what doesn't work as well." For example, one of the class's goals was that every student would earn 90 percent or better on the weekly vocabulary test. To help ensure this, the students decided to take their words to the lunch room and study them together after they finished eating. The weeks they used that strategy, the class met its goal. So the strategy went on the strategy board.

All This—And More

Of course, in addition to the characteristics I've mentioned, effective teachers display professionalism, are exceptional communicators with all stakeholders, and don't watch the clock. As I sit here rocking on my porch, I count myself fortunate to have known so many of them.

POSTNOTE

This reflection by a retired teacher and principal makes several telling points about good education. In particular, two themes recur: colleagueship and imperfection. While teachers usually ply their craft alone with their assigned students, they are, in fact, part of a team. Good schooling is a "corporate effort." In good schools, teachers share what they have learned about the craft of teaching, about the content they are teaching and their insights about their students. They take responsibility not just for their classroom and their students, but for the success of the total enterprise, whether it is the academic achievement of the school's students or maintaining the rules that support a civil and positive environment. Good teaching is a "team sport."

As a career, teaching is hard on a perfectionist. Surgeons, accountants and high-wire acrobats need to be perfectionists. Of necessity, things have to go "just right." And while teachers occasionally dream of classes and school-years going "just right," those dreams rarely, if ever, come true. Human nature, theirs and their students', keeps rearing is all-too-human head. The perfect class where the content rolled out of the teacher's mouth flawlessly and entered the heads and memory banks of all the students with absolute accuracy is an unreachable allusion. We believe our author would urge us to strive for perfection, but settle for high, but realistic, performance standards.

DISCUSSION QUESTIONS

1. Of the several characteristics of good teachers mentioned in this article, which do you feel is most important? Why?
2. Which of these characteristics do you feel you possess and which do you feel you need to develop?

3

Elevating the Teaching Profession

Arne Duncan

Arne Duncan, the Secretary of the U.S. Department of Education, is the former Chief Executive Officer of the Chicago Public Schools.

Elevating the Teaching Profession by Arne Duncan, 2009. http://www.ed.gov/news/speeches/call-teaching

FOCUS QUESTION

What is the U.S. educational leader's reform vision for the nation?

InTASC
Standards 9 and 10

KEY TERMS

- Compensation
- Professional development
- Race to the Top

A little more than a half-century ago, in 1958, Senator John F. Kennedy penned a piece for the *NEA Journal*. In it, the future president urged a number of reforms to the teaching profession. As a longtime supporter of the NEA, Kennedy felt that higher pay and more classrooms were not enough—"more and better teachers are also needed." To strengthen the teaching profession, JFK wrote, "we must find better means for providing better rewards for our better teachers. We must make actual use of probationary periods to retain only those with satisfactory performance records, and we must demonstrate concretely to young beginners in the field that real opportunities for advancement await those whose contribution is of the highest caliber."

Flash forward a quarter century, and Al Shanker, the legendary head of the American Federation of Teachers, was echoing JFK's warning. In his 1984 address to the AFT Convention, Shanker suggested that "one possibility is that we will improve the profession ourselves and find ways of selecting and training teachers—and yes, even some ways of removing people who shouldn't be in the profession." Shanker recognized that change would not be easy or happen overnight. But he declared that "the professionalization of teaching in the next 10 or 20 years is life or death for the future of public education."

Unfortunately, JFK's and Al Shanker's calls to strengthen the teaching profession ring all too familiar today. Like President Kennedy and Al Shanker, President Obama and I believe deeply that good teachers are unsung heroes. We know exemplary teachers toil late into the night on lesson plans, shell out of their own pocket to pay for supplies, and wake up worrying when one of their students seems headed for trouble.

People remember their favorite teacher decades later because great teachers change the course of a student's life. They light a lifelong curiosity, teaching students to solve problems like a scientist, write like a novelist, listen like a poet, see like an artist, and observe like a journalist. It is no surprise that the single biggest influence on student growth is the quality of the teacher standing in the front of the classroom.

Teaching, in short, should be one of the nation's most revered professions. Teachers should be amply compensated, fairly evaluated, and supported by topnotch professional development. Yet teachers today are not accorded the respect they deserve—and teaching is still not treated as a profession on par with other highly skilled professions. The unavoidable question is, why? Why, 25 years after Al Shanker's admonition and 50 years after JFK's plea, are teachers still not treated like true professionals?

The answer, I believe, is that we have a broken system—a system of training, induction, evaluation, professional development, and promotion that is an artifact from an earlier era. As Al Shanker pointed out, schools today are still largely stuck in the factory model of the industrial age. Students, in classrooms that look uncannily like the classrooms of a century ago, move through 13 years of schooling beginning at age five, attending school 180 days a year, and taking five subjects a day in timed periods similar to what the Carnegie Foundation recommended in 1910.

Teacher promotion and compensation policies are based on equally outdated conceptions of K–12 education. This year marks the 100th anniversary of the first tenure law, passed by New Jersey in 1909. The single-salary pay schedule got its start in 1921, nearly 90 years ago, in Des Moines and Denver.

In the factory model of education, teachers are treated as interchangeable widgets who keep the educational assembly line moving. Teachers today are not paid based on their skill in the classroom or the difficulty of their teaching assignments. If two teachers have comparable experience and credentials, they are paid the same—even if one teacher is the Teacher of the Year and the other instructor is the weakest teacher at her school. As Al Shanker summed up, teachers continue to be treated "as workers in an old fashioned factory who may not exercise judgment and discretion, [and] who are supervised and directed by everyone from the state legislature down to the school principal. Our schools are organized today exactly the way they were a century ago."

A century ago, when teachers could be fired willy-nilly, tenure protection and the single-salary schedule provided teachers with vital safeguards against arbitrary dismissals by principals and school boards. Yet in 2009, while teachers still need processes that assure fair treatment, it no longer makes sense to treat teachers as widgets. The teaching profession will never receive the respect it deserves, so long as teachers are perceived as indistinguishable components of the educational assembly line.

The Obama administration is committed to strengthening the teaching profession, from teacher preparation, to induction, professional development, and retention, especially in high-poverty schools and for high-needs students. In fact, much of our teacher quality agenda draws on what teachers and union leaders tell us needs to change to better support teachers and elevate the profession.

During the last year, I undertook a Listening and Learning Tour that took me to more than 30 states. During that tour, and in the seven preceding years when I was CEO of the Chicago Public Schools, I had hundreds of conversations with talented teachers. Virtually every teacher I spoke to told me the same thing, expressing a conviction borne out repeatedly in teacher surveys: Teachers want to challenge the status quo and they want to be treated as skilled professionals.

Most teachers are not content with their preservice preparation. Novice teachers and veterans alike say they were not adequately prepared for the realities of managing a classroom of diverse learners. Once in the classroom, teachers found they lacked consistent, high-quality mentoring from an experienced teacher.

Nor do teachers get enough time to collaborate and plan with their colleagues, discuss problem students, and learn from their peers. Professional development is generally of poor quality, and often fails to develop a teacher's skills. Drop-by evaluations by principals are superficial. Single-salary compensation policies offer few incentives to teachers to take on leadership responsibilities in their schools—and almost no encouragement to attract, reward, and recognize effective teachers in high-needs schools.

Today, union leaders committed to challenging the status quo are courageously and candidly speaking out about the need to move beyond their comfort zones. For example, AFT president Randi Weingarten is an outspoken critic of current teacher evaluation systems. "For too long and in too many places," she says, "teacher evaluation has ranged from hollow to harmful. For most teachers, the process of evaluation is a ritual in which a principal spends 15 minutes in their classroom once a year checking off a grocery list of minimum competencies. This process does not improve teaching [or] learning."

NEA president Dennis Van Roekel testified recently that "we can all agree that our public schools need a wholesale transformation." Dennis concluded that "if states and/or the federal government are to make a serious commitment to ensuring a quality teacher for every child … attention should be placed on how best to advance the professionalism of teaching."

So how does the administration plan to advance the teaching profession? As the President and I have stated, we start from the presumption that far-reaching reforms to the teaching profession can only take hold with the support and guidance of teachers and their unions. That is one reason why our teaching quality agenda adopts many of the policies that teachers themselves told us are essential to elevating the profession.

No area of the teaching profession is more plainly broken today than that of teacher evaluation and professional development. In district after district, more than 95 percent of teachers are rated as good or superior, even in schools that are chronically underperforming year after year. Worse yet, evaluations typically fail to take any account of a teacher's impact on student learning.

The truth is that students and teachers don't live in mythic Lake Wobegon, where everyone is above average. Yet we have an evaluation system today that pretends otherwise. As a result, great teachers don't get recognized, don't get rewarded, and don't help their peers grow. The teachers in the middle of the skills spectrum don't get the support they need to improve. And the teachers at the bottom don't get the support they need either, and if they do and still don't improve, they need to be counseled out of the profession. It's not just students who suffer; as Al Shanker pointed out, "teachers have to live with the results of other people's bad teaching—the students who don't know anything." To continue tinkering around the edges of such a dysfunctional system is a waste.

All of the department's new or redesigned programs provide powerful incentives for states and districts to make far-reaching changes to teacher evaluation and professional development—from Race to the Top, to the 2009 School Improvement Grants, the Teacher Incentive Fund, and Title I and IDEA funds under the American Recovery and Reinvestment Act. Our guiding principle is simply that teachers should be treated as professionals: They should have the support, tools, and opportunities to perform at their full potential by having timely and accurate data about their students to inform instruction; they should have time to consult and collaborate with their peers; and they should be evaluated, compensated, and advanced based in part on student learning.

Student growth and gain, not absolute test scores, are what we are most interested in—how much are students improving each year, and what are teachers, schools, school districts, and states doing the most to accelerate student achievement?

The $4.3 billion Race to the Top program recognizes that strong teachers and leaders are the heart of educational improvement, and it places more weight on this factor than any other in its grant competition. The final Race to the Top application emphasizes that professional collaboration and planning time, individualized professional development plans, training and support to use assessment data, classroom observations with timely and constructive feedback, and other activities are critical to developing high-quality evaluation systems and professional development.

The Race to the Top competition also recognizes that teacher effectiveness cannot be assessed solely on student test scores. Instead, teacher effectiveness should be evaluated based on multiple measures, provided that student academic growth over the course of the year is a significant factor. I am pleased that both Dennis Van Roekel and Randi Weingarten recognized and applauded a number of these elements in the final Race to the Top guidelines.

It defies common sense to bar all consideration of student learning from teacher evaluation. But it is time to move past the over-reliance on fill-in-the-bubble tests to richer assessments of successful teaching and learning—and the department will be pursuing such reforms in its $350 million competition for a new generation of assessments when it moves forward with reauthorizing the Elementary and Secondary Education Act in 2010. Those new assessments will be aligned to common college and career-ready standards being developed by states—which the NEA and AFT have endorsed, and which, eventually, should reduce curricular turmoil and instability for teachers.

Finally, teachers need high-quality, timely information about the progress of their students. Through the State Longitudinal Data Systems program and Race to the Top, we're providing hundreds of millions of dollars to states and districts to develop data systems that deliver this information in a timely and useful format. When teachers get better data on student growth, including results from interim assessments, they have the chance to tailor classroom instruction to the needs of their students and drive a cycle of continuous improvement.

Not all teachers have experience using data to improve instruction. But the department is asking states that apply for Race to the Top grants to develop plans for professional development to help teachers and principals get training in how to use data to inform instruction.

We want to continue working with teachers and unions to elevate the teaching profession. With that kind of collaboration, it is possible to turn battlegrounds into common ground. I am encouraged by the NEA's new $6 million initiative to recruit more topnotch teachers in high-needs schools and hard-to-staff subjects like science and mathematics, and specialties like special education and English language acquisition. I am heartened as well by the AFT's support of pay-for-performance initiatives in the AFT's Innovation Fund, and the AFT's innovative contract in New Haven, Connecticut.

As we move ahead to reform the teaching profession, we'll have disagreements and make mistakes along the way. But we cannot let the perfect become the enemy of the good. The need for reform, both for students and teachers, is urgent. Students cannot afford to wait another decade, while adults tinker with issues of teacher quality. It's time to stop tweaking the system. It's time, once and for all, to make teaching the revered profession it should be.

POSTNOTE

Reforming the way we are preparing and supporting teachers could be compared to trying to change the course of an aircraft carrier while it is steaming through the ocean. The captain can call out to the helmsman to change course, and the helmsman can obediently swing the wheel. However, it takes miles before the course is actually changed. In this article, Arne Duncan, the country's current Secretary of Education, is calling for a dramatic change in the way we educate, place, and support the nation's teachers.

While we support Duncan's change agenda, we need to point out a few difficulties.

First, American education is more like a vast flotilla of small ships than one large carrier. So, too, with the education of teachers, which takes place at some twelve hundred colleges and universities. These "educational ships" have to take their orders from many sources—from state departments of education to boards of trustees and from professional associations to faculty committees. The same holds true for the in-service and staff development efforts designed to improve the work of practicing teachers.

Educational change has many captains and steering wheels. Much can, and undoubtedly, will be done to improve the lot of teachers. However, as the article's title, "Elevating the Teaching Profession," acknowledges, teaching is a *profession*. Teachers, unlike a sales force, factory workers, or a military unit, are members of a profession. As a professional, each of us has a personal responsibility to "elevate" ourselves, to improve our knowledge and skills and to ensure that we are growing as people and professionals. First and foremost, the job is ours. As Pogo said, "We have met the enemy and he is us!'

DISCUSSION QUESTIONS

1. What are the key challenges Secretary Duncan presented to the teachers, unions in the article above?
2. What are the core incentives of the federal Race to the Top program?
3. Do you believe that the Secretary's activist stance and federal educational programs will undermined the U.S.'s traditional local control policy? Why or why not?

RELATED WEBSITE RESOURCES AND VIDEO CASES

WEB RESOURCES:

Strengthening Teaching at the U.S. Department of Education. Available at:

http://www.ed.gov/teaching.

News, information on grants and study opportunity can be accessed at this site, along with videotaped interviews with the Secretary of Education.

▶❙❙ TEACHSOURCE VIDEO CASE

NO CHILD LEFT BEHIND (NCLB): GOOD INTENTIONS, REAL PROBLEMS

In this video case, the Secretary of Education, Arne Duncan, and Jonathan Kozol, an education activist, discuss the No Child Left Behind Law. Go to the website for the Education Media Library at CengageBrain.com to watch the video clips, study the artifacts in the case, and reflect on the following questions.

1. What are Secretary Duncan's key criticisms of NCLB?
2. What are Mr. Kozol's primary complaints?
3. Where, if anywhere, do you see common ground between them?

4

The Power of Personal Relationships

Thomas S. Mawhinney and Laura L. Sagan

Thomas S. Mawhinney is an associate professor at Touro College in New York. He is a former high school principal, an education consultant, a teacher trainer, and the president of Leading for Learning, Inc., Poughkeepsie, New York. **Laura L. Sagan** is Director of Curriculum for Humanities in the Lakeland School District in Shrub Oak, New York.

"The Power of Personal Relationships," by Thomas S. Mawhinney and Laura L. Sagan, *Phi Delta Kappan 88,* no. 6 (February 2007), pp. 460–464. Reprinted with permission of Phi Delta Kappa International, www.pdkintl.org. All rights reserved.

Donta stayed after class a few minutes to ask her teacher for help. As she hurried to get to her next class on time her boyfriend cornered her and questioned her about a rumor he had heard involving Donta and her best friend. She could not get away. She was torn because she had been late for this class several times before and did not want to disappoint her teacher again.

When Donta finally got to her class, she was obviously nervous. Her teacher simply said, "Donta, how nice to see you. Come on in and take a seat." Donta smiled and felt relieved. She loved this class because the teacher made her feel important. "Why couldn't all teachers treat kids this way?" she thought.

Donta had just experienced the power of personal-relationship building. Her teacher could have demanded a pass, interrogated her in front of the class, greeted her with a sarcastic remark, or embarrassed her in some other way. Instead, she made her feel welcome. Donta was in a frame of mind ready to learn.

There are many children who make up their minds on the first day of class whether they are going to succeed or fail—sometimes consciously and sometimes not. How can this be, one might ask? Simply put, the initial student/teacher encounter often determines how well or poorly a child will perform throughout the school year. Likewise, a positive teacher/student relationship creates the classroom atmosphere necessary to maximize a student's mental state of readiness.

Picture the teacher who, in an attempt to establish control from the beginning, spends the first day describing classroom rules and routines and emphasizes what will happen if they are not followed. Coercive classrooms are

FOCUS QUESTION

What does a teacher need to do to establish the proper personal relationship with students?

InTASC

Standards 2, 5, 6, and 9

KEY TERMS

- Empathetic listening
- Fight-or-flight response
- Pedagogic caring

not conducive to learning, yet many teachers continue to believe that a dominating relationship such as that between a parent and child ensures student compliance. How often have instructional leaders advised the first-year teacher to be tough in the beginning and loosen up later—that one can never do it in reverse? Well, after that first day of toughness, many students have "downshifted" into a fight-or-flight mode. In doing so they have bypassed much of their capacity for higher-order thinking or creative thought, and it is hard to learn when your bodily functions are focused on survival. We now understand that higher-level thinking is more likely to occur in the brain of a student who is emotionally secure than in the brain of a student who is scared, upset, anxious, or stressed.

Researchers continue to report that the teacher has a significant impact on student achievement. Based on an extensive analysis of research, Robert and Jana Marzano claim that "the quality of teacher-student relationships is the keystone for all other aspects of classroom management."[1] As former secondary school principals, we feel that personal-relationship building is one of the most important skills a teacher can possess and continue to refine. In this article, we intend to describe the many dimensions of this skill.

Personal-Relationship Building

We first encountered the term "personal-relationship building" as the title of the shortest chapter in *The Skillful Teacher,* by Jon Saphier and Robert Gower.[2] The authors classify this skill under the broader category of motivation and supply a two-part definition: "the variety of ways teachers have of contacting students' personal worlds and the traits of teachers that seem to engender affection and regard in a relationship."[3]

We will use this framework in an attempt to paint a clear picture of this powerful tool in a teacher's pedagogical "bag of tricks." We do not expect even great teachers to have all the skills and characteristics we will describe. Adding one or two to one's repertoire each year will put the self-renewing teacher on a path to canonization.

Ways of Contacting Students' Personal Worlds

A beginning teacher gets only one chance to make a first impression. As we noted above, despite the advice commonly given to new teachers to be tough in the beginning, one does not want to scare off the marginal students or those students who need a caring and nurturing environment to survive and prosper. Teachers can create such an environment by consciously engaging in particular practices and behaviors.

Knowing Your Students and Allowing Them to Know You

Differentiating instruction—planning varied lessons according to students' interests—is an important skill. Therefore we recommend that teachers spend the first few days of the school year or new semester getting to know their students by using interest surveys or other activities to discover the ways in which each one of them is unique.

We also support those teachers who allow their students to know them. Teachers who offer their students "genuineness and self-disclosure"[4] reveal "aspects of themselves that allow [the] image of authority figure to be tempered by images of teacher-as-a-real-person."[5] Steven Wolk believes that "teachers need to allow students to see them as complete people with emotions, opinions, and lives outside of school. A good way for a teacher to get students to treat him or her as a human being is to act like one."[6]

Two of our most beloved teachers are women who, when faced with child-care problems, bring their young children to school for short periods of time. Whenever this happens, secondary and middle school students flock to them. While some schools frown on teachers using the workplace as a backup day-care facility, we find that the practice allows students to get a peek at the other side of a teacher's life. Not only does it improve relationships, it forms a long-lasting bond between the students and the teacher's own children.

Reestablishing Contact and High Expectations

Reestablishing contact with a student with whom one has had a negative interaction is one of the most difficult things a teacher can do. Yet if that student is ever to feel a sense of belonging again, the teacher must somehow have a positive interaction with the student around some other issue. No apology is needed, but the message that the negative incident is in the past and that it is time to move on must be clear. How often have you heard students claim that they are doing poorly in a class because the teacher "hates" them? We believe that students have an innate sense that adults hold grudges and it is not clear to them when an incident of misbehavior has been forgotten. Therefore, we feel that teachers—and schools, for that matter—need to consciously apply techniques to bring closure to discipline problems, so that students understand that "everyone makes mistakes. You need to learn from it, and move on."

There is an abundance of research on the academic benefits of high expectations for students. High expectations are a crucial ingredient in personal-relationship building. In our years of administrative experience, we have seen the damage that low expectations can do even before a student walks through the classroom door for the first time. We fought in our respective schools for heterogeneous grouping, yet many days we were butting up against a wall of long-held teacher beliefs in the efficiency of sorting and separating students. We encountered one teacher who had special education students coloring rather than participating in a writing assignment with the rest of the class. You can imagine how demeaned those children felt. We will leave it at this: a student—especially a young person who has experienced the negative effects of low expectations over time—can sense when a teacher has high expectations for all students.

Active and Empathetic Listening

Active listening not only helps build personal relationships but is a powerful teaching strategy as well.

James Stronge places this practice under the more general category of caring.[7] We feel that it deserves special mention, having observed its effect on student participation in the classroom as well as the expressions on the faces of those students who are the recipients of this potent form of attention from the teacher.

Active listening serves to:

- reaffirm to the speaker the content of his or her remark;
- confirm to the students that they have been heard in a nonjudgmental way;
- restate or infer the feeling state of the speaker; and, most important,
- send a message to the students that their comments or responses are important to the teacher.[8]

You can imagine the look on an insecure student's face when the teacher refers to an answer he or she gave earlier in the class—"as Jimmy said at the beginning of class, one of the main causes of the Civil War was …." Even using students' names when repeating or rephrasing a comment is a powerful teaching and personal-relationship-building move. We cannot encourage teachers enough to use active listening in their classrooms.

Involvement

For more than 30 years, first as teachers and then as administrators, we have enjoyed being involved with students, whether chaperoning a dance, overseeing a field trip, or watching a school sporting or other extracurricular event. School staff members who appear at activities taking place outside the normal school day are those with whom students most easily connect. Many veteran teachers feel that they have paid their dues with respect to this aspect of school life and pass on such duties to their younger colleagues. Yet we find that students appreciate the fact that *any* teacher attends an event or chaperones an activity. We ourselves showed up at so many events that students began to ask why we were not at every activity—too much of a good thing, perhaps?

Teacher Traits That Engender Affection and Regard

In addition to using particular practices, teachers who successfully build personal relationships with students exhibit certain attitudes and qualities.

Respect, Courtesy, and Fairness

One of the most respected teachers that we have observed was a traditional, veteran teacher. Year after year, students would affirm that he was one of the best teachers they had ever had. In his classroom, you had to pay particular attention to understand why. He was courteous, always saying please and thank you. He frequently gave students one last chance to increase their grades on a quiz or exam. He insisted that those who did not do well see him for help. He never got mad or raised his voice. He used humor but was never sarcastic. He was loyal to the absent, never speaking of other students in front of their peers or with his fellow teachers. He disciplined students privately; he never did so publicly. He is our "poster child" for the category of respect, courtesy, and fairness.

We believe that these basic human qualities are often lost in secondary schools. As adults, we bring to school scripts that we learned, not from teacher training, but from our experiences as parents and as children being parented. Under pressure, we often revert to these scripts. Take the example of a teacher we overheard when one of her students walked out of her class in anger. The teacher followed the student into the hall, asking, "Who do you think you are?" How is the student supposed to answer that question?

Respect, courtesy, and fairness cover a wide variety of teacher behaviors. A teacher can demonstrate respect by:

- using students' interests in class activities,
- allowing students to express ideas without criticism,
- correcting errors without putdowns,
- balancing corrective feedback with recognition of strengths,

- displaying student products, and
- using specific praise.[9]

According to students, fairness on the part of the teacher includes:

- treating students as people,
- refraining from ridicule and from creating situations that cause students to lose the respect of their peers,
- being consistent and giving students opportunities to have input into the classroom, and
- providing opportunities for all students to participate and succeed.[10]

A teacher displays courtesy by:

- smiling often,
- being polite,
- not interrupting,
- exhibiting simple kindnesses such as picking up a dropped item or holding a door, and
- greeting students when they arrive and wishing them well when they leave.

Caring and Understanding

Caring too much can be dangerous for teachers. We all have heard stories of teachers who have blurred the line between their professional and personal lives. It is possible to develop unhealthy relationships that are damaging to both the teacher and the child. Yet not caring can be equally debilitating. How often do youths who drop out of school complain that no one cares about them or even cares if they exist? We believe that the right kind of caring is the secret to developing students' motivation to achieve.

Nancy Hoffman asserts, "There is a great deal to be done to make the caring work of teachers less elusive, to name it among our expectations, to study how it works, and to reward it as a substantial component of excellence in teaching."[11] While teachers cannot possibly involve themselves completely in the lives of all their students, they can exhibit a burning interest in student achievement by using effective praise and by showing an almost parental pride in exceptional student work.

Hoffman uses the term "pedagogic caring," which she defines as a passion for learning that emanates from the teacher. It is easy to gauge the level of this type of caring by observing the display of student work in and around a teacher's room or office.

We think Peter Senge sums it up well: "When people genuinely care, they are actively committed. They are doing what they truly want to do. They are full of energy and enthusiasm. They persevere, even in the face of frustration and setbacks, because what they are doing is what they must do. It is their work."[12]

When we speak of "understanding" on the part of teachers, we are referring primarily to empathy, defined as "the ability to vicariously feel what another person is feeling, to understand and connect where that person is."[13] We agree with Arnold Goldstein that this capacity to understand/empathize is positively associated with a broad range of prosocial behaviors, such as cooperation, sociability, and interpersonal competence, and negatively associated with aggressive behavior.[14] It is so important for the teacher to know that each of her students is walking through the door with a myriad of social experiences from neglect to overindulgence. "While we do not advocate for the lessening of standards or expectations for students who may not be having a good day, we do think that getting inside a child's head and empathizing with what is there will go a long way toward fostering the kinds of relationships that promote higher achievement."

Humor

According to Rita Dunn, students who are global processors—those who see the big picture and learn better through anecdotes—need humor to function more effectively.[15] Roland Barth states that his personal vision of a great school is one that is characterized by humor, and we concur.[16] But teachers need to be aware that there is a fine line between appropriate and inappropriate humor. Poking fun at someone in an attempt to win students' favor is inappropriate. The ability to see humor in situations, and to laugh at oneself is key. Appropriate

humor makes people smile, it creates warmth in a classroom, it relaxes students, and it reverses the "fight-or-flight" response that many troubled students take with them into every class they enter.

Love of Children

It would seem obvious that all teachers must possess this quality to work in education. Unfortunately, we have encountered teachers and other staff members who leave us scratching our heads, wondering how and why these individuals ever chose—and were hired—to work with children. There are adults in our schools who do not like "other people's children" and do not like being around them. We absolutely have to prevent these individuals from entering the profession, or, if we mistakenly hire them, we must have the courage to weed them out.

Risking Closeness

Andy Hargreaves refers to the "emotional geographies of teaching"—the patterns of closeness and distance that shape the emotions we experience.[17] In his discussion of professional distance, he observes, "School teaching has become an occupation with a feminine caring ethic that is trapped within a rationalized and bureaucratic structure." This is the problem for educators working in politically sensitive environments. Teachers and administrators are often directed to distance themselves from children in order to avoid the risks of personal relationships. As Hargreaves notes, "The dilemma for teachers is that although they are supposed to care for their students, they are expected to do so in a clinical and detached way—to mask their emotions."[18] We know there is validity in establishing closeness, yet there are land mines all about the countryside. We can be safe and sterile or take a chance and create a warm, loving community of learners.

We wrote this article because we deeply believe in the concept of personal-relationship building. We wanted to add to the knowledge base regarding this valuable skill and to describe it in a way that makes it real—something you can see and feel, something that is coachable, and, above all, something that plays a key role in the teaching act. There used to be a myth that good teachers are born, not made, and that there is nothing one can do to help the unfortunate who do not have this natural ability. We disagree and believe that "being skillful means you can do something that can be seen; it means different levels of skill may be displayed by different individuals; and it means, above all, that you can learn how to do it and continue to improve at it."[19]

Notes

1. Robert J. Marzano and Jana S. Marzano, "The Key to Classroom Management," *Educational Leadership,* September 2003, p. 6.
2. Jon Saphier and Robert Gower, *The Skillful Teacher: Building Your Teaching Skills,* 5th ed. (Acton, Mass.: Research for Better Teaching, 1997).
3. Ibid, p. 345.
4. Richard P. Dufour and Robert E. Eaker, *Fulfilling the Promise of Excellence: A Practitioner's Guide to School Improvement* (Westbury, N.Y.: J. L. Wilkerson, 1987), p. 144.
5. Saphier and Gower, p. 348.
6. Steven Wolk, "Hearts and Minds: Classroom Relationships and Learning Interact," *Educational Leadership,* September 2003, p. 18.
7. James H. Stronge, *Qualities of Effective Teachers* (Alexandria, Va.: Association for Supervision and Curriculum Development, 2002).
8. Saphier and Gower, op. cit.
9. Ibid.
10. Stronge, op. cit.
11. Nancy Hoffman, "Toughness and Caring," *Education Week,* 28 March 2001, p. 42.
12. Peter M. Senge, *The Fifth Discipline* (New York: Doubleday, 1990), p. 148.
13. David A. Levine, *Teaching Empathy: A Social Skills Resource* (Accord, N.Y.: Blue Heron Press, 2000), p. 13.
14. Arnold P. Goldstein, *The Prepare Curriculum: Teaching Prosocial Competencies* (Champaign, Ill.: Research Press, 1999).
15. Rita S. Dunn, "The Dunn and Dunn Learning-Style Model and Its Theoretical Cornerstone," in Rita S. Dunn and Shirley A. Griggs, eds., *Synthesis of the Dunn and Dunn Learning-Style Model Research: Who, What, When, Where, and So What?* (Jamaica, N.Y.: St. John's University, 2003).
16. Roland S. Barth, "A Personal Vision of a Good School," *Phi Delta Kappan,* March 1990, pp. 512–16.
17. Andy Hargreaves, "Emotional Geographies of Teaching," *Teachers College Record,* vol. 103, 2000, pp. 1056–80.
18. Ibid., p. 1069.
19. Saphier and Gower, p. 3.

POSTNOTE

This article, written by two experienced administrators, makes several useful and practical points. It summarizes in vivid fashion important research on teacher-student relationships. In addition, it catalogs many attitudes and behaviors, such as teacher sarcasm and aloofness, that build barriers between teachers and their students. As such, the article can serve as a "teacher's self-evaluation" tool. That said, we do, however, raise one caveat.

One of the besetting mistakes of new teachers is in this area of teacher-student relationships. Further, much of the struggle and uncertainty experienced by first-year teachers is finding and becoming comfortable with a productive social distance between themselves and their students. A "productive" social distance is one that "produces" good results: students learn and feel good about themselves; and teachers achieve their learning goals and feel good about themselves. However, one very human flaw often gets in the way of beginning teachers. Instead of looking for the signs that their students are learning, they are looking for signs that their students *like* them. They are [often unknowingly] seeking love rather than respect. As the song says, they are "lookin' for love in all the wrong places." Settle for respect, and good relationships will most likely follow.

DISCUSSION QUESTIONS

1. What are the advantages and disadvantages of spending initial class time establishing rules and procedures?

2. Which method of "contacting students' personal world" do you admire most?

3. The authors speak of the dangers of involving oneself too closely in the personal lives of students. What are your views on this issue? In your own school experience, did you observe problematic examples of this?

RELATED WEBSITE RESOURCES AND VIDEO CASES

WEB RESOURCES:

Questia's Teacher-Student Relationship site. Available at:

http://www.questia.com/library/education/classroom-management/teacher-student-relationship.jsp.

This site is a treasure trove of books and articles on teacher-student relationships and many, many related topics.

 TEACHSOURCE VIDEO CASE

SECONDARY CLASSROOM MANAGEMENT: BASIC STRATEGIES

In this clip, James Turner, an American history teacher, discusses personal classroom management strategies, which are also demonstrated in the clips of his teaching. Go to the website for the Education Media Library at CengageBrain.com to watch the video clips, study the artifacts in the case, and reflect on the following questions.

1. How does the teacher in this video case handle teacher-student relationships?

2. Does the teacher remaining calm and firm in the face of violations of classroom rules help or hinder the situation?

5

Fostering Reflection

Lana M. Danielson

Lana M. Danielson is Chair of Teacher Education at the University of Nebraska, Omaha. 402-554-3465; ldanielson@unomaha.edu.

"Fostering Reflection," by Lana M. Danielson, 2009, *Educational Leadership* 66(5), Online. © 2009 by ASCD. Reprinted with permission. Learn more about ASCD at www.ascd.org.

FOCUS QUESTION

What is the role of reflection in the professional life of the teacher?

InTASC

Standard 9

KEY TERMS

- Deliberate Thinking
- Dialectical Thinking
- Situational Thinking
- Technological Thinking

Great teachers know when to make decisions quickly and when to step back and reflect.

Teachers face a myriad of daily choices: how to organize classrooms and curriculums, how to interpret students' behaviors, how to protect learning time, and so forth. Many choices involve matters so routine that a teacher can make and implement decisions automatically. Teachers make other decisions in the midst of an evolving situation after quickly reviewing the situation and recalling what has worked in similar scenarios. But teaching also involves complex choices about difficult problems that, if left unaddressed, often escalate. A different type of thinking is needed to address such choices. Tough choices call for teachers to engage in sophisticated reflection—including self-reflection.

Expert teachers adjust their thinking to accommodate the level of reflection a situation calls for. Their teaching is characterized by an intentional competence that enables them to identify and replicate best practice, refine serendipitous practice, and avoid inferior practice. Because of their ability to reflect, great teachers know not only *what* to do, but also why. Research (Constantino & De Lorenzo, 2001; Danielson & McGreal, 2000; Glickman, 2002; Lambert, 2003) substantiates the role of reflection in teachers' professional growth. A disposition toward reflection—and a good sense of when the teacher needs to step back and think deeply—should be part of all teachers' repertoires. How can we nurture this habit of mind?

Understanding Reflective Thinking

Reflective thinking in teaching is associated with the work of Dewey (1933, 1938), who suggested that reflection begins with a dilemma. Effective teachers suspend making conclusions about a dilemma in order to gather information, study the problem, gain new knowledge, and come to a sound decision. This deliberate contemplation brings about new learning.

In the 1970s, Lortie (1975) described how failing to reflect on teaching decisions leads to teaching by imitation rather than intentionality. People who enter the profession have already gone through 16 years of "apprenticeship of observation" as students themselves and have developed preconceived ideas of what teaching is through having watched others do it. They may sense *what* teachers do but have no grasp of *why* they do it. Other researchers (Clift, Houston, & Pugach, 1990; Hargreaves & Fullan, 1992) have reinforced how important it is for teachers to examine their own beliefs about their classroom practices.

Four Modes of Thinking

To understand the complexity of reflection, consider the four modes of thinking Grimmett proposed: technological, situational, deliberate, and dialectical (Danielson, 1992; Grimmett, Erickson, Mackinnon, & Riecken, 1990). I see these modes in a hierarchy from the lower-level reflection useful for making routine decisions to the higher-level reflection needed for complex dilemmas.

Each mode requires an increasing degree of conscious analysis and data seeking. Expert teachers adapt their reflective thinking to the situation, recognizing when each level of thought is sufficient to address a concern and when they need to move to the next mode.

The following teacher journal entries (drawn from my research) show examples of a teacher using each mode of thinking, sometimes inappropriately (Danielson, 1992).

Technological (or Formulaic) Thinking

Technological or formulaic thinking is based on prepackaged knowledge from an external source. It relies on practices that have proven efficient and effective. For example, teachers might adopt general policies and rules that are part of a school culture. In deciding how to teach a concept, curriculum teams might adopt standardized instructional procedures they believe will result in greater student learning.

Formulaic thinking works for many routine decisions: how a classroom teacher takes attendance,

transitions students from subject to subject, implements emergency drills, and so on. As long as routines function effectively, there is no need to change them. Likewise, there may be instructional practices that demand that the teacher follows a prescribed set of steps.

The following scenario, however, shows a teacher relying on formulaic thinking to make decisions when a more reflective style would suit her purpose better. Mary[1] is a novice teacher who has been given a plethora of curriculum materials. She shared her approach to lesson planning:

> When I start working on a unit, I just gather resource materials and start taking notes. I do outlines and headings of all the areas … [students] need to know about. I have here a whole stack of notes and things; it's not broken down into specific lessons. I see how far I get with it and how they handle it. When I thought about today's lesson, I was thinking about reviewing what I had already covered to jog their memories. I also try to highlight some realistic examples that they would find interesting and that would draw them in more, as attention getters.… I'm still dealing with the issue of how to get kids to respond to questions that I know they know the answers to.

Mary was conscientious in providing her students information she thought they needed to know and she used teaching techniques she had seen described in research articles: activating prior knowledge, including relevant examples, and asking questions. However, Mary's comments indicate that she didn't fully understand *why* these techniques might work or *how* she might use them more effectively.

For example, Mary reviewed the previous day's lesson "to jog their memories" but she didn't explicitly tie this material to the new lesson so students would see the connection. She asked questions she knew her students could answer, implying that she was thinking of questioning as another "attention-getting" technique rather than a strategy to ignite thinking. Mary's words indicate that she was not skilled at determining how to engage students actively in their own learning. By applying rules and procedures identified with good teaching in a formulaic way, Mary used her knowledge to direct, but not inform, her teaching.

Situational Thinking

When teachers make decisions using situational thinking, they focus only on information embedded in a specific context at a specific time, such as student behavior they are observing in the moment. They reflect quickly and act on a problem immediately. A teacher's day is full of appropriate opportunities for situational thinking. For example, when a student's behavior is off-task, the teacher might use a low level of intervention such as eye contact to remind the student to focus on work.

But situational thinking doesn't look beyond the surface to consider root causes of problems. If a teacher is unable to look beyond the realities of the immediate, frustrating situation, situational thinking can lead to spinning one's wheels rather than to quick reflection that halts a problem in its tracks.

In the following scenario, Teresa expresses frustration about make-up work and late assignments:

> Already many students have missed days so that they have make-up work. With all the responsibilities teachers have, worrying about make-up work is a real problem. Renee [Teresa's mentor] always tries to write down the things we do in class on a slip of paper for absent students so they have a list of what they missed for the class, but it just seems impossible to keep up with it. First of all, you have to mark in the grade book so that you remember they were gone, and then you have to remember that their assignment will probably not be on time again… . If parents realized this, they would be less likely to pull their children out for such trivial reasons as a vacation.

Teresa's mode of thinking is situational. She identified the problem of student absences by listing its immediately observable effects. She attributes all absences to "trivial" family activities and concludes that parents need better judgment. Although she does mention the effect absences have on students' learning, she doesn't explore alternatives for

addressing the problem, focusing more on the teacher's burden. Teresa needs to ask different questions that might lead to better results. In short, she needs a higher level of reflection.

Deliberate Thinking

With deliberate thinking, an educator purposefully seeks more information than the immediate context provides by, for example, revisiting theory, talking with colleagues, interviewing students or reviewing student records. The goal is to learn more to better understand the dilemma.

One of Beth's students resisted participating in class. Tony attended class regularly but sat removed from his peers and said little. Yet he did not appear shy, and Beth learned that he was quite verbal in other classes.

In thinking about what was going on with Tony, Beth looked beyond his immediate, irritating resistance. She listened to information from another teacher and considered her own teaching behaviors in a new light:

> Today I was working with this group on a short story. Every time I asked Tony a question, I'd get "I don't know." When my eyes left him, I guess he grinned at another kid. After about three rounds of this, Jane [Beth's mentor] took him to the hall to talk with him. After much prodding, he finally blurted out "She treats us like we're stupid! I know those dumb vocabulary words, and the stories we read are stupid 3rd grade stories."
>
> When Jane told me what Tony said, I felt awful. I kept thinking, "If I treat kids like they're stupid, that defeats my purpose." … This situation brings up the larger question. What do you do in a class [where] there are about five kids with average skills, about four who have low skills, and then about three who are simply behavior problems?

Beth did not blame Tony for being in a class that didn't challenge him. She generated possible reasons for Tony's conduct and comments. And she used his behavior as a prompt to assess her teaching and the ways she might be contributing to a less than ideal learning environment. Instead of becoming defensive or deciding that Tony's placement in a remedial class was the explanation for his stonewalling, she asked herself questions that led to new insights.

Although the scenarios discussed so far have highlighted problems, reflection is also a powerful way for teachers to understand why some kinds of instruction work so they can replicate them. If Beth's probing into how Tony was doing had shown he was actually making progress, deliberate thinking might have validated her current practices. However, when deliberate thinking generates more questions or indicates a change is needed, move to a higher level of reflection.

Dialectical Thinking

The dialectical mode builds on deliberate thinking to gain understanding of a situation and generate solutions. The greater a teacher's ability to suspend judgment and the broader the repertoire of pedagogical strategies, the more flexible dialectical thinking will be.

In the following scenario, Emily identifies a weakness in her instructional repertoire—her conferencing skills with student writers:

> In discussing each student's goals, I had a difficult time with eye contact. I was so nervous that I was forcing myself to look at [the students], and they started to get nervous and fidgety. Second, I talked so fast that there was no way they could have understood, but they pretended. The blank look and questioning eyes were a dead giveaway ... so one of my goals is to improve one-on-one dialogues.

In thinking about her first writing conferences, Emily employed situational thinking to describe the experience and identify weaknesses. Later, she engaged in deliberate thinking to gather information that would help her refine her skills. Talking with more experienced teachers and rereading texts on writers workshop process

helped her plan for the next conferences. A few weeks later, Emily wrote:

> I held miniconferences with my kids. We went over their journal entries, and I concentrated on praise. I searched for originality in my comments to each student, and it really was easier than before. I found myself asking more than telling, which is a much better approach and much more meaningful to them.

Dialectical thinking is characterized by a change in how the thinker conceptualizes a particular episode that results in new teaching behaviors. Emily used dialectical thinking to transform her teaching, implementing changes that brought about more productive writing conferences.

Refining the Skill of Reflection

All teachers can develop habits of mind conducive to effective decision making. Reflection is a skill that is best fostered with colleagues. Coworkers who demonstrate expertise in posing and solving problems often prove to be good mentors. They usually have the ability to listen analytically—focusing on key information that helps clarify what needs to be explored—and they have expanded repertoires of options.

Mentors should pose questions that lead their colleagues to ask productive questions themselves, to consider other sources of information that might provide additional insight, and to generate their own possible solutions. If the colleagues collaborate in drafting a plan for implementing change and formally schedule follow-up discussions, this will encourage the less experienced teacher to self-monitor and reflect further.

Another way to help teachers become better at reflection is to create study groups that introduce teachers to these four modes of thinking and explore which aspects of teaching call for each mode. Discussions and role-plays can help teachers see which routine decisions can be made through technological or situational thinking and which may require the deliberate or dialectical modes.

Identifying when different kinds of thinking are appropriate helps teachers use their time and mental energies wisely.

Finally, to foster higher levels of reflection, encourage teachers to ask themselves questions about their classroom practice. Prompts like the following promote frequent reflection:

- What worked in this lesson? How do I know?
- What would I do the same or differently if I could reteach this lesson? Why?
- What root cause might be prompting or perpetuating this student behavior?
- What do I believe about how students learn? How does this belief influence my instruction?
- What data do I need to make an informed decision about this problem?
- Is this the most efficient way to accomplish this task?

The four modes of thinking enable teachers to connect reflection to practical classroom applications. When the modes are used appropriately, they also help educators understand their own practice and, ultimately, foster the intentional competence necessary for accomplished teaching.

References

Clift, R. T., Houston, W. R., & Pugach, M. C. (Eds.). (1990). *Encouraging reflective practice in education: An analysis of issues and programs.* New York: Teachers College Press.

Constantino, P. M., & De Lorenzo, M. N. (2001). *Developing a professional teaching portfolio: A guide for success.* Boston: Allyn and Bacon.

Danielson, C., & McGreal, T. L. (2000). Teacher evaluation to enhance professional practice. Alexandria, VA: ASCD.

Danielson, L. M. (1992). *Exploring modes of thinking: A study of how student teachers reflect on their practice.* Unpublished doctoral dissertation, University of Iowa, Iowa City.

Danielson, L. M. (2008). Making reflective practice more concrete through reflective decision making. *The Educational Forum, 72,* 129–137.

Dewey, J. (1933). How we think: A restatement of the relation of reflective thinking to the educative process. New York: D.C. Heath.

Dewey, J. (1938). *Experience and education.* New York: MacMillan.

Glickman, C. D. (2002). Leadership for learning: How to help teachers succeed. Alexandria, VA.: ASCD.

Grimmett, P. P., Erickson, G. L., Mackinnon, A. A., & Riecken, T. J. (1990). Reflective practice in teacher education. In R. T. Clift, W. R. Houston, & M. C. Pugach (Eds.), *Encouraging reflective practice in education: An analysis of issues and programs* (pp. 20–38). New York: Teachers College Press.

Hargreaves, A., & Fullan, M. G. (1992). *Understanding teacher development.* New York: Teachers College Press.

Lambert, L. (2003). Leadership capacity for lasting school improvement. Alexandria, VA: ASCD.

Lortie, D. C. (1975). *Schoolteacher: A sociological study.* Chicago: University of Chicago Press.

Note

1. All names in this article are pseudonyms.

POSTNOTE

There is an old story about a braggart teacher trying to impress a new teacher with his vast professional experience. "I should know because I've had twenty-two years of classroom experience!" To which a colleague tartly responded, "Yeah, twenty-two years of repeating your first year of teaching over and over again."

Teaching, like most occupations, can become routine. We find some ways to reach our goals and settle in. Like golfers or tennis players, we develop an array of passable strokes and stop improving. In effect, we keep practicing our inadequate strokes or teaching behaviors. Besides being unfulfilling, such a situation is soul-killingly dull. This article points the way out of an all-too-common condition in education: settling for adequacy.

Reflective thinking or reflection is a habit of the mind, particularly the dialectical reflection described above. As with other habits, such as eating, exercising, relaxing, we can consciously take control and strengthen it. The most important steps are acknowledging the need for reflection on our teaching and committing hours to acquiring the habit. How and when to reflect on our work is a matter of personal circumstance and disposition. Many teachers regularly reflect in a journal that becomes a record of what worked and what didn't work. Others reflect in structured conversations with a colleague. And still others set aside a time daily for a quiet cup of coffee or tea to systematically review the day's experiences. What matters most, though, is establishing the habit.

DISCUSSION QUESTIONS

1. Why is dialectical reflection more valuable than the other three types?
2. What are the major barriers in a teacher's life to developing the habit of reflective thinking?

RELATED WEBSITE RESOURCES AND VIDEO CASES

WEB RESOURCES:

Becoming a Reflective Practitioner. Available at: http://www.education.umd.edu/teacher_education/sthandbook/reflection.html.

This site provides a useful primer for individuals who want to acquire the habit of reflective thinking.

Demonstrating Capacity for Reflective Practice: The Reflective Practitioner. Available at: http://www.lcsc.edu/education/teacherprep/standards/rp.shtml.

Focused on a number of issues, the Division of Education of Lewis-Clark State College maintains this site for its students and the profession in general.

▶❚❚ TEACHSOURCE VIDEO CASE

MENTORING FIRST-YEAR TEACHERS: KEYS TO PROFESSIONAL SUCCESS

In this video case, you will see a new teacher, Dania Diaz, working with a mentor teacher, Abdi Ali. First, Dania lays out her expectations to students for an upcoming lesson. Then we watch Dania raise a question in a faculty meeting about plagiarism. Related to the theme of this article, notice how Dania is developing the habit of reflecting on her practice. Go to the website for the Education Media Library at CengageBrain.com to watch the video clips, study the artifacts in the case, and reflect on the following questions.

1. Dania keeps a "reflective journal." Do you think it would be useful for her to regularly share her journal with her mentor, Abdi?
2. Having viewed Dania's interaction with her mentor, how comfortable do you believe you would be "opening up" your teaching to a mentor teacher?

6

Why New Teachers Leave …

Leslie Baldacci

Leslie Baldacci was a Teach For America teacher in the Chicago Public Schools from 1999 to 2005. She has been a reporter for the *Chicago Sun-Times*.

FOCUS QUESTION

What should a first-year teacher expect?

My classroom was just one deck chair on the Titanic. The kids ran wild. They swore, fought, refused to work. At assemblies they booed the principal. The only punishment was suspension, and that wasn't so terrible. As one of my students, Cortez, put it, "At least it's better than having to come up here."

This was seventh and eighth grade in a poverty-level, urban school on the South Side of Chicago. Our classes were bursting at the seams with 35, 36, and 37 kids apiece. Tough kids, many of them raising themselves in tough circumstances. There was barely room to walk around the classrooms for all the desks. When the kids were in the room, there was no room left. The noise and heat levels were like a steel mill.

I understand the teacher shortage and why one-third of new teachers quit after three years and nearly half bail out after five years. I believe my experience was more typical than extraordinary.

What was not typical about my experience was my background. As a newspaperwoman for 25 years, I had reported on Chicago's education crises long before the city's "school reform" effort started in the late 1980s. By 1999, Chicago's schools had improved their finances, halted a disastrous cycle of teacher strikes, fixed crumbling buildings, and put up new ones. Student test scores were beginning to improve. Yet, Mayor Daley worried about sustaining the momentum. He asked, "How do you know that we set the foundation and it's not going to fall back?"

I believed the answer lay in the front-line troops, teachers. So, after being accepted to the alternative certification program called Teachers For Chicago, I turned in my press credentials to become a teacher. The program would pay for my master's degree, minimize the requirements for entering graduate school, and put me in a classroom immediately as a teacher, with a mentor looking over my shoulder and working with me daily. I would earn $24,000 a year.

★ ★ ★

My school had two buildings—a beautiful old yellow brick school, built like a fortress in 1925, and another from the 1970s, a poured-concrete prefab shell three stories high. Built as a temporary solution to overcrowding, it had long ago outlived its intended lifespan. Over time, the windows had become a cloudy opaque, impossible to see in or out.

I walked in a side door, past a security guard who did not question me, and introduced myself to the ladies in the office as "the new Teachers For Chicago intern."

"Hello!" they said, friendly and smiling.

They paged the principal, who came right away and took me into his office to chat. He looked weary. His eyes were bloodshot. Above his desk, tufts of pink insulation poked through a hole where ceiling tiles were missing. Other tiles were water-stained.

When I asked the principal for copies of the books I'd be using when school started in eight weeks, he sighed heavily and folded his hands on his desk. It wasn't that simple, he said. He wasn't sure what grade I'd be teaching. He was still working on his organizational lineup for fall. He assured me that my Teachers For Chicago mentor would be in touch and help me with the details of getting set up.

In late July, when I stopped by the school again, the principal emerged from behind closed doors to level his bloodshot eyes at me and tell me he still wasn't sure what grade I was going to get, but it would definitely be fifth grade or higher. Two more teachers had quit, I later learned, and he had requested four additional Teachers For Chicago interns to fill the many empty spots on his organizational chart. The school's first experience with the nine-year-old internship program would place interns in eight of his classrooms. The poor man looked beleaguered. Running a school with 900 kids, 89 percent from poverty-level homes, had to be tough. Student achievement was low: At third grade, 86 percent of the student body was below grade level standards in reading and 79 percent was below

grade level in math. On top of that, experienced teachers were bailing out right and left.

It was precisely the setting I wanted. The optimist in me, by virtue of a scant six weeks of education training, thought, "What if this turns out to be a turning point for the school? What if all these new people coming in with their energy and ideas make a difference?"

"I'm counting on you," he told me. I pledged my allegiance with a handshake.

"Put me where you need me," I told him. I sent up a simple prayer, "Thy will be done."

About two weeks before school started I finally heard from my mentor; I would be teaching seventh grade in Room 118.

Room 118 was painted seafoam green, which didn't look nearly as putrid with the dark woodwork as the pink in the library across the hall. The ceilings were so high the room echoed. My desk had four drawers; my chair was broken. The cupboards were full of junk I would never use, coated with years of dust. There were 40 desks, which seemed excessive.

All the maps and the AV screen were pulled down. What was behind them? I clomped and creaked over the wood floors to the far corner of the room and tried to roll up the AV screen. A huge chunk of blackboard, ancient, heavy slate, jagged and lethal, lunged forward behind the screen, threatening to slash right through it. Behind the slate was exposed brick, internal walls, vintage 1925. Behind the maps were unsightly chalk boards ruined by years of wear and subsequent efforts to cover them with contact paper and other sticky stuff. What a mess.

★ ★ ★

I had never seen kids act like that in a classroom with an adult present. Throughout the first week, they talked incessantly. They shouted to be heard over the talking. They didn't do their work. They got up out of their seats without permission and wandered around, touching and bothering each other on their way. They shouted out questions and comments, including, "This is stupid." Any little ripple set off a chain reaction. Someone passed gas and everyone leapt from his seat fanning the air and jumping around. They threw things. They hit. I had broken up two fist fights already. They yelled out the window to their gang-banger friends and relatives, who gathered outside at dismissal time. They swore like sailors. I felt like the old woman who lived in the shoe; I had so many children I didn't know what to do. In addition to the 35 students in my homeroom, more than 100 other students, seventh- and eighth-graders, called me their English teacher.

And where was my backup? What were the consequences? Everyone I sent to the office bounced right back in. There was no detention. There had been no suspensions, even for fighting. I was beginning to think "alternative" schools for poorly behaved students were a myth made up by the board of education. Was my school an alternative school and no one told me about it?

All good questions, but ones I could not resolve. These were issues I needed to discuss with an experienced hand, but I had not seen much of my mentor. I felt like a prisoner in solitary confinement, thrown into a cell and forgotten. I was lucky to get to the bathroom in the course of a day.

★ ★ ★

A five-week reorganization brought new levels of angst. I had never heard of such a thing. My children had always had the same teacher from the first day of school to the last. There were no switcheroos unless someone had a baby or got sick. But apparently a principal has a right to shake things up through the fifth week of school. He can move teachers around and fine-tune the operation if things aren't going well. This, it seems, is an annual event at some schools.

That is how my colleague Astrid got switched from seventh-grade social studies to a sixth-grade, self-contained classroom and how Mr. Diaz joined the seventh- and eighth-grade team. Jennifer, an intern with a third-grade class, got switched to second grade.

Astrid was devastated at leaving her seventh-graders and starting over with a sixth-grade class. New faces, new books, new routines. And she had to teach every subject! Her seventh-graders gave her a farewell party. They took a collection and raised $13.00. Donna went to Sam's Club and bought a cake decorated with "Movin' On Up!" Astrid's new classroom was on the second floor.

When one intern explained to her third-graders that they were getting a new teacher, a student asked, "Why are you giving us up?" The enormity of the question caused the first-year teacher to lose her composure. She started to cry. Then the kids all started bawling. They spent the rest of the day watching a video. "We couldn't do anything else," she said. "We were wrecked."

Besides disrupting children's classroom situations, no one seemed to have given any thought to which children should or shouldn't be together. Most of the kids had been together since they were tiny. They had history together. Yet no teachers seemed to have been asked for insight on the group dynamic. At my children's public school, teachers met at the end of the school year to make their lists with an eye toward who worked well with whom and who needed to be separated.

Then again, at a school like mine with a 40 percent mobility rate, who knew who would be back? Year to year, five weeks into the year, changes came.

★ ★ ★

My students were ignorant of geography. They didn't know the states; they had vague ideas of continents. I decided to craft a research project around travel so they'd get some geography along with language arts. The project was planning their dream trip. I went to a couple of travel agents and grabbed every glossy brochure I could get my hands on.

They had to decide where they wanted to go and how far it was from Chicago. They had to determine the cost, pack a suitcase, and write an itinerary of sightseeing and other activities specific to their destination. They had to find out the currency, the language, what different foods they might eat, and what were good souvenirs to buy. They had to convert currency and account for time zones.

Destinations included Mexico, Jamaica, Africa, Wyoming, Florida, California, and England. The dream trip project, with its cross-curricular integrations of math and social studies, came in handy when, two days before first-quarter report card pickup, our principal informed Mr. Diaz and me that our worst fear had been realized: The seventh and eighth grades would no longer be departmentalized. No more changing classes. Each of us would teach all subjects to our homerooms. Starting that day.

Apparently, he had decided this some weeks before. He had informed the eighth-grade teachers the week before. "I should have told you, too. My fault. Apologies," he said curtly before turning on his heel and walking away.

We were in shock. Suddenly, we were on the hook for lesson plans in all subjects, coming up to speed on the curriculum, and teaching the lessons. But that was only a week-by-week crisis. The deeper crisis was whether or not we were up to the task of teaching our students in all subjects. Seventh-grade standardized test scores determine a child's high school options. What if my ineptitude kept someone from getting into an accelerated program or a better high school? I'd become comfortable with language arts. This new responsibility was daunting.

When my graduate school advisor came to observe just a few days later, she was so upset that she called for the mentor and the principal. "This is a joke," she informed them. She reminded the mentor that her job was to spend an hour each day in each intern's room, co-teaching and modeling for us how to teach. The mentor replied that she was the "disciplinarian."

"You're the mentor," my advisor told her. "If you can't do that job, maybe someone else should. And maybe if this school can't give these interns the support they need, Teachers For Chicago doesn't belong in this school."

I prayed they wouldn't pull us out. There were so many things I had learned already but much I still needed to find out. Why weren't there any television sets or VCRs? Why were there so few books in the library? Why didn't the upper grades get time in the computer lab? Were chronic, truly dangerous kids ever sent to alternative schools?

The bottom line was, I couldn't leave the class. The upset of the reorganization made me realize how desperately they needed continuity. There had to be some value in coming back day after day, trying hard, doing my best, even if my best was woefully inadequate. Those were the only terms under which I could ask the same from them.

After my advisor left, the principal and mentor returned to my room.

"Where's your fire escape plan?" asked my mentor.

"Hanging right there, by the door," I said, pointing to the pink sheets. The children watched, rapt.

"Where's your schedule?"

"Nichelle, please put up the map at the back of the room. The schedule is behind it."

"Where's your grading scale?"

"Bulletin board, lower right corner."

"Where's your time distribution chart?"

"I don't know what that is."

"You should have it posted in the classroom," she said. "Have it on my desk at eight o'clock tomorrow morning."

They turned and left.

★ ★ ★

Near the end of the school year, the principal informed me that I would be teaching second grade the following year. I assured him I would do my best.

I walked back to my classroom with conflicting emotions. We had filled out wish lists and I had asked for seventh grade again, feeling I could do better now that I knew the pitfalls. My second choice was sixth grade, my third choice fourth. Being sent to second grade, clearly not what I desired, looked like a punishment. Had I been such a dismal failure with my seventh-graders, self-contained in the largest classroom in the school with all of our personalities and problems? Surely someone else would have been a better teacher for them than I was. Was it criminal to leave them with me all year? Would I be equally as dismal with second-graders? My eyes were watery with tears.

★ ★ ★

While the whole group of interns was exhausted, as the oldest I may have been feeling it more than the others. And the fatigue was not just physical. It was mental as well. I was drained more every day by the limits of poverty, the unprofessional manner in which our school was run, the criticism, the nitpicking, the zero encouragement or respect. No one ever told you when you did a good job. It was like no other job situation I had ever experienced.

Toward the end of my second year of teaching, I did a mental count of the teacher interns who had come through the doors and who had left. By my tally, 16 interns came on board in my two years. All but five left in one circumstance or another. I had to find a more supportive school where I was viewed as competent and dedicated.

I made only one effort to find another job. I wrote to a principal who had come up to me after a speech I gave to the Annenberg Foundation a year before, a woman with a short blond Afro and fantastic jewelry who told me, "When you're done with your internship, call me. I like your attitude." Her school was known throughout the city as an exciting school that works for kids.

She called me soon after she received my letter to set up an interview. When I returned her call at 5:40 A.M., she answered the office phone herself. I was not surprised. By then, I understood the extraordinary dedication it took to be a strong school leader.

I set my sights on this school and this leader.

With bags under my eyes, wearing a ridiculous flowered dress and a jean jacket, I went for my interview at the new school. The day happened to be the day of the annual school carnival. I arrived as students were being dismissed. I couldn't believe how many children's names the principal knew. As the students left the building, they were walking, not running. Most were quiet, but if they were talking, it was in normal conversational tones, not screaming. At least 20 kids said to their principal as they left, "Thanks for the carnival."

The principal, vice principal, and I talked for nearly two hours. About teaching children. About testing. About assessment. About curriculum integration. About teams of teachers working collaboratively. The school, with corridors that looked like a museum of African art, had three bands, sports teams, afterschool dance and art programs, an entrepreneurship initiative and video club and book clubs, among other programs. We talked about a school paper and what they would like to see on a fifth-grade reading list.

I realized that I was poised on the brink of an excellent opportunity to see in action the kind of leadership that made this school stand out among 700 elementary schools in our city. I very much wanted to be part of an organization working hard, plowing forward. The faculty was dedicated, innovative, bright. Initiative was applauded. Everyone wore many hats. There were responsibilities to serve on committees, to formulate policies and philosophies. It was a unique team, constantly evolving, positive.

"I'm going to do something strange and forgo the secret conference with the vice principal and listen to my heart," the principal said. "I'm going to offer you the job right now."

I accepted the position on the spot, with sincere gratitude and humility.

POSTNOTE

Like the first year in many occupations (medicine, sales, the law), the career of teaching often has a taxing break-in period. This is complicated by the fact that new teachers are shocked by the strangeness of something that is quite familiar: being in school. The issue, and the problem, is that new teachers are in an entirely different role. Being on "the other side of the desk" can be a world away. One of the most difficult aspects of the work for many new teachers is being "in charge." They know about school. They know their subjects. They know what their students should be doing. They don't, however, know how to get them to do it. They have not had much experience being the boss or "the responsible person." Neither have they had much experience with directing others or with what the military would call giving orders. Necessity, however, is still the mother of invention, and most new teachers adapt in time.

Ms. Baldacci's experience, however, was particularly challenging. With minimal training and little support, she was assigned to an extremely difficult teaching situation. It would be dangerous to generalize from Ms. Baldacci's experiences, as many beginning teachers make the transition to teacher with success and joy.

DISCUSSION QUESTIONS

1. As a student, what memorable experiences did you have with new teachers? Describe them.
2. If and when you become a new teacher, what do you believe will be your most vulnerable areas?
3. What can you learn from this teacher's experience that may mitigate problems of your first year of teaching?

RELATED WEBSITE RESOURCES AND VIDEO CASES

WEB RESOURCES:

Teachers First. Available at:

http://www.teachersfirst.com.

This website is an extremely useful source of information, good ideas, lesson plans, and even humor. It is well organized and easy to search for the topic or need of choice.

 TEACHSOURCE VIDEO CASE

TEACHING AS A PROFESSION: COLLABORATION WITH COLLEAGUES

In this video case, you will hear teachers talk about the importance and the "how-to" of collaborating with colleagues. You will also see a formal collaborative work group in action. Go to the website for the Education Media Library at CengageBrain.com to watch the video clips, study the artifacts in the case, and reflect on the following questions.

1. How do the teachers' definitions of collaboration fit with your understanding of the concept?
2. Does the idea of the type of collaboration exhibited in this video case appeal to you? Why or why not?

 The companion website for this text includes useful study tools and resources. Go to CengageBrain.com to access links to relevant websites, glossaries, flashcards, an article review form, and more.

Students

Teaching is one of life's most complex activities. So much is involved: knowledge, attitudes, values, and skills to be learned; the process of instruction; and the management of the learning environment. To teach well, to be an effective educator, demands so much of our attention that an essential element in the teaching-learning process may be lost: the student.

The entire purpose of teaching is to make positive change in students. They are the main event, but sometimes teachers lose focus. We become so involved in the knowledge to be conveyed or in the process of instruction that we often lose sight of our students. We need to remind ourselves continually that the entire enterprise of education fails if the student is ill served. In addition, we need to remind ourselves constantly that each student has a different set of needs, preferences, and goals.

One thing that should help us stay attuned to the student is the fact that modern life regularly requires us all to become students. No longer is the term *student* reserved for a relatively few young people receiving formal education. With the explosion of education in the last quarter century, people continually move in and out of student status. A knowledge-based and information-oriented society such as ours requires continuous education. Whether it is acquiring computer literacy or learning how to run cooperative learning groups, we all return to being students from time to time. Having to struggle with new information or trying to master a new skill may be the best thing we can do to improve our teaching.

7

Why Don't Students *Like* School? Because the Mind Is Not Designed for Thinking

Daniel T. Willingham

Daniel T. Willingham is professor of cognitive psychology at the University of Virginia and author of numerous articles, including his regular "Ask the Cognitive Scientist" articles for *American Educator*. To read more of his work on education, go to www.danielwillingham.com. This article is excerpted from his new book,

FOCUS QUESTION

Why is "school thinking" so hard?

InTASC

Standards 1, 2, 3, 5, and 9

KEY TERMS

- Curiosity
- Long-term memory
- Thinking
- Working memory

Question: Most of the teachers I know entered the profession because they loved school as children. They want to help their students feel the same excitement and passion for learning that they did. They are understandably dejected when they find that some of their pupils don't like school much, and that they, the teachers, have great difficulty inspiring them. Why is it difficult to make school enjoyable for students?

Answer: Contrary to popular belief, the brain is not designed for thinking. It's designed to save you from having to think, because the brain is actually not very good at thinking. Thinking is slow and unreliable. Nevertheless, people enjoy mental work if it is successful. People like to solve problems, but not to work on unsolvable problems. If schoolwork is always just a bit too difficult for a student, it should be no surprise that she doesn't like school much. The cognitive principle that guides this article is: *People are naturally curious, but they are not naturally good thinkers; unless the cognitive conditions are right, people will avoid thinking.* The implication of this principle is that teachers should reconsider how they encourage their students to think in order to maximize the likelihood that students will get the pleasurable rush that comes from successful thought.

What is the essence of being human? What sets us apart from other species? Many would answer that it is our ability to reason—birds fly, fish swim, and humans think. (By "thinking," I mean solving problems, reasoning, reading something complex, or doing any mental work that requires some effort.) Shakespeare extolled our cognitive ability in *Hamlet*: "What a piece of work is man! How noble in reason!" Some 300 years later, however, Henry Ford more cynically observed, "Thinking is the hardest work there is, which is the probable reason why so few people engage in it."

They both had a point. Humans are good at certain types of reasoning, particularly in comparison with other animals. But we exercise that ability infrequently. A cognitive scientist would add another observation. Humans don't think very often because our brains are designed not for thought, but for the avoidance of thought. Thinking is not only effortful, as Ford noted, it's also slow and unreliable.

Your brain serves many purposes, and thinking is not the one it does best. Your brain also supports the ability to see and to move, for example, and these functions operate much more efficiently and reliably than our ability to think. It's no accident that most of your brain's real estate is devoted to them. The extra brain power is needed because seeing is actually more difficult than playing chess or solving calculus problems.

Compared with your ability to see and move, thinking is slow, effortful, and uncertain. To get a feel for why I say that, try this problem: In an empty room are a candle, some matches, and a box of tacks. The goal is to have the lit candle about five feet off the ground. You've tried melting some of the wax on the bottom of the candle and sticking it to the wall, but that wasn't effective. How can you get the lit candle to be five feet off the ground without your having to hold it there? Twenty minutes is the usual maximum time allowed and few people are able to solve it by then, although once you hear the answer you realize that it's not especially tricky. You dump the tacks out of the box, tack the box to the wall, and use it as a platform for the candle.

This problem illustrates three properties of thinking. First, thinking is *slow*. Your visual system instantly takes in a complex scene. When you enter a friend's backyard, you don't think to yourself, "Hmm … there's some green stuff. Probably grass, but it could be some other ground cover … and what's that rough brown object sticking up there? A fence, perhaps?" You take in the whole scene—lawn, fence, flower beds, gazebo—at a glance. Your

thinking system does not instantly calculate the answer to a problem the way that your visual system immediately takes in a visual scene.

Second, thinking is *effortful*; you don't have to try to see, but thinking takes concentration. You can perform other tasks while you see, but you can't think about something else while you work on a problem.

Third, thinking is *uncertain*. Your visual system seldom makes mistakes, and when it does, you usually think you see something similar to what is actually out there—you're close, if not exactly right. Your thinking system might not even get you close; your solution to a problem may be far from correct. In fact, your thinking system may not produce an answer at all, which is what happens to most people when they try the candle problem.

If we're all so bad at thinking, how does anyone hold down a job, or manage his money? How does a teacher make the hundreds of decisions necessary to get through her day? The answer is that, when we can get away with it, we don't think. Instead, we rely on memory. Most of the problems you face are ones you've solved before, so you just do what you've done in the past. For example, suppose next week a friend gives you the candle problem. You would immediately say, "Oh, right. I've heard this one. You tack the box to the wall." Just as your visual system takes in a scene and, without any effort on your part, tells you what is in the environment, so too your memory system immediately and effortlessly recognizes that you've heard the problem before and provides the answer. Most people think that they have a terrible memory, and it's true that your memory is not as reliable as your visual or movement systems—but your memory system is much more reliable than your thinking system, and provides answers quickly and with little effort.

We normally think of memory as storing personal events (e.g., memories of my wedding) and facts (e.g., George Washington was the first president of the United States). Your memory also stores procedures to guide what you should do: where to turn when you're driving home, how to handle a minor dispute when you're monitoring recess, what to do when a pot on the stove starts to boil over. For the vast majority of decisions you make, you don't stop to consider what you might do, reason about it, anticipate possible consequences, and so on. You do take such steps when faced with a new problem, but not when faced with a problem you've already encountered many times. That's because one more way that your brain saves you from having to think is by changing.

If you repeat the same thought-demanding task again and again, it will eventually become automatic; your brain will change so that you can complete the task without thinking about it. When you feel as though you are "on autopilot," even if you're doing something rather complex, such as driving home from your school, it's because you are using memory to guide your behavior. Using memory doesn't require much of your attention, so you are free to daydream, even as you're stopping at red lights, passing cars, watching for pedestrians, and so on.

For education, the implications of this section sound rather grim. If people are bad at thinking and try to avoid it, what does that say about their attitudes toward school? Fortunately, despite the fact that we're not that good at it, we actually *like* to think. But because thinking is so hard, the conditions have to be right for this curiosity to thrive, and we quit thinking rather readily. The next section explains when we like to think and when we don't.

People Are Naturally Curious, But Curiosity Is Fragile

Even though our brains are not set up for very efficient thinking, people actually enjoy mental activity, at least in some circumstances. They have hobbies like solving crossword puzzles or scrutinizing maps. They watch information-packed documentaries. They pursue careers—such as teaching—that offer greater mental challenge than competing careers, even if the pay is lower. Not only are they willing to think, they intentionally seek out situations that demand thought.

Solving problems brings pleasure. When I say "problem solving" here, I mean any cognitive work that succeeds; it might be understanding a difficult passage of prose, planning a garden, or sizing up an investment opportunity. There is a sense of satisfaction, of fulfillment, in successful thinking. In the last 10 years, neuroscientists have discovered that there is overlap in the brain areas and chemicals that are important in learning and those that are important in the brain's natural reward system. Many neuroscientists suspect that the two systems are related, even though they haven't worked out the explicit tie between them yet. It's notable too that the pleasure is in the *solving* of the problem. Working on a problem with no sense that you're making progress is not pleasurable. In fact, it's frustrating. And there's not great pleasure in simply knowing the answer either. I told you the solution to the candle problem; did you get any fun out of it? Think how much more fun it would have been if you had solved it yourself—in fact, the problem would have seemed more clever, just as a joke that you get is funnier than a joke that has to be explained. Even if someone doesn't tell you the answer to a problem, once you've had too many hints you lose the sense that *you've* solved the problem and getting the answer doesn't bring the same mental snap of satisfaction.

Mental work appeals to us because it offers the opportunity for that pleasant feeling when it succeeds. But not all types of thinking are equally attractive. People choose to work crossword puzzles, but not algebra problems. A biography of the vocalist Bono is more likely to sell well than a biography of the poet Keats. What characterizes the mental activity that people enjoy? The answer most people would give may seem obvious. "I think crossword puzzles are fun and Bono is cool, but math is boring and so is Keats." In other words, it's the content that matters. But I don't think that content drives interest. We've all attended a lecture or watched a TV show (perhaps against our will) about a subject we thought we weren't interested in, only to find ourselves fascinated. And it's easy to get bored even when you usually like the topic. I'll never forget my anticipation for the day my middle school teacher was to talk about sex. As a teenage boy in a staid 1970s suburban culture, I fizzed with anticipation of any talk about sex, anytime, anywhere. But when the big day came, my friends and I were absolutely disabled with boredom. It's not that the teacher talked about flowers and pollination, he really did talk about human sexuality, but somehow it was still dull. I actually wish I could remember how he did it; boring a bunch of hormonal teenagers with a sex talk is quite a feat.

So if content is not enough to keep your attention, when does curiosity have staying power? The answer may lie in the difficulty of the problem. If we get a little burst of pleasure from solving a problem, then there's no point in working on a problem that is too easy—there'll be no pleasure when it's solved because it didn't feel like much of a problem in the first place. Then too, when you size up a problem as very difficult, you are judging that you're unlikely to solve it, and therefore unlikely to get the satisfaction that would come with the solution. So there is no inconsistency in claiming that people avoid thought and in claiming that people are naturally curious—curiosity prompts people to explore new ideas and problems, but when they do, they quickly evaluate how much mental work it will take to solve the problem. If it's too much or too little, people stop working on the problem if they can.

Our analysis of the sorts of mental work that people seek out or avoid provides one answer to why more students don't like school. Working on problems that are at the right level of difficulty is rewarding, but working on problems that are too easy or too difficult is unpleasant. Students can't opt out of these problems the way that adults often can. If the student routinely gets work that is a bit too difficult, it's little wonder that he doesn't care much for school. So what's the solution? Give the student easier work? You could, but of course you'd have to be careful not to make it so easy that the student would be bored. And anyway, wouldn't it be better to boost the student's ability a little bit? Instead of making the work easier, is it possible to make thinking easier?

How Thinking Works

Understanding a bit about how thinking happens will help you understand what makes thinking hard. That, in turn, will help you understand how to make thinking easier for your students, and therefore help them enjoy school more.

Just about the simplest model of the mind possible

★ ★ ★

Environment ⟶ **Working Memory**
(site of awareness
and thinking)

↓

Long-Term Memory
(factual knowledge and
procedural knowledge)

Let's begin with a very simple model of the mind. The figure above shows the environment on the left, full of things to see and hear, problems to be solved, and so on. On the right is one component of your mind that scientists call *working memory*; it holds the stuff that you're thinking about and is the part of your mind where you are aware of what is around you: the sight of a shaft of light falling on a dusty table, the sound of a dog barking in the distance, and so forth. Of course, you can also be aware of things that are not currently in the environment; for example, you can recall the sound of your mother's voice, even if she's not in the room (or indeed, no longer living). *Long-term memory* is the vast storehouse in which you maintain your factual knowledge of the world: that ladybugs have spots, that triangles are closed figures with three sides, that your 3-year-old surprised you yesterday by mentioning kumquats, and so on. All of the information in long-term memory resides outside of awareness. It lies quietly until it is needed, and then enters working memory, and so becomes conscious.

Thinking occurs when you combine information (from the environment and from long-term memory) in new ways. That combination happens in working memory. To get a feel for this process, think back to what you did as you tried to solve the candle problem. You began by taking information from the environment—the scenario described in the problem—and then you imagined ways to solve it.

Knowing *how* to combine and rearrange ideas in working memory is essential to successful thinking. If you hadn't seen the candle problem before, you probably felt like you were pretty much guessing. You didn't have any information in long-term memory to guide you. But if you have had experience with a particular type of problem, then you likely have information in long-term memory about how to solve it, even if the information is not foolproof. For example, try to work this math problem in your head:

18

×7

You know just what to do for this problem. Your long-term memory not only contains factual information, such as the value of 8 × 7, it also contains what we'll call *procedural knowledge*, which is your knowledge of the mental procedures necessary to execute tasks. If "thinking" is combining information in working memory, then procedural knowledge is a list of what to combine and when—it's like a recipe to get a particular type of thought accomplished. You might have stored procedures for the steps needed to calculate the area of a triangle, or to duplicate a computer file using Windows, or to drive from your home to work.

It's pretty obvious that having the appropriate procedure stored in long-term memory helps a great deal when we're thinking. That's why it was easy to solve the math problem and hard to solve the candle problem. But how about factual knowledge? Does that help you think as well? It does, in several different ways. Note that solving the math problem required the retrieval of factual information, such as the fact that 8 × 7 = 56 or the fact that 18 can be broken into 10 and 8. Oftentimes, the information provided in the environment is not sufficient to solve a problem—you

need to supplement it with information from long-term memory.

There's a final necessity for thinking: sufficient space in working memory. Thinking becomes increasingly difficult as working memory gets crowded. A math problem requiring lots of steps, for example, would be hard to solve in your head because the steps would occupy so much space in working memory that it would be difficult to keep them all in mind.

In sum, successful thinking relies on four factors: information from the environment, facts in long-term memory, procedures in long-term memory, and space in working memory. If any one of them is inadequate, thinking will likely fail.

What Does This Mean for the Classroom?

Let's begin with the question that opened this article: what can teachers do to make school enjoyable for students? From a cognitive perspective, an important factor is whether a student consistently experiences the pleasurable rush of solving a problem. So, what can teachers do to ensure that each student gets that pleasure?

Be Sure That There Are Problems to Be Solved

By "problem," I don't necessarily mean a question posed to the class by the teacher, or a mathematical puzzle. I mean cognitive work that presents a moderate challenge, including things like understanding a poem or thinking of novel uses for recyclable materials. This sort of cognitive work is, of course, the main stuff of teaching—we want our students to think. But without some attention, a lesson plan can become a long string of teacher explanations, with little opportunity for students to solve problems. So scan each lesson plan with an eye toward the cognitive work that students will be doing. How often does such work occur? Is it intermixed with cognitive breaks? When you have identified the challenges, consider whether they are open to negative outcomes like the students failing to understand what they are to do, or students being unlikely to solve the problem, or students simply trying to guess what you would like them to say or do.

Respect Students' Limited Knowledge and Space in Working Memory

When trying to develop effective mental challenges for your students, bear in mind the cognitive limitations discussed here. For example, suppose you began a history lesson with a question: "You've all heard of the Boston Tea Party; why do you suppose the colonists dressed as Indians and dumped tea in the Boston harbor?" Do your students have the necessary background knowledge in memory to consider this question? What do they know about the relationship of the colonies and the British crown in 1773? Do they know about the social and economic significance of tea? Could they generate reasonable alternative courses of action? If they lack the appropriate background knowledge, the question you pose will quickly be judged as "boring." If students lack the background knowledge to engage with a problem, save it for another time when they have the knowledge they need.

Equally important is the limit on working memory. Remember that people can only keep so much information in mind at once. Overloads to working memory are caused by things like multistep instructions, lists of unconnected facts, chains of logic more than two or three steps long, and the application of a just-learned concept to new material (unless the concept is quite simple). The solution to working memory overloads is straightforward: slow the pace and use memory aids, such as writing on the blackboard, that save students from keeping as much information in working memory.

Identify Key Questions and Ensure That Problems Are Solvable

How can you make the problem interesting? A common strategy is to try to make the material "relevant" to students. This strategy sometimes works well, but it's hard to use for some material. I remember my daughter's math teacher telling me that he liked to use "real world" problems to capture his students' interest, and gave an example from geometry that entailed a ladder propped against a house. I didn't think that would do much for my 14-year-old. Another difficulty is that a teacher's class may include two football fans, a doll collector, a NASCAR enthusiast, a horseback riding competitor—you get the idea. Our curiosity is provoked when we perceive a problem that we believe we can solve. What is the question that will engage students and make them want to know the answer?

One way to view schoolwork is as a series of *answers*. We want students to know Boyle's law, or three causes of the U.S. Civil War, or why Poe's raven kept saying "Nevermore." Sometimes I think that we, as teachers, are so eager to get to the answers that we do not devote sufficient time to developing the question. But it's the *question* that piques people's interest. Being told an answer doesn't do anything for you. When you plan a lesson, you start with the information you want students to know by its end. As a next step, consider what the key question for that lesson might be, and how you can frame that question so that it will be of the right level of difficulty to engage your students, and will respect your students' cognitive limitations.

Reconsider When to Puzzle Students

Teachers often seek to draw students in to a lesson by presenting a problem that they believe interests students, or by conducting a demonstration or presenting a fact that they think students will find surprising. In either case, the goal is to puzzle students, to make them curious. This is a useful technique, but it's worth considering whether these strategies might also be used not at the beginning of a lesson, but *after* the basic concepts have been learned. For example, a classic science demonstration is to put a burning piece of paper in a milk bottle and then put a boiled egg over the bottle opening. After the paper burns, the egg is sucked into the bottle. Students will no doubt be astonished, but if they don't know the principle behind it, the demonstration is like a magic trick—it's a momentary thrill, but one's curiosity to understand may not be long lasting. Another strategy would be to conduct the demonstration after students know that warm air expands and that cooling air contracts, potentially forming a vacuum. That way they can use their new knowledge to think about the demonstration, which is no longer just a magic trick.

Act on Variations in Student Preparation

I don't accept that some students are "just not very bright." But it's naïve to pretend that all students come to your class equally prepared to excel; they have had different preparation, as well as different levels of support at home, and they will, therefore, differ in their current abilities. If that's true, and if what I've said in this article is true, it is self-defeating to give all of your students the same work or to offer all of them the same level of support. To the extent that you can, I think it's smart to assign work to individuals or groups of students that is appropriate to their current level of competence, and/or to offer more (or less) support to students depending on how challenging you think they will find the assignment. Naturally, one wants to do this in a sensitive way, minimizing the extent to which these students will perceive themselves as behind the others. But the fact is that they *are* behind the others; giving them work that is beyond them is unlikely to help

them catch up, and is likely to make them fall still further behind.

Change the Pace

Change grabs attention, as you no doubt know. When you change topics, start a new activity, or in some other way show that you are shifting gears, virtually every student's attention comes back to you. So plan these shifts and monitor your class's attention to see whether you need to make them more often or less frequently.

Keep a Diary

The core idea presented in this article is that solving a problem gives people pleasure, but the problem must be easy enough to be solved yet difficult enough that it takes some mental effort. Finding this sweet spot of difficulty is not easy. Your experience in the classroom is your best guide. But don't expect that you will remember how well a lesson plan worked a year later. When a lesson goes brilliantly well or down in flames, it feels at the time that we'll never forget what happened; but the ravages of memory can surprise us, so write it down. Even if it's just a quick scratch on a sticky note, try to make a habit of recording your success in gauging the level of difficulty in the problems you pose for your students.

For Further Reading

Mihaly Csikszentmihalyi, *Flow: The Psychology of Optimal Experience* (New York: Harper Perennial, 1990). The author describes the ultimate state of interest, when one is completely absorbed in what one is doing to the point that time itself stops. The book does not tell you how to enter this state yourself, but is an interesting read in its own right.

Steven Pinker, *How the Mind Works* (New York: W. W. Norton, 1997). This book covers not only thinking, but emotion, visual imagery and other related topics. Pinker is a wonderful writer, and draws in references from many academic fields, and from pop culture. Not for the fainthearted, but great fun if the topic appeals to you.

Why Don't Students *Like* School? Because the Mind Is Not Designed for Thinking

47

POSTNOTE

Let's face it. Stuffing twenty or so energetic, stimulation-hungry children in classrooms for six or seven hours a day is ... well ... "unnatural." Their natures call out for excitement and action. In the long history of mankind, packing children into desks for hours and hours, month after month and subjecting them to instruction is a recent idea. Before the invention of schools, children learned at their parent's knee or from other adults in the village. As life has become more complex and people need to know more and be able to perform more complex task (e.g., how to reads the manual for a new tractor, download software to their computer or work their way through the income tax form), schools, classrooms and, yes, teachers seemed to be an efficient social solution. Whether the school, as we currently know it, is the most efficient way to educate in the coming age of high-tech, computer-delivered education is a question which will be answered in the next decade or so.

In the meantime, this essay provides an array of useful principles and suggestions for dealing with a current and widespread condition: children who are bored, frustrated or otherwise turned off by school. While hardly a new phenomenon, the situation has been enhanced in recent years by children's extensive exposure to television, the Internet and other electronic media. Years ago, media guru Marshall McLuhan claimed that when children come to school, they interrupt their "first education," their media-delivered education. Professor Willingham's distillation of principles from recent research in cognitive psychology is welcome information as teachers try to reach and engage students in mastering all the "boring, unexciting stuff" they will need to succeed in the world today. Work toward a good question, rather than a good answer.

DISCUSSION QUESTIONS

1. How do you evaluate the author's analysis of why so many students don't like school?
2. What are his key solutions to more fully engage students in learning?
3. Consider some content you may want to teach. Now, how would you apply the author's suggestions to teach that particular content?

RELATED WEBSITE RESOURCES

WEB RESOURCES:

Daniel T. Willingham. Available at:

http://www.danielwillingham.com/index.html.

This website provides a great deal of information about the thoughts of Professor Willingham. It links to his recent writings, his biography and several excellent lectures on current educational topics.

Mihaly Csikszentmihalyi on flow. TED: Ideas Worth Spreading. Available at:

http://www.ted.com/talks/mihaly_csikszentmi halyi_on_flow.html.

Professor Mihaly Csikszentmihalyi in this lecture describes the ultimate state of interest, when one is completely absorbed in what one is doing to the point that time itself stops.

8

How We Treat One Another in School

Donna M. San Antonio and Elizabeth A. Salzfass

Donna M. San Antonio is the Executive Director of Appalachian Mountain Teen Project, in Wolfeboro, New Hampshire. **Elizabeth A. Salzfass** is program and evaluation coordinator for Responsive Advocacy for Life and Learning in Youth (RALLY), and community service learning coordinator with Peace Games, Boston, Massachusetts.

"How We Treat One Another in School," by Donna M. San Antonio and Elizabeth A. Salzfass, 2007, *Educational Leadership* 64(8), pp. 32–38. © 2007 by ASCD. Reprinted with permission. Learn more about ASCD at www.ascd.org.

FOCUS QUESTION

Why do so many students experience the effects of bullying?

InTASC
Standards 2, 3, 5, and 6

KEY TERM

- Cyberbullying

When rising middle school students are asked to name their biggest worry about going to a new school, they most often answer, "That I will not have any friends" or "That people will make fun of me" (San Antonio, 2004). The prospect of being friendless or getting teased looms large for many students at this age and can profoundly affect their sense of affiliation with school. Students tell us with heartbreaking regularity of the pain and anger they feel when their peers do not see them, include them, or care about them. At the extreme, some students not only are treated with indifference but also become targets of bullying.

Devastating Effects

Olweus (1993) defines bullying as verbal, physical, or psychological abuse or teasing accompanied by real or perceived imbalance of power. Bullying most often focuses on qualities that students (and the broader society) perceive to be different from the established norm, such as expected gender specific behavior for boys and girls, dress and physical appearance, and manner of speaking. Bullying is connected to diversity, and reducing bullying means taking steps to make the community and the school safe for diversity of all kinds.

Research indicates that bullying—with its accompanying fear, loss of self-efficacy, anger, and hurt—negatively affects the school environment and can greatly diminish students' ability to engage actively in learning (Hoover & Oliver, 1996). Being bullied has been linked with high rates of school absence (Fried & Fried, 1996); dropping out of school (Weinhold & Weinhold, 1998); and low self-esteem, anxiety, and depression (Banks, 1997). A U.S. Department of Education study (1998) found that students who had experienced sustained threats and verbal and physical peer aggression carried out two-thirds of school shootings.

Some researchers and practitioners believe that the impact of bullying is as devastating and life changing as that of other forms of trauma, such as physical abuse. The effects of bullying may linger long into the victims' adulthood (Kaltiala-Heino, Rimpelae, Rantanen, & Rimpelae, 2000). Recent research has documented increased levels of depression and anxiety in adults who had been bullied in their youth (Gladstone, Parker, & Malhi, 2006).

Because of the documented harmful effects of bullying—as well as other forms of social isolation—on school climate and student achievement, educators are taking this problem seriously. Many schools have explored the benefits of implementing school-wide programs to promote social and emotional learning, prevent bullying, and nurture positive peer relationships. A survey of middle school students that we recently conducted in three schools provides information on bullying behavior that can inform such programs.

A Middle School Survey on Bullying

To measure students' experience with physical, verbal, and relational[1] bullying, we administered surveys in spring 2006 to 211 7th and 8th grade students in three K–8 schools in New England. The three schools differ significantly by race, socioeconomic status, and urbanicity. Rural School,[2] located in a small town, serves a student population that is socioeconomically diverse but is 94 percent white; 25 percent of the students are eligible for free or reduced-price lunch. Big City School is located in a low-income urban neighborhood and serves primarily Latino (65 percent) and black (33 percent) students; 93 percent are eligible for free or reduced-price lunch. Small City School has a socioeconomically and ethnically diverse student body composed of 40 percent white, 36 percent black, 11 percent Latino, and 10 percent Asian students; 30 percent of the students are eligible for free or reduced-price lunch.

We surveyed nearly all the students in each grade, with the exception of 8th graders at Rural School, where we were able to survey only half of the class. The surveys included multiple-choice and open-ended questions. Respondents were evenly split between boys and girls. Most of our findings were consistent with what other research has found and what middle grades teachers know about bullying in the adolescent years. Some of our most significant findings follow.

Extent of Bullying

Most students (76.5 percent) felt safe most of the time. However, students at Big City School reported feeling safe much less often than did their peers at the other two schools (65 percent, compared with 83 percent at Small City School and 81 percent at Rural School). They also feared bullying more, even though students at Rural School reported seeing it occur more often. We believe this reflects the greater incidence of community violence to which Big City School students are exposed.

Rural School was the only school in which a majority of students (about 2 in 3) said that bullying was a serious problem. Many of the respondents from Rural School spoke about the difference between physical and emotional safety. As one 7th grade girl said, "I feel safe physically but my emotions take a blow here."

In terms of grade level, bullying was more common for 7th graders than for 8th graders at the three schools we surveyed, with two notable exceptions: Verbal bullying affected 8th grade girls more than any other subgroup at Small City School, and physical violence affected 8th grade boys and girls more than 7th graders at Big City School.

Finally, across schools, boys and girls experienced physical and verbal bullying to a similar extent, but girls experienced more relational bullying than boys did. Girls at all three schools worried more often than boys that if they did or said something wrong, their friends would gang up on them and decide not to be their friends. This problem appeared to be most dire for girls at Rural School: A full 72 percent of them reported suffering relational bullying either "every once in a while," "often," or "every day," compared with 58 percent of girls at Big City School and 48 percent at Small City School. This finding raises the question of the effect of socioeconomic status and cultural background on the bullying phenomenon. The almost entirely white population of girls at the school with the widest gap between wealthy and poor students was the group most at risk of relational aggression.

Boys were more likely to admit to bullying other students than girls were (which may have something to do with the way bullying is traditionally defined), but no significant gender difference was expressed overall when we asked students whether boys or girls bullied other students more. We also found that boys bullied both boys and girls, whereas girls typically only bullied other girls. We were troubled by girls' graphic narrative responses that demonstrated that boys often bullied girls with demeaning comments about the girls' appearance and demands for sexual interactions, particularly oral sex.

Location of Bullying

In all three schools, bullying happened most frequently in the hallways. When asked how to mitigate bullying at their school, many students suggested putting more adult supervisors in the hallways between classes. The second most common place in which bullying occurred differed across the three schools. At Big City School, bullying tended to happen in the bathrooms, where there was generally no adult supervision. At Small City School and Rural School, bullying happened on the playground and in the cafeteria, both places where adults were on duty.

Reasons Students Are Bullied

Students at all three schools perceived that "being overweight" and "not dressing right" were the most common reasons an individual might be bullied. At Small City School and Rural School, the second most common reason stated was being

perceived as gay, which suggests rigid behavior expectations for boys and girls. Many students commented that someone might be a target for bullying if they look or act "different" or "weird."

Students' Reactions to Bullying

The most common strategies students reported using when confronted by bullies were walking away, saying mean things back, hitting back, or telling the bully to stop. The least common strategy was telling an adult at the school. Hitting back was a particularly popular response to bullying at Big City and Small City Schools, particularly among the boys. Given steadily increasing numbers of violent deaths over the last few years in many urban communities, we believe that this finding highlights the importance that urban youth put on maintaining a tough appearance to survive, as well as a perceived lack of options for nonviolent conflict resolution.

Student reactions to bullying also differed according to gender. More boys than girls believed that they had the right to use violence to protect themselves from physical violence or someone hurting their feelings or reputations. Girls reported being more likely to help a victim of bullying than boys did and more often said that bullying is wrong.

Inadequate Adult Response

Most students said they were not confident that adults could protect them from being bullied. Students at Rural School had more faith that their teachers could stop the bullying when they were told about it than did students at the other two schools. However, students in this school agreed with their urban peers that teachers did not seem to notice bullying and did not take it seriously enough. Most students said they wanted teachers to be more aware of all types of bullying and to intervene more often. These findings are consistent with past research in which students reported that most bullying goes undetected by school staff (Skiba & Fontanini, 2000).

When we talk with students in a variety of settings, they have many thoughts about how adults can help to make school safer and stop bullying. They frequently answer with statements like these: "Watch out for us and don't ignore us." "Pay attention." "Just ask us what's wrong." "Talk to the students who have been bullied to see how to stop it." "Start caring more." "Believe us." "Punish the bullies." "Do something instead of nothing." One thing seems certain: Most students want adults to see what is going on in their world and respond to bullying in caring, effective, and firm ways.

What Schools Can Do

The following recommendations for a schoolwide approach to bullying prevention are derived from our review of the literature, our survey findings, and a report generated by Northwest Regional Educational Laboratory (Railsback & Brewster, 2001). All sources agree that schoolwide strategies must complement classroom curriculum. Schools should not frame the issue of how students and educators treat one another as an issue of behavior. Instead, they should opt for a more comprehensive set of goals that address social and moral development, school and classroom climate, teacher training, school policies, and community values, along with student behavior.

Conduct an Assessment

The first step toward creating an effective schoolwide antibullying program is identifying where, when, and how students experience bullying at a particular school. As our study demonstrated, different types of bullying occur with different frequency and magnitude among different populations in different school settings; therefore, a one-size-fits-all approach is not an appropriate solution. Schoolwide bullying intervention programs are more purposeful and relevant when they are informed by students' views. We strongly recommend using a participatory action research approach that involves students in framing a problem statement; constructing a survey; summarizing, analyzing, and reporting the results; and

generating ideas for how staff and students can respond to the issues uncovered by the survey.

Create a Committee to Focus on School Relationships

A committee involving students, parents, and community members along with school staff should focus on schoolwide relationships, not only on student bullying. This committee will assist the school in generating developmentally and culturally sound prevention and intervention ideas.

Implement an Antibullying Policy

When asked what teachers could do to stop bullying, many of the students we surveyed said that teachers should be stricter with bullies. An effective policy should be developed through collaboration among students, teachers, parents, and administrators.

Pepler and Craig (2000) say that a whole-school policy is the foundation of antibullying interventions, and they recommend that a policy include the following: a schoolwide commitment to address bullying; a statement of rights and responsibilities for all members of the school community; a definition of bullying, including types and dynamics; the process for identifying and reporting bullying; expected ways for students and staff to respond to bullying; strategies that will be implemented; and a way to assess the effectiveness of antibullying efforts.

Train All School Employees

Bullying can be subtle and hard to detect, making it challenging for adults to intervene effectively. To stop bullying, school staff (including custodians, clerical staff, bus drivers, and lunchroom staff) must first have an opportunity to discuss the various ways and locations in which bullying occurs. From there, they can develop structures for communicating across roles within a school district and decide on an appropriate unified response. Considering that the majority of students in our study did not believe they could count on adults to protect them from being bullied, ongoing training and communication in this area is key. For students to develop positive attitudes toward school, they need to know that all staff members are committed to making it a safe and friendly environment.

Help the Bullied and the Bullies

Another step in implementing a schoolwide antibullying program involves providing resources for those most affected by bullying. Many of the students we surveyed who had experienced bullying said that they wanted adults to listen to their stories. Some schools have had success with facilitating groups in which students address issues directly with their peers. The PALS program at Rocky Mountain Middle School in Idaho trains teachers to facilitate these groups, which increase communication and social skills and give stigmatized students a chance to experience a positive interpersonal connection with others and with the school.

Some students who are highly involved in bullying (either as perpetrators or victims) will need one-to-one support. It is important to involve parents and provide referrals for mentoring or counseling. Journaling with a teacher or counselor who reads and replies to concerns and issues may help particularly reticent students. Connecting students to after-school and summer programs will enable them to socialize with their peers outside of the school and form new friendships.

When children have been treated unfairly or violently in their primary relationships, it can be difficult for them to understand why they and their peers should be treated with respect. Nakkula and Selman (1991) describe an effective intervention called *pair counseling* as a way for two children who have difficult peer relationships to come together with the help of a counselor to negotiate differences and learn how to be a friend.

Recognize and Name All Forms of Bullying

Be aware of the relationships among students and of shifts in cliques and friendships as much as possible. Look for subtle signs of relational aggression that may occur between students, such as whispering, spreading rumors, and exclusion. Let students know that comments and actions against any racial, ethnic, or social group will not be tolerated. Be prepared to explain your ethical position to your students. The students we surveyed suggested that teachers ask students what would benefit them and help students generate realistic and effective ideas. On this topic, one 7th grade girl wrote,

> Teachers do everything, I think, in their power, but if they would just listen to the person who says they're being bullied, instead of just saying "stay away from them" or "ignore it" maybe we would see some change.

Reclaim Goodness

School classrooms and corridors contain a full spectrum of behavior, from countless everyday small acts of kindness to serious acts of aggression. In our effort to mitigate negative student behavior, a commonly overlooked but essential aspect of creating emotionally and socially safe environments is noticing, acknowledging, and actively drawing out acts of kindness. Schools are places of tremendous courage, generosity, and thoughtfulness. Some students risk their own social standing by being kind to an "unpopular" classmate. Some students talk with others who appear lonely and try to offer friendship; they speak up when they see injustice because, in the words of one student, they "don't think it is right to judge people by how they dress." In past research (San Antonio, 2004) and in the survey we describe here, students frequently spoke with admiration about teachers who actively intervened against stereotyping and teasing based on gender, social class, race, and learning needs. Naming and reclaiming goodness in the school community is an important step toward reducing bullying.

Integrate Social-Emotional Education into the Curriculum

An effective curriculum for social, emotional, and ethical learning addresses bullying as a social and moral development issue. Activities in such a program

Choosing a Social-Emotional Learning Curriculum

Look for a curriculum that

- Becomes part of a schoolwide and communitywide discussion (with parents) about values, beliefs about how to treat one another, and policies that reflect these values.

- Poses developmentally and culturally appropriate social dilemmas or discussion.

- Challenges the idea that aggression and bullying are inevitable and expected behavior. Demonstrates how people can resolve tensions and disagreements without losing face by giving detailed examples of people who responded to violence in an actively nonviolent manner.

- Encourages students to express their feelings and experiences concerning bullying and enables students to generate realistic and credible ways to stay safe.

- Supports critical analysis of the issues and rejects explanations of behavior based on stereotypes (such as the idea that boys will use physical violence and girls will use relational violence).

- Helps children and teens become critical consumers of popular culture.

- Addresses all types of bullying.

- Discusses how bullying reflects broader societal injustice.

- Gives ideas for what the adults in the school can do as part of a whole-school effort.

Beware of any curriculum that

- Ignores such issues as injustice, stereotype and imbalance of power regarding gender, race, social class, and sexual orientation.

- Focuses on the victim's behavior as the reason for being a target of bullying.

- Focuses on student behavior without addressing schoolwide climate.

- Emphasizes having students tell the teacher about the bullying and ignoring bullying assaults.

- Focuses on either bullying only or victimization only.

- Portrays victims or bullies as unpopular misfits.

- Promotes simplistic or trendy solutions (for example, "boys will be boys").

- Promotes good solutions, such as peer mediation, but does not provide clear guidelines for when these strategies should and should not be used.

- Lacks evidence-based, population-specific suggestions for design, implementation, training, and evaluation.

---

focus on self-understanding, understanding of others, appreciation for diversity, and responsibility to the community. By encouraging empathy, respect, and acceptance and giving students tools for communicating their feelings and confronting conflict positively, an effective social–emotional learning curriculum will likely improve school climate and culture beyond just the mitigation of bullying. (See Choosing a Social-Emotional Learning Curriculum.)

Educators Set the Tone

As a primary social environment for young people, classrooms and schools are uniquely good places to learn how to treat others and how to tell others the way we want them to treat us. Dozens of times a

day, people in schools negotiate interpersonal exchanges with others from diverse backgrounds, making schools a premier learning environment for social, emotional, and ethical learning. Nel Noddings (2002) has long held that a key purpose of schooling is to educate moral people:

> An emphasis on social relationships in classrooms, students' interest in the subject matter to be studied and the connections between classroom life and that of the larger world provides the foundation of our attempts to produce moral people. As educators we must make it possible and desirable for students to be good. (p. 85)

Of course, students behave in aggressive or submissive ways for a variety of reasons that are not always easy to discern or manage. Some students may posture aggressively because they face violent behavior at home or in their neighborhoods, some have problems reading social cues or controlling their impulses, and some are simply scared. But in our work with schools, we have found that when educators take students' concerns seriously, teach them alternative ways to communicate their needs assertively but not violently, and provide adult guidance, vigilance, safety, good role models, and support, students are more likely to interact positively with their peers.

The findings from the survey we conducted among middle grade students support the concept that educators *can* influence the social and emotional climate of schools. Students' written comments on the survey make it clear that they value fairness, respectful communication, and adults who make them feel physically and emotionally safe and cared for. By implementing an effective social-emotional learning curriculum and addressing the systemic factors that determine school climate, we can create schools where bullying is rare and where all students are ready to learn.

References

Banks, R. (1997). *Bullying in schools*. Champaign, IL: ERIC Clearinghouse on Elementary and Early Childhood Education. (ERIC No. ED407154)

Crick, N. R., & Bigbee, M. A. (1998). Relational and overt forms of peer victimization: A multi-informant approach. *Journal of Consulting and Clinical Psychology, 66*, 337–347.

Fried, S., & Fried, P. (1996). *Bullies and victims: Helping your child survive the schoolyard battlefield*. New York: M. Evans and Company.

Gladstone, G., Parker, G. B., & Malhi, G. S. (2006). Do bullied children become anxious and depressed adults? A cross-sectional investigation of the correlates of bullying and anxious depression. *Journal of Nervous and Mental Disease, 194*(3), 201–208.

Hoover, J. H., & Oliver, R. (1996). *The bullying prevention handbook: A guide for principals, teachers, and counselors*. Bloomington, IN: National Educational Service.

Kaltiala-Heino, R., Rimpelae, M., Rantanen, P., & Rimpelae, A. (2000). Bullying at school: An indicator of adolescents at risk for mental disorders. *Journal of Adolescence, 23*(6), 661–674.

Nakkula, M., & Selman, B. (1991). How people "treat" each other: Pair therapy as a context for the development of interpersonal ethics. In W. M. Kurtines & J. Gewirtz (Eds.), *Handbook of moral behavior and development* (Vol. 3, pp. 179–210). Hillsdale, NJ: Erlbaum.

Noddings, N. (2002). *Educating moral people: A caring alternative to character education*. New York: Teachers College Press.

Olweus, D. (1993). *Bullying at school: What we know and what we can do*. Malden, MA: Blackwell.

Pepler, D. J., & Craig, W. (2000). *Making a difference in bullying* (Report #60). Toronto, Ontario: La Marsh Centre for Research on Violence and Conflict Resolution.

Railsback, J., & Brewster, C. (2001). *Schoolwide prevention of bullying*. Portland, OR: Northwest Regional Education Laboratory. Available: www.nwrel.org/request/dec01

San Antonio, D. M. (2004). *Adolescent lives in transition: How social class influences adjustment to middle school*. Albany: State University of New York Press.

Skiba, N., & Fontanini, A. (2000). *Fast facts: Bullying prevention*. Bloomington, IN: Phi Delta Kappa International. Available: www.pdkintl.org/newsroom/newsletters/fastfacts/ffl2.pdf

U.S. Department of Education. (1998). *Preventing bullying: A manual for schools and communities*. Washington, DC: Author.

Weinhold, B. K., & Weinhold, J. B. (1998). Conflict resolution: The partnership way in schools. *Counseling and Human Development, 30*(7), 1–2.

Endnotes

1. *Physical bullying* includes hitting, kicking, or otherwise physically attacking the victim, as well as taking or damaging the victim's possessions. *Verbal bullying* includes name-calling, aggressive teasing, or making insulting comments designed to humiliate the victim. *Relational bullying* includes any behavior that intimidates and hurts the victim by harming or threatening to harm relationships or feelings of friendship and belonging (Crick & Bigbee, 1998). *Cyberbullying* involves the use of information and communication technologies, such as e-mail, cell phone and pager text messages, instant messaging, and Web sites to deliberately harm others (www.cyberbullying.org).

2. To preserve confidentiality, schools are identified by community type rather than by name.

POSTNOTE

Although bullying has probably existed ever since schools were created, the issue has generated considerable discussion of late. Reports of children skipping school or even committing suicide because of bullying occur commonly in both professional literature and news coverage. A relatively new form of bullying, *cyberbullying*, is of growing concern. Cyberbullying refers to bullying through information and communication technologies, such as mobile phone text messages, e-mail messages, Internet chat rooms, and social networking websites such as MySpace or Facebook. Recent surveys show that fully one-third of teenagers have had mean, threatening, or embarrassing things said about them online. Ten percent of teenagers were threatened online with physical harm. The results of such cyberbullying can cause shame, embarrassment, depression, anger, withdrawal, and, again, even lead to suicide.

As the article indicates, by developing a heightened awareness of bullying and its negative consequences, teachers can take actions that can transform schools and classrooms from places of suffering to places of happiness and success for bullied children.

DISCUSSION QUESTIONS

1. Have you or any of your friends experienced firsthand the effects of bullying? If so, how did you cope with it?

2. If you, as a teacher, witnessed one child picking on another one, how would you handle the situation? What would you do?

3. What kind of information or skills do you believe you still need to be effective in preventing bullying? How will you get that information or develop those skills?

RELATED WEBSITE RESOURCES AND VIDEO CASES

WEB RESOURCE:

Connect for Kids. Available at:

http://sparkaction.org/node/614.

This website provides a list of various resources useful in preventing bullying and much more.

▶❚❚ **TEACHSOURCE VIDEO CASE**

SOCIAL AND EMOTIONAL DEVELOPMENT: THE INFLUENCE OF PEER GROUPS

Although not dealing directly with the issue of bullying, this video case examines the issue of peer pressure. A sixth-grade teacher, Voncille Ross, has students use drama to better understand real-life situations, the choices they can make, and the potential consequences of those choices. Go to the website for the Education Media Library at CengageBrain.com to watch the video clips, study the artifacts in the case, and reflect on the following questions.

1. What insights did you gain from listening to students discuss peer pressure? How might these insights influence your teaching?

2. In the bonus segment, "A Real Story About Bullying," the teacher describes two students who are bullied for reading books during lunch period. The students say that while they are comfortable with being smart, they still want to fit in with everyone else and not stand out. How can you help students realize that they can be strong academically and still fit in socially?

9

The Perils and Promises of Praise

Carol Dweck

Carol S. Dweck is the Lewis and Virginia Eaton Professor of Psychology at Stanford University.

"The Perils and Promises of Praise," by Carol S. Dweck, 2007, *Educational Leadership* 65(2), pp. 34–39. © 2007 by ASCD. Reprinted with permission. Learn more about ASCD at www.ascd.org.

We often hear these days that we've produced a generation of young people who can't get through the day without an award. They expect success because they're special, not because they've worked hard.

Is this true? Have we inadvertently done something to hold back our students?

I think educators commonly hold two beliefs that do just that. Many believe that (1) praising students' intelligence builds their confidence and motivation to learn, and (2) students' inherent intelligence is the major cause of their achievement in school. Our research has shown that the first belief is false and that the second can be harmful—even for the most competent students.

As a psychologist, I have studied student motivation for more than 35 years. My graduate students and I have looked at thousands of children, asking why some enjoy learning, even when it's hard, and why they are resilient in the face of obstacles. We have learned a great deal. Research shows us how to praise students in ways that yield motivation and resilience. In addition, specific interventions can reverse a student's slide into failure during the vulnerable period of adolescence.

Fixed or Malleable?

Praise is intricately connected to how students view their intelligence. Some students believe that their intellectual ability is a fixed trait. They have a certain amount of intelligence, and that's that. Students with this fixed mind-set become excessively concerned with how smart they are, seeking tasks that will prove their intelligence and avoiding ones that might not (Dweck, 1999, 2006). The desire to learn takes a backseat.

Other students believe that their intellectual ability is something they can develop through effort and education. They don't necessarily believe that anyone can become an Einstein or a Mozart, but they do understand that even Einstein and Mozart had to put in years of effort to become who they were. When students believe that they can develop their intelligence, they focus on

FOCUS QUESTION

What are the different effects of teacher praise on student motivation and learning?

InTASC
Standards 2, 3, 4, 5, and 6

KEY TERMS

- Fixed mind-set
- Growth mind-set

doing just that. Not worrying about how smart they will appear, they take on challenges and stick to them (Dweck, 1999, 2006).

More and more research in psychology and neuroscience supports the growth mind-set. We are discovering that the brain has more plasticity over time than we ever imagined (Doidge, 2007); that fundamental aspects of intelligence can be enhanced through learning (Sternberg, 2005); and that dedication and persistence in the face of obstacles are key ingredients in outstanding achievement (Ericsson, Charness, Feltovich, & Hoffman, 2006).

Alfred Binet (1909/1973), the inventor of the IQ test, had a strong growth mind-set. He believed that education could transform the basic capacity to learn. Far from intending to measure fixed intelligence, he meant his test to be a tool for identifying students who were not profiting from the public school curriculum so that other courses of study could be devised to foster their intellectual growth.

The Two Faces of Effort

The fixed and growth mind-sets create two different psychological worlds. In the fixed mind-set, students care first and foremost about how they'll be judged: smart or not smart. Repeatedly, students with this mind-set reject opportunities to learn if they might make mistakes (Hong, Chiu, Dweck, Lin, & Wan, 1999; Mueller & Dweck, 1998). When they do make mistakes or reveal deficiencies, rather than correct them, they try to hide them (Nussbaum & Dweck, 2007).

They are also afraid of effort because effort makes them feel dumb. They believe that if you have the ability, you shouldn't need effort (Blackwell, Trzesniewski, & Dweck, 2007), that ability should bring success all by itself. This is one of the worst beliefs that students can hold. It can cause many bright students to stop working in school when the curriculum becomes challenging.

Finally, students in the fixed mind-set don't recover well from setbacks. When they hit a setback in school, they *decrease* their efforts and consider cheating (Blackwell et al., 2007). The idea of fixed intelligence does not offer them viable ways to improve.

Let's get inside the head of a student with a fixed mind-set as he sits in his classroom, confronted with algebra for the first time. Up until then, he has breezed through math. Even when he barely paid attention in class and skimped on his homework, he always got *A*s. But this is different. It's hard. The student feels anxious and thinks, "What if I'm not as good at math as I thought? What if other kids understand it and I don't?" At some level, he realizes that he has two choices: try hard, or turn off. His interest in math begins to wane, and his attention wanders. He tells himself, "Who cares about this stuff? It's for nerds. I could do it if I wanted to, but it's so boring. You don't see CEOs and sports stars solving for *x* and *y*."

By contrast, in the growth mind-set, students care about learning. When they make a mistake or exhibit a deficiency, they correct it (Blackwell et al., 2007; Nussbaum & Dweck, 2007). For them, effort is a *positive* thing: It ignites their intelligence and causes it to grow. In the face of failure, these students escalate their efforts and look for new learning strategies.

Let's look at another student—one who has a growth mind-set—having her first encounter with algebra. She finds it new, hard, and confusing, unlike anything else she has ever learned. But she's determined to understand it. She listens to everything the teacher says, asks the teacher questions after class, and takes her textbook home and reads the chapter over twice. As she begins to get it, she feels exhilarated. A new world of math opens up for her.

It is not surprising, then, that when we have followed students over challenging school transitions or courses, we find that those with growth mind-sets outperform their classmates with fixed mind-sets—even when they entered with equal skills and knowledge. A growth mind-set fosters the growth of ability over time (Blackwell et al., 2007; Mangels, Butterfield, Lamb, Good, & Dweck, 2006; see also Grant & Dweck, 2003).

The Effects of Praise

Many educators have hoped to maximize students' confidence in their abilities, their enjoyment of learning, and their ability to thrive in school by praising their intelligence. We've studied the effects of this kind of praise in children as young as 4 years old and as old as adolescence, in students in inner-city and rural settings, and in students of different ethnicities—and we've consistently found the same thing (Cimpian, Arce, Markman, & Dweck, 2007; Kamins & Dweck, 1999; Mueller & Dweck, 1998): Praising students' intelligence gives them a short burst of pride, followed by a long string of negative consequences.

In many of our studies (see Mueller & Dweck, 1998), 5th grade students worked on a task, and after the first set of problems, the teacher praised some of them for their intelligence ("You must be smart at these problems") and others for their effort ("You must have worked hard at these problems"). We then assessed the students' mind-sets. In one study, we asked students to agree or disagree with mind-set statements, such as, "Your intelligence is something basic about you that you can't really change." Students praised for intelligence agreed with statements like these more than students praised for effort did. In another study, we asked students to define intelligence. Students praised for intelligence made significantly more references to innate, fixed capacity, whereas the students praised for effort made more references to skills, knowledge, and areas they could change through effort and learning. Thus, we found that praise for intelligence tended to put students in a fixed mind-set (intelligence is fixed, and you have it), whereas praise for effort tended to put them in a growth mind-set (you're developing these skills because you're working hard).

We then offered students a chance to work on either a challenging task that they could learn from or an easy one that ensured error-free performance. Most of those praised for intelligence wanted the easy task, whereas most of those praised for effort wanted the challenging task and the opportunity to learn.

Next, the students worked on some challenging problems. As a group, students who had been praised for their intelligence *lost* their confidence in their ability and their enjoyment of the task as soon as they began to struggle with the problem. If success meant they were smart, then struggling meant they were not. The whole point of intelligence praise is to boost confidence and motivation, but both were gone in a flash. Only the effort-praised kids remained, on the whole, confident and eager.

When the problems were made somewhat easier again, students praised for intelligence did poorly, having lost their confidence and motivation. As a group, they did worse than they had done initially on these same types of problems. The students praised for effort showed excellent performance and continued to improve.

Finally, when asked to report their scores (anonymously), almost 40 percent of the intelligence-praised students lied. Apparently, their egos were so wrapped up in their performance that they couldn't admit mistakes. Only about 10 percent of the effort-praised students saw fit to falsify their results.

Praising students for their intelligence, then, hands them not motivation and resilience but a fixed mind-set with all its vulnerability. In contrast, effort or "process" praise (praise for engagement, perseverance, strategies, improvement, and the like) fosters hardy motivation. It tells students what they've done to be successful and what they need to do to be successful again in the future. Process praise sounds like this:

- You really studied for your English test, and your improvement shows it. You read the material over several times, outlined it, and tested yourself on it. That really worked!
- I like the way you tried all kinds of strategies on that math problem until you finally got it.
- It was a long, hard assignment, but you stuck to it and got it done. You stayed at your desk, kept up your concentration, and kept working. That's great!
- I like that you took on that challenging project for your science class. It will take a lot of work—

doing the research, designing the machine, buying the parts, and building it. You're going to learn a lot of great things.

What about a student who gets an *A* without trying? I would say, "All right, that was too easy for you. Let's do something more challenging that you can learn from." We don't want to make something done quickly and easily the basis for our admiration.

What about a student who works hard and *doesn't* do well? I would say, "I liked the effort you put in. Let's work together some more and figure out what you don't understand." Process praise keeps students focused, not on something called ability that they may or may not have and that magically creates success or failure, but on processes they can all engage in to learn.

Motivated to Learn

Finding that a growth mind-set creates motivation and resilience—and leads to higher achievement—we sought to develop an intervention that would teach this mind-set to students. We decided to aim our intervention at students who were making the transition to 7th grade because this is a time of great vulnerability. School often gets more difficult in 7th grade, grading becomes more stringent, and the environment becomes more impersonal. Many students take stock of themselves and their intellectual abilities at this time and decide whether they want to be involved with school. Not surprisingly, it is often a time of disengagement and plunging achievement.

We performed our intervention in a New York City junior high school in which many students were struggling with the transition and were showing plummeting grades. If students learned a growth mind-set, we reasoned, they might be able to meet this challenge with increased, rather than decreased, effort. We therefore developed an eight-session workshop in which both the control group and the growth-mind-set group learned study skills, time management techniques, and memory strategies (Blackwell et al., 2007). However, in the growth-mind-set intervention, students also learned about their brains and what they could do to make their intelligence grow.

They learned that the brain is like a muscle—the more they exercise it, the stronger it becomes. They learned that every time they try hard and learn something new, their brain forms new connections that, over time, make them smarter. They learned that intellectual development is not the natural unfolding of intelligence, but rather the formation of new connections brought about through effort and learning.

Students were riveted by this information. The idea that their intellectual growth was largely in their hands fascinated them. In fact, even the most disruptive students suddenly sat still and took notice, with the most unruly boy of the lot looking up at us and saying, "You mean I don't have to be dumb?"

Indeed, the growth-mind-set message appeared to unleash students' motivation. Although both groups had experienced a steep decline in their math grades during their first months of junior high, those receiving the growth-mind-set intervention showed a significant rebound. Their math grades improved. Those in the control group, despite their excellent study skills intervention, continued their decline.

What's more, the teachers—who were unaware that the intervention workshops differed—singled out three times as many students in the growth-mindset intervention as showing marked changes in motivation. These students had a heightened desire to work hard and learn. One striking example was the boy who thought he was dumb. Before this experience, he had never put in any extra effort and often didn't turn his homework in on time. As a result of the training, he worked for hours one evening to finish an assignment early so that his teacher could review it and give him a chance to revise it. He earned a *B* on the assignment (he had been getting *C*s and lower previously).

Other researchers have obtained similar findings with a growth-mind-set intervention. Working with junior high school students, Good, Aronson, and Inzlicht (2003) found an increase in math and English achievement test scores; working with college students, Aronson, Fried, and Good (2002) found an increase in students' valuing of academics, their enjoyment of schoolwork, and their grade point averages.

To facilitate delivery of the growth-mind-set workshop to students, we developed an interactive computer-based version of the intervention called *Brainology*. Students work through six modules, learning about the brain, visiting virtual brain labs, doing virtual brain experiments, seeing how the brain changes with learning, and learning how they can make their brains work better and grow smarter.

We tested our initial version in 20 New York City schools, with encouraging results. Almost all students (anonymously polled) reported changes in their study habits and motivation to learn resulting directly from their learning of the growth mind-set. One student noted that as a result of the animation she had seen about the brain, she could actually "picture the neurons growing bigger as they make more connections." One student referred to the value of effort: "If you do not give up and you keep studying, you can find your way through."

Adolescents often see school as a place where they perform for teachers who then judge them. The growth mind-set changes that perspective and makes school a place where students vigorously engage in learning for their own benefit.

Going Forward

Our research shows that educators cannot hand students confidence on a silver platter by praising their intelligence. Instead, we can help them gain the tools they need to maintain their confidence in learning by keeping them focused on the *process* of achievement.

Maybe we have produced a generation of students who are more dependent, fragile, and entitled than previous generations. If so, it's time for us to adopt a growth mind-set and learn from our mistakes. It's time to deliver interventions that will truly boost students' motivation, resilience, and learning.

References

Aronson, J., Fried, C., & Good, C. (2002). Reducing the effects of stereotype threat on African American college students by shaping theories of intelligence. *Journal of Experimental Social Psychology, 38,* 113–125.

Binet, A. (1909/1973). *Les idées modernes sur les enfants* [Modern ideas on children]. Paris: Flamarion. (Original work published 1909)

Blackwell, L., Trzesniewski, K., & Dweck, C. S. (2007). Implicit theories of intelligence predict achievement across an adolescent transition: A longitudinal study and an intervention. *Child Development, 78,* 246–263.

Cimpian, A., Arce, H., Markman, E. M., & Dweck, C. S. (2007). Subtle linguistic cues impact children's motivation. *Psychological Science, 18,* 314–316.

Doidge, N. (2007). *The brain that changes itself: Stories of personal triumph from the frontiers of brain science.* New York: Viking.

Dweck, C. S. (1999). *Self-theories: Their role in motivation, personality and development.* Philadelphia: Taylor and Francis/Psychology Press.

Dweck, C. S. (2006). *Mindset: The new psychology of success.* New York: Random House.

Ericsson, K. A., Charness, N., Feltovich, P. J., & Hoffman, R. R. (Eds.). (2006). *The Cambridge handbook of expertise and expert performance.* New York: Cambridge University Press.

Good, C., Aronson, J., & Inzlicht, M. (2003). Improving adolescents' standardized test performance: An intervention to reduce the effects of stereotype threat. *Journal of Applied Developmental Psychology, 24,* 645–662.

Grant, H., & Dweck, C. S. (2003). Clarifying achievement goals and their impact. *Journal of Personality and Social Psychology, 85,* 541–553.

Hong, Y. Y., Chiu, C., Dweck, C. S., Lin, D., & Wan, W. (1999). Implicit theories, attributions, and coping: A meaning system approach. *Journal of Personality and Social Psychology, 77,* 588–599.

Kamins, M., & Dweck, C. S. (1999). Person vs. process praise and criticism: Implications for contingent self-worth and coping. *Developmental Psychology, 35,* 835–847.

Mangels, J. A., Butterfield, B., Lamb, J., Good, C. D., & Dweck, C. S. (2006). Why do beliefs about intelligence influence learning success? A social–cognitive–neuroscience model. *Social, Cognitive, and Affective Neuroscience, 1*, 75–86.

Mueller, C. M., & Dweck, C. S. (1998). Intelligence praise can undermine motivation and performance. *Journal of Personality and Social Psychology, 75*, 33–52.

Nussbaum, A. D., & Dweck, C. S. (2007). Defensiveness vs. remediation: Self-theories and modes of self-esteem maintenance. *Personality and Social Psychology Bulletin.*

Sternberg, R. (2005). Intelligence, competence, and expertise. In A. Elliot & C. S. Dweck (Eds.), *The handbook of competence and motivation* (pp. 15–30). New York: Guilford Press.

POSTNOTE

Most of us probably grew up thinking that praise was a good thing to receive. However, research by Carol Dweck and others shows praise to be a more complicated issue. Depending on a student's mind-set, praising students for being smart can actually be harmful in developing their confidence and motivation to learn. Seeing intellect as a fixed entity—either you're smart or you're not—can cause students to decline opportunities to learn if there is a chance they might fail. Students who view their intelligence as something that can grow and develop seek opportunities to learn and meet new challenges. Rather than praising students for their intelligence, teachers should encourage students to try hard and to learn something new, even if they don't succeed right away. In this way, students can develop their intelligence through effort and learning.

It was not too many years ago when psychologists ridiculed the quite prevalent idea that "the mind is a muscle." Tied to this conception had been admonitions of the "use-it-or-lose-it" variety from teachers and parents. Psychologists saw intelligence as a fixed attribute, which led to a "you-have-it-or-you-don't" attitude. The break-through work of the author and her research team establishing that "brain is a muscle" suggests that we have come full circle. For educators, this is a much more positive and constructive starting point.

DISCUSSION QUESTIONS

1. Were there any findings in this article that surprised you? If so, what were they?
2. Which mind-set, growth or fixed, do you think you have? Why do you think this?
3. How might you incorporate the findings of this research into your own classroom?

RELATED WEBSITE RESOURCES AND VIDEO CASES

WEB RESOURCES:

Po Bronson, "How Not to Talk to Your Kids,"
New Yorker Magazine (February 12, 2007). Available at:

http://nymag.com/news/features/27840/.

A good summary of some of Carol Dweck's research, as seen applied to a particular child.

Jennifer Henderlong and Mark R. Lepper, "The Effects of Praise on Children's Intrinsic Motivation: A Review and Synthesis," *Psychological Bulletin* 2002, Vol. 128, No. 5, 774–795. Available at:

http://www.inner-cityarts.org/documents/resources/
EffectsofPraiseonMotivationHenderlongLepper.pdf.

An excellent review of the effects of praise on children.

▶❚❚ TEACHSOURCE VIDEO CASE

SCHOOLS USE EFFECTIVE SCHOOLS CORRELATES

This video show how students in KIPP (Knowledge is Power) schools are learning and the methods teachers use to promote that learning. Go to the website for the Education Media Library at CengageBrain.com to watch the video clips, study the artifacts in the case, and reflect on the following questions.

1. What are the techniques that teachers use to engage their students in learning?

2. Could these approaches be used in regular public schools? Why or why not?

3. What is the moral and ethical nature of the KIPP schools seen in this video?

10

How To Create Discipline Problems

M. Mark Wasicsko and Steven M. Ross

M. Mark Wasicsko is currently Dean, College of Education and Human Services and holds the Bank of Kentucky Endowed Chair in Educational Leadership at Northern Kentucky University. **Steven M. Ross** is executive director at The Center for Research in Educational Policy (CREP) and is a professor of Educational Psychology and Research at The University of Memphis.

"How To Create Discipline Problems," by M. Mark Wasicisko and Steven M. Ross, *The Clearing House*, May/June 1994. Reprinted by permission of the publisher. Taylor & Francis Group, http://www.informaworld.com.

FOCUS QUESTION

What is the classroom philosophy inherent in the authors' suggestions?

InTASC
Standards 2, 3, 4, and 5

KEY TERMS

- Discipline problems
- Teacher expectations

Creating classroom discipline problems is easy. By following the ten simple rules listed you should be able to substantially improve your skill at this popular teacher pastime.

1. ***Expect the worst from kids.*** This will keep you on guard at all times.
2. ***Never tell students what is expected of them.*** Kids need to learn to figure things out for themselves.
3. ***Punish and criticize kids often.*** This better prepares them for real life.
4. ***Punish the whole class when one student misbehaves.*** All the other students were probably doing the same thing or at least thinking about doing it.
5. ***Never give students privileges.*** It makes students soft and they will just abuse privileges anyway.
6. ***Punish every misbehavior you see.*** If you don't, the students will take over.
7. ***Threaten and warn kids often.*** "If you aren't good, I'll keep you after school for the rest of your life."
8. ***Use the same punishment for every student.*** If it works for one it will work for all.
9. ***Use school work as punishment.*** "Okay, smarty, answer all the questions in the book for homework!"
10. ***Maintain personal distance from students.*** Familiarity breeds contempt, you know.

We doubt that teachers would deliberately follow any of these rules, but punishments are frequently dealt out without much thought about their effects. In this article we suggest that many discipline problems are caused and sustained by teachers who inadvertently use self-defeating discipline strategies. There are, we believe, several simple, concrete methods to reduce classroom discipline problems.

Expect the Best from Kids

That teachers' expectations play an important role in determining student behavior has long been known. One author remembers two teachers who, at first glance, appeared similar. Both were very strict, gave mountains of homework, and kept students busy from the first moment they entered the classroom. However, they differed in their expectations for students. One seemed to say, "I know I am hard on you, but it is because I know you can do the work." She was effective and was loved by students. The other conveyed her negative expectations, "If I don't keep these kids busy they will stab me in the back." Students did everything they could to live up to each teacher's expectations. Thus, by conveying negative attitudes toward students, many teachers create their own discipline problems.

A first step in reducing discipline problems is to demonstrate positive expectations toward students. This is relatively easy to do for "good" students but probably more necessary for the others. If you were lucky, you probably had a teacher or two who believed you were able and worthy, and expected you to be capable even when you presented evidence to the contrary. You probably looked up to these teachers and did whatever you could to please them (and possibly even became a teacher yourself as a result). Now is the time to return the favor. Expect the best from *each* of your students. Assume that *every* child, if given the chance, will act properly. And, most important, if students don't meet your expectations, *don't give up!* Some students will require much attention before they will begin to respond.

Make the Implicit Explicit

Many teachers increase the likelihood of discipline problems by not making their expectations about proper behavior clear and explicit. For example, how many times have you heard yourself saying, "Now class, BEHAVE!"? You assume everyone knows what you mean by "behave." This assumption may not be reasonable. On the playground, for example, proper behavior means running, jumping, throwing things (preferably balls, not rocks), and cooperating with other students. Classroom teachers have different notions about proper behavior, but in few cases do teachers spell out their expectations carefully. Sad to say, most students must learn the meaning of "behave" by the process of elimination: "Don't look out the window.... Don't put hands on fellow students.... Don't put feet on the desk ... don't ... don't ... don't...."

A preferred approach would be to present rules for *proper* conduct on the front end (and try to phrase them positively: "Students should ..."). The teacher (or the class) could prepare a poster on which rules are listed. In that way, rules are clear, explicit, and ever present in the classroom. If you want to increase the likelihood that rules will be followed, have students help make the rules. Research shows that when students feel responsible for rules, they make greater efforts to live by them.

Rewards, Yes! Punishments, No!

A major factor in creating classroom discipline problems is the overuse of punishments as an answer to misbehavior. While most teachers would agree with this statement, recent research indicates that punishments outweigh rewards by at least 10 to 1 in the typical classroom. The types of punishments identified include such old favorites as The Trip to the Office and "Write a million times, 'I will not....'" But punishments also include the almost unconscious (but frequent) responses made for minor infractions: the "evil eye" stare of disapproval and the countless pleas to "Face front," "Stop talking," "Sit down!" and so on.

Punishments (both major and minor) have at least four consequences that frequently lead to increased classroom disruption: 1) Punishment brings attention to those who misbehave. We all know the adage, "The squeaky wheel gets greased." Good behavior frequently leaves a student nameless and unnoticed, but bad behavior can bring the undivided attention of the teacher before an audience of classmates! 2) Punishment has negative side effects such as aggression, depression, anxiety, or embarrassment. At the least, when a child is punished he feels worse about himself, about you and your class, or about school in general. He may even try to reduce the negative side effects by taking it out on another child or on school equipment. 3) Punishment only temporarily suppresses bad behavior. The teacher who rules with an iron ruler can have students who never misbehave in her presence, but who misbehave the moment she leaves the room or turns her back. 4) Punishment disrupts the continuity of your lessons and reduces the time spent on productive learning. These facts, and because punishments are usually not premeditated (and frequently do not address the real problems of misbehavior such as boredom, frustration, or physical discomfort), usually work to increase classroom discipline problems rather than to reduce them.

In view of these factors, the preferred approach is to use rewards. Rewards bring attention to *good* behaviors: "Thank you for being prepared." Rewards provide an appropriate model for other students, and make students feel positive about themselves, about you, and about your class. Also, reinforcing positive behaviors reduces the inclination toward misbehavior and enhances the flow of your lesson. You stay on task, get more student participation, and accentuate the correct responses.

Let the Punishment Fit the Crime

When rewards are inappropriate, many teachers create discipline problems by using short-sighted or ineffective punishments. The classic example is the "whole class punishment." "Okay, I said if anyone talked there would be no recess, so we stay in today!" This approach frustrates students (especially the ones who were behaving properly) and causes more misbehavior.

Research indicates that punishments are most effective when they are the natural consequences of the behavior. For example, if a child breaks a window, it makes sense to punish him with clean-up responsibilities and by making him pay for damage. Having him write 1,000 times, "I will not break the window," or having him do extra math problems (!) does little to help him see the relationship between actions and consequences.

In reality, this is one of the hardest suggestions to follow. In many cases, the "natural consequences" are obscure ("Okay, Steve, you hurt Carlton's feelings by calling him fat. For your punishment, you will make him feel better."). So, finding an appropriate punishment is often difficult. We suggest that after racking your brain, you consult with the offenders. They may be able to come up with a consequence that at least appears to them to be a fit punishment. In any case, nothing is lost for trying.

If You Must Punish, Remove Privileges

In the event that there are no natural consequences that can serve as punishments, the next best approach is to withdraw privileges. This type of punishment fits in well with the actual conditions in our society. In "real life" (located somewhere outside the school walls) privileges and responsibilities go hand in hand. People who do not act responsibly quickly lose freedoms and privileges. Classrooms provide a great opportunity to teach this lesson, but there is one catch: *There must be privileges to withdraw!* Many privileges already exist in classrooms and many more should be created. For example, students who finish their work neatly and on time can play an educational game, do an extra credit math sheet, work on homework, or earn points toward fun activities and free time. The possibilities are limitless. The important point, however, is that those who break the rules lose out on the privileges.

"Ignor"ance Is Bliss

One of the most effective ways to create troubles is to reward the very behaviors you want to eliminate. Many teachers do this inadvertently by giving attention to misbehaviors. For example, while one author was observing a kindergarten class, a child uttered an expletive after dropping a box of toys. The teachers quickly surrounded him and excitedly exclaimed, "That's nasty! Shame! Shame! Don't ever say that nasty word again!" All the while the other kids looked on with studied interest. So by lunch time, many of the other students were chanting, "... (expletive deleted) ..." and the teachers were in a frenzy! Teachers create similar problems by bringing attention to note passing, gum chewing, and countless other minor transgressions. Such problems can usually be avoided by ignoring minor misbehaviors and, at a later time, talking to the student individually. Some minor misbehavior is probably being committed by at least one student during every second you teach! Your choice is to spend your time trying to correct (and bring attention to) each one *or* to go about the business of teaching.

Consistency Is the Best Policy

Another good way to create discipline problems is to be inconsistent with rules, assignments, and punishments. For example, one author's daughter was given 750 math problems to complete over the Christmas holidays. She spent many hours (which she would rather have spent playing with friends) completing the task. As it turned out, no one else completed the assignment, so the teacher extended the deadline by another week. In this case, the teacher was teaching students that it is all right to skip assignments. When events like this recur, the teacher loses credibility and students are taught to procrastinate, which they may continue to do throughout their lives.

Inconsistent punishment has a similar effect. By warning and rewarning students, teachers actually cultivate misbehavior. "The next time you do that, you're going to the office!" Five minutes pass and then, "I'm warning you, one more time and you are gone!" And later, "This is your last warning!" And finally, "Okay, I have had it with you, go stand in the hall!" In this instance, a student has learned that a punishment buys him/her a number of chances to misbehave (she/he might as

well use them all), and that the actual punishment will be less severe than the promised one (not a bad deal).

To avoid the pitfalls of inconsistency, mean what you say, and, when you say it, follow through.

Know Each Student Well

Discipline problems can frequently be caused by punishing students we intended to reward and vice versa. When a student is told to clean up the classroom after school, is that a reward or punishment? It's hard to tell. As we all know, "One person's pleasure is another's poison."

One author remembers the difficulty he had with reading in the fourth grade. It made him so anxious that he would become sick just before reading period in the hope that he would be sent to the clinic, home, or anywhere other than to "the circle." One day, after helping the teacher straighten out the room before school, the teacher thanked him with, "Mark, you've been so helpful, you can be the first to read today." The author made sure he was never "helpful" enough to be so severely punished again.

The opposite happens just as often. For example, there are many class clowns who delight in such "punishments" as standing in the corner, leaving the room, or being called to the blackboard. The same author recalls having to stand in the school courtyard for punishment. He missed math, social studies, and English, and by the end of the day had entertained many classmates with tales of his escapades.

The key to reducing discipline problems is to know your students well; know what is rewarding and what is punishing for each.

Use School Work as Rewards

One of the worst sins a teacher can commit is to use school work as punishments. There is something sadly humorous about the language arts teacher who punishes students with, "Write 1,000 times, I will not . . ." or the math teacher who assigns 100 problems as punishment. In cases like these we are actually punishing students with that which we want them to use and enjoy! Teachers can actually reduce discipline problems (and increase learning) by using their subjects as rewards. This is done in subtle and sometimes indirect ways, through making lessons meaningful, practical, and fun. If you are teaching about fractions, bring in pies and cakes and see how fast those kids can learn the difference between ½, ¼, and ⅛. Reading teachers should allow free reading as a reward for good behavior. Math teachers can give extra credit math sheets (points to be added to the next test) when regular assignments are completed. The possibilities are endless and the results will be less misbehavior and a greater appreciation for both teacher and subject.

Treat Students with Love and Respect

The final suggestion for reducing discipline problems is to treat students kindly. It is no secret that people tend to respond with the same kind of treatment that they are given. If students are treated in a cold or impersonal manner, they are less likely to care if they cause you grief. If they are treated with warmth and respect they will want to treat you well in return. One of the best ways to show you care (and thus reduce discipline problems) is to surprise kids. After they have worked particularly hard, give them a treat. "You kids have worked so hard you may have 30 minutes extra recess." Or have a party one day for no good reason at all. Kids will come to think, "This school stuff isn't so bad after all!" Be careful to keep the surprises unexpected. If kids come to expect them,

surprises lose their effectiveness. Recently, one author heard a student pay a teacher the highest tribute. He said, "She is more than just a teacher; she is our friend." Not surprisingly, this teacher is known for having few major discipline problems.

Final Thoughts

When talking about reducing discipline problems, we need to be careful not to suggest that they can or should be totally eliminated. When children are enthusiastic about learning, involved in what they are doing, and allowed to express themselves creatively, "discipline problems" are apt to occur. Albert Einstein is one of numerous examples of highly successful people who were labeled discipline problems in school. It was said of Einstein that he was "the boy who knew not merely which monkey wrench to throw in the works, but also how best to throw it." This led to his expulsion from school because his "presence in the class is disruptive and affects the other students." For dictators and tyrants, robot-like obedience is a major goal. For teachers, however, a much more critical objective is to help a classroom full of students reach their maximum potential as individuals.

The theme of this article has been that many teachers create their own discipline problems. Just as we teach the way we were taught, we tend to discipline with the same ineffectual methods that were used on us. By becoming aware of this and by following the simple suggestions presented above, learning and teaching can become more rewarding for all involved.

POSTNOTE

A friend of ours, Ernie Lundquist, claims that as a student he actually saw a sign on his principal's door that read, "The beatings will continue until the morale improves." While over the years Ernie has not proved to be a particularly reliable source

in these matters, his reported sign-sighting underlines the point that student misbehavior often brings out the very worst in educators. In dealing with disruptive, misbehaving students, we who are supposed to stand for the use of intelligence, compassion, and imagination all too often demonstrate stupidity, insensitivity, and a complete lack of imagination.

Maintaining classroom control or discipline, as it is usually called by teachers, is perhaps the greatest challenge for new teachers. Its elusive presence or absence can be the difference between success or failure for a teacher. However, being able to maintain good classroom discipline is not a magical quality, but rather it is a learned set of skills.

Like many skills of teaching, success comes with intelligent practice.

The authors of this essay take the problem of discipline and turn it inside out, suggesting how we can create discipline problems for ourselves. But the real answer they offer us, and one the teacher frequently forgets in the heat of dealing with a discipline problem, is to *be creative!* We expect creativity from our students. Why not show a little in dealing with our discipline problems?

DISCUSSION QUESTIONS

1. Which of the authors' "ten simple rules" have you seen demonstrated most frequently in our schools?
2. What do you believe is the central message of this article?
3. What, in your judgment, are the three most practical suggestions offered by the authors? Why?

RELATED WEBSITE RESOURCES AND VIDEO CASES

WEB RESOURCE:

Education World. Available at:

http://educationworld.com/a_cur/archives/ classmanagement.shtml.

This website includes a fine menu of teacher resources related to classroom management.

▶❚❚ TEACHSOURCE VIDEO CASE

CLASSROOM MANAGEMENT: HANDLING A STUDENT WITH BEHAVIOR PROBLEMS

In this video you will see how two teachers, working with a student-support coach, design strategies and interventions to cope with particular students' disruptive behavior.

Go to the website for the Education Media Library at CengageBrain.com to watch the video clips, study the artifacts in the case, and reflect on the following questions.

1. What concerns about your own ability to work with students who have emotional or behavioral problems did this video raise? How can you prepare yourself to deal with these kinds of problems?

2. What do you see as the strongest points of the strategies and interventions that Ellen Henry, the student-support coach, suggests?

11

At Risk for Abuse: A Teacher's Guide for Recognizing and Reporting Child Neglect and Abuse

Dennis L. Cates, Marc A. Markell, and Sherrie Bettenhausen

At the time this article was written, **Dennis L. Cates** was an assistant professor in Programs in Special Education at the University of South Carolina in Columbia. Currently, he is the pastor of the Woodland and Martin Memorial United Methodist Churches in Texarkana, Texas. **Marc A. Markell** is currently a professor in the Department of Special Education at St. Cloud State University in St. Cloud, Minnesota. **Sherrie Bettenhausen** died in August 2003. At the time this article was written, she was a professor in the Special Education Department of the University of Charleston.

"At Risk for Abuse: A Teacher's Guide for Recognizing and Reporting Child Neglect and Abuse," by Dennis L. Cates, Marc A. Markell, and Sherrie Bettenhausen, *Preventing School Failure*, vol. 39, no. 2, Winter 1995. Reprinted by permission of the publisher Taylor & Francis Group, http://www.informaworld.com.

FOCUS QUESTION

Child abuse is becoming increasingly common in our society. What exactly are the classroom teacher's responsibilities?

InTASC

Standards 2, 3, and 4

KEY TERMS

- Behavioral indicators of child abuse
- Child abuse
- Physical indicators of child abuse

In 1992, 2.9 million children were reported as suspected victims of abuse or neglect, an increase of 8% from 1991 (Children, Youth, & Families Department [CYFD], 1993). [Editor's note: In 2006, 3.6 million incidents of child abuse or neglect were reported, and 905,000 of these reported cases were sustained "Child Maltreatment 2006," U.S. Department of Health and Human Services, Administration for Children & Families. Available at: http://www.acf.hhs.gov/programs/cb/pubs/cm06/chapter3.htm#subjects.] The exact number of children who are abused is, of course, difficult to determine because many cases of abuse go unreported and the definition of abuse varies from state to state (Winters Communication, Inc. [WCI], 1988). Not only does the definition of abuse differ among states, but professionals also define abuse in different ways (Pagelow, 1984). An additional reason for the difficulty in determining an accurate rate is that there may be a failure to recognize and report child abuse among professionals. Giovannoni (1989) stated that the failure to uncover child abuse and neglect is generally a result of three factors: (a) failure to detect injury caused by abuse, particularly when parents use different medical treatment facilities each time or do not seek medical treatment; (b) failure to recognize the indicators of abuse and neglect, especially for middle- and upper-income families; and (c) failure to report the case to the appropriate agency when injury is detected and recognized as abuse or neglect.

Although exact numbers for children who are abused are not available, it is known that an alarming number of children are abused each year. These children are in our classrooms throughout the United States.

Child abuse can lead to the development of a full range of problems in children, from poor academic performance and socialization to a variety of physical and cognitive disabilities. Because children are required to attend school, teachers and other educators are faced with the responsibility of maintaining a protective and vigilant posture in relation to their students' well-being.

Studies have shown that children with disabilities are at greater risk for abuse and neglect than are nondisabled children (Ammerman, Lubetsky, Hersen, & Van Hasselt, 1988). Meier and Sloan (1984) suggested that "most certifiably abused children have been identified as suffering from various developmental handicaps" (p. 247). They further stated that "it is seldom clear whether or not the handicapping conditions are a result of inflicted trauma or, because of a misreading of the child's abilities by parents, such disappointing delays precipitate further abuse" (pp. 247–248). Blacher (1984) suggested that children with disabilities are more likely to supply the "trigger mechanism" for abuse or neglect. It has further been indicated that parents who abuse often describe their children as being backward, hyperactive, continually crying, or difficult to control.

The premise that a disability, developmental delay, or problem adjusting to the school environment may be directly linked to an abusive home environment requires that educators must be especially vigilant in dealing with those children who are at risk for the development of educational disabilities or poor school performance. Because many children will not report abuse directly, teachers need to be aware of specific behavioral and physical indicators that may indicate that abuse has occurred (Parent Advocacy for Educational Rights [PACER], 1989). The purpose of this article is to provide teachers with potential indicators of abuse, guidelines in dealing with child abuse in at-risk

children, and information related to their legal responsibilities in reporting suspected child abuse.

Definitions and Extent of the Problem

The Child Abuse Prevention and Treatment Act of 1974 defines child abuse and neglect as follows:

> the physical or mental injury, sexual abuse or exploitation, negligent treatment, or maltreatment of a child under the age of eighteen, or the age specified by the child protection law of the state in question, by a person who is responsible for the child welfare under the circumstances which indicate that the child's health or welfare is harmed or threatened thereby. (42 U.S.C. § 5102)

Maltreatment of a child can be further described in terms of neglect and physical, verbal, emotional, and sexual abuse.

Neglect typically involves a failure on the part of a parent, guardian, or other responsible party to provide for the child's basic needs, such as food, shelter, medical care, educational opportunities, or protection and supervision. Further, neglect is associated with abandonment and inadequate supervision (Campbell, 1992).

Verbal abuse may involve excessive acts of derision, taunting, teasing, and mocking. Verbal abuse also involves the frequent humiliation of the child as well as a heavy reliance on yelling to convey feelings. Physical abuse can involve shaking, beating, or burning.

Emotional abuse is a pattern of behavior that takes place over an extended period of time, characterized by intimidating, belittling, and otherwise damaging interactions that affect a child's emotional development (PACER, 1989). It may be related to an intent to withhold attention or a failure to provide adequate supervision, or relatively normal living experiences. Sensory deprivation and long periods of confinement are also related to emotional abuse. Emotional abuse is very difficult to define or categorize.

Sexual abuse of children is also referred to as child sexual abuse and child molesting. It is typically defined in terms of the criminal laws of a state and involves intent to commit sexual acts with minors or to sexually exploit children for personal gratification (Campbell, 1992). Sexual intercourse need not take place and, in fact, is rare in prepubertal children. Sexual abuse involves coercion, deceit, and manipulation to achieve power over the child (PACER, 1989).

In Table 1, we provide possible physical and behavioral indicators of neglect and physical, emotional, and sexual abuse. A child who persistently shows several of these characteristics *may* be experiencing the symptoms of abuse or neglect.

TABLE 1   Physical and Behavioral Indicators of Possible Neglect and Abuse

PHYSICAL INDICATORS	BEHAVIORAL INDICATORS
EMOTIONAL ABUSE AND NEGLECT	
• Height and weight significantly below age level • Inappropriate clothing for weather, scaly skin • Poor hygiene, lice, body odor • Child left unsupervised or abandoned • Lack of safe and sanitary shelter • Unattended medical or dental needs • Developmental lags • Habit disorders	• Begging or stealing food • Constant fatigue • Poor school attendance • Chronic hunger • Dull, apathetic appearance • Running away from home • Child reports that no one cares for/looks after him/her • Sudden onset of behavioral extremes (conduct problems, depression)
PHYSICAL ABUSE	
• Frequent injuries such as cuts, bruises, or burns • Wearing long sleeves in warm weather • Pain despite lack of evident injury • Inability to perform motor skills because of injured hands • Difficulty walking or sitting	• Poor school attendance • Refusing to change clothes for physical education • Finding reasons to stay at school and not go home • Frequent complaints of harsh treatments by parents • Fear of adults
SEXUAL ABUSE	
• Bedwetting or soiling • Stained or bloody underclothing • Venereal disease • Blood or purulent discharge from genital or anal area • Difficulty walking or sitting • Excessive fears, clinging	• Unusual, sophisticated sexual behavior/knowledge • Sudden onset of behavioral extremes • Poor school attendance • Finding reasons to stay at school and not go home

© Cengage Learning, 2013.

It is important to note that the physical and behavioral indicators of neglect and emotional, sexual, and physical abuse *suggest* or *indicate* that abuse *may* have taken place. They *do not prove* that abuse has occurred and may be indicators of other situations happening in the child's life. Additionally, educators need to be cognizant of the fact that children who are motorically delayed or impaired may be prone to accidents and as a result have bruises, scrapes, cuts, or other minor injuries. This may also be true of children with severely limited vision. Children with diagnosed medical conditions may develop symptoms that result in a change of demeanor or physical appearance. It is important that teachers who serve these children become familiar with the child's condition and be well acquainted with the child's family. Frequent meetings, by telephone and in person, will assist the teacher in keeping up to date with changing medical conditions and aid in monitoring changes in family life patterns.

A teacher who is equipped with knowledge of the symptoms of child abuse and neglect and the characteristics of the child and the family will be able to better determine whether an at-risk learner or child with a disability is a victim of abuse.

Legal Obligations

Children who are at risk for developmental delays are at greater risk for child abuse than children who are not. Teachers who work with these students should, therefore, be aware of their responsibilities relative to child abuse and neglect.

Child abuse cannot be legally ignored by school officials. Teachers and administrators are required by law in all 50 states to report suspected child abuse (Fossey, 1993; Trudell & Whatley, 1988). In most jurisdictions, it is a criminal offense for a person to fail to report abuse when he or she is required by law to do so (Fossey, 1993). Therefore, failure to act may result in the filing of criminal charges or civil suits. The courts have also ruled against teachers for delaying their actions (McCarthy & Cambron-McCabe, 1992). The possibility of criminal or civil proceedings may give

many teachers pause and result in undue anxiety or overreaction to the problem. Educators must, therefore, become aware of their legal and administrative responsibilities.

The state laws governing the reporting of child abuse generally require teachers, doctors, school counselors, nurses, dentists, and police, to name a few, to report suspected child abuse to those human services agencies responsible for child welfare. Generally, teachers are required only to have a reasonable suspicion that child abuse has occurred before they are required to report it. Reasonable suspicion suggests that one is relieved of the responsibility of researching a case or of having specific facts related to the incidence of abuse. Given teachers' training in child behavior and their daily contact with children, they are in a position to recognize unusual circumstances. Exercising prudence in reporting suspected abuse will generally protect the teacher from criminal or civil action. Persons who report abuse and neglect *in good faith* to the appropriate state agency are immune from civil liability (Fossey, 1993). Laws vary from state to state in this regard, however.

Reporting laws in all states give final authority to investigate abuse charges to agencies other than the schools (Fossey, 1993). The advantage of reporting suspected abuse to agencies other than the school lies in the fact that the burden of gathering facts does not rest with the school. These agencies can research each case objectively and determine the need for action. Teachers may report child abuse to law enforcement officials; however, most states require them to report to local service agencies such as children's protective services, child abuse hotlines, local welfare departments, local social service agencies, public health authorities, school social workers, nurses, or counselors. In extreme cases, teachers may be required to report cases to hospital emergency rooms. Questions often arise, however, about the procedures for reporting abuse.

Should teachers report suspected abuse directly to the appropriate human service agency or to their building principal or immediate supervisor? These questions may be difficult to answer if specific policies and procedures have not been outlined. If no policy exists, and a teacher reports suspected abuse to the principal, and the principal fails or refuses to report the case to the proper authorities, both teacher and principal may be subject to legal action. In such a case, a teacher may be held responsible depending upon specific circumstances involved.

A specific policy or procedure for reporting abuse should protect the teacher from legal liability if those procedures are followed. A policy requiring a teacher to report to the principal or school counselor relieves the teacher of the need to second-guess the system. Teachers are encouraged to familiarize themselves with existing law as well as district policies related to child abuse. If policies do not exist or are not clear, teachers should work through their professional organizations to help promote institutionalization of such policies.

McCarthy and Cambron-McCabe (1992) suggest that low levels of reporting by teachers may be related to the lack of clearly defined administrative policy. Additionally, they recommend the development of in-service programs to acquaint teachers with their legal responsibilities as well as the signs of abuse.

Even though specific laws may require the person suspecting abuse to report specific information, the following suggestions from PACER (1989), CYFD (1992), and WCI (1988) should answer many questions a teacher may have concerning the reporting of suspected abuse.

1. *To whom should I report suspected child abuse?* If the teacher suspects that a child has been abused, she or he must report the suspected abuse to the local social service agency, the local police, or the local county sheriff's department. Reporting the suspected abuse to another teacher or the school principal may not be enough to fulfill the requirements of mandatory reporting.

2. *Should I tell the parents or alleged abuser of my suspicion of child abuse?* The teacher should not disclose the suspicion of abuse or neglect of a child to either the parents, the caregiver, or the alleged perpetrators. The teacher should report the suspected abuse to the local social service agency, the local police, or the county sheriff's department.

3. *What should I report?* The teacher should report the following information (if known):
   - identifying information about the child (name, age, grade, address, and names of parents)
   - name of the person responsible for the abuse
   - where the alleged abuse took place
   - description of the child, any relevant statements made by the child, and any observations made
   - how long ago the incident described took place
   - the reporter's name, address, and phone number
   - if the child has a disability, any information that may be helpful to the officials (i.e., if the child has difficulty with communication, uses a hearing aid, has mental retardation, emotional, or behavioral difficulties, or has a learning disability that indicates special needs)

Summary

To ensure that accurate information is reported to the appropriate human service agency, teachers who serve children at risk for the development of educational problems must be prudent in their efforts to know their children and their families well. Parents who abuse or neglect their children often exhibit characteristics that may be heightened or triggered during family crises. This is of critical importance to teachers of children at risk for developing educational problems because of the additional stress that often results from the child's presence. Parents who abuse or neglect their child may exhibit low self-esteem or appear to be isolated from the community. They typically fail to appear for parent–teacher conferences and are often defensive when questioned about their child. Their child's injuries are often blamed on others or unsatisfactorily explained. The child may relate stories of abuse or unusual behavior by his or her parents. Limited parenting skills may be a result of lack of education, experience, or maturity. Parents may lack patience and be overly demanding of a child who, because of developmental difficulties, is unable to meet their demands in a timely manner. Often, parents who abuse their children were abused themselves.

In determining whether a child is subject to abuse or neglect, the teacher should make note of consistent behaviors or physical evidence, being aware that one incident may not be evidence of child abuse. An isolated incident should be recorded for future reference but should not necessarily be reported immediately. This will depend, of course, on the severity of the injury or the effect on the child's behavior. Knowing the parents well will certainly aid in making a decision relative to reporting of abuse and neglect.

Recognizing abuse and reporting it to the appropriate agency is expected of all teachers and administrators. The experienced teacher makes the extra effort to gather information about the family, to become well acquainted with the parents, and to monitor all of his or her students' physical and behavioral conditions. Teachers must know their students if they intend to effectively deal with child abuse and neglect.

In addition to understanding the procedures for reporting abuse and neglect, teachers may also contribute to improved parent–student relations by participating in the development of parenting education programs or in setting up a more flexible schedule for parent conferences. Efforts should be made to help parents see the advances and improvements made by their children. As parents develop a more realistic view of their child's abilities and potential, they may become more patient and understanding of their child's actions. Teachers should preface a note home with a friendly telephone call or an informal letter discussing the child's overall performance in school. Given a

situation in which abuse is present, a teacher's first note home detailing a disciplinary action may precipitate undue punishment. One key to reduced child abuse is improved parent–teacher communication. Teachers cannot afford to wait for the parent to initiate contact. Open lines of communication must be established and supported by the school's administration.

Children at risk for the development of educational problems are at greater risk for abuse and neglect than those children who develop normally. Teachers who serve these children must be aware of this and be able to recognize the warning signs. They must also have a complete understanding of the legal and administrative procedures for reporting abuse. Most important, they must know their students and work to establish effective parent–teacher communication. To stem the tide of abuse and neglect among disabled and at-risk children, teachers must be vigilant, understanding, observant, prudent, and effective record keepers.

Acknowledgment

We wish to thank Dr. J. David Smith and Dr. Mitchell L. Yell for their editorial assistance in the preparation of this manuscript.

References

Ammerman, R., Lubetsky, M., Hersen, M., & Van Hasselt, V. (1988). Maltreatment of children and adolescents with multiple handicaps: Five case examples. *Journal of the Multihandicapped Person*, *1*, 129–139.

Blacher, J. (1984). A dynamic perspective on the impact of a severely handicapped child on the family. In J. Blacher (Ed.), *Severely handicapped young children and their families: Research in review* (pp. 3–50). New York: Academic Press.

Campbell, R. (1992). Child abuse and neglect. In L. Bullock (Ed.), *Exceptionalities in children and youth* (pp. 470–475). Boston: Allyn and Bacon.

Child Abuse Prevention and Treatment Act of 1974, 42 U.S.C. § 5101 et. seq.

Children, Youth, and Families Department (CYFD). (1993). *Stop child abuse/neglect: Prevention and reporting kit*. Available from Children, Youth and Families Department, Social Services Division, Child Abuse Prevention Unit, 300 San Mateo NE, Suite 802, Albuquerque, NM 87108-1516.

Fossey, R. (1993). Child abuse investigations in the public school: A practical guide for school administrators. *Education Law Reporter*. St. Paul, MN: West.

Giovannoni, J. (1989). Definitional issues in child maltreatment. In D. Cicchitti & V.Carlson (Eds.), *Child maltreatment: Theory and research on the causes and consequences of child abuse and neglect* (pp. 48–50). New York: Cambridge University Press.

McCarthy, M., & Cambron-McCabe, N. (1992). *Public school law: Teachers' and students' rights*. Boston: Allyn and Bacon.

Meier, J., & Sloan, M. (1984). The severely handicapped and child abuse. In J. Blacher (Ed.), *Severely handicapped*

young children and their families: Research in review (pp. 247–272). New York: Academic Press.

Pagelow, M. D. (1984). *Family violence*. New York: Praeger Publishing.

Parent Advocacy for Educational Rights (PACER). (1989). *Let's prevent abuse: An informational guide for educators*. Available from PACER Center, Inc., 4826 Chicago Avenue South, Minneapolis, Minnesota 55407-1055.

Trudell, B., & Whatley, M. H. (1988). School sexual abuse prevention: Unintended consequences and dilemmas. *Child Abuse and Neglect, 12*, 103–113.

Winters Communication, Inc. (WCI). (1988). *Child abuse and its prevention*. Available from Winters Communication, Inc., 1007 Samy Drive, Tampa, Florida 33613.

POSTNOTE

The abuse (or, more accurately stated, the torture) of a helpless child by an adult is one of those crimes that truly cries out for attention. The effects of abuse usually spill over into a child's school life and can make him or her impervious to the best schooling. Recently, greater attention has been given to child abuse in the hope of alerting teachers and other youth workers to the problem and of sensitizing adults to its long-term harm. Nevertheless, every year the abuse and torment of thousands of children go unreported by teachers who turned away from the evidence before their eyes. Confronting the signs discussed in this article and reporting them takes courage. Fortunately, now every state provides complete protection to whistle-blowing teachers who stand up to this terrible evil.

DISCUSSION QUESTIONS

1. Describe a case of child abuse you know of personally or through media accounts. What was the outcome of the case for all parties involved?
2. What legal responsibilities do teachers have in your state for reporting child abuse? Do they have any legal protection (such as anonymity) once they have reported a case? How comfortable are you with the possibility of meeting these responsibilities?
3. What services are available in your area for children who have been abused? Consider child protection or welfare services as well as law enforcement agencies at the state, county, and city levels.

RELATED WEBSITE RESOURCES AND VIDEO CASES

WEB RESOURCE:

How to Report Suspected Child Maltreatment, U.S. Department of Health and Human Services. Available at: http://www.childwelfare.gov/responding/how.cfm.

This website provides statistics, research, programs, and many other resources on children, including information on reporting child abuse and neglect.

 TEACHSOURCE VIDEO CASE

STUDENTS WITH SPECIAL NEEDS: THE IMPORTANCE OF HOME-SCHOOL PARTNERSHIPS

In this video you will see a middle school teacher, Sophia Boyer, recall the ways she worked with the parents of two former students with special needs. Note the impact of early identification and intervention on the lives of students. Go to the website for the Education Media Library at CengageBrain.com to watch the video clips, study the artifacts in the case, and reflect on the following questions.

1. How would you describe the effect of this home-school partnership on the lives of these students?

2. What are the barriers to this type of successful home-school partnership?

 The companion website for this text includes useful study tools and resources. Go to CengageBrain.com to access links to relevant websites, glossaries, flashcards, an article review form, and more.

Schools

Schools and schooling in the United States have been under intense scrutiny and considerable criticism in recent years. Disappointing test scores, disciplinary problems, violence, and a lack of clear direction are all points of tension. In the past decade or so, there has been a shift in what educators, legislators, and critics say schools must do to address these and other problems. There is a sense that schools have drifted away from their most important purpose—that is, to prepare students academically and intellectually for the future. Schools have lost sight, some say, of a sense of excellence.

Some of the following selections consider this emphasis, whereas others pose alternative solutions. The topics include how to increase academic achievement, what constitutes a good school, the size of schools, cheating, and bringing parents to school.

12

What Makes a Good School?

Joan Lipsitz and Teri West

Joan Lipsitz is co-founder of the National Forum to Accelerate Middle-Grades Reform as well as the Schools to Watch Initiative and currently serves as a senior fellow at MDC, Inc. **Teri West** is the senior program officer at the Academy for Educational Development.

What Makes a Good School? Identifying Excellent Middle Schools, *Phi Delta Kappan*, September 2006, pp. 57–66. Reprinted with permission of Phi Delta Kappa International, www.pdkintl.org. All rights reserved.

FOCUS QUESTION

What should you look for if you are trying to identify a high-performance school?

InTASC

Standards 1, 2, 3, 5, 7, 8, 9, and 10

KEY TERMS

- Developmentally responsive
- High-performing school
- Socially equitable

Excellent schools have a sense of purpose that drives every facet of practice and decision making. But what are the critical priorities that fuel that sense of purpose? The National Forum to Accelerate Middle-Grades Reform is a group of educators who believe that young adolescents are capable of learning and achieving at high levels and who are dedicated to improving schools for middle-grades students across the country. Believing that there is nothing as practical as a vision, the first step taken by the members of the forum was to develop a vision statement that would both answer the question posed above and express our shared convictions about school excellence. Through this process, we identified three interlocking priorities that are critical to the sense of purpose that permeates all aspects of successful schools. Briefly, high-performing schools with middle grades are:

- academically excellent—they challenge all of their students to use their minds well;
- developmentally responsive—they are sensitive to the unique developmental challenges of early adolescence and respectful of students' needs and interests; and
- socially equitable, democratic, and fair—they provide every student with high-quality teachers, resources, learning opportunities, and supports and make positive options available to all students.

The forum also concluded that in order to pursue these priorities, high-performing schools must be learning organizations that establish norms, structures, and organizational arrangements that will support and sustain their trajectory toward excellence.

There isn't anything in the forum's work that is exclusive to the middle grades; we believe our vision applies to all schools teaching all grade levels. However, the forum was created to advocate for dramatically improved schools for young adolescents, and, therefore, our emphasis is on the middle grades.

After developing and adopting our vision statement by unanimous consent, we all celebrated—but only briefly. We recognized that for our work to be practical, the forum would need to turn the vision statement into specific criteria for evaluating schools. We needed to develop an instrument that identified the qualities to examine and the questions to ask when assessing a middle-grades school. Could we come up with a set of criteria that would be as useful to a team of classroom teachers as it would be to a group of community members on a school governance committee, or to citizens advocating for school improvement, or to individual parents seeking a good school for their children? And would this set of criteria help the forum identify high-performing schools that others could visit and learn from?

The forum identified a set of criteria on which to evaluate each of the three priorities for high-performing middle-grades schools. The priorities and their criteria are complementary and interdependent. So, for example, an academically excellent school is one in which all students are learning to use their minds well in challenging classrooms where the curriculum, instruction, and assessments are responsive to children's developmental needs. The truly high-performing school sits at the intersection of academic excellence, developmental responsiveness, and social equity.

It is extremely difficult to find schools that excel in all three areas, as the forum discovered in 1999 when it launched its Schools to Watch (STW) program to identify, recognize, and learn from exemplary schools. Since the vision was developed, STW has become a national movement in middle-level education. Fourteen states have recognized 87 STWs, and new states and schools are being added each year. Far more important, the forum's Schools to Watch have become models from which many other schools can learn to "get it right."

In the pages that follow, we describe a selection of the criteria for each of our three priorities for excellent schools. We offer this selection to give readers examples of our approach to assessing schools and to share specific bits and pieces from our observations of four schools. We also describe a sampling of criteria for evaluating a school's organizational structures and processes.[1] Our purpose in presenting the forum's construct of high performance is both to shape the way that readers think about school excellence and to give them explicit guidelines for action when they answer the question "Is this a good school?"

Academic Excellence

Criteria

At high-performing schools, curriculum, instruction, and assessment are aligned with high standards, and all students are expected to meet or exceed those standards. These schools provide a coherent vision of what students should know and be able to do. They use instructional strategies that include a variety of challenging and engaging activities that are clearly related to the concepts and skills being taught.

When talking to teachers in an academically excellent school, it quickly becomes clear that they hold high expectations for all of their students and insist that all of their students can master the curriculum. Teachers at such schools say things like, "We don't let up on the students," "We want everyone to achieve," and "We are a no-excuses school." Likewise, the principal expects a great deal from all the teachers at the school, holding them responsible for improving the quality of student work over time.

The curriculum at high-performing schools follows a coherent plan that builds systematically on instruction from earlier grades—what students learn is neither haphazard nor random. When we ask teachers at such schools how they decide what to teach, they report spending a great deal of their planning time working individually or with their colleagues to incorporate the best of professional and state standards in their content-area lessons. Vibrant displays of student work in the halls reflect students' care in meeting those standards. In one school held accountable by high-stakes testing, teachers insist that, because the state test is based on state and national standards, preparing students for the state test is not "teaching to the test" but rather "teaching to the standards." When we ask these teachers what accounts for the rising test scores in such unusual schools, they talk about highly focused and energetic teaching.

When we ask students what they are learning, they not only express their enthusiasm but also can describe the content and purpose of the lesson. For instance, students in a language arts class said they were learning how to analyze a short story and predict its outcome. They were able to recognize that the lesson called for inference and "higher-order thinking skills." In other words, the students were aware of how they were thinking, and, though they did not know it, they were learning about metacognition.

We ask students how they know if they are doing a good job. In some cases, the students are aware of and understand the performance standards because their teachers have told them what they are expected to master before starting a major activity. In some classes, students help develop the rubrics for judging the quality of their work. In one inter-disciplinary classroom that integrates art, math, and science, we observed students preparing a group presentation on empathy. When asked how they would be assessed, the students reported that they and their teacher had designed a grading rubric. These rubrics are often posted on the classroom walls, or the students are given a copy to keep in their notebooks. In all cases, the rubrics are explicit and make sense to the students—the criteria for good work are not a mystery.

When we ask students if they have opportu-nities to investigate and solve problems that inter-est them, they like to talk about the projects they have designed. For instance, in a seventh-grade math lab, each student was to choose an area in which to become proficient. The students were given a choice of topics drawn from the state's learning goals for seventh-graders, including bar graphs, fractions, perimeter, the Pythagorean the-orem, and volume. The students' task was to study their chosen topic and then teach it to their classmates using a PowerPoint presentation of their own design. The goal was for all students to master a set of mathematical concepts while, at the same time, learning a useful application of technology. The students in this class were deeply engaged in becoming proficient in their chosen areas.

When evaluating schools on these criteria, ask yourself:

- Do I see zest for learning among both the teachers and the students?
- Are students expected to meet high academic standards? How are these standards communicated?
- Can students explain what they are doing in their classes and why it is important?
- How is the school's curriculum selected? Who is involved in the process, and what guidelines do they use? Do teachers know why they are teaching what they are teaching?
- Does the school's assessment program support its vision for curriculum and instruction?

Criteria

The school provides opportunities for teachers and other instructional staff to plan for, select, and engage in professional development that is aligned with nationally recognized standards. They have regular opportunities to work with their colleagues to deepen their knowledge and improve their practice. They collaborate in making decisions about substantive and challenging curriculum and effective instructional methods.

When the forum members visit schools, we ask teachers and administrators to define professional development in the context of their school. Invari-ably, they first tell us what it is not. As one principal says, "It does not occur once in the summer and go away. It keeps coming back and back and back." They also stress that professional development takes place during team meetings, in which teachers meet to discuss their practice and how to improve it. During such meetings, the teachers plan and reflect together about ways to deepen instruction in individual content areas or in interdisciplinary units. To teachers in high-performing schools, pro-fessional development is an integral part of everyday life in the school. Professional development also occurs in divisional meetings, in which teachers come together to analyze student progress. In some schools, professional development occurs as a result of teachers' individual growth plans. One principal said, "I think we grow more across the year through nudges, conversations, and lesson planning than we ever do on professional development days."

In one school, one of the teams constructed the year's curriculum around interdisciplinary units. The team members decided what topics they would explore and then designed and developed the unit together using district standards. While we were visiting this school, the team was in the process of developing a unit on inventions. One of the teachers shared materials and resources from an inventions convention she had just attended. The teachers on the team were excited about planning this unit, and they shared ideas freely and gave one another feedback without fear of judgment. They were honest with one another when an idea didn't seem right or if they felt it might create a problem.

In the social studies and language arts segments of the unit, the students were asked to explore the legal issues around inventions, to learn the difference between a copyright and a patent, and to investigate the history of inventions in the United States. In the math and science segments, students were challenged to design and build their own inventions in small groups of two or three. The teachers had brainstormed about the kinds of reading and writing students would do in this unit. They wanted their students to design inventions for real-world problems or needs. The unit was to culminate with the students presenting their work to the school and community at their own invention convention.

When the forum visits schools, we ask teachers what help they have received in aligning their curriculum with state and national standards. In one school, the mathematics curriculum is driven by the state's learning goals, which, according to one of the mathematics teachers, encourage a balance of skill building and application. All the mathematics teachers at this school worked together closely to align the curriculum with the state standards. After aligning the curriculum, the teachers then piloted three textbooks but were not satisfied with any. After discussing what worked well and what didn't, they finally decided to use a combination of teacher-developed curriculum units, a pre-algebra textbook, and Connected Math, which offers a range of hands-on activities.

The teachers at this school had administrative support during this intensive planning period from the school's learning coordinator, who facilitated their conversations. They now meet each grading quarter with the coordinator and the principal to review where they are and to make further decisions. In addition, the teachers meet regularly to refine their curriculum.

When evaluating a school on these criteria, ask yourself:

- Does the principal support professional development opportunities for teachers and staff members?
- How does the school's professional development plan help increase teachers' knowledge and skills?
- Does the professional development challenge teachers' current beliefs and assumptions?
- Does it provide classroom support and coaching?
- How is professional development related to the school's improvement plan?

Developmental Responsiveness

Criterion

The school provides access to comprehensive services that foster healthy physical, social, emotional, and intellectual development.

In *high-performing schools,* the adults work together to provide a web of emotional and social support for the students, not just in the services the school provides but in the attitudes and relationships the adults establish with students. When visiting schools, we ask students where they go if they are having a problem. In almost all of the schools, students mention the names of one or two teachers with whom they have a good relationship. We can see signs of these relationships when we walk through the halls and sit in classrooms. Students have smiles on their faces and laugh with their teachers and their friends. During the change of classes at one school, a teacher who is clearly one of the favorites is surrounded by a half-dozen students, all wanting to share something about themselves or their families.

The affection and genuine caring between the students and faculty at this school is expressed in the way one principal puts her arm around a student to reprimand him about shouting a profanity in the hall. It is also expressed in the way students affectionately refer to members of the staff as "Mom" and to the school as a "second home." In one School to Watch, the principal collected money from teachers and parents in order to buy presents for the students who were living in the local youth home during the winter holidays. She spent one night and more than $1,000 on gifts for these children. The teachers and administrators in these schools care about the details of their students' lives.

Understanding that the faculty and staff do not have the capacity to attend to all of their students' needs, one school seeks out partnerships with a local agency that can provide social services and programs to students with demonstrated need. The agency provides guidance; a creative arts program; individual, family, group, and crisis counseling; support for the school's parent involvement program; and classroom and faculty support services. The agency works only with schools that are committed to the partnership and able to make a financial contribution, albeit a small one. At this particular school, the partnership with the agency is written into the School Improvement Plan, and faculty members are identified to work with agency staff. Together, the teachers and agency staff members review the criteria for the partnership and then develop the kinds of programs and services that are most needed in the school.

Another school responded to its teen pregnancy rate by investing in a program designed to give young adolescents a sense of what being the primary caretaker for an infant is like. While the program is designed to help students make intelligent physical and emotional choices, the ultimate goal is to prevent teen pregnancy.

The school invested in 23 baby simulators, and every student is required take a simulator home for at least one weekend during his or her two years at the school. These lifelike dolls are computer programmed to look, weigh, and behave like three-month-old infants. They need to be fed, picked up, held, and cuddled. They cry when they are hungry or need affection, when their diapers need changing, or when their head is not supported correctly. Sometimes they cry inconsolably for no apparent reason. The only way to stop the baby from crying is to turn a key a certain way to respond to the baby's particular need. The keys are locked onto students' wrists so they cannot give their 24-hour-a-day responsibility to anyone else. Sometimes, particularly during the night, parents want to help, but that would break the rules. The parents report how the weight of parenthood starts descending upon their children as the weekend progresses. The youth service agency worker says that most students are eager to take the baby home with them, but they are even more eager to bring it back. The students are sadder, wiser, and much more tired.

Another issue that the forum looks at when evaluating schools on this criterion is how they address conflicts between students. In most schools, when a conflict between two students escalates, a fight breaks out, and students are suspended. And time out of the classroom is not time well spent. At each of the schools we visited, there was some form of peer mediation in which students learn to address and solve problems before they escalate. In this way, the schools help foster students' social and emotional development. At one school, 20 students are selected by their peers and trained to be peer mediators. They are required to take a six-hour training program that focuses on rules and standards for mediation, leadership, and being accountable for what occurs in sessions. This school, which averages one peer mediation session per day, has seen a dramatic reduction in the number of discipline referrals to the principal's office. At another school, the eighth-grade student conflict managers developed a presentation about the school's peer mediation program for the seventh-graders in order to identify and begin to train the peer mediators for the following year.

When evaluating a school on this criterion, ask yourself:

- Where can students go when they are having a problem?
- Does every student in the school feel there is an adult he or she trusts and can turn to?
- How do the adults in the building relate to the students? Is there evidence of strong and respectful relationships between adults and students? Is there a feeling of warmth and genuine caring between teachers and their students? Are students smiling and laughing?
- What does respecting students' needs and interests mean to the faculty, staff, and administration? How does this fit into the school's overall mission? Do the school's programs and practices reflect this understanding?
- What programs, services, and support systems are in place to address students' needs?
- Does the school have a network of health care providers, counselors, education and job training specialists, and other providers that is available to serve students and families? Does the school publicize this network well? Do students and families feel comfortable using these services?

Criterion

The school develops alliances with families to enhance and support the well-being of students. It regards families as partners in their children's education, keeping them informed, involving them in their children's learning, and including them in decision making.

When we visit schools, we hear over and over again that when children get to middle school, parents tend to "drop out" of school involvement. This happens just when young adolescents are beginning to seek greater autonomy from their parents and to crave acceptance from their peers. But parent involvement in the middle grades is crucial to student success. Therefore, schools must do more than invite parents into the school; they must reach out into their communities and make parents feel needed and welcomed. They also must help parents see the value to their children of being active in the middle school. High-performing schools create structures and systems to facilitate parent involvement. We ask principals what the school does to make parents feel that they are an integral part of the school.

In one school with a student population of around 570, about 70 parents are actively involved under the leadership of a volunteer coordinator. Parents at this school donated over 5,000 academic hours in one year as part of the parent volunteer program. This level of parental activity does not happen by chance. A parent volunteer coordinator is trained by the district's central office for the position; in turn, the coordinator trains the school volunteers. Parents fill out applications to volunteer, indicating their available hours. The parent volunteer coordinator calls the parents, who must be fingerprinted, have criminal background checks, and get a TB skin test prior to volunteering. The parent volunteers take part in an orientation session, in which they receive training in areas as diverse as student confidentiality and running the copying machines. Most important, the parents become an integral part of the school's aspirations for student development and achievement. A father at this school summed up parent involvement this way: "At this school the child is in the center of a circle, and everyone is around that child to reach out and help him or her mature and learn."

We ask parents what they think is the key to increasing parent involvement, and they often mention the responsiveness of staff members and the welcoming environment of the school. Many parents we speak with say that it means a lot to them when the principal greets them by name when they walk in the school door. These details are important to parents and communicate to them that they are valued members of the school. One parent said, "Parents are accepted as full partners in the school. We are welcomed with open arms."

Parents also appreciate that the school shares information with them. At one school, parents can call into an information-on-demand system. Using a PIN number, they have immediate access to their child's academic, attendance, and discipline records. A homework hotline gives parents access to their child's homework assignments on any given night. At another school, parents can access their child's homework assignments through the school's website. Some teachers communicate with parents via e-mail during the course of the day. If a problem comes up or if there is something positive the teachers want to share with parents, they can do so immediately and at their convenience. In these various ways, schools help parents gain access to information and be more involved in their children's education.

When evaluating a school on this criterion, ask yourself:

- Are there many parents in the school? Do they have lunch with the students and talk to the teachers and counselors?
- Is there a family center in the school, and do parents run it?
- What communication systems does the school have to make sure that every family is contacted at least once a month?
- Does the principal know many family members by name?
- What does the school do to ensure that parents and family members play meaningful roles, for instance, on the school council and school committees?

Social Equity

Criteria

Faculty and administrators expect high-quality work from all students and are committed to helping each student produce it. Evidence of this commitment includes tutoring, mentoring, offering special adaptations, and other supports. All students have equal access to valued knowledge in all classes and school activities.

When the forum visits schools, we are especially interested in how accessible academic and extracurricular programs are to students with disabilities. Inclusion for students with special needs means more than simply including them in the same classes as regular students. It often means adapting curriculum, instruction, and assessment to their special needs. For a socially equitable school, ensuring that all students have access to academic and extracurricular programs, having high expectations for all students, and providing the support to help them meet those expectations are paramount.

When evaluating a school, we ask the teachers and principal about the kinds of support they provide for students with disabilities and special needs. At one school, students with diagnosed learning and behavioral disabilities are included in classes that are co-taught by regular teachers and special education teachers. In this school, students with learning disabilities and their teachers are not relegated to an out-of-the-way room; they are an integral part of the school community. The special education teachers are equal partners in the design and delivery of classroom instruction. They collaborate with subject-matter teachers in designing instructional units and share the responsibility of teaching classes. The special education teachers are consulted by many teachers in the school and are valued for their knowledge about teaching students with learning disabilities.

In another school, students with severe cognitive or behavioral disabilities cannot be included in regular academic classes. Nonetheless, these students participate in school life to the greatest extent possible and are held accountable for their work. Their teacher believes it is important for these students to be expected to accomplish a great deal in their self-contained class. So, for example, when this teacher reads his students a story, they know they are going to be assessed on it the next day.

Another thing that we look at when evaluating schools is how they support those students who are at risk academically. In an otherwise heterogeneously grouped school we visited, the principal had instituted a program called "Academic Connections" to help students achieve the required standards and beyond. In this program, students are divided into three groups according to their achievement test scores and are provided with instruction specifically geared to their skill levels. Another school offers two after-school programs that provide additional instructional time to students who are not meeting academic standards. The student/teacher ratio in the after-school classes is low—about 12 students per teacher—in order to allow for more individualized instruction. The participating teachers meet with one another to determine which students will receive additional tutorial time based on the students' needs. At yet another school, the resource room is open to all students for additional tutorials in reading and math. While some students are assigned to the reading and math resource tutorials, all students have the option to drop in voluntarily.

Principals and teachers at socially equitable schools foster an atmosphere of inclusion by ensuring that all students have access to the richest and most challenging programs—programs that are usually available to only some students. Many schools across the country have mandated special programs for their highest-achieving students. One principal who believes that all her students should have access to the enriched learning opportunities offered in these programs is in the process of ensuring that all her teachers become certified in instruction for the gifted and talented. So far, 50% of her faculty has earned this certification. This principal also allows any student who has the motivation, the will, and parental permission to do so to take an advanced class in math or language arts.

When evaluating a school on these criteria, ask yourself:

- Is there evidence that all students are being held accountable to high standards? Are students with disabilities and limited English proficiency held to those same standards?
- Do students have access to supports and programs to help them meet or exceed the standards?
- Do teachers work together to identify the students who need additional support? Do teachers share their knowledge and expertise with one another about the best ways to provide support to struggling students?
- Are special education teachers, extracurricular teachers, and others who deliver services to students seen as equal partners in the education of all students? Are their special skills and expertise valued in the school?
- Is there evidence of tracking or low-level classes with watered-down curricula in the school? Are students grouped by skill level for the purposes of instruction?

- If the school has a mandated program for the gifted and talented, how are students selected for this program? How do students and teachers who are not participating benefit from the program?

Criterion

The school's suspension rate is low, and students from specific demographic groups are not disproportionately represented among the suspended.

Each school's suspension rate became a critical factor in our evaluation—actually rising to the level of "deal breaker" in deciding whether to designate a school an STW. This is because we believe that when a school has a high suspension rate or suspends students from particular groups at a grossly higher rate than others and has no plan for addressing these problems, it is a sign that the school does not have the same expectations for all students.

Suspended students miss valuable classroom time, and the time they spend in in-school suspension is generally a waste. Therefore, a crucial factor in our evaluations of schools is what students are required to do during suspensions. Are they expected to complete the work they are missing in their classes? Do their teachers visit them to keep them up-to-date on assignments? If the students need counseling in order to get back on track, do they receive it from a school counselor or social worker? Is the school aware of the obstacles and barriers the students may be facing outside of school, and do school personnel intervene to help these students get assistance or counseling? While in order to ensure students' safety all schools must have a discipline code that establishes clear consequences for students who break rules, the way a school understands and tries to change patterns of suspension ultimately reflects its beliefs about social equity.

One school we visited disaggregated its suspension data manually by race, socioeconomic status, and gender because its district did not have the technological capacity to provide this service. As a result of their data analysis, which identified unacceptably high suspension rates, the staff members of this school zeroed in on reducing the amount of instructional time missed. Staff members tracked the amount of time that passed from the moment a student was referred to the administration for disciplinary action until a decision about consequences was made. As a result of this exercise, students no longer waste instructional time sitting in the office waiting for administrative disposition. In addition, the school registers student demographic information for each referral (e.g., gender, race, free/reduced-priced-lunch status, length of time in the school), the name of the student's teacher, and other categories of information. Administrators share this information at faculty meetings, and the staff discusses why the referral happened and what to do about it. Through this process the principal and her staff also found a positive correlation between discipline referrals and reading failure. They instituted a schoolwide reading program to address problems in reading and, consequently, to help reduce the school's suspension rate. This kind of data gathering and school-wide effort bears dramatic results: in just one year this school reduced its suspension rate by one-third.

When evaluating a school on this criterion, ask yourself:

- What is the school's suspension rate, and are particular groups of students disproportionately represented among the suspended?
- Do key people in the school know its suspension rates?
- What are students required to do during in-school suspension?
- Does the school examine data related to suspension rates? What does it do with the data?
- If the school's suspension rates are high, particularly among a racial or ethnic group, what are the principal and the faculty doing to lower these rates?

Organizational Structures and Processes

In order for schools to be academically excellent, developmentally responsive, and socially equitable, there must be appropriate structures and processes in place. When evaluating schools, the forum looks at whether these structural factors are in place to allow the school to excel.

Criterion

Someone in the school has the responsibility and authority to oversee the school improvement enterprise and move it forward. This person or group has the knowledge and the ability to conduct the daily coordination, strategic planning, and communication needed to improve a school.

There is just no getting around it, to become excellent a school must have a risk-taking, visionary, practical leader. One of the STW principals likes to quote Joel Barker: "A leader is a person you would follow to a place you wouldn't go to by yourself."[2]

When evaluating a school, we ask the principal what he or she finds lacking in the school. We then ask the action question: What steps will you take to address the problem? Invariably, the principal has a plan on the drawing boards. In one school, for instance, the principal believes her students are being short-changed technologically. Her action plan includes:

- *Studying.* She and her teachers will look at outstanding programs across the state.
- *Training.* She will draw on the expertise of the district's curriculum director, who is a proponent of instructional technology. The director has a train-the-trainers process that the principal would like to adopt in her school so that the teachers can teach one another.
- *Monitoring.* She will require her teachers to report how their specific plans to use technology will improve instruction and increase student performance.

We ask principals about their sources of inspiration. Excellent school leaders can answer this question articulately. For instance, one principal, who is an ardent proponent of school-based decision making, was influenced by John Goodlad's school renewal plan. This principal organized her school staff into Goodlad's five cadres: planning, curriculum and instruction, communication, school climate, and staff development. (She later added a technology cadre.) Each cadre chooses by consensus co-leaders who constitute the "campus advisory team," which is the school's shared-decision-making committee. This is not process for the sake of process; the purpose is to create a structure and climate for school improvement. All staff members must serve on the cadres so that, as the principal says, everyone is "part of the solution. No one can sit back and whine."

When we ask principals what their goals were when they first came to their schools, they have no trouble rattling them off. One principal's three major goals were to strengthen the school's academics, improve the learning environment, and increase parent participation. Over the course of her first year at the school, this principal met with her staff to turn these goals into manageable objectives for their school improvement plan. She wanted staff members both to see the big picture and to be able to focus on what was doable. In her second year, she and the staff developed specific goals in all three areas, which have driven the school ever since.

We ask principals to tell us very specific anecdotes that illustrate their leadership styles. Here is one such story, in which the principal's leadership combines strategic thinking, inclusiveness, and humor. At the outset of her administration, this principal took the building itself under her wing as part of an effort to get an unruly school back under control. While the building needed repairs—even the water fountains were broken—the custodial staff argued that the students would destroy anything they fixed. The principal disagreed and, in order to quickly accomplish a visual change—what she calls "the image of discipline"—she had the school facilities fixed and cleaned.

From the beginning of her principalship, she wove the contributions of community partners into the school's goals. To encourage teachers to help keep the building clean by getting their hands dirty picking things up from the floors, the principal got Target, a new school partner, to contribute 100 bottles of hand cleaner, which she dispensed to a surprised staff during a faculty meeting.

We also ask principals to list the top three to five things they would do if moving to another school. This is one of the principals favorite questions, because it challenges them to evaluate their work to date and fantasize about starting over. One principal came up with the following:

1. Communicate a vision for student success very early on, continually articulate the vision throughout the year, and have a plan for realizing it. Staff members need to see very early on how high the bar is raised, what the expectations are, and what needs to be done to get there.

2. Look at how the school collects data, in which areas, and how the data are used for planning. What guides schoolwide initiatives? It is extremely important to collect data, formally and informally, to support the school's goals. There is no other way to be able to assess accurately the school's strengths and weaknesses.

3. Look at how each schoolwide initiative is tied into the school improvement plan. It is easy to get off track quickly. Before you know it, there is so much going on in the school that things can quickly become disconnected.

4. Continually encourage the staff in the great things they are already doing and give them the latitude and flexibility to try something new and different.

5. Open the school and its classrooms to external critical friends. We constantly talk about the need for accountability as well as the need for continuous school improvement. What a great way to achieve both by having professionals in the field with specific expertise come into the school to observe our teaching practices in the classroom and review our supports for students and provide feedback.

When evaluating a school on this criterion, ask yourself:

- Does the school look like what it wants to be?
- Does it have a single, thorough, credible plan for reaching its vision?
- Does everyone know what the plan is? Do they respect it? Do they endorse it enthusiastically? Can they articulate it?
- Is the plan a healthy stretch for faculty and students?

Criteria

The school holds itself accountable for its students' success rather than blaming others for its shortcomings. The school collects, analyzes, and uses data as a basis for making decisions, including school-generated evaluation data that it uses to identify areas for more extensive and intensive improvement. The school delineates benchmarks and insists upon evidence and results. The school intentionally and explicitly reconsiders its vision and practices when data call them into question.

We ask high-performing schools how they know if they are meeting their behavioral and academic goals. Their answers invariably have to do with "sleuthing their data." The data the administration and staff collect and analyze serve as the basis for decisions about areas needing more focused attention and changes in practice. Data provide evidence of need, improvement, and success or failure.

One school collects student work, sometimes monthly and sometimes biweekly, as evidence of whether its school improvement plan is leading to higher student achievement. The school has developed what it calls a "crate system." All teachers submit a crate of examples of high-, medium-, and low-level student work along with lesson plans that they propose to help improve their students' knowledge and skills. A curriculum committee meets monthly to evaluate the content of the crates. The information from this evaluation is compiled into what the school calls a "Vital Signs Report."

In addition, at least once every nine weeks, "content leaders" facilitate a content-area meeting—a time for all teachers of the same subject matter to evaluate student work and student progress. Information from this "impact check," along with the "vital signs report," is forwarded to the school's decision-making council, where schoolwide decisions affecting continuous improvement are made. Teachers' data collection improves their day-to-day instructional practice; it also ties the school's governance structure to the school's achievement goals.

We ask schools what they do when their data analysis tells them they are not meeting their goals. We have observed a school that uses staff development days to go over students' state test data by subject area. Test data have become one of several lenses for understanding the strengths and weaknesses of every student and teacher and for setting improvement strategies. Together, the principal and the teachers study state data, objective by objective, and then take action. For instance, when only 53% of the school's students were skilled in summarization,

teachers focused on that objective schoolwide. In this school, analysis of test data makes the test serve the school's instructional goals.

Data analysis is not a dry affair in these schools. One principal has studied patterns of teacher absences to learn which times of the year absences are greatest and to devise morale-building strategies for those times. Running the numbers helps her meet the needs of the adults in her school so that her teachers are energized to work with their students.

When evaluating a school on these criteria, ask yourself:

- What tools and processes does the school use to set high standards for progress?
- Does the school continually collect and use data to seek evidence that it is meeting its goals?
- Does the school avoid blaming others for its shortfalls?
- Are there examples of ways that the school changed its approach in response to an examination of its data?

Conclusion

Using a construct for assessing schools concentrates the mind on their mission, accomplishments, and failures. But using evaluation criteria as part of a rigid checklist can lead to looking at the parts disconnected from the whole—or the soul—of the school. The ethos of the school—its personality, its environment, its spirit—is every bit as important as its particular practices and structures. High-performing schools are places where adults and children live, grow, and learn well. These schools are driven by a sense of purpose about children's intellectual, ethical, social, and physical development. These schools are also vibrant adult learning communities. The intellectual ante is high, and a can-do spirit pervades the school, from the janitors and cafeteria workers to the parents, students, teachers, and administrators. The work ethic is palpable. Relationships between adults and students are relaxed, demanding, and caring. The corridors and cafeteria are noisy but peaceable, the adults are energetic and enthusiastic, and the students are attentive and expressive. These schools are a part of, not apart from, their communities. One leaves these schools with a renewed sense of hopefulness about the power of the teaching/learning contract between adults and students.

It is a joy to visit these schools. You may not be able to quantify "joy," but look for it within both the school and yourself. It is the most important criterion of all.

Notes

1. The full set of criteria for each priority and for assessing the organizational structure of a school can be viewed at the forum's website, **www.schoolstowatch.org**.

2. Joel Barker, *Paradigms* (New York: HarperCollins, 1992).

POSTNOTE

The authors of this comprehensive article are reporting on their research on middle schools. However, as they acknowledge, the various criteria and factors related to high-performing schools they identify also have relevance to elementary and high schools. As such, the article provides a rich bank of questions that educators can use as they reflect on their own school or as school observers.

The question, "Which of the three divisions, elementary, middle, or high school, is most important?" is difficult to determine. Various "blue ribbon" educational reports and the views of individual experts do not provide a clear consensus. However, the middle school years, particularly in the early years, appear to be a time when many students "disengage" from the educational mission. They become frustrated with the academic work, distracted by outside concerns, or both. While they continue to show up for school, academic knowledge and skills are hardly on their priority list. This often casual and "below-the-radar" choice they make has a profound impact on their futures.

As the authors note, a high-performing school is not one that simply caters to eager and cooperative students. Rather, the teachers and administrators in such a school go after the potentially "lost sheep." They make special efforts to keep these vulnerable students engaged and moving forward.

DISCUSSION QUESTIONS

1. The authors identify three priorities of high-performing schools. What are they? In your view, what is their order of importance, and why?

2. Toward the end of the article, the authors report on five questions a principal (or any educator) might ask about a school to which he or she might move. What are they?

3. What does the term *sleuthing the data* mean, and how might it be used to improve the performance of a school?

RELATED WEBSITE RESOURCE

WEB RESOURCE:

The National Forum to Accelerate Middle-Grade Reform. Available at:

http://www.mgforum.org/ImprovingSchools/tabid/56/Default.aspx.

This organization, which one of the authors has been associated with, maintains a school improvement website which addresses many of the issues raised by this article.

13

A Tale of Two Schools

Larry Cuban

Larry Cuban is an emeritus professor of education at Stanford University, Stanford, California. Prior to university teaching, Cuban had a rich career as a teacher, trainer of Peace Corps volunteers, principal, and school superintendent. His major contributions to the field include his studies of urban education and his historical perspectives on school curricula.

"A Tale of Two Schools," by Larry Cuban, Education Week, Vol. 17, No. 20, January 28, 1998. Reprinted by permission of the author.

FOCUS QUESTION

Can schools with seemingly divergent philosophies of education nevertheless prepare their students to be good citizens in a democracy?

InTASC

Standards 1, 2, 3, 4, 7, 8, and 10

KEY TERMS

- "Good" school
- Progressive school
- Traditional school

For this entire century, there has been conflict among educators, public officials, researchers, and parents over whether traditionalist or progressive ways of teaching reading, math, science, and other subjects are best. Nowhere has this unrelenting search for the one best way of teaching a subject or skill been more obvious than in the search for "good" schools. Progressives and traditionalists each have scorn for those who argue that there are many versions of "good" schools. Partisan debates have consumed policymakers, parents, practitioners, and researchers, blocking consideration of the unadorned fact that there is more than one kind of "good" school.

What follows is a verbal collage of two elementary schools I know well. School A is a quiet, orderly school where the teacher's authority is openly honored by both students and parents. The principal and faculty seek out students' and parental advice when making schoolwide decisions. The professional staff sets high academic standards, establishes school rules that respect differences among students, and demands regular study habits from the culturally diverse population. Drill and practice are parts of each teacher's daily lesson. Report cards with letter grades are sent home every nine weeks. A banner in the school says: "Free Monday through Friday: Knowledge— Bring Your Own Container." These snippets describe what many would call a "traditional" school.

School B prizes freedom for students and teachers to pursue their interests. Most classrooms are multiage (6- to 9-year-olds and 7- to 11-year-olds). Every teacher encourages student-initiated projects and trusts children to make the right choices. In this school, there are no spelling bees; no accelerated reading program; no letter or numerical grades. Instead, there is a year-end narrative in which a teacher describes the personal growth of each student. Students take only those standardized tests required by the state. A banner in the classroom reads: "Children need a place to run! explore! a world to discover." This brief description describes what many would call a "progressive" school.

I will argue that both Schools A and B are "good" schools. What parents, teachers, and students at each school value about knowledge, teaching, learning, and freedom differs. Yet both public schools have been in existence for 25 years. Parents have chosen to send their children to the schools. Both schools have staffs that volunteered to work there. And both schools enjoy unalloyed support: Annual surveys of parent and student opinion have registered praise for each school; each school has had a waiting list of parents who wish to enroll their sons and daughters; teacher turnovers at each school have been virtually nil.

Moreover, by most student-outcome measures, both schools have compiled enviable records. In academic achievement, measured by standardized tests, School A was in the top 10 schools in the entire state. School B was in the upper quartile of the state's schools.

These schools differ dramatically from one another in how teachers organize their classrooms, view learning, and teach the curriculum. Can both of them be "good"? The answer is yes.

What makes these schools "good"? They have stable staffs committed to core beliefs about what is best for students and the community, parents with beliefs that mirror those of the staffs, competent people working together, and time to make it all happen. Whether one was traditional or progressive was irrelevant. The century-long war of words over traditional vs. progressive schooling is a cul-de-sac, a dead end argument that needs to be retired once and for all.

What partisans of each fail to recognize is that this pendulum-like swing between traditional and progressive schooling is really a deeper political conflict over what role schools should play in society. Should schools in a democracy primarily concentrate on making citizens who fulfill their civic duties? Should schools focus on efficiently preparing students with skills credentials to get jobs and maintain a healthy economy? Honor individual excellence yet treat everyone equally? Or should schools do everything they can to develop the personal and social capabilities of each and every child? For almost two centuries of tax-supported public schooling in the United States, all of these goals have been viewed as both important and achievable.

The war of words between progressives and traditionalists has been a proxy for this political struggle over goals. Progressive vs. traditionalist battles over discipline in schools, national tests, tracking students by their performance, and school uniforms mask a more fundamental tension in this country over which goals for public schools should have priority.

The problem lies not in knowing how to make schools better. Many parents and educators already know what they want and possess the requisite knowledge and skills to get it. Schools A and B are examples of that knowledge in action. The problem is determining what goals public schools should pursue, given the many goals that are desired and inescapable limits on time, money, and people.

Determining priorities among school goals is a political process of making choices that involves policymakers, school officials, taxpayers, and parents. Deciding what is important and how much should be allocated to it is at the heart of the process. Political parties, lobbies, and citizen groups vie for voters' attention. Both bickering and deliberation arise from the process. Making a school "good" is not a technical problem that can be solved by experts or scientific investigation into traditional or progressive approaches. It is a struggle over values that are worked out in elections for public office, tax referendums, and open debate in civic meetings, newspapers, and TV talk shows. Yet these simple distinctions between the political and the technical, between goals for schools and the crucial importance of the democratic process determining which goals should be primary, seem to have been lost in squabbles over whether progressive or traditional schools are better.

And that is why I began with my descriptions of the two schools. They represent a way out of this futile struggle over which kind of schooling is better than the other. I argue that both these schools are "good."

One is clearly traditional in its concentration on passing on to children the best knowledge, skills, and values in society. The other is progressive in its focus on students' personal and social development. Each serves different goals, each honors different values. Yet—and this is the important point that I wish to drive home—these seemingly different goals are not inconsistent. They derive from a deeply embedded, but seldom noticed, common framework of what parents and taxpayers want their public schools to achieve.

What is different, on the surface, are the relative weights that each "good" school gives to these goals, how they go about putting into practice what they seek, and the words that they use to describe what they do. The common framework I refer to is the core duty of tax-supported public schools in a democracy to pass on to the next generation democratic attitudes, values, and behaviors. Too often we take for granted the linkage between the schools that we have and the kind of civic life that we want for ourselves and our children. What do I mean by democratic attitudes, values, and behaviors? A few examples may help:

- Open-mindedness to different opinions and a willingness to listen to such opinions.
- Respect for values that differ from one's own.
- Treating individuals decently and fairly, regardless of background.
- A commitment to talk through problems, reason, deliberate, and struggle toward openly arrived-at compromises.

I doubt whether partisans for traditional and progressive schools, such as former U.S. Secretary of Education William J. Bennett, educator Deborah Meier, and academics like Howard Gardner and E. D. Hirsch, Jr., would find this list unimportant.

Tax-supported public schools in this country were not established 150 years ago to get jobs for graduates. They were not established to replace the family or church. They were established to make sure that children grew into literate adults who respected authority, could make reasoned judgments, accept differences of opinions, and fulfill their civic duties to participate in the political life of their communities. Over time, of course, as conditions changed, other responsibilities were added

to the charter of public schools. But the core duty of schools, teachers, and administrators—past and present—has been to turn students into citizens who can independently reason through difficult decisions, defend what they have decided, and honor the rule of law. Our traditional and progressive schools each have been working on these paramount and essential tasks.

Consider such democratic values as individual freedom and respect for authority. In School A, students have freedom in many activities, as long as they stay within the clear boundaries established by teachers on what students can do and what content they must learn. Staff members set rules for behavior and academic performance, but students and parents are consulted; students accept the limits easily, even enjoying the bounded freedom that such rules give them. School A's teachers and parents believe that students' self-discipline grows best by setting limits on freedom and learning what knowledge previous generations counted as important. From these will evolve students' respect for the rule of law and their growth into active citizens.

In School B, more emphasis is placed on children's individual freedom to create, diverge from the group, and work at their own pace. Students work on individually designed projects over the year. They respect teachers' authority but often ask why certain things have to be done. The teacher gives reasons and, on occasion, negotiates over what will be done and how it will be done. School B's teachers and parents believe that students' self-discipline, regard for authority, and future civic responsibility evolve out of an extended, but not total, freedom.

Thus, I would argue, both of these schools prize individual freedom and respect for authority, but they define each value differently in how they organize the school, view the curriculum, and engage in teaching. Neither value is ignored. Parents, teachers, and students accept the differences in how their schools put these values into practice. Moreover, each school, in its individual way, cultivates the deeper democratic attitudes of open-mindedness, respect for others' values, treating others decently, and making deliberate decisions.

Because no researcher could ever prove that one way of schooling is better than the other, what matters to me in judging whether schools are "good" is whether they are discharging their primary duty to help students think and act democratically. What we need to talk about openly in debates about schooling is not whether a traditional school is better or worse than a progressive one, but whether that school concentrates on instilling within children the virtues that a democratic society must have in each generation. Current talk about national goals is *not* about this core goal of schooling. It is about being first in the world in science and math achievement; it is about preparing students to use technology to get better jobs. Very little is said about the basic purpose of schooling except in occasional one-liners or a paragraph here and there in speeches by top public officials.

What are other criteria for judging goodness? I have already suggested parent, student, and teacher satisfaction as reasonable standards to use in determining how "good" a school is. I would go further and add: To what degree has a school achieved its own explicit goals? By this criterion, School A is a clear success. Parents and teachers want children to become literate, respectful of authority, and responsible. Although School B scores well on standardized tests, parents and teachers are less interested in test results. What School B wants most are students who can think on their own and work together easily with those who are different from themselves; students who, when faced with a problem, can tackle it from different vantage points and come up with solutions that are creative. Parents and teachers have plenty of stories about students' reaching these goals, but there are few existing tests or quantitative measures that capture these behaviors.

So, another standard to judge "goodness" in a school is to produce graduates who possess these democratic behaviors, values, and attitudes. This is, and always has been, the common, but often ignored, framework for our public schools. It has been lost in the battle of words and programs between public officials and educators who champion either traditional or progressive schools. A "good" school, I would argue, even in the face of the technological revolution and globalization of the U.S. economy in this century, is one that has students who display those virtues in different situations during their careers as students and afterwards as well.

My criteria, then, for determining good schools are as follows: Are parents, staff, and students satisfied with what occurs in the school? Is the school achieving the explicit goals it has set for itself? And, finally, are democratic behaviors, values, and attitudes evident in the students?

Why is it so hard to get past the idea that there is only one kind of "good" school? Varied notions of goodness have gotten mired in the endless and fruitless debate between traditionalists and progressives. The deeply buried but persistent impulse in the United States to create a "one best system," a solution for every problem, has kept progressives and traditionalists contesting which innovations are best for children, while ignoring that there are more ways than one to get "goodness" in schools.

Until Americans shed the view of a one best school for all, the squabbles over whether a traditional schooling is better than a progressive one will continue. Such a futile war of words ignores the fundamental purpose of public schooling as revitalizing democratic virtues in each generation and, most sadly, ignores the good schools that already exist.

POSTNOTE

We select this article as a classic because of the profound importance of its message: a call to educators to rise above ideological squabbles and get on with the serious business of educational excellence.

What one defines as a "good" school depends on what one values, says Larry Cuban, which makes perfectly sound sense. A person's educational philosophy will determine how that person views schooling, teaching, and curriculum. Thus, many different types of good schools can—and do—exist.

Cuban's point argues for giving parents choices about the kinds of school their children attend. By offering different kinds of school that represent different educational philosophies and by allowing parents to select the school of their choice, school boards can better satisfy parents' educational preferences. In this way, more parents will be more committed to the school they have selected as well as inclined to believe their children attend good schools.

DISCUSSION QUESTIONS

1. Of the two schools that Cuban describes in his article, would you prefer to teach in School A or School B? Why?
2. Describe the characteristics of the kind of school that you would consider to be "good."
3. Do you agree with Cuban's assertion that the common framework of public schools should be to "pass on to the next generation democratic attitudes, values, and behaviors"? Is there anything else that you would add to this common framework?

RELATED WEBSITE RESOURCES

WEB RESOURCES:

American Philosophical Association (APA).
Available at:

http://www.apaonline.org/.

This excellent website provides basic information and reference material on many branches and schools of philosophy.

The Society for Philosophical Inquiry (SPI).
Available at:

www.philosopher.org.

SPI is a grassroots nonprofit organization devoted to supporting philosophical inquirers of all ages and walks of life. There are a number of ways to get involved, such as its Socrates Cafe program.

"As Though They Owned the Place": Small Schools as Membership Communities

Deborah Meier

Deborah Meier is a senior scholar at New York University and the MacArthur Award-winning founder of Central Park East School in East Harlem, New York. She has spent more than thirty years working in public education as a teacher, principal, and writer. As reflected in this essay, her primary focus has been finding ways to make schools work.

"As Though They Owned the Place": Small Schools as Membership Communities, by Deborah Meier, Phi Delta Kappan 87, no. 9 (May 2006), pp. 657–662. Reprinted by permission of the author.

Small schools were once the norm. When I was born, there were 200,000 school districts in North America. Schools generally averaged under a hundred students. Most people—above all in the vast majority of communities that had only one or two schools in the district—knew their schools and school board members well. Accountability was a thing very close to home and often highly contentious. If you were a member of a community, you had a say—however irritating it might be to your neighbors.

Today, there are fewer than 15,000 school districts serving nearly three times as many children, and most districts have relatively little say over matters that were once their primary responsibility. More and more decisions lie in hands far removed from communities, families, teachers, and kids.

This change has happened within my lifetime. The reasons have been many—including the greater importance of education itself in the future of both individuals and the nation and the struggle for equity and civil rights that reshaped school law with regard to race, gender, and the rights of the handicapped. The change went hand in hand with the diminishing of the role of local life in so many matters, as it has seemed more appropriate to handle more decisions on a state, regional, or national level. Whether all of these changes necessitated larger schools and larger school districts and whether some of the tradeoffs made were truly necessary are issues worth examining.

The pendulum has swung too far away from the face-to-face quality of old-time accountability ("vote the rascals out") and the potential for strong parent and community involvement that went more naturally with greater

FOCUS QUESTION

What have we lost by all this "bigness" in schooling?

InTASC
Standards 1, 2, 3, 7, 9, and 10

local voice. The question we face today is how to determine the value of small schools in redressing some of the negative consequences associated with large schools and districts without sacrificing the benefits that came along with them.

If a central, nonnegotiable function of public schooling in the U.S. is to strengthen our democracy, then we must examine all the issues that affect the ability of schools to do so, many of which are at the heart of why we need small schools. Students learn from us; the robustness of our school community, its capacity to exercise judgment on important matters, and its inclusiveness are all part of young people's education. Where else might kids learn about the tradeoffs, critical judgments, and responsibilities inherent in democratic life—including when and how to resist? If educating young people to make judgments based on credible evidence, reasoning, and collaboration with others is essential to our task, then we must create schools that have the intention of practicing these arts and the time to do so. In order to align the means with the ends, we must ask more probing questions about the ends we desire for our schools. If we seek only to improve scores on tests of standards determined by others, then educating students for democratic life is not necessary—and maybe small schools aren't either.

Some of the consequences of consolidating small schools into larger schools and districts have not only been bad for democracy but have also made all forms of serious intellectual rigor in schools more, not less, difficult to address. The kinds of relationships that can develop in a small school between students and their teachers and between teachers and the school's community turn out to be critical in determining what can be effectively demanded of its students.

While small schools can have a significant impact on the education of our kids, it is not ordained that small schools will achieve the ends we seek. We can have small schools that behave like big ones, or we can have small schools that take advantage of their size to improve the learning that goes on within them in terms of intellectual standards and the development of responsible citizens.

The official distribution of power within a school is always a difficult issue to discuss. But when we fail to do so, we tend to overlook that the unofficial powers often end up undermining the official ones. For example, kids and teachers have the power to sabotage and resist the best intentions of reformers. When a big school, especially if it is in a big district, decides to go small, it is often responding to a struggle over power. Control and accountability with regard to money, safety, personnel, and educational outcomes—far removed these days from the daily life of the school and its immediate constituents—will be more difficult to keep track of and monitor if we quadruple the number of schools. Too often, having more small schools becomes a nuisance instead of an asset and leads to new forms of resistance and new efforts to monitor and control. Are we prepared to tackle this problem?

Small schools are an idea that will work only if we are prepared to open up and examine the contents of other cans of worms. Is the district ready to reconsider where each of a wide range of decisions is made? How money is distributed? What the line of command is? We've had a history of fads that sputter out because we tend to simply pile one reform on top of another without looking carefully at the foundation. Let me share what I call the "big five" issues that those considering a move to smaller schools would do well to consider.

1. *Acknowledge that there will be tradeoffs.* If we opt for small schools, we are making choices, accepting tradeoffs that big schools do not have to make. The big comprehensive high school can teach five foreign languages, even if no one really learns any of them. They can have honors tracks and semi-vocational tracks large enough so that each segment can feel like a school of its own, not a marginalized group. Large schools can afford orchestras, bands, a newspaper, and lots of other exciting stuff—even if only a small elite group of students actually experiences the wide range of electives and extracurricular activities. Each of these "extras" has a constituency ready to go to the mat for it.

Small schools force us to ask: What matters most? What are kids not getting in the larger educational world of media/TV/screen/etc. or from their busy families that is essential to the good health of the public sphere? What's altogether out of balance now without the intervention of schools? What aspects of being "well educated" must the school provide in order to create an appropriate balance? For example, schools can provide inter-generational relationships; thoughtful and long-standing personal ties; communication across other-wise alienated and separated communities of heart and mind; direct, authentic experience with the nat-ural world; experience with books, with writing, with scientific tools and experimentation; the nuan-ces of mathematics; civil debate and disagreement; experience with compromise; and on and on. None of these come to us naturally today, but they are all naturals for small schools. But at what price? And it is a price that must be considered so that it doesn't spark a backlash that we're unprepared for.

2. *Pay attention to genuine outcomes.* We should assess and graduate kids based on their real capacity to show us what they know and can do. Real-life projects, portfolios, auditions, exhibitions, oral defenses, and so on are natural demonstrations of solid academic work, well suited to small schools. In addition, building our assessment around long-term impacts is another obvious approach that has been neglected. But even if the roots of such practices predate standardized tests, we will need to sort out the proper balance between these types of assessment and the ones most communities are now accustomed to.

We must keep coming back to the basics. The power of smallness lies in the effectiveness of learn-ing through the company one keeps—the oldest teaching method on earth. We know that most important adult occupations have historically been passed on in just this way. We abandoned the apprenticeship model of learning at a price that we needn't have paid.

Smallness allows young people to learn again in the company of powerful adults. Learning to be a citizen, like learning math or science, is best accom-plished by observing adults engaged in the same kinds of activity. Young people today have little experience seeing what makes adults powerful and effective. But even here the realities need to be monitored. How do

we know that ownership of learning is being shared? Or that kids are interested in the adults (and vice versa)? Is there the same percentage of kids who are not noticed and fall through the cracks in a small school as in a big school, or are there fewer of them? In short, the forms of accountability need to be broadened to embrace the school's mission.

3. *Be sure important constituents are on board.* If not, go slower or offer choices. Even if you can "make 'em," it doesn't last.

Start only as many small schools as you have people to staff them and families to choose them. Avoid choices that divide haves from have-nots or the "gifted" from the "others." Otherwise, go for whatever is legal and exciting, even if it's just a group of adults who want to work together. Give those involved maximum autonomy, which is what will grease the wheels for otherwise reluctant fac-ulty members and maybe even for families. People will tend to exploit their capacities to the fullest in the interests of proving that their own ideas work. Above all, give schools their own per-capita bud-gets, so that they can make choices that reflect their own priorities. And don't believe it when people say such changes won't cost any more. At least for starters, they will.

4. *Avoid false efficiencies.* Speaking of money, start counting what a small school costs not per student but per graduate. Remember, a new prac-tice that drives up the dropout rate is anything but an efficient use of scarce dollars. Be sure that the methods you have for keeping track are consistent with your purposes.

5. *Reassure the recalcitrant.* Tell folks that over the next decade you expect to gradually increase the number of small schools and the range of choices—but only as people are persuaded to want them. There may always be room for one big school in a district with 25 small ones. Don't, I repeat, don't mandate smallness so that everyone must do it. Who knows? Let the old schools and the new schools speak for themselves. If I'm right about small schools, it will get easier and easier to persuade folks.

But even if you keep these big five principles in mind, going small still will not be easy. Here are some other hints for getting a change to small schools off on the right foot.

It takes time. How long? Three to five years, at least. And don't start with a whole school at once. Begin with one age group of 60 to 80 kids and three or four adults, with a plan to grow, year by year, into a school of 200 or so. Or start with a sixth and ninth grade and let the school grow over the years until it includes grades 6–12. Set a realistic time line for when you expect to have the start-up glitches fixed. It can easily take three to five years for you to grow a school to its full size, build communitywide understanding of its mission, and tweak it as needed. It will require a few more years to make sure a school's approach doesn't need more than tweaking. This is where external school reviews are so useful in giving the public some feedback.

The importance of continuity. Make sure a school has a plan to enroll kids for four or more years. Such grade spans as K–3, K–6, K–8, 4–8, 5–12, etc., can all work. It's in knowing kids year after year, and gaining in the process the trust of families and the understanding in the larger community, that big changes become possible—and successful. This continuity allows reforms to be sustained.

Be inclusive. Make sure each school has a plan that can handle both those students who make running a school easier and those who make it harder. It's okay to have a focus or theme, but not one that rules out kids who might be hard to teach. (Figuring out how to be sure every kid has real freedom of choice is the district's task.) From the start, think through what small schools can offer to the full range of kids and which kids, if any, might be better served separately. Be sure the funds for special needs go with the kids.

Physical space. Small schools waste space. Of necessity. So bear that in mind when planning. Make sure each small school has turf to call its own— including a bathroom and a way to get into and out of the building without bothering others. Make sure that the offices aren't all centralized; guidance staff and school heads need to be close to the action. If necessary, settle for science labs that are less fancy, so that each school has its own labs. Create spaces where different constituencies and different ages can interact—large faculty rooms where everyone has a desk or "central" offices with computers, copying machines, and phones in which principal, office manager, parents, teachers, and kids can congregate. This kind of use of space creates a sense of community and ownership.

Don't be missionaries. Make sure that new and fragile schools are not expected to carry the burden of convincing others—beyond their own community of kids and families—that they are doing good work. Those who are struggling to create a good small school can't be proselytizers for the small schools movement. That's the district's job. When the time seems ripe, arrange for visiting days, led by parents and kids as well as by staff members.

Keep lines of communication open. Be sure to build in ways for the new schools to interact with one another and with the schools not in the project. Arrogance can kill the whole program off. Beware the "one true way," and don't abandon the ones "left behind" in the traditional schools—or they'll get their revenge.

Keep lots of data. Keep a wide range of data— who signs on, who leaves and for what reason (kids and teachers), what the evidence is for student achievement, who gets in trouble. Pay attention to trends. Since longitudinal data on cohorts of kids are the only truly reliable data, build in a way to collect such data right from the start. And keeping in touch with families and kids who leave the school or who graduate is the best source of feedback a faculty and other families can get. Make sure it's in the district's plans to shoulder part of this burden of accounting for results.

Different data are needed for different audiences. For kids and their parents, data drawn from a sample of students won't do; this audience needs information about individual students. On the other hand, the larger, more anonymous public wants information on the overall performance of schools, so sample data are appropriate because they provide a richer and more accurate picture of student achievement across schools.

Accountability. The kind of data a school and district keep will determine the kind of accountability that can be pursued. Make sure that the form of accountability recognizes the special nature of these new schools. So be sure that standardized test scores are only part of, not the complete definition of, the school's standards. Make sure that the school says up front what it's aiming for and works out within a few years some ways to provide evidence of its success or failure. Schools should also report the means they are using to improve practice when faults and flaws are discovered.

School review can be a form of accountability. From the start, build in a process for reviewing school progress that's consistent with the reform itself. This means that you will need some form of school review that allows judges to get to know a school well enough to comment knowledgeably on its strengths and weaknesses and to have access to a wide range of evidence. Such a process is more costly than just printing out test scores, but it's the district's most critical task.

In Boston, the new, small Pilot schools are reviewed every four years by five educators from different fields and areas of expertise. They examine specified documents ahead of time and spend three days visiting a school. Then they prepare a document for the school's own board and for Boston's superintendent, who has ultimate authority. The process leads to one of three ratings: all's well; the school should be placed in a probationary status while certain specific issues are addressed; or the district should consider closing or reorganizing the school.

Professional development. No plan is any better than what's actually happening inside schools—first and foremost in classrooms, but also in all those shared spaces and the places where key actors interact and at meetings with families. Keep large-scale districtwide (or even buildingwide) professional development to a minimum—at least at first. Instead, give schools the time to build a community of adults as well as youngsters. That means providing time for staff to meet daily—even for a short time. Also provide for more extended weekly gatherings and for less frequent prolonged "retreats." Since faculty stability is at the heart of building a school culture (and constantly recycling staff is costly and inefficient), having the funds required for internal professional development is key. Make sure professionals have a week to talk

among themselves before the school year, as well as a week during the year and one afterward. This is a practice any summer camp thinks necessary, but many schools don't. Involve faculty members in the selection of their colleagues, as well as in observing and critiquing one another. Treat staff morale as central; it is not a luxury item.

The union. Don't start off by assuming that union leaders won't love this idea. In many places, unions have been the initiators of small school reform. As long as the development of small schools doesn't become a tactic for union busting or for undermining teachers' collective power, it can be viewed as a perfect tool for providing a strong professional base for teacher unions. Make sure to have an understanding with the union of what a living contract could be like—one that leaves most details to the school site and can be changed as conditions change. School staff members need to be able to shape aspects of the contract to match their school's design and governance style. Bring these issues down to the school level, where all parties can reach the best understanding of how strong unions lead to good teaching and learning.

Leadership. The success of small school reform depends on a different kind of school-based leadership, a kind more collegial than administrative. There are many different models of such leadership, but all require principals who think more like teachers than they do in big schools and teachers who think more like principals. There must be co-ownership of the reform. Teachers and principals must be eager to see what their colleagues are up to. Most would-be principals have never experienced such co-leadership and will need help in doing so. If we don't provide models, they may view such a style as "weak" leadership. They need to interact with colleagues in the same situation: handling the problems that come with being half colleague and half school head. We need new forms of training in leadership for small schools.

It's also important, as small schools are phased in, that one strong and respected member of the district-level team be there as a trusted ally and resource for the school-level leaders. Having a strong advocate in the central office is key to making sure folks feel they are being heard.

Parent involvement. If parents are to be our allies—which is possible when they know their children's teachers well—we need to tackle another can of worms. In the past, when we've decried the lack of parent involvement, we've mostly not meant it. Few school people really feel comfortable when a group of parents starts hanging around asking questions and wanting a voice in decisions. We want parents there when we need them, but we don't spend a lot of time imagining what it would require if we were to be there when they need us. We need a different view of time. How can we ensure that parents will have the time to attend to their children's school issues without losing their jobs? What would we need to put in place so that parents could reach us easily and comfortably with information about family emergencies or just to share their worries about their children? While some of the necessary changes will be at least partly beyond our control, they ought to be on our agenda. However, one thing within our control is reducing the number of adults parents must get to know well to one or two individuals over two, three, or more years.

Probably each school will find that what it needs is not more guidance counselors, but a wise family/school coordinator, trained to help allies with different kinds of tunnel vision to work well together. This position is not a throwaway to hand over to an active parent as a reward. It requires real skill and training. At best, it requires someone with experience as a family therapist and as a consultant and advisor to organizations.

Buildingwide issues. Finally, never let small details go unnoticed. One that sometimes gets overlooked when small schools share a building is: who's minding the physical plant?

A plethora of details will crop up daily as different autonomous schools with different styles share a building. How kids and adults who attend different schools in the same building relate to one another is important. It helps a lot if the students are not all of the same age, so wherever possible schools serving different age groups should be placed in the same building. Sometimes parents worry about this idea. Can young children be assigned to the same building as teenagers? Actually, in my experience, this almost always is mutually beneficial to both groups.

It helps if the heads of all the small schools in a building meet regularly to discuss shared issues, with someone responsible (perhaps on a rotating basis) for following up on decisions made. A plant manager will probably be needed to deal with the kitchen, security, and custodial issues. It also helps to figure out how to use shared spaces and to remember that any decision must be sufficiently flexible to allow for the kinds of lives that schools live—full of emergencies, unexpected crises, joyful celebrations, and more.

These fledgling new schools need to see one another as allies—even though at times they may bump into one another. They need to take pride in the "complex"—the site—as a whole and in all its parts. They need to appreciate their diversity, not their sameness. There are some practices that may help in this regard, such as common sports teams and after-school activities or shared fundraisers to build a common photo lab, ceramics studio, or dance room.

Putting all of this down on paper scares me. I hope it doesn't scare readers. It's a lot to do at once. Fortunately, some of it will come naturally, while other aspects will bedevil you for years. And who knows which will prove to be which?

But this much I know: it will be exciting, and kids will thrive in the excitement of being part of a new venture. A colleague at a new small school in San Francisco complained to me recently, "The trouble is the kids walk around the school like they own it." And then after a pause she added, "And I suppose that's the good thing too. But it takes time to get used to it and get the balance right." Ditto for parents and, blessedly, for teachers too. And that's why it works.

The more complex, centralized, distanced, virtual, and diverse the larger world, the more important it is for young people, their parents, and their teachers to feel the power of their own ideas; to embrace their own capacity to influence and have an impact; to learn to hear, to listen, and to argue; to check out abstractions through metaphors that they have experienced together. It's the solid foundation they need in order to move into the larger world with confidence, "as though they owned the place."

POSTNOTE

Americans are an innovative and restless people. These characteristics are seen in the way we "do" education. We love our schools, but continually criticize them. We seem to be constantly in search of the "new new thing." One of the newest movements in American schooling is "smallness." Large high schools are being reconfigured into "schools within schools" with separate faculties and student bodies. Where once a community would build one big elementary school, now they will build three small schools. "Small" is in!

This article is a classic because the author's ideas were instrumental in challenging the educational status quo. Deborah Meier is one of the pioneers of this movement toward smaller schools. However, she is no one-sided cheerleader. Her reflections here, based on her own experience and having observed many new efforts to convert to smaller schools, provide balance and direction to teachers and administrators. Her title, "'As Though They Owned the Place': Small Schools as Membership Communities," captures the "two-edged" quality of many small schools: an environment of personal connectedness. One of the major criticisms of our large schools is that they breed impersonal relationships among teachers, students, administrators, and parents. The complaint is that the "connective tissue" among these groups is weak and thin. In small schools, however, people know one another and, in turn, are known. There is an environment of personal accountability and a shared sense of ownership. This places demands on all concerned, but the benefits are looking increasingly attractive.

DISCUSSION QUESTIONS

1. What are the major educational advantages for students in small school settings?
2. What are the major advantages for teachers?
3. On the other hand, what is lost? Or rather, what are the advantages of large schools?

RELATED WEBSITE RESOURCES AND VIDEO CASE

WEB RESOURCES

Planning Resources for Teachers in Small High Schools. Available at:

http://www.smallschoolsproject.org.

The Small Schools Project, founded and funded by the Gates Foundation, has many resources on this site for educators to maximize the impact of small schools.

Small Schools Workshop. Available at:

http://www.smallschoolsworkshop.org.

This site has several links to subtopics, such as arguments for small schools, ways to increase students' achievement, and small-school-related research.

▶❚❚ TEACHSOURCE VIDEO CASE

SOCIAL AND EMOTIONAL DEVELOPMENT: UNDERSTANDING ADOLESCENTS

In this video case, you will see how Shania Martinez, a guidance counselor, helps a group of seventh-grade boys deal with the anger they feel in everyday life. Go to the website for the Education Media Library at CengageBrain.com to watch the video clips, study the artifacts in the case, and reflect on the following questions.

1. What do you think of the ideas students generate in how to deal with frustration?
2. One student, Alan, advises teachers to really listen to their students. Can you recall any of your teachers who were particularly good listeners? Was their listening effective? In what ways?

15

Who's Cheating Whom?

Alfie Kohn

Alfie Kohn, the author of the book *The Schools Our Children Deserve*, is a highly praised writer and speaker on education, human behavior, and social theory.

FOCUS QUESTION

Is cheating more a sign of flaws in the education system than in a student's character?

InTASC
Standards 1, 2, 3, 6, 9, and 10

An article about cheating practically writes itself. It must begin, of course, with a shocking statistic or two to demonstrate the pervasiveness of the problem, perhaps accompanied by a telling anecdote or a quotation from a shrugging student ("Well, sure, everyone does it"). This would be followed by a review of different variants of unethical behavior and a look at who is most likely to cheat. Finally, a list of ideas must be provided for how we can deter or catch cheaters, along with a stern call for greater vigilance.

Just about everyone agrees that cheating is bad and that we need to take steps to prevent it. But it is precisely this overwhelming consensus that makes me uneasy. Whenever a conclusion seems so obvious and is accepted so uncritically, it's probably time to take a fresh look. That doesn't mean we're obligated to give equal time to arguments in favor of cheating, but it may make sense to reconsider what the term actually signifies and examine what leads students to do what they're not supposed to—and what that tells us about their schooling.

In the 1970s, Lee Ross, a social psychologist at Stanford University, attracted some attention (at least within his field) by coining the term "fundamental attribution error." He defined this as a tendency to "underestimate the impact of situational factors and to overestimate the role of dispositional factors in controlling behavior."[1] Ross was summarizing what a number of experiments had already demonstrated: we frequently pay so much attention to character, personality, and individual responsibility that we overlook how profoundly the social environment affects what we do and who we are.

There are surely examples of this error to be found everywhere, but it may be particularly prevalent in a society where individualism is both a descriptive reality and a cherished ideal. We Americans are stubbornly resistant to the simple truth that another eminent social psychologist, Philip Zimbardo, recently summarized in a single sentence: "Human behavior is more influenced by things outside us than inside."[2] Specifically, we're apt to assume that people who commit crimes are morally deficient, that the have-nots in our midst are lazy (or at least insufficiently resourceful), that children who fail to learn simply aren't studying hard enough (or have unqualified teachers). In other words, we treat each instance of illegality, poverty, or academic difficulty as if it had never happened before and as if the individual in question were acting out of sheer perversity or incompetence.

Cheating is a case in point because most discussions of the subject attribute the problem to the cheaters themselves. The dominant perspective on the issue, as educational psychologist Bruce Marlowe recently remarked, "is all about 'Gotcha!'"[3] This continues to be true even though we've known for quite some time that the environment matters at least as much as individual character when trying to predict the occurrence of various types of cheating.

Nearly 80 years ago, in a study that has come to be regarded as a classic work of social science, a group of researchers at Teachers College, Columbia University, investigated almost 11,000 children between the ages of 8 and 16 over a period of five years and found that "even slight changes in the situation affect individual behavior in unpredictable ways." As a result, the correspondence between what any given child would do in two different circumstances was "lower than would be required for accurate prediction of individual behavior." Cheating, the researchers concluded, "is as much a function of the particular situation in which [the student] is placed as it is of his own inner experience and training, his general ideas and ideals, his fears, ambition, and purposes."[4]

Since the publication of that report, a fair amount of research has accumulated to illuminate the situations in which students are most likely to cheat and to help us understand the reasons they do so. First, we've learned that when teachers don't seem to have a real connection with their students, or when they don't seem to care much about them, students are more inclined to cheat.[5] That's a very straightforward finding, and not a particularly surprising one, but if taken seriously it has the effect of shifting our attention and reshaping the discussion.

So, too, does a second finding—cheating is more common when students experience the academic tasks they've been assigned as boring, irrelevant, or overwhelming. In two studies of ninth- and 10th-graders, for example, "Perceived likelihood of cheating was uniformly relatively high … when

a teacher's pedagogy was portrayed as poor."[6] To put this point positively, cheating is relatively rare in classrooms where the learning is genuinely engaging and meaningful to students and where a commitment to exploring significant ideas hasn't been eclipsed by a single-minded emphasis on "rigor." The same is true in "democratic classes where [students'] opinions are respected and welcomed."[7] List the classroom practices that nourish a disposition to find out about the world, the teaching strategies that are geared not to covering a prefabricated curriculum but to discovering the significance of ideas, and you will have enumerated the conditions under which cheating is much less likely to occur. (Interestingly, one of the mostly forgotten findings from that old Teachers College study was that "progressive school experiences are less conducive to deception than conventional school experiences"—a result that persisted even after the researchers controlled for age, I.Q., and family background. In fact, the more time students spent in either a progressive school or a traditional school, the greater the difference between the two in terms of cheating.[8])

Third, "when students perceive that the ultimate goal of learning is to get good grades, they are more likely to see cheating as an acceptable, justifiable behavior," as one group of researchers summarized their findings in 2001.[9] Cheating is particularly likely to flourish if schools use honor rolls and other incentives to heighten the salience of grades or if parents offer financial inducements for good report cards.[10] In other words, cheating is more likely if students are not merely rewarded for academic success, but are also rewarded for being rewarded.

Grades, however, are just the most common manifestation of a broader tendency on the part of schools to value product more than process, results more than discovery, achievement more than learning. If students are led to focus on *how well* they're doing more than on *what* they're doing, they are more inclined to do whatever they think is necessary to make it look as though they're succeeding. Thus a recent study of more than 300 students in two California high schools confirmed that the more classrooms drew attention to students' academic performance, the more the students "engaged in various types of cheating."[11]

The goal of acing a test, getting a good mark, making the honor roll, or impressing the teacher is completely different from—indeed, antithetical to—the goal of figuring out what makes some objects float and some sink or why the character in that play we just read is so indecisive.[12] When you look at the kind of schooling that's all about superior results and "raising the bar," you tend to find a variety of unwelcome consequences: less interest in learning for its own sake, less willingness to take on challenging tasks (since the point is to produce good results, not to take intellectual risks), more superficial thinking ..., and more cheating.

That is exactly what Eric Anderman, a leading expert on the subject, and his colleagues have observed. In a 1998 study of middle school students, they found that those who "perceived that their schools emphasized performance [as opposed to learning] goals were more likely to report engaging in cheating behaviors." Six years later, Anderman turned his attention to the transition from eighth to ninth grade and looked at the culture of individual classrooms. The result was essentially the same: more cheating took place when teachers emphasized good grades, high test scores, and being smart; there was less cheating when teachers made it clear that the point was to enjoy the learning, when understanding mattered more than memorizing, and when mistakes were accepted as a natural result of exploration.[13] Interestingly, these studies found that even students who acknowledged that it's wrong to cheat were more likely to do so when the school culture placed a premium on results.

It makes perfect sense when you think about it. Cheating can help you to get a good grade and look impressive (assuming you don't get caught), so it's a strategy that might well appeal to students with those goals. But it would be pointless to cheat if you were interested in the learning itself because cheating can't help you understand an idea.[14] How, then, do students *develop* certain goals? What leads them to display an interest in what they're doing as

opposed to a concern about how well they're doing it? Individual dispositions count for something; obviously, all students don't behave identically even in the same environment. But that environment—the values and policies of a classroom, a school, or a society—is decisive in determining how pervasive cheating will be.[15] It affects students' behaviors at the moment and shapes their values and attitudes over time. What the data are telling us, like it or not, is that cheating is best understood as a symptom of problems with the priorities of schools and the practices of educators. To lose sight of that fact by condemning the kids who cheat and ignoring the context is to fall into the trap that Lee Ross warned us about.

One major cause of cheating, then, is an academic environment in which students feel pressured to improve their performance even if doing so involves methods that they, themselves, regard as unethical. But when you look carefully at the research that confirms this discovery, you begin to notice that the worst environments are those in which the pressure is experienced in terms of one's standing *relative to others*.

Competition is perhaps the single most toxic ingredient to be found in a classroom, and it is also a reliable predictor of cheating. Grades are bad enough, but the practice of grading on a curve—or ranking students against one another—is much worse. Similarly, while it's destructive to lean on students to raise their test scores, it's even more damaging to lead them to think about how their scores compare to those of other students (in another school or another country). And while using *rewards* to "motivate" people is generally counterproductive,[16] the negative effects are intensified with *awards*—which is to say, the practice of making recognition artificially scarce so that students must try to triumph over one another.

Competitive schools are those where, by design, all students cannot succeed.[17] To specify the respects in which that arrangement is educationally harmful may help us understand its connections to cheating.

Competition typically has an adverse impact on relationships because each person comes to look at everyone else as obstacles to his or her own success. Competition often contributes to a loss of intrinsic motivation because the task itself, or the act of learning, becomes a means to an end—the end being victory. (Competition may "motivate" some people, but only in the sense of supplying an extrinsic inducement; at best this fails to promote interest in the task, but more often interest in the task actually diminishes.) Competition often erodes academic self-confidence (even for winners)—partly because students come to think of their competence as dependent on how many people they've beaten and partly because the dynamics of competition really do interfere with the development of higher-order thinking.[18] In each case, cheating becomes more likely, as students feel unsupported, uninterested, and incompetent, respectively.

In short, a competitive school is to cheating as a warm, moist environment is to mold—except that in the latter case we don't content ourselves with condemning the mold spores for growing. Moreover, competition is the ultimate example of focusing on performance rather than on learning, so it's no wonder that "cheating qualifies as part of the unhealthy legacy that results from having tied one's sense of worth to achieving competitively," as the eminent psychologist Martin Covington explained. In an early investigation, he heard echoes of this connection from the students themselves. One told him, "Kids don't cheat because they are bad. They are afraid that they aren't smart and [of] what will happen if they don't do good." Another said that students who cheat "feel really bad but it is better than being yelled at for bad grades." And from a third: "People cheat because they are afraid of doing poorer than other kids and feeling miserable for being different and behind. Some do it to be the best in class or move to the next group."[19] How ironic, then, that some of the adults who most vociferously deplore cheating also support competitive practices—and confuse competitiveness with excellence—with the result that cheating is more likely to occur.

Because competition, a relentless focus on achievement, and bad pedagogy aren't new, it stands to reason that cheating isn't exactly a recent development either. In 1928, the Teachers College group had no shortage of examples to study. In fact, Elliot Turiel compared surveys of students from the 1920s with those conducted today and found that about the same percentage admitted to cheating in both eras—an interesting challenge to those who view the past through a golden haze and seem to take a perverse satisfaction in thinking of our times as the worst ever.[20]

But let's assume for a moment that the alarmists are right. If it's true that cheating or at least some versions of it really are at all-time highs, that may well be because pressures to achieve are increasing, competitiveness is more rampant and virulent, and there is a stronger incentive to cut corners or break rules. In fact, we're currently witnessing just such pressures not only on children but on teachers and administrators who are placed in an environment where everything depends on their students' standardized test scores.[21]

If schools focus on relative achievement and lead students to do the same, it may be because they exist in a society where education is sometimes conceived as little more than a credentialing ritual. Schools then become, in the words of educational historian David Labaree, "a vast public subsidy for private ambition," places where "self-interested actors [seek] opportunities for gaining educational distinctions at the expense of each other." And if the point is just to get ahead, he continues, individuals may seek "to gain the highest grade with the minimum amount of learning."[22] Cheating could be seen as a rational choice in a culture of warped values.

A deep analysis of cheating may lead us to investigate not only the situations that give rise to it but the process by which we decide what will be classified as cheating in the first place. Even a careful examination of the social context usually assumes that cheating, almost by definition, is unethical. But perhaps things are more complicated. If cheating is defined as a violation of the rules, then we'd want to know whether those rules are reasonable, who devised them, and who stands to benefit by them. Yet these questions are rarely asked.

Some kinds of cheating involve actions that are indisputably objectionable. Plagiarism is one example. While it's not always clear in practice where to draw the line between an idea that has been influenced by the work of other writers and one that clearly originated with someone else (and ought to be identified as such),[23] we should be able to agree that it's wrong to use a specific concept or a verbatim passage from another source without giving credit if the objective is to deceive the reader about its origin.[24]

More interesting, though, and perhaps just as common, are those cases where what is regarded as cheating actually consists of a failure to abide by restrictions that may be arbitrary and difficult to defend. It's not just that questionable educational practices may *cause* students to cheat; it's that such practices are responsible for *defining* certain behaviors as cheating. In the absence of those practices and the ideology supporting them, such behaviors would not be regarded as illegitimate.

This unsettling possibility enjoys a prima facie plausibility because there are plenty of other things we regard as facts of life whose existence actually turns out to be dependent on social context. Sportsmanship, for example, is an artificial concept that wouldn't exist at all except for competition: only in activities where people are attempting to defeat one another is it meaningful to talk about doing so in a graceful or virtuous fashion. (People who play cooperative games don't require reminders to be "good sports" because they're working *with* one another toward a common goal.) Likewise, theft does not exist in cultures where there is no private property—not because people refrain from stealing but because the idea literally has no meaning if people's possessions are not off-limits to one another. There is no such thing as leisure unless work is experienced as alienating or unfulfilling. You cannot commit blasphemy unless you believe there is a God to be profaned. And jaywalking is a meaningless concept in Boston, where I live, because there is simply no expectation that pedestrians should cross only at intersections.

On what, then, does the concept of cheating depend for *its* existence? One answer was supplied by a scandal at the Massachusetts Institute of Technology in the early 1990s. More than 70 students were punished for "cheating" because they worked in small groups to write computer programs for fear that they would otherwise be unable to keep up with their class assignments. "Many feel that the required work is clearly impossible to do by straightforward"—that is, solitary—"means," observed the faculty member who chaired MIT's Committee on Discipline.[25]

The broader context in which to understand this episode is that cooperative learning, beyond helping students deal with an overwhelming workload, also provides a number of benefits when compared with individual or competitive instructional models. By working together, students not only are able to exchange information and divide up tasks but typically end up engaging in more sophisticated problem-solving strategies, which, in turn, results in more impressive learning on a range of measures. Structured cooperation in the classroom also proves beneficial in terms of self esteem, relationships, and motivation to learn.[26]

The problem, however, is that, aside from the occasional sanctioned group project, the default condition in most American classrooms—particularly where homework and testing are concerned—is reflected in that familiar injunction heard from elementary school teachers: "I want to see what you can do, not what your neighbor can do." (Or, if the implications were spelled out more precisely, "I want to see what you can do all by yourself, deprived of the resources and social support that characterize most well-functioning real-world environments, rather than seeing how much more you and your neighbors could accomplish together.") Whether, and under what circumstances, it might make more sense to have students learn, and to assess their performance, in groups is an issue ripe for analysis. Alas, most collaboration is simply classified as cheating. End of discussion.

By the same token, students may be disciplined if they consult reference sources during any sort of assessment in which the teacher has forbidden the practice. But what does it say about the instructor, and the education system, that assessment is geared largely to students' ability to memorize? What pedagogical purpose is served by declaring that students will be judged on this capacity and must therefore spend a disproportionate amount of time attempting to cram dates, definitions, and other facts into their short-term memories? How else might we have encouraged them to spend that time? And what is the purpose of this sort of assessment? Is information being collected about students' capacity to remember what they've read or heard for the purpose of helping them to learn more effectively—or is the exercise more about sorting them (comparing students to one another) or controlling them (using assessment to elicit compliance)?

It may well be that students who use "unauthorized" materials or assistance thereby compromise the teacher's preferred method of assessment. But perhaps this should lead us to question the legitimacy of that plan and ask why those materials have been excluded. Similarly, if "cheating hinders standardization," as one group of academics warned,[27] should we condemn the cheaters or question the value of a standardized education? Again, we can expect lively debate on these questions; but again, what is troubling is the absence of such debate—the result of uncritically accepting conventional definitions and assumptions. Consulting a reference source during an exam (or working with one's peers on an assignment) will be classified as cheating in one classroom, with all the grave implications and practical repercussions attendant on that label, while it will be seen as appropriate, even admirable, in another. Students unlucky enough to find themselves in the first classroom stand condemned of cheating, with little attention paid to the nature of the rules they broke. To that extent, *their actions have violated a purely conventional set of prohibitions, but they are treated as though guilty of a* moral *infraction.*

Moreover, any student who offered just such a defense, perhaps arguing that her action was actually less problematic than the instructor's requirements, or that what she did was more like entering a lecture hall through a door marked "exit" than like lying or stealing, would probably be accused of engaging in denial, attempting to displace responsibility for what she has done, or trying to rationalize her behavior. Once we've decided that the student's action is morally wrong, her efforts to challenge that premise, no matter how well reasoned, merely serve to confirm our view of her immorality.

In 2006, a front-page story in the *New York Times* described how instructors and administrators are struggling to catch college students who use ingenious high-tech methods of cheating. In every example cited in the article, the students were figuring out ways to consult their notes during exams; in one case, a student was caught using a computer spell-check program. The implication here, which is that students even at the university level are being tested primarily on their capacity to memorize, was noted neither by the reporter nor by any of his sources. Only a single sentence dealt with the nature of the assessments: "Several professors said they tried to write exams on which it was hard to cheat, posing questions that outside resources would not help answer."[28] Even here, the intent appeared to be foiling cheaters rather than improving the quality of assessment and instruction. Or, to put it differently, the goal was to find ways to prevent students from being *able* to cheat rather than addressing the reasons they *wanted* to cheat or what the instructors *regarded* as cheating.

These distinctions are important. An Alabama student, quoted in another article, pointed out that "you can cheat if all you are going to be tested on are facts, but it is much harder to cheat when you are asked to … write an essay." However, this student went on to make a much more significant point: "Maybe a bigger problem is that teachers require students to memorize instead of teaching them how to think."[29] The deficiencies of the curriculum, in other words, go well beyond whether they facilitate or discourage cheating. Dudley Barlow, a retired high school teacher and education columnist, recalled assigning a research paper about El Salvador. One student began with some facts about the country

and then went on to describe how General William Booth and his band of followers worked diligently to help the downtrodden by spreading the gospel of Christ. I was absolutely stumped about the paper until I realized the student had sat in a library copying from an encyclopedia about El Salvador, and he had inadvertently turned two pages at one time. Without even realizing it, he began copying text about the Salvation Army.

This story presents us with a kind of projective test, notable for what our reactions to it reveal about us. It's not just that some will be appalled and others will find it funny; it's that some will regard it as a reflection on the student while others will zero in on what the teacher had assigned the student (and his classmates) to do. Fortunately, Barlow himself had the courage to adopt the latter point of view. "That student," he concluded, "finally convinced me that the kinds of research papers I had customarily assigned were not accomplishing what I had in mind."[30] What he had in mind, presumably, was helping students to learn as well as to take pleasure in doing so. And detecting or deterring cheating more effectively, as one language arts teacher explains, fails to address the "educational damage" caused by whatever systemic forces have taught students that "the final product takes precedence over learning."[31]

Let us suppose that cheating could be at least partly curtailed by tightly monitoring and regulating students or by repeatedly announcing the dire penalties that await anyone who breaks the rules. Would this result be worth the cost of creating a climate of mistrust, undermining a sense of community, and perhaps leading students to become less enthusiastic about learning? Rebecca Moore Howard, who teaches writing at Syracuse University, put it this way:

> In our stampede to fight what some call a "plague" of plagiarism, we risk becoming the enemies rather than the mentors of our students; we are replacing the student-teacher relationship with the criminal-police relationship.... Worst of all, we risk not recognizing that our own pedagogy needs reform... [if it] encourages plagiarism because it discourages learning.[32]

It is sometimes said that students who take forbidden shortcuts with their homework will just end up "cheating themselves" because they will not derive any intellectual benefits from doing the assignment. This assertion, too, is often accepted on faith and doesn't prompt us to ask just how likely it is that the assignment really would prove valuable if it had been completed in accordance with instructions. A review of the available evidence on the effects of homework fails to support widely held beliefs about its benefits.[33] To that extent, we're forced to confront the possibility that students' violation of the instructor's rules not only may fail to constitute a moral infraction but also may not lead to any diminution of learning. Outraged condemnations of cheating, at least in such instances, may turn out to have more to do with power than with either ethics or pedagogy. Perhaps what actually elicits that outrage is not a lack of integrity on the part of students so much as a lack of conformity.[34]

A penetrating analysis of cheating will at least raise these possibilities, even if it may not always lead to these conclusions. It will invite us to reexamine what comes to be called cheating and to understand the concept as a function of the context in which the label is used. Even if the reality of cheating is unquestioned, however, its causes will lead us to look at the actions of teachers as well as the (re)actions of students and at classroom and cultural structures as well as individual behaviors. Such a perspective reminds us that how we educate students is the dog; cheating is just the tail.

Notes

1. Lee Ross, "The Intuitive Psychologist and His Shortcomings: Distortions in the Attribution Process," in Leonard Berkowitz, ed., *Advances in Experimental Social Psychology* (New York: Academic Press, 1977), vol. 10, p. 183.
2. Philip Zimbardo, quoted in Claudia Dreifus, "Finding Hope in Knowing the Universal Capacity for Evil," *New York Times*, 3 April 2007, p. D-2.

3. Marlowe teaches at Roger Williams University in Rhode Island. Personal communication, August 2006.

4. Character Education Inquiry, *Studies in Deceit*, Studies in the Nature of Character, Vol. 1 (New York Macmillan, 1928), Book 1, pp. 381, 400.

5. See the research conducted with undergraduates and high school students by Gregory Schraw et al., "Interest and Academic Cheating," in Eric M. Anderman and Tamera B. Murdock, eds., *Psychology of Academic Cheating* (Burlington, Mass.: Elsevier Academic Press, 2007), pp. 59–86.

6. Tamera B. Murdock, Angela Miller, and Julie Kohlhardt, "Effects of Classroom Context Variables on High School Students' Judgments of the Acceptability and Likelihood of Cheating," *Journal of Educational Psychology*, vol. 96, 2004, p. 775. See also the research reviewed by Schraw et al., pp. 60–65.

7. This finding by Kay Johnston of Colgate University was described in Lynley H. Anderman, Tierra M. Freeman, and Christian E. Mueller, "The 'Social' Side of Social Context: Interpersonal and Affiliative Dimensions of Students' Experiences and Academic Dishonesty," in Anderman and Murdock, p. 207.

8. Character Education Inquiry, Book 2, p. 184.

9. This paraphrase of a conclusion by Donald McCabe of Rutgers University and his colleagues in an article called "Cheating in Academic Institutions: A Decade of Research" is taken from Eric M. Anderman, "The Effects of Personal, Classroom, and School Goal Structures on Academic Cheating," in Anderman and Murdock, p. 95.

10. Schraw et al., p. 69.

11. Jason M. Stephens and Hunter Gehlbach, "Under Pressure and Underengaged: Motivational Profiles and Academic Cheating in High School," in Anderman and Murdock, p. 127. See also the review of other research in Anderman, op. cit.

12. For more on the research behind this distinction and on the detrimental effects of overemphasizing academic performance, see Alfie Kohn, *The Schools Our Children Deserve* (Boston: Houghton Mifflin, 1999), chap. 2.

13. Eric M. Anderman, Tripp Griesinger, and Gloria Westerfield, "Motivation and Cheating During Early Adolescence," *Journal of Educational Psychology*, vol. 90, 1998, pp. 84–93; and Eric M. Anderman and Carol Midgley, "Changes in Self-Reported Academic Cheating Across the Transition from Middle School to High School," *Contemporary Educational Psychology*, vol. 29, 2004, pp. 499–517.

14. On this point, see Anderman, p. 93.

15. See, for example, Anderman, Griesinger, and Westerfield, op. cit.; and Angela D. Miller et al., "Who Are All These Cheaters?: Characteristics of Academically Dishonest Students," in Anderman and Murdock, p. 20.

16. Alfie Kohn, *Punished by Rewards*, rev. ed. (Boston: Houghton Mifflin, 1999).

17. This is also true of international rankings of student performance. Even putting aside the question of whether standardized tests should be accepted as valid indicators, when competence in math or literacy is framed in competitive terms, the goal is for American students to triumph over their peers. The accomplishments of children who happen to live in other lands are therefore viewed as troubling; we are encouraged to want those children to fail, at least in relative terms. For this reason alone, educational "competitiveness" is a deeply flawed idea. See Alfie Kohn, "Against Competitiveness," *Education Week*, September 19, 2007.

18. Alfie Kohn, *No Contest: The Case Against Competition*, rev. ed. (Boston: Houghton Mifflin, 1992).

19. Martin Covington, *Making the Grade: A Self-Worth Perspective on Motivation and School Reform* (Cambridge: Cambridge University Press, 1992), p. 91.

20. See Susan Gilbert, "Scientists Explore the Molding of Children's Morals," *New York Times*, 18 March 2003, p. D-5.

21. For an excellent review of the prevalence of, reasons for, and moral ambiguity surrounding cheating by educators in the context of high-stakes testing, see Sharon L. Nichols and David C. Berliner, *Collateral Damage: How High-Stakes Testing Corrupts America! Schools* (Cambridge, Mass.: Harvard Education Press, 2007), esp.

chap. 2. See also Thomas M. Haladyna, Susan Bobbit Nolen, and Nancy S. Haas, "Raising Standardized Achievement Test Scores and the Origins of Test Pollution," *Educational Researcher*, June/July 1991, pp. 2–7; and Claudia Kolker, "Texas Offers Hard Lessons on School Accountability," *Leangles Times*, 14 April 1999.

22. David F. Labaree, *How to Succeed in School Without Really Learning: The Credentials Race in American Education* (New Haven: Yale University Press, 1997), pp. 258, 32, and 259.

23. "Encouraged by digital dualisms, we forget that plagiarism means many different things: downloading a term paper, failing to give proper credit to the source of an idea, copying extensive passages without attribution, inserting someone else's phrases or sentences – perhaps with small changes – into your own prose, and forgetting to supply a set of quotation marks. If we ignore these distinctions, we fail to see that most of us have violated the plagiarism injunctions in one way or another, large or small, intentionally or inadvertently, at one time or another. The distinctions are just not that crisp," writes Rebecca Moore Howard in "Forget About Policing Plagiarism. Just *Teach*," *Chronicle of Higher Education*, 16 November 2001, p. B-24.

24. The intent to deceive is critical because plagiarism is sometimes unconscious. It's not uncommon for people to borrow someone else's work while genuinely believing it's their own. In fact, this happens often enough that it's been given a name ("cryptomnesia") and become a subject for social psychological research. See, for example, Alan S. Brown and Dana R. Murphy, "Cryptomnesia Delineating Inadvertent Plagiarism," *Journal of Experimental Psychology: Learning, Memory, and Cognition*, vol. 15, 1989, pp. 432–42; and Jesse Preston and Daniel M. Wegner, "The Eureka Error: Inadvertent Plagiarism by Misattributions of Effort," *Journal of Personality and Social Psychology*, vol. 92, 2007, pp. 575–84.

25. Quoted in Fox Butterfield, "Scandal over Cheating at M.I.T. Stirs Debate on Limits of Teamwork," *New York Times*, 22 May 1991, p. A-23.

26. See, for example, the research reviewed in David W. Johnson and Roger T. Johnson, *Cooperation and Competition: Theory and Research* (Edina, Minn.: Interaction Books, 1989); and in Kohn, *No Contest*. For a recent meta-analysis of the effects of cooperative learning and peer tutoring in elementary school, see Marika D. Ginsburg-Block, Cynthia A. Rohrbeck, and John W. Fantuzzo, "A Meta-Analytic Review of Social, Self-Concept, and Behavioral Outcomes of Peer-Assisted Learning," *Journal of Educational Psychology*, vol. 98, 2006, pp. 732–49.

27. Linda Garavalia et al., "How Do Students Cheat?," in Anderman and Murdock, p. 35.

28. Jonathan D. Glater, "Colleges Chase as Cheats Shift to Higher Tech," *New York Times*, 18 May 2006, pp. A-1, A-24.

29. This student is quoted in Paris S. Strom and Robert D. Strom, "Cheating in Middle School and High School," *Educational Forum*, Winter 2007, p. 112.

30. Dudley Barlow, "Cut, Paste, and Get Caught: Plagiarism and the Internet," *Education Digest*, May 2006, p. 40.

31. Lisa Renard, "Cut and Paste 101: Plagiarism and the Net," *Educational Leadership*, December 1999/January 2000, p. 41.

32. Howard, op. cit.

33. Alfie Kohn, *The Homework Myth: Why Our Kids Get Too Much of a Bad Thing* (Cambridge, Mass.: Da Capo Press, 2006).

34. The same motive appears to be on display when students who clearly have mastered the material in a course are nevertheless given a lower grade because they failed to complete all the homework. Here the student has implicitly disconfirmed the hypothesis that homework is necessary for successful learning, and the teacher responds by saying, in effect, that the point isn't to learn so much as it is to do what one is told.

POSTNOTE

In a Duke University study, 75 percent of high school students admitted to cheating. If copying another student's homework is included in the definition of cheating, that number climbed to 90 percent. We used to think that academically weak students were the ones who cheated; however, the Duke study found that 80 percent of honors and advanced placement (AP) students cheat on a regular basis.

Alfie Kohn, the author of this article, believes that the practices and mores of schools are as much to blame for cheating as the students themselves. When schools promote competition, reward students for good grades, and often provide boring instruction, Kohn says cheating should be expected.

He believes major changes to school practices would take care of what we label as "cheating."

DISCUSSION QUESTIONS

1. Do you agree or disagree with Kohn's perspective that cheating may have as much to do with the rules and procedures of schools as with the students themselves? Support your position.

2. Do you believe that by encouraging competition, schools may unwittingly be encouraging cheating? Why or why not?

3. What do you think are the most effective steps you can take to curb cheating by your students?

RELATED WEBSITE RESOURCE

WEB RESOURCE:

Plagiarism and the Web. Available at:

http://www.wiu.edu/users/mfbhl/wiu/plagiarism.htm.

This website, created by Professor Bruce Leland at Western Illinois University, is designed to help teachers deal with plagiarism.

16

Piece by Piece: How Schools Solved the Achievement Puzzle and Soared

Karin Chenoweth

Karin Chenoweth, an experienced educational writer, currently is a senior editor for the Education Trust. Prior to her current position, she also served as an education columnist for the *Washington Post* and before that was the senior writer and executive editor of *Black Issues in Higher Education* (now *Diverse*).

This article was adapted from her book, *"How It's Being Done": Academic Success in Unexpected Schools* (Harvard University Press, 2009).

Karin, Chenoweth, "Piece by Piece: How Schools solved the Achievement Puzzle and Soared," American Educator, Fall 2009. Reprinted by permission of the author.

FOCUS QUESTION

What are the keys to first-class education in urban schools?

InTASC

Standards 1, 2, 3, 7, 9, and 10

KEY TERMS

- Formative assessment
- Summative assessment

Most schools have traditionally been organized so that individual teachers operate in isolation, with no recognized standards for what or how to teach, and with only an occasional supervisor wandering through to criticize kids' behavior or teachers' bulletin boards.[1] Good principals have taken great care in hiring teachers, but traditionally, a principal's job has been widely understood within the education world to be handling and preventing crises, staving off parents by keeping them busy raising money for the school, and—at the high school level—producing winning sports teams. Superintendents are pretty much expected to do the same thing on a larger scale, which means they try to keep their school boards mostly focused on athletic fields and bond referenda instead of what and whether kids are learning.

That all sounds grim, but it gets worse. In general, teachers pretty much sink or swim—that is, become bad or good teachers—on their own, with very little help from their colleges' teacher preparation programs, little help from principals and colleagues, and shockingly little guidance on what they are actually supposed to teach.[2] "Teachers are born, not made," the old saw goes, implying that there is not really a body of knowledge and skill teachers need to master. Many a social studies teacher has been assigned to teach high school algebra with little more help than the airy sentiment, "A good teacher can teach anything."

As far as what they are supposed to teach, teachers have pretty much had to make it up. They have rarely been provided a systematic plan of instruction that allows them to know what a student should have learned before getting to their classroom, what each student needs to learn in their classroom, and what the student will learn once he or she leaves their classroom. If they're lucky, they have colleagues who take pity on them and help out, but even then, the solutions are idiosyncratic, leaving far too many kids studying the rain forest and *Charlotte's Web* multiple times in their school careers without ever studying animal classification and *Tom Sawyer*.

By operating without clear standards for what they are supposed to teach or good information about how to ensure students learn, teachers—particularly inexperienced ones—are left to hope their kids arrive knowledgeable, disciplined, organized, and able to understand material the first time it is presented. Kids, being kids, rarely come in pre-educated, and children who grow up in poverty or isolation often arrive significantly behind in vocabulary, background knowledge, and organizational wherewithal. When kids arrive behind, they need much more skilled instruction than most middle-class kids require. The resulting disconnect between teacher hopes and reality leads to endless teacher frustration and is at least part of the reason so many young teachers flee high-poverty, high-minority schools in search of "better" kids or abandon the profession altogether.[3]

The sense that low student achievement in high-poverty and high-minority schools is the fault of the students themselves—and their families—has permeated the education profession. As a result, not only many teachers but also many principals, superintendents, academics, and even much of the public have come to think that there is little schools can do to help low-income students and students of color achieve at levels comparable to their more privileged peers. I disagree.

For the past five years, I have been visiting high-poverty and high-minority schools that have demonstrated success through their student achievement data.

Each school's reading, math, and science achievement data have been thoroughly examined to ensure that not only are the schools doing well in the aggregate, but that each group of students is also doing well. In these schools, achievement gaps are narrow or, in some cases, nonexistent. Aside from a few rudimentary checks to ensure that they have achieved their success legitimately, I simply ask

the educators in those schools to describe what they do to achieve their success. My assumption is that they are the experts in their success, and that we need to learn what they have to teach. So it is all the more significant that I saw and heard about the same essential elements again and again.

Different principals and teachers list those elements in a different order and might use different words, but Molly Bensinger-Lacy, principal of Graham Road Elementary School in Falls Church, Virginia,[*] was particularly succinct: "The strategies for educating students to high standards are pretty much the same for all kids: teacher collaboration; a laserlike focus on what we want kids to learn; formative assessment to see if they learned it; data-driven instruction; personal relationship building."

In my new book, *How It's Being Done,* from which this article is drawn, I explore those essential elements and how I saw them play out in different schools and different contexts.

Anyone looking for simple answers will not find them here. As many of the teachers and administrators in these schools, which I call "It's Being Done" schools, have told me, there is no magic bullet—there is no single program, policy, or practice that will ensure all schools and all students will be successful. Educating children is a complex task, and when children live in poverty or isolation, the task is even more complex. If our nation is to have an educated citizenry, we must be very thoughtful and deliberate about the way we structure all children's educational experiences, All the elements described below work together to fundamentally change how we go about educating all students.

Teacher Collaboration

Many teachers, reading Bensinger-Lacy's recommendations for high standards of education, may say something along the lines of, "When are we

---

[*]All of the schools mentioned in this article are profiled in either my new book, *How It's Being Done: Urgent Lessons from Unexpected Schools* (Harvard Education Press, 2009), or it my 2007 book, *It's Being Done: Academic Success in Unexpected Schools* (Harvard Education Press).

supposed to collaborate? I teach all day, and during my planning times, I plan lessons and grade papers." Others may say, "We 'collaborate' [imagine air quotes and sarcastic tone], and it is such a waste of time. Then I have to go home and prepare lessons and grade papers until late at night." Both reactions are understandable in schools that do not provide the structures to make sure teacher collaboration is both possible and productive.

So let's begin at the beginning. The point of teacher collaboration is to improve instruction for students and to ensure that all students learn. No one teacher can be an expert in all aspects of the curriculum, all possible ways to teach it, and every child who sits in his or her class. But every teacher should have expertise that can be tapped by other teachers to improve their knowledge of their subject, their teaching skill, and their knowledge of their students.

It should be said, however, that learning from colleagues is not something that is built into the field of American teaching. It sometimes springs up because teachers organize themselves to work together, but it has not been integral to teacher professional development or school organization. When teachers advise each other, consult with experts, think deeply about new ways to teach the material, and examine existing research in a systematic way in order to help all their students learn the material, they are working in sharp contrast to the way teachers have traditionally been expected to work. They are working in schools that have the structures and systems in place that make collaboration meaningful.

Let's examine the conditions necessary for the kind of collaboration I saw in It's Being Done schools.

Time

I'm starting with the obvious, but that doesn't make it any less important. To make their time with students effective and worthwhile, teachers must have time to think about their lessons, observe each others' classes, examine student work, learn from colleagues and outside experts, and do all the other things that are subsumed under the term *collaboration.*

It's Being Done schools make sure that teachers have regular meeting times, usually during the course of the school day. The schools squeeze in the time where they can. Elementary schools generally schedule "specials"—that is, art, music, counseling, and physical education—so that all the students from a particular grade have them at one time, permitting the grade-level teachers time to meet. Some schools close early once a week to permit cross-grade collaborations. Others have aides start the school day, supervising the putting away of coats and boots, collecting homework and lunch money, and distributing backpack notices while teachers meet together. Many secondary schools schedule planning time so that the teachers can meet with their departments or teams. If possible, schools find money to pay teachers to stay after school or come in on Saturdays.

At Ware Elementary School in Fort Riley, Kansas, principal Deb Gustafson told me that when she speaks to other educators, the lack of available time to meet "is usually one of the biggest excuses." Since all schools have roughly the same amount of time, "The message needs to be that it has to be captured; creativity must be employed," she said.

The schools I visit are, for the most part, Title I schools, meaning that they receive federal funds aimed at high-poverty schools. As a result, they often have a bit more resources than non–Title I schools have to pay teachers to meet outside school hours or hire substitute teachers to allow for classroom observations. Not coincidentally, It's Being Done schools work hard to make sure that time with substitutes is not a waste of time for children. In Steubenville, Ohio, substitutes must get a minimum of one day of training in reading instruction and one day in math. In addition, each elementary school in the district is allocated 100 days of a substitute teacher; Wells Elementary hired a recently retired teacher for that part-time position.

One way or another, all of the schools carefully carve out time for teacher collaboration. But time is not enough. The time has to be well spent.

Rules of Engagement

To make teacher collaboration time productive, cultural norms about how that time will be spent must be established.

- *If you don't say it in the meeting, don't say it in the parking lot.* At Oakland Heights Elementary in Russellville, Arkansas, principal Sheri Shirley made this an explicit rule. Shirley wasn't looking to quell disagreements, but to ensure that they saw the light of day and didn't fester. Note, however, that this must be matched with openness on the part of the leader to hear things he or she might not want to hear.
- *Focus discussions on the things the school can control rather than what it can't.* Molly Bensinger-Lacy of Graham Road uses a graphic organizer for teachers to fill out all the causes of a given problem—and then together they cross out anything they don't have control over, from the poverty of the kids to the testing schedule of the district.
- *Focus on specific objectives related to instruction.* According to Ware Elementary's principal, Deb Gustafson, "meetings and requirements must be well organized, focused, agenda-driven, and contain specific expectations." Meetings should not be filled with the administrative trivia of new roll-call systems, hall-duty assignments, or anything else that could be handled by e-mail.

At the beginning of the school improvement process, principals often will sit in on the teacher collaboration meetings to make sure the sessions are productive; once teachers have begun to internalize the norms, teachers usually meet on their own. Often principals will require that specific products result from these meetings, such as a curriculum map, formative assessment, or group of lesson plans complete with assignments.

And when teachers observe other classrooms, it is often with a specific aim in mind, In Elmont, New York, I learned about Elmont Memorial Junior-Senior High School's evaluation process, in which an "action plan" is formulated to help teachers improve. Here's one example: "By observing Ms. McDonnell, you will take note of smooth transitions between lesson activities that will enable you to maintain student attention. From Ms. Smith, you will see the perfect implementation and enforcement of sound opening strategies. Finally, from Mr. Schuler you will observe the benefits reaped from a well-structured activity." This is not simply sending teachers off to wander and possibly pick up some tips from more experienced teachers, but rather a highly structured way of making sure teachers learn from each other.

Good Teachers Willing to Collaborate to Improve Student Achievement

Again, so obvious you want to say, "Duh." But that doesn't make this an unimportant point. "You've got to have master teachers," said Susan Brooks, the principal who led the improvement of Lockhart Junior High School, in Lockhart, Texas, "it's all about teachers."

It's Being Done principals warn prospective teachers that they will he expected to work collaboratively. "Our interviews take a really long time," Bensinger-Lacy says, because she lays out in great detail the collaborative environment teachers will be expected to participate in. This has not made it difficult to recruit; on the contrary, as word gets around and success builds, most It's Being Done schools have found it easier to find applicants.

Although It's Being Done schools hire carefully—and occasionally counsel out teachers unwilling or unable to work collaboratively—they also give good, experienced teachers time to get used to working in the kind of public way these schools require. One of the difficult issues involved in school improvement is that many veteran teachers are used to seeing a parade of one unsuccessful principal after another (not to mention superintendents), many of whom talk big before fizzling out. Those teachers need to be convinced that changing will be meaningful and not just another heartbreaking waste of time. That means there needs to be a commitment on the part of school leaders—who need the support of their superintendents—to stay in place for the improvement process. How long that takes depends on the school, but It's Being Done principals have told me that although there should be some signs of improvement, particularly in the school atmosphere, almost immediately, improvements in instruction might take as long as two or three years to be reflected in state test scores. To go from being the first school in Kansas to be put "on improvement" to one of the best schools in the state took Ware about six years; to go from being in the bottom third to the top third of schools in California took Imperial High School about as long.

Because the point of teacher collaboration is to improve student achievement, teachers in It's Being Done schools recognize that the students who struggle the most need the best teachers. At Wells Elementary, for example, one of the most accomplished reading teachers (in a building full of accomplished reading teachers) is assigned to teach the "lowest" class of struggling first-graders. This is in direct contrast to ordinary schools, where the best teachers are often rewarded with the "best" students, who are usually defined as those students who easily master new material with or without expert teachers.

While It's Being Done schools seek out accomplished teachers for tough assignments, they also recognize that someone just entering the profession, whether from a traditional or an alternative certification program, needs a great deal of support, "We got him as a baby, first rattle out," is the way Lockhart Junior High's Brooks described Jeffrey Knickerbocker, who came into teaching after working as a geophysicist. He himself said that when he first started, he was a "terrible teacher." But he got the help and support he needed and is now widely acknowledged both by his colleagues and by students to be among the best teachers in the school.

Common Goals

Meaningful collaboration requires teachers to have meaningful things to collaborate about, and that is the subject of the next section. But even before that, teachers need to share the goal that every

student be successful. Sometimes this means having the vision to see past their students' childhood and adolescent goofiness. English teacher José Maldonado at Granger High School in Granger, Washington, said this about his students, many of whom are tempted by the gangs that dominate the Yakima Valley: "I try to look beyond where they are now and see them for who they will be."

A Laserlike Focus on What We Want Kids to Learn

For generations, teaching has been an isolated activity, and teachers pretty much decided what they would teach. At the same time, teachers have long been whipsawed from one fad to another about *how* to teach. Teachers were told to keep their students seated in neat rows and columns, then they were told to have them sit in circles, and then in cooperative learning groups. They were told to have quiet classrooms, and then they were told to have lively yet controlled classrooms. And so on. Yet through all that, most teachers were still allowed to decide whether kids would learn about dinosaurs or the Bill of Rights. This is exactly backward. Teachers should be the experts in *how* to teach, but on their own, they should not be deciding *what* to teach.

After all, the reason we have schools is to impart the knowledge and skills that our society as a whole has deemed important. This means that decisions about what knowledge and skills children learn are of concern to all of us. That doesn't mean that there shouldn't always be room in a school day or year for teachers to share their passion for the more obscure plays of William Shakespeare. But the bulk of the curriculum should be devoted to the knowledge and skills that we as a society have decided are essential for students to become educated citizens.

Today, we are converging on the idea that every high school graduate should be ready for college or the workplace. The more we study what this actually means, the more we realize that the two are pretty much the same. To be ready for, say, a plumbing apprenticeship or to get a job on an automobile assembly line or as a sales representative requires that students have fairly high reading and writing levels and have mastered math at least through Algebra II. In other words, students who are entering the workforce after high school require the same educational level as students who are ready for credit-bearing classes in college—at least if they want the kind of job that has traditionally offered paid vacation and health insurance.

The last 20 years has seen the beginning of agreement about what should be taught. For the most part, this has taken the form of states bringing together groups of teachers and content experts to set standards for what students are expected to know and be able to do by the time they graduate; then the groups work backward through the grades. The real problem is that too few states have done the hard job of developing clear, teachable standards. Some states have shied away from paring down what they want students to learn, so their standards tend to be impossibly large compendia of knowledge and skills. Other states have stuck with incredibly vague standards that do not offer any real guidance. Even in a field as seemingly definite as mathematics, the lack of clarity in standards has led to math curricula that are, as scholar William Schmidt says, "a mile wide and an inch deep."

By being too broad and expecting too much, many states essentially push the decisions of what to teach back onto individual teachers, who find themselves picking and choosing among standards rather than trying to teach all of them—because teaching all of them is impossible. (In contrast, by paring down the vast array of human knowledge into a relatively manageable yet ambitious set of standards, Massachusetts made a real contribution, and it did so long enough ago that those standards have really started permeating Massachusetts schools. Massachusetts now has the highest overall performance in reading and math on the National Assessment of Educational Progress.)

Many It's Being Done educators hope that all states and schools will eventually share the same ambitious national standards. As Ware's Gustafson told me in an e-mail: "National standards would help the students most in need, those with the highest mobility." She added that the difficulties of moving from school to school are compounded "by making the requirements different everywhere a student lands."

Even once common standards are embraced, however, teachers still have a lot of work to do. It's Being Done schools often have to build their own curriculum from scratch, and most spend quite a lot of time building "curriculum maps" or other documents that clearly delineate what each grade will study when. Roxbury Prep in Roxbury, Massachusetts, has teachers come in three weeks ahead of the students, in part to build that year's curriculum map. Graham Road Elementary School has daylong teacher retreats while students are taught by substitutes so that teachers can build their curriculum map, and Imperial High School has slowly built its curriculum map, subject by subject, over the years.

Once that initial planning is done, teachers don't have to start from scratch in subsequent years, but can work on improvements and refinements each year. For this, they will often use the results on state tests. If their students didn't do well on measurement, for example, the teachers will revise their instructional strategies and may add time to that subject. If all the students have mastered standard punctuation, the teachers might decide to spend a little less time on that subject so they can add time to teaching students how to write research papers.

Teachers then work on how students should demonstrate their knowledge of the curriculum. To make this effective, teachers need to agree on a good assessment, what constitutes meeting standards, and what constitutes exceeding standards. Teachers often need help in learning how to do this work—which is known as proficiency setting or range finding—and in making sure that they are aiming at high standards (more on this topic in the next section, "Formative Assessments").

Even now, teachers are not yet ready to walk into the classroom. A curriculum with assessments still isn't sufficient guidance for a teacher to know what he or she is doing tomorrow. Teachers in It's Being Done schools work together on lesson plans.

This is where all their hard work in collaborating pays off for teachers. Because they work together so closely and because they are working on the same things at the same times, they are able to share the work of developing individual lessons. Outside the teaching profession, not everyone understands what a huge and complex burden lesson planning is—particularly for new teachers. At Lockhart Junior High School, new teachers are handed their entire first year of lessons so that they don't have to worry about planning. As Susan Brooks, the former principal, said, it takes so much effort to learn about the school's routines, culture, colleagues, and students —as well as to establish good classroom management and build relationships with their students—that new teachers simply don't have the time and energy to plan lessons. After their first year, they are welcomed into the collaborative process of lesson development. Far from feeling undermined, the new teachers I spoke to said they felt supported by this system.

Formative Assessments

Students have always had regular assessments—I had weekly spelling and arithmetic tests all through my elementary school years, in addition to the big chapter tests, unit tests, and, of course, the norm-referenced standardized tests most of us took growing up. But for the most part, those assessments were used as "summative assessments." That is, they were used to gauge what students knew, assign grades, and ultimately, sort kids into "high," "middle," and "low" reading or math groups in elementary school and tracks in secondary school.

Formative assessments are not designed to assign a grade but to gauge what students know about a particular topic or what they are able to do. In this way, teachers can understand where students are, what weaknesses or misunderstandings the students have, or whether they need additional enrichment or extension.

Some teachers may say, "We already have the state tests—we don't need more assessments." But that's not how the educators in It's Being Done schools think. They see state tests as useful end-of-year or midyear assessments that make sure schools and students are on track. But most state tests, for a variety of reasons, are not sufficient to guide day-to-day instruction. For one thing, results usually don't come back in anything under a couple of months. And, of course, most state tests are pretty low level. It's Being Done schools are aiming high, and they need to be able to see whether their students understand the material they are presenting and are meeting rigorous standards. For that, the schools need their own formative assessments. At Lockhart Junior High, teachers give quizzes in each core academic class once a week—students who score below 75 percent are immediately scheduled into "rescue classes" so that master teachers can figure out where the misunderstandings lie. At Graham Road, teachers go over every wrong test answer with every student so that they, too, can understand what led to the wrong answer. Sometimes it is just inattention; sometimes it is a misunderstanding of a word or a lack of background knowledge. In this way, teachers catch small problems before they grow.

It's Being Done schools also often use the formative tests as a way to ensure that their students are ready for both the format and the content of state tests. This is not the same as "teaching to the test." It is more along the lines of teaching students "test sophistication," as Valarie Lewis, principal of Osmond A. Church School in Queens, New York, calls it. Graham Road's Bensinger-Lacy is forthright about saying that children need help acculturating themselves to state tests. "I have no apologies for doing for our kids what middle-class families do for their kids. I'm hoping that when SATs come around, they'll understand how to take that kind of test." But the emphasis in all these schools is not on test-taking strategies but on ensuring that students understand the material represented in high-level standards.

Data-Driven Instruction

In It's Being Done schools, data are certainly used to identify which students need help and which need greater challenges. But there is another, more profound, way data are used as well: to see patterns that aren't always visible to teachers in their day-to-day teaching. So, for example, kindergarten teachers at Graham Road pore over color-coded charts to try to see patterns of achievement. In her first year, teacher Laura Robbins saw from the charts that in comparison with the students in other classes, her students didn't have many sight words. She asked her fellow teachers what they were doing to help their students. This is the kind of crucial interaction among teachers that has led to more students at Graham Road achieving at high levels than in most schools in Virginia.

Similarly, at Imperial High School, teachers spend a day before each school year looking for such patterns. One year they found that vocabulary was the weakest area for all groups of students—not just the English language learners. Once they identified that pattern, they were able to address the issue of vocabulary acquisition in a schoolwide way. Had the teachers simply been focused on their own students, they might never have noticed that even the highest-achieving students in the school still had weaknesses in their vocabularies.

Personal Relationship Building

It's hard for me to fully convey the atmosphere in It's Being Done schools and how different it is from ordinary schools. In essence, It's Being Done schools have an atmosphere of respect and caring that emanates from the teachers and principals. As Ware Elementary teacher Lisa Akard said, "We're a kind school. We really care about each other. The teachers care about the children." That caring is reciprocated by the students. So, for example, I could not find a student at Imperial High School who did not have good things to say about the school and his or her teachers. In comparing Imperial to his previous school, student Israel Ramos said, "The teachers there were just getting through the year—here they really care if you do your work and do well." Imperial's principal, Lisa Tabarez, expressed it this way: "It's not just about being successful in high school. We work for a greater accomplishment.

We work for students to be successful, to take care of themselves and take part in society." Students respond powerfully to that commitment to their overall well-being.

When I say that It's Being Done schools are respectful, that doesn't mean that they put up with disruptive behavior on the part of students—they do not. They do not let the learning of their students be disrupted for any reason, even another student. But they remain respectful, even of disruptive students. When John Capozzi, who is now principal of Elmont Memorial Junior-Senior High School, was assistant principal, he was in charge of discipline. His then-principal, Al Harper, said, "I've seen John suspend a student [and then] the student thanks him." That's how respectful the atmosphere is.

At Imperial High School, staff often have to explicitly train students, particularly new students, in the Imperial way of operating. "We start with where they are," assistant principal Aimee Queen says. One student, who had just transferred in and was completely unused to an orderly school, was given the initial goal of not getting thrown out of class. When he managed a whole day without disruption, Queen celebrated with him and gave him a pencil. They then started working on his being prepared for class with a notebook and pencil, until finally, the expectation was that he was doing his work well and competently, complete with good grades in a college-preparatory curriculum. As in just about everything in It's Being Done schools, the ultimate standard was kept well in view, even as students and teachers worked on the many necessary interim steps.

These schools also have a respectful way of being honest about shortcomings without allowing them to be debilitating. Teachers work with administrators on improvement plans. And they speak candidly with students about their reading levels and academic accomplishments—or lack thereof—without the demeaning sense that if the students have failed at a task, it means they are and always will be failures. Failure merely means that students—and teachers—have more work to do before they can be successful.

So, for example, at Norfork Elementary in Norfolk, Arkansas, third-grade students who were very marginal readers were told that they needed to improve dramatically to be promoted to fourth grade, and they were given a special reading class dedicated to improving their decoding, fluency and vocabulary. In the spring, when it was clear all of them would be prepared to move to the next grade, the teacher brought the principal in to celebrate. They were celebrating very real accomplishments by the students, who could feel genuine satisfaction that they had met a tough standard. The children weren't being pumped up with phony self-esteem-building exercises—they were building genuine self-esteem based on the hard work of accomplishment.

It takes a great deal of work to establish the right kind of tone and atmosphere in It's Being Done schools. But once it is established, students feel safe and able to learn; teachers feel safe and able to teach; and, not incidentally, administrators who in ordinary schools would spend all their time on discipline are able to turn their attention to other issues, such as improving instruction.

I have described at some length the five elements of school reform as listed by Molly Bensinger-Lacy: teacher collaboration; a laserlike focus on what we want kids to learn; formative assessment to see if they learned it; data-driven instruction; and personal relationship building, all within the context of outside assessment.

There is something else that she didn't mention—something that I hope to explore more fully in future work—and that is leadership. Principals of It's Being Done schools set a vision for their schools and then helped teachers work toward it. And teachers set another version of that vision in their individual classrooms and then help their students work toward it.

All those leaders have embraced as a goal something that American public schools never before were asked to do: to educate all students to a meaningful standard. They all understand that to make that goal anything more than a pipe dream requires an enormous shift in how schools are organized and how they operate.

By making sure that everyone understands what children need to learn and then figuring out how to teach them, teachers and principals in It's Being Done schools have gone a long way toward devising the organizational structures that can help all students become educated citizens.

In contrast, the tradition of isolation that has characterized school organization has meant that too many children have gone to schools where there are no systems to ensure that they learn what they need. Affluent children, many of whom can draw on outside resources ranging from family dinner conversations to individual private tutoring, are often able to compensate for weaknesses in their school experiences. But children who live in poverty or isolation have fewer such resources to draw on, making them more dependent on schools and more dependent on educators figuring out how to ensure they learn.

It goes without saying that no school is perfect. Even the most successful have their mistakes, failures, and weaknesses. All have ways they can improve. This is, after all, difficult work requiring a lot of thought, skill, and effort—but educating all students can be done, and successful schools are showing us the way.

Endnotes

1. Probably the best description of how schools are organized is by Harvard University's Richard F. Elmore, "Building a New Structure for School Leadership," *American Educator* 23, no. 4 (Winter 1999–2000): 6–13, 42–44, www.aft.org/pubs-reports/american_educator/winter99–00/NewStructure Win99_00.pdf.

2. On teacher preparation programs, see, for example, the indictment by Art Levine (former president of Teachers College at Columbia University) of just about all such programs in *Educating School Teachers* (Washington, DC: Education Schools Project, 2006). www.edschools.org/teacher_report.htm. On colleague support, see, for example, Richard Kahlenberg's description of Albert Shanker's first year as a teacher in *Tough Liberal: Albert Shanker and the Battles Over Schools, Unions, Race, and Democracy* (New York: Columbia University Press. 2007). On teaching

standards, see, for example, "There's a Hole in State Standards: And New Teachers Like Me Are Falling Through," by an anonymous second-year teacher, *American Educator* 32, no. 1 (Spring 2008): 6–7, www.aft.org/pubs–reports/american_educator/issues/spring2008/newteacher.htm.

3. For some insight into the disconnect between teacher hopes and reality, see "Pursuing a Sense of Success: New Teachers Explain Their Career Decisions," *American Education Research Journal* 40, no. 3 (2003), which contains the results of a survey of 50 Massachusetts teachers.

POSTNOTE

There is much hand-wringing and dismal talk about urban education and the schools serving our minority populations. Also, much of the research and reportage on urban schools provides chilling evidence of failing students and frustrated educators. Ms. Chenoweth's article, based on extensive "embedded" reporting, tells a different story. Urban schools may have severe challenges, but they are hardly hopeless. Her article again reminds us that focusing on the essentials of learning—that is, high expectations for students and focusing support on students in need—will bear results.

Among the excellent issues raised by this article is the attention given to teacher collaboration and the conditions necessary for successful collaboration to occur. Few teachers themselves come from the troubled urban classrooms. Few have had adequate preparation for the problems and issues they encounter in these schools. Therefore, teacher collaboration and opportunities to plan together are important ingredients in order for them to develop into effective teachers.

Although the author tells us, "no school is perfect," she offers us valuable insights into the pieces of the puzzle for making urban schools successful.

DISCUSSION QUESTIONS

1. Of the several principles or characteristics of how to make urban schools successful, which two do you think are most important? Why?
2. Based on this article, what is your disposition to teaching in schools serving the urban poor?
3. Do you have other suggestions or ideas for how to solve the achievement puzzle that could be added to the author's list? What are they?

RELATED WEBSITE RESOURCES

WEB RESOURCES:

National Institute for Urban School Improvement. Available at:

http://urbanschools.org/.

This site is a deep and varied resource on many aspects of urban education compiled from free learning modules and informative articles.

FOCUS. Available at:

http://www.focusdc.org/.

FOCUS, or Friends of Choice in Urban Schools, is a site primarily devoted to supporting educators interested in or involved in the charter school movement.

17

Why Some Parents Don't Come to School

Margaret Finders and Cynthia Lewis

Margaret Finders is director of the School of Education and associate dean of the University of Wisconsin–LaCrosse's College of Liberal Studies.

Cynthia Lewis is director of graduate studies and professor in the Department of Curriculum and Instruction at the University of Minnesota.

"Why Some Parents Don't Come to School," by Margaret Finders and Cynthia Lewis, 1994, Educational Leadership 51(8), pp. 50–54. (c) 1994 by ASCD. Reprinted with permission. Learn more about ASCD at www.ascd.org.

FOCUS QUESTION

Why is it that some parents just won't come to their children's schools?

InTASC
Standard 10

KEY TERM

- Institutional perspective

In our roles as teachers and as parents, we have been privy to the conversations of both teachers and parents. Until recently, however, we did not acknowledge that our view of parental involvement conflicts with the views of many parents. It was not until we began talking with parents in different communities that we were forced to examine our own deeply seated assumptions about parental involvement.

From talking with Latino parents and parents in two low-income Anglo neighborhoods, we have gained insights about why they feel disenfranchised from school settings. In order to include such parents in the educational conversation, we need to understand the barriers to their involvement from their vantage point, as that of outsiders. When asked, these parents had many suggestions that may help educators re-envision family involvement in the schools.

The Institutional Perspective

The institutional perspective holds that children who do not succeed in school have parents who do not get involved in school activities or support school goals at home. Recent research emphasizes the importance of parent involvement in promoting school success (Comer 1984, Lareau 1987). At the same time, lack of participation among parents of socially and culturally diverse students is also well documented (Clark 1983, Delgado-Gaitan 1991).

The model for family involvement, despite enormous changes in the reality of family structures, is that of a two-parent, economically self-sufficient nuclear family, with a working father and homemaker mother (David 1989). As educators, we talk about "the changing family," but the language we use has changed little. The institutional view of nonparticipating parents remains based on a deficit model. "Those who *need* to come, don't come," a teacher explains, revealing an assumption that one of the main reasons for involving parents is to remediate them. It is assumed that involved parents bring a body of knowledge about the purposes of schooling to match institutional knowledge. Unless they bring such knowledge to the school, they themselves are thought to need education in becoming legitimate participants.

Administrators, too, frustrated by lack of parental involvement, express their concern in terms of a deficit model. An administrator expresses his bewilderment:

> Our parent-teacher group is the foundation of our school programs…. This group (gestures to the all-Anglo, all-women group seated in the library) is the most important organization in the school. You know, I just don't understand why *those other parents* won't even show up.

Discussions about family involvement often center on what families lack and how educators can best teach parents to support instructional agendas at home (Mansbach 1993). To revise this limited model for interaction between home and school, we must look outside of the institutional perspective.

The Voices of "Those Other Parents"

We asked some of "those other parents" what they think about building positive home/school relations. In what follows, parents whose voices are rarely heard at school explain how the diverse contexts of their lives create tensions that interfere with positive home/school relations. For them, school experiences, economic and time constraints, and linguistic and cultural practices have produced a body of knowledge about school settings that frequently goes unacknowledged.

Diverse School Experiences Among Parents

Educators often don't take into account how a parent's own school experiences may influence school relationships. Listen in as one father describes his son's school progress:

> They expect me to go to school so they can tell me my kid is stupid or crazy. They've been telling me that for three years, so why should I go and hear it again? They don't do anything. They just tell me my kid is bad.
>
> See, I've been there. I know. And it scares me. They called me a boy in trouble but I was a troubled boy. Nobody helped me because they liked it when I didn't show up. If I was gone for the semester, fine with them. I dropped out nine times. They wanted me gone.

This father's experiences created mistrust and prevent him from participating more fully in his son's education. Yet, we cannot say that he doesn't care about his son. On the contrary, his message is urgent.

For many parents, their own personal school experiences create obstacles to involvement. Parents who have dropped out of school do not feel confident in school settings. Needed to help support their families or care for siblings at home, these individuals' limited schooling makes it difficult for them to help their children with homework beyond the early primary level. For some, this situation is compounded by language barriers and lack of written literacy skills. One mother who attended school through 6th grade in Mexico, and whose first language is Spanish, comments about homework that "sometimes we can't help because it's too hard." Yet the norm in most schools is to send home schoolwork with little information for parents about how it should be completed.

Diverse Economic and Time Constraints

Time constraints are a primary obstacle for parents whose work doesn't allow them the autonomy and flexibility characteristic of professional positions. Here, a mother expresses her frustrations:

> Teachers just don't understand that I can't come to school at just any old time. I think Judy told you that we don't have a car right now…. Andrew catches a different bus than

Dawn. He gets here a half an hour before her, and then I have to make sure Judy is home because I got three kids in three different schools. And I feel like the teachers are under pressure, and they're turning it around and putting the pressure on me cause they want me to check up on Judy and I really can't.

Often, parents work at physically demanding jobs, with mothers expected to take care of child-care responsibilities as well as school-related issues. In one mother's words:

What most people don't understand about the Hispanic community is that you come home and you take care of your husband and your family first. Then if there's time you can go out to your meetings.

Other parents work nights, making it impossible to attend evening programs and difficult to appear at daytime meetings that interfere with family obligations and sleep.

At times, parents' financial concerns present a major obstacle to participation in their child's school activities. One mother expresses frustration that she cannot send eight dollars to school so her daughter can have a yearbook to sign like the other girls.

I do not understand why they assume that everybody has tons of money, and every time I turn around it's more money for this and more money for that. Where do they get the idea that we've got all this money?

This mother is torn between the pressures of stretching a tight budget and wanting her daughter to belong. As is the case for others, economic constraints prevent her child from full participation in the culture of the school. This lack of a sense of belonging creates many barriers for parents.

Diverse Linguistic and Cultural Practices

Parents who don't speak fluent English often feel inadequate in school contexts. One parent explains that "an extreme language barrier" prevented her own mother from ever going to anything at the school. Cultural mismatches can occur as often as linguistic conflicts. One Latino educator explained that asking young children to translate for their parents during conferences grates against a cultural norm. Placing children in a position of equal status with adults creates dysfunction within the family hierarchy.

One mother poignantly expresses the cultural disconnect she feels when communicating with Anglo teachers and parents:

[In] the Hispanic culture and the Anglo culture things are done different and you really don't know—am I doing the right thing? When they call me and say, "You bring the plates" [for class parties], do they think I can't do the cookies, too? You really don't know.

Voicing a set of values that conflicts with institutional constructions of the parent's role, a mother gives this culturally-based explanation for not attending her 12-year-old's school functions:

It's her education, not mine. I've had to teach her to take care of herself. I work nights, so she's had to get up and get herself ready for school. I'm not going to be there all the time. She's gotta do it. She's a tough cookie.... She's almost an adult, and I get the impression that they want me to walk her through her work. And it's not that I don't care either. I really do. I think it's important, but I don't think it's my place.

This mother does not lack concern for her child. In her view, independence is essential for her daughter's success.

Whether it is for social, cultural, linguistic, or economic reasons, these parents' voices are rarely heard at school. Perhaps, as educators, we too readily categorize them as "those other parents" and fail to hear the concern that permeates such conversations. Because the experiences of these families vary greatly from our own, we operate on assumptions that interfere with our best intentions. What can be done to address the widening gap between parents who participate and those who don't?

Getting Involved: Suggestions from Parents

Parents have many suggestions for teachers and administrators about ways to promote active involvement. Their views, however, do not always match the role envisioned by educators. Possessing fewer economic resources and educational skills to participate in traditional ways (Lareau 1987), these parents operate at a disadvantage until they understand how schools are organized and how they can promote systemic change (Delgado-Gaitan 1991).

If we're truly interested in establishing a dialogue with the parents of all of our nation's students, however, we need to understand what parents think can be done. Here are some of their suggestions.

Clarify How Parents Can Help

Parents need to know exactly how they can help. Some are active in church and other community groups, but lack information about how to become more involved in their children's schooling. One Latina mother explains that most of the parents she knows think that school involvement means attending school parties.

As Concha Delgado-Gaitan (1991) points out "… the difference between parents who participate and those who do not is that those who do have recognized that they are a critical part of their children's education." Many of the parents we spoke to don't see themselves in this capacity.

Encourage Parents to Be Assertive

Parents who do see themselves as needed participants feel strongly that they must provide their children with a positive view of their history and culture not usually presented at school.

Some emphasize the importance of speaking up for their children. Several, for instance, have argued for or against special education placement or retention for their children; others have discussed with teachers what they saw as inappropriate disciplinary procedures. In one parent's words:

> Sometimes kids are taken advantage of because their parents don't fight for them. I say to parents, if you don't fight for your child, no one's going to fight for them.

Although it may sound as if these parents are advocating adversarial positions, they are simply pleading for inclusion. Having spent much time on the teacher side of these conversations, we realize that teachers might see such talk as challenging their positions as professional decision makers. Yet, it is crucial that we expand the dialogue to include parent knowledge about school settings, even when that knowledge conflicts with our own.

Develop Trust

Parents affirm the importance of establishing trust. One mother attributes a particular teacher's good turnout for parent/teacher conferences to her ability to establish a "personal relationship" with parents. Another comments on her need to be reassured that the school is open, that it's OK to drop by "anytime you can."

In the opportunities we provide for involvement, we must regularly ask ourselves what messages we convey through our dress, gestures, and talk. In one study, for example, a teacher described her school's open house in a middle-class neighborhood as "a cocktail party without cocktails" (Lareau 1987). This is the sort of "party" that many parents wouldn't feel comfortable attending.

Fear was a recurrent theme among the parents we interviewed: fear of appearing foolish or being misunderstood, fear about their children's academic standing. One mother explained:

> Parents feel like the teachers are looking at you, and I know how they feel, because I feel like that here. There are certain things and places where I still feel uncomfortable, so I won't go, and I feel bad, and I think maybe it's just me.

This mother is relaying how it feels to be culturally, linguistically, and ethnically different.

Her body of knowledge does not match the institutional knowledge of the school and she is therefore excluded from home/school conversations.

Build on Home Experiences

Our assumptions about the home environments of our students can either build or serve as links between home and school. An assumption that "these kids don't live in good environments" can destroy the very network we are trying to create. Too often we tell parents what we want them to do at home with no understanding of the rich social interaction that already occurs there (Keenan et al. 1993). One mother expresses her frustrations:

> Whenever I go to school, they want to tell me what to do at home. They want to tell me how to raise my kid. They never ask me what I think. They never ask me anything.

When we asked parents general questions about their home activities and how these activities might build on what happens at school, most thought there was no connection. They claimed not to engage in much reading and writing at home, although their specific answers to questions contradicted this belief. One mother talks about her time at home with her teenage daughter:

> My husband works nights and sometimes she sleeps with me.... We would lay down in bed and discuss the books she reads.

Many of the parents we spoke to mentioned Bible reading as a regular family event, yet they did not see this reading in relation to schoolwork. In one mother's words:

> I read the Bible to the children in Spanish, but when I see they're not understanding me, I stop (laughing). Then they go and look in the English Bible to find out what I said.

Although the Bible is not a text read at public schools, we can build on the literacy practices and social interactions that surround it. For instance, we can draw upon a student's ability to compare multiple versions of a text. We also can include among the texts we read legends, folktales, and mythology —literature that, like the Bible, is meant to teach us about our strengths and weaknesses as we strive to make our lives meaningful.

As teachers, of course, we marvel at the way in which such home interactions do, indeed, support our goals for learning at school; but we won't know about these practices unless we begin to form relationships with parents that allow them to share such knowledge.

Use Parent Expertise

Moll (1992) underscores the importance of empowering parents to contribute "*intellectually* to the development of lessons." He recommends assessing the "funds of knowledge" in the community, citing a teacher who discovered that many parents in the Latino community where she taught had expertise in the field of construction. Consequently, the class developed a unit on construction, which included reading, writing, speaking, and building, all with the help of responsive community experts—the children's parents.

Parents made similar suggestions—for example, cooking ethnic foods with students, sharing information about multicultural heritage, and bringing in role models from the community. Latino parents repeatedly emphasized that the presence of more teachers from their culture would benefit their children as role models and would help them in home/ school interactions.

Parents also suggested extending literacy by writing pen pal letters with students or involving their older children in tutoring and letter writing with younger students. To help break down the barriers that language differences create, one parent suggested that bilingual and monolingual parents form partnerships to participate in school functions together.

An Invitation for Involvement

Too often, the social, economic, linguistic, and cultural practices of parents are represented as serious problems rather than valued knowledge. When we reexamine our assumptions about parental absence, we may find that our interpretations of parents who care may simply be parents who are like us, parents who feel comfortable in the teacher's domain.

Instead of operating on the assumption that absence translates into noncaring, we need to focus on ways to draw parents into the schools. If we make explicit the multiple ways we value the language, culture, and knowledge of the parents in our communities, parents may more readily accept our invitations.

References

Clark, R. M. (1983). *Family Life and School Achievement: Why Poor Black Children Succeed or Fail.* Chicago: University of Chicago Press.

Comer, J. P. (1984). "Home-School Relationships as They Affect the Academic Success of Children." *Education and Urban Society* 16: 323–337.

David, M. E. (1989). "Schooling and the Family." In *Critical Pedagogy, the State, and Cultural Struggle*, edited by H. Giroux and P. McLaren. Albany, N.Y.: State University of New York Press.

Delgado-Gaitan, C. (1991). "Involving Parents in the Schools: A Process of Empowerment." *American Journal of Education* 100: 20–46.

Keenan, J. W., J. Willett, and J. Solsken. (1993). "Constructing an Urban Village: School/Home Collaboration in a Multicultural Classroom." *Language Arts* 70: 204–214.

Lareau, A. (1987). "Social Class Differences in Family-School Relationships: The Importance of Cultural Capital." *Sociology of Education* 60: 73–85.

Mansbach, S. C. (February/March 1993). "We Must Put Family Literacy on the National Agenda." *Reading Today*: 37.

Moll, L. (1992). "Bilingual Classroom Studies and Community Analysis: Some Recent Trends." *Educational Researcher* 21: 20–24.

POSTNOTE

Much research supports the principle that children whose parents are active in their schools are more likely to succeed in school, whereas children whose parents are not involved are more apt to do poorly. Some parents are eager to work as partners with schools to be certain that their children are well prepared for the life and career choices they will make. Other parents are almost never involved with the school.

This article is useful to educators working at schools where parental involvement is less than what they hoped for. By understanding why some parents never show up at schools, educators can take steps to help overcome the parents' reluctance.

Remember, teachers need parents to help them succeed.

DISCUSSION QUESTIONS

1. List some of the main reasons Finders and Lewis give for parents not coming to school. Which of these reasons do you find compelling? Do any of the reasons surprise you?
2. Can you identify any additional reasons for parents to stay away from school besides those given by the authors?
3. What strategies for involving parents in school have you seen employed, and how successful were they?

RELATED WEBSITE RESOURCES AND VIDEO CASE

WEB RESOURCES:

Parent-Teacher Conferences. Available at:

http://www.nea.org/tools/36079.htm.

This National Education Association website is an excellent resource on preparing for and conducting parent-teacher conferences.

Building Successful Partnerships. Available at:

http://www.pta.org/local_leadership_subprogram_
1116958575937.html.

This website, supported by the Parent-Teacher Association, provides helpful insights and information from the parents' perspective.

▶❚❚ TEACHSOURCE VIDEO CASE

HOME-SCHOOL COMMUNICATIONS: THE PARENT-TEACHER CONFERENCE

In this video case, you will meet teacher Jim St. Clair. His approach weaves actual examples of the child's work and his own observations into a discussion of the child's strengths and weaknesses. You will also see Jim listen and respond to a mother's concerns. Go to the website for the Education Media Library at CengageBrain.com to watch the video clips, study the artifacts in the case, and reflect on the following questions.

1. Why might a teacher ask family members what the student says about school when they are at home? What is the value in asking this?

2. What, if anything, would you do differently in parent–teacher conferences to reflect the age of students you teach and your own personal teaching style?

 The companion website for this text includes useful study tools and resources. Go to CengageBrain.com to access links to relevant websites, glossaries, flashcards, an article review form, and more.

Curriculum and Standards

The bedrock question of education is this: What knowledge is most worth knowing? This question goes right to the heart of individual and social priorities. As our world has become more and more drenched with information—information pouring out at us from many different media—the question of what is worth our limited time and attention has increased in importance. It is the quintessential curriculum question.

In recent years, however, policymakers and educators have attempted to improve our schools by establishing what should be learned through state-mandated curriculum standards and by enforcing those standards through regular testing. The federal No Child Left Behind Act of 2001 requires states to test students in reading and mathematics each year in grades 3–8. This effort has dramatically affected what is going on in today's classrooms.

The question of what is most worth knowing, however, begets others. What is the purpose of knowledge? To make a great deal of money? To become a wise person? To prepare oneself for important work? To contribute to the general good of society?

This difficult question becomes more and more complex, and swiftly takes us into the realm of values. Nevertheless, it is a question communities must regularly address in our decentralized education system. In struggling with curriculum issues, a community is really making a bet on the future needs of society and of the young people who will have to live in that society. Behind the choice of a new emphasis on foreign language instruction or on computer literacy is a social gamble, and the stakes are high. Offering students an inadequate curriculum is like sending troops into battle with popguns.

The Saber-Tooth Curriculum

J. Abner Peddiwell

J. Abner Peddiwell is the pseudonym for Harold W. Benjamin, a professor of education who was a prominent figure in 20th-century education in the U.S. He died in 1969.

FOCUS QUESTION

As you read this article, think of what subjects, if any, in the current school curriculum you believe are outmoded and should be replaced.

The first great educational theorist and practitioner of whom my imagination has any record (began Dr. Peddiwell in his best professional tone) was a man of Chellean times whose full name was *New-Fist-Hammer-Maker* but whom, for convenience, I shall hereafter call *New-Fist*.

New-Fist was a doer, in spite of the fact that there was little in his environment with which to do anything very complex. You have undoubtedly heard of the pear-shaped, chipped-stone tool which archaeologists call the *coup-de-poing* or fist hammer. New-Fist gained his name and a considerable local prestige by producing one of these artifacts in less rough and more useful form than any previously known to his tribe. His hunting clubs were generally superior weapons, moreover, and his fire-using techniques were patterns of simplicity and precision. He knew how to do things his community needed to have done, and he had the energy and will to go ahead and do them. By virtue of these characteristics he was an educated man.

New-Fist was also a thinker. Then, as now, there were few lengths to which men would not go to avoid the labor and pain of thought. More readily than his fellows, New-Fist pushed himself beyond those lengths to the point where cerebration was inevitable. The same quality of intelligence which led him into the socially approved activity of producing a superior artifact also led him to engage in the socially disapproved practice of thinking. When other men gorged themselves on the proceeds of a successful hunt and vegetated in dull stupor for many hours thereafter, New-Fist ate a little less heartily, slept a little less stupidly, and arose a little earlier than his comrades to sit by the fire and think. He would stare moodily at the flickering flames and wonder about various parts of his environment until he finally got to the point where he became strongly dissatisfied with the accustomed ways of his tribe. He began to catch glimpses of ways in which life might be made better for himself, his family, and his group. By virtue of this development, he became a dangerous man.

This was the background that made this doer and thinker hit upon the concept of a conscious, systematic education. The immediate stimulus which put him directly into the practice of education came from watching his children at play. He saw these children at the cave entrance before the fire engaged in activity with bones and sticks and brightly colored pebbles. He noted that they seemed to have no purpose in their play beyond immediate pleasure in the activity itself. He compared their activity with that of the grown-up members of the tribe. The children played for fun; the adults worked for security and enrichment of their lives. The children dealt with bones, sticks, and pebbles; the adults dealt with food, shelter, and clothing. The children protected themselves from boredom; the adults protected themselves from danger.

"If I could only get these children to do the things that will give more and better food, shelter, clothing, and security," thought New-Fist, "I would be helping this tribe to have a better life. When the children became grown, they would have more meat to eat, more skins to keep them warm, better caves in which to sleep, and less danger from the striped death with the curving teeth that walks these trails at night."

Having set up an educational goal, New-Fist proceeded to construct a curriculum for reaching that goal. "What things must we tribesmen know how to do in order to live with full bellies, warm backs, and minds free from fear?" he asked himself.

To answer this question, he ran various activities over in his mind. "We have to catch fish with our bare hands in the pool far up the creek beyond that big bend," he said to himself. "We have to catch fish with our bare hands in the pool right at the bend. We have to catch them in the same way in the pool just this side of the bend. And so we catch them in the next pool and the next and the next. And we catch them with our bare hands."

Thus New-Fist discovered the first subject of the first curriculum—fish-grabbing-with-the-bare-hands.

"Also we club the little woolly horses," he continued with his analysis. "We club them along the bank of the creek where they come down to drink. We club them in the thickets where they lie down to sleep. We club them in the upland meadow where they graze. Wherever we find them we club them."

So woolly-horse-clubbing was seen to be the second main subject of the curriculum.

"And finally, we drive away the saber-tooth tigers with fire," New-Fist went on in his thinking. "We drive them from the mouth of our caves with fire. We drive them from our trail with burning branches. We wave firebrands to drive them from our drinking hole. Always we have to drive them away, and always we drive them with fire."

Thus was discovered the third subject—saber-tooth-tiger-scaring-with-fire.

Having developed a curriculum, New-Fist took his children with him as he went about his activities. He gave them an opportunity to practice these three subjects. The children liked to learn. It was more fun for them to engage in these purposeful activities than to play with colored stones just for the fun of it. They learned the new activities well, and so the educational system was a success.

As New-Fist's children grew older, it was plain to see that they had an advantage in good and safe living over other children who had never been educated systematically. Some of the more intelligent members of the tribe began to do as New-Fist had done, and the teaching of fish-grabbing, horse-clubbing, and tiger-scaring came more and more to be accepted as the heart of real education.

For a long time, however, there were certain more conservative members of the tribe who resisted the new, formal educational system on religious grounds. "The Great Mystery who speaks in thunder and moves in lightning," they announced impressively, "the Great Mystery who gives men life and takes it from them as he wills—if that Great Mystery had wanted children to practice fish-grabbing, horse-clubbing, and tiger-scaring before they were grown up, he would have taught them these activities himself by implanting in their natures instincts for fish-grabbing, horse-clubbing, and tiger-scaring. New-Fist is not only impious to attempt something the Great Mystery never intended to have done; he is also a damned fool for trying to change human nature."

Whereupon approximately half of these critics took up the solemn chant, "If you oppose the will of the Great Mystery, you must die," and the remainder sang derisively in unison, "You can't change human nature."

Being an educational statesman as well as an educational administrator and theorist, New-Fist replied politely to both arguments. To the more theologically minded, he said that, as a matter of fact, the Great Mystery had ordered this new work done, that he even did the work himself by causing children to want to learn, that children could not learn by themselves without divine aid, that they could not learn at all except through the power of the Great Mystery, and that nobody could really understand the will of the Great Mystery concerning fish, horses, and saber-tooth tigers unless he had been well grounded in three fundamental subjects of the New-Fist school. To the human-nature-cannot-be-changed shouters, New-Fist pointed out the fact that paleolithic culture had attained its high level by changes in human nature and that it seemed almost unpatriotic to deny the very process which had made the community great.

"I know you, my fellow tribesmen," the pioneer educator ended his argument gravely, "I know you as the humble and devoted servants of the Great Mystery. I know that you would not for one moment consciously oppose yourselves to his will. I know you as intelligent and loyal citizens of the great cave-realm, and I know that your pure and noble patriotism will not permit you to do anything which will block the development of that most cave-realmish of all our institutions— the paleolithic educational system. Now that you understand the true nature and purpose of this institution, I am serenely confident that there are no reasonable lengths to which you will not go in its defense and its support."

By this appeal the forces of conservatism were won over to the side of the new school, and in due time everybody who was anybody in the community knew that the heart of good education lay in the three subjects of fish-grabbing, horse-clubbing, and tiger-scaring. New-Fist and his contemporaries grew older and were gathered by the Great Mystery to the Land of the Sunset far down the creek. Other men followed their educational ways more and more, until at last all the children of the tribe were practiced systematically in the three fundamentals. Thus the tribe prospered and was happy in the possession of adequate meat, skins, and security.

It is to be supposed that all would have gone well forever with this good educational system if conditions of life in that community had remained forever the same. But conditions changed, and life which had once been so safe and happy in the cave-realm valley became insecure and disturbing.

A new ice age was approaching in that part of the world. A great glacier came down from the neighboring mountain range to the north. Year after year it crept closer and closer to the head-waters of the creek which ran through the tribe's valley, until at length it reached the stream and began to melt into the water. Dirt and gravel which the glacier had collected on its long journey were dropped into the creek. The water grew muddy. What had once been a crystal-clear stream in which one could see easily to the bottom was now a milky stream into which one could not see at all.

At once the life of the community was changed in one very important respect. It was no longer possible to catch fish with the bare hands. The fish could not be seen in the muddy water. For some years, moreover, the fish in the creek had been getting more timid, agile, and intelligent. The stupid, clumsy, brave fish, of which originally there had been a great many, had been caught with the bare hands for fish generation after fish generation, until only fish of superior intelligence and agility were left. These smart fish, hiding in the muddy water under the newly deposited glacial boulders, eluded the hands of the most expertly trained fish-grabbers. Those tribesmen who had studied advanced fish-grabbing in the secondary school could do no better than their less well-educated fellows who had taken only an elementary course in the subject, and even the university graduates with majors in ichthyology were baffled by the problem. No matter how good a man's fish-grabbing education had been, he could not grab fish when he could not find fish to grab.

The melting waters of the approaching ice sheet also made the country wetter. The ground became marshy far back from the banks of the creek. The stupid woolly horses, standing only five or six hands high and running on four-toed front feet and three-toed hind feet, although admirable objects for clubbing, had one dangerous characteristic. They were ambitious. They all wanted to learn to run on their middle toes. They all had visions of becoming powerful and aggressive animals instead of little and timid ones. They dreamed of a far-distant day when some of their descendants would be sixteen hands high, weigh more than half a ton, and be able to pitch their would-be riders into the dirt. They knew they could never attain these goals in a wet, marshy country, so they all went east to the dry, open plains, far from the paleolithic hunting grounds. Their places were taken by little antelopes who came down with the ice sheet and were so shy and speedy and had so keen a scent for danger that no one could approach them closely enough to club them.

The best trained horse-clubbers of the tribe went out day after day and employed the most efficient techniques taught in the schools, but day after day they returned empty-handed. A horse-clubbing education of the highest type could get no results when there were no horses to club.

Finally, to complete the disruption of paleolithic life and education, the new dampness in the air gave the saber-tooth tigers pneumonia, a disease to which these animals were peculiarly susceptible and to which most of them succumbed. A few moth-eaten specimens crept south to the desert, it is true, but they were pitifully few and weak representatives of a once numerous and powerful race.

So there were no more tigers to scare in the paleolithic community, and the best tiger-scaring techniques became only academic exercises, good in themselves, perhaps, but not necessary for tribal security. Yet this danger to the people was lost only to be replaced by another and even greater danger, for with the advancing ice sheet came ferocious glacial bears which were not afraid of fire, which walked the trails by day as well as by night, and which could not be driven away by the most advanced methods developed in the tiger-scaring course of the schools.

The community was now in a very difficult situation. There was no fish or meat for food, no

hides for clothing, and no security from the hairy death that walked the trails day and night. Adjustment to this difficulty had to be made at once if the tribe was not to become extinct.

Fortunately for the tribe, however, there were men in it of the old New-Fist breed, men who had the ability to do and the daring to think. One of them stood by the muddy stream, his stomach contracting with hunger pains, longing for some way to get a fish to eat. Again and again he had tried the old fish-grabbing technique that day, hoping desperately that at last it might work, but now in black despair he finally rejected all that he had learned in the schools and looked about him for some new way to get fish from that stream. There were stout but slender vines hanging from trees along the bank. He pulled them down and began to fasten them together more or less aimlessly. As he worked, the vision of what he might do to satisfy his hunger and that of his crying children back in the cave grew clearer. His black despair lightened a little. He worked more rapidly and intelligently. At last he had it—a net, a crude seine. He called a companion and explained the device. The two men took the net into the water, into pool after pool, and in one hour they caught more fish— intelligent fish in muddy water—than the whole tribe could have caught in a day under the best fish-grabbing conditions.

Another intelligent member of the tribe wandered hungrily through the woods where once the stupid little horses had abounded but where now only the elusive antelope could be seen. He had tried the horse-clubbing technique on the antelope until he was fully convinced of its futility. He knew that one would starve who relied on school learning to get him meat in those woods. Thus it was that he too, like the fishnet inventor, was finally impelled by hunger to new ways. He bent a strong, springy young tree over an antelope trail, hung a noosed vine therefrom, and fastened the whole device in so ingenious a fashion that the passing animal would release a trigger and be snared neatly when the tree jerked upright. By setting a line of these snares, he was able in one night to secure more meat and skins than a dozen horse-clubbers in the old days had secured in a week.

A third tribesman, determined to meet the problem of the ferocious bears, also forgot what he had been taught in school and began to think in direct and radical fashion. Finally, as a result of this thinking, he dug a deep pit in a bear trail, covered it with branches in such a way that a bear would walk on it unsuspectingly, fall through to the bottom, and remain trapped until the tribesmen could come up and dispatch him with sticks and stones at their leisure. The inventor showed his friends how to dig and camouflage other pits until all the trails around the community were furnished with them. Thus the tribe had even more security than before and in addition had the great additional store of meat and skins which they secured from the captured bears.

As the knowledge of these new inventions spread, all the members of the tribe were engaged in familiarizing themselves with the new ways of living. Men worked hard at making fish nets, setting antelope snares, and digging bear pits. The tribe was busy and prosperous.

There were a few thoughtful men who asked questions as they worked. Some of them even criticized the schools.

"These new activities of net-making and operating, snare-setting, and pit-digging are indispensable to modern existence," they said. "Why can't they be taught in school?"

The safe and sober majority had a quick reply to this naive question. "School!" they snorted derisively. "You aren't in school now. You are out here in the dirt working to preserve the life and happiness of the tribe. What have these practical activities got to do with schools? You're not saying lessons now. You'd better forget your lessons and your academic ideals of fish-grabbing, horse-clubbing, and tiger-scaring if you want to eat, keep warm, and have some measure of security from sudden death."

The radicals persisted a little in their questioning. "Fishnet-making and using, antelope-snare construction and operation, and bear-catching and killing," they pointed out, "require intelligence and

skills—things we claim to develop in schools. They are also activities we need to know. Why can't the schools teach them?"

But most of the tribe, and particularly the wise old men who controlled the school, smiled indulgently at this suggestion. "That wouldn't be *education*," they said gently.

"But why wouldn't it be?" asked the radicals.

"Because it would be mere training," explained the old men patiently. "With all the intricate details of fish-grabbing, horse-clubbing, and tiger-scaring—the standard cultural subjects—the school curriculum is too crowded now. We can't add these fads and frills of net-making, antelope-snaring, and—of all things—bear-killing. Why, at the very thought, the body of the great New-Fist, founder of our paleolithic educational system, would turn over in its burial cairn. What we need to do is to give our young people a more thorough grounding in the fundamentals. Even the graduates of the secondary schools don't know the art of fish-grabbing in any complete sense nowadays, they swing their horse clubs awkwardly too, and as for the old science of tiger-scaring—well, even the teachers seem to lack the real flair for the subject which we oldsters got in our teens and never forgot."

"But, damn it," exploded one of the radicals, "how can any person with good sense be interested in such useless activities? What is the point of trying to catch fish with the bare hands when it just can't be done any more? How can a boy learn to club horses when there are no horses left to club? And why in hell should children try to scare tigers with fire when the tigers are dead and gone?"

"Don't be foolish," said the wise old men, smiling most kindly smiles. "We don't teach fish-grabbing to grab fish; we teach it to develop a generalized agility which can never be developed by mere training. We don't teach horse-clubbing to club horses; we teach it to develop a generalized strength in the learner which he can never get from so prosaic and specialized a thing as antelope-snare-setting. We don't teach tiger-scaring to scare tigers; we teach it for the purpose of giving that noble courage which carries over into all the affairs of life and which can never come from so base an activity as bear-killing."

All the radicals were silenced by this statement, all except the one who was most radical of all. He felt abashed, it is true, but he was so radical that he made one last protest.

"But—but anyway," he suggested, "you will have to admit that times have changed. Couldn't you please *try* these other, more up-to-date activities? Maybe they have *some* educational value after all?"

Even the man's fellow radicals felt that this was going a little too far.

The wise old men were indignant. Their kindly smiles faded. "If you had any education yourself," they said severely, "you would know that the essence of true education is timelessness. It is something that endures through changing conditions like a solid rock standing squarely and firmly in the middle of a raging torrent. You must know that there are some eternal verities, and the saber-tooth curriculum is one of them!"

POSTNOTE

The Saber-Tooth Curriculum is one of the greatest classic curriculum articles ever written; its message is timeless. One might think that it had been written by a modern-day critic of the public school curriculum instead of someone writing in 1939. It is virtually impossible to read this selection without drawing parallels to courses and curricula we have experienced. Fish-grabbing-with-the-bare-hands has not disappeared. It still exists today in many American schools, but it is called by a different name. And the same arguments used by the elders to defend the saber-tooth curriculum are used today to defend subjects that many say have outlived their right to remain in the curriculum. Why do they remain?

DISCUSSION QUESTIONS

1. What is the main message of this excerpt from *The Saber-Tooth Curriculum?*
2. What subjects, if any, in the current school curriculum would you equate with fish-grabbing-with-the-bare-hands? Why?
3. What new subjects would you suggest adding to the school curriculum to avoid creating our own saber-tooth curriculum? Why?

19

CLASSIC

Teaching What We Hold to Be Sacred

John I. Goodlad

John I. Goodlad, professor emeritus at the University of Washington, is also president of the Institute for Educational Inquiry and a founder of the Center for Educational Renewal at the University of Washington. He was Dean of the Graduate School of Education at UCLA for a number of years, and is known as one of America's advocates and experts on educational renewal.

"Teaching What We Hold To Be Sacred," by John I. Goodlad, 2004, *Educational Leadership 61*(4), pp.18–21. © 2004 by ASCD. Reprinted with permission. Learn more about ASCD at www.ascd.org.

FOCUS QUESTION

As you read this article, try to think of the various ways schools can address social inequality to promote social justice.

InTASC
Standards 2, 7, and 10

KEY TERMS
- Moral ecology
- Social justice

On February 1, 1994, the U.S. Postal Service added a new postage stamp honoring Allison Davis to its Black Heritage Series. An important figure in psychology, social anthropology, and education for more than 40 years, Davis was the first person from the field of education to be elected to the American Academy of Arts and Sciences (Unicover, 2003).

In the 1940s, Davis became the first African American ever appointed to a tenured position at a major "white" university, the University of Chicago. His appointment was controversial. Ralph Tyler, chairman of the department of education, and Robert M. Hutchins, president of the university, overcame the opposition's pretext of lack of funds for hiring Davis by securing private funding to underwrite Davis's salary and related expenses for the first three years.

Even so, Davis did not gain access to the amenities that his colleagues took for granted. He unsuccessfully sought housing in the surrounding Hyde Park neighborhood. He was ineligible for membership in the university's Quadrangle Club until women, too, finally gained admittance in 1948. And he could not find living quarters and mixed-race meeting places when conducting field research in the South and the Southwest (Finder, 2004).

Much of Davis's research centered on the effects of the color-caste system in U.S. society, particularly on the ways in which biases in standardized intelligence tests unfairly stigmatized poor and minority students. With colleague Robert Havighurst, Davis produced a series of papers arguing that the American social class system actually prevents the vast majority of children of the working classes, or of the slums, from learning any culture but that of their own groups (cited in University of Chicago, 2003).

Davis and Havighurst challenged the conventional wisdom of their day that claimed that social inequalities resulted from racial biological inferiority. They envisioned a day in which this misconception would be replaced by the knowledge that inequalities in achievement stemmed from environmental factors, such as widespread denial of educational and economic opportunities to people of color.

In the ensuing years, innumerable researchers and thinkers have confirmed Davis's message, including James B. Conant (1961), who documented the shameful differences between the relatively lavish provisions for schooling in the suburbs and the shamefully shabby provisions in the inner cities.

Unfortunately, the biological causation thesis as an explanation of social inequality has had a stubborn longevity. As Stephen J. Gould tells us in *The Mismeasure of Man* (1981), researchers (of a sort) have extended this thesis beyond race. Gould's account of the efforts to assign lower levels of intelligence to women because of their generally smaller craniums is eerily hilarious. He cites the French anthropologist Hervé, who savaged women and black men with one stroke in 1881: "Men of the black races have a brain scarcely heavier than that of white women" (p. 3). As Gould points out, attempts to rank people—whether by brain size or by an IQ test score—have consistently recorded "little more than social prejudice" (p. 28).

History demonstrates that people will find ingenious ways and develop elaborate constructs to create and harden categories of status and privilege among the diverse groups that constitute humankind. And they will produce a litany of justifications to convince the populace that these inequalities are natural and right.

One might argue that a more enlightened era has, in part, arrived. The end of legal racial segregation, improved access to higher education for minorities, and increased economic opportunities have improved individual lives. But the caste system is still entrenched in society; social prejudices and injustices remain.

Our Moral Ecology

Will humankind ever manage—or want—to do away with social inequality? The apparent inevitability and tenacity of caste as a way of life may make us feel hopeless about trying to eliminate this system. Why try to reform what exists? To quote the 19th century British politician, Lord Thomas Macaulay, "Reform, reform, don't speak to me of reform. We have enough problems already."

Nonetheless, the history of civilization reveals that in every era, some people, somewhere, have envisioned gaining freedom from the caste system. The themes of enlightenment have been argued from both the rational and the divine perspectives. The two perspectives have come together to form a central core of common principles. This evolving center, never static, takes on a kind of cultural sacredness, an abstract moral ecology. It provides, in Seymour Sarason's words, a "sense of interconnections among the individual, the collectivity, and ultimate purpose and meaning of human existence" (1986, p. 899).

In societies seeking to balance the private and public good, we might well consider what we commonly hold sacred. If our moral ecology encompasses equality and social justice, and if we want that moral ecology to guide our society, then equality and social justice must be taught—carefully taught.

Many people assign to our schools the task of nurturing these values in the populace. In its much lauded experiment, universal schooling, the United States set as a major purpose the enculturation of the young—specifically the children of immigrants—into a social and political democracy.

But when we place this responsibility entirely on schools, we forget that between the years of 6 and 18, young people spend approximately 55 percent of their time in activities other than school and sleep. We give little critical thought to the cacophony of teaching that now surrounds our young throughout the day, and nearly all of which is driven by economic ends rather than by the ideals of education that we espouse in the rhetoric of school and college graduation ceremonies.

Political scientist Benjamin Barber brings our attention sharply to the daunting task that schools undertake when they attempt to develop students' democratic character amid the ubiquitous culture that surrounds young people throughout the day:

> We honor ambition, we reward greed, we celebrate materialism, we worship acquisitiveness,

we cherish success, and we commercialize the classroom—and then we bark at the young about the gentle art of the spirit. (1993, p. 42)

The Role of Schools

In spite of the obstacles, it would be the height of folly for our schools not to have as their central mission educating the young in the democratic ideals of humankind, the freedoms and responsibilities of a democratic society, and the civil and civic understandings and dispositions necessary to democratic citizenship. And yet here we are, hardening into place the caste categories linked to test scores, a practice that directly impedes such a mission. When polls ask people what they want of their schools, the people say over and over that the personal and social development of their children is just as important to them as vocational and academic development. As the accumulating body of knowledge about cognition clearly reveals, test scores do not correlate at all with the other attributes that people believe their schools should develop in students.

But not to worry. High test scores will get your offspring into a college or university if the money is available from family resources or scholarships. Forget those who dominate among the low scorers, such as low-income children whose late-in-the-year birthdays kept them out of kindergarten for most of an additional year, during which their families had no resources to send them to preschool. Funding for Head Start did not quite embrace their neighborhoods. And, oh yes, those children in the inner cities who had substitute teachers for every year of their schooling did not reach the upper levels of test scores, either. But let us keep the system, anyway—it offers special rewards for those who succeed and who then join the upper levels of the layers of power.

We need to pay increased attention to the commonalities that bind humankind. Our schools are not lacking in the rhetoric of "respecting diversity" and social studies texts extolling "understanding other people." What *other* people?

We all belong to one species—humankind. There is only one ongoing conversation—the human conversation, consisting of the work, play, parenting, conversing, and imagining in which we all engage and of the beliefs, hopes, and aspirations that we hold. To be sure, within those commonalities there is rich diversity—not only in the rainbow of colors to which the Reverend Jesse Jackson refers, but also in all human characteristics. The diversity in color, language, song, ceremony, religion, games, flora, and fauna that exists among us adds to the miracle of life. Why else do we travel to other parts of the world?

But if we begin with the concept of one humankind and then add the concept of diversity in addressing such democratic essentials as liberty and justice for all, we embark on a slippery slope. Some years ago, a critic attacked the late Ernest Boyer's book, *High School* (1983), and my book, *A Place Called School* (1984), on the grounds that we did not address special education. A specialist in the field defended us by pointing out that we *had* addressed special education—by advocating individualized education for all students.

A few years later, Thomas Lovitt and I were gently taken to task for our advocacy of integrating general and special education (Goodlad & Lovitt, 1993). Critics argued that the road to bringing attention—some of it now required by federal law—to students who require substantial deviations from the norms of schooling had been a rocky one. Many of the hard-won gains could be wiped out if schools eliminated special education as a separate service, even with the best intentions of providing for the individual differences and education needs of all children. We agreed with their assessment. Our agreement did not change our basic argument for the benefits of bringing general and special education together in classrooms, but it did caution us to emphasize that exceptional provisions are sometimes necessary to provide equal opportunity in education. The same perspective applies to our efforts to provide equal education opportunities to diverse students, no matter what type of diversity we mean.

Beyond Social Caste

The struggle for justice, equity, respect, and appreciation for human diversity has been long and often troubled. It continues to be so. The human race's proclivity for arranging its members in hierarchies of strongly maintained status and privilege is likely to continue as a malaise that can become cancerous.

The answer, we know, is education. But education, despite our honoring the concept, is not in itself good. We must intentionally and even passionately inject morality into education (Goodlad, 1999).

Winston Churchill said, "Democracy is the worst form of government except for all those others that have been tried." If we agree, we must do more than teach students only about the political structures of democracy. We must teach students the ideals of democracy and social equality and give our young people opportunities to practice those ideals in their daily lives, both in and out of school.

Unless we work simultaneously as a society to eliminate in our schools and society a caste system harboring and even fostering beliefs and practices that contradict these ideals, our hypocrisy will become transparent. We are all participants in the informal education that goes on outside of schools. The larger community must ensure a democracy that protects and supports the democratic education that needs to go on inside of schools. The clear purpose of schooling, then, becomes attending to all those educational matters that the larger community does not address, especially enculturating the young into satisfying, responsible citizens in a social and political democracy.

Once formal education inside of schools and informal education outside of schools, working together, make morally grounded democratic behavior routine—as John Dewey said it must become—such principles as justice, equity, and freedom for everyone will need no special advocacy. But when we parcel them out into the tiers of caste privilege, as we often do today, we endanger these precious principles.

References

Barber, B. R. (1993, November). America skips school. *Harper's Magazine, 286,* 42.

Boyer, E. L. (1983). *High school.* New York: Harper & Row.

Conant, J. B. (1961). *Slums and suburbs: A commentary on schools in metropolitan areas.* New York: McGraw-Hill.

Finder, M. (2004). *Educating America: The extraordinary career of Ralph W. Tyler.* New York: Praeger.

Goodlad, J. I. (1984). *A place called school.* New York: McGraw-Hill.

Goodlad, J. I. (1999). Convergence. In R. Soder, J. I. Goodlad, & T. J. McMannon (Eds.), *Developing Democratic Character in the Young* (pp. 1–25). San Francisco: Jossey-Bass.

Goodlad, J. I., & Lovitt, T. C. (Eds.). (1993). *Integrating general and special education.* New York: Merrill.

Gould, S. J. (1981). *The mismeasure of man.* New York: W. W. Norton.

Sarason, S. B. (1986, August). And what is the public interest? *American Psychologist, 41,* 899.

Unicover. (2003). *U.S. proof card: 29¢ Dr. Allison Davis: Black heritage series* [Online]. Available: www.unicover.com/EA4PAD1J.htm

University of Chicago. (2003). *The University of Chicago faculty: A centennial view—Allison Davis/Education* [Online]. Available: www.lib.uchicago.edu/projects/centcat/centcats/fac/facch25_01.html

POSTNOTE

John I. Goodlad is one of the elder statesmen of education, which is why we have identified this article as Classic. He has written on many different topics throughout his career, such as teacher education, curriculum, and instruction. On all of these topics, he focuses on the important, salient features and never becomes bogged down in details. In this article, he addresses one of the ultimate purposes of public schooling in a democratic society, ensuring that principles of equality and social justice are carefully taught.

With our current focus on content standards, high-stakes testing, and other accountability features, Goodlad reminds us that most parents want more from our schools than this emphasis on acquiring knowledge. They want their children to learn the freedoms and responsibilities of living in a democracy. Sometimes, we lose sight of this most important goal of schooling. As Socrates said, education has a dual responsibility: to make people smart and to make people good.

DISCUSSION QUESTIONS

1. In your own schooling, did you receive specific instruction or lessons on social justice or civic responsibility? If so, can you describe them?
2. Can you think of any events you observed in school that violated the concept of social justice and equality? Was anything done about them? If so, what?
3. If you were to design a school that focused strongly on civic responsibility, social justice, and equality, what would be some of its practices?

RELATED WEBSITE RESOURCE

WEB RESOURCE:

Website:

http://www.ieiseattle.org/.

This site of the Institute for Educational Inquiry contains links to other affiliated organizations that promote educational efforts in a democracy.

20

E Pluribus Unum

Deborah Meier and Chester E. Finn, Jr.

Deborah Meier was the founder of New York City's Central Park East Schools and the author of *The Power of Their Ideas: Lessons for America from a Small School in Harlem*.

Chester E. Finn, Jr. is a senior fellow at Stanford's Hoover Institution and chairman of Hoover's Koret Task Force on K–12 Education. Finn is also president of the Thomas B. Fordham Foundation and Thomas B. Fordham Institute and senior editor of *Education Next*.

Deborah Meier and Chester E. Finn, Jr., "E Pluribus Unum," *Education Next*, Spring 2009, Vol. 9, No. 2. Available at: http://educationnext.org/e-pluribus-unum-2/.

The push for a national curriculum is gaining momentum as reformers press states to acknowledge "world class" benchmarks for student achievement. The topic had been dormant since Clinton-era efforts to promote "voluntary national standards" yielded little more than charges of political correctness. With No Child Left Behind now stirring concerns about disparate state assessments and sometimes incoherent state standards, has the time come for the new president and Congress to press forward on a national curriculum? Chester E. Finn Jr., Education Next senior editor and longtime champion of standards-based reform, says unequivocally "Yes!" and lays out his vision of what it should look like and how it should work. Deborah Meier, founder of New York City's Central Park East Schools and author of *The Power of Their Ideas: Lessons for America from a Small School in Harlem*, is equally vehement in arguing "No!" while providing her own set of strategies for improving our nation's schools.

Education Next: Should the United States have a national curriculum?

Chester Finn: Absolutely, positively yes, provided that we properly define "curriculum," and ensure that the states' participation remains voluntary. In the core subjects of English, math, science, and history (including geography and civics, never say "social studies"), there is absolutely no reason why we ought not ask all young Americans to learn most of the same things while in the elementary and secondary grades. That doesn't mean all teachers should follow identical lesson plans, that everybody needs to read the same poems and plays, or that a rigid "scope and sequence" should be clamped onto all schools and school systems. But the basic content of, say, 4th-grade English or 6th-grade math or 8th-grade science should be the same from Portland, Maine, to Portland, Oregon. And that content should be married to national standards of "proficiency" in these subjects at these grade levels, and joined to national exams by which we determine how well and by whom this is being accomplished.

FOCUS QUESTION

Should the United States have a national curriculum like most other countries?

InTASC
Standards 4, 5, and 7

KEY TERMS

- Achieve
- Coalition of Essential Schools (CES)
- Core Knowledge Curriculum
- International Baccalaureate (IB)
- National Assessment of Educational Progress (NAEP)
- National Board for Professional Teaching Standards (NBPTS)
- National Council for the Accreditation of Teacher Education (NCATE)

The curriculum should cover grades K–12 and leave plenty of room for state, local, and building- and classroom-level variation and augmentation. Particularly in grades 11 and 12, it would make sense to offer (as high schools do today) some choice among courses in science, history, and English; one English class might focus on drama, another on creative writing. A charter or magnet school might specialize in art and music, while another concentrates on science and math, in addition to the academic core.

One way to picture the core is the "1,000 question" approach, which blends standards, curriculum, and assessment. Here's a simple version: The testing body (perhaps a consortium of states, possibly a spin-off from the National Assessment of Educational Progress [NAEP]) would publish—this is all totally transparent—maybe 1,000 possible exam questions dealing with, say, 7th-grade science. A generous portion would be open-response and deep-thought queries that probe a student's ability to make sense of what he or she is learning, not just parrot it back or fill in bubbles. The national end-of-course exam in 7th-grade science would consist of a subset of those questions. Any student able to answer all 1,000 would likely get a perfect score on the exam.

But 1,000 is obviously too many to drill students on, so effective teaching of 7th-grade science would cover most if not all of the subject matter spanned by those questions. The teacher would be free to cover it however she likes—any sequence, any course structure, any instructional materials. If the state or school system or charter school wants to systematize this (and assist its teachers) by setting forth a scope and sequence, textbooks, units, mid-course assessments, and such, that's fine, too.

Obviously, the testing body needs to ensure that there's a logical, sequential relationship between the 7th-grade science questions and the 8th-grade questions and so forth. Indeed, the questions would surely overlap in part—and would cumulate, over the 13 grades, to a solid science education.

That's pretty much the way the best extant national curriculum works, at least through grade 8. Of course I'm thinking of the Core Knowledge Curriculum developed by University of Virginia professor and Cultural Literacy author E. D. Hirsch. (Alas, it doesn't yet include the high school grades.) Hirsch says it's supposed to occupy roughly half of the school day. That feels about right to me. Maybe even two-thirds.

The national curriculum would cover only content, not pedagogy or instruction. For that we depend on professionals, and we assume and expect that they will differ from one another in their skills, enthusiasms, preferences, and values. One school might rely heavily on "virtual" instruction, for example, making extensive use of Internet offerings and opportunities. Others may team teach several subjects via two or three teachers who like working together and whose subjects lend themselves to blending. Still others will resemble the traditional self-contained-classroom schools of yesteryear. This is as it should be. The United States has some 54 million school kids, 3 million teachers, and 100,000 schools. They differ in many ways and ought to. But today the absence of a common core is a critical handicap, particularly for the neediest kids, weakest teachers, and least advantaged schools. Equity demands that we rectify this.

Most successful modern nations have something akin to a national curriculum, whether explicitly or through their exam systems. Japan has "national curriculum standards" and insists that individual schools use them as the basis for planning what they will actually teach and how they teach it. Singapore publishes syllabi for each major course or subject, usually divided between primary and secondary. England spells it all out in considerable detail, and France famously standardizes even its lesson plans. To my knowledge, no two nations do this in quite the same way—and some of the other "federal" countries, such as Australia and Canada, are still working on how to do it at all. In Canada, for example, several provincial education ministries have voluntarily joined together to develop "pan-Canadian" curricula, starting with science.

Rather than starting with a federal mandate, a consortium of states and private organizations (such as some combination of Achieve, the state school "chiefs," and the governors) could develop the curricula and tests, ideally with initial support from major national foundations. States would then be free to join if they like. Possibly we'll wind up with more than one consortium, and states would have choices among them. Picture the Southern Regional Education Board spearheading the second of these. Maybe the four small New England states that have already joined forces on testing will become the starting point for a third. (The Brits do something like this with their multiple testing bodies.) Uncle Sam's role is to encourage movement in this direction, probably by giving states that join such consortia some breaks on No Child Left Behind (NCLB) and its successors, perhaps a bit more money, perhaps automatic approval of their standards and tests without further inspection or negotiation.

I don't expect every state will join, at least not soon, so the federal government's additional responsibility is to maintain NAEP as the external auditor of all states. We'll find out over time whether kids in schools and states that join in the common curricula and exams do better (or worse) than in those that maintain their curricular independence.

Deborah Meier: I have five concerns with Chester Finn's proposal for a national curriculum.

First, what's (positively) special about the U.S.A. is that it doesn't have an official line, above all, on ideological and intellectual matters. This is part of our unusual history and reflects tolerance for diverse origins and beliefs. It has always been a struggle, never quite won, but it is a strength that is always tempting for us to abandon. Doing so would be at a cost we would someday rue.

Second, there is no way in which a federally approved curriculum can avoid the trap of selection bias—no matter who might design it. Even if I were to design my ideal history curriculum, whatever I decided to spend more time on or (God forbid) omit altogether will be influenced by my biases. The sources I require my students to be familiar with; the differences of opinion I tolerate versus those I feel compelled to correct; how I "simplify" without losing the most important truths—all these are fraught with inevitable biases. What I believe everyone must know may be different from what you believe. Do we vote

on "the truth" and then put a camera in each classroom to ensure it's carried out?

I truly cannot imagine how supporters of a federally approved curriculum solve these issues. It's not merely political bias, mind you, but academic and intellectual views that may or may not have political implications. Historians at my graduate school differed on whether history was a science or a field of humanities, for example. So they offered both! Not an insignificant difference of opinion. Biologists and physicists may have different views about which science is more critical, and within each field there are controversies about the nature of science and which scientific ideas are more important.

A panel of righteous and well-educated people is not an answer. So, you might ask, are multiple bodies of righteous and well-educated people any better? Yes, because it leaves the door open for more controversy; offers escape hatches for unexpected views; and leaves contenders, alternatives, and authority in many hands.

Third, attempting to avoid bias by including everyone's biases only generates more problems. Precisely in order to avoid charges of bias, the tendency of textbooks (and curricula and tests) is already to include snippets of all viewpoints, thus becoming long-winded and boring. The effort of the national science community a decade or so ago to outline what every 18-year-old should know about science was so extensive that it invited either rote memorization (in defiance of the heart of science instruction being recommended) or studying nothing but science in order to cover it all. The science teachers at my old high school admitted that they were only secure in their knowledge of one or at most two of the fields covered. What part of the fascinating study of mathematics is a "must" for 18-year-olds? What knowledge of music or art?

The focus on testing also has an interesting side effect: it makes it hard for wise educators to take advantage of the teachable moment in their concern to stick with the stuff that will appear on the test. For example, teachers should be able to use the recent election as a moment for understanding our political system or the financial crisis to examine how money and finance works.

My fourth problem is that any curriculum leads—as Finn acknowledges—to assessment issues. My colleague Diane Ravitch suggests we decouple the two ideas. I think, as Finn does, that the one inevitably follows the other. At that point the best intentions of a good curriculum come screeching to a halt. In reality, the test becomes the curriculum, and the scoring guide for the test becomes the bible.

Of course, we can do our best to develop tests that are more nuanced, that require strong written and oral exposition, opportunities to defend one's ideas, to think critically and persuasively, etc. But it's highly unlikely, almost utopian, to imagine we could do it on a national scale, and far more likely are precisely the kinds of assessment tools that undermine a strong education.

But my greatest concern is none of the above!

I'm concerned that all of this is a way to avoid a real conversation about the purposes of public education and then to acknowledge our ignorance about "ensuring" success. Our own children are worth more than money can buy, but no parent can offer a guarantee.

Whether the first discussion might ever lead to a substantial consensus I don't know. What math must we "all" know, and why? Like music, mathematics is a subject of beauty, as well as a practical study of import. But which aspects of math must we all—as citizens—have at our fingertips regardless of our vocational goals? In this debate not only experts in math must have a voice.

So, too, with debating what literature is indispensable. How tempting it is to add a little bit of everything to please all camps rather than engaging with a few works in great depth. The development of a "taste" for literature—fiction and nonfiction alike—is hardly something we're good at teaching, not to mention the dilemma about how to teach literacy of the new media that will constitute the bulk of the next generation's "reading."

Perhaps we can reach agreement that one purpose stands apart from the rest—that the indispensable core purpose of a public education system is that it prepares people for public life in a democracy, with all that this implies. But even that would be far from settling matters. How we define democracy, and what constitutes the intellectual underpinnings of a democracy are open to endless discourse. But it's the "litmus" test.

I also know that the second question—how to make it work—is equally knotty and that no one has a monopoly on the right answers.

EN: What should be taught, in your view, and how will educators figure out effective ways to do this?

CF: If I were king, I'd probably install Core Knowledge in the primary and middle grades and the International Baccalaureate (IB) in high schools. I don't think it's any coincidence that the most highly respected high school courses in America today are Advanced Placement (AP) and IB courses, which have quite a lot of nationwide prescription as to their content. (It's true that AP shuns a prescribed "syllabus," but veteran AP teachers are clear as to what they must cover in order to prepare their pupils for those exams—and the College Board isn't shy about clueing in new teachers.)

With these standards and assessments in place, the question reasonably arises, where do educators find the curricular materials that best help them tackle the standards? Some will develop their own or pull them off the Internet. I think we can be confident that major publishing companies will develop and market commercial versions. I'd favor staging a competition among prospective curriculum suppliers, maybe have a jury evaluate and grade their products. Perhaps then we could make all their products available to states, districts, and schools, and let the market select among them. Wikipedia-style (or Zagat-style) open-source rating systems will enable product users to rate and comment on what works best in what circumstances. Having a national curriculum doesn't mean we need confine ourselves to just one option.

Textbook publishers (and their modern-day successors, such as virtual-curriculum developers) will align their products with the national standards rather than with the whims of California and Texas. (That assumes California and Texas join the multistate ventures, of course.) The total amount of testing should diminish and, if it doesn't, it will have to be better aligned to the end-of-course expectations and exams that states will administer. Commercial tests such as the Stanford and Iowa may evolve into something more like formative assessments meant to assist teachers rather than be used for external accountability.

Teacher preparers and professional developers, and those who try to set standards for them (e.g., National Council for Accreditation of Teacher Education, National Board for Professional Teaching Standards), will need to take seriously the obligation to align their expectations for instructors with the common expectations for students. All this is mostly good—and, yes, a little bit risky, if the national standards go squishy or the national curriculum falls into the hands of zealots. That's why it needs to stay voluntary, so any jurisdiction that can't abide it need not stick with it.

A big grown-up country in the 21st century needs common (and ambitious!) curricular standards for all its children, at least in core subjects, and it needs common assessments, too. If we've learned anything from the NCLB experience (and its antecedent "Goals 2000" and "Improving America's Schools" legislation), it's that having these things vary from state to state produces mediocrity, cacophony, waste, duplication, and confusion. Survey after survey makes clear that (if the question is asked correctly) parents favor national standards and tests. Instead of letting "That's the first step toward a national curriculum" serve as a conversation stopper, let's deploy it as a conversation starter. Let's acknowledge that "curriculum," loosely defined, is supposed to be aligned with standards and appraised by assessments.

Let me note, finally, that I'm unimpressed by Meier's "habits of mind" alternative to content (see below). It's wonderfully seductive, but the serious psychologists with whose work I'm acquainted (see, for example, "Reframing the Mind," check the facts, Summer 2004) don't put much stock in this Howard Gardner–originated proposition that youngsters can learn skills devoid of content. It's the absence of essential core content from her view of schooling that lies at the heart of our curricular disagreement.

EN: What other options are there for bringing our nation's public education system to a higher level?

DM: At the schools I led for nearly 40 years, as part of the work of the Coalition of Essential Schools, we spent a lot of time exploring the "why" questions and developing an approach that was aimed at answering them. This discussion was at the heart of the school's existence and included all parties to it. Like Coalition founder Ted Sizer, we figured if we could grab hold of that, we'd see how much else we could teach and, more importantly, how everything we taught and did helped to reinforce "the essentials," influencing not only our students' hours in school (or doing homework), but every waking hour of their lives. We even saw misbehavior as an opening, an opportunity to teach such habits and not an obstacle to it.

We boiled it down to five "habits of mind" that we claimed (somewhat pompously) underlay all the academic disciplines as well as the mental and social disciplines needed for living in a complex modern society: (1) How do you know what you know? What's the nature of your evidence? How credible is it? Compared to what? (2) Are there other perspectives? What affects our points of view? How otherwise might this be seen? (3) Are there patterns there? A sequence? A theory of cause and effect? (4) Could it be otherwise? What would happen if? Supposing that x had not happened? and (5) Who cares? Why does it matter? As you can see, they blend into each other and, in a way, just define a mind state of skepticism and informed empathy. It suggests having to take seriously the idea that one might be wrong, and so could others. We added "habits of work" like meeting deadlines and being on time and "habits of the heart" like caring about one's impact on others.

We developed rubrics that spelled out specific formats in which students could demonstrate their proficiency in each discipline. The diploma from our high school rested on convincing an internal and external evaluation committee that the student met the standards set by the faculty. Students' oral presentations and defenses were based on written essays and other performances in each of the major disciplines as well as subjects of the student's and faculty's choice.

Could the five habits of mind become a national curriculum? Democratic habits of the sort we laid out at Central Park East can be taught in the process of learning math with its powerful logical habits, its attentiveness to patterns, as well as its multiple approaches to getting "right answers." They can be taught in science, with its scrupulous attention to detail, specificity, and evidence, not to mention its humility in the face of the unknown. They can be taught in literature through our capacity to empathize with otherwise unacceptable protagonists, connecting us to people and worlds we otherwise would or could never choose. They can be taught in the way one handles discipline!

Isn't democratic culture best served if all citizens are accustomed to such habitual ways of thinking, not just knowing how to do various things? I know how to do a lot of things—like putting my keys in the right compartment in my purse—that I don't practice, especially in times of stress. What would it mean to teach so well that we'd hang on to such "habits of mind" in times of stress? Are our five a fair representation of what democratic intellectual habits amount to? Fair questions.

A school community that holds itself to high standards must risk such everlasting debate among, at the very least, the adults in charge and ideally all members of the community. But nothing I've said works if it's simply adopted to try to "cover" the likely contents of a test with which ordinary teachers, families, and students cannot argue or differ. The habit of mind of "supposing that" is best learned from adults who are in a position to choose, revise, and rethink their own viewpoints in the presence of the young.

POSTNOTE

Unlike most other developed nations, the United States does not have a national curriculum. The U.S. Constitution reserves for the states and the people rights that are not specifically granted to the federal government, and the Constitution does not mention education. Consequently, the education of the young has been overseen by each individual state, which has led to varying quality from state to state. Recently, led by the National Governors Association and the Council of Chief State School Officers, a coalition of organizations has begun to develop a Common Core of State Standards and assessments in the fields of English/language arts and mathematics. To date, over forty states have committed themselves to implementing these common standards. However, it should be noted that committing themselves to a set of common standards is not the same as having a common curriculum. States could develop different curricula that would address the common standards.

In this article, Chester Finn and Deborah Meier debate the pros and cons of having a national curriculum. This debate is likely to continue for many years.

DISCUSSION QUESTIONS

1. Whose arguments—Finn or Meier—did you find most persuasive, and why?
2. What do you think is the single strongest argument in favor of a national curriculum, and which is the single strongest argument against a national curriculum?
3. Can you think of any other arguments either for or against a national curriculum that were not mentioned by either Finn or Meier?

RELATED WEBSITE RESOURCE

WEB RESOURCE:

Common Core Standards. Available at:

http://www.corestandards.org/.

This website describes the Common Core State Standards and the efforts made to implement them.

21

National Education Standards: To Be or Not to Be?

Paul E. Barton

Paul E. Barton is an education writer and consultant and senior associate in the Policy Information Center at Educational Testing Service.

"National Education Standards: To Be or Not to Be?" by Paul E. Barton, 2010, *Educational Leadership 67*(7), pp. 22–29. © 2010 by ASCD. Reprinted with permission. Learn more about ASCD at www.ascd.org.

Should the United States have national standards for our education system? Americans have been debating this question for the last quarter of a century. If you are trying to make up your own mind and think the decision should be simple, you're likely to be surprised.

In a system in which localities and states pay about 93 percent of the cost of schooling and the federal government has no constitutional role in education, the nation has flirted with the idea of injecting broader national control into education policy. The United States has seen historic episodes of federal or national initiatives in education. These episodes include efforts to bolster math and science capability in response to Sputnik, the quest for racial and ethnic equity through the courts, efforts to equalize resources in public schools, and an outright seizure of control in crucial areas of policy and practice through No Child Left Behind (NCLB).

In parallel efforts since the mid-1980s, policymakers have made sporadic attempts to raise achievement levels by creating both a national definition of what students should be taught and a national test to see whether schools were successfully bolstering achievement. This effort was touched off by the 1983 report of the National Commission on Educational Excellence, which found the nation "at risk," although its corrective recommendations were directed at local and state governments.

By 1989, concern about the U.S. education system's worldwide status had risen so high that President George H.W. Bush gathered the nation's governors for a summit to establish goals for the United States to achieve by 2000. Other calls for national intervention included the National Council on Education Standards and Tests, the National Education Standards and Assessment Council, the Clinton administration's Goals 2000 legislation, and that administration's partial development of a voluntary national test, which Congress soon abandoned.

This condensed history conveys the continuing desire for action at the national level, the failure to bring that desire to fruition, and a lack of

FOCUS QUESTION

Should the United States have national education standards like most other countries?

InTASC
Standards 1, 4, 5, 6, and 7

KEY TERMS

- Education Testing Service
- National Assessment of Educational Progress (NAEP)
- No Child Left Behind Act

agreement and enthusiasm for this level of federal intervention. America has clearly been of two minds about bringing change to our locally based public education system.

One reason we lack agreement is that people place different degrees of value on schools' traditional local control and diversity, show different degrees of willingness to take the risks involved, and come to different conclusions about whether accompanying challenges can be overcome. Perhaps most basic, people have different mind-sets about what "national standards" means.

What Are "National Standards"?

When people say they are for or against national standards, they often harbor quite different views of what they want to create—or protest. Some people have in mind setting standards for the content of what is taught in any grade or subject in school. For some, establishing content standards means increasing the rigor of instruction; for others, it means "standardizing" what knowledge is taught. These two goals are related but different. An extreme example of the latter goal would be the uniformity in France, where at almost any hour, all students are studying the same thing.

Some supporters of standards envision a single national test that all students would be required to take. Others want both prescribed course content and a national test. There are those who claim that standards should be voluntary and those who believe that we should subject all students to them. Goals vary: Some want standards to give teachers information that will improve instruction, whereas others want a national test to measure performance in an NCLB-like accountability system.

Differences also exist on the "how." Some people clearly want standards to be national but to be created and enforced by some agency other than the federal government (although possibly with government funding); others want the federal government to develop and prescribe standards. In another version, both standards and tests would emanate from outside the federal government, but

they would be used to enforce a federal accountability system—a scenario that I believe would effectively federalize such a test.

Before we can fruitfully discuss issues involved in setting national standards, everyone will have to agree on what we are after. Although the options that individuals or groups might propose would still entail differing challenges, issues, and values, all parties would at least then be on the same page.

Surprising Variation

One complication to developing standards is the extensive variation in our education landscape. A 2009 report I wrote for the Educational Testing Service reveals huge variations in content of instruction, states' performance standards, and student achievement levels across the nation. We could look at this high rate of variation in two ways: as a sign that the obstacles to standardization are insurmountable or as evidence for why a single set of standards is needed.

The amount and degree of variation throughout our education system may surprise many readers. Let's consider three major areas of variation: (1) the content of instruction from place to place, (2) the performance standards states have set, and (3) student achievement.

Variation in Content

Throughout U.S. history, certain forces have worked to produce uniformity in curriculum, and others have pushed toward increasing variation. Historian Daniel Boorstein has pointed out that early U.S. schoolmarms taught a standard English; therefore, unlike British citizens, Americans could understand one another wherever they went in the country. McGuffey readers were widespread in schools throughout the 19th century, and standardized tests have long been in use.

One would expect textbooks to exert pressure toward uniformity. Schools in all 50 states generally choose from only a handful of textbooks for any particular subject or grade. However, there is great variation in the levels of student achievement in any grade across the country, and there are large differences among district and state prescriptions of what should be taught. So if textbook publishers are to market themselves well, they must span a wide diversity of instructional objectives. A detailed review of prescribed content for 4th grade instruction in 10 U.S. states, for instance, revealed 108 possible learning outcomes, only four of which were common to all 10 states (Reys, as cited in Beatty, 2008). Publishers are pushed in the direction of covering a vast number of objectives. If we hope to set common standards, we must address the forces that produce this tremendous variability.

Variation in Performance Standards

The U.S. Secretary of Education recently said that we don't need 50 different goal-posts, a reference to NCLB's provision that each state can set its own performance standards. So how much variation is there? A lot. Each test's performance standard is simply a cut point on the state test that represents the level at which a test taker is deemed proficient. The stringency of standards is difficult to compare because each state has its own tests.

However, the cut points for each state test have been "mapped" onto the national score scale for the National Assessment of Educational Progress (NAEP), and the Department of Education has published tables showing where each state's cut point falls on that scale. The percentage of students meeting or exceeding the score that NAEP has set as representing proficiency ranges from 18 percent in Hawaii and Mississippi to 38 percent in New Jersey (Barton, 2009, p. 18).

States differ greatly, of course, in average income, the richness of students' experiences before they start school, and the size of the state's tax base. Do these differences account for some of the variation in how high they set their requirements for student achievement? One way to examine this would be to map the cut points on each state's test onto that state's own NAEP scale rather than

the national NAEP scale to see how states compare in reaching their own cut points for their student populations. I did this mapping and found that the disparity on this basis was greater, not less: The percentage of students reaching or exceeding the cut point ranges from 30 percent in South Carolina to 88 percent in North Carolina—two adjoining states with identical average NAEP scores (see Barton, 2009, p. 18). So the dynamics are complicated. A lot of carpentry will be required to make all goal-posts the same height.

Variation in Achievement

Broad variation exists in student achievement for any particular grade level and school subject. The degree of variation makes a huge difference in the effort it will take to raise all U.S. students to the same level. Figure 1 (p. 152) provides a panorama of student scores on the reading portion of the 1990 and 2004 NAEP assessments at ages 9, 13, and 17 for all racial and ethnic subgroups. If you place a ruler across the chart at the point showing 9-year-olds scoring in the 90th percentile to see what percentile it reaches for the scores of 17-year-olds, you'll see that the bottom fourth of 17-year-olds read no better than the top tenth of 9-year-olds.

To gauge the magnitude of this variation, consider that the spread of scores *within* any one grade level is as great as, or greater than, the difference in the average scores from the 4th grade to the 12th. This is a lot of variation to deal with.

Commonality Versus Tolerance for Diversity

The United States is a diverse society created by people from many cultures, religions, and parts of the world. We live in communities and neighborhoods with extremes in wealth and income. These extreme differences have been well tolerated by Americans because we are a land of opportunity. And, because we believe that opportunity depends a lot on education, we want to reduce inequality in our school system.

FIGURE 1   Percentile Distributions of NAEP Reading Scores by Age
and Racial/Ethnic Group, 1990 and 2004

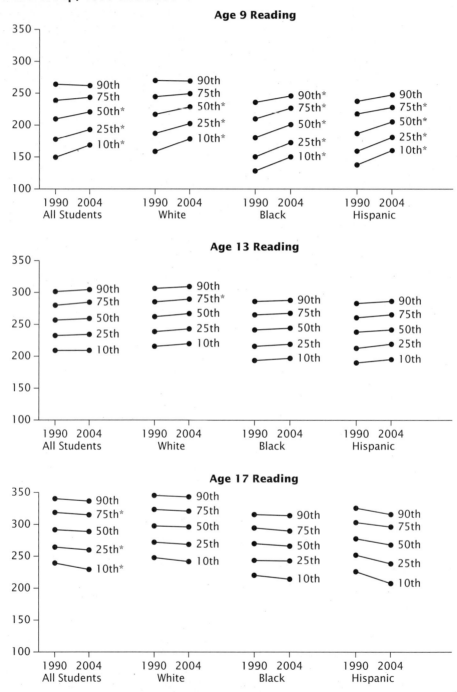

* Indicates a statistically significant difference 1990 to 2004.

Source: Data from the National Assessment of Educational Progress analyzed by Educational Testing Service.

The American experience has always accommodated a great deal of disagreement about what to teach, how to teach it, and when to teach it. As late as March 2009, a panel appointed by President George W. Bush tried—again—to put to rest what the *New York Times* called "the long, heated debate over math teaching methods" (Lewin, 2008). Debates over how to teach reading are still divisive. Controversies over teaching evolution and other topics still flare up around the country—at times even involving literal textbook fires, such as in West Virginia in the 1970s.

All this diversity and disagreement is like a coil-spring mattress; the weight pressing on one area of the mattress is tolerated without affecting the rest of the mattress. When we try to settle basic differences about education at a national level, however, we elevate the stakes. We open the door for national-level organizations to bring pressures and counter-pressures to bear. As U.S. citizens balance a desire for commonality against tolerance for differences, we face the question of how strongly we want to raise such issues to a court of national settlement.

Up the Hill Again?

Beginning in March 2009, signs emerged that supporters of national standards were making another effort to storm the hill under a new banner: Common Standards. If the word *federal* has become tarnished in connection with standards, so has the word *national*; both words suggest requirements emanating from on high, even if not from the federal government. The National Governors Association, the National Council of Chief State School Officers, Achieve, the College Board, and ACT have organized into a strong coalition. That coalition moved quickly to get most states to sign an agreement to unite around a set of common standards. At this point, this means common content standards for the subject matter to be taught at each grade level.

The starting point has been to write standards for what U.S. students should know when they leave high school to be ready for college and career.

As this article went to press, the coalition had drafted standards in math and reading and was putting those drafts through a process of "validation" by a committee that the coalition appointed. The next step will be to write standards for each grade level. Then the question will be whether the coalition moves on to create a common test for each grade in math and reading and advances to other subject areas.

At this stage, there is substantial momentum. As of August 2009, 49 states had signed on. Although this "sign on" has been from the chief state school officials and governors, many state legislatures have been heavily involved in the standards-setting movement. It remains to be seen whether they will go along or balk. In 2007, the National Conference of State Legislatures adopted a measure against national standards that favored higher standards developed for—and by—each state.

Another element in the mix is the fact that at the end of January, states applied for a share of the $48.6 billion in economic stimulus funds to be distributed under the American Recovery and Reimbursement Act. The selection process, underway as this article goes to press, takes into account whether each applying state is engaged in collaborative efforts with other states to develop common standards—a considerable incentive to get with the program.

Learning From Experience

Years of experience with "standards-based reform" and its transformation into test-based accountability tells us that there is more trouble in Accountability City than just lack of commonality. A consideration of our current accountability landscape and our past attempts raises four questions.

How Can We Develop High-Quality Content Standards and Tests?

There are quality problems with current content standards, as evaluations by independent researchers and evaluators have shown. The tests that accompany them are typically "cheapies" that do not get far enough below the surface in terms of content instruction. Content standards, created through compromises among committee members, are far broader than what can be covered in a nine-month school year. And when tests are constructed that merely sample this broad content—as most do—such tests are not sensitive to the actual instruction teachers deliver. Nor do they pick up changes in achievement that follow improvements in instruction.

How Can Schools Serve the Highest and Lowest Achievers?

The selection of a single cut point provides incentives for teachers and schools to overfocus on students near that cut point, to avoid sanctions. Because results are reported in terms of the cut point, teachers know nothing about how students who are far below—or above—that cut point are doing.

Should We Contemplate Standards Across a Range of Subjects?

Standards now concentrate on math and reading. The incentive this creates for distorting the curriculum has been widely discussed; many people are concerned about cutting back on social studies, music, and art. We must reflect on whether to extend standards to other disciplines to keep the curriculum broad.

How Can We Measure Gains in Student Achievement?

We now test students at a single point in time to establish the effectiveness of schools. But that test actually measures *all* a student knows, including learning generated in early childhood, out of school, or even in different schools. To achieve true test-based accountability for schools, we need to measure the effectiveness of what a student learned *while in that school* in addition to what the student knows in total.

Even if we achieve commonality in curriculum and performance standards, these questions will remain. We should ask ourselves, Do we want a common version of the current operating model, or do we want to work more on the model?

Teachers have seen the locus of power move up the governmental hierarchy over the past few decades. Educators at all levels should stay tuned and use their on-the-ground experience and judgment to determine what is good for students—and for educational equity—as we consider whether national standards are to be or not to be.

References

Barton, P. E. (2009). *National education standards: Getting beneath the surface*. Princeton, NJ: Educational Testing Service, Policy Information Center. Available: www.ets.org/Media/Research/pdf/PICNATEDSTAND.pdf

Beatty, A. (2008). *Common standards for K–12 education? Considering the evidence*. Washington, DC: National Academy Press.

Lewin, T. (2008, March 13). Report urges changes in teaching math. *The New York Times*. Available: www.nytimes.com/2008/03/14/education/14math.html

POSTNOTE

The Constitution of the United States does not mention education, thus by the 10th Amendment, which reserves for the states or the people that which is not specifically designated to the federal government, education has remained the province of each state. As a result, we have varied and variable systems of education across the different states. As part of the K–12 curriculum, some states have established strong content standards and rigorous assessments to measure these standards, while other states get by with less than rigorous standards and assessments. With concern for how the United States will fare in the global marketplace in the future, advocates for a set of national education standards believe that such standards will work toward raising the quality of education across the states. Some opponents of national standards fear too much involvement of the federal government and relish the rights of states to determine education decisions.

As of late 2011, 45 states voluntarily have signed on to a set Common Core State Standards in English/language arts and mathematics. These states will work to devise common standards and assessment measures, making it possible to compare student achievement across these states. Proponents of the common standards believe that the quality of education will rise significantly across the United States as a result of these common standards. Why, they argue, should we have different state standards in English and mathematics? Shouldn't English and mathematics be the same in Louisiana and Massachusetts, for example?

It seems unlikely, however, that common agreement can come about in the subject areas of social studies and science. Hot-button topics like religion and evolution provoke differing views, which will make reaching a consensus on what to teach very difficult.

DISCUSSION QUESTIONS

1. Do you believe that the United States should or should not have national content standards for K–12 education? Give reasons for your position.
2. What arguments can you make in opposition to your position? Which argument do you think is strongest?
3. Visit the web site of the Common Core State Standards initiative: http://www.corestandards. org/. Browse through the web site. What questions do you have after visiting the web site?

RELATED WEBSITE RESOURCE

WEB RESOURCE:

http://www.corestandards.org/.

This website of the Common Core State Standards initiative lists the standards for English/language arts and mathematics.

Creating a Curriculum for the American People

E. D. Hirsch, Jr.

E. D. Hirsch, Jr. is professor emeritus in education and humanities from the University of Virginia, and he is the founder of the Core Knowledge Foundation. Among his most widely known books are *Cultural Literacy, The Schools We Need and Why We Don't Have Them, The Knowledge Deficit,* and *The Making of Americans.*

Hirsch is an elected member of both the American Academy of Arts and Sciences and the International Academy of Education.

E. D. Hirsch, Jr., "Creating a Curriculum for the American People," *American Educator,* Winter 2009–2010. Reprinted by permission of the author.

FOCUS QUESTION

Should the United States have national education standards like most other countries?

InTASC
Standards 1, 2, 4, 5, and 7

KEY TERM

• Common Core Curriculum

I was wrenched from my comfortable life as a conference-going literary theorist almost four decades ago. I was doing experiments on reading and writing, first with students at the University of Virginia and then with students at J. Sargeant Reynolds Community College, a predominantly African American institution in Richmond. What shocked me into school reform was the discovery that the community college students could comprehend written text just as well as the University of Virginia students when the topic was roommates or car traffic, but they could not understand passages about Robert E. Lee's surrender to Ulysses S. Grant They had graduated from the schools of Richmond, the erstwhile capital of the Confederacy, and were ignorant of the most elementary facts of the Civil War and other basic information normally taken for granted in the United States. They had not been taught the things they needed to know to understand texts addressed to a general audience. What had the schools been doing? I decided to switch careers and devote myself to helping right the wrong being done to these students. It soon became clear that for most students, the primary determinant of whether they ended up at the community college or at the University of Virginia was not innate ability or family background—it was knowledge. More important, it was knowledge that could be learned at school.

America's three biggest educational problems are our low academic achievement relative to other nations, our lack of equality of educational opportunity, and our failure to perpetuate a strong sense of loyalty to the national community and its civic institutions. A single, radical reform will go far in solving all three: a content-rich core curriculum in the early grades.

A lack of knowledge, both civic and general, is the most significant deficit in most American students' education. For the most part, our students (and teachers) are bright, idealistic, well meaning, and good natured. Many students and teachers are working harder in school than their counterparts did a decade ago. Yet most students still lack basic information that high school and college teachers once took for granted. In this article, I'll explain why this lack of knowledge is even more important than most people realize and why a content-rich core curriculum is the *only* viable remedy.

Shared Knowledge Is Essential to Language Comprehension

Back in the 1970s, when I was doing research on reading and writing, the field of psycholinguistics was just beginning to emphasize that the chief factor in the comprehension of language is relevant knowledge about the topic at hand. That finding has since been replicated many times, in different ways and with varying constraints, both in the laboratory and in the classroom.

The specific knowledge dependence of reading comprehension becomes obvious when we take the time to reflect on what any given bit of text assumes the reader already knows. For a simple example, here is a passage from a sample 10th-grade Florida state test of reading comprehension:[1]

> The origin of cotton is something of a mystery. There is evidence that people in India and Central and South America domesticated separate species of the plant thousands of years ago. Archaeologists have discovered fragments of cotton cloth more than 4,000 years old in coastal Peru and at Mohenjo Daro in the Indus Valley. By A.D. 1500, cotton had spread across the warmer regions of the Americas, Eurasia, and Africa.
>
> Today cotton is the world's major nonfood crop, providing half of all textiles. In 1992, 80 countries produced a total of 83 million bales, or almost 40 billion pounds. The business revenue generated—some 50 billion dollars in the United States alone—is greater than that of any other field crop.

It would take many pages to indicate even a significant fraction of the tacit knowledge needed to understand this passage. The main subject, cotton, is not defined. The reader must already know what it is, a reasonable assumption. It also helps to have an idea of how it grows, and how it is harvested and then put into bales. (What's a bale?) Then consider the throwaway statement that different people "domesticated separate species of the plant thousands of years ago." To domesticate a species of a plant is not an action that is self-evident from everyday knowledge. Ask a group of 10th-graders what it means to domesticate a plant, and chances are that most will not know. Of course, they *should* know. Domestication of plants is fundamental to human history. But I suspect most do not, and so they will not understand that part of the passage. The writer of this passage (which was, the state of Florida informs us, taken from *National Geographic*) clearly expected his readers to know what cotton is and what plant domestication is. He expected them to know that the Indus Valley is many thousands of miles from Peru. (How many 10th-graders know *that*?)

This passage illustrates the way reading comprehension works in the real world of magazines, training manuals, textbooks, newspapers, Web sites, books, etc. Writers assume that readers know some things but not others. In this case, readers were expected to know some geography and history, and something about agriculture, but not how long human beings have used cotton—the new information supplied in the passage. That is exactly how new information is always offered: it is embedded in a mountain of knowledge that readers are expected to have already in their long-term memories. That is the way language *always* works. And it is the way language must work. Just imagine how cumbersome your newspaper would be if, in reporting on a baseball game, it did not assume you already knew what "pitching" "being at bat," and "hitting a home run" mean. Instead of a short synopsis of last night's game, you'd get paragraph after paragraph that (boringly) explained the basics of the game. Of course, if you didn't know anything about baseball, a short synopsis of the game wouldn't make any sense (no matter how many comprehension strategies you had mastered).

Not convinced? Give this passage on cricket, from the online site of the British newspaper the *Guardian*, a try:[2]

> Much depended on Ponting and the new wizard of Oz, Mike Hussey, the two overnight batsmen. But this duo perished either side of lunch—the latter a little unfortunate to be adjudged leg-before—and with Andrew Symonds, too, being shown the dreaded finger off an inside edge, the inevitable beckoned, bar the pyrotechnics of Michael Clarke and the ninth wicket.

This is perfectly understandable for virtually all British readers, but at the dim edge of comprehensibility for most American readers. Yet the words are familiar enough. There is not a single word except maybe "leg-before" that I could not use effectively in a sentence. Comprehension is not just a matter of knowing words—and it is certainly not a matter of mastering comprehension strategies. What makes the passage incomprehensible to me is that I don't know much about cricket.

In language use, there is always a great deal that is left unsaid and must be inferred. This means that communication depends on both sides, writer and reader, sharing a great deal of *unspoken* knowledge. This large body of tacit knowledge is precisely what our students are *not* being adequately taught in our schools. Specific subject-matter knowledge over a broad range of domains is the key to language comprehension—and, as a result, to a broad ability to learn new things. It is the cornerstone of competence and adaptability in the modern world. (Cognitive scientist Daniel T. Willingham thoroughly explained this in the Spring 2006 issue of *American Educator*. See "How Knowledge Helps: It Speeds and Strengthens Reading Comprehension, Learning—and Thinking," available online at www.aft.org/pubs.reports/american_educator/issues/spring06/index.htm.)

If we want students to read and write well, we cannot take a laissez-faire attitude to the content of their schooling. Rather, we must specify the content that adults are assumed to have (e.g., to comprehend a newspaper or serve on a jury), and be sure to teach it to our children.

But much more is at stake in ensuring that all students have access to this knowledge than just enabling our students to make higher scores on reading comprehension tests. Those scores do correlate with a student's ability to learn and to earn a good living,[3] but they also connect with something less tangible: a sense of belonging to a wider community and a feeling of solidarity with other Americans. When we acquire enough knowledge to become full members of the American speech community, we belong to a wider group toward which we feel a sense of loyalty.

Shared Knowledge Is Essential to Democracy

When Benjamin Franklin was leaving the Constitutional Convention of 1787, a lady asked him, "Well, Doctor, what have we got, a monarchy or a republic?" to which Franklin famously replied, "A republic, madam, if you can keep it." It's hard for us to recapture that state of mind, but it is instructive to do so. The causes of our Founders' concern for preserving the republic have not suddenly disappeared with the emergence of American economic and military power. We are still a nation of immigrants, social stratification, and disparate beliefs held together chiefly by a shared devotion to freedom and democracy.

Anxiety about maintaining the republic runs through the writings of all our earliest thinkers about American education. Thomas Jefferson, John Adams, James Madison, Franklin, and their colleagues consistently alluded to the fact that republics have been among the least stable forms of government, and were always collapsing from their internal antagonisms and self-seeking citizens.

The most famous example was the republic of ancient Rome, which was taken over by the unscrupulous Caesars and destroyed by what the American founders called "factions."[4] Internal conflicts were seen to be the chief danger we faced—Germans against English, state against state, region against region, local interests against national interests, party against party, personal ambition against personal ambition, religion against religion, poor against rich, uneducated against educated. If uncontrolled, these hostile factions would subvert the common good, breed demagogues, and finally turn the republic into a military dictatorship, just as in ancient Rome.

To keep that from happening, we would need far more than checks and balances in the structure of the national government. We would also need a special new brand of citizens who, unlike the citizens of Rome and other failed republics, would subordinate their local interests to the common good.

Our early thinkers about education believed the only way we could create such virtuous, civic-minded citizens was through common schooling. By the phrase "common school," our early educational thinkers meant several things: Elementary schools were to be universal and egalitarian. All children were to attend the same schools, with rich and poor studying in the same classrooms. The schools were to be supported by taxes and to have a common, statewide system of administration. And the early grades were to have a common core curriculum that would foster patriotism, solidarity, and civic peace as well as enable effective commerce, rule of law, and politics.[5]

For example, George Washington bequeathed a portion of his estate to education in order "to sprd systematic ideas through all parts of this rising Empire, thereby to do away local attachments and State prejudices."[6] Thomas Jefferson's plan for the common school aimed to secure not only the peace and safety of the republic, but also social fairness and the best leaders. He outlined a system of elementary schooling that required all children, rich and poor, to go to the same schools so that they would get an equal chance regardless of who their parents happened to be.

Such notions about the civic necessity of the common school animated American thinkers far into the 19th century and had a profound effect on Abraham Lincoln. Lincoln believed that the center of children's upbringing and schooling in the United States should be instruction in a *religious*

devotion to democracy. Like the Founders from whom he took his inspiration, Lincoln was sensitive to the fragility of peace and harmony in a country where people of different religious faiths and ethnic origins bound themselves into one federation. His tragic sense of how precarious that unity is brought him very early to the view that parents and schools must diligently teach a common creed in order to sustain the union. His great Lyceum speech on that subject, "The Perpetuation of Our Political Institutions," dates to 1838—long before he became the central figure in preserving the unity of a nation riven by the issue of slavery. The urgency conveyed in this speech came not from the single issue of slavery but more broadly from his perception of the need to put solidarity, equality, freedom, and civic peace above all other principles—a public "political religion" that transcended all sectarian religions.[7]

> Let reverence for the laws, be breathed by every American mother, to the lisping babe, that prattles on her lap—let it be taught in schools, in seminaries, and in colleges;—let it be written in Primmers, spelling books, and in Almanacs;—let it be preached from the pulpit, proclaimed in legislative halls, and enforced in courts of justice. And, in short, let it become the *political religion* of the nation; and let the old and the young, the rich and the poor, the grave and the gay, of all sexes and tongues, and colors and conditions, sacrifice unceasingly upon its altars.

Lincoln conceived that America needed to be held together by a secular religion called "Democracy" that would be taught in our schools and would supersede all other religions. This religious conception was not a mere analogy or rhetorical flourish. With his accustomed profundity, he went directly from the writings of the Founders to the center of the American idea. Garry Wills has shown in his dazzling book *Lincoln at Gettysburg* how concisely Lincoln reformulated the American creed as an extension of the Declaration of Independence.[8] In his Lyceum speech, he did no less for the basic theory of American schooling.

Fundamental to this idea of making democracy America's secular religion was the sharp distinction the Founders drew between the public and private spheres of life.[9] We operate in the public sphere whenever we vote, serve in the military, transact business, become a member of a jury or a defendant at a jury's mercy, write for a big unseen audience, or encounter any situation where we wish to be understood by strangers. This public sphere is where common laws and a common language are needed. The private sphere is a much broader realm, especially in tolerant America with its protections against intrusive government and its freedoms of association, speech, and action. It is neither literally private nor purely individual. "Private" associations are private only in the sense of being out of the reach of government and enjoyed peacefully apart from our legal, civic, and moral duties as members of the wider public community.

From the nation's founding to today, American schools have played a critical role in our attempt to accommodate different groups and ethnicities in a peaceful and harmonious unity without requiring them to abandon their private identities. The elementary school has a special place in this great political experiment because it is the institution that prepares children to participate effectively in the public sphere. Our ambition as a nation has been to give children from any and all origins a chance to participate in the pubic sphere as equals, no matter who their parents are, or what language or religion they practice in their homes.

Equality—both equality before the law and equality of opportunity—is not only a core American value but also a core requisite for a peaceable public sphere. In America, universal schooling has always been understood as critical to our ideal of equality. In the introduction to his 1817 bill for an Elementary School Act in Virginia, the aging Thomas Jefferson, the most consistent of the Founders in stressing the importance of public education, succinctly stated the grounds for equality of opportunity. An educational system that offered it would "avail the commonwealth of those talents and virtues which nature has sown as liberally among the poor as rich."[10]

The early school curriculum needs to offer enough commonality of content to connect each American with the larger community of citizens. Students need to leave school with a good understanding of the civic principles under which the United States operates and with an emotional commitment to making this political experiment continue to work. They need to possess the specific, concrete knowledge that will enable them to communicate with one another in the standard language across time and space. That much substantial content is required for our civic life to function.

An initiation into this public sphere does *not* require students to reject the private sphere that nurtured them. Membership in this public sphere means mastery of the formal codes of speech and of the tacit knowledge that makes formal speech intelligible—shared information about football, civics, Shakespeare, Rosa Parks, Diego Rivera, and so on.

In the early grades of schooling in a democracy, the public sphere *should* take priority. No matter what special talents and interests we may encourage in a young child, all of us have to learn the same base-10 system of arithmetic; the same 26–letter alphabet; the same grammar, spelling, and connotations of words; and the same basic facts about the wider community to which we belong. Most modern nations impose that kind of compulsory early education because neither a democracy nor a modern economy can function properly without citizens who have enough shared knowledge to be loyal, competent, and able to communicate with one another.

Under this founding conception, the early curriculum can be viewed as a set of concentric circles. At the core are the knowledge and skills all citizens should have. Beyond that is the knowledge, such as state history, that each state wants children to possess. Beyond that may be the knowledge and values agreed on by the locality. And finally, beyond that, are the activities and studies that fulfill the needs, talents, and interests of each individual student. From the standpoint of the public good, what must be imparted most clearly and explicitly are the central core elements common to all citizens of the republic. These need to be set forth specifically, grade by grade, so that one grade can build cumulatively on the prior one, allowing school time to be used effectively and putting all students in a given grade level on an equal footing.

We *all* have a stake in promoting an effective public sphere and a vibrant economy through our schools. The distinction between the private and public spheres is a founding conception that has made the United States a haven for freedom and an outstanding political success. But the public sphere cannot exist as a democratic vehicle for everyone unless everyone is schooled to participate in it. That goal requires a common core curriculum in the early grades. There is no practical way around that necessity.

All of our earliest educational thinkers agreed that precisely because we were a big, diverse country, our schools should offer many common topics to bring us together; if schools did so, they felt, we would be able to communicate with one another, act as a unified republic, and form bonds of loyalty and patriotism among our citizens.

The kind of education that will enable all our young people to access the public sphere and develop a sense of national solidarity is precisely the kind that will narrow the achievement gaps among demographic groups and raise the nation's average level of achievement.

Shared Knowledge Should Be Taught Using a Shared Curriculum

The policy implications of this article and my new book, *The Making of Americans,* can be boiled down to this: institute in your district or state an explicit, knowledge-rich, grade-by-grade core curriculum in grades K–8 that takes up at least 50 percent of school time. There are no good educational arguments against a coherent, content-specific core curriculum that could possibly outweigh its superior efficacy and fairness. Nevertheless, prejudices against commonality, and indeed against any set curriculum, continue to dominate American education.

In discussions of a common curriculum, the main question is always the conversation stopper, "Who will decide?" The problem has been

solved in other multicultural liberal democracies. In fact, no high-performing and fair educational system has failed to solve it. If an American core curriculum can meet two criteria—*acceptability* and *effectiveness*—then the political problem can be solved, and there will be a real chance to reverse decades of American educational decline.★

Acceptability: We know from surveys that the public generally likes the idea of a common core and wants the schools to teach the traditions that hold the country together—traditions such as respect for those laws, institutions, and ideals of freedom and equality that Abraham Lincoln exhorted American schools to promote in order to preserve the union as the "last best hope of earth." Lincoln's view is seconded by most citizens. In the Public Agenda report *A Lot to Be Thankful For,* 84 percent of parents said they wanted their children to learn about America's political institutions, history, and ideals of freedom and equality. Concerning civics, then, the American public has clearly decided the core-curriculum question. Moreover, few sensible people will wish to launch a campaign against a core curriculum in math and science, which are the same in China as in Chattanooga. But there is a lot more to elementary education than civics, math, and science. We also need agreement on a common core for history, art, music, and literature—a more daunting task that leads to the second characteristic a common core must exhibit: effectiveness.

Effectiveness: An explicit curriculum would he accepted in the United States if it were shown to be highly effective in imparting an ability to read, write, and learn at a high level. Hence the answer to the question "Who decides?" is "The community that makes up the public sphere has already largely decided." A core curriculum that

---

★Other, more technical attributes are that the early core curriculum must be highly specific, and outlined grade by grade. Without specificity there can be no commonality, and then we fall into the vagueness trap of current state stanards. Grade-by-grade definiteness is needed because the school year is the key time unit for the student, who usually moves to a new teacher at each new grade level.

systematically imparts this content will be optimally effective in developing reading, writing, and learning ability, and in giving all children equal access to the public sphere.

In 1987, I ventured to set down an index to some of the knowledge students needed to possess to be proficient in the American standard language and full participants in the public sphere.[11] In the two decades since then, my colleagues and I at the Core Knowledge Foundation have transformed that list into a coherent core curriculum that is now being followed by hundreds of schools. Unsurprisingly, reading comprehension scores at these schools have soared.[12]

Other sequences that put the same basic knowledge in a different order could be equally effective.[†] But the substance of any such curriculum would need to be very similar to the Core Knowledge curriculum, because the taken-for-granted knowledge in the American public sphere is finite and definable. Core Knowledge did not decide what students should learn—it inventoried and then organized the knowledge that the public sphere assumes adults know.

Any effective curriculum would also need to be, like ours, grade-specific. This is a critical point for the following reasons:

1. Specifying core content by year enables the teacher at each grade level to know what students already know, making it possible to communicate with the whole class and bring the group forward together. As Harold Stevenson and James Stigler pointed out in their pathbreaking book *The Learning Gap*, the American classroom's lack of productivity is not chiefly caused by diversity of ethnic and family background but by diversity of

academic preparation. Without a common core curriculum, the disparity in student readiness increases with each successive grade, slowing down progress and making the teacher's task ever more difficult. In core-curriculum nations such as Finland and France, the disparity in students' knowledge, skills, and readiness to learn new material decreases over time.[13]

2. When critical knowledge gaps (for some students) and boring repetitions (for others) are avoided, student interest and motivation are enhanced and progress in learning speeds up. Many American teachers say that they spend several weeks at the start of each year in review. That is, they offer a minicourse in the things students need to know to go forward. To students who already know those things, the review is an occasion to start shooting spitballs. To students who are so far behind that they lack the knowledge needed to make sense of the review, it is an occasion for spitballs, too, because they are lost.

3. Instituting a common core curriculum is especially helpful for disadvantaged students who change schools. By third grade, some 50 to 60 percent of low-income students have changed schools, many in the middle of the year.[14]

4. Specific, grade-by-grade planning allows the entire curriculum to be integrated. The history of a period can be integrated with its literature, art, and music. Such integration leads to better retention and fuller understanding.

I have not encountered any cogent arguments against these reasons for greater commonality and specificity in the curriculum.

The need for a common core curriculum in the early grades is far greater in the United States than in other nations that actually have one. Americans move from one place to another in greater numbers than do residents of any other country. As a transethnic nation, we have a greater need for an *invented* common public sphere that is determined not by blood and soil, or hearth and home, but by transethnic traditions concerning our history, laws, and freedoms. The medium of this public sphere is language, which cannot be disentangled from specific, commonly shared knowledge. Such a

---

[†]An alternative example with excellent results is the Roxbury Preparatory Charter School, a public school for grades 6–8 (see www.roxburyprep.org). The school has developed a highly specific, grade-by-grade curriculum basen on an analysis of the Massachusetts state standards (among the best in the country) and the kinds of knowledge probed by the state tests. It is a tremedous credit to this school that it has undertaken the immense labor required to create this curriculum.

curriculum is critical to the United States continuing to be, in Lincoln's words, "the last best hope of earth."[15]

Endnotes

1. Florida Department of Education, *2009 Florida Comprehensive Assessment Test, Reading Sample Test and Answer Book, Grade 10* (Tallahassee: Florida Department of Education, 2008), 9, http://fcat.fldoe.org/pdf/sample/0809/reading/FL09_STIV_R_STB_G'D_WT_00".pdf.

2. Ashis Ray, "Australia Brought Down to Earth," *Guardian Online*, January 20, 2008, http://fcat.fldoe.org/pdf/sample/0809/reading/FL09_STIV_R_STB_G'D_WT_00".pdf.

3. William R. Johnson and Derek Neal, "Basic Skills and the Black-White Earnings Gap," in *The Black-White Test Score Gap*, ed. Christopher Jencks and Meredith Phillips (Washington, DC: Brookings Institution Press, 1998), 480–497.

4. See Gordon S. Wood, *The Radicalism of the American Revolution* (New York: Vintage, 1993), esp. 102–103.

5. Carl F. Kaestle, *Pillars of the Republic: Common Schools and American Society: 1780–1880* (New York: Hill and Wang, 1983).

6. From George Washington's last will and testament: "It has been my ardent wish to see a plan devised on a liberal scale, which would have a tendency to sprd systematic ideas through all parts of this rising Empire, thereby to do away local attachments and State prejudices, as far as the nature of things would, or indeed ought to admit, from our National Councils." George Washington, "The Will," in *The Papers of George Washington, Retirement Series*, ed. W.W. Abbot, vol. 4, April–December 1799 (Charlottesville: University Press of Virginia, 1999), 477–492.

7. "Address before the Young Men's Lyceum, Springfield, Illinois, January 27, 1838," in *The Collected Works of Abraham Lincoln*, vol. 1, ed. Roy P. Basier (New Brunswick, NJ: Rutgers University Press, 1953), 112.

8. Garry Wills, *Lincoln at Gettysburg: The Words That Remade America* (New York: Simon and Schuster, 1992).

9. See Jeff Weintraub and Krishan Kumar, eds., *Public and Private in Thought and Practice: Perspectives on a Grand Dichortomy* (Chicago: University of Chicago Press, 1997).

10. Andrew A. Lipscomb and Albert Ellery Bergh, eds., *The Writings of Thomas Jefferson,* vol. 17 (Washington, DC: Thomas Jefferson Memorial Association, 1905), 440.

11. E. D. Hirsch, Jr., *Cultural Literacy: What Every American Needs to Know* (Boston: Houghton Mifflin, 1987).

12. Georgia J. Kosmoski, Geneva Gay, and Edward L. Vockell, "Cultural Literacy and Academic Achievement," *Journal of Experimental Education* 58 (1990): 265–272; and Joseph F. Pentony, "Cultural Literacy: A Concurrent Validation," *Educational and Psychological Measurement* 52 (1992): 967–972. For a summary of research reports, see http://coreknowledge.org/CK/about/research/index.htm.

13. Harold W. Stevenson and James W. Stigler, *The Learning Gap: Why Our Schools Are Falling and What We Can Learn from Japanese and Chinese Education* (New York: Summit, 1992): and Jean-Pierre Jarousse, Alain Mingat, and Marc Richard, "La Scolarisation Maternelle a Deus Ans: Effets Pedagogiques et Sociaux," *Education et Formations* 31 (1992): 3–9. See also M. Duthoit, "L'enfant et L'école: Aspects Synthetiques du Sulvt d'un Echamillon de Vingt Mille Eleves des Ecoles," *Education of Formations* 16 (1988): 3–13.

14. David T. Burkam, Valerie E. Lee, and Julie Dwyer, *School Mobility in the Early Elementary Grades: Frequency and Impact from Nationally-Representative Data* (paper prepared for the Workshop on the impact of Mobility and Change on the Lives of Young Children, Schools, and Neighborhoods, June 29–30, 2009); and U.S. General Accounting Office, *Elementary School Children: Many Change Schools Frequently, Harming Their Education,* GAO/HEHS-94-45 (Washington, DC: U.S. General Accounting Office, 1994).

15. Abraham Lincoln, "Annual Message to Congress" (Washington, DC, December 1, 1862). Concluding remarks, including this quote, are available at http://showcase.netins.net/web/creative/lincoln/speeches/congress.htm.

POSTNOTE

In 1987, E. D. Hirsch, Jr., published the enormously successful book, *Cultural Literacy: What Every American Needs to Know.* In that book, Hirsch argues that Americans need to possess cultural literacy—that is, knowledge of the persons, events, literature, and science that forms the basis of shared knowledge in American culture.

Since the publication of *Cultural Literacy*, Hirsch has worked with educators to develop his Core Knowledge curriculum for the elementary grades. It is currently being implemented in hundreds of schools. In a series of books, Hirsch and his collaborators have set forth the cultural knowledge that they believe should be taught at each grade level. Hirsch believes that children from advantaged homes have always had access to this knowledge but that children from disadvantaged homes have not. By teaching children a common core of knowledge in school, Hirsch believes that the barriers to adult literacy can be overcome.

In spite of careful attention to including cultural knowledge from many facets of American society in his Core Knowledge Curriculum, some people still believe Hirsch promotes Western European culture over other cultures represented in our society. Examine *What Every First Grader Needs to Know*, as well as other similarly titled books for grades 2 through 8, and decide for yourself.

DISCUSSION QUESTIONS

1. Why doesn't the United States have a common national curriculum as many other countries do?
2. Do you agree or disagree with Hirsch's contention that shared knowledge is important in sustaining a democracy? Why?
3. What concerns, if any, do you have about all Americans experiencing a shared curriculum?

RELATED WEBSITE RESOURCE

WEB RESOURCE:

Core Knowledge Foundation. Available at:

http://coreknowledge.org/CK/index.htm.

This foundation's official website contains many resources and answers to questions about core knowledge.

The Relevance of Religion to the Curriculum

Warren A. Nord

... n A. Nord works in the philosophy of the humanities, the philosophy of religion, the philosophy of education (especially moral education), and the relationship of religion and education. He is the author of two books: *Religion and American Education: Rethinking a National Dilemma* (1995); and, with

Charles C. Haynes, *Taking Religion Seriously Across the Curriculum* (1998).

Reprinted with permission from the January 1999 issue of The School Administrator magazine, published by the American Association of School Administrators.

For some time now, public school administrators have been on the front lines of our culture wars over religion and education—and I expect it would be music to their ears to hear that peace accords have been signed.

Unfortunately, the causes of war are deep-seated. Peace is not around the corner.

At the same time, however, it is also easy to overstate the extent of the hostilities. At least at the national level—but also in many communities across America—a large measure of common ground has been found. The leaders of most major national educational, religious and civil liberties organizations agree about the basic principles that should govern the role of religion and public schools. No doubt we don't agree about everything, but we agree about a lot.

For example, in 1988, a group of 17 major religious and educational organizations—the American Jewish Congress and the Islamic Society of North America, the National Association of Evangelicals and the National Council of Churches, the National Education Association and American Federation of Teachers, the National School Boards Association and AASA among them—endorsed a statement of principles that describes the importance of religion in the public school curriculum.

The statement, in part, says this: "Because religion plays significant roles in history and society, study about religion is essential to understanding both the nation and the world. Omission of facts about religion can give students the false impression that the religious life of humankind is insignificant or unimportant. Failure to understand even the basic symbols, practices and concepts of the various religions makes much of history, literature, art and contemporary life unintelligible."

> **FOCUS** QUESTION
>
> *What, if anything, should public schools teach about religion?*

A Profound Problem

As a result of this (and other "common ground" statements) it is no longer controversial to assert that the study of religion has a legitimate and important place in the public school curriculum.

Where in the curriculum? In practice, the study of religion has been relegated almost entirely to history texts and courses, for it is widely assumed that religion is irrelevant to every other subject in the curriculum—that is, to understanding the world here and now.

This is a deeply controversial assumption, however. A profoundly important educational problem lingers here, one that is almost completely ignored by educators.

Let me put it this way. Several ways exist for making sense of the world here and now. Many Americans accept one or another religious interpretation of reality; others accept one or another secular interpretation. We don't agree—and the differences among us often cut deeply.

Yet public schools systematically teach students to think about the world in secular ways only. They don't even bother to inform them about religious alternatives—apart from distant history. That is, public schooling discriminates against religious ways of making sense of the world. This is no minor problem.

An Economic Argument

To get some sense of what's at issue, let's consider economics.

One can think about the economic domain of life in various ways. Scriptural texts in all religious traditions address questions of justice and morality, poverty and wealth, work and stewardship, for example. A vast body of 20th century literature in moral theology deals with economic issues. Indeed most mainline denominations and ecumenical agencies have official statements on justice and economics. What's common to all of this literature is the claim that the economic domain of life cannot be understood apart from religion.

Needless to say, this claim is not to be found in economics textbooks. Indeed, if we put end to end all the references to religion in the 10 high school economics texts I've reviewed in the past few years, they would add up to about two pages—out of 4,400 pages combined (and all of the references are to premodern times). There is but a single reference to religion—a passing mention in a section on taxation and nonprofit organizations—in the 47 pages of the new national content standards in economics. Moreover, the textbooks and the standards say virtually nothing about the problems that are the major concern of theologians—problems relating to poverty, justice, our consumer culture, the Third World, human dignity and the meaningfulness of work.

The problem isn't just that the texts ignore religion and those economic problems of most concern to theologians. A part of the problem is what the texts do teach—that is, neoclassical economic theory. According to the texts, economics is a science, people are essentially self-interested utility-maximizers, the economic realm is one of competition for scarce resources, values are personal preferences and value judgments are matters of cost-benefit analysis. Of course, no religious tradition accepts this understanding of human nature, society, economics and values.

That is, the texts and standards demoralize and secularize economics.

An Appalling Claim

To be sure, they aren't explicitly hostile to religion; rather they ignore it. But in some ways this is worse than explicit hostility, for students remain unaware of the fact that there are tensions and conflicts between their religious traditions and what they are taught about economics.

In fact, the texts and the standards give students no sense that what they are learning is controversial. Indeed, the national economics standards make it a matter of principle that students be kept in the dark about alternatives to neoclassical theory. As the editors put it in their introduction, the standards were developed to convey a single conception of eco-nomics, the "majority paradigm" or neoclassical model of economic behavior. For, they argue, to include "strongly held minority views of economic processes [would only risk] confusing and frustrat-ing teachers and students who are then left with the responsibility of sorting the qualifications and alter-natives without a sufficient foundation to do so."

This is an appalling statement. It means, in effect, that students should be indoctrinated; they should be given no critical perspective on neoclas-sical economic theory.

The problem with the economics texts and standards is but one aspect of the much larger prob-lem that cuts across the curriculum, for in every course students are taught to think in secular ways that often (though certainly not always) conflict with religious alternatives. And this is always done uncritically.

Even in history courses, students learn to think about historical meaning and causation in exclusively secular ways in spite of the fact that Judaism, Christianity and Islam all hold that God acts in history, that there is a religious meaning to history. True, they learn a few facts about reli-gion, but they learn to think about history in secular categories.

Nurturing Secularity

Outside of history courses and literature courses that use historical literature, religion is rarely even mentioned, but even on those rare occasions when it is, the intellectual context is secular. As a result, public education nurtures a secular mentality. This marginalizes religion from our cultural and intellec-tual life and contributes powerfully to the secular-ization of our culture.

Ignoring religious ways of thinking about the world is a problem for three important reasons.

- *It is profoundly illiberal.*

Here, of course, I'm not using the term "liberal" to refer to the left wing of the Democratic Party. A liberal education is a broad education, one that provides students with the perspective to think

critically about the world and their lives. A good liberal education should introduce students—at least older students—to the major ways humankind has developed for making sense of the world and their lives. Some of those ways of thinking and living are religious and it is illiberal to leave them out of the discussion. Indeed, it may well constitute indoctrination—secular indoctrination.

We indoctrinate students when we uncritically initiate them into one way of thinking and system-atically ignore the alternatives. Indeed, if students are to be able to think critically about the secular ways of understanding the world that pervade the curriculum, they must understand something about the religious alternatives.

- *It is politically unjust.*

Public schools must take the public seriously. But religious parents are now, in effect, education-ally disenfranchised. Their ways of thinking and living aren't taken seriously.

Consider an analogy. A generation ago text-books and curricula said virtually nothing about women, blacks and members of minority subcul-tures. Hardly anyone would now say that that was fair or just. We now—most of us—realize this was a form of discrimination, of educational disenfranchisement. And so it is with religious subcultures (though, ironically, the multicultural movement has been almost entirely silent about religion).

- *It is unconstitutional.*

It is, of course, uncontroversial that it is consti-tutionally permissible to teach about religion in public schools when done properly. No Supreme Court justice has ever held otherwise. But I want to make a stronger argument.

The court has been clear that public schools must be neutral in matters of religion—in two senses. Schools must be neutral among religions (they can't favor Protestants over Catholics or Christians over Jews), and they must be neutral between religion and nonreligion. Schools can't promote religion. They can't proselytize. They can't conduct religious exercises.

Of course, neutrality is a two-edged sword. Just as schools can't favor religion over nonreligion, neither can they favor nonreligion over religion. As Justice Hugo Black put it in the seminal 1947 *Everson* ruling, "State power is no more to be used so as to handicap religions than it is to favor them."

Similarly, in his majority opinion in *Abington* v. *Schempp* in 1963, Justice Tom Clark wrote that schools can't favor "those who believe in no religion over those who do believe." And in a concurring opinion, Justice Arthur Goldberg warned that an "untutored devotion to the concept of neutrality [can lead to a] pervasive devotion to the secular and a passive, or even active, hostility to the religious."

Of course this is just what has happened. An untutored, naïve conception of neutrality has led educators to look for a smoking gun, an explicit hostility to religion, when the hostility has been philosophically rather more subtle—though no less substantial for that.

The only way to be neutral when all ground is contested ground is to be fair to the alternative. That is, given the Supreme Court's longstanding interpretation of the Establishment Clause, public schools must require the study of religion if they require the study of disciplines that cumulatively lead to a pervasive devotion to the secular—as they do.

Classroom Practices

So how can we be fair? What would a good education look like? Here I can only skim the surface—and refer readers to *Taking Religion Seriously Across the Curriculum,* in which Charles Haynes and I chart what needs to be done in some detail.

Obviously a great deal depends on the age of students. In elementary schools students should learn something of the relatively uncontroversial aspects of different religions—their traditions, holidays, symbols and a little about religious histories, for example. As students mature, they should be initiated into the conversation about truth and goodness that constitutes a good liberal education. Here a two-prong approach is required.

First, students should learn something about religious ways of thinking about any subject that is religiously controversial in the relevant courses. So, for example, a biology text should include a chapter in which scientific ways of understanding nature are contrasted with religious alternatives. Students should learn that the relationship of religion and science is controversial, and that while they will learn what most biologists believe to be the truth about nature, not everyone agrees.

Indeed, every text and course should provide students with historical and philosophical perspective on the subject at hand, establishing connections and tensions with other disciplines and domains of the culture, including religion.

This is not a balanced-treatment or equal-time requirement. Biology courses should continue to be biology courses and economics courses should continue to be economics courses. In any case, given their competence and training, biology and economics teachers are not likely to be prepared to deal with a variety of religious ways of approaching their subject. At most, they can provide a minimal fairness.

A robust fairness is possible only if students are required to study religious as well as secular ways of making sense of the world in some depth, in courses devoted to the study of religion.

A good liberal education should require at least one year-long high school course in religious studies (with other courses, I would hope, available as electives). The primary goal of such a course should be to provide students with a sufficiently intensive exposure to religious ways of thinking and living to enable them to actually understand religion (rather than simply know a few facts about religion). It should expose students to scriptural texts, but it also should use more recent primary sources that enable students to understand how contemporary theologians and writers within different traditions think about those subjects in the curriculum—morality, sexuality, history, nature, psychology and the economic world—that they will be taught to interpret in secular categories in their other courses.

Of course, if religion courses are to be offered, there must be teachers competent to teach them. Religious studies must become a certifiable field in public education, and new courses must not be offered or required until competent teachers are available.

Indeed, all teachers must have a much clearer sense of how religion relates to the curriculum and, more particularly, to their respective subjects. Major reforms in teacher education are necessary—as is a new generation of textbooks sensitive to religion.

Some educators will find it unrealistic to expect such reforms. Of course several decades ago textbooks and curricula said little about women and minority cultures. Several decades ago, few universities had departments of religious studies. Now multicultural education is commonplace and most universities have departments of religious studies. Things change.

Stemming an Exodus

No doubt some educators will find these proposals controversial, but they will be shortsighted if they do. Leaving religion out of the curriculum is also controversial. Indeed, because public schools don't take religion seriously many religious parents have deserted them and, if the Supreme Court upholds the legality of vouchers, as they may well do, the exodus will be much greater.

In the long run, the least controversial position is the one that takes everyone seriously. If public schools are to survive our culture wars, they must be built on common ground. But there can be no common ground when religious voices are left out of the curricular conversation.

It is religious conservatives, of course, who are most critical of public schooling—and the most likely to leave. But my argument is that public schooling doesn't take any religion seriously. It marginalizes all religion—liberal as well as conservative, Catholic as well as Protestant, Jewish, Muslim and Buddhist as well as Christian. Indeed, it contributes a great deal to the secularization of American culture—and this should concern any religious person.

But, in the end, this shouldn't concern religious people only. Religion should be included in the curriculum for three very powerful secular reasons. The lack of serious study of religion in public education is illiberal, unjust and unconstitutional.

POSTNOTE

Parents rightfully want to pass on to their children their most deeply held beliefs. Many of these beliefs about what constitutes a good life, and what is a person's true nature, are theological questions that are embedded in their religious convictions. For a variety of reasons, many of which are touched on in this article, the public schools have ignored and marginalized religion.

This was not always the case. During the 18th and 19th centuries, religious teaching was commonplace in American public schools, but the U.S. Supreme Court, through a number of rulings, has had a chilling effect on teachers and administrators. Rather than get involved with what is clearly a set of controversial issues, many public educators have tended to discourage any expression or even mention of religious issues and topics. Besides the educational implications of this policy, the impact on the public support of public schools is beginning to show.

America is a religious nation, founded on religious principles ("In God we trust" and "All men are created equal"). Also, about 80 percent of American adults describe themselves as belonging to some religion. It would seem, then, that the current condition of the two powerful educational influences on children, the media and the public school system, being areligious or anti-religious is bound to have political consequences. Because parents can do little to punish Hollywood, the temptation to take out their resentments on the local, tax-supported schools is strong, and has led many parents to either home school their children or send them to private schools.

DISCUSSION QUESTIONS

1. Warren Nord ends his essay with the words, "The lack of serious study of religion in public education is illiberal, unjust and unconstitutional." What is your reaction to this statement?
2. Has your previous school experience strengthened, undermined, or had no effect on your religious convictions?
3. What solutions to the problem he has outlined does Nord offer? Do you agree with them? Why? Why not?

Teaching Themes of Care

Nel Noddings

Noddings is among the leading figures in the ... of Educational Philosophy. She is Lee L. Jacks Professor of Child Education Emerita at Stanford University. She is a past president of the National Academy of Education, the Philosophy of Education Society and the John Dewey Society. Noddings has written extensively on the culture of care and education.

"Teaching Themes of Care," by NelNoddings, Phi Delta Kappan, May 1995. Reprinted with permission of Phi Delta Kappa International, www.pdkintl.org. All rights reserved.

Some educators today—and I include myself among them—would like to see a complete reorganization of the school curriculum. We would like to give a central place to the questions and issues that lie at the core of human existence. One possibility would be to organize the curriculum around themes of care— caring for self, for intimate others, for strangers and global others, for the natural world and its nonhuman creatures, for the human-made world, and for ideas.[1]

A realistic assessment of schooling in the present political climate makes it clear that such a plan is not likely to be implemented. However, we can use the rich vocabulary of care in educational planning and introduce themes of care into regular subject-matter classes. In this article, I will first give a brief rationale for teaching themes of care; second, I will suggest ways of choosing and organizing such themes; and, finally, I'll say a bit about the structures required to support such teaching.

Why Teach Caring?

In an age when violence among schoolchildren is at an unprecedented level, when children are bearing children with little knowledge of how to care for them, when the society and even the schools often concentrate on materialistic messages, it may be unnecessary to argue that we should care more genuinely for our children and teach them to care. However, many otherwise reasonable people seem to believe that our educational problems consist largely of low scores on achievement tests. My contention is, first, that we should want more from our educational efforts than adequate academic achievement and, second, that we will not achieve even that meager success unless our children believe that they themselves are cared for and learn to care for others.

There is much to be gained, both academically and humanly, by including themes of care in our curriculum. First, such inclusion may well expand our

FOCUS QUESTION

As you read this article, ask yourself whether our schools need to give more attention to caring as part of the curriculum and, if so, how such themes of caring could be implemented.

InTASC
Standards 1, 2, 3, 4, 5, 7, 8, and 10

students' cultural literacy. For example, as we discuss in math classes the attempts of great mathematicians to prove the existence of God or to reconcile a God who is all good with the reality of evil in the world, students will hear names, ideas, and words that are not part of the standard curriculum. Although such incidental learning cannot replace the systematic and sequential learning required by those who plan careers in mathematically oriented fields, it can be powerful in expanding students' cultural horizons and in inspiring further study.

Second, themes of care help us to connect the standard subjects. The use of literature in mathematics classes, of history in science classes, and of art and music in all classes can give students a feeling of the wholeness in their education. After all, why should they seriously study five different subjects if their teachers, who are educated people, only seem to know and appreciate one?

Third, themes of care connect our students and our subjects to great existential questions. What is the meaning of life? Are there gods? How should I live?

Fourth, sharing such themes can connect us person-to-person. When teachers discuss themes of care, they may become real persons to their students and so enable them to construct new knowledge. Martin Buber put it this way:

> Trust, trust in the world, because this human being exists—that is the most inward achievement of the relation in education. Because this human being exists, meaninglessness, however hard pressed you are by it, cannot be the real truth. Because this human being exists, in the darkness the light lies hidden, in fear salvation, and in the callousness of one's fellow-man the great love.[2]

Finally, I should emphasize that caring is not just a warm, fuzzy feeling that makes people kind and likable. Caring implies a continuous search for competence. When we care, we want to do our very best for the objects of our care. To have as our educational goal the production of caring, competent, loving, and lovable people is not anti-intellectual. Rather, it demonstrates respect for the full range of human talents. Not all human beings are good at or

interested in mathematics, science, or British literature. But all humans can be helped to lead lives of deep concern for others, for the natural world and its creatures, and for the preservation of the human-made world. They can be led to develop the skills and knowledge necessary to make positive contributions, regardless of the occupation they may choose.

Choosing and Organizing Themes of Care

Care is conveyed in many ways. At the institutional level, schools can be organized to provide continuity and support for relationships of care and trust.[3] At the individual level, parents and teachers show their caring through characteristic forms of attention: by cooperating in children's activities, by sharing their own dreams and doubts, and by providing carefully for the steady growth to the children in their charge. Personal manifestations of care are probably more important in children's lives than any particular curriculum or pattern of pedagogy.

However, curriculum can be selected with caring in mind. That is, educators can manifest their care in the choice of curriculum, and appropriately chosen curriculum can contribute to the growth of children as carers. Within each large domain of care, many topics are suitable for thematic units: in the domain of "caring for self," for example, we might consider life stages, spiritual growth, and what it means to develop an admirable character; in exploring the topic of caring for intimate others, we might include units on love, friendship, and parenting; under the theme of caring for strangers and global others, we might study war, poverty, and tolerance; in addressing the idea of caring for the human-made world, we might encourage competence with the machines that surround us and a real appreciation for the marvels of technology. Many other examples exist. Furthermore, there are at least two different ways to approach the development of such themes: units can be constructed by interdisciplinary teams, or themes can be identified by individual teachers and addressed periodically throughout a year's or semester's work.

The interdisciplinary approach is familiar in core programs, and such programs are becoming more and more popular at the middle school level. One key to a successful interdisciplinary unit is the degree of genuinely enthusiastic support it receives from the teachers involved. Too often, arbitrary or artificial groupings are formed, and teachers are forced to make contributions that they themselves do not value highly. For example, math and science teachers are sometimes automatically lumped together, and rich humanistic possibilities may be lost. If I, as a math teacher, want to include historical, biographical, and literary topics in my math lessons, I might prefer to work with English and social studies teachers. Thus it is important to involve teachers in the initial selection of broad areas for themes, as well as in their implementation.

Such interdisciplinary arrangements also work well at the college level. I recently received a copy of the syllabus for a college course titled "The Search for Meaning," which was co-taught by an economist, a university chaplain, and a psychiatrist.[4] The course is interdisciplinary, intellectually rich, and aimed squarely at the central questions of life.

At the high school level, where students desperately need to engage in the study and practice of caring, it is harder to form interdisciplinary teams. A conflict arises as teachers acknowledge the intensity of the subject-matter preparation their students need for further education. Good teachers often wish there were time in the day to co-teach unconventional topics of great importance, and they even admit that their students are not getting what they need for full personal development. But they feel constrained by the requirements of a highly competitive world and the structures of schooling established by that world.

Is there a way out of this conflict? Imaginative, like-minded teachers might agree to emphasize a particular theme in their separate classes. Such themes as war, poverty, crime, racism, or sexism can be addressed in almost every subject area. The teachers should agree on some core ideas related to caring that will be discussed in all classes, but beyond the central commitment to address themes of care, the topics can be handled in whatever way seems suitable in a given subject.

Consider, for example, what a mathematics class might contribute to a unit on crime. Statistical information might be gathered on the location and number of crimes, on rates for various kinds of crime, on the ages of offenders, and on the cost to society; graphs and charts could be constructed. Data on changes in crime rates could be assembled. Intriguing questions could be asked: Were property crime rates lower when penalties were more severe—when, for example, even children were hanged as thieves? What does an average criminal case cost by way of lawyers' fees, police investigation, and court processing? Does it cost more to house a youth in a detention center or in an elite private school?

None of this would have to occupy a full period every day. The regular sequential work of the math class could go on at a slightly reduced rate (e.g., fewer textbook exercises as homework), and the work on crime could proceed in the form of interdisciplinary projects over a considerable period of time. Most important would be the continual reminder in all classes that the topic is part of a larger theme of caring for strangers and fellow citizens. It takes only a few minutes to talk about what it means to live in safety, to trust one's neighbors, to feel secure in greeting strangers. Students should be told that metal detectors and security guards were not part of their parents' school lives, and they should be encouraged to hope for a safer and more open future. Notice the words I've used in this paragraph: caring, trust, safety, strangers, hope. Each could be used as an organizing theme for another unit of study.

English and social studies teachers would obviously have much to contribute to a unit on crime. For example, students might read *Oliver Twist,* and they might also study and discuss the social conditions that seemed to promote crime in 19th-century England. Do similar conditions exist in our country today? The selection of materials could include both classic works and modern stories and films. Students might even be introduced to some of the mystery stories that adults read so avidly on airplanes and beaches, and teachers should be engaged in lively discussion about the comparative value of the various stories.

Science teachers might find that a unit on crime would enrich their teaching of evolution. They could bring up the topic of social Darwinism, which played such a strong role in social policy during the late 19th and early 20th centuries. To what degree are criminal tendencies inherited? Should children be tested for the genetic defects that are suspected of predisposing some people to crime? Are females less competent than males in moral reasoning? (Why did some scientists and philosophers think this was true?) Why do males commit so many more violent acts than females?

Teachers of the arts can also be involved. A unit on crime might provide a wonderful opportunity to critique "gangsta rap" and other currently popular forms of music. Students might profitably learn how the control of art contributed to national criminality during the Nazi era. These are ideas that pop into my mind. Far more various and far richer ideas will come from teachers who specialize in these subjects.

There are risks, of course, in undertaking any unit of study that focuses on matters of controversy or deep existential concern, and teachers should anticipate these risks. What if students want to compare the incomes of teachers and cocaine dealers? What if they point to contemporary personalities from politics, entertainment, business, or sports who seem to escape the law and profit from what seems to be criminal behavior? My own inclination would be to allow free discussion of these cases and to be prepared to counteract them with powerful stories of honesty, compassion, moderation, and charity.

An even more difficult problem may arise. Suppose a student discloses his or her own criminal activities? Fear of this sort of occurrence may send teachers scurrying for safer topics. But, in fact, any instructional method that uses narrative forms or encourages personal expression runs this risk. For example, students of English as a second language who write proudly about their own hard lives and new hopes may disclose that their parents are illegal immigrants. A girl may write passages that lead her teacher to suspect sexual abuse. A boy may brag about objects that he has "ripped off." Clearly, as we use these powerful methods that encourage students to initiate discussion and share their experiences, we must reflect on the ethical issues involved, consider appropriate responses to such issues, and prepare teachers to handle them responsibly.

Caring teachers must help students make wise decisions about what information they will share about themselves. On the one hand, teachers want their students to express themselves, and they want their students to trust in and consult them. On the other hand, teachers have an obligation to protect immature students from making disclosures that they might later regret. There is a deep ethical problem here. Too often educators assume that only religious fundamentalists and right-wing extremists object to the discussion of emotionally and morally charged issues. In reality, there is a real danger of intrusiveness and lack of respect in methods that fail to recognize the vulnerability of students. Therefore, as teachers plan units and lessons on moral issues, they should anticipate the tough problems that may arise. I am arguing here that it is morally irresponsible to simply ignore existential questions and themes of care; we must attend to them. But it is equally irresponsible to approach these deep concerns without caution and careful preparation.

So far I have discussed two ways of organizing interdisciplinary units on themes of care. In one, teachers actually teach together in teams; in the other, teachers agree on a theme and a central focus on care, but they do what they can, when they can, in their own classrooms. A variation on this second way—which is also open to teachers who have to work alone—is to choose several themes and weave them into regular course material over an entire semester or year. The particular themes will depend on the interests and preparation of each teacher.

For example, if I were teaching high school mathematics today, I would use religious/existential questions as a pervasive theme because the biographies of mathematicians are filled with accounts of their speculations on matters of God, other dimensions, and the infinite—and because these topics fascinate me. There are so many wonderful stories to be told: Descartes's proof of the existence of God, Pascal's famous wager, Plato's world of forms, Newton's attempt to verify Biblical chronology, Leibnitz' detailed theodicy, current attempts to describe a divine domain in terms of metasystems, and mystical speculations on the infinite.[5] Some of these stories can be told as rich "asides" in five minutes or less. Others might occupy the better part of several class periods.

Other mathematics teachers might use an interest in architecture and design, art, music, or machinery as continuing themes in the domain of "caring for the human-made world." Still others might introduce the mathematics of living things. The possibilities are endless. In choosing and pursuing these themes, teachers should be aware that they are both helping their students learn to care and demonstrating their own caring by sharing interests that go well beyond the demands of textbook pedagogy.

Still another way to introduce themes of care into regular classrooms is to be prepared to respond spontaneously to events that occur in the school or in the neighborhood. Older teachers have one advantage in this area: they probably have a greater store of experience and stories on which to draw. However, younger teachers have the advantage of being closer to their students' lives and experiences; they are more likely to be familiar with the music, films, and sports figures that interest their students.

All teachers should be prepared to respond to the needs of students who are suffering from the death of friends, conflicts between groups of students, pressure to use drugs or to engage in sex, and other troubles so rampant in the lives of today's children. Too often schools rely on experts—"grief counselors" and the like—when what children really need is the continuing compassion and presence of adults who represent constancy and care in their lives. Artificially separating the emotional, academic, and moral care of children into tasks for specially designated experts contributes to the fragmentation of life in schools.

Of course, I do not mean to imply that experts are unnecessary, nor do I mean to suggest that some matters should not be reserved for parents or psychologists. But our society has gone too far in compartmentalizing the care of its children. When we ask whose job it is to teach children how to care, an appropriate initial response is "Everyone's." Having accepted universal responsibility, we can then ask about the special contributions and limitations of various individuals and groups.

Supporting Structures

What kinds of schools and teacher preparation are required, if themes of care are to be taught effectively? First, and most important, care must be taken seriously as a major purpose of our schools; that is, educators must recognize that caring for students is fundamental in teaching and that developing people with a strong capacity for care is a major objective of responsible education. Schools properly pursue many other objectives—developing artistic talent, promoting multicultural understanding, diversifying curriculum to meet the academic and vocational needs of all students, forging connections with community agencies and parents, and so on. Schools cannot be single-purpose institutions. Indeed, many of us would argue that it is logically and practically impossible to achieve that single academic purpose if other purposes are not recognized and accepted. This contention is confirmed in the success stories of several inner-city schools.[6]

Once it is recognized that school is a place in which students are cared for and learn to care, that recognition should be powerful in guiding policy. In the late 1950s, schools in the U.S., under the guidance of James Conant and others, placed the curriculum at the top of the educational priority list. Because the nation's leaders wanted schools to provide high-powered courses in mathematics and science, it was recommended that small high schools be replaced by efficient larger structures complete with sophisticated laboratories and specialist teachers. Economies of scale were anticipated, but the main argument for consolidation and regionalization centered on the curriculum. All over the country, small schools were closed, and students were herded into larger facilities with "more offerings." We did not think carefully about schools as communities and about what might be lost as we pursued a curriculum-driven ideal.

Today many educators are calling for smaller schools and more family-like groupings. These are good proposals, but teachers, parents, and students should be engaged in continuing discussion about what they are trying to achieve through the new arrangements. For example, if test scores do not immediately rise, participants should be courageous in explaining that test scores were not the main object of the changes. Most of us who argue for caring in schools are intuitively quite sure that children in such settings will in fact become more competent learners. But, if they cannot prove their academic competence in a prescribed period of time, should we give up on caring and on teaching them to care? That would be foolish. There is more to life and learning than the academic proficiency demonstrated by test scores.

In addition to steadfastness of purpose, schools must consider continuity of people and place. If we are concerned with caring and community, then we must make it possible for students and teachers to stay together for several years so that mutual trust can develop and students can feel a sense of belonging in their "school-home."[7]

More than one scheme of organization can satisfy the need for continuity. Elementary school children can stay with the same teacher for several years, or they can work with a stable team of specialist teachers for several years. In the latter arrangement, there may be program advantages; that is, children taught by subject-matter experts who get to know them well over an extended period of time may learn more about the particular subjects. At the high school level, the same specialist teaching might work with students throughout their years in high school. Or, as Theodore Sizer has suggested, one teacher might teach two subjects to a group of 30 students rather than one subject to 60 students, thereby reducing the number of different adults with whom students interact each day.[8] In all the suggested arrangements, placements should be made by mutual consent whenever possible. Teachers and students who hate or distrust one another should not be forced to stay together.

A policy of keeping students and teachers together for several years supports caring in two essential ways: it provides time for the development of caring relations, and it makes teaching themes of care more feasible. When trust has been established, teachers and students can discuss matters that would be hard for a group of strangers to approach, and classmates learn to support one another in sensitive situations.

The structural changes suggested here are not expensive. If a high school teacher must teach five classes a day, it costs no more for three of these classes to be composed of continuing students than for all five classes to comprise new students—i.e., strangers. The recommended changes come directly out of a clear-headed assessment of our major aims and purposes. We failed to suggest them earlier because we had other, too limited, goals in mind.

I have made one set of structural changes sound easy, and I do believe that they are easily made. But the curricular and pedagogical changes that are required may be more difficult. High school textbooks rarely contain the kinds of supplementary material I have described, and teachers are not formally prepared to incorporate such material. Too often, even the people we regard as strongly prepared in a liberal arts major are unprepared to discuss the history of their subject, its relation to other subjects, the biographies of its great figures, its connections to the great existential questions, and the ethical responsibilities of those who work in that discipline. To teach themes of care in an academically effective way, teachers will have to engage in projects of self-education.

At present, neither liberal arts departments nor schools of education pay much attention to connecting academic subjects with themes of care. For example, biology students may learn something of the anatomy and physiology of mammals but nothing at all about the care of living animals; they may never be asked to consider the moral issues involved in the annual euthanasia of millions of pets. Mathematics students may learn to solve quadratic equations but never study what it means to live in a mathematicized world. In enlightened history classes, students may learn something about the problems of racism and colonialism but never hear anything about the evolution of childhood, the contributions of women in both domestic and public caregiving, or the connection between the feminization of caregiving and public policy. A liberal education that neglects matters that are central to a fully human life hardly warrants the name,[9] and a professional education that confines itself to technique does nothing to close the gaps in liberal education.

The greatest structural obstacle, however, may simply be legitimizing the inclusion of themes of care in the curriculum. Teachers in the early grades have long included such themes as a regular part of their work, and middle school educators are becoming more sensitive to developmental needs involving care. But secondary schools—where violence, apathy, and alienation are most evident—do little to develop the capacity to care. Today, even elementary teachers complain that the pressure to produce high test scores inhibits the work they regard as central to their mission: the development of caring and competent people. Therefore, it

would seem that the most fundamental change required is one of attitude. Teachers can be very special people in the lives of children, and it should be legitimate for them to spend time developing relations of trust, talking with students about problems that are central to their lives, and guiding them toward greater sensitivity and competence across all the domains of care.

Notes

1. For the theoretical argument, see Nel Noddings, *The Challenge to Care in Schools* (New York: Teachers College Press, 1992); for a practical example and rich documentation, see Sharon Quint, *Schooling Homeless Children* (New York: Teachers College Press, 1994).
2. Martin Buber, *Between Man and Man* (New York: Macmillan, 1965), p. 98.
3. Noddings, chap. 12.
4. See Thomas H. Naylor, William H. Willimon, and Magdalena R. Naylor, *The Search for Meaning* (Nashville, Tenn.: Abingdon Press, 1994).
5. For many more examples, see Nel Noddings, *Educating for Intelligent Belief and Unbelief* (New York: Teachers College Press, 1993).
6. See Deborah Meier, "How Our Schools Could Be," *Phi Delta Kappan,* January 1995, pp. 369–73; and Quint, op.cit.
7. See Jane Roland Martin, *The Schoolhome: Rethinking Schools for Changing Families* (Cambridge, Mass.: Harvard University Press, 1992).
8. Theodore Sizer, *Horace's Compromise: The Dilemma of the American High School* (Boston: Houghton Mifflin, 1984).
9. See Bruce Wilshire, *The Moral Collapse of the University* (Albany: State University of New York Press, 1990).

POSTNOTE

Getting over selfishness and self-preoccupation is a major task of one's early years. As Nel Noddings demonstrates in this article, schools have a responsibility to help children develop the habit of caring for others. She makes a strong case for giving this task a more prominent place in our educational planning. Because of her national prominence in the field of educational philosophy, we have deemed this article to be a Classic.

As children grow older, however, they need to develop some sterner virtues to complement caring. They need to acquire self-discipline and self-control. They need to acquire the habit of persistence at hard tasks. They need, too, to learn how to strive for individual excellence and to compete against others without hostility. We could argue that both a strong individual and a strong nation need a balance of strengths. To pursue one strength, such as caring, without developing the full spectrum of human virtues, leaves both the individual and the nation incomplete.

DISCUSSION QUESTIONS

1. Do you agree with the primacy given to caring by the author? Why or why not?
2. What obstacles does the author identify and what additional ones can you name that would stand in the way of implementing themes of care in the school curriculum?
3. What practical classroom suggestions to advance caring have you gleaned from this article?

 The companion website for this text includes useful study tools and resources. Go to CengageBrain.com to access links to relevant websites, glossaries, flashcards, an article review form, and more.

Instruction

What should we teach? is the fundamental question. But next in importance is: How do we teach it? Instructional questions range from the very nature of students as learners to how to organize a third-grade classroom.

In this section, we present a palette of new and old ideas about how to organize classrooms and schools to meet the needs of new students and a new society. A number of the most high-profile topics in education—such as cooperative learning, classroom management, assessment, constructivism, and differentiated instruction—are presented. It is important to realize, however, as you read about an instructional methodology or a set of procedures, that each represents a view of what the teaching-learning process is and what students are like. So, as you read these articles, we urge you to probe for their foundational ideas.

25

For Openers: How Technology Is Changing School

Curtis J. Bonk

Curtis J. Bonk is Professor of Instructional Systems Technology at Indiana University. He is the author of *The World Is Open: How Web Technology Is Revolutionizing Education*. He blogs at TravelinEdMan (http://travelinedman.blogspot.com).

"For Openers: How Technology is Changing School," by Curtis J. Bonk, 2010, *Educational Leadership 67*(7), pp. 60–65. © 2010 by ASCD. Reprinted with permission. Learn more about ASCD at www.ascd.org.

FOCUS QUESTION

What effect are new technologies having on schooling?

InTASC

Standards 1, 2, 3, 4, 5, 7, and 8

KEY TERM

• Mobile learning

Sometimes it takes a major catastrophe to transform how we deliver schooling. In 2005, in the aftermath of Hurricanes Katrina and Rita, Web sites went up in Louisiana, Texas, and Mississippi to help educators, students, families, and school districts deal with the crisis. The Mississippi Department of Education (2005) announced free online courses at the high school level, and institutions from 38 states provided more than 1,300 free online courses to college students whose campuses had been affected by the hurricanes (Sloan-C, 2006).

Health emergencies in recent years have also caused educators to ponder the benefits of the Web. In 2003, during the SARS epidemic in China, government officials decided to loosen restrictions on online and blended learning (Huang & Zhou, 2006). More recently, as concerns about the H1N1 virus mounted, many U.S. schools piloted new educational delivery options, such as free online lessons from Curriki (www.curriki.org) and Smithsonian Education (www.smithsonianeducation.org). Microsoft has even offered its Microsoft Office Live free of charge to educators dealing with H1N1. The software enables teachers to share content, lesson plans, and other curriculum components, while students access the virtual classroom workspace, chat with one another on discussion topics, and attend virtual presentations.

Blended Learning Is Here

The focus today is on continuity of learning, whether learning is disrupted because of a hurricane or the flu—or because of other factors entirely. Schools may have difficulty serving students who live in rural areas; reduced budgets may limit the range of learning that a school can offer; people young and old involved in serious scholarly, artistic, or athletic pursuits may find it difficult to adhere to the traditional school structure.

In light of these developments, some school districts are resorting to blended learning options. They are using tools like Tegrity (www.tegrity. com); Elluminate (www.elluminate.com); and Adobe Connect Pro (www.Adobe.com/products/ acrobatconnectpro) to provide online lectures. Many are developing procedures for posting course content and homework online. Some are trying phone conferencing with Skype (www.skype. com) or Google Talk (www.google.com/talk). Others are evaluating digital textbooks and study guides. Still others are sharing online videos from places like Link TV (www.linktv.org); FORA.tv (http://fora.tv); or TeacherTube (www.teacher-tube.com), with teachers often asking students to post their reflections in blogs or online discussion forums. Many schools have begun to foster teamwork by using Google Docs (http://docs.google. com) and wikis. Although some schools use e-mail to communicate messages districtwide, others are experimenting with text messaging or Twitter (http://twitter.com).

The wealth of information available online is also changing teaching practices. Teachers can access free online reference material, podcasts, wikis, and blogs, as well as thousands of free learning portals, such as the Periodic Table of Videos (www.periodicvideos.com) for chemistry courses and the Encyclopedia of Life (www.eol.org) for biology. Science teachers can use portals devoted to Einstein (www.alberteinstein.info); Darwin (www.darwin-online.org.uk); or Goodall (www. janegoodall.org). English teachers can find similar content repositories on Poe (www.eapoe.org); Shakespeare (http://shakespeare.mit.edu); and Austen (www.janeausten.org), to name just a few.

High School—Online

Tools like these enable great flexibility in learning. When I take a break from work and jog across my campus, smack in the middle of it I come to Owen Hall, home of the Indiana University High School

(http://iuhighschool.iu.edu). Indiana University High School (IUHS) students can take their courses online or through correspondence or some combination of the two. Students range from those who live in rural settings to those who are homebound, homeschooled, pregnant, or gifted. Some are Americans living in other countries; some are natives of other countries whose parents want them to have a U.S. education. Some are dropouts or students academically at risk. Still others are teenagers about to enter college who need advanced placement courses or adults who want to finish their high school degrees (Robbins, 2009). Across the board, many of the 4,000 students enrolled in IUHS simply did not fit in the traditional U.S. high school setting.

Take 16-year-old Evren Ozan (www. ozanmusic.com), the Native American flute prodigy whose music I've enjoyed for several years. I'm listening to him as I write this sentence. Many of Evren's vast accomplishments—he's been recording music since he was 7 years old—would not have been possible without the online and distance education experiences he benefited from during his teen years when most of his peers were attending traditional high schools. Also attending IUHS is 15-year-old Ania Filochowska, a Polish-born violinist who has studied with several great masters of the violin in New York City since 2005. Similarly, Kathryn Morgan enrolled in IUHS so she could continue her quest to become a professional ballerina. With the flexibility of online courses and degrees, Kathryn danced full-time and pursued an apprenticeship with the New York City Ballet.

Then there is the amazing story of Bridey Fennell. Bridey completed four IUHS courses while enjoying a five-month sailboat journey with her parents and two sisters from Arcaju, Brazil, to Charleston, South Carolina. Ship dock captains and retired teachers proctored her exams in port, and she practiced her French lessons on different islands of the Caribbean. Her sister Caitlin posted updates about their daily activities to her blog, and elementary students in the Chicago area monitored the family's journey and corresponded with Caitlin.

We All Learn

All this raises the question of why so many people only see the benefits of online learning for musicians, dancers, athletes, and other performers or for those affected by some calamity. I personally benefited from nontraditional education a quarter of a century ago when I was taking correspondence and televised courses from the University of Wisconsin. Back then, I was a bored accountant, and distance learning was my only way out. It got me into graduate school and changed my life. I now speak, write books, and teach about the benefits of distance learning.

The 21st century offers us far more options to learn and grow intellectually. Today, more than a million people in the United States alone are learning online.

To make sense of the vast array of Web-based learning opportunities possible today, I have developed a framework based on 10 *openers*—10 technological opportunities that have the potential to transform education by altering where, when, and how learning takes place. The openers form the acronym WE-ALL-LEARN.[1] They include

- **W**eb searching in the world of e-books.
- **E**-learning and blended learning.
- **A**vailability of open-source and free software.
- **L**everaged resources and open courseware.
- **L**earning object repositories and portals.
- **L**earner participation in open information communities.
- **E**lectronic collaboration.
- **A**lternate reality learning.
- **R**eal-time mobility and portability.
- **N**etworks of personalized learning.

Online and blended learning opportunities are just one opener (opener #2). Let's look at two more.

Web Searching in the World of e-Books

A decade ago, books were limited to being physical objects. Today, all that has changed. Government, nonprofit, and corporate initiatives are placing greater emphasis on digital book content.

The digital textbook project in Korea (www.dtbook.kr/eng), for instance, is being piloted in 112 schools with hopes of making textbooks free for all Korean schools by 2013. Digital textbooks include such features as dictionaries, e-mail applications, forum discussions, simulations, hyperlinks, multimedia, data searching, study aids, and learning evaluation tools.

Right behind Korea is California, which is steeped in a huge deficit. Governor Arnold Schwarzenegger is seeking ways out. One direction is a greater emphasis on digital education (Office of the Governor, 2009). By using digital books, California not only addresses its budgetary problems, but also assumes a leadership role in online learning. Officials in the state plan to download digital textbooks and other educational content into mobile devices that they will place in the hands of all students.

Some digital book initiatives are taking place at the district level. Vail School District in Arizona has adopted an approach called Beyond Textbooks (http://beyondtextbooks.org), which encourages the use of Web resources and shared teacher lesson plans geared to meet state standards (Lewin, 2009). Rich online videos, games, and portals of Web materials as well as podcasts of teacher lectures extend learning at Vail in directions not previously possible.

Innovative companies and foundations are also finding ways to offer free textbooks. Flat World Knowledge (www.flatworldknowledge.com) offers free online textbooks and also sells print-on-demand softcover textbooks, audio textbooks, and low-cost ancillary or supplemental materials, such as MP3 study guides, online interactive quizzes, and digital flashcards connected to each book. Using an open-content, Web-based collaborative model, the CK-12 Foundation (http://ck12.org) is pioneering the idea of free FlexBooks that are customizable to state standards.

Digital books on mobile devices will move a significant chunk of learning out of traditional classroom settings. Hundreds of thousands of free e-books are now available online. You can search for them at places like Google; Many-Books.net (http://manybooks.net); LibriVox (www.librivox.org); the World Public Library (http://worldlibrary.net); the Internet Archive (www.archive.org); Bookyards.com (www.bookyards.com); and other e-book sites. Ironically, the majority of the top 25 best sellers on the Kindle are actually free (Kafka, 2009). We have entered the era of free books.

Real-Time Mobility and Portability

Mobile learning is the current mantra of educators. More than 60,000 people around the planet get mobile access to the Internet each hour (Iannucci, 2009), with 15 million people subscribing each month in India alone (Telecom Regulatory Authority of India, 2009). Also, if just one percent of the 85,000 applications for the iPhone (Marcus, 2009) are educational, thousands of possible learning adventures are at one's fingertips. It's possible to access grammar lessons, language applications, Shakespearean plays or quotes, physics experiments, musical performances, and math review problems with a mobile phone.

Online classes and course modules as well as teacher professional development are now delivered on mobile devices. As mobile learning advocate John Traxler (2007) points out, mobile professional development options are especially important in developing countries in Africa.

Mobile learning is not restricted to phones, of course. Laptops, iPods, MP3 players, flash memory sticks, digital cameras, and lecture recording pens all foster mobile learning pursuits as well as greater learning engagement. Educators need to thoughtfully consider where, when, and how to use such devices.

For instance, rather than ban mobile technologies, school officials might encourage students to record lectures with their pens or digital devices and listen to them while studying for quizzes and final exams. Or teachers might make available snippets of content that students can download to their mobile devices—such as French grammar lessons or quick guides to concepts in the study of chemistry, the human nervous system, or cell biology (Bonk, 2009).

When we think about mobile learning, we often just think of a mobile learner. But the deliverer of the learning might also be mobile. With the Web, our learning content might come from a climb up Mount Everest, expeditions to the Arctic or Antarctic, research at the bottom of an ocean, NASA flights far above us, or sailing adventures across the planet.

Michael Perham (www.sailmike.com) and Zac Sunderland (www.zacsunderland.com), for instance, each blogged and shared online videos of their record-setting solo sailing journeys around the globe. Amazingly, they each completed their adventures last summer at the tender age of 17. I could track their daily experiences and post comments in their blogs. They were my highly mobile teachers. I also learn from Jean Pennycook, a former high school science teacher who now brings scientific research on penguins in the Antarctic to classrooms around the world (see www.windows.ucar.edu/tour/link=/people/postcards/penguin_post.html).

Trends in the Open World

Given these myriad learning opportunities on the Web, you might wonder what is coming next. Here are some predictions.

- *Free as a book.* Digital books will not only be free, but readers will also be able to mix and match several of their components. E-books and classrooms will increasingly embed shared online video, animations, and simulations to enhance learning.
- *The emergence of super e-mentors and e-coaches.* Super e-mentors and e-coaches, working from computer workstations or from mobile devices, will provide free learning guidance. As with the gift culture that we have seen in the open source movement over the past two decades, some individuals will simply want to share their expertise and skills, whereas others may want practice teaching. Many will be highly educated individuals who have always wanted opportunities to teach, coach, or mentor but who work

in jobs that do not enable them to do so. Those with the highest credibility and in the most demand will have human development or counseling skills (perhaps a master's degree in counseling); understand how to use the Web for learning; and have expertise in a particular domain, such as social work, nursing, accounting, and so forth.

- *Selecting global learning partners.* Peers don't need to live down the street; they could be anywhere on the planet. Tools like Ning (www.ning.com) and Google Docs and resources like ePals (www.epals.com) and iEARN (International Education and Research Network; www.iearn.org) make global interactions ubiquitous. Global peer partners will form mini-school communities and unique school-based social networking groups. Projects might include learning how to cope with natural disasters, engaging in cultural exchanges, designing artwork related to human rights, exploring the effects of global warming, and learning about threats to animal habitats.

- *Teachers everywhere.* Soon students will be able to pick their teachers at a moment's notice. Want a teacher from Singapore, the Philippines, the United Kingdom, or Israel? They will be available in online teacher or mentor portals as well as preselected and approved by local school districts or state departments. Some will be displayed on a screen as students walk into school; students might consult this individual during a study hall period or review session.

- *Teacher as concierge.* The notion of a teacher will shift from a deliverer of content to that of a concierge who finds and suggests education resources as learners need them.

- *Informal = formal.* Informal learning will dramatically change the idea of "going to school," with a greater percentage of instructors being informal ones who offer content, experiences, and ideas to learners of all ages. Such individuals will include explorers on expeditions, researchers in a science lab, and practitioners in the workplace.

- *International academic degrees.* Consortia of countries will band together to provide international education using online courses and activities with the goal of offering a high school or community college degree.

- *Dropouts virtually drop back in.* The U.S. government will offer free online courses for high school dropouts and those needing alternative learning models (Jaschik, 2009). Such courses, as well as multiple options for learning, may lure students back to pick up a secondary or postsecondary degree. Interactive technology enhancements will appeal to teenagers and young adults savvy with emerging tools for learning.

- *The rise of the super blends.* As schools are faced with continued budgetary constraints and with the plethora of free courses, learning portals, and delivery technologies available, blended learning will become increasingly prevalent in K–12 education. Determining the most effective blend will be a key part of effective school leadership.

- *The shared learning era.* In the coming decade, the job of a K–12 teacher will include the willingness to share content with teachers in one's school district as well as with those far beyond. Teachers will also be called on to evaluate shared content.

- *Personalized learning environments.* Open educational resources (OER) and technologies like shared online videos, podcasts, simulations, and virtual worlds will be available to enhance or clarify any lesson at any time (Bonk & Zhang, 2008). For example, Wendy Ermold, a researcher and field technician for the University of Washington Polar Science Center, conducts research in Greenland and in other northern locations on this planet. While out on the icebreakers or remote islands, she listens to lectures and reviews other OER content from MIT, Stanford, Seattle Pacific University, and Missouri State University to update her knowledge of physics and other content areas. The expansion of such free and open course content options will personalize learning according to particular learner needs or preferences.

- *Alexandrian Aristotles.* Learners will emerge who have the modern-day equivalent of the entire ancient library of Alexandria on a flash memory stick in their pocket or laptop. They will spend a significant amount of time learning from online tools and resources, will be ideal problem finders and solvers, and will set high personal achievement standards.

Open for Business

The world is open for learning. In addition to blended learning, e-books, and mobile learning, we are witnessing an increase in learner generation of academic content, collaboration in that content generation, and customization of the learning environment at significantly reduced costs and sometimes for free.

The 10 openers I suggest push educators to rethink models of schooling and instruction. They are converging to offer the potential for a revolution in education—which is already underway.

References

Bonk, C. J. (2009). *The world is open: How Web technology is revolutionizing education.* San Francisco: Jossey-Bass.

Bonk, C. J., & Zhang, K. (2008). *Empowering online learning: 100+ activities for reading, reflecting, displaying, and doing.* San Francisco: Jossey-Bass.

Huang, R., & Zhou, Y. (2006). Designing blended learning focused on knowledge category and learning activities: Case studies from Beijing. In C. J. Bonk & C. R. Graham (Eds.), *Handbook of blended learning: Global perspectives, local designs* (pp. 296–310). San Francisco: Pfeiffer.

Iannucci, B. (2009, January 7). *Connecting everybody to everything.* Nokia Research Center, Stanford University POMI (Programmable Open Mobile Internet), NSF research advisory meeting.

Jaschik, S. (2009, June 29). U.S. push for free online courses. *Inside Higher Ed.* Available: www.insidehighered.com/news/2009/06/29/ccplan

Kafka, P. (2009, December). The secret behind the Kindle's best-selling e-books: They're not for sale. *CNET News.* Available: http://news.cnet.com/8301-1023_310422538-93.html

Lewin, T. (2009, August 9). In a digital future, textbooks are history. *The New York Times.* Available: www.nytimes.com/2009/08/09/education/09textbook.html

Marcus, M. B. (2009, October 5). Pull yourself from that iPhone and read this story. *USA Today.* Available: www.usatoday.com/printedition/life/20091005/appaddiction05_st.art.htm

Mississippi Department of Education. (2005, September). *Katrina recovery information.* Available: www.mde.k12.ms.us/Katrina

Office of the Governor. (2009, May 6). Gov. Schwarzenegger launches first-in-nation initiative to develop free digital textbooks for high school students (Press Release). Sacramento, CA: Author. Available: http://gov.ca.gov/press-release/12225/

Robbins, R. (2009, June 9). Distance students are "a varied and interesting lot." *Herald Times Online.* Available: www.heraldtimesonline.com/stories/2009/06/08/schoolnews.qp-2930970.sto

Sloan-C. (2006, August 8). The Sloan Consortium honored for post-hurricane delivery of online courses. The Sloan semester. Available: www.sloan-c.org/sloansemester

Telecom Regulatory Authority of India. (2009, June). Information note to the press (Press Release No 54/2009). Available: www.trai.gov.in/WriteReadData/trai/upload/PressReleases/687/pr1june09no54.pdf

Traxler, J. (2007, June). Defining, discussing, and evaluating mobile learning: The moving finger writes and having writ … *International Review of Research in Open and Distance Learning, 8*(1). Available: www.irrodl.org/index.php/irrodl/article/view/346/875

Note

1. For a full discussion of the We-All-Learn framework, see my book, *The World Is Open: How Web Technology Is Revolutionizing Education* (Jossey-Bass, 2009).

POSTNOTE

For much of the last decade, schools have emphasized the acquisition of technology hardware as a major objective. Educators have now reached the point where their goal should not be just to acquire technology. Instead, they should ask how technologies should be used to help students reach the higher standards being developed by states and to prepare students for the world they will enter when they leave school.

Although most educators, policymakers, and business leaders believe that technology has the potential to alter dramatically how teachers teach and students learn, there are some who remain skeptical that technology will have a significant impact on education. These skeptics cite as historical evidence the "hype" that accompanied previous technologies, such as television, that failed to deliver on their promises.

It is clear that if computers and other related technologies are to transform educational practice, much time and effort must go into working with teachers. They need to understand the capabilities of technology and to develop the skills necessary to deliver those capabilities. They need to know how to integrate appropriate technologies into the content they teach. If this teacher development does not occur, then the latest educational technology, like some earlier ones, will prove to be a bust.

DISCUSSION QUESTIONS

1. Which technologies do you believe offer the most promise for active student engagement? Why?
2. In what ways have schools yet to take advantage of some of the newer technologies mentioned by the author?
3. What technology skills do you possess that you think will be useful to you as a teacher? What skills do you need to develop?

RELATED WEBSITE RESOURCES AND VIDEO CASES

WEB RESOURCES:

International Society for Technology in Education (ISTE), ISTE's Electronic Resources. Available at:

http://www.iste.org/resources.

A superb list of links that cover a wide range of issues, including standards, the "digital divide," professional development, and technology integration.

Alliance for Childhood: Computers and Children. Available at:

http://www.allianceforchildhood.net/projects/computers/computers_reports.htm.

A series of reports on children and their use of technology.

▶❚❚ TEACHSOURCE VIDEO CASE

USING TECHNOLOGY TO PROMOTE DISCOVERY LEARNING: HIGH SCHOOL GEOMETRY LESSON

In this high school geometry class, you will see how teacher Gary Simons uses a technological tool that allows students to investigate problems and create their own "conjectures." Go to the website for the Education Media Library at CengageBrain.com to watch the video clips, study the artifacts in the case, and reflect on the following questions.

1. Mr. Simons maintains that technology is an essential tool for promoting discovery learning. Is his statement consistent with your experiences? Why or why not?

2. What aspect of using technology tools to support discovery learning do you think will be most challenging to you as a new teacher? How will you approach this challenge?

3. What other technologies might Gary Simons have used in teaching his lesson?

▶❚❚ TEACHSOURCE VIDEO CASE

TEACHING TECHNOLOGY SKILLS: AN ELEMENTARY SCHOOL LESSON ON POWERPOINT

In this video case, you will meet two teachers who teach students how to create their own PowerPoint slide shows in order to present what they have learned about the Civil Rights movement. Go to the website for the Education Media Library at CengageBrain.com to watch the video clips, study the artifacts in the case, and reflect on the following questions.

1. Would the author of this article agree or disagree with the way technology is being used in this video case? Support your position.

2. How else might you teach this lesson using some of the newer technologies mentioned in this article?

26

Confronting the Achievement Gap

David Gardner

David Gardner retired from the classroom in 2005 and is now head teacher for Explorations in Math, a nonprofit group working with the Seattle schools.

"Confronting the Achievement Gap," by David Gardner, *Phi Delta Kappan*, March 2007, pp. 542–546. Reprinted with permission of Phi Delta Kappa International, www.pdkintl.org. All rights reserved.

FOCUS QUESTION

What causes so many children of color to underachieve throughout school, and what can be done to remedy this problem?

InTASC

Standards 1, 2, 3, 7, 8, and 10

KEY TERM

• Achievement gap

Over the course of 33 years, I have taught in schools with high concentrations of low-income families, children of color, and students and families who speak little or no English, and I have taught in schools in mostly affluent, white neighborhoods. The difference in achievement levels will surprise no one: high in the affluent, white schools; much lower in schools where poverty is common.

The question is, Why is this so? Why do so many urban minority students come into fifth grade with low skills in virtually every area? Many cannot add or subtract accurately; they don't know their multiplication and division facts; they can't write a decent paragraph or, in some cases, a decent sentence. Why do they have so much trouble reasoning out problems?

For example, during a discussion in an American history class made up of students from the South End of Seattle, I handed out tables that showed how much money was spent to educate white children in the South in the 1920s as opposed to how much was spent for black children. One of the tables showed a breakdown by county in Mississippi. I asked my students to find the difference in the amount spent for white students and black students in each county. Most of the students had a very difficult time even understanding what I wanted them to do. When they did grasp the concept, they had still more difficulty using the table to determine the answer. And even then most of the answers were wrong because of problems with subtraction. I posed questions about another table, asking students to identify a particular state. Most answered with dollar amounts.

When I ask why this should be so, I'm repeating a question that continues to be asked by educators, schools, parents, and communities across the country. Why is there such a large achievement gap between so many children of color and their white peers?

Of course, this quandary is nothing new. The gap dates back to the first mass-administered achievement tests given by the U.S. Army in World War I. Even as crude as those tests were, they measured an achievement gap between black recruits and white recruits that persists today, in spite of everything we have tried.

The first and most obvious response to my question is almost always unequal funding. Throughout most of our history the funding disparities between white schools and those serving children of color have been enormous. Scott Nearing, in *Black America* (from which I took the tables I used in the history lesson above), first published in 1929, documented these disparities as they existed in the South in the 1920s.[1] For example, in 1927, South Carolina spent $2.74 per "Negro" student and $27.88 per white student. Or even more astoundingly, Mississippi counties in 1926 averaged $3.59 a year per black student as opposed to $68.15 per white student. Nearing cited 162 kindergartens for white children in eight southern cities, but just eight for black children. All eight were in Kentucky: seven of them in Louisville, one in Lexington.

While disparities of that magnitude no longer exist, it's still true that affluent districts outspend their poorer counterparts. Ironically, though, even as funding disparities are reduced, the playing field for students of color remains badly tilted. Spending the same amount of money on each individual student harks back to a time when teachers would say, "I treat every student exactly the same." We know that notion has been discredited: all students are *not* the same, and to treat them as if they were does them a disservice. Funding schools as if all populations faced the same problems and had the same needs is an equally ineffective means of addressing the achievement gap.

My own district of Seattle instituted a weighted student funding formula several years ago. This formula distributes money to schools based on a number of factors, including such things as the number of students on free or reduced-price lunch, the number of special education students, and the number of English-language learners. Schools with greater needs receive more money per student. Has this approach made a difference? There has been some slight, but by no means significant, movement toward closing the achievement gap. But there has been no way to tell how much of that change is the result of the funding formula and how much is the result of other efforts the district has undertaken.

Soon after the funding answer to my question has been proposed, another common response—this one spoken more softly—is that children of color must be inherently less capable, less intelligent. I'm tempted to dismiss this as utter nonsense, except for the tremendous harm such thinking has caused and continues to cause. To believe it is to say we might as well give up on these children. Except for the occasional anomaly, they'll never make it. As a result of an at least tacit belief in this answer, many teachers, schools, and even whole communities *have* given up on children of color. When this belief prevails, teachers can transfer much of the responsibility for the failure to learn from their own shoulders to those of their students. Teachers go through the motions of educating these children, pay lip service to the ideals, but don't believe, deep down, that these children will ever catch up. And if teachers don't believe in them, how in the world will the children ever believe in themselves?

Let me parse the problem into two separate questions and deal with each one separately: What causes so many children of color to underachieve throughout school? And what are the remedies?

Why the Achievement Gap?

The reasons for the achievement gap are as varied as the students who pass through my classes every year. First, many come from a background of poverty. One of the detrimental effects of growing up in poverty is receiving inadequate nourishment at a time when bodies and brains are rapidly developing. Proper human development requires a steady and healthy diet. Poor children rarely get such a diet. Add to that the fact that poor mothers-to-be are rarely well nourished themselves and don't often receive adequate prenatal care, and you have a recipe for lower achievement among the children.

Poverty also means that there are fewer resources in the home for the child to draw on. Parents (or other caretakers) often work two or more jobs, or they work a night shift, either of which takes away time they might spend with their children. In such circumstances, parents can't be as involved with their children's education as they need to be or would like to be.

Poverty can also make it difficult to develop a child's self-esteem. Poor children have fewer opportunities for enriching experiences. Poor people don't take trips to Europe or Africa; indeed, some rarely leave their neighborhoods. They may have trouble even taking trips to the zoo or art museum or library. This is not to say that poor children have no enriching experiences, for they clearly do. However, their experiences may not be the kind valued by the larger community. When the greater society does not value a child's culture, what is his or her likely response? Anger. Resentment. Loss of trust. Seeing school as an obstacle rather than a way out. These factors drive down motivation, drive down confidence. Many poor children are stuck in this cycle.

Still another factor that can adversely affect a child's learning is the parents' own experiences with school and teachers. For many poor parents, these experiences were negative. These parents will thus be more reluctant to come to school, to participate in school events, to contact teachers, or to place any confidence in the school and the education system. Add to the mix the large and increasing number of people who are new to the country—who do not speak English, are unfamiliar with the culture, and in many cases are themselves minimally educated—and the problems are magnified.

Still another reason for the achievement gap has to do with what in academic circles is called "locus of control." People with an internal locus of control see themselves as primarily responsible for their successes and failures. People with an external locus of control tend to attribute their successes and failures to outside factors: luck, fate, the boss likes me, the teacher doesn't like me, etc. A great example of external locus of control can be seen in a "Peanuts" comic strip in which Peppermint Patty bemoans the F she got on a test. "I think I got an F," she tells Franklin, "because I have a big nose. Sometimes a teacher just doesn't like the way a kid looks. I've got a big nose so I fail. It's as simple as that."

Research shows that many people of color have an external locus of control. And there are some good reasons for that. People of color generally experience success (promotions, raises, upward mobility) at lower and slower rates than do whites. They may work as hard or harder and be just as competent, but their efforts are not routinely rewarded. Does this affect their children? It seems entirely possible. After all, they see their parents struggling, year after year, and they hear their parents talking about the difficulty or impossibility of getting ahead. Then they come to school, work as hard as other students, and see that they, too, fail to achieve at the same rate as their white and Asian peers. They deduce, not unreasonably, that external factors, things beyond their control, must be responsible. This conclusion leads them to reduce their effort and resign themselves to not doing well.

Finally, the long-term effects of racism on the achievement gap should not be underestimated. Schooling for whites in this country extends back for several centuries. Though not equally distributed even among whites, free public education has nonetheless an expectation that education leads to success—at least for those in the majority. For people of color no such centuries-long positive history exists. From the slave codes that forbade educating those who were enslaved, to the Jim Crow laws that followed, to the institutional racism that has only been weakened, not eliminated, all have had a devastatingly negative impact on the education of children of color, an impact that continues to this day.

In all of this, can any blame be assigned to today's schools and teachers? Sadly, the answer is yes, for there's plenty of blame to go around. There are bad schools, and there are incompetent teachers. And, once again, both are all too often found in African American neighborhoods or in the barrios or on the reservations. And in these locales, even the good schools with good teachers are affected by an undercurrent of racism that undermines what we try to do. This is not intentional racism; it is racism that we're not even aware of practicing. It's a colleague who stands, smiles, and shakes hands with white parents at the start of a parent/teacher conference but fails to show the same courtesies to black parents in the next conference. The teacher is doubtless unaware of the differential treatment. But the unconscious stereotypes and expectations we carry around with us can and do affect how we teach. You can hear those stereotypes just beneath the surface of the frequently voiced assumption that minority parents don't care as much about education as white parents.

For all of these reasons, closing the achievement gap presents us with an extremely difficult problem. However, the idea that schools alone are responsible for the existence of this gap and so bear sole responsibility for closing it is disingenuous at best. And attributing blame to the schools, which has been going on for at least a decade, has simply made teachers defensive while failing to improve the situation. Hundreds of millions of dollars are expended on the problem every year. Expensive programs are implemented, attempted for a couple of years, and then tossed out when they fail to produce results, like the long line of failed efforts that preceded them. School staffs attend workshop after workshop in an effort to acquire the skills and the attitudes needed to close the achievement gap, but their efforts are doomed before they start, as long as schools alone are deemed to be responsible for the problem. The achievement gap and the problems that continue to feed it are a reflection of society and its attitudes. And until these change, we will meet with little success.

What Is the Solution?

The solution to the problem of the achievement gap lies within each one of us as citizens and within each of us who teaches. This is not the kind of problem that is going to be eliminated by an institutional response. No school system and no state or federal department of education will ever be able to mandate a solution.

The achievement gap will begin to disappear when attitudes in this country begin to change, when eliminating poverty becomes a national priority. It will begin to disappear when racism is recognized as the pervasive and insidious cancer that it is and when Americans are united in their willingness to do something about it.

The only way this kind of change will happen is for each of us, individually, to want it to happen and to be willing to make it happen. As a teacher, I do many things that are designed to help my students change their attitudes toward themselves and toward school and learning. They, too, need to be a part of a national change of heart. Here are two places to start, places that are within the ability of each individual educator to control.

First, I believe in my kids. I *know* they are capable, and so I'm not reluctant to set high standards for them. But believing in them isn't enough; they need to *know* that I believe in them. I communicate that belief to them every day, and I do it in many ways, both explicitly and implicitly. Explicitly, I tell them they're capable. I tell them I believe in them. I tell them each of them has a good brain and is capable of doing what I ask of them. I tell them I have high expectations of them, that I will not accept poor work, and that I will return slipshod work to them to be redone.

I routinely refuse to answer the standard "I don't get this. How do you do it?" lament when it's about a problem or question that I know a student can figure out. And I let students know that they must do their part. I draw analogies for them: body builders develop their muscles by gradually increasing the weight they lift. Students increase their abilities by accepting the challenges posed by their teachers to do work that steadily increases in difficulty. I also challenge them to take risks. There are no wrong answers, I tell them. If you give me a wrong answer, it tells me two good things about you. One, you're paying attention. And two, you're thinking. If you're doing those two things, you can't help but learn.

I talk to my students explicitly about failure. I tell them that failure is not only okay, it's critical to learning. When you were learning to ride a bike, you fell. And every fall marked a failure in learning to ride a bike. When you were learning to skate, you fell, and every fall marked a failure in learning to skate. But those failures guided your learning, and persistence paid off. The same thing happens when you're learning at school. You're going to fail before you succeed. Long division, writing a decent paragraph, thinking through a difficult problem, success in any of these comes about only after failures. At first, you'll get wrong answers more often than not in long division, but your failures let you see what you need to do differently. You'll write many bad paragraphs before you write a good one. You'll stumble over difficult problems before you're able to solve them. If you're willing to work at it, success will come through these failures. Children need to hear these messages regularly, because they're afraid of failure, which means they're afraid to take risks. And when they don't take risks, of course, they do fail, only they fail in a much more significant and dangerous way: they lose the opportunity to learn a skill, and they reinforce their own feelings of deficiency. To get them out of that self-defeating loop, I do everything in my power to get them to believe in themselves. Once that happens, they will begin to close the achievement gap on their own.

Another critical step in helping students to do well is to make learning fun. Think about it: the things we all do well tend to be the things we enjoy doing. But when I say learning must be fun, that doesn't mean it comes without effort. When learning is fun, it is interesting, challenging, and rewarding. Drill and kill, rote memorization, round-robin reading, dull textbooks, a 100% teacher-centered classroom, all of these are poisonous to learning because they do not engage students. On the contrary, students are turned off and tuned out, the first steps on the road to falling behind and dropping out. Just as bad, they are obstacles to closing and eliminating the achievement gap.

How does a good teacher go about making learning fun? It may sound like an oxymoron, but making learning fun is hard work. You need to be prepared to discard much of the conventional wisdom of teaching and most of the commercially produced texts and worksheets. And you'll have to deal with the dual anxiety that can come from not having a manual to guide you while you do have a principal who insists that you use the prescribed texts.

Then, too, to make learning fun you'll have to be willing to bust your brain thinking up better ways—more interesting, more challenging, more rewarding, more enjoyable ways—of covering the curriculum in each content area. This means scrounging for materials in the stockroom, in vacant classrooms, in garage sales and flea markets, in stores that sell school supplies, and in many other places. This means making many of your own teaching materials, such as graphs, posters, and charts. It means creating your own worksheets for each lesson, tailoring them to fit both the specific objectives you have in mind and the needs of your students. It means being creative and flexible. It means giving students more autonomy and a greater say in how they're going to learn. It means that humor and laughter are integral parts of the classroom environment, an environment that leads to achievement rather than boredom.

Making learning fun means using games and manipulatives. And for me, a key part of making learning fun is interspersing brain games and other short, quick activities throughout the day. For example, after I take attendance and we listen to the opening announcements each day, my class solves some kind of puzzle on the board, or we engage in some brainteasers. We always have time for two or three students chosen randomly to do "Acting in a Can" (like charades), to play Taboo® (using the words from the commercially produced game), or to play categories. Throughout the day, when there are a few minutes to fill, we do mental math or mental spelling and play word games or "Guess My Number." I put a premium on humor, imagination, and creativity. All of these activities engage students and keep them coming back for more.

Believing in my students and letting them know I believe in them and making school a place they find rewarding will not, in and of themselves, eliminate the achievement gap. But these measures are within our control as educators, and they will have a positive effect on our students, both now and in the future.

Note

1. Scott Nearing, *Black America* (1929; reprint, New York: Schocken, 1969), pp. 61–63, 268–69.

POSTNOTE

Many people see the academic achievement problem of students from urban poverty schools as being intractable. Poverty is too great … parents don't care … drugs and violence take a toll. Gardner argues that the major remedy lies in eliminating both poverty and attitudes that expect less from children of color. With high standards, a challenging curriculum, and good teachers, children from poverty schools can learn, and at surprisingly high levels. As Jaime Escalante demonstrated at Garfield High School in East Los Angeles, poor Latino youths could learn calculus well enough to score at high levels on AP exams. He set high standards and made serious demands on students. His success is celebrated in the Academy Award–nominated movie *Stand and Deliver*. Marva Collins, in Chicago, also demonstrated that poor African American children could learn a classical curriculum at high levels.

DISCUSSION QUESTIONS

1. Was there anything in this article that surprised you? If so, what?
2. Do you agree with the author's assertion that poverty and institutional racism are the major deterrents for children of color to achieve comparably with middle class white students? Why or why not?
3. In addition to the author's suggestions, what do you believe can be done to improve the quality of schools serving the urban poor?

RELATED WEBSITE RESOURCES

WEB RESOURCES:

Education Trust. Available at:

http://www.edtrust.org.

The Education Trust works to ensure high academic achievement for all students. The website contains many resources toward that end.

Children's Defense Fund. Available at:

http://www.childrensdefense.org.

The Children's Defense Fund provides a voice for all children, paying particular attention to the needs of poor and minority children and those with disabilities. The website contains policy positions, research, and papers on issues related to children.

27

Students Need Challenge, Not Easy Success

Margaret M. Clifford

At the time this article was written, **Margaret M. Clifford** was professor emeritus of educational psychology, College of Education, University of Iowa, Iowa City. She died in 2003.

"Students Need Challenge, Not Easy Success," by Margaret M. Clifford, 1990, *Educational Leadership 48*(1), pp. 32–36. © 1990 by ASCD. Reprinted with permission. Learn more about ASCD at www.ascd.org.

FOCUS QUESTION

What are the psychological principles advocated by the author that enhance the likelihood of motivating students to succeed?

InTASC

Standards 1, 2, 3, 4, 5, 6, 7, and 8

KEY TERMS

- Formative evaluation
- Intrinsic motivation
- Summative evaluation

Hundreds of thousands of apathetic students abandon their schools each year to begin lives of unemployment, poverty, crime, and psychological distress. According to Hahn (1987), "Dropout rates ranging from 40 to 60 percent in Boston, Chicago, Los Angeles, Detroit, and other major cities point to a situation of crisis proportions." The term *dropout* may not be adequate to convey the disastrous consequences of the abandonment of school by children and adolescents; *educational suicide* may be a far more appropriate label.

School abandonment is not confined to a small percentage of minority students, or low ability children, or mentally lazy kids. It is a systemic failure affecting the most gifted and knowledgeable as well as the disadvantaged, and it is threatening the social, economic, intellectual, industrial, cultural, moral, and psychological well-being of our country. Equally disturbing are students who sever themselves from the flow of knowledge while they occupy desks, like mummies.

Student apathy, indifference, and under-achievement are typical precursors of school abandonment. But what causes these symptoms? Is there a remedy? What will it take to stop the waste of our intellectual and creative resources?

To address these questions, we must acknowledge that educational suicide is primarily a motivational problem—not a physical, intellectual, financial, technological, cultural, or staffing problem. Thus, we must turn to motivational theories and research as a foundation for examining this problem and for identifying solutions.

Curiously enough, modern theoretical principles of motivation do not support certain widespread practices in education. I will discuss four such discrepancies and offer suggestions for resolving them.

Moderate Success Probability Is Essential to Motivation

The maxim, "Nothing succeeds like success," has driven educational practice for several decades. Absolute success for students has become the means *and* the end of education: It has been given higher priority than learning, and it has obstructed learning.

A major principle of current motivation theory is that tasks associated with a moderate probability of success (50 percent) provide maximum satisfaction (Atkinson 1964). Moderate probability of success is also an essential ingredient of intrinsic motivation (Lepper and Greene 1978, Csikszentmihalyi 1975, 1978). We attribute the success we experience on easy tasks to task ease; we attribute the success we experience on extremely difficult tasks to luck. Neither type of success does much to enhance self-image. It is only success at moderately difficult or truly challenging tasks that we explain in terms of personal effort, well-chosen strategies, and ability; and these explanations give rise to feelings of pride, competence, determination, satisfaction, persistence, and personal control. Even very young children show a preference for tasks that are just a bit beyond their ability (Danner and Lonky 1981).

Consistent with these motivational findings, learning theorists have repeatedly demonstrated that moderately difficult tasks are a prerequisite for maximizing intellectual development (Fischer 1980). But despite the fact that moderate challenge (implying considerable error-making) is essential for maximizing learning and optimizing motivation, many educators attempt to create error-proof learning environments. They set minimum criteria and standards in hopes of ensuring success for all students. They often reduce task difficulty, overlook errors, de-emphasize failed attempts, ignore faulty performances, display "perfect papers," minimize testing, and reward error-free performance.

It is time for educators to replace easy success with challenge. We must encourage students to reach beyond their intellectual grasp and allow them the privilege of learning from mistakes. There must be a tolerance for error-making in every classroom, and gradual success rather than continual success must become the yardstick by which learning is judged. Such transformations in educational practices will not guarantee the elimination of educational suicide, but they are sure to be one giant step in that direction.

External Constraints Erode Motivation and Performance

Intrinsic motivation and performance deteriorate when external constraints such as surveillance, evaluation by others, deadlines, threats, bribes, and rewards are accentuated. Yes, even rewards are a form of constraint! The reward giver is the General who dictates rules and issues orders; rewards are used to keep the troops in line.

Means-end contingencies, as exemplified in the statement, "If you complete your homework, you may watch TV" (with homework being the means and TV the end), are another form of external constraint. Such contingencies decrease interest in the first task (homework, the means) and increase interest in the second task (TV, the end) (Boggiano and Main 1986).

Externally imposed constraints, including material rewards, decrease task interest, reduce creativity, hinder performance, and encourage passivity on the part of students—even preschoolers (Lepper and Hodell 1989)! Imposed constraints also prompt individuals to use the "minimax strategy"—to exert the minimum amount of effort needed to obtain the maximum amount of reward (Kruglanski et al. 1977). Supportive of these findings are studies showing that autonomous behavior—that which is self-determined, freely chosen, and personally controlled—elicits high task interest, creativity, cognitive flexibility, positive emotion, and persistence (Deci and Ryan 1987).

Unfortunately, constraint and lack of student autonomy are trademarks of most schools. Federal and local governments, as well as teachers, legislate academic requirements; impose guidelines; create rewards systems; mandate behavioral contracts; serve warnings of expulsion; and use rules, threats, and punishments as routine problem-solving strategies. We can legislate school attendance and the conditions for obtaining a diploma, but we cannot legislate the development of intelligence, talent, creativity, and intrinsic motivation—resources this country desperately needs.

It is time for educators to replace coercive, constraint-laden techniques with autonomy-supportive techniques. We must redesign instructional and evaluation materials and procedures so that every assignment, quiz, text, project, and discussion activity not only allows for, but routinely *requires,* carefully calculated decision making on the part of students. Instead of minimum criteria, we must define multiple criteria (levels of minimum, marginal, average, good, superior, and excellent achievement), and we must free students to choose criteria that provide optimum challenge. Constraint gives a person the desire to escape; freedom gives a person the desire to explore, expand, and create.

Prompt, Specific Feedback Enhances Learning

A third psychological principle is that specific and prompt feedback enhances learning, performance, and motivation (Ilgen et al. 1979, Larson 1984). Informational feedback (that which reveals correct responses) increases learning (Ilgen and Moore 1987) and also promotes a feeling of increased competency (Sansone 1986). Feedback that can be used to improve future performance has powerful motivational value.

Sadly, however, the proportion of student assignments or activities that are promptly returned with informational feedback tends to be low. Students typically complete an assignment and then wait one, two, or three days (sometimes weeks) for its return. The feedback they do get often consists of a number or letter grade accompanied by ambiguous comments such as "Is this your best?" or "Keep up the good work." Precisely what is good or what needs improving is seldom communicated.

But, even if we could convince teachers of the value of giving students immediate, specific, informational feedback, our feedback problem would still be far from solved. How can one teacher provide 25 or more students immediate feedback on their tasks? Some educators argue that the solution to the feedback problem lies in having a tutor or teacher aide for every couple of students. Others argue that adequate student feedback will require an increased use of computer technology. However, there are less expensive alternatives. First, answer keys for students should be more plentiful. Resource books containing review and study activities should be available in every subject area, and each should be accompanied by a key that is available to students.

Second, quizzes and other instructional activities, especially those that supplement basic textbooks, should be prepared with "latent image" processing. With latent image paper and pens, a student who marks a response to an item can watch a hidden symbol emerge. The symbol signals either a correct or incorrect response, and in some instances a clue or explanation for the response is revealed. Trivia and puzzle books equipped with this latent image, immediate feedback process are currently being marketed at the price of comic books.

Of course, immediate informational feedback is more difficult to provide for composition work, long-term projects, and field assignments. But this does not justify the absence of immediate feedback on the learning activities and practice exercises that are aimed at teaching concepts, relationships, and basic skills. The mere availability of answer keys and latent image materials would probably elicit an amazing amount of self-regulated learning on the part of many students.

Moderate Risk Taking Is a Tonic for Achievement

A fourth motivational research finding is that moderate risk taking increases performance, persistence, perceived competence, self-knowledge, pride, and satisfaction (Deci and Porac 1978, Harter 1978,

Trope 1979). Moderate risk taking implies a well-considered choice of an optimally challenging task, willingness to accept a moderate probability of success, and the anticipation of an outcome. It is this combination of events (which includes moderate success, self-regulated learning, and feedback) that captivates the attention, interest, and energy of card players, athletes, financial investors, lottery players, and even juvenile video arcade addicts.

Risk takers continually and freely face the probability of failing to attain the pleasure of succeeding under specified odds. From every risk-taking endeavor—whether it ends in failure or success—risk takers learn something about their skill and choice of strategy, and what they learn usually prompts them to seek another risk-taking opportunity. Risk taking—especially moderate risk taking—is a mind-engaging activity that simultaneously consumes and generates energy. It is a habit that feeds itself and thus requires an unlimited supply of risk-taking opportunities.

Moderate risk taking is likely to occur under the following conditions.

- The success probability for each alternative is clear and unambiguous.
- Imposed external constraints are minimized.
- Variable payoff (the value of success increases as risk increases) in contrast to fixed payoff is available.
- The benefits of risk taking can be anticipated.

My own recent research on academic risk taking with grade school, high school, and college students generally supports these conclusions. Students do, in fact, freely choose more difficult problems (a) when the number of points offered increases with the difficulty level of problems, (b) when the risk-taking task is presented within a game or practice situation (i.e., imposed constraint or threat is minimized), and (c) when additional opportunities for risk taking are anticipated (relatively high risk taking will occur on a practice exercise when students know they will be able to apply the information learned to an upcoming test). In the absence of these conditions we have seen students choose tasks that are as much as one-and-a-half years

below their achievement level (Clifford 1988). Finally, students who take moderately high risks express high task interest even though they experience considerable error making.

In summary, risk-taking opportunities for students should be (a) plentiful, (b) readily available, (c) accompanied by explicit information about success probabilities, (d) accompanied by immediate feedback that communicates competency and error information, (e) associated with payoffs that vary with task difficulty, (f) relatively free from externally imposed evaluation, and (g) presented in relaxing and nonthreatening environments.

In today's educational world, however, there are few opportunities for students to engage in academic risk taking and no incentives to do so. Choices are seldom provided within tests or assignments, and rarely are variable payoffs made available. Once again, motivational theory, which identifies risk taking as a powerful source of knowledge, motivation, and skill development, conflicts with educational practice, which seeks to minimize academic risk at all costs.

We must restructure materials and procedures to encourage moderate academic risk taking on the part of students. I predict that if we fill our classrooms with optional academic risk-taking materials and opportunities so that all students have access to moderate risks, we will not only lower our educational suicide rate, but we will raise our level of academic achievement. If we give students the license to take risks and make errors, they will likely experience genuine success and the satisfaction that accompanies it.

Using Risk Can Ensure Success

Both theory and research evidence lead to the prediction that academic risk-taking activities are a powerful means of increasing the success of our educational efforts. But how do we get students to take risks on school-related activities? Students will choose risk over certainty when the consequences of the former are more satisfying and informative. Three basic conditions are needed to ensure such outcomes.

- First, students must be allowed to freely select from materials and activities that vary in difficulty and probability of success.
- Second, as task difficulty increases, so too must the payoffs for success.
- Third, an environment tolerant of error making and supportive of error correction must be guaranteed.

The first two conditions can be met rather easily. For example, on a 10-point quiz, composed of six 1-point items and four 2-point items, students might be asked to select and work only 6 items. The highest possible score for such quizzes is 10 and can be obtained only by correctly answering the four 2-point items and any two 1-point items. Choice and variable payoff are easily built into quizzes and many instructional and evaluation activities.

The third condition, creating an environment tolerant of error making and supportive of error correction, is more difficult to ensure. But here are six specific suggestions.

First, teachers must make a clear distinction between formative evaluation activities (tasks that guide instruction during the learning process) and summative evaluation activities (tasks used to judge one's level of achievement and to determine one's grade at the completion of the learning activity). Practice exercises, quizzes, and skill-building activities aimed at acquiring and strengthening knowledge and skills exemplify formative evaluation. These activities promote learning and skill development. They should be scored in a manner that excludes ability judgments, emphasizes error detection and correction, and encourages a search for better learning strategies. Formative evaluation activities should generally provide immediate feedback and be scored by students. It is on these activities that moderate risk taking is to be encouraged and is likely to prove beneficial.

Major examinations (unit exams and comprehensive final exams) exemplify summative evaluation; these activities are used to determine course grades. Relatively low risk taking is to be expected on such tasks, and immediate feedback may or may not be desirable.

Second, formative evaluation activities should be far more plentiful than summative. If, in fact, learning rather than grading is the primary object of the school, the percentage of time spent on summative evaluation should be small in comparison to that spent on formative evaluation (perhaps about 1:4). There should be enough formative evaluation activities presented as risk-taking opportunities to satisfy the most enthusiastic and adventuresome learner. The more plentiful these activities are, the less anxiety-producing and aversive summative activities are likely to be.

Third, formative evaluation activities should be presented as optional; students should be enticed, not mandated, to complete these activities. Enticement might be achieved by (a) ensuring that these activities are course-relevant and varied (e.g., scrambled outlines, incomplete matrices and graphs, exercises that require error detection and correction, quizzes); (b) giving students the option of working together; (c) presenting risk-taking activities in the context of games to be played individually, with competitors, or with partners; (d) providing immediate, informational, nonthreatening feedback; and (e) defining success primarily in terms of improvement over previous performance or the amount of learning that occurs during the risk-taking activity.

Fourth, for every instructional and evaluation activity there should be at least a modest percentage of content (10 percent to 20 percent) that poses a challenge to even the best students completing the activity. Maximum development of a country's talent requires that *all* individuals (a) find challenge in tasks they attempt, (b) develop tolerance for error making, and (c) learn to adjust strategies when faced with failure. To deprive the most talented students of these opportunities is perhaps the greatest resource-development crime a country can commit.

Fifth, summative evaluation procedures should include "retake exams." Second chances will not only encourage risk taking but will provide good reasons for students to study their incorrect responses made on previous risk-taking tasks. Every error made on an initial exam and subsequently corrected on a second chance represents real learning.

Sixth, we must reinforce moderate academic risk taking instead of error-free performance or excessively high or low risk taking. Improvement scores, voluntary correction of errors, completion of optional risk-taking activities—these are behaviors that teachers should recognize and encourage.

Toward a New Definition of Success

We face the grim reality that our extraordinary efforts to produce "schools without failure" have not yielded the well-adjusted, enthusiastic, self-confident scholars we anticipated. Our efforts to mass-produce success for every individual in every educational situation have left us with cheap reproductions of success that do not even faintly represent the real thing. This overdose of synthetic success is a primary cause of the student apathy and school abandonment plaguing our country.

To turn the trend around, we must emphasize error tolerance, not error-free learning; reward error correction, not error avoidance; ensure challenge, not easy success. Eventual success on challenging tasks, tolerance for error making, and constructive responses to failure are motivational fare that school systems should be serving up to all students. I suggest that we engage the skills of researchers, textbook authors, publishers, and educators across the country to ensure the development and marketing of attractive and effective academic risk-taking materials and procedures. If we convince these experts of the need to employ their creative efforts toward this end, we will not only stem the tide of educational suicide, but we will enhance the quality of educational success. We will witness self-regulated student success and satisfaction that will ensure the intellectual, creative, and motivational well-being of our country.

References

Atkinson, J. W. (1964). *An Introduction to Motivation.* Princeton, N.J.: Van Nostrand.

Boggiano, A. K., and D. S. Main. (1986). "Enhancing Children's Interest in Activities Used as Rewards: The Bonus Effect." *Journal of Personality and Social Psychology* 51: 1116–1126.

Clifford, M. M. (1988). "Failure Tolerance and Academic Risk Taking in Ten- to Twelve-Year-Old Students." *British Journal of Educational Psychology* 58: 15–27.

Csikszentmihalyi, M. (1975). *Beyond Boredom and Anxiety.* San Francisco: Jossey-Bass.

Csikszentmihalyi, M. (1978). "Intrinsic Rewards and Emergent Motivation." In *The Hidden Costs of Reward,* edited by M. R. Lepper and D. Greene. Hillsdale, N.J.: Lawrence Erlbaum Associates.

Danner, F. W., and D. Lonky. (1981). "A Cognitive-Developmental Approach to the Effects of Rewards on Intrinsic Motivation." *Child Development* 52: 1043–1052.

Deci, E. L., and J. Porac. (1978). "Cognitive Evaluation Theory and the Study of Human Motivation." In *The Hidden Costs of Reward,* edited by M. R. Lepper and D. Greene. Hillsdale, N.J.: Lawrence Erlbaum Associates.

Deci, E. L., and R. M. Ryan. (1987). "The Support of Autonomy and the Control of Behavior." *Journal of Personality and Social Psychology* 53: 1024–1037.

Fischer, K. W. (1980). "Learning as the Development of Organized Behavior." *Journal of Structural Learning* 3: 253–267.

Hahn, A. (1987). "Reaching Out to America's Drop-outs: What to Do?" *Phi Delta Kappan* 69: 256–263.

Harter, S. (1978). "Effective Motivation Reconsidered: Toward a Developmental Model." *Human Development* 1: 34–64.

Ilgen, D. R., and C. F. Moore. (1987). "Types and Choices of Performance Feedback." *Journal of Applied Psychology* 72: 401–406.

Ilgen, D. R., C. D. Fischer, and M. S. Taylor. (1979). "Consequences of Individual Feedback on Behavior in Organizations." *Journal of Applied Psychology* 64: 349–371.

Kruglanski, A., C. Stein, and A. Riter. (1977). "Contingencies of Exogenous Reward and Task Performance: On the 'Minimax' Strategy in Instrumental Behavior." *Journal of Applied Social Psychology* 2: 141–148.

Larson, J. R., Jr. (1984). "The Performance Feedback Process: A Preliminary Model." *Organizational Behavior and Human Performance* 33: 42–76.

Lepper, M. R., and D. Greene. (1978). *The Hidden Costs of Reward.* Hillsdale, N.J.: Lawrence Erlbaum Associates.

Lepper, M. R., and M. Hodell. (1989). "Intrinsic Motivation in the Classroom." In *Motivation in Education, Vol. 3,* edited by C. Ames and R. Ames. New York: Academic Press.

Sansone, C. (1986). "A Question of Competence: The Effects of Competence and Task Feedback on Intrinsic Motivation." *Journal of Personality and Social Psychology* 51: 918–931.

Trope, Y. (1979). "Uncertainty Reducing Properties of Achievement Tasks." *Journal of Personality and Social Psychology* 37: 1505–1518.

POSTNOTE

In the 1980s, educators and their many critics recognized that our schools were failing many of our students and that our students were failing many of our schools. An avalanche of reports, books, television specials, and columns lambasted the schools' performance. In response, standards have been raised, graduation requirements increased, and more rigorous courses of study implemented.

However, as an old adage says, "You can lead a horse to water, but you can't make it drink." Vast numbers of students still commit "educational suicide," and student apathy, indifference, and underachievement are widespread. Margaret Clifford's remedy first takes a realistic look at the mismatch between the student and the school and then suggests quite tangible modifications to match the student's motivational system with the goals of schooling.

DISCUSSION QUESTIONS

1. This article pinpoints student motivation as a major source of school problems. Do you agree with this assessment? Why or why not?

2. What are the most important remedies Clifford offers for our schools' ills? In your judgment, will these remedies solve the problem?

3. What is the author's new definition of *success*? Do you agree with it? Why or why not?

RELATED WEBSITE RESOURCES

WEB RESOURCES:

Center for Teaching at Vanderbilt University. Available at:

http://cft.vanderbilt.edu/teaching-guides/interactions/motivating-students/.

Although targeted for university teachers, the theories and strategies are also applicable for elementary and secondary schools.

Center for Research on Learning and Teaching. Available at:

http://www.crlt.umich.edu/tstrategies/tsms.php.

This particular website has links to other websites dealing with teaching strategies for motivating students.

The Key to Classroom Management

Robert J. Marzano and Jana S. Marzano

Robert J. Marzano, PhD, is cofounder and CEO of Marzano Research Laboratory in Englewood, Colorado. He is a speaker, trainer, and author of more than 30 books and 150 articles on topics such as instruction, assessment, writing and implementing standards, cognition, effective leadership, and school intervention.

Jana S. Marzano is a licensed professional counselor in private practice in Greenwood, Colorado.

"The Key to Classroom Management," by Robert J. Marzano and Jana S. Marzano, 2003, *Educational Leadership 61*(1), pp. 6–13. © 2003 by ASCD. Reprinted with permission. Learn more about ASCD at www.ascd.org.

Today, we know more about teaching than we ever have before. Research has shown us that teachers' actions in their classrooms have twice the impact on student achievement as do school policies regarding curriculum, assessment, staff collegiality, and community involvement (Marzano, 2003a). We also know that one of the classroom teacher's most important jobs is managing the classroom effectively.

A comprehensive literature review by Wang, Haertel, and Walberg (1993) amply demonstrates the importance of effective classroom management. These researchers analyzed 86 chapters from annual research reviews, 44 handbook chapters, 20 government and commissioned reports, and 11 journal articles to produce a list of 228 variables affecting student achievement. They combined the results of these analyses with the findings from 134 separate meta-analyses. Of all the variables, classroom management had the largest effect on student achievement. This makes intuitive sense—students cannot learn in a chaotic, poorly managed classroom.

Research not only supports the importance of classroom management, but it also sheds light on the dynamics of classroom management. Stage and Quiroz's meta-analysis (1997) shows the importance of there being a balance between teacher actions that provide clear consequences for unacceptable behavior and teacher actions that recognize and reward acceptable behavior. Other researchers (Emmer, Evertson, & Worsham, 2003; Evertson, Emmer, & Worsham, 2003) have identified important components of classroom management, including beginning the school year with a positive emphasis on management; arranging the room in a way conducive to effective management; and identifying and implementing rules and operating procedures.

In a recent meta-analysis of more than 100 studies (Marzano, 2003b), we found that the quality of teacher-student relationships is the keystone for all other aspects of classroom management. In fact, our meta-analysis indicates that on average, teachers who had high-quality relationships with their

FOCUS QUESTION

As you read this article, note the teacher behaviors that establish effective teacher-student relationships—a key for effective classroom management and student achievement.

InTASC

Standards 1, 2, 3, 4, 5, 7, 8, and 9

KEY TERMS

- Assertive behavior
- Dominance

students had 31 percent fewer discipline problems, rule violations, and related problems over a year's time than did teachers who did not have high-quality relationships with their students.

What are the characteristics of effective teacher-student relationships? Let's first consider what they are not. Effective teacher-student relationships have nothing to do with the teacher's personality or even with whether the students view the teacher as a friend. Rather, the most effective teacher-student relationships are characterized by specific teacher behaviors: exhibiting appropriate levels of dominance; exhibiting appropriate levels of cooperation; and being aware of high-needs students.

Appropriate Levels of Dominance

Wubbels and his colleagues (Wubbels, Brekelmans, van Tartwijk, & Admiral, 1999; Wubbels & Levy, 1993) identify appropriate dominance as an important characteristic of effective teacher-student relationships. In contrast to the more negative connotation of the term *dominance* as forceful control or command over others, they define dominance as the teacher's ability to provide clear purpose and strong guidance regarding both academics and student behavior. Studies indicate that when asked about their preferences for teacher behavior, students typically express a desire for this type of teacher-student interaction. For example, in a study that involved interviews with more than 700 students in grades 4–7, students articulated a clear preference for strong teacher guidance and control rather than more permissive types of teacher behavior (Chiu & Tulley, 1997). Teachers can exhibit appropriate dominance by establishing clear behavior expectations and learning goals and by exhibiting assertive behavior.

Establish Clear Expectations and Consequences

Teachers can establish clear expectations for behavior in two ways: by establishing clear rules and procedures, and by providing consequences for student behavior.

The seminal research of the 1980s (Emmer, 1984; Emmer, Sanford, Evertson, Clements, & Martin, 1981; Evertson & Emmer, 1982) points to the importance of establishing rules and procedures for general classroom behavior, group work, seat work, transitions and interruptions, use of materials and equipment, and beginning and ending the period or the day. Ideally, the class should establish these rules and procedures through discussion and mutual consent by teacher and students (Glasser, 1969, 1990).

Along with well-designed and clearly communicated rules and procedures, the teacher must acknowledge students' behavior, reinforcing acceptable behavior and providing negative consequences for unacceptable behavior. Stage and Quiroz's research (1997) is instructive. They found that teachers build effective relationships through such strategies as the following:

- Using a wide variety of verbal and physical reactions to students' misbehavior, such as moving closer to offending students and using a physical cue, such as a finger to the lips, to point out inappropriate behavior.
- Cuing the class about expected behaviors through prearranged signals, such as raising a hand to indicate that all students should take their seats.
- Providing tangible recognition of appropriate behavior—with tokens or chits, for example.
- Employing group contingency policies that hold the entire group responsible for behavioral expectations.
- Employing home contingency techniques that involve rewards and sanctions at home.

Establish Clear Learning Goals

Teachers can also exhibit appropriate levels of dominance by providing clarity about the content and expectations of an upcoming instructional unit. Important teacher actions to achieve this end include

- Establishing and communicating learning goals at the beginning of a unit of instruction.
- Providing feedback on those goals.

- Continually and systematically revisiting the goals.
- Providing summative feedback regarding the goals.

The use of rubrics can help teachers establish clear goals. To illustrate, assume that a teacher has identified the learning goal "understanding and using fractions" as important for a given unit. That teacher might present students with the following rubric:

4 points. You understand the characteristics of fractions along with the different types. You can accurately describe how fractions are related to decimals and percentages. You can convert fractions to decimals and can explain how and why the process works. You can use fractions to understand and solve different types of problems.

3 points. You understand the basic characteristics of fractions. You know how fractions are related to decimals and percentages. You can convert fractions to decimals.

2 points. You have a basic understanding of the following, but have some small misunderstandings about one or more: the characteristics of fractions; the relationships among fractions, decimals, and percentages; how to convert fractions to decimals.

1 point. You have some major problems or misunderstandings with one or more of the following: the characteristics of fractions; the relationships among fractions, decimals, and percentages; how to convert fractions to decimals.

0 points. You may have heard of the following before, but you do not understand what they mean: the characteristics of fractions; the relationships among fractions, decimals, and percentages; how to convert fractions to decimals.

The clarity of purpose provided by this rubric communicates to students that their teacher can provide proper guidance and direction in academic content.

Exhibit Assertive Behavior

Teachers can also communicate appropriate levels of dominance by exhibiting assertive behavior. According to Emmer and colleagues, assertive behavior is

the ability to stand up for one's legitimate rights in ways that make it less likely that others will ignore or circumvent them. (2003, p. 146)

Assertive behavior differs significantly from both passive behavior and aggressive behavior. These researchers explain that teachers display assertive behavior in the classroom when they

- Use assertive body language by maintaining an erect posture, facing the offending student but keeping enough distance so as not to appear threatening and matching the facial expression with the content of the message being presented to students.
- Use an appropriate tone of voice, speaking clearly and deliberately in a pitch that is slightly but not greatly elevated from normal classroom speech, avoiding any display of emotions in the voice.
- Persist until students respond with the appropriate behavior. Do not ignore an inappropriate behavior; do not be diverted by a student denying, arguing, or blaming, but listen to legitimate explanations.

Appropriate Levels of Cooperation

Cooperation is characterized by a concern for the needs and opinions of others. Although not the antithesis of dominance, cooperation certainly occupies a different realm. Whereas dominance focuses on the teacher as the driving force in the classroom, cooperation focuses on the students and teacher functioning as a team. The interaction of these two dynamics—dominance and cooperation—is a central force in effective teacher-student relationships. Several strategies can foster appropriate levels of cooperation.

Provide Flexible Learning Goals

Just as teachers can communicate appropriate levels of dominance by providing clear learning goals, they can also convey appropriate levels of cooperation by providing flexible learning goals. Giving students the opportunity to set their own objectives at the beginning of a unit or asking students what they would like to learn conveys a sense of cooperation. Assume, for example, that a teacher has identified the topic of fractions as the focus of a unit of instruction and has provided students with a rubric. The teacher could then ask students to identify some aspect of fractions or a related topic that they would particularly like to study. Giving students this kind of choice, in addition to increasing their understanding of the topic, conveys the message that the teacher cares about and tries to accommodate students' interests.

Take a Personal Interest in Students

Probably the most obvious way to communicate appropriate levels of cooperation is to take a personal interest in each student in the class. As McCombs and Whisler (1997) note, all students appreciate personal attention from the teacher. Although busy teachers—particularly those at the secondary level—do not have the time for extensive interaction with all students, some teacher actions can communicate personal interest and concern without taking up much time. Teachers can

- Talk informally with students before, during, and after class about their interests.
- Greet students outside of school—for instance, at extracurricular events or at the store.
- Single out a few students each day in the lunchroom and talk with them.
- Be aware of and comment on important events in students' lives, such as participation in sports, drama, or other extracurricular activities.
- Compliment students on important achievements in and outside of school.
- Meet students at the door as they come into class; greet each one by name.

Use Equitable and Positive Classroom Behaviors

Programs like Teacher Expectations and Student Achievement emphasize the importance of the subtle ways in which teachers can communicate their interest in students (Kerman, Kimball, & Martin, 1980). This program recommends many practical strategies that emphasize equitable and positive classroom interactions with all students. Teachers should, for example,

- Make eye contact with each student. Teachers can make eye contact by scanning the entire room as they speak and by freely moving about all sections of the room.
- Deliberately move toward and stand close to each student during the class period. Make sure that the seating arrangement allows the teacher and students clear and easy ways to move around the room.
- Attribute the ownership of ideas to the students who initiated them. For instance, in a discussion a teacher might say, "Cecilia just added to Aida's idea by saying that...."
- Allow and encourage all students to participate in class discussions and interactions. Make sure to call on students who do not commonly participate, not just those who respond most frequently.
- Provide appropriate wait time for all students to respond to questions, regardless of their past performance or your perception of their abilities.

Awareness of High-Needs Students

Classroom teachers meet daily with a broad cross-section of students. In general, 12–22 percent of all students in school suffer from mental, emotional, or behavioral disorders, and relatively few receive mental health services (Adelman & Taylor, 2002). The Association of School Counselors notes that 18 percent of students have special needs and require extraordinary interventions and treatments that go beyond the typical resources available to the classroom (Dunn & Baker, 2002).

Although the classroom teacher is certainly not in a position to directly address such severe problems, teachers with effective classroom management skills are aware of high-needs students and have a repertoire of specific techniques for meeting some of their needs (Marzano, 2003b). Table 1 summarizes five categories of high-needs students and suggests classroom strategies for each category and subcategory.

- *Passive* students fall into two subcategories: those who fear *relationships* and those who fear *failure*. Teachers can build strong relationships with these students by refraining from criticism, rewarding small successes, and creating a classroom climate in which students feel safe from aggressive people.
- The category of *aggressive* students comprises three subcategories: *hostile, oppositional,* and *covert.* Hostile students often have poor anger control, low capacity for empathy, and an inability to see the consequences of their actions. Oppositional students exhibit milder forms of

TABLE 1   **Categories of High-Needs Students**

CATEGORY	DEFINITIONS & SOURCE	CHARACTERISTICS	SUGGESTIONS
Suggestion	Behavior that avoids the domination of others or the pain of negative experiences. The child attempts to protect self from criticism, ridicule, or rejection, possibly reacting to abuse and neglect. Can have a biochemical basis, such as anxiety.	**Fear of relationships:** Avoids connection with others, is shy, doesn't initiate conversations, attempts to be invisible. **Fear of failure:** Gives up easily, is convinced he or she can't succeed, is easily frustrated, uses negative self-talk.	Provide safe adult and peer interactions and protection from aggressive people. Provide assertiveness and positive self-talk training. Reward small successes quickly. Withhold criticism.
Aggressive	Behavior that overpowers, dominates, harms, or controls others without regard for their well-being. The child has often taken aggressive people as role models. Has had minimal or ineffective limits set on behavior. Is possibly reacting to abuse and neglect. Condition may have a biochemical basis, such as depression.	**Hostile:** Rages, threatens, or intimidates others. Can be verbally or physically abusive to people, animals, or objects. **Oppositional:** Does opposite of what is asked. Demands that others agree or give in. Resists verbally or nonverbally. **Covert:** Appears to agree but then does the opposite of what is asked. Often acts innocent while setting up problems for others.	Describe the student's behavior clearly. Contract with the student to reward corrected behavior and set up consequences for uncorrected behavior. Be consistent and provide immediate rewards and consequences. Encourage and acknowledge extracurricular activities in and out of school. Give student responsibilities to help teacher or other students to foster successful experiences.

(continued)

TABLE 1　(Continued)

CATEGORY	DEFINITIONS & SOURCE	CHARACTERISTICS	SUGGESTIONS
Attention problems	Behavior that demonstrates either motor or attentional difficulties resulting from a neurological disorder. The child's symptoms may be exacerbated by family or social stressors or biochemical conditions, such as anxiety, depression, or bipolar disorders.	**Hyperactive:** Has difficulty with motor control, both physically and verbally. Fidgets, leaves seat frequently, interrupts, talks excessively. **Inattentive:** Has difficulty staying focused and following through on projects. Has difficulty with listening, remembering, and organizing.	Contract with the student to manage behaviors. Teach basic concentration, study, and thinking skills. Separate student in a quiet work area. Help the student list each step of a task. Reward successes; assign a peer tutor.
Perfectionist	Behavior that is geared toward avoiding the embarrassment and assumed shame of making mistakes. The child fears what will happen if errors are discovered. Has unrealistically high expectations of self. Has possibly received criticism or lack of acceptance while making mistakes during the process of learning.	Tends to focus too much on the small details of projects. Will avoid projects if unsure of outcome. Focuses on results and not relationships. Is self-critical.	Ask the student to make mistakes on purpose, then show acceptance. Have the student tutor other students.
Socially inept	Behavior that is based on the misinterpretation of nonverbal signals of others. The child misunderstands facial expressions and body language. Hasn't received adequate training in these areas and has poor role modeling.	Attempts to make friends but is inept and unsuccessful. Is forced to be alone. Is often teased for unusual behavior, appearance, or lack of social skills.	Teach the student to keep the appropriate physical distance from others. Teach the meaning of facial expressions, such as anger and hurt. Make suggestions regarding hygiene, dress, mannerisms, and posture.

Source: Marzano, R. J. (2003). *What works in schools: Translating research into action* (pp. 104–105). Alexandria, VA: ASCD.

behavior problems, but they consistently resist following rules, argue with adults, use harsh language, and tend to annoy others. Students in the covert subcategory may be quite pleasant at times, but they are often nearby when trouble starts and they never quite do what authority figures ask of them. Strategies for helping aggressive students include creating behavior contracts and providing immediate rewards and consequences. Most of all, teachers must keep in mind that aggressive students, although they may appear highly resistant to behavior change, are still children who are experiencing a significant amount of fear and pain.

- Students with *attention* problems fall into two categories: *hyperactive* and *inattentive*. These students may respond well when teachers contract with them to manage behaviors; teach them basic concentration, study, and thinking skills; help them divide tasks into manageable parts; reward their successes; and assign them a peer tutor.
- Students in the *perfectionist* category are driven to succeed at unattainable levels. They are self-critical, have low self-esteem, and feel inferior. Teachers can often help these students by encouraging them to develop more realistic standards, helping them to accept mistakes, and giving them opportunities to tutor other students.
- *Socially inept* students have difficulty making and keeping friends. They may stand too close and touch others in annoying ways, talk too much, and misread others' comments. Teachers can help these students by counseling them about social behaviors.

School may be the only place where many students who face extreme challenges can get their needs addressed. The reality of today's schools often demands that classroom teachers address these severe issues, even though this task is not always considered a part of their regular job.

In a study of classroom strategies (see Brophy, 1996; Brophy & McCaslin, 1992), researchers examined how effective classroom teachers interacted with specific types of students. The study found that the most effective classroom managers did not treat all students the same; they tended to employ different strategies with different types of students. In contrast, ineffective classroom managers did not appear sensitive to the diverse needs of students. Although Brophy did not couch his findings in terms of teacher–student relationships, the link is clear. An awareness of the five general categories of high-needs students and appropriate actions for each can help teachers build strong relationships with diverse students.

Don't Leave Relationships to Chance

Teacher-student relationships provide an essential foundation for effective classroom management—and classroom management is a key to high student achievement. Teacher-student relationships should not be left to chance or dictated by the personalities of those involved. Instead, by using strategies supported by research, teachers can influence the dynamics of their classrooms and build strong teacher-student relationships that will support student learning.

References

Adelman, H. S., & Taylor, L. (2002). School counselors and school reform: New directions. *Professional School Counseling, 5*(4), 235–248.

Brophy, J. E. (1996). *Teaching problem students*. New York: Guilford.

Brophy, J. E., & McCaslin, N. (1992). Teachers' reports of how they perceive and cope with problem students. *Elementary School Journal, 93,* 3–68.

Chiu, L. H., & Tulley, M. (1997). Student preferences of teacher discipline styles. *Journal of Instructional Psychology, 24*(3), 168–175.

Dunn, N. A., & Baker, S. B. (2002). Readiness to serve students with disabilities: A survey of elementary school counselors. *Professional School Counselors, 5*(4), 277–284.

Emmer, E. T. (1984). *Classroom management: Research and implications.* (R & D Report No. 6178). Austin, TX: Research and Development Center for Teacher Education, University of Texas. (ERIC Document Reproduction Service No. ED251448)

Emmer, E. T., Evertson, C. M., & Worsham, M. E. (2003). *Classroom management for secondary teachers* (6th ed.). Boston: Allyn and Bacon.

Emmer, E. T., Sanford, J. P., Evertson, C. M., Clements, B. S., & Martin, J. (1981). *The classroom management improvement study: An experiment in elementary school classrooms.* (R & D Report No. 6050). Austin, TX: Research and Development Center for Teacher Education, University of Texas. (ERIC Document Reproduction Service No. ED226452)

Evertson, C. M., & Emmer, E. T. (1982). Preventive classroom management. In D. Duke (Ed.), *Helping teachers manage classrooms* (pp. 2–31). Alexandria, VA: ASCD.

Evertson, C. M., Emmer, E. T., & Worsham, M. E. (2003). *Classroom management for elementary teachers* (6th ed.). Boston: Allyn and Bacon.

Glasser, W. (1969). *Schools without failure.* New York: Harper and Row.

Glasser, W. (1990). *The quality school: Managing students without coercion.* New York: Harper and Row.

Kerman, S., Kimball, T., & Martin, M. (1980). *Teacher expectations and student achievement.* Bloomington, IN: Phi Delta Kappa.

Marzano, R. J. (2003a). *What works in schools.* Alexandria, VA: ASCD.

Marzano, R. J. (with Marzano, J. S., & Pickering, D. J.). (2003b). *Classroom management that works.* Alexandria, VA: ASCD.

McCombs, B. L., & Whisler, J. S. (1997). *The learner-centered classroom and school.* San Francisco: Jossey-Bass.

Stage, S. A., & Quiroz, D. R. (1997). A meta-analysis of interventions to decrease disruptive classroom behavior in public education settings. *School Psychology Review, 26*(3), 333–368.

Wang, M. C., Haertel, G. D., & Walberg, H. J. (1993). Toward a knowledge base for school learning. *Review of Educational Research, 63*(3), 249–294.

Wubbels, T., Brekelmans, M., van Tartwijk, J., & Admiral, W. (1999). Interpersonal relationships between teachers and students in the classroom. In H. C. Waxman & H. J. Walberg (Eds.), *New directions for teaching practice and research* (pp. 151–170). Berkeley, CA: McCutchan.

Wubbels, T., & Levy, J. (1993). *Do you know what you look like? Interpersonal relationships in education.* London: Falmer Press.

POSTNOTE

No issue is of greater concern to beginning teachers than classroom management. New teachers worry that they may not be effective because of their inability to maintain discipline. The authors point out that being an effective teacher is not a function of your personality or being a friend to students. Rather, establishing effective teacher-student relationships is the key to effective management and instruction, and the authors identify specific teacher behaviors that characterize effective relationships: appropriate levels of dominance, appropriate levels of cooperation, and awareness of high-needs students. Work on developing these behaviors, and you will experience greater success and fewer discipline problems. There are a number of excellent books, based on research, to guide you in becoming a good classroom manager, some of which are mentioned in the references of this article.

DISCUSSION QUESTIONS

1. Think of some teachers you have had who could not maintain discipline in their classrooms. What made them ineffective in managing the classroom?

2. Conversely, think of some teachers who were very effective in maintaining order and had good relations with students. What made them so effective?

3. Are there any points in the article with which you disagree? Are there other aspects to effective classroom management that you think should have been discussed? If so, what are they?

RELATED WEBSITE RESOURCES AND VIDEO CASES

WEB RESOURCES:

Education World. Available at:

http://educationworld.com/a_curr/archives/class management.shtml.

This website presents a range of information concerning classroom management, including a database of teacher resources.

Learning Network. Available at:

http://www.teachervision.fen.com/classroom-management/resource/5776.html.

This section of the website presents advice from experienced teachers and specialists regarding various aspects of behavior management.

 TEACHSOURCE VIDEO CASE

CLASSROOM MANAGEMENT: BEST PRACTICES

In this video case, several teachers discuss their rules and how they establish the classroom culture. Go to the website for the Education Media Library at CengageBrain.com to watch the video clips, study the artifacts in the case, and reflect on the following questions.

1. The first teacher emphasizes the length of time it takes for students to understand classroom rules and procedures. Were you surprised by her time estimate? How long do you think it will take your students to internalize rules and procedures?

2. How will you establish a feeling of "community" in your classes?

 TEACHSOURCE VIDEO CASE

CLASSROOM MANAGEMENT: HANDLING A STUDENT WITH BEHAVIOR PROBLEMS

This video case shows two teachers working with a student support coach to design strategies and interventions to cope with a particular student's disruptive behavior. Go to the website for the Education Media Library at CengageBrain.com to watch the video clips, study the artifacts in the case, and reflect on the following questions.

1. The support coach mentions the importance of helping students feel a sense of belonging. What are some ways you hope to help your students feel they belong?

2. The support coach also mentions the importance of noticing and appreciating students. What are some specific ways in which you might be able to notice your students?

Seven Practices for Effective Learning

Jay McTighe and Ken O'Connor

Jay McTighe is an education consultant who has held a variety of positions in Maryland, including having served as the director of the Maryland Assessment Consortium. **Ken O'Connor** is an educational consultant who was formerly the Curriculum Coordinator with the Toronto District School Board in Ontario, Canada.

"Seven Practices for Effective Learning," by Jay McTighe and Ken O'Connor, 2005, *Educational Leadership 63*(3), pp. 10–17. © 2005 by ASCD. Reprinted with permission. Learn more about ASCD at www.ascd.org.

FOCUS QUESTION

When assessing students, what information do you need and what will you do with it?

InTASC
Standards 1, 2, 3, 6, 7, and 8

KEY TERMS

- Benchmarks
- Diagnostic assessment
- Feedback
- Formative assessment
- Performance assessment
- Rubric
- Summative assessment

Classroom assessment and grading practices have the potential not only to measure and report learning but also to promote it. Indeed, recent research has documented the benefits of regular use of diagnostic and formative assessments as feedback for learning (Black, Harrison, Lee, Marshall, & Wiliam, 2004). Like successful athletic coaches, the best teachers recognize the importance of ongoing assessments and continual adjustments on the part of both teacher and student as the means to achieve maximum performance. Unlike the external standardized tests that feature so prominently on the school landscape these days, well-designed classroom assessment and grading practices can provide the kind of specific, personalized, and timely information needed to guide both learning and teaching.

Classroom assessments fall into three categories, each serving a different purpose. *Summative* assessments summarize what students have learned at the conclusion of an instructional segment. These assessments tend to be evaluative, and teachers typically encapsulate and report assessment results as a score or a grade. Familiar examples of summative assessments include tests, performance tasks, final exams, culminating projects, and work portfolios. Evaluative assessments command the attention of students and parents because their results typically "count" and appear on report cards and transcripts. But by themselves, summative assessments are insufficient tools for maximizing learning. Waiting until the end of a teaching period to find out how well students have learned is simply too late.

Two other classroom assessment categories—diagnostic and formative—provide fuel for the teaching and learning engine by offering descriptive feedback along the way. *Diagnostic* assessments—sometimes known as *pre-assessments*—typically precede instruction. Teachers use them to check students' prior knowledge and skill levels, identify student misconceptions, profile learners' interests, and reveal learning-style preferences. Diagnostic assessments provide information to assist teacher planning and guide differentiated instruction. Examples of diagnostic assessments include prior knowledge and skill checks and interest or learning preference sur-veys. Because pre-assessments serve diagnostic pur-poses, teachers normally don't grade the results.

Formative assessments occur concurrently with instruction. These ongoing assessments provide spe-cific feedback to teachers and students for the pur-pose of guiding teaching to improve learning. Formative assessments include both formal and informal methods, such as ungraded quizzes, oral questioning, teacher observations, draft work, think-alouds, student-constructed concept maps, learning logs, and portfolio reviews. Although teach-ers may record the results of formative assessments, we shouldn't factor these results into summative evaluation and grading.

Keeping these three categories of classroom assessment in mind, let us consider seven specific assessment and grading practices that can enhance teaching and learning.

Practice 1: Use Summative Assessments to Frame Meaningful Performance Goals

On the first day of a three-week unit on nutrition, a middle school teacher describes to students the two summative assessments that she will use. One assess-ment is a multiple-choice test examining student knowledge of various nutrition facts and such basic skills as analyzing nutrition labels. The second assessment is an authentic performance task in which each student designs a menu plan for an upcoming two-day trip to an outdoor education facility. The menu plan must provide well-balanced and nutritious meals and snacks.

The current emphasis on established content standards has focused teaching on designated knowledge and skills. To avoid the danger of view-ing the standards and benchmarks as inert content to "cover," educators should frame the standards and benchmarks in terms of desired performances and ensure that the performances are as authentic as possible. Teachers should then present the summa-tive performance assessment tasks to students at the beginning of a new unit or course.

This practice has three virtues. First, the summative assessments clarify the targeted standards and benchmarks for teachers and learners. In standards-based education, the rubber meets the road with assessments because they define the evi-dence that will determine whether or not students have learned the content standards and benchmarks. The nutrition vignette is illustrative: By knowing what the culminating assessments will be, students are better able to focus on what the teachers expect them to learn (information about healthy eating) and on what they will be expected to do with that knowledge (develop a nutritious meal plan).

Second, the performance assessment tasks yield evidence that reveals understanding. When we call for authentic application, we do not mean recall of basic facts or mechanical plug-ins of a mem-orized formula. Rather, we want students to transfer knowledge—to use what they know in a new situa-tion. Teachers should set up realistic, authentic con-texts for assessment that enable students to apply their learning thoughtfully and flexibly, thereby demon-strating their understanding of the content standards.

Third, presenting the authentic performance tasks at the beginning of a new unit or course provides a meaningful learning goal for students. Consider a sports analogy. Coaches routinely con-duct practice drills that both develop basic skills and purposefully point toward performance in the game. Too often, classroom instruction and assessment overemphasize decontextualized drills and provide too few opportunities for students to actually "play the game." How many soccer players would practice corner kicks or run exhausting wind sprints if they weren't preparing for the upcoming game? How many competitive swimmers would log endless laps if there were no future swim meets? Authentic performance tasks provide a worthy goal and help learners see a reason for their learning.

Practice 2: Show Criteria and Models in Advance

A high school language arts teacher distributes a summary of the summative performance task that students will complete during the unit on research, including the rubric for judging the performance's quality. In addition, she shows examples of student work products collected from previous years (with student names removed) to illustrate criteria and performance levels. Throughout the unit, the teacher uses the student examples and the criteria in the rubric to help students better understand the nature of high-quality work and to support her teaching of research skills and report writing.

A second assessment practice that supports learning involves presenting evaluative criteria and models of work that illustrate different levels of quality. Unlike selected-response or short-answer tests, authentic performance assessments are typically open-ended and do not yield a single, correct answer or solution process. Consequently, teachers cannot score student responses using an answer key or a Scantron machine. They need to evaluate products and performances on the basis of explicitly defined performance criteria.

A rubric is a widely used evaluation tool consisting of criteria, a measurement scale (a 4-point scale, for example), and descriptions of the characteristics for each score point. Well-developed rubrics communicate the important dimensions, or elements of quality, in a product or performance and guide educators in evaluating student work. When a department or grade-level team—or better yet, an entire school or district—uses common rubrics, evaluation results are more consistent because the performance criteria don't vary from teacher to teacher or from school to school.

Rubrics also benefit students. When students know the criteria in advance of their performance, they have clear goals for their work. Because well-defined criteria provide a clear description of quality performance, students don't need to guess what is most important or how teachers will judge their work.

Providing a rubric to students in advance of the assessment is a necessary, but often insufficient, condition to support their learning. Although experienced teachers have a clear conception of what they mean by "quality work," students don't necessarily have the same understanding. Learners are more likely to understand feedback and evaluations when teachers show several examples that display both excellent and weak work. These models help translate the rubric's abstract language into more specific, concrete, and understandable terms.

Some teachers express concern that students will simply copy or imitate the example. A related worry is that showing an excellent model (sometimes known as an exemplar) will stultify student creativity. We have found that providing multiple models helps avoid these potential problems. When students see several exemplars showing how different students achieved high-level performance in unique ways, they are less likely to follow a cookie-cutter approach. In addition, when students study and compare examples ranging in quality—from very strong to very weak—they are better able to internalize the differences. The models enable students to more accurately self-assess and improve their work before turning it in to the teacher.

Practice 3: Assess Before Teaching

Before beginning instruction on the five senses, a kindergarten teacher asks each student to draw a picture of the body parts related to the various senses and show what each part does. She models the process by drawing an eye on the chalkboard. "The eye helps us see things around us," she points out. As students draw, the teacher circulates around the room, stopping to ask clarifying questions ("I see you've drawn a nose. What does the nose help us do?"). On the basis of what she learns about her students from this diagnostic pre-test, she divides the class into two groups for differentiated instruction. At the conclusion of the unit, the teacher asks students to do another drawing, which she collects and compares with their original pre-test as evidence of their learning.

Diagnostic assessment is as important to teaching as a physical exam is to prescribing an appropriate medical regimen. At the outset of any unit of study, certain students are likely to have already mastered some of the skills that the teacher is about to introduce, and others may already understand key concepts. Some students are likely to be deficient in prerequisite skills or harbor misconceptions. Armed with this diagnostic information, a teacher gains greater insight into *what to teach,* by knowing what skill gaps to address or by skipping material previously mastered; into *how to teach,* by using grouping options and initiating activities based on preferred learning styles and interests; and into *how to connect* the content to students' interests and talents.

Teachers can use a variety of practical pre-assessment strategies, including pre-tests of content knowledge, skills checks, concept maps, drawings, and K-W-L (*Know-Want* to learn-*Learn*) charts. Powerful pre-assessment has the potential to address a worrisome phenomenon reported in a growing body of literature (Bransford, Brown, & Cocking, 1999; Gardner, 1991): A sizeable number of students come into school with misconceptions about subject matter (thinking that a heavier object will drop faster than a lighter one, for example) and about themselves as learners (assuming that they can't and never will be able to draw, for example). If teachers don't identify and confront these misconceptions, they will persist even in the face of good teaching. To uncover existing misconceptions, teachers can use a short, nongraded true-false diagnostic quiz that includes several potential misconceptions related to the targeted learning. Student responses will signal any prevailing misconceptions, which the teacher can then address through instruction. In the future, the growing availability of portable, electronic student-response systems will enable educators to obtain this information instantaneously.

Practice 4: Offer Appropriate Choices

As part of a culminating assessment for a major unit on their state's history and geography, a class of 4th graders must contribute to a classroom museum display. The displays are designed to provide answers to the unit's essential question: How do geography, climate, and natural resources influence lifestyle, economy, and culture? Parents and students from other classrooms will view the display. Students have some choice about the specific products they will develop, which enables them to work to their strengths. Regardless of students' chosen products, the teacher uses a common rubric to evaluate every project. The resulting class museum contains a wide variety of unique and informative products that demonstrate learning.

Responsiveness in assessment is as important as it is in teaching. Students differ not only in how they prefer to take in and process information but also in how they best demonstrate their learning. Some students need to "do"; others thrive on oral explanations. Some students excel at creating visual representations; others are adept at writing. To make valid inferences about learning, teachers need to allow students to work to their strengths. A standardized approach to classroom assessment may be efficient, but it is not fair because any chosen format will favor some students and penalize others.

Assessment becomes responsive when students are given appropriate options for demonstrating knowledge, skills, and understanding. Allow choices—but always with the intent of collecting needed and appropriate evidence based on goals. In the example of the 4th grade museum display project, the teacher wants students to demonstrate their understanding of the relationship between geography and economy. This could be accomplished through a newspaper article, a concept web, a PowerPoint presentation, a comparison chart, or a simulated radio interview with an expert. Learners often put forth greater effort and produce higher-quality work when given such a variety of choices. The teacher will judge these products using a three-trait rubric that focuses on accuracy of content, clarity and thoroughness of explanation, and overall product quality.

We offer three cautions. First, teachers need to collect appropriate evidence of learning on the basis of goals rather than simply offer a "cool" menu of assessment choices. If a content standard calls for proficiency in written or oral presentations, it would be inappropriate to provide performance options other than those involving writing or speaking, except in the case of students for whom such goals are clearly inappropriate (a newly arrived English language learner, for example). Second, the options must be worth the time and energy required. It would be inefficient to have students develop an elaborate three-dimensional display or an animated PowerPoint presentation for content that a multiple-choice quiz could easily assess. In the folksy words of a teacher friend, "With performance assessments, the juice must be worth the squeeze." Third, teachers have only so much time and energy, so they must be judicious in determining when it is important to offer product and performance options. They need to strike a healthy balance between a single assessment path and a plethora of choices.

Practice 5: Provide Feedback Early and Often

Middle school students are learning watercolor painting techniques. The art teacher models proper technique for mixing and applying the colors, and the students begin working. As they paint, the teacher provides feedback both to individual students and to the class as a whole. She targets common mistakes, such as using too much paint and not enough water, a practice that reduces the desired transparency effect. Benefiting from continual feedback from the teacher, students experiment with the medium on small sheets of paper. The next class provides additional opportunities to apply various watercolor techniques to achieve such effects as color blending and soft edges. The class culminates in an informal peer feedback session. Skill development and refinement result from the combined effects of direct instruction, modeling, and opportunities to practice guided by ongoing feedback.

It is often said that feedback is the breakfast of champions. All kinds of learning, whether on the practice field or in the classroom, require feedback based on formative assessments. Ironically, the quality feedback necessary to enhance learning is limited or nonexistent in many classrooms.

To serve learning, feedback must meet four criteria: It must be timely, specific, understandable

to the receiver, and formed to allow for self-adjustment on the student's part (Wiggins, 1998). First, feedback on strengths and weaknesses needs to be prompt for the learner to improve. Waiting three weeks to find out how you did on a test will not help your learning.

In addition, specificity is key to helping students understand both their strengths and the areas in which they can improve. Too many educators consider grades and scores as feedback when, in fact, they fail the specificity test. Pinning a letter (B-) or a number (82%) on a student's work is no more helpful than such comments as "Nice job" or "You can do better." Although good grades and positive remarks may feel good, they do not advance learning.

Specific feedback sounds different, as in this example:

> Your research paper is generally well organized and contains a great deal of information on your topic. You used multiple sources and documented them correctly. However, your paper lacks a clear conclusion, and you never really answered your basic research question.

Sometimes the language in a rubric is lost on a student. Exactly what does "well organized" or "sophisticated reasoning" mean? "Kid language" rubrics can make feedback clearer and more comprehensible. For instance, instead of saying, "Document your reasoning process," a teacher might say, "Show your work in a step-by-step manner so the reader can see what you were thinking."

Here's a simple, straightforward test for a feedback system: Can learners tell *specifically* from the given feedback what they have done well and what they could do next time to improve? If not, then the feedback is not specific or understandable enough for the learner.

Finally, the learner needs opportunities to act on the feedback—to refine, revise, practice, and retry. Writers rarely compose a perfect manuscript on the first try, which is why the writing process stresses cycles of drafting, feedback, and revision as the route to excellence. Not surprisingly, the best feedback often surfaces in the performance-based subjects—such as art, music, and physical education—and in extra-curricular activities, such as band and athletics. Indeed, the essence of coaching involves ongoing assessment and feedback.

Practice 6: Encourage Self-Assessment and Goal Setting

Before turning in their science lab reports, students review their work against a list of explicit criteria. On the basis of their self-assessments, a number of students make revisions to improve their reports before handing them in. Their teacher observes that the overall quality of the lab reports has improved.

The most effective learners set personal learning goals, employ proven strategies, and self-assess their work. Teachers help cultivate such habits of mind by modeling self-assessment and goal setting and by expecting students to apply these habits regularly.

Rubrics can help students become more effective at honest self-appraisal and productive self-improvement. In the rubric in Figure 1, students verify that they have met a specific criterion—for a title, for example—by placing a check in the lower left-hand square of the applicable box. The teacher then uses the square on the right side for his

or her evaluation. Ideally, the two judgments should match. If not, the discrepancy raises an opportunity to discuss the criteria, expectations, and performance standards. Over time, teacher and student judgments tend to align. In fact, it is not unusual for students to be harder on themselves than the teacher is.

The rubric also includes space for feedback comments and student goals and action steps. Consequently, the rubric moves from being simply an evaluation tool for "pinning a number" on students to a practical and robust vehicle for feedback, self-assessment, and goal setting.

Initially, the teacher models how to self-assess, set goals, and plan improvements by asking such prompting questions as,

- What aspect of your work was most effective?
- What aspect of your work was least effective?
- What specific action or actions will improve your performance?
- What will you do differently next time?

Questions like these help focus student reflection and planning. Over time, students assume greater responsibility for enacting these processes independently.

FIGURE 1   Analytic Rubric for Graphic Display of Data

	Title	Labels	Accuracy	Neatness
3	The graph contains a title that clearly tells what the data show.	All parts of the graph (units of measurement, rows, etc.) are correctly labeled. ✓	All data are accurately represented on the graph. ✓✓	The graph is very neat and easy to read.
2	The graph contains a title that suggests what the data show.	Some parts of the graph are inaccurately labeled. ✓✓	Data representation contains minor errors.	The graph is generally neat and readable. ✓
1	The title does not reflect what the data show OR the title is missing. ✓	The graph is incorrectly labeled OR labels are missing. ✓	The data are inaccurately represented, contain major errors, OR are missing.	The graph is sloppy and difficult to read.

Comments: _____

Goals/Actions: _____

Source: Richard Ingersoll, cited in "No Dream Denied: A Pledge to America's Children," by the National Commission on Teaching and America's Future and the National Center for Education Statistics.

Educators who provide regular opportunities for learners to self-assess and set goals often report a change in the classroom culture. As one teacher put it,

> My students have shifted from asking, "What did I get?" or "What are you going to give me?" to becoming increasingly capable of knowing how they are doing and what they need to do to improve.

Practice 7: Allow New Evidence of Achievement to Replace Old Evidence

A driver education student fails his driving test the first time, but he immediately books an appointment to retake the test one week later. He passes on his second attempt because he successfully demonstrates the requisite knowledge and skills. The driving examiner does not average the first performance with the second, nor does the new license indicate that the driver "passed on the second attempt."

This vignette reveals an important principle in classroom assessment, grading, and reporting: New evidence of achievement should replace old evidence. Classroom assessments and grading should focus on *how well*—not on when—the student mastered the designated knowledge and skill.

Consider the learning curves of four students in terms of a specified learning goal (see Figure 2). Bob already possesses the targeted knowledge and skill and doesn't need instruction for this particular goal. Gwen arrives with substantial knowledge and skill but has room to improve. Roger and Pam are true novices who demonstrate a high level of achievement by the *end* of the instructional segment as a result of effective teaching and diligent learning. If their school's grading system truly documented learning, all these students would receive the same grade because they all achieved the desired results over time. Roger and Pam would receive lower grades than Bob and Gwen, however, if the teacher factored their earlier performances into the final evaluation. This practice, which is typical of the grading approach used in many classrooms, would misrepre-

FIGURE 2   Student Learning Curves

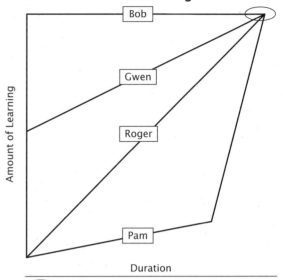

⬭ Represents several (2 or 3) pieces of evidence.

Source: Copyright © Ken O'Connor. Reprinted with permission.

sent Roger and Pam's ultimate success because it does not give appropriate recognition to the real—or most current—level of achievement.

Two concerns may arise when teachers provide students with multiple opportunities to demonstrate their learning. Students may not take the first attempt seriously once they realize they'll have a second chance. In addition, teachers often become overwhelmed by the logistical challenges of providing multiple opportunities. To make this approach effective, teachers need to require their students to provide some evidence of the corrective action they will take—such as engaging in peer coaching, revising their report, or practicing the needed skill in a given way—before embarking on their "second chance."

As students work to achieve clearly defined learning goals and produce evidence of their achievement, they need to know that teachers will not penalize them for either their lack of knowledge at the beginning of a course of study or their initial attempts at skill mastery. Allowing new evidence to replace old conveys an important message to students—that teachers care about their successful learning, not merely their grades.

Motivated to Learn

The assessment strategies that we have described address three factors that influence student motivation to learn (Marzano, 1992). Students are more likely to put forth the required effort when there is

- *Task clarity*—when they clearly understand the learning goal and know how teachers will evaluate their learning (Practices 1 and 2).
- *Relevance*—when they think the learning goals and assessments are meaningful and worth learning (Practice 1).
- *Potential for success*—when they believe they can successfully learn and meet the evaluative expectations (Practices 3–7).

By using these seven assessment and grading practices, all teachers can enhance learning in their classrooms.

References

Black, P., Harrison, C., Lee., C., Marshall, B., & Wiliam, D. (2004). Working inside the black box: Assessment for learning in the classroom. *Phi Delta Kappan, 86*(1), 8–21.

Bransford, J. D., Brown, A. L., & Cocking, R. R. (Eds.). (1999). *How people learn: Brain, mind, experience, and school.* Washington, DC: National Research Council.

Gardner, H. (1991). *The unschooled mind.* New York: BasicBooks.

Marzano, R. (1992). *A different kind of classroom: Teaching with dimensions of learning.* Alexandria, VA: ASCD.

Wiggins, G. (1998). *Educative assessment: Designing assessments to inform and improve student performance.* San Francisco: Jossey-Bass.

POSTNOTE

Assessment is a vital part of the instructional process. Finding out what students already know and don't know (diagnostic assessment) is an important step before beginning instruction. Finding out what students are learning during the midst of instruction (formative assessment) provides guidance to the teacher on how to proceed. Finding out what students have learned after instruction is over (summative assessment) lets the teacher know how successful he/she and the students have been.

Unfortunately, policymakers seem much more interested in assessments for accountability purposes, that is, holding educators and students accountable for student learning by offering rewards to those who succeed and punishment to those who don't. The high-stakes testing that accompanies most states' standards of learning are usually worthless as guides to teachers for adjusting instructional decisions to help particular students. The results

come months after the students have taken the tests and don't provide enough information to guide students in self-assessments to improve their learning. The authors of this article give the reader practical advice on how to make the diagnostic, formative, and summative forms of assessment vital to improving student learning.

DISCUSSION QUESTIONS

1. Thinking back on your own educational experiences, have you ever experienced assessments (e.g., tests, papers, projects) that motivated you to want to learn more? If so, what made them so exceptional?
2. Describe the most creative assessment you ever completed as a student. What made it creative?
3. What questions about assessment do you have? How will you get them answered?

RELATED WEBSITE RESOURCES AND VIDEO CASE

WEB RESOURCES:

The National Center for Research on Evaluation, Standards, and Student Testing. Available at:

http://www.cse.ucla.edu/.

This website contains numerous articles and reports that discuss current assessment and evaluation issue.

Yahoo's Directory of K-12 Lesson Plans. Available at:

http://dir.yahoo.com/Education/Standards_and_Testing.

This website contains a wide variety of resources for testing, assessment, measurement, and benchmarking.

▶❙❙ TEACHSOURCE VIDEO CASE

ASSESSMENT IN THE ELEMENTARY GRADES: FORMAL AND INFORMAL LITERARY ASSESSMENT

In this video case, you will see how Chris Quinn, a second-grade teacher, administers both a formal assessment (a standardized test on phonics) and an informal literacy assessment (a running record) to her students. Go to the website for the Education Media Library at CengageBrain.com to watch the video clips, study the artifacts in the case, and reflect on the following questions. (Alternatively, you could watch *Assessment in the Middle Grades: Measurement of Student Learning*.)

1. How do you anticipate combining formal and informal assessments in your classroom?

2. How does this teacher show that she is using assessment as a key part of instruction?

3. Do you agree that students should help determine the assessment process? Why or why not?

The Courage to Be Constructivist

Martin G. Brooks and Jacqueline Grennon Brooks

Martin Brooks, Ed.D., is executive director of the Tri-State Consortium (New York, Connecticut, and New Jersey). **Jacqueline Grennon Brooks, Ed.D.,** is Professor of Teaching, Literacy, and Leadership at Hofstra University, New York.

"The Courage to be Constructivist," by Martin G. Brooks and Jacqueline Grennon Brooks, 1999, *Educational Leadership* 57(3), pp. 18–24. © 1999 by ASCD. Reprinted with permission. Learn more about ASCD at www.ascd.org.

For years, the term *constructivism* appeared only in journals read primarily by philosophers, epistemologists, and psychologists. Nowadays, *constructivism* regularly appears in the teachers' manuals of textbook series, state education department curriculum frameworks, education reform literature, and education journals. Constructivism now has a face and a name in education.

A theory of learning that describes the central role that learners' ever-transforming mental schemes play in their cognitive growth, constructivism powerfully informs educational practice. Education, however, has deep roots in other theories of learning. This history constrains our capacity to embrace the central role of the learner in his or her own education. We must rethink the very foundations of schooling if we are to base our practice on our understandings of learners' needs.

One such foundational notion is that students will learn on demand. This bedrock belief is manifested in the traditional scope and sequence of a typical course of study and, more recently, in the new educational standards and assessments. This approach to schooling is grounded in the conviction that all students can and will learn the same material at the same time. For some students, this approach does indeed lead to the construction of knowledge. For others, however, it does not.

The people working directly with students are the ones who must adapt and adjust lessons on the basis of evolving needs. Constructivist educational practice cannot be realized without the classroom teacher's autonomous, ongoing, professional judgment. State education departments could and should support good educational practice. But too often they do not.

Their major flaw is their focus on high-stakes accountability systems and the ramifications of that focus on teachers and students. Rather than set standards for professional practice and the development of local capacity to enhance student learning, many state education departments have placed even greater weight on the same managerial equation that has failed repeatedly in the past: State Standards = State Tests; State Test Results = Student Achievement; Student Achievement = Rewards and Punishments.

FOCUS QUESTION

What does it mean to be a constructivist teacher?

InTASC
Standards 1, 2, 3, 4, 5, 6, 7, and 8

KEY TERMS

- Constructivism
- High-stakes accountability
- Performance-based assessment

We are not suggesting that educators should not be held accountable for their students' learning. We believe that they should. Unfortunately, we are not holding our profession accountable for learning, only for achievement on high-stakes tests. As we have learned from years of National Assessment of Educational Progress research, equating lasting student learning with test results is folly.

The Emerging Research from Standards-Driven States

In recent years, many states have initiated comprehensive educational reform efforts. The systemic thinking that frames most standards-based reform efforts is delectably logical: Develop high standards for all students; align curriculum and instruction to these standards; construct assessments to measure whether all students are meeting the standards; equate test results with student learning; and reward schools whose students score well on the assessments and sanction schools whose students don't.

Predictably, this simple and linear approach to educational reform is sinking under the weight of its own flaws. It is too similar to earlier reform approaches, and it misses the point. Educational improvement is not accomplished through administrative or legislative mandate. It is accomplished through attention to the complicated, idiosyncratic, often paradoxical, and difficult to measure nature of learning.

A useful body of research is emerging from the states. With minor variations, the research indicates the following:

- Test scores are generally low on the first assessment relating to new standards. Virginia is an extreme example of this phenomenon: More than 95 percent of schools failed the state's first test. In New York, more than 50 percent of the state's 4th graders were deemed at risk of not graduating in 2007 after taking that state's new English language arts test in 1999.
- Failure, or the fear of failure, breeds success on subsequent tests. After the first administration of most state assessments, schools' scores rise because educators align curriculum closely with the assessments, and they focus classroom instruction directly on test-taking strategies.
- To increase the percentages of students passing the state assessments—and to keep schools off the states' lists of failing schools—local district spending on student remediation, student test-taking skills, and faculty preparation for the new assessments increases.
- Despite rising test scores in subsequent years, there is little or no evidence of increased student learning. A recent study by Kentucky's Office of Educational Accountability (Hambleton et al., 1995) suggests that test-score gains in that state are a function of students' increasing skills as test takers rather than evidence of increased learning.

When Tests Constrict Learning

Learning is a complex process through which learners constantly change their internally constructed understandings of how their worlds function. New information either transforms their current beliefs—or doesn't. The efficacy of the learning environment is a function of many complex factors, including curriculum, instructional methodology, student motivation, and student developmental readiness. Trying to capture this complexity on paper-and-pencil assessments severely limits knowledge and expression.

Inevitably, schools reduce the curriculum to only that which is covered on tests, and this constriction limits student learning. So, too, does the undeviating, one-size-fits-all approach to teaching and assessment in many states that have crowned accountability king. Requiring all students to take the same courses and pass the same tests may hold political capital for legislators and state-level educational policymakers, but it contravenes what years of painstaking research tells us about student learning. In discussing the inordinate amount of time and energy devoted to preparing students to take and pass high-stakes tests, Angaran (1999) writes

Ironically, all this activity prepares them for hours of passivity. This extended amount of seat time flies in the face of what we know about how children learn. Unfortunately, it does not seem to matter. It is, after all, the Information Age. The quest for more information drives us forward. (p. 72)

We are not saying that student success on state assessments and classroom practices designed to foster understanding are inherently contradictory. Teaching in ways that nurture students' quests to resolve cognitive conflict and conquer academic challenges fosters the creative problem solving that most states seek. However, classroom practices designed to prepare students for tests clearly do not foster deep learning that students apply to new situations. Instead, these practices train students to mimic learning on tests.

Many school districts question the philosophical underpinnings of the dominant test-teach-test model of education and are searching for broader ways for students to demonstrate their knowledge. However, the accountability component of the standards movement has caused many districts to abandon performance-based assessment practices and refocus instead on preparing students for paper-and-pencil tests. The consequences for districts and their students are too great if they don't.

Constructivism in the Classroom

Learners control their learning. This simple truth lies at the heart of the constructivist approach to education.

As educators, we develop classroom practices and negotiate the curriculum to enhance the likelihood of student learning. But controlling what students learn is virtually impossible. The search for meaning takes a different route for each student. Even when educators structure classroom lessons and curriculums to ensure that all students learn the same concepts at the same time, each student still constructs his or her own unique meaning through his or her own cognitive processes. In other words, as educators we have great control over what we teach, but far less control over what students learn.

Shifting our priorities from ensuring that all students learn the same concepts to ensuring that

we carefully analyze students' understandings to customize our teaching approaches is an essential step in educational reform that results in increased learning. Again, we must set standards for our own professional practice and free students from the anti-intellectual training that occurs under the banner of test preparation.

The search for understanding motivates students to learn. When students want to know more about an idea, a topic, or an entire discipline, they put more cognitive energy into classroom investigations and discussions and study more on their own. We have identified five central tenets of constructivism (Grennon Brooks & Brooks, 1993).

- First, constructivist teachers seek and value students' points of view. Knowing what students think about concepts helps teachers formulate classroom lessons and differentiate instruction on the basis of students' needs and interests.
- Second, constructivist teachers structure lessons to challenge students' suppositions. All students, whether they are 6 or 16 or 60, come to the classroom with life experiences that shape their views about how their worlds work. When educators permit students to construct knowledge that challenges their current suppositions, learning occurs. Only through asking students what they think they know and why they think they know it are we and they able to confront their suppositions.
- Third, constructivist teachers recognize that students must attach relevance to the curriculum. As students see relevance in their daily activities, their interest in learning grows.
- Fourth, constructivist teachers structure lessons around big ideas, not small bits of information. Exposing students to wholes first helps them determine the relevant parts as they refine their understandings of the wholes.
- Finally, constructivist teachers assess student learning in the context of daily classroom investigations, not as separate events. Students demonstrate their knowledge every day in a variety of ways. Defining understanding as only that which is capable of being measured

by paper-and-pencil assessments administered under strict security perpetuates false and counter-productive myths about academia, intelligence, creativity, accountability, and knowledge.

Opportunities for Constructing Meaning

Recently, we visited a classroom in which a teacher asked 7th graders to reflect on a poem. The teacher began the lesson by asking the students to interpret the first two lines. One student volunteered that the lines evoked an image of a dream. "No," he was told, "that's not what the author meant." Another student said that the poem reminded her of a voyage at sea. The teacher reminded the student that she was supposed to be thinking about the first two lines of the poem, not the whole poem, and then told her that the poem was not about the sea. Looking out at the class, the teacher asked, "Anyone else?" No other student raised a hand.

In another classroom, a teacher asked 9th graders to ponder the effect of temperature on muscle movement. Students had ice, buckets of water, gauges for measuring finger-grip strength, and other items to help them consider the relationship. The teacher asked a few framing questions, stated rules for handling materials safely, and then gave the students time to design their experiments. He posed different questions to different groups of students, depending on their activities and the conclusions that they seemed to be drawing. He continually asked students to elaborate or posed contradictions to their responses, even when they were correct.

As the end of the period neared, the students shared initial findings about their investigations and offered working hypotheses about the relationship between muscle movement and temperature. Several students asked to return later that day to continue working on their experiments.

Let's consider these two lessons. In one case, the lesson was not conducive to students' constructing deeper meaning. In the other case, it was. The 7th grade teacher communicated to her students that there is one interpretation of the poem's meaning, that she knew it, and that only that interpretation was an acceptable response. The students' primary quest, then, was to figure out what the teacher thought of the poem.

The teacher spoke to her students in respectful tones, acknowledging each one by name and encouraging their responses. However, she politely and calmly rejected their ideas when they failed to conform to her views. She rejected one student's response as a misinterpretation. She dismissed another student's response because of a procedural error: The response focused on the whole poem, not on just the designated two lines.

After the teacher told these two students that they were wrong, none of the other students volunteered interpretations, even though the teacher encouraged more responses. The teacher then proceeded with the lesson by telling the students what the poet really meant. Because only two students offered comments during the lesson, the teacher told us that a separate test would inform her whether the other students understood the poem.

In the second lesson, the teacher withheld his thoughts intentionally to challenge students to develop their own hypotheses. Even when students' initial responses were correct, the teacher challenged their thinking, causing many students to question the correctness of their initial responses and to investigate the issue more deeply.

Very few students had awakened that morning thinking about the relationship between muscle movement and temperature. But, as the teacher helped students focus their emerging, somewhat disjointed musings into a structured investigation, their engagement grew. The teacher provoked the students to search for relevance in a relationship they hadn't yet considered by framing the investigation around one big concept, providing appropriate materials and general questions, and helping the students think through their own questions. Moreover, the teacher sought and valued his students' points of view and used their comments to assess their learning. No separate testing event was required.

What Constructivism Is and Isn't

As constructivism has gained support as an educational approach, two main criticisms have emerged. One critique of constructivism is that it is overly permissive. This critique suggests that constructivist teachers often abandon their curriculums to pursue the whims of their students. If, for example, most of the students in the aforementioned 9th grade science class wished to discuss the relationship between physical exercise and muscle movement rather than pursue the planned lesson, so be it. In math and science, critics are particularly concerned that teachers jettison basic information to permit students to think in overly broad mathematical and scientific terms.

The other critique of constructivist approaches to education is that they lack rigor. The concern here is that teachers cast aside the information, facts, and basic skills embedded in the curriculum—and necessary to pass high-stakes tests—in the pursuit of more capricious ideas. Critics would be concerned that in the 7th grade English lesson described previously, the importance of having students understand the one true main idea of the poem would fall prey to a discussion of their individual interpretations.

Both of these critiques are silly caricatures of what an evolving body of research tells us about learning. Battista (1999), speaking specifically of mathematics education, writes,

> Many ... conceive of constructivism as a pedagogical stance that entails a type of nonrigorous, intellectual anarchy that lets students pursue whatever interests them and invent and use any mathematical methods they wish, whether those methods are correct or not. Others take constructivism to be synonymous with "discovery learning" from the era of "new math," and still others see it as a way of teaching that focuses on using manipulatives or cooperative learning. None of these conceptions is correct. (p. 429)

Organizing a constructivist classroom is difficult work for the teacher and requires the rigorous intellectual commitment and perseverance of students. Constructivist teachers recognize that students bring their prior experiences with them to each school activity and that it is crucial to connect lessons to their students' experiential repertoires. Initial relevance and interest are largely a function of the learner's experiences, not of the teacher's planning. Therefore, it is educationally counterproductive to ignore students' suppositions and points of view. The 7th grade English lesson is largely nonintellectual. The 9th grade science lesson, modeled on how scientists make state-of-the-art science advancements, is much more intellectually rigorous.

Moreover, constructivist teachers keep relevant facts, information, and skills at the forefront of their lesson planning. They usually do this within the context of discussions about bigger ideas. For example, the dates, battles, and names associated with the U.S. Civil War have much more meaning for students when introduced within larger investigations of slavery, territorial expansion, and economics than when presented for memorization without a larger context.

State and local curriculums address *what* students learn. Constructivism, as an approach to education, addresses *how* students learn. The constructivist teacher, in mediating students' learning, blends the *what* with the *how*. As a 3rd grader in another classroom we visited wrote to his teacher, "You are like the North Star for the class. You don't tell us where to go, but you help us find our way." Constructivist classrooms demand far more from teachers and students than lockstep obeisance to prepackaged lessons.

The Effects of High-Stakes Accountability

As we stated earlier, the standards movement has a grand flaw at the nexus of standards, accountability, and instructional practice. Instructional practices designed to help students construct meaning are being crowded out of the curriculum by practices designed to prepare students to score well on state assessments. The push for accountability is eclipsing the intent of standards and sound educational practice.

Let's look at the effects of high-stakes accountability systems. Originally, many states identified higher-order thinking as a goal of reform and promoted constructivist teaching practices to achieve this goal. In most states, however, policymakers dropped this goal or subsumed it into other goals because it was deemed too difficult to assess and quantify. Rich evidence relating to higher-order thinking is available daily in classrooms, but this evidence is not necessarily translatable to paper-and-pencil assessments. High-stakes accountability systems, therefore, tend to warp the original visions of reform.

Education is a holistic endeavor. Students' learning encompasses emerging understandings about themselves, their relationships, and their relative places in the world. In addition to academic achievement, students develop these understandings through nonacademic aspects of schooling, such as clubs, sports, community service, music, arts, and theater. However, only that which is academic and easily measurable gets assessed, and only that which is assessed is subject to rewards and punishments. Jones and Whitford (1997) point out that Kentucky's original educational renewal initiative included student self-sufficiency and responsible group membership as goals, but these goals were dropped because they were deemed too difficult to assess and not sufficiently academic.

Schools operating in high-stakes accountability systems typically move attention away from principles of learning, student-centered curriculum, and constructivist teaching practices. They focus instead on obtaining higher test scores, despite research showing that higher test scores are not necessarily indicative of increased student learning.

Historically, many educators have considered multiple-choice tests to be the most valid and reliable form of assessment—and also the narrowest form of assessment. Therefore, despite the initial commitment of many states to performance assessment, which was to have been the cornerstone of state assessment efforts aligned with broader curriculum and constructivist instructional practices, multiple-choice questions have instead remained the coin of the realm. As Jones and Whitford (1997) write about Kentucky,

> The logic is clear. The more open and performance based an assessment is, the more variety in the responses; the more variety in the responses, the more judgment is needed in scoring; the more judgment in scoring, the lower the reliability.... At this point, multiple-choice items have been reintroduced, performance events discontinued. (p. 278)

Ironically, as state departments of education and local newspapers hold schools increasingly accountable for their test results, local school officials press state education departments for greater guidance about material to be included on the states' tests. This phenomenon emboldens state education departments to take an even greater role in curriculum development, as well as in other decisions typically handled at the local level, such as granting high school diplomas, determining professional development requirements for teachers, making special education placements, and intervening academically for at-risk students. According to Jones and Whitford (1997),

> [In Kentucky] there has been a rebound effect. Pressure generated by the state test for high stakes accountability has led school-based educators to pressure the state to be more explicit about content that will be tested. This in turn constrains local school decision making about curriculum. This dialectical process works to increase the state control of local curriculum. (p. 278)

Toward Educational Reform

Serious educational reform targets cognitive changes in students' thinking. Perceived educational reform targets numerical changes in students' test scores. Our obsession with the perception of reform, what Ohanian (1999) calls "the mirage theory of education," is undermining the possibility of serious reform.

History tells us that it is likely that students' scores on state assessments will rise steadily over the next decade and that meaningful indexes of student learning generally will remain flat. It is also likely that teachers, especially those teaching in the grades in which high-stakes assessments are administered, will continue to narrow their curriculum to match what is covered on the assessments and to use instructional practices designed to place testing information directly in their students' heads.

We counsel advocacy for children. And vision. And courage.

Focus on student learning. When we design instructional practices to help students construct knowledge, students learn. This is our calling as educators.

Keep the curriculum conceptual. Narrowing curriculum to match what is covered on state assessments results in an overemphasis on the rote memorization of discrete bits of information and pushes aside big ideas and intellectual curiosity. Keep essential principles and recurring concepts at the center.

Assess student learning within the context of daily instruction. Use students' daily work, points of view, suppositions, projects, and demonstrations to assess what they know and don't know, and use these assessments to guide teaching.

Initiate discussions among administrators, teachers, parents, school boards, and students about the relationship among the state's standards, the state's assessments, and your district's mission. Ask questions about what the assessments actually assess, the instructional practices advocated by your district, and the ways to teach a conceptual curriculum while preparing students for the assessments. These are discussions worth having.

Understand the purposes of accountability. Who wants it, and why? Who is being held accountable, and for what? How are data being used or misused? What are the consequences of accountability for all students, especially for specific groups, such as special education students and English language learners?

Students must be permitted the freedom to think, to question, to reflect, and to interact with ideas, objects, and others—in other words, to construct meaning. In school, being wrong has always carried negative consequences for students. Sadly, in this climate of increasing accountability, being wrong carries even more severe consequences. But being wrong is often the first step on the path to greater understanding.

We observed a 5th grade teacher return a test from the previous day. Question 3 was, "There are 7 blue chips and 3 green chips in a bag. If you place your hand in the bag and pull out 1 chip, what is the probability that you will get a green chip?" One student wrote, "You probably won't get one." She was "right"—and also "wrong." She received no credit for the question.

References

Angaran, J. (1999, March). Reflection in an age of assessment. *Educational Leadership, 56,* 71–72.

Grennon Brooks, J., & Brooks, M. G. (1993). *In search of understanding: The case for constructivist classrooms.* Alexandria, VA: ASCD.

Hambleton, R., Jaeger, R. M., Koretz, D., Linn, R. L., Millman, J., & Phillips, S. E. (1995). *Review of the measurement quality of the Kentucky instructional results information system 1991–1994.* (Report prepared for the Kentucky General Assembly.) Frankfort, KY: Office of Educational Accountability.

Jones, K., & Whitford, B. L. (1997, December). Kentucky's conflicting reform principles: High stakes accountability and student performance assessment. *Phi Delta Kappan, 78*(4), 276–281.

Ohanian, S. (1999). *One size fits few.* Portsmouth, NH: Heinemann.

POSTNOTE

This article was chosen as a classic because the topic of constructivism has become such a dominant instructional philosophy in American education. Research from cognitive scientists has taught us that when confronted with new learning, human beings "construct" new understandings of relationships and phenomena, rather than simply receiving others' understandings. Learners are always fitting new information into the schemas they carry in their heads, or else they adjust or change the schema to fit the new information. As the authors of this article state, students bring their prior experiences with them so teachers need to design lessons that connect to students' experiential repertoires.

The implications for teachers are enormous. Constructivism suggests that educators should invite students to explore the world's complexity, proposing situations for students to think about and observing how students use their prior knowledge to confront the problems. When students make errors, teachers can analyze the errors to understand better just how the students are approaching the matter. Throughout the process, teachers must accept that there is no single "right" way to solve a problem.

DISCUSSION QUESTIONS

1. In what ways does constructivism challenge your ideas about how people learn?
2. How do you think constructivism will affect what goes on in classrooms? Describe a scenario in which a teacher conducts a lesson, using constructivist principles similar to those presented by the authors. Choose any subject or grade level you wish.
3. How does constructivism dispute the notion of a fixed world that students need to understand?

RELATED WEBSITE RESOURCE AND VIDEO CASE

WEB RESOURCE:

Constructivism. Available at:

http://www.innovativelearning.com/teaching/constructivism.html.

This website by Martin Ryder contains multiple links to definitions and readings on constructivism.

▶❚❚ TEACHSOURCE VIDEO CASE

CONSTRUCTIVIST TEACHING IN ACTION: A HIGH SCHOOL CLASSROOM DEBATE

In this video case you'll see how teacher Sarabinh Levy-Brightman sets the stage for students to become expert on the topic of Jeffersonian democracy, figure out how best to express opposing ideas, and evaluate their own effectiveness. Go to the website for the Education Media Library at CengageBrain.com to watch the video clips, study the artifacts in the case, and reflect on the following questions.

1. In what ways is this teacher's approach consistent with constructivist learning philosophy?
2. Describe the process the students use in preparing for the debate. What are some of its advantages and possible drawbacks?

Orchestrating Multiple Intelligences

Seana Moran, Mindy Kornhaber, and Howard Gardner

Seana Moran is a research fellow in Education at Stanford University.

Mindy Kornhaber is an Associate Professor in the College of Education at The Pennsylvania State University.

Howard Gardner, the originator of the theory of multiple intelligences, is the John H. and Elisabeth A. Hobbs Professor of Cognition and Education at the Harvard

Graduate School of Education and Senior Director of Harvard Project Zero.

"Orchestrating Multiple Intelligences," by Seana Moran, Mindy Kornhaber, and Howard Gardner, 2006, *Educational Leadership 64*(1), pp. 22–29. © 2006 by ASCD. Reprinted with permission. Learn more about ASCD at www.ascd.org.

Education policymakers sometimes go astray when they attempt to integrate multiple intelligences theory into schools. They mistakenly believe that teachers must group students for instruction according to eight or nine different intelligence scores. Or they grapple with the unwieldy notion of requiring teachers to prepare eight or nine separate entry points for every lesson.

Multiple intelligences theory was originally developed as an explanation of how the mind works—not as an education policy, let alone an education panacea. Moreover, when we and other colleagues began to consider the implications of the theory for education, the last thing we wanted to do was multiply educators' jobs ninefold. Rather, we sought to demonstrate that because students bring to the classroom diverse intellectual profiles, one "IQ" measure is insufficient to evaluate, label, and plan education programs for all students.

Adopting a multiple intelligences approach can bring about a quiet revolution in the way students see themselves and others. Instead of defining themselves as either "smart" or "dumb," students can perceive themselves as potentially smart in a number of ways.

Profile Students, Don't Score Them

Multiple intelligences theory proposes that it is more fruitful to describe an individual's cognitive ability in terms of several relatively independent but interacting cognitive capacities rather than in terms of a single "general" intelligence. Think of LEGO building blocks. If we have only one kind of block to play with, we can build only a limited range of structures. If we have a number of different block shapes that can interconnect to create a variety of patterns and structures, we can accomplish more nuanced and complex designs. The eight or nine intelligences work the same way.

FOCUS QUESTION

How can the theory of multiple intelligences be implemented in classrooms?

InTASC
Standards 1, 2, 3, 4, 6, 7, and 8

KEY TERM

- Multiple Intelligences theory

The greatest potential of a multiple intelligences approach to education grows from the concept of a *profile* of intelligences. Each learner's intelligence profile consists of a combination of relative strengths and weaknesses among the different intelligences: linguistic, logical-mathematical, musical, spatial, bodily-kinesthetic, naturalistic, interpersonal, intrapersonal, and (at least provisionally) existential (Gardner, 2006).

Most people have jagged profiles; they process some types of information better than other types. Students who exhibit vast variation among their intelligences—with one or two intelligences very strong and the others relatively weak—have what we call a *laser* profile. There students often have a strong area of interest and can follow a clear path to success by developing their peak intelligences. Given the ubiquity of high-stakes testing, educators' challenge with laser-profile students is deciding whether to accentuate the students' strengths through advanced opportunities to develop their gifts or to bolster their weak areas through remediation so that they can pass the tests. Policy and funding currently favor the second option unless the student is gifted in the traditional academic areas.

Other students have a *searchlight* profile: They show less pronounced differences among intelligences. The challenge with searchlight-profile students is to help them choose a career and life path. Time and resource limitations often preclude developing all intelligences equally, so we need to consider which intelligences are most likely to pay off for a particular student. Policy and funding currently favor developing primarily linguistic and logical-mathematical intelligences at the expense of the others.

Intelligences are not isolated; they can interact with one another in an individual to yield a variety of outcomes. For example, a successful dancer must combine musical, spatial, and bodily kinesthetic intelligences; a science fiction novelist must use logical-mathematical, linguistic, interpersonal, and some existential intelligences; an effective trial lawyer must combine linguistic and interpersonal intelligences; a skillful waiter uses linguistic, spatial, interpersonal, and bodily-kinesthetic intelligences; and a marine biologist needs strong naturalistic and logical-mathematical intelligences. In the education setting, the different intelligences can interact in two ways: within the student and across students.

An Internal Orchestra

Just as the sounds of string, woodwind, and percussion instruments combine to create a symphony, the different intelligences intermix within a student to yield meaningful scholastic achievement or other accomplishments. And as in an orchestra, one intelligence (instrument) in an individual can interfere with others, compensate for others, or enhance others.

Interference

Intelligences may not always work in harmony; sometimes they create discord. For example, even a student who has good social skills (strong interpersonal intelligence), may have trouble making friends if she cannot talk with others easily because she has weak linguistic intelligence. Another student who loves to read and receives frequent praise in English class may sit in the back row and bury her head in a novel during math class, where she feels less confident. Thus, her linguistic strength is a bottleneck for the development of her logical-mathematical intelligence. A third student's weakness in intrapersonal intelligence, which makes it difficult for him to regulate his moods or thoughts, may prevent him from completing his math homework consistently and thus mask his strong logical-mathematical intelligence.

Compensation

Sometimes one intelligence compensates for another. A student may give great class presentations because he can effectively use his body posture and gestures even though his sentence structure is somewhat convoluted. That is, his bodily-kinesthetic intelligence compensates for his linguistic limitations. (We can think of more than one U.S. president who fits this profile.) Or a student may earn a high mark on a paper for writing with a powerful rhetorical voice, even though her argument is not quite solid: Her linguistic intelligence compensates for her logical-mathematical limitations.

Enhancement

Finally, one intelligence may jump-start another. Strong spatial intelligence may improve a student's ability to conceptualize a mathematical concept or problem. This was certainly the case with Einstein. Strong musical intelligence may stimulate interest and playfulness in writing poetry. Understanding how intelligences can catalyze one another may help students—and teachers—make decisions about how to deploy the intellectual resources they have at their disposal.

The profile approach to multiple intelligences instruction provides teachers with better diagnostic information to help a particular student who is struggling. Before providing assistance, we need to ask *why* the student is having difficulty. For example, consider three beginning readers who have trouble comprehending a story. The first is struggling because of poor reading comprehension skills (a linguistic intelligence challenge). The second has poor social understanding of the dynamics among the story's characters (an interpersonal intelligence challenge). The third has such strong spatial intelligence that he has trouble seeing beyond the physical pattern of the letter symbols (a challenge that Picasso, for example, faced in his early years). More reading practice, which is often the default intervention, may not help all of these students.

A student's potential is not the sum of his or her intelligence "scores," as some multiple intelligence inventory measures on the market imply. If one intelligence is a bottleneck for others, then the student's overall potential may be lower than the straight sum. If intelligences are compensating for or enhancing one another, the student's overall potential may be higher than the straight sum. Intelligences have multiplicative as well as additive effects.

An Effective Ensemble

Intelligences can also work across students. The information explosion has greatly escalated the amount of information that each person must assimilate and understand—frequently beyond what we can handle by ourselves. Work teams, institutional partnerships, and interdisciplinary projects have increasingly become the norm. These ensembles support individuals as they seek to learn, understand, and perform well.

Multiple intelligences theory encourages collaboration across students. Students with compatible profiles (exhibiting the same patterns of strengths and weaknesses) can work together to solidify and build on strengths. For example, two students highly capable in storytelling can support each other by moving beyond the basics of plot to explore and develop twists in the narrative. A group of students who are skilled in numerical computation might extend a statistics lesson beyond mean, median, mode, and range to understand correlation or regression.

Students with complementary profiles (in which one student's weak areas are another student's strengths) can work together to compensate for one another. Such students can approach material in different but equally valid ways. For example, a student who is strong in logical-mathematical intelligence and sufficient in spatial intelligence might be able to translate abstract math problems into dance choreography or sculpture contexts to make them understandable to a student with strong spatial and bodily-kinesthetic intelligences.

Provide Rich Experiences

The eminent psychologist L. S. Vygotsky (1978) emphasized that *experience*—the idiosyncratic way each individual internalizes the environment's information—is important in both cognitive and personality development. If we give all students the same material, each student will have a different experience according to his or her background, strengths, and challenges. Thus, to promote learning across student intelligence profiles, teachers need to offer students rich experiences—activities in which they can engage with the material personally rather than just absorb it in an abstract, decontextualized way.

Rich experiences enable students to learn along several dimensions at once—socially, spatially, kinesthetically, self-reflectively, and so on. Often, these experiences cross subject-area lines. At Searsport Elementary School in Searsport, Maine, a 5th grade teacher who had strong storytelling abilities and an avid interest in history joined forces with her colleague, an expert in hands-on science, to develop an archaeology unit. Students studied history and geography as well as scientific method and archaeology techniques. They investigated local history, conducted a state-approved archaeological dig, identified and classified objects, and displayed the artifacts in a museum exhibit that met real-world curatorial standards (Kornhaber, Fierros, & Veenema, 2004).

Rich experiences also provide diagnostic information. Teachers can observe student performances to find root causes of misunderstandings and to figure out how students can achieve superior understandings. One small group of 2nd and 3rd graders in Chimene Brandt's class at Pittsburgh's McCleary Elementary School produced a mural depicting a rainy street scene. Their spatial portrayal of material was ambiguous: The connection to the unit's topic of rivers and the lesson's topic of the water cycle laws was not obvious. The students' understanding came through linguistically, however, when they presented in class how the water from the street would evaporate, condense into clouds, and again produce rain. By giving the students multiple ways to express the concepts, Brandt was able to confirm that the students understood the material even though their linguistic skills outstripped their spatial skills (Kornhaber, Fierros, & Veenema, 2004).

Two programs exemplify how rich experiences can serve as venues for developing and assessing multiple intelligences. The first, Project Spectrum, is an interactive assessment process for preschool children developed in the 1980s at Harvard Project Zero (Gardner, Feldman, & Krechevsky, 1998). This process evaluates each intelligence directly, rather than funneling the information through a linguistic paper-and-pencil test. Spatial orientation and manipulation tasks evaluate spatial intelligence; group tasks evaluate interpersonal intelligence; self-assessments paired with the other assessments evaluate intrapersonal

intelligence. Project Spectrum environments do not segment tasks strictly into one intelligence or another. Instead, they set up situations in which a student can interact with rich materials—and teachers can observe these interactions—to see which intelligences come to the fore and which are relegated to the background.

A naturalist's corner provides biological specimens for students to touch and move (using bodily-kinesthetic intelligence), arrange (naturalistic), create relationships among (logical-mathematical), tell stories about (linguistic), or even compare themselves with (intra-personal). In a storytelling area, students can tell tales (linguistic), arrange props and character figurines (spatial and possibly bodily-kinesthetic), make characters interact (interpersonal), and design their own storyboards (spatial). Fifteen other activities provide opportunities for evaluating intelligences through reliable scoring rubrics that have been used widely in early childhood education in the United States, Latin America, Europe, and Asia (Gardner, Feldman, & Krechevsky, 1998).

Another environment providing rich experiences using a multiple intelligences approach is the Explorama at Danfoss Universe, a science park in Nordborg, Denmark (see www.danfossuniverse. com). Designed according to multiple intelligences theory, this interactive museum is used by people of all ages—from school groups to corporate teams. The designers have devised separate exhibits, games, and challenges for each intelligence and for numerous combinations of intelligences. One experience asks participants to balance themselves (bodily-kinesthetic); another asks them to balance in a group (bodily-kinesthetic and interpersonal). A computer program encourages participants to add, subtract, or combine different musical qualities and see on screen how the tone frequencies change, tapping into musical, spatial, and logical-mathematical intelligences.

Three activities deserve particular attention for their innovativeness in assessing several intelligences concurrently and in emphasizing intelligences that are often neglected in mainstream academic testing. One game involves manipulating a joystick to control a robot that can lift and move a cube to a target space. When played alone, this exhibit primarily assesses bodily-kinesthetic and spatial intelligence. But when two to four people each control a different joystick—one that controls the left wheel of the robot, another that controls the right wheel, another that raises the cube, and another that lowers the cube—they must coordinate their play to accomplish the task, employing linguistic, logical-mathematical, and interpersonal intelligences.

Another game has two players sitting opposite each other at a table, with a ping-pong ball in the center. Each player tries to move the ball toward the opponent by relaxing. Relaxing reduces the player's stress level, creating alpha waves in the brain that sensors pick up to move the ball forward. This task requires self-control, and thus taps into intrapersonal intelligence. However, the players must also employ interpersonal intelligence, paying attention to each other and trying to produce more alpha waves than the opponent does.

A third notable Explorama activity is a computerized questionnaire in which participants assess their own intelligence profiles. Participants take the self-assessment before entering the Explorama and again after they have engaged in the various activities and tasks. Participants thus get an idea of how well they know their own capabilities. They also can compare their self-assessments before and after the Explorama experience to learn whether their self-perceptions stayed constant or changed. This process develops participants' intrapersonal intelligence.

Get Personal

The orientation toward profiles, interactions, and experience emphasizes a need to develop, in particular, the two personal intelligences.

Intrapersonal intelligence involves knowing yourself—your talents, energy level, interests, and so on. Students who strengthen their intrapersonal intelligence gain a better understanding of areas in which they can expect to excel, which helps them plan and govern their own learning.

Interpersonal intelligence involves understanding others through social interaction, emotional reactions, conversation, and so on. An individual's interpersonal intelligence affects his or her ability to work in groups. Group projects can create environments for students to improve their interpersonal intelligence as they develop other skills and knowledge.

Donna Schneider, a 3rd grade teacher at the John F. Kennedy Elementary School in Brewster, New York, developed a real-world publishing company

Gardner's Multiple Intelligences

Linguistic. Ability to understand and use spoken and written communication. Ideal vocation: poet.*

Logical-mathematical. Ability to understand and use logic and numerical symbols and operations. Ideal vocation: computer programmer.

Musical. Ability to understand and use such concepts as rhythm, pitch, melody, and harmony. Ideal vocation: composer.

Spatial. Ability to orient and manipulate three-dimensional space. Ideal vocation: architect.

Bodily-kinesthetic. Ability to coordinate physical movement. Ideal vocation: athlete.

Naturalistic. Ability to distinguish and categorize objects or phenomena in nature. Ideal vocation: zoologist.

Interpersonal. Ability to understand and interact well with other people. Ideal vocation: politician; salesperson.

Intrapersonal. Ability to understand and use one's thoughts, feelings, preferences, and interests. Ideal vocation: autobiographer; entrepreneur. (Although high intrapersonal intelligence should help in almost any job because of its role in self-regulation, few paid positions reward a person solely for knowing himself or herself well.)

Existential. Ability to contemplate phenomena or questions beyond sensory data, such as the infinite and infinitesimal. Ideal vocation: cosmologist; philosopher.

in her classroom: "Schneider's Ink." Each spring when the school puts on performances and events, Schneider's 3rd graders create programs, banners, advertisements, and other publicity materials for their clients, the sponsoring teachers. Each student assumes a different job—editor, sales manager, typist, accountant, customer service representative, or designer. Before taking on a given position, each student writes a resumé and cover letter, obtains letters of recommendation, and is interviewed by the teacher. Students explore their own strengths and become aware of how those strengths can enable them to succeed in various jobs.

Schneider's Ink also engages students' interpersonal intelligence. For example, the quality-control manager, who is responsible for handling customer complaints, has to work with both clients and the editor to review problems. As company employees, the students juggle simultaneous print orders, coordinating the sequencing of tasks among themselves to produce high-quality work on time. They must understand others through social interaction, emotional reactions, and conversation. Through this process, students acquire a better understanding of the interdependence of individual strengths (Kornhaber, Fierros, & Veenema, 2004).

Building Active Learners

The multiple intelligences approach does not require a teacher to design a lesson in nine different ways so that all students can access the material. Rather, it involves creating rich experiences in which students with different intelligence profiles can interact with the materials and ideas using their particular combinations of strengths and weaknesses.

Often, these experiences are collaborative. As the amount of information that students—and adults—must process continues to increase dramatically, collaboration enables students to learn more by tapping into others' strengths as well as into their own. In ideal multiple intelligences instruction, rich experiences and collaboration provide a context for students to become aware of their own intelligence profiles, to develop self-regulation, and to participate more actively in their own learning.

References

Gardner, H. (2006). *Multiple intelligences: New horizons*. New York: BasicBooks.

Gardner, H., Feldman, D. H., & Krechevsky, M. (Eds.). (1998). *Project Zero frameworks for early childhood education: Volume 1. Building on children's strengths: The experience of Project Spectrum*. New York: Teachers College Press.

Kornhaber, M., Fierros, E., & Veenema, S. (2004). *Multiple intelligences: Best ideas from research and practice*. Boston: Pearson.

Vygotsky, L. S. (1978). *Mind in society: The development of higher psychological processes*. Cambridge, MA: Harvard University Press.

Endnote

★ Most vocations involve several intelligences.

POSTNOTE

Howard Gardner's theory of multiple intelligences refutes the widely accepted idea that there is a single, general intelligence. The eight or nine intelligences—*linguistic, logical-mathematical, musical, spatial, bodily-kinesthetic, interpersonal, intrapersonal, naturalist,* and perhaps, *existentialist*—that he has identified appeal greatly to many educators, who see them as ways that schools can reach more students. In Gardner's theory, abilities in diverse areas would be valued as indicators of intelligence and would be considered worthy of further nurturance and development in school. If teachers provide multiple ways for students to be taught and assessed that recognize and value the kinds of differences that exist among students, then greater numbers of students will succeed and receive recognition. As a result, fewer students are likely to think of themselves as failures. Acknowledging and fostering individual abilities in a variety of areas, as suggested in this article, is a way that teachers can help students succeed.

Teachers of gifted and talented students also see the theory of multiple intelligences as broadening conceptions of who is gifted or talented. The concept of giftedness can embrace dancers, athletes, musicians, artists, or naturalists, and programs can be established to help foster these talents. Gardner raises the issue of whether or not these abilities should be called intelligence or talent. He argues that to call linguistic or logical-mathematical ability intelligence, but spatial or musical ability talent, elevates certain types of ability and devalues others. Gardner's argument is not generally accepted, as society and most schools seem to value language and mathematical capabilities over other types of abilities. (Except, of course, for NFL and NBA athletes!) Howard Gardner's influence on how we think about human intelligence has earned him our designation as a Classic author.

DISCUSSION QUESTIONS

1. Do you believe the different types of intelligences identified by Gardner are valued equally in our society? Why or why not do you think this is the case?
2. Which of the intelligences are strengths of yours? How do you know this?
3. What challenges would you anticipate in trying to orchestrate attention to multiple intelligences in your classroom?

RELATED WEBSITE RESOURCE AND VIDEO CASE

WEB RESOURCE:

ASCD. Available at:

http://www.ascd.org.

ASCD has many resources on multiple intelligences and learning styles. Click on Education Topics, Multiple Intelligences, for more resources on this topic.

▶❙❙ TEACHSOURCE VIDEO CASE

MULTIPLE INTELLIGENCES: ELEMENTARY SCHOOL INSTRUCTION

In this fourth-grade classroom, you'll see how teacher Frederick Won Park draws upon Multiple Intelligences theory to help his students improve their writing abilities. Go to the website for the Education Media Library at CengageBrain.com to watch the video clips, study the artifacts in the case, and reflect on the following questions.

1. How does this teacher's emphasis on the ability to solve problems compare to general-ability theories of intelligence?
2. How does the writing activity link multiple intelligences with one another?
3. In your opinion, does this teacher use multiple intelligences activities in a way that supports standard learning goals or in a way that detracts from achievement standards? Why do you think so?

Power of Story—To Teach, to Reach, to Inspire

Ann Unkovich

Ann Unkovich is the co-author of *Chicken Soup for the Soul in the Classroom* (HCI, 2007) and education director for Pay It Forward Foundation, San Luis Obispo, California.

"The Power of Story–To Teach, to Reach, to Inspire," *Phi Delta Kappan*, v.92, no. 6, March 2011, pp. 58–62.

FOCUS QUESTION

Is reading stories in the classroom a legitimate form of education?

InTASC
Standards 1, 4, 5, and 8

KEY TERMS

- Bloom's Taxonomy
- Emotional literacy

Perhaps the most powerful tool I found in my 35-year teaching career was the *story*—telling a story, reading a story, using a story to teach a concept, to make a connection, or to inspire a group of students.

In hindsight, it all started in 3rd grade when Mrs. Ferguson read a chapter a day from the *Little House on the Prairie* book series. I could hardly wait to get to school to find out what was happening to the Ingalls family. That launched my love of story, a passion for reading, and a view of school as a wonderful place to be.

For Mrs. Ferguson, it was a *knowingness* about the power of a good tale. I doubt that she had any specific training on reading strategies to promote students' overall success in school and in life. Teaching elementary school in the 1950s, she hadn't read Jim Burke's books on the importance of reading (1999, 2000). Nor did she have Jim Trelease's *Read Aloud Handbook* (2001) to guide her to the best stories for age-appropriate concepts to be learned. She didn't have access to the plethora of research that focuses on reading and achievement that is now available.

She just *knew* that it was good teaching. Throughout history, stories have taught us custom, tradition, culture, and diversity. Stories have conjured mental images, sparked imaginations, and tapped into emotions. A good story connects us with the deepest core of our self, with other students, teachers, family, and with all of humanity. A good story takes us anywhere in time and space and introduces us to a wealth of experiences we will never have in real life. A good story is a good friend.

Long before books, and in many indigenous cultures, stories were the only way to share history and lessons about life. In fact, history *is* a story of how we came to be—as a person, a society, or a world.

To Teach …

Across all age groups, stories are an easy and natural way to learn and to get students to use their critical cogitative expertise. If you look to Bloom's Taxonomy (Bloom 1956), you can find every level of thinking skill evidenced in a good story and its follow-up questions. A teacher can lead a student from simple knowledge (Who was the main character?) through comprehension, application, analysis, synthesis, and to evaluation (Why did the main character do what she did? What choice would you have made?). Or, to use the updated terminology: *remembering, understanding, applying, analyzing, evaluating, and creating.*

When given in a lecture format, higher-level skills can overwhelm many students. When placed in the context of a story, students naturally make choices and decisions that challenge their thinking. The story forms pathways in the brain and promotes thinking habits that carry over to other situations, other classrooms, and into students' daily lives. When students are presented with words, not visual images, they must fill in the gaps with all of the sensory details that make for a good story; they must develop their imaginations. Teachers who read to their students at every grade level offer opportunities to develop this inventive, innovative, creative part of their brains. Furthermore, reading to students may give youngsters some balance with the high-speed visual images that flash before them in this world filled with technology.

We've long known the value of a good story and of learning how to read. Reading is so important that we require it of students in every year of their schooling. However, much *required* reading today consists of catastrophic, dark, depressing, problem novels. Stories for elementary students are more often filled with humor, play, or fantasy, which are comforting elements for youngsters of any age. Yet prescribed reading at the secondary level rarely has these joyful elements (Feinberg 2004/2005: 16). Is it any wonder that our youths have become aliterates, persons who *choose not to read,* unlike the *illiterate* persons who are *unable to read*?

With hope, we look to the success of the *Harry Potter* books or to the plethora of fiction for young adults that captures their imaginations and carries them away to places of dragons and magic, of charm and illusion. Or to nonfiction that takes them back in history to learn the real lives and real challenges of people like Winston Churchill, Rosa Parks, or Cesar Chavez.

I'm not suggesting that all problem novels, painful stories, or classics be pulled from classroom shelves. But I am recommending a balance that provides young people with stories that create a sense of well-being and a *desire* to pick up a good book and to find friendship in a good story. In addition to creating an appetite to read, stories that touch children's hearts and souls create a longing to make a difference in the world.

Fast forward to me as a teacher in the 1990s and well into my career. The situation was a teacher's nightmare—five minutes left in the class period with a rowdy group of 7th graders. I looked at the clock, looked at my students, looked at the clock, and looked at my desk for anything that might magically fill the minutes. Sitting there was a Christmas present—a book of motivational short stories. I grabbed it, randomly opened it, and began reading.

I finished the story moments before the dismissal bell, breathed a sigh of relief, and thought nothing more of the matter. The next day, several students walked into class requesting more. So I gathered together short stories with messages of hope, determination, kindness, laughter, love, and life. Thus began a classroom journey that had some very surprising side effects.

To Reach …

After a week of reading stories to students, I polled all of my classes, grades 7–12, to get their reactions to this daily fare. When I received a unanimous response, I acted on this teachable moment. Since each story took only two or three minutes to read, I felt it was not taking significant time away from content. And I knew students were often unaware that they were learning something important. An added benefit was that even my most disruptive students settled down for this story routine that ended each class period.

I was creating what we now call "emotional literacy." Without realizing it, by reading these stories each day, I was creating a classroom environment where it was safe to access and express feelings. Even more important, I was modeling this behavior for my students. If I read a sad story, I cried. Initially, my students were mortified to see a teacher crying. Later, they would occasionally request a "cry story." There were some stories that would make us laugh so hard we would almost pee our pants!

Without ever talking about it, we were sharing our feelings on a daily basis, much as a family would do. And slowly, we became a family. Each of my five classes developed its own unique classroom bond.

Weeks passed, and I saw that my students were treating each other more respectfully. Within months, I noticed changes in the hallways throughout the school. Following a story about a potential suicide, I saw several students stop to help pick up dropped books, rather than to kick them down the hallway, laughing. The mother of a learning disabled student chased me down in a parking lot. "What have you done to my daughter? She *hates to read*, and now she wants me to buy her a book. What's up with that?" Nonreaders were becoming readers because they couldn't wait until the next day for me to read them a story.

As a result of this classroom family, I spent significantly less time on discipline and more time on task. Students were more interested in course content. And learning a difficult task became easier when using a story. I found that students might forget a lecture in a matter of minutes, yet would relate to me a detailed classroom story as much as 30 years later!

To Inspire ...

Educators must realize that they're significant role models for many students. Together with parents, they offer the greatest impact on a youngster's school success by the examples they set.

We can almost universally acknowledge the importance of reading, yet our children aren't testing well on it. They've been raised on technology, and at every juncture they've been exposed to videos and television programs designed to capture the attention of our very youngest learners. In a special report in *Time* magazine (Jan. 16, 2006), it is suggested that these products *do* capture the eyes and ears of infants, despite the American Academy of Pediatrics' recommendation of no television viewing of *any* kind before age two. I'm suggesting less technology and more human interaction for a child's optimal development—try reading them a story.

Many of today's youngsters are coming from classroom environments that are test-driven and anxiety-ridden. For some, their home life is even worse. A story may well be the best *friend* a child will ever have. As educators, we have a duty to help youngsters to choose high-quality *friends*.

The Ending to This Story

Stories can be used solely for the purpose of learning, but they can also be used for pure pleasure and for inspiring students to read. Don't underestimate either version.

Teachers can tell stories, or they can read stories. A story that is *told* has the advantage of full eye contact with audiences, allowing for awareness of body language and adjustments to suit their interest levels. A story that is *read* provides an example for students to follow. When significant role models demonstrate the beauty and power of a good story, youngsters identify with that and feel that they, too, can enjoy reading a book. To begin, choose the approach that you are most comfortable with until you can provide a balance of both telling and reading stories to students.

One of the most important things teachers can give to their students is a passion for the written word. By using stories that touch youngsters' hearts and minds, teachers can make words come alive and can light a fire for reading that will live with them forever. I welcome you on this journey!

References

Armstrong, Thomas. *Seven Kinds of Smart: Identifying and Developing Your Many Intelligences.* New York: Plume, 1999.

Armstrong, Thomas. *Multiple Intelligences in the Classroom,* 3rd ed. Alexandria, Va.: ASCD, 2009.

Bloom, Benjamin S., ed. *Taxonomy of Educational Objectives: The Classification of Educational Goals by a Committee of College and University Examiners. Handbook 1: Cognitive Domain.* New York: Longman, 1956.

Burke, Jim. *I Hear America Reading: Why We Read, What We Read.* Portsmouth, N.H.: Heinemann, 1999.

Burke, Jim. *Reading Reminders.* Portsmouth, N.H.: Heinemann–Boynton/Cook, 2000.

Feinberg, Barbara. *"Reflections on the Problem Novel." American Educator* (Winter 2004/2005). www.aft.org/newspubs/periodicals/ae/winter0405/feinberg.cfm.

Forehand, Mary. *"Bloom's Taxonomy: Original and Revised." In Emerging Perspectives on Learning, Teaching, and Technology,* ed. Orey Michael. Bloomington, Ind.: Association for Educational Communications and Technology, 2005. www.coe.uga.edu/epltt/bloom.htm.

Gardner, Howard. *Frames of Mind: The Theory of Multiple Intelligences.* New York: Basic Books, 1983.

Trelease, Jim. *The Read-Aloud Handbook.* New York: Penguin Books, 2001.

POSTNOTE

"Once upon a time …" Just hearing those familiar words is enough to wake us up. They alert us, and, as the author says, "welcome us to a journey." This news that we are going to hear a story signals to us that for a while we will able to get out of our own skins and see new worlds. It means a "time-out" from our own lives and that we can safely sit back and experience the feelings, thoughts and situations of others.

It has been said that human beings are "people of the story." Storytelling is the oldest form of education, of our coming to understand who we are and what the strange world around us really means. Anthropologists have conjured up images of primitive tribesmen huddled around hillside fires, listening to the leader telling stories to explain the howling wild, the surrounding dark, and those strange beings over the next mountain. Throughout much of human history, storytelling was the primary form of teaching.

In the current 21st-century educational crush to prepare students for life in our complex world, storytelling as a teaching device has been somewhat crowded out. It has lost ground to inquiry techniques, questioning skills, cooperative learning and many others methodologies. The great value of this article is that it brings back to the attention of educators the importance of stories and the art of storytelling. Wise teachers have known for years that students from kindergarten to graduate school straighten up and pay attention when the teacher utters those enchanting words, "Once upon a time …"

DISCUSSION QUESTIONS

1. Are you personally attracted to storytelling as a form of learning?
2. Do you remember teachers who were good storytellers or who used stories effectively in their teaching?
3. How skillful do you believe you are as a storyteller?

RELATED WEBSITE RESOURCES

WEB RESOURCES:

Education Resources Section of Pay It Forward Foundation. Available at:

http://www.payitforwardfoundation.org/educators/index.html.

This site, which is directed by the author of this article, has classroom ideas and resources for both elementary and secondary teachers.

Digital Storytelling in the Classroom. Available at:

http://www.microsoft.com/education/teachers/guides/digital_storytelling.aspx

This Microsoft-sponsored site to aids teachers in using stories in their classrooms and promotes storytelling among students.

Tim Sheppard's Story Links for Story Tellers. Available at:

http://www.timsheppard.co.uk/story/tellinglinks.html.

This is a splendid "link of links" that leads to many useful aspects of narrative teaching. The creator, Tim Sheppard, is a sometimes circus clown and sometimes teacher who has committed himself to spreading the power of story.

Making Cooperative Learning Work

David W. Johnson and Roger T. Johnson

David W. Johnson and **Roger T. Johnson** are professors of education and codirectors of the Cooperative Learning Center at the University of Minnesota. They have been pioneers in the development of and research on cooperative learning.

"Making Cooperative Learning Work," by David W Johnson and Roger T. Johnson, *Theory Into Practice*, Spring 1999. Reprinted by permission of the publisher Taylor & Francis Group, http://www.informaworld.com.

Sandy Koufax was one of the greatest pitchers in the history of baseball. Although he was naturally talented, he was also unusually well trained and disciplined. He was perhaps the only major-league pitcher whose fastball could be heard to hum. Opposing batters, instead of talking and joking around in the dugout, would sit quietly and listen for Koufax's fastball to hum. When it was their turn to bat, they were already intimidated.

There was, however, a simple way for Koufax's genius to have been negated: by making the first author of this article his catcher. To be great, a pitcher needs an outstanding catcher (his great partner was Johnny Roseboro). David is such an unskilled catcher that Koufax would have had to throw the ball much slower in order for David to catch it. This would have deprived Koufax of his greatest weapon.

Placing Roger at key defensive positions in the infield or outfield, furthermore, would have seriously affected Koufax's success. Sandy Koufax was not a great pitcher on his own. Only as part of a team could Koufax achieve greatness. In baseball and in the classroom, it takes a cooperative effort. Extraordinary achievement comes from a cooperative group, not from the individualistic or competitive efforts of an isolated individual.

In 1966 David began training teachers at the University of Minnesota in how to use small groups for instructional purposes. In 1969 Roger joined David at Minnesota, and the training of teachers in how to use cooperative learning groups was extended into teaching methods courses in science education. The formation of the Cooperative Learning Center soon followed to focus on five areas:

1. Summarizing and extending the theory on cooperation and competition.
2. Reviewing the existing research in order to validate or disconfirm the theory and establish what is known and unknown.
3. Conducting a long-term program of research to validate and extend the theory and to identify (a) the conditions under which cooperative,

FOCUS QUESTION

What are the benefits of employing cooperative learning strategies in classrooms?

InTASC

Standards 1, 2, 3, 4, 5, 6, 7, and 8

KEY TERM

• Cooperative learning

competitive, and individualistic efforts are effective and (b) the basic elements that make cooperation work.

4. Operationalizing the validated theory into a set of procedures for teachers and administrators to use.

5. Implementing the procedures in classes, schools, school districts, colleges, and training programs.

These five activities result in an understanding of what is and is not a cooperative effort, the different types of cooperative learning, the five basic elements that make cooperation work, and the outcomes that result when cooperation is carefully structured.

What Is and Is Not a Cooperative Effort

Not all groups are cooperative. There is nothing magical about working in a group. Some kinds of learning groups facilitate student learning and increase the quality of life in the classroom. Other types of learning groups hinder student learning and create disharmony and dissatisfaction. To use cooperative learning effectively, one must know what is and is not a cooperative group (Johnson, Johnson, & Holubec, 1998b).

1. *Pseudo learning group:* Students are assigned to work together but they have no interest in doing so and believe they will be evaluated by being ranked from the highest to the lowest performer. Students hide information from each other, attempt to mislead and confuse each other, and distrust each other. The result is that the sum of the whole is less than the potential of the individual members. Students would achieve more if they were working alone.

2. *Traditional classroom learning group:* Students are assigned to work together and accept that they have to do so. Assignments are structured so that students are evaluated and rewarded as individuals, not as members of the group. They seek each other's information but have no motivation to teach what they know to group-mates. Some students seek a free ride on the efforts of group-mates,

who feel exploited and do less. The result is that the sum of the whole is more than the potential of some of the members, but the more hard working and conscientious students would perform higher if they worked alone.

3. *Cooperative learning group:* Students work together to accomplish shared goals. Students seek outcomes that are beneficial to all. Students discuss material with each other, help one another understand it, and encourage each other to work hard. Individual performance is checked regularly to ensure that all students are contributing and learning. The result is that the group is more than a sum of its parts, and all students perform higher academically than they would if they worked alone.

4. *High-performance cooperative learning group:* This is a group that meets all the criteria for being a cooperative learning group and outperforms all reasonable expectations, given its membership. The level of commitment members have to each other and the group's success is beyond that of most cooperative groups. Few groups ever achieve this level of development.

How well any small group performs depends on how it is structured. Seating people together and calling them a cooperative group does not make them one. Study groups, project groups, lab groups, homerooms, and reading groups are groups, but they are not necessarily cooperative. Even with the best of intentions, teachers may be using traditional classroom learning groups rather than cooperative learning groups. To ensure that a group is cooperative, educators must understand the different ways cooperative learning may be used and the basic elements that need to be carefully structured within every cooperative activity.

Types of Cooperative Learning

Two are better than one, because they have a good reward for toil. For if they fall, one will lift up his fellow; but woe to him who is alone when he falls and has not another to lift him up.... And though a man might prevail against one who is alone, two will withstand him.

A threefold cord is not quickly broken. (Ecclesiastes 4:9–12)

Cooperative learning is a versatile procedure and can be used for a variety of purposes. Cooperative learning groups may be used to teach specific content (formal cooperative learning groups), to ensure active cognitive processing of information during a lecture or demonstration (informal cooperative learning groups), and to provide long-term support and assistance for academic progress (cooperative base groups) (Johnson, Johnson, & Holubec, 1998a, 1998b).

Formal cooperative learning consists of students working together, for one class period or several weeks, to achieve shared learning goals and complete specific tasks and assignments (e.g., problem solving, writing a report, conducting a survey or experiment, learning vocabulary, or answering questions at the end of the chapter) (Johnson, Johnson, & Holubec, 1998b). Any course requirement or assignment may be structured cooperatively. In formal cooperative learning groups, teachers:

1. Make a number of *preinstructional decisions.* Teachers specify the objectives for the lesson (both academic and social skills) and decide on the size of groups, the method of assigning students to groups, the roles students will be assigned, the materials needed to conduct the lesson, and the way the room will be arranged.

2. *Explain* the task and the positive interdependence. A teacher clearly defines the assignment, teaches the required concepts and strategies, specifies the positive interdependence and individual accountability, gives the criteria for success, and explains the social skills to be used.

3. *Monitor* students' learning and *intervene* within the groups to provide task assistance or to increase students' interpersonal and group skills. A teacher systematically observes and collects data on each group as it works. When needed, the teacher intervenes to assist students in completing the task accurately and in working together effectively.

4. *Assess* students' learning and help students process how well their groups functioned. Students' learning is carefully assessed and their performances evaluated. Members of the learning groups then discuss how effectively they worked together and how they can improve in the future.

Informal cooperative learning consists of having students work together to achieve a joint learning goal in temporary, ad-hoc groups that last from a few minutes to one class period (Johnson, Johnson, & Holubec, 1998a; Johnson, Johnson, & Smith, 1998). During a lecture, demonstration, or film, informal cooperative learning can be used to (a) focus student attention on the material to be learned, (b) set a mood conducive to learning, (c) help set expectations as to what will be covered in a class session, (d) ensure that students cognitively process the material being taught, and (e) provide closure to an instructional session.

During direct teaching the instructional challenge for the teacher is to ensure that students do the intellectual work of organizing material, explaining it, summarizing it, and integrating it into existing conceptual structures. Informal cooperative learning groups are often organized so that students engage in 3–5 minute focused discussions before and after a lecture and 2–3 minute turn-to-your-partner discussions interspersed throughout a lecture.

Cooperative base groups are long-term, heterogeneous cooperative learning groups of 3–4 members with stable membership (Johnson, Johnson, & Holubec, 1998a; Johnson, Johnson, & Smith, 1998). Base groups give the support, help, encouragement, and assistance each member needs to make academic progress (attend class, complete all assignments, learn) and develop cognitively and socially in healthy ways. Base groups meet daily in elementary school and twice a week in secondary school (or whenever the class meets). They are permanent (lasting from one to several years) and provide the long-term caring peer relationships necessary to influence members consistently to work hard in school.

The use of base groups tends to improve attendance, personalize the work required and the school experience, and improve the quality and quantity of learning. School and classroom management is enhanced when base groups are given the responsibility for conducting a year-long service project to improve the school. The larger the class or school and the more complex and difficult the subject matter, the more important it is to have base groups. Base groups are also helpful in structuring homerooms and when a teacher meets with a number of advisees.

Example of Integrated Use of Cooperative Learning

An example of the integrated use of the cooperative learning procedures is as follows. Students arrive at class and meet in their base groups to welcome each other, check each student's homework to make sure all members understand the academic material and are prepared for the class session, and tell each other to have a great day.

The teacher then begins a lesson on the limitations of being human (Billion-Dollar Being, 1974). To help students cognitively organize in advance what they know about the advantages and disadvantages of being human, the teacher uses informal cooperative learning. The teacher asks students to form a triad and ponder, "What are five things you cannot do with your human limitations that a billion-dollar being might be designed to do?" Students have 4 minutes to do so. In the next 10 minutes, the teacher explains that while the human body is a marvelous system, we (like other organisms) have very specific limitations. We cannot see bacteria in a drop of water or the rings of Saturn unaided. We cannot hear as well as a deer or fly like an eagle. Humans have never been satisfied being so limited and, therefore, we have invented microscopes, telescopes, and our own wings. The teacher then instructs students to turn to the person next to them and answer the questions, "What are three limitations of humans, what have we invented to

overcome them, and what other human limitations might we be able to overcome?"

Formal cooperative learning is now used in the lesson. The teacher has the 32 students count off from 1 to 8 to form groups of four randomly. Group members sit in a semicircle so they can face each other and still be facing the teacher. Each member is assigned a role: researcher/runner, summarizer/timekeeper, collector/recorder, and technical adviser (role interdependence). Every group gets one large (2 × 3-feet) piece of paper, a marking pen, a rough draft sheet for designing the being, an assignment sheet explaining the task and cooperative goal structure, and four student self-evaluation checklists (resource interdependence). The task is to design a billion-dollar being that overcomes the human limitations thought of by the class and the group. The group members are to draw a diagram of the being on the scratch paper and, when they have something they like, transfer it to the larger paper.

The teacher establishes positive goal interdependence by asking for one drawing from the group that all group members contribute to and can explain. The criterion for success is to complete the diagram in the 30-minute time limit. The teacher observes each group to ensure that members are fulfilling their roles and that any one member can explain any part of the being at any time. The teacher informs students that the expected social skills to be used by all students are encouraging each other's participation, contributing ideas, and summarizing. She defines the skill of encouraging participation and has each student practice it twice before the lesson begins.

While students work in their groups, the teacher monitors by systematically observing each group and intervening to provide academic assistance and help in using the interpersonal and small group skills required to work together effectively. At the end of the lesson, the groups hand in their diagrams of the billion-dollar being to be assessed and evaluated. Group members then process how well they worked together by identifying actions each member engaged in that helped the group succeed and one thing that could be added to improve their group next time.

The teacher uses informal cooperative learning to provide closure to the lesson by asking students to meet in new triads and write out six conclusions about the limitations of human beings and what we have done to overcome them. At the end of the class session, the cooperative base groups meet to review what students believe is the most important thing they have learned during the day, what homework has been assigned, what help each member needs to complete the homework, and to tell each other to have a fun afternoon and evening.

The Cooperative School

Teachers are not the only ones who need to carefully structure cooperation. Administrators need to create a learning community by structuring cooperation at the school level (Johnson & Johnson, 1994, 1999). In addition, they have to attend to the cooperation among faculty, between the school and parents, and between the school and the community.

Administrators, for example, may structure three types of cooperative faculty teams. Collegial teaching teams are formed to increase teachers' instructional expertise and success. They consist of 2–5 teachers who meet weekly and discuss how to better implement cooperative learning within their classrooms. Teachers are assigned to task forces to plan and implement solutions to school-wide issues and problems such as curriculum adoptions and lunchroom behavior. Ad hoc decision-making groups are used during faculty meetings to involve all staff members in important school decisions.

The use of cooperative teams at the building level ensures that there is a congruent cooperative team-based organizational structure within both classrooms and the school. Finally, the superintendent uses the same types of cooperative teams to maximize the productivity of district administrators.

Basic Elements of Cooperation

In order for an activity to be cooperative, five basic elements are essential and need to be included (Johnson & Johnson, 1989; Johnson, Johnson, & Holubec, 1998a). The five essential elements are as follows.

1. *Positive interdependence:* Positive interdependence is the perception that we are linked with others in a way so that we cannot succeed unless they do. Their work benefits us and our work benefits them. Within every cooperative lesson, positive goal interdependence must be established through mutual learning goals (learn the assigned material and make sure that all members of your group learn the assigned material). In order to strengthen positive interdependence, joint rewards (if all members of your group score 90 percent correct or better on the test, each will receive 5 bonus points), divided resources (giving each group member a part of the total information required to complete an assignment), and complementary roles (reader, checker, encourager, elaborator) may also be used.

2. *Individual accountability:* Individual accountability exists when the performance of each individual student is assessed and the results are given back to the group and the individual. The purpose of cooperative learning groups is to make each member a stronger individual. Students learn together so that they can subsequently perform higher as individuals. To ensure that each member is strengthened, students are held individually accountable to do their share of the work. Common ways to structure individual accountability include (a) giving an individual test to each student, (b) randomly selecting one student's product to represent the entire group, or (c) having each student explain what they have learned to a classmate.

3. *Face-to-face promotive interaction:* Individuals promote each other's success by helping, assisting, supporting, encouraging, and praising each other's efforts to achieve. Certain cognitive activities and interpersonal dynamics only occur when students get involved in promoting each other's learning. These include orally explaining how to solve problems, discussing the nature of the concepts being learned, teaching one's knowledge to classmates, and connecting present with past learning. Accountability to peers, ability to influence each other's reasoning and conclusions, social modeling, social support, and interpersonal rewards all increase as the face-to-face interactions among group members increase.

In addition, the verbal and nonverbal responses of other group members provide important information concerning a student's performance. Silent students are uninvolved students who are not contributing to the learning of others as well as themselves. To obtain meaningful face-to-face interaction, the size of groups needs to be small (2–4 members).

4. *Social skills:* Contributing to the success of a cooperative effort requires interpersonal and small group skills. Placing socially unskilled individuals in a group and telling them to cooperate does not guarantee that they will be able to do so effectively. Persons must be taught the leadership, decision-making, trust-building, communication, and conflict-management skills just as purposefully and precisely as academic skills. Procedures and strategies for teaching students social skills may be found in Johnson (1997) and Johnson and F. Johnson (1997).

5. *Group processing:* Group processing exists when group members discuss how well they are achieving their goals and maintaining effective working relationships. Groups need to describe what member actions are helpful and unhelpful and make decisions about what behaviors to continue or change. When difficulties in relating to each other arise, students must engage in group processing and identify, define, and solve the problems they are having working together effectively.

Understanding these five basic elements and developing skills in structuring them allows teachers to (a) adapt cooperative learning to their unique circumstances, needs, and students, (b) fine tune their use of cooperative learning, and (c) prevent and solve problems students have in working together.

What Do We Know About Cooperative Efforts?

> Everyone has to work together; if we can't get everybody working toward common goals, nothing is going to happen. (Harold K. Sperlich, president, Chrysler Corporation)

A great deal of research has been conducted comparing the relative effects of cooperative, competitive, and individualistic efforts on instructional outcomes. During the past 100 years, over 550 experimental and 100 correlational studies have been conducted by a wide variety of researchers in different decades with different age subjects, in different subject areas, and in different settings (see Johnson & Johnson, 1989, for a complete listing and review of these studies).

The type of interdependence structured among students determines how they interact with each other, which, in turn, largely determines instructional outcomes. Structuring situations cooperatively results in students interacting in ways that promote each other's success, structuring situations competitively results in students interacting in ways that oppose each other's success, and structuring situations individualistically results in no interaction among students. These interaction patterns affect numerous instructional outcomes, which may be subsumed within the three broad and interrelated categories of effort exerted to achieve, quality of relationships among participants, and participants' psychological adjustment and social competence (see Figure 1) (Johnson & Johnson, 1989).

Achievement

> Achievement is a we thing, not a me thing, always the product of many hands and heads. (John Atkinson)

Regarding the question of how successful competitive, individualistic, and cooperative efforts are in promoting productivity and achievement, over 375 studies have been conducted in the past 100 years (Johnson & Johnson, 1989). Working together to achieve a common goal produces higher achievement and greater productivity than does working alone. This is so well confirmed by so much research that it stands as one of the strongest principles of social and organizational psychology.

Cooperative learning, furthermore, results in process gain (i.e., more higher-level reasoning, more frequent generation of new ideas and solutions), greater transfer of what is learned within

FIGURE 1 Outcomes of Cooperative Learning

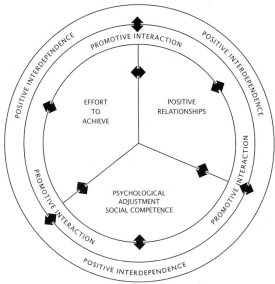

Source: Johnson, 1999.

one situation to another (i.e., group to individual transfer), and more time on task than does competitive or individualistic learning. The more conceptual the task, the more problem solving required; the more higher-level reasoning and critical thinking, the more creativity required; and the greater the application required of what is being learned to the real world, the greater the superiority of cooperative over competitive and individualistic efforts.

Cooperative learning ensures that all students are meaningfully and actively involved in learning. Active, involved students do not tend to engage in disruptive, off-task behavior. Cooperative learning also ensures that students are achieving up to their potential and are experiencing psychological success, so they are motivated to continue to invest energy and effort in learning. Those who experience academic failure are at risk for tuning out and acting up, which often leads to physical or verbal aggression.

Interpersonal Relationships

A faithful friend is a strong defense, and he that hath found him, hath found a treasure. (Ecclesiastes 6:14)

Over 180 studies have been conducted since the 1940s on the relative impact of cooperative, competitive, and individualistic experiences on interpersonal attraction (Johnson & Johnson, 1989). The data indicate that cooperative experiences promote greater interpersonal attraction than do competitive or individualistic ones. Cooperative learning promotes the development of caring and committed relationships for every student. Even when individuals initially dislike each other or are obviously different from each other, cooperative experiences have been found to promote greater liking than is found in competitive and individualistic situations.

Cooperative groups help students establish and maintain friendships with peers. As relationships become more positive, there are corresponding improvements in productivity, morale, feelings of personal commitment and responsibility to do the assigned work, willingness to take on and persist in completing difficult tasks, and commitment to peers' success and growth. Absenteeism and turnover of membership decreases. Students who are isolated or alienated from their peers and who do not have friends are more likely to be at risk for violent and destructive behavior than students who experience social support and a sense of belonging.

Psychological Health and Social Competence

Working cooperatively with peers, and valuing cooperation, results in greater psychological health, higher self-esteem, and greater social competencies than does competing with peers or working independently. When individuals work together to complete assignments, they interact (improving social skills and competencies), promote each other's success (gaining self-worth), and form personal as well as professional relationships (creating the basis for healthy social development).

Cooperative efforts with caring people tend to increase personal ego-strength, self-confidence, independence, and autonomy. They provide the opportunity to share and solve personal problems, which increases an individual's resilience and ability to cope with adversity and stress. The more individuals work cooperatively, the more they see themselves as worthwhile and as having value and the more autonomous and independent they tend to be.

Cooperative groups provide an arena in which individuals develop the interpersonal and small group skills needed to work effectively with diverse schoolmates. Students learn how to communicate effectively, provide leadership, help the group make good decisions, build trust, repair hurt feelings, and understand others' perspectives. Even kindergartners can practice social skills each day in cooperative activities. Cooperative experiences are not a luxury. They are a necessity for the healthy social and psychological development of individuals who can function independently.

Conclusion

Cooperative learning is the instructional use of small groups in which students work together to maximize their own and each other's learning. Cooperative learning may be differentiated from pseudo groups and traditional classroom learning groups. There are three types of cooperative learning: formal cooperative learning, informal cooperative learning, and cooperative base groups. The basic elements that make cooperation work are positive interdependence, individual accountability, promotive interaction, appropriate use of social skills, and periodic processing of how to improve the effectiveness of the group.

When efforts are structured cooperatively, there is considerable evidence that students will exert more effort to achieve (learn more, use

higher-level reasoning strategies more frequently, build more complete and complex conceptual structures, and retain information learned more accurately), build more positive and supportive relationships (including relationships with diverse individuals), and develop in more healthy ways (psychological health, self-esteem, ability to manage stress and adversity).

References

Billion-Dollar Being. (1974). *Topics in applied science.* Golden, CO: Jefferson County Schools.

Johnson, D. W. (1997). Reaching out: Interpersonal effectiveness and self-actualization (6th ed.). Boston: Allyn & Bacon.

Johnson, D. W., & Johnson, F. (1997). *Joining together: Group theory and group skills* (6th ed.). Boston: Allyn & Bacon.

Johnson, D. W., & Johnson, R. (1989). *Cooperation and competition: Theory and research.* Edina, MN: Interaction Book Co.

Johnson, D. W., & Johnson, R. (1994). Leading the cooperative school (2nd ed.). Edina, MN: Interaction Book Co.

Johnson, D. W., & Johnson, R. (1999). The three Cs of classroom and school management. In H. Freiberg (Ed.), *Beyond behaviorism: Changing the classroom management paradigm.* Boston: Allyn & Bacon.

Johnson, D. W., Johnson, R., & Holubec, E. (1998a). *Advanced cooperative learning* (3rd ed.). Edina, MN: Interaction Book Co.

Johnson, D. W., Johnson, R., & Holubec, E. (1998b). *Cooperation in the classroom* (7th ed.). Edina, MN: Interaction Book Co.

Johnson, D. W., Johnson, R., & Smith, K. (1998). *Active learning: Cooperation in the college classroom* (2nd ed.). Edina, MN: Interaction Book Co.

POSTNOTE

The authors have been researching and championing cooperative learning for many years, and their efforts have made a major contribution to American education. Cooperative learning has become a staple in both pre-service and in-service teacher education. David and Roger Johnson's contributions in developing and researching cooperative learning strategies have placed them among our classic selections.

Although most educators applaud the idea of cooperative learning, few use it on a regular basis. Many young teachers read about cooperative learning, become advocates, try it a few times with few of the positive results discussed in this article, then put it away in a mental closet (labeled "Great Ideas from the Ivory Tower That Don't Work in the Trenches") and go on to more traditional "sage on the stage" instructional approaches. The key to a more widespread use of cooperative learning may be captured by the well-known story of the tourist in New York City who stops a native and asks: "Sir, how do I get to Carnegie Hall?" The New Yorker doesn't stop, but yells over his shoulder, "Practice! Practice! Practice!" From personal experiences, we know that becoming skillful at cooperative learning takes more than just knowledge of it. Like Sandy Koufax, knowing the mechanics of throwing a fastball is hardly enough. Our advice: Practice! Practice! Practice!

DISCUSSION QUESTIONS

1. Describe the experiences you, as a student, have had with cooperative learning.
2. Do you agree or disagree with the common criticism that cooperative learning is unfair because it slows down the progress of the academically gifted?
3. Which aspects of cooperative learning are most appealing? Which are least appealing?

RELATED WEBSITE RESOURCES AND VIDEO CASES

WEB RESOURCES:

The Cooperative Learning Center (CLC) at the University of Minnesota. Available at:

http://www.cooplearn.org.

Provided by the CLC, this website contains descriptions of center work; essays and research reports by Johnson and Johnson and others; and book and supply catalogues.

The Jigsaw Classroom. Available at:

http://www.jigsaw.org.

Developed by Eliot Aronson and the Social Psychology Network, this website contains "how-to" explanations, research summaries, implementation tips, and related links.

▶II TEACHSOURCE VIDEO CASE

COOPERATIVE LEARNING IN THE ELEMENTARY GRADES: JIGSAW MODEL

In this fifth-grade class, students use the Jigsaw model of cooperative learning to study the ancient Olympics. Go to the website for the Education Media Library at CengageBrain.com to watch the video clips, study the artifacts in the case, and reflect on the following questions.

1. How does this teacher manage the classroom environment during cooperative learning?

2. How are group composition and group-skills training important to the success of these groups?

3. What new things about cooperative learning did you learn from this video case?

▶II TEACHSOURCE VIDEO CASE

COOPERATIVE LEARNING: HIGH SCHOOL HISTORY LESSON

In this high school classroom, the teacher demonstrates great sensitivity to group dynamics as students are assigned to groups to analyze texts and respond to the question of what it means to be a human being. Go to the website for the Education Media Library at CengageBrain.com to watch the video clips, study the artifacts in the case, and reflect on the following questions.

1. What do you think of Jake's description of the benefits of cooperative learning? Do his comments ring true to you?

2. What advice about setting up *ad hoc* cooperative groups does the teacher offer in the bonus video, "The Benefits of Ad Hoc Cooperative Learning Groups"? What do you consider to be important criteria for setting up partners and groups?

34

The Goals of Differentiation

Carol Ann Tomlinson

Carol Ann Tomlinson is the William Clay Parrish, Jr. Professor in the Curry School of Education, University of Virginia, and Chair of the Department of Leadership, Foundations, and Policy. She is the author of many articles and books on gifted education and differentiated instruction.

"The Goals of Differentiation," by Carol Ann Tomlinson, 2008, *Educational Leadership* 66(3), pp. 26–30. © 2008 by ASCD. Reprinted with permission. Learn more about ASCD at www.ascd.org.

After visiting a high school biology class, I asked the teacher why she thought it was worth her effort to set up that day's lab so that students could complete it in several different ways. She looked puzzled at the question, but her answer was direct: "Why do I do this? Because it makes me a better teacher and it makes my students more successful learners."

Knowing this teacher, I'm fairly certain that her concept of making her students "more successful learners" extended beyond covering more content knowledge. The ultimate aim of the work that went into preparing for the lab—her detailed knowledge of her students and her efforts to differentiate instruction to meet their individual needs—was to help her students become focused, motivated, and independent learners. Much more than instruction in biology was going on in that classroom.

Differentiated instruction is student-aware teaching. It is guided by the premise that schools should maximize student potential, not simply bring students to an externally established norm on a test. To grow as much and as rapidly as possible, students must not only learn essential content, but also increasingly take charge of their own lives as learners.

> **FOCUS** QUESTION
>
> *How does differentiated instruction address the needs of individual learners?*

InTASC
Standards 1, 2, 3, 4, 5, 6, 7, and 8

KEY TERM

- Differentiated instruction

It's Only Logical

There's logic in differentiated instruction when we use it to ensure student mastery of content. Differentiation calls for teachers to have clear learning goals that are rooted in content standards but crafted to ensure student engagement and understanding. If teachers are uncertain about the learning destination, their students are adrift. We want students to go into the world fully possessed of the power of knowledge. Yet what we teach must engage learners, or we've lost them before we've begun.

Thus, differentiation also proposes that teachers must know their students. As one educator noted, it's virtually impossible to make content relevant for learners whom you don't know (Littky, 2004). For many students, lack of connection with the teacher spells academic failure.

Further, differentiation calls on teachers to vigilantly monitor student proximity to content goals throughout a learning cycle. The teacher needs to know what each student knows and can do at a given moment. How else could we plan instruction to increase the likelihood that students stay on course toward the destination?

Differentiation also counsels that—armed with assessment information and other knowledge about a student—the teacher should adapt teaching plans to attend to learner readiness, interest, and preferred modes of learning. Once we understand what a student knows (and doesn't know), what motivates that student to learn, and how the student learns best, differentiation is simply what comes next (Earl, 2003).

So differentiated instruction is a logical way to achieve the goal of content acquisition. But there's a parallel logic in differentiation that functions at a deeper level. Differentiation enables teachers to go beyond the question, How can I make sure a student masters a body of information? asking instead, How can I help create a real learner? As teachers address this question, they need to consider four elements that help students take charge of their own learning and thus take charge of their lives: trust, fit, voice, and awareness.

Building Trust

Trust begins when students believe that the teacher is on their side—when they realize that the teacher views them as persons of worth, believes in their capacity to succeed, and works in their best interest. Trust develops as students become aware that what goes on in the classroom supports their success individually and as a group. This kind of trust creates a partnership of striving for excellence.

In the 2004 summer Olympics, an athlete from an emerging country qualified to compete in swimming because he was the best from his country, a place where training for top-level swimming competition was simply not available. Before he arrived at the Olympic venue, he had never even seen an Olympic-size pool. In his initial heat, he flailed at the water with a stroke so awkward it was painful to watch. As the race progressed, he was clearly out of breath and gasping for air. Spectators feared he would drown. Nonetheless, he swam the entire race. Later in an interview, he confirmed that he, too, was afraid for his safety as he swam. "Why did you continue?" asked the interviewer. "Why didn't you just stop?" Without a pause the young man answered, "Because the people in the stands were clapping so hard for me. I just didn't want to let them down."

That's an apt metaphor for the classroom. When the people around us are pulling for us, when we feel buoyed by their expectations and partnership, we persevere.

Teachers build trust through an accumulation of small, positive exchanges with individual students. They build trust when they take a minute or two each day to share experiences with the class and to build memories, when they listen to student responses with respect, and when they provide ample time for practice and feedback before the judgment of grading. They build trust when they ensure that classroom routines exist to support student success and when they enlist students as partners in implementing those routines. Differentiation provides a structure that supports trust by enabling teachers to actively and optimistically support each student's learning.

Ensuring Fit

A second element that gives students ownership of their learning is making sure that the learning fits the student. Fit suggests that we ask students to do only what they are ready to do. If work is consistently beyond a student's reach, that student becomes more occupied with escaping possible danger or humiliation than with learning. If work is consistently too easy for a student, the student develops strategies for marking time rather than for addressing challenge. In both instances, the student's willingness to persist in the face of difficulty diminishes.

Fit also requires that what we ask students to learn connects with what they care about. When knowledge, understanding, and skill help students make sense of their world, do things they want to do, or develop a sense of personal agency, students will give whatever it takes to succeed.

Further, fit implies that students have the opportunity to learn and to express learning in ways that facilitate their success. Such opportunities make learning efficient rather than cumbersome and enhance the likelihood that students' efforts will lead to success.

Sarah Kajder (2006) found that a large number of students in her high school classroom were discouraged with school and alienated from learning. They didn't read, they told her. They couldn't, and they weren't going to. Meeting them where they were in readiness, interests, and learning modes, she asked the students to find images on the Internet that reflected their feelings about reading. One student brought in a picture of a bulldozer and wrote about how reading tore him apart and destroyed his chances of success. To counteract these feelings, Kajder used graphic novels, digital word walls and flash cards, and online journals to build students' competencies, connect with their worlds, and nurture their expression. Later in the year, one of her students wrote,

> I don't know what it is about this assignment but I have never taken so much time to read something before. I think maybe it's because I'm taking the time to allow the picture to unfold in my head. (p. 90)

Teachers in differentiated classrooms create fit by using small-group instruction, reading partners, text at varied reading levels, personalized rubrics, miniworkshops, learning contracts, product and task options with common learning goals, independent studies, varied homework assignments, and a host of other strategies—not for the sake of using them, but to make learning work for each student. These teachers are flexible with time, seating arrangements, working conditions, student groupings, and other classroom elements. They assiduously study their students. They use ongoing assessment to understand what a student needs next, and they adjust their teaching in response to what they discover.

When curriculum, instruction, and classroom environment fit a student, the student's sense of possibility increases. The balance of challenge and support, the sense of personal relevance, and the opportunity to learn and express learning in ways that work for the student enhance the student's willingness to risk the hard work of real learning.

Strengthening Voice

Voice, the third element, is an extension and refinement of thought that gives students power over their own destinies as learners. As Parker Palmer (1998) wrote,

> Learning doesn't happen when students are unable to express their ideas, emotions, confusion, ignorance, and prejudices. In fact, only when people can speak their minds does education have a chance to happen. (p. 74)

Teachers honor student voice by inviting, encouraging, affirming, supporting, mentoring, and responding with honesty.

A pair of high school teachers asked their classes to complete a set of probing questions about the effectiveness of their class so that the teachers could become "their best selves." The teachers shared with their classes the percentage of students who chose each answer as well as some elaborative student responses. The teachers then explained to the students how particular responses would help them adjust instruction. To observers of the class sessions in which student feedback was sought, shared, and acted on, it was clear that students understood the power of their voice (Tomlinson, Brimijoin, & Narvaez, 2008).

Because differentiated instruction enables teachers to individualize so they can better respond to student needs, it provides a nurturing environment for student voice to grow. Teachers cultivate student voice when, among other approaches, they effectively use dialogue journals; make time for student discussions; problem solve with individuals, small groups, and the whole class; ask for student input in developing classroom rules and routines; provide guided choice for tasks and ways of accomplishing them; conduct morning meetings; have students conduct parent conferences; provide opportunities for students to review one another's work using clear criteria; and listen to students' experiences and connect them with content.

Elementary teacher Stephen Levy (1996) explained how he listened to student voices as he crafted curriculum to engage students' minds and spirits:

> We made all our decisions by consensus. We sat in a circle on the floor, and each person had a chance to state an opinion or pass. After all opinions were heard, students were invited to defend their idea or to explain how their opinion had been modified by what they had heard. Most discussions were very civil, and consensus was clear. (pp. 56–57)

In Levy's class, students owned their learning. Trust and fit, also evident in his classes, are intertwined with voice.

Developing Awareness

Awareness is the final element. Real learners understand how learning works. They know how to make sense of text, how to listen, and how to ask questions. They know how to gauge their work based on criteria for success. They understand how to capitalize on their learning strengths and how to compensate for their weaknesses. They know how to plan, follow through with plans, modify plans when necessary, and evaluate the effectiveness of their planning. Through those avenues, they come to believe that they are captains of their own fate as learners. Teachers who differentiate for student ownership of learning guide each student in developing these abilities.

Monica Harrold, then a 1st grade teacher, frequently led her students to analyze a piece of work they were about to begin with a partner or small group. After she described the task, she'd say, "Now tell me what skills are necessary to do this work really well." Gradually, her young students became proficient at naming the skills the assignment called for. Next, she'd ask them to think

about which of the necessary skills they had and which ones they'd need to be sure someone else in the group had. In my observations of Monica's classroom, it was common to hear a student say, "I can draw and I can write, but I'm not very good at finding information so I'll need to work with someone who can do that." At age 6, these students were already becoming metacognitively aware. They were learning to position themselves as successful learners by controlling their working conditions.

Teachers build student awareness as they talk about what they observe in their students, how they plan, why they teach as they do, and how they solve problems in their own work. They use rubrics that are carefully constructed to support student thinking about the quality of their work instead of merely awarding points for completed work. They help students analyze their points of entry in the rubrics and set goals for next steps. They have students keep track of their own skill development, feedback, and grades. They give students opportunities to reflect on their work through exit cards, journals, or plus/minus/delta charts that aid them in thinking about their strengths, their weaknesses, and the changes they will make as they approach future work.

Academic awareness builds academic success. Success inevitably sends an invitation writ large to pursue further success and to own both its processes and its products.

A Dual Goal

Differentiated instruction is a way of thinking about teaching. Certainly one of its goals is increased student mastery of essential content and skills. But few students will become dedicated learners because their standardized test scores increase. Differentiation, fully understood, is concerned with developing not only content mastery but also student efficacy and ownership of learning.

In a differentiated classroom, even as students grapple with fractions, French verbs, names of explorers, and the periodic table, their teachers strive to build trust, ensure fit, strengthen voice, and develop awareness. These elements help students build a sturdy platform to support the kind of learning that enriches life. Teachers in effectively differentiated classes help students participate in the formation of their own identity as learners. As students come to trust that process, they develop the power and agency they need to become intellectual beings and thus to own the process of learning.

References

Earl, L. (2003). *Assessment as learning: Using classroom assessment to maximize student learning.* Thousand Oaks, CA: Corwin.

Kajder, S. (2006). *Bringing the outside in: Visual ways to support reluctant readers.* Portland, ME: Stenhouse.

Levy, S. (1996). *Starting from scratch: One classroom builds its own curriculum.* Portsmouth, NH: Heinemann.

Littky, D. (2004). *The big picture: Education is everyone's business.* Alexandria, VA: ASCD.

Palmer, P. (1998). *The courage to teach: Exploring the inner landscape of a teacher's life.* San Francisco: Jossey-Bass.

Tomlinson, C., Brimijoin, K., & Narvaez, L. (2008). The *differentiated school: Making revolutionary changes in teaching and learning.* Alexandria, VA: ASCD.

POSTNOTE

The term *differentiated instruction* is relatively new in education circles, but its practice is as old as teachers and classrooms. Teachers know that their classrooms contain students with tremendous diversity—ethnic, cultural, racial, academic, learning styles, to name but a few of the diverse characteristics. How can teachers plan and deliver instruction and assessment that will respond to these forms of diversity to help students learn better? Differentiated instruction is teaching with student variance in mind and using practical ways to respond to learner needs. Instead of presuming that all of your students are essentially alike, differentiated instruction means starting where the students are and planning varied approaches to what individual students need to learn, how they will learn it, and how they can express what they have learned. The idea of differentiated or personalized instruction has great appeal to teachers and teacher educators, but its implementation may seem overwhelming, particularly for new teachers. In other writings, Carol Ann Tomlinson advises that teachers start the process slowly and gradually expand differentiation as they feel comfortable and have the time. Most important is making a commitment to the process of responding to student differences.

DISCUSSION QUESTIONS

1. If you could ask the author one question, what would it be?
2. What concerns or questions do you have regarding differentiated instruction?
3. Did you have a teacher who used differentiated instruction particularly successfully? Describe what he or she did that made the instruction successful.

RELATED WEBSITE RESOURCES AND VIDEO CASE

WEB RESOURCES:

ASCD. Available at:

http://www.ascd.org.

This educational leadership organization website contains numerous articles on differentiation.

Reaching All Students. Available at:

http://www.openc.k12.or.us/reaching/tag/dcsamples.html.

The Reaching All Students website contains many sample lesson plans that use differentiated instruction.

 TEACHSOURCE VIDEO CASE

ACADEMIC DIVERSITY: DIFFERENTIATED INSTRUCTION

In this third-grade classroom, the teacher tries to design instruction that meets the needs of different types of learners. Go to the website for the Education Media Library at CengageBrain.com to watch the video clips, study the artifacts in the case, and reflect on the following questions.

1. How are all students held accountable for mastering the same writing-skills content, even though they approach the task differently?

2. Building on students' strengths when planning instruction is essential, according to the teacher in this video. Can you recall examples of teachers you had who built on your strengths? What were your learning results?

 The companion website for this text includes useful study tools and resources. Go to CengageBrain.com to access links to relevant websites, glossaries, flashcards, an article review form, and more.

Foundations

As a career, education is a practical field like medicine or criminal justice. It is not a discipline or content area, such as anthropology, physics, or English literature. However, education draws on these various disciplines and fields of knowledge to guide teachers in their work.

The term *foundations* as used in *educational foundations* is a metaphor, suggesting that as a house is built upon a foundation, so should the practice of education rest on a solid foundation of basic knowledge. The primary intellectual foundations for the practice of education include philosophy, history, psychology, and sociology. The articles selected for this section demonstrate the contribution of foundational scholarship to the practice of teaching.

35

CLASSIC

My Pedagogic Creed

John Dewey

John Dewey (1859–1952) was a philosopher, educator, and clearly the most influential single figure in the history of American educational thought. He denounced classical approaches to learning and stressed teaching students *how* to use knowledge rather than simply pursue "learning for learning's sake." Although honored as the founder of the Progressive Education movement, his theories receive more lip service than practice.

Dewey John, (1897) "My pedagogic creed" *The School Journal*, Volume LIV, Number 3 (January 16, 1897), pages 77–80.

Article I—What Education Is

FOCUS QUESTION

What did the "Father of Progressive Education" actually believe?

KEY TERMS

- Continuous reconstruction of experience
- Social reconstruction

I BELIEVE THAT

- all education proceeds by the participation of the individual in the social consciousness of the race. This process begins unconsciously almost at birth, and is continually shaping the individual's powers, saturating his consciousness, forming his habits, training his ideas, and arousing his feelings and emotions. Through this unconscious education the individual gradually comes to share in the intellectual and moral resources which humanity has succeeded in getting together. He becomes an inheritor of the funded capital of civilization. The most formal and technical education in the world cannot safely depart from this general process. It can only organize it or differentiate it in some particular direction.

- the only true education comes through the stimulation of the child's powers by the demands of the social situations in which he finds himself. Through these demands he is stimulated to act as a member of a unity, to emerge from his original narrowness of action and feeling, and to conceive of himself from the standpoint of the welfare of the group to which he belongs. Through the responses which others make to his own activities he comes to know what these mean in social terms. The value which they have is reflected back into them. For instance, through the response which is made to the child's instinctive babblings the child comes to know what those babblings mean; they are transformed into articulate language, and thus the child is introduced into the consolidated wealth of ideas and emotions which are now summed up in language.

- this educational process has two sides—one psychological and one sociological—and that neither can be subordinated to the other, or neglected, without evil results following. Of these two sides, the psychological is the basis. The child's own instincts and powers furnish the material and give the starting-point for all education. Save as the efforts of the educator connect with some activity which the child is carrying on of his own initiative independent of the educator, education becomes reduced to a pressure from without. It may, indeed, give certain external results, but cannot truly be called educative. Without insight into the psychological structure and activities of the individual the educative process will, therefore, be haphazard and arbitrary. If it chances to coincide with the child's activity it will get a leverage; if it does not, it will result in friction, or disintegration, or arrest of the child-nature.

- knowledge of social conditions, of the present state of civilization, is necessary in order properly to interpret the child's powers. The child has his own instincts and tendencies, but we do not know what these mean until we can translate them into their social equivalents. We must be able to carry them back into a social past and see them as the inheritance of previous race activities. We must also be able to project them into the future to see what their outcome and end will be. In the illustration just used, it is the ability to see in the child's babblings the promise and potency of a future social intercourse and conversation which enables one to deal in the proper way with that instinct.
- the psychological and social sides are organically related, and that education cannot be regarded as a compromise between the two, or a superimposition of one upon the other. We are told that the psychological definition of education is barren and formal—that it gives us only the idea of a development of all the mental powers without giving us any idea of the use to which these powers are put. On the other hand, it is urged that the social definition of education, as getting adjusted to civilization, makes of it a forced and external process, and results in subordinating the freedom of the individual to a preconceived social and political status.
- each of these objections is true when urged against one side isolated from the other. In order to know what a power really is we must know what its end, use, or function is,

and this we cannot know save as we conceive of the individual as active in social relationships. But, on the other hand, the only possible adjustment which we can give to the child under existing conditions is that which arises through putting him in complete possession of all his powers. With the advent of democracy and modern industrial conditions, it is impossible to foretell definitely just what civilization will be twenty years from now. Hence it is impossible to prepare the child for any precise set of conditions. To prepare him for the future life means to give him command of himself; it means so to train him that he will have the full and ready use of all his capacities; that his eye and ear and hand may be tools ready to command, that his judgment may be capable of grasping the conditions under which it has to work, and the executive forces be trained to act economically and efficiently. It is impossible to reach this sort of adjustment save as constant regard is had to the individual's own powers, tastes, and interests—that is, as education is continually converted into psychological terms.

In sum, I believe that the individual who is to be educated is a social individual, and that society is an organic union of individuals. If we eliminate the social factor from the child we are left only with an abstraction; if we eliminate the individual factor from society, we are left only with an inert and lifeless mass. Education, therefore, must begin with a psychological insight into the child's capacities, interests, and habits. It must be controlled at every point by reference to these same considerations. These powers, interests, and habits must be continually interpreted—we must know what they mean. They must be translated into terms of their social equivalents—into terms of what they are capable of in the way of social service.

Article II—What the School Is

I BELIEVE THAT

- the school is primarily a social institution. Education being a social process, the school is simply that form of community life in which all those agencies are concentrated that will be most effective in bringing the child to share in the inherited resources of the race, and to use his own powers for social ends.

- education, therefore, is a process of living and not a preparation for future living.
- the school must represent present life—life as real and vital to the child as that which he carries on in the home, in the neighborhood, or on the playground.
- that education which does not occur through forms of life, forms that are worth living for their own sake, is always a poor substitute for the genuine reality, and tends to cramp and to deaden.
- the school, as an institution, should simplify existing social life; should reduce it, as it were, to an embryonic form. Existing life is so complex that the child cannot be brought into contact with it without either confusion or distraction; he is either overwhelmed by the multiplicity of activities which are going on, so that he loses his own power of orderly reaction, or he is so stimulated by these various activities that his powers are prematurely called into play and he becomes either unduly specialized or else disintegrated.
- as such simplified social life, the school life should grow gradually out of the home life; that it should take up and continue the activities with which the child is already familiar in the home.
- it should exhibit these activities to the child, and reproduce them in such ways that the child will gradually learn the meaning of them, and be capable of playing his own part in relation to them.
- this is a psychological necessity, because it is the only way of securing continuity in the child's growth, the only way of giving a background of past experience to the new ideas given in school.
- it is also a social necessity because the home is the form of social life in which the child has been nurtured and in connection with which

he has had his moral training. It is the business of the school to deepen and extend his sense of the values bound up in his home life.

- much of the present education fails because it neglects this fundamental principle of the school as a form of community life. It conceives the school as a place where certain information is to be given, where certain lessons are to be learned, or where certain habits are to be formed. The value of these is conceived as lying largely in the remote future; the child must do these things for the sake of something else he is to do; they are mere preparations. As a result they do not become a part of the life experience of the child and so are not truly educative.
- the moral education centers upon this conception of the school as a mode of social life, that the best and deepest moral training is precisely that which one gets through having to enter into proper relations with others in a unity of work and thought. The present educational systems, so far as they destroy or neglect this unity, render it difficult or impossible to get any genuine, regular moral training.
- the child should be stimulated and controlled in his work through the life of the community.
- under existing conditions far too much of the stimulus and control proceeds from the teacher, because of neglect of the idea of the school as a form of social life.
- the teacher's place and work in the school is to be interpreted from this same basis. The teacher is not in the school to impose certain ideas or to form certain habits in the child, but is there as a member of the community to select the influences which shall affect the child and to assist him in properly responding to these influences.
- the discipline of the school should proceed from the life of the school as a whole and not directly from the teacher.
- the teacher's business is simply to determine, on the basis of larger experience and riper wisdom, how the discipline of life shall come to the child.
- all questions of the grading of the child and his promotion should be determined by reference to the same standard. Examinations are of use

only so far as they test the child's fitness for social life and reveal the place in which he can be of the most service and where he can receive the most help.

Article III—The Subject-Matter of Education

I BELIEVE THAT

- the social life of the child is the basis of concentration, or correlation, in all his training or growth. The social life gives the unconscious the unity and the background of all his efforts and of all his attainments.
- the subject-matter of the school curriculum should mark a gradual differentiation out of the primitive unconscious unity of social life.
- we violate the child's nature and render difficult the best ethical results by introducing the child too abruptly to a number of special studies, of reading, writing, geography, etc., out of relation to this social life.
- the true center of correlation on the school subjects is not science, nor literature, nor history, nor geography, but the child's own social activities.
- education cannot be unified in the study of science, or so-called nature study, because apart from human activity, nature itself is not a unity; nature in itself is a number of diverse objects in space and time, and to attempt to make it the center of work by itself is to introduce a principle of radiation rather than one of concentration.
- literature is the reflex expression and interpretation of social experience; that hence it must follow upon and not precede such experience. It, therefore, cannot be made the basis, although it may be made the summary of unification.
- history is of educative value in so far as it presents phases of social life and growth. It must be controlled by reference to social life. When taken simply as history it is thrown into the distant past and becomes dead and inert.

Taken as the record of man's social life and progress it becomes full of meaning. I believe, however, that it cannot be so taken excepting as the child is also introduced directly into social life.

- the primary basis of education is in the child's powers at work along the same general constructive lines as those which have brought civilization into being.
- the only way to make the child conscious of his social heritage is to enable him to perform those fundamental types of activity which make civilization what it is.
- the so-called expressive or constructive activities are the center of correlation.
- this gives the standard for the place of cooking, sewing, manual training, etc., in the school.
- they are not special studies which are to be introduced over and above a lot of others in the way of relaxation or relief, or as additional accomplishments. I believe rather that they represent, as types, fundamental forms of social activity, and that it is possible and desirable that the child's introduction into the more formal subjects of the curriculum be through the medium of these activities.
- the study of science is educational in so far as it brings out the materials and processes which make social life what it is.
- one of the greatest difficulties in the present teaching of science is that the material is presented in purely objective form, or is treated as a new peculiar kind of experience which the child can add to that which he has already had. In reality, science is of value because it gives the ability to interpret and control the experience already had. It should be introduced, not as so much new subject-matter, but as showing the factors already involved in previous experience and as furnishing tools by which that experience can be more easily and effectively regulated.
- at present we lose much of the value of literature and language studies because of our elimination of the social element. Language is almost always treated in the books of pedagogy simply

as the expression of thought. It is true that language is a logical instrument, but it is fundamentally and primarily a social instrument. Language is the device for communication; it is the tool through which one individual comes to share the ideas and feelings of others. When treated simply as a way of getting individual information, or as a means of showing off what one had learned, it loses its social motive and end.

- there is, therefore, no succession of studies in the ideal school curriculum. If education is life, all life has, from the outset, a scientific aspect, an aspect of art and culture, and an aspect of communication. It cannot, therefore, be true that the proper studies for one grade are mere reading and writing, and that at a later grade, reading, or literature, or science, may be introduced. The progress is not in the succession of studies, but in the development of new attitudes towards, and new interests in, experience.
- education must be conceived as a continuing reconstruction of experience; that the process and the goal of education are one and the same thing.
- to set up any end outside of education, as furnishing its goal and standard, is to deprive the educational process of much of its meaning, and tends to make us rely upon false and external stimuli in dealing with the child.

Article IV—The Nature of Method

I BELIEVE THAT

- the question of method is ultimately reducible to the question of the order of development of the child's powers and interests. The law for presenting and treating material is the law implicit within the child's own nature. Because this is so I believe the following statements are of supreme importance as determining the spirit in which education is carried on:
- the active side precedes the passive in the development of the child-nature; that expression comes before conscious impression; that

the muscular development precedes the sensory; that movements come before conscious sensation; I believe that consciousness is essentially motor or impulsive; that conscious states tend to project themselves in action.

- the neglect of this principle is the cause of a large part of the waste of time and strength in school work. The child is thrown into a passive, receptive, or absorbing attitude. The conditions are such that he is not permitted to follow the law of nature; the result is friction and waste.
- ideas (intellectual and rational processes) also result from action and devolve for the sake of the better control of action. What we term reason is primarily the law of orderly and effective action. To attempt to develop the reasoning powers, the powers of judgment, without reference to the selection and arrangement of means in action, is the fundamental fallacy in our present methods of dealing with this matter. As a result we present the child with arbitrary symbols. Symbols are a necessity in mental development, but they have their place as tools for economizing effort; presented by themselves they are a mass of meaningless and arbitrary ideas imposed from without.
- the image is the great instrument of instruction. What a child gets out of any subject presented to him is simply the images which he himself forms with regard to it.
- if nine-tenths of the energy at present directed towards making the child learn certain things were spent in seeing to it that the child was forming proper images, the work of instruction would be indefinitely facilitated.
- much of the time and attention now given to the preparation and presentation of lessons might be more wisely and profitably expended in training the child's power of imagery and in seeing to it that he was continually forming definite, vivid, and growing images of the various subjects with which he comes in contact in his experience.
- interests are the signs and symptoms of growing power. I believe that they represent dawning capacities. Accordingly the constant and careful

observation of interests is of the utmost importance for the educator.

- these interests are to be observed as showing the state of development which the child has reached.
- they prophesy the stage upon which he is about to enter.
- only through the continual and sympathetic observation of childhood's interests can the adult enter into the child's life and see what it is ready for, and upon what material it could work most readily and fruitfully.
- these interests are neither to be humored nor repressed. To repress interest is to substitute the adult for the child, and so to weaken intellectual curiosity and alertness, to suppress initiative, and to deaden interest. To humor the interests is to substitute the transient for the permanent. The interest is always the sign of some power below; the important thing is to discover this power. To humor the interest is to fail to penetrate below the surface, and its sure result is to substitute caprice and whim for genuine interest.
- the emotions are the reflex of actions.
- to endeavor to stimulate or arouse the emotions apart from their corresponding activities is to introduce an unhealthy and morbid state of mind.
- if we can only secure right habits of action and thought, with reference to the good, the true, and the beautiful, the emotions will for the most part take care of themselves.
- next to deadness and dullness, formalism and routine, our education is threatened with no greater evil than sentimentalism.
- this sentimentalism is the necessary result of the attempt to divorce feeling from action.

Article V—The School and Social Progress

I BELIEVE THAT

- education is the fundamental method of social progress and reform.
- all reforms which rest simply upon enactment of law, or the threatening of certain penalties, or upon changes in mechanical or outward arrangements, are transitory and futile.
- education is a regulation of the process of coming to share in the social consciousness; and that the adjustment of individual activity on the basis of this social consciousness is the only sure method of social reconstruction.
- this conception has due regard for both the individualistic and socialistic ideals. It is duly individual because it recognizes the formation of a certain character as the only genuine basis of right living. It is socialistic because it recognizes that this right character is not to be formed by merely individual precept, example, or exhortation, but rather by the influence of a certain form of institutional or community life upon the individual, and that the social organism through the school, as its organ, may determine ethical results.
- in the ideal school we have the reconciliation of the individualistic and the institutional ideals.
- the community's duty to education is, therefore, its paramount moral duty. By law and punishment, by social agitation and discussion, society can regulate and form itself in a more or less haphazard and chance way. But through education society can formulate its own purposes, can organize its own means and resources, and thus shape itself with definiteness and economy in the direction in which it wishes to move.
- when society once recognizes the possibilities in this direction, and the obligations which these possibilities impose, it is impossible to conceive of the resources of time, attention, and money which will be put at the disposal of the educator.
- it is the business of every one interested in education to insist upon the school as the primary and most effective interest of social progress and reform in order that society may be awakened to realize what the school stands for, and aroused to the necessity of endowing the educator with sufficient equipment properly to perform his task.
- education thus conceived marks the most perfect and intimate union of science and art conceivable in human experience.

- the art of thus giving shape to human powers and adapting them to social service is the supreme art; one calling into its service the best of artists; that no insight, sympathy, tact, executive power, is too great for such service.
- with the growth of psychological service, giving added insight into individual structure and laws of growth; and with growth of social science, adding to our knowledge of the right organization of individuals, all scientific resources can be utilized for the purpose of education.
- when science and art thus join hands the most commanding motive for human action will be

reached, the most genuine springs of human conduct aroused, and the best service that human nature is capable of guaranteed.
- the teacher is engaged, not simply in the training of individuals, but in the formation of the proper social life.
- every teacher should realize the dignity of his calling; that he is a social servant set apart for the maintenance of proper social order and the securing of the right social growth.
- in this way the teacher always is the prophet of the true God and the usherer in of the true kingdom of God.

POSTNOTE

This article is a classic because it outlines the core beliefs of John Dewey, the American who has had the most powerful impact on our schools. Dewey, the father of progressivism, was the most influential educational thinker of the last 100-plus years. Many of the beliefs expressed in this article (originally published in 1897) have greatly affected educational practice in America. What we find most curious is how current some of these statements still are. On the other hand, many seem dated and clearly from another era. Those that appeal to altruism and idealism have a particularly old-fashioned ring to them. The question remains, however: Which is "out of sync"—the times or the appeals to idealism and altruism? And another lingering question: If John Dewey is the most revered and influential thinker

about American education, why is there so little evidence of his ideas being put into practice in our schools?

DISCUSSION QUESTIONS

1. How relevant do you believe Dewey's statements are today? Why?
2. Which of Dewey's beliefs do you personally agree or disagree with? Why?
3. How does Dewey's famous statement that "education ... is a process of living and not a preparation for future living" square with what your parents, guidance counselors, and teachers have told you over the years? If it is different, how do you explain this?

RELATED WEBSITE RESOURCES AND VIDEO CASE

WEB RESOURCES:

Center for Dewey Studies. Available at:

http://www.siu.edu/~deweyctr/.

This center, located on the campus of the University of Illinois at Carbondale, is a font of valuable insight and information on Dewey and his philosophy of education.

John Dewey: Philosophy of Education. Available at:

http://wilderdom.com/experiential/JohnDewey PhilosophyEducation.html.

This site, maintained by James Neill, is an outstanding repository of John Dewey's educational thought as well as commentary on his work.

▶❚❚ TEACHSOURCE VIDEO CASE

MOTIVATING ADOLESCENT LEARNERS: CURRICULUM BASED ON REAL LIFE

In this video clip, sixth-grade math teacher Kelly Franklin breathes new life into her class by having her students start and operate a school store. Her intention is to instill in her students the value of knowing fractions and other math concepts. Go to the website for the Education Media Library at CengageBrain.com to watch the video clips, study the artifacts in the case, and reflect on the following questions.

1. What do you see as the benefits and the costs of employing this curricular strategy?

2. How is Kelly Franklin's teaching strategy consistent with the views of John Dewey in the previous article?

36

Personal Thoughts on Teaching and Learning

Carl Rogers

Carl Rogers (1902–1987) had a powerful influence on American education. As a psychotherapist, he pioneered nondirective, client-centered theory and the actualizing tendency, the built-in motivation present in every life form to develop its potentials to the fullest extent possible. When applied to formal education, the theory suggests that each of us already possesses the important knowledge. The role of the teacher is to help the student uncover and bring to the surface what he or she already knows. This theory had its profoundest impact on American education in the form of values clarification.

FOCUS QUESTION

One of the twentieth century's most influential psychologists asks the question, "What can teachers really teach us?"

KEY TERMS

- Inconsequential learning
- Self-discovered learning

I wish to present some very brief remarks, in the hope that if they bring forth any reaction from you, I may get some new light on my own ideas.

I find it a very troubling thing to *think*, particularly when I think about my own experiences and try to extract from those experiences the meaning that seems genuinely inherent in them. At first such thinking is very satisfying, because it seems to discover sense and pattern in a whole host of discrete events. But then it very often becomes dismaying, because I realize how ridiculous these thoughts, which have much value to me, would seem to most people. My impression is that if I try to find the meaning of my own experience it leads me, nearly always, in directions regarded as absurd.

So in the next three or four minutes, I will try to digest some of the meanings which have come to me from my classroom experience and the experience I have had in individual and group therapy. They are in no way intended as conclusions for someone else, or a guide to what others should do or be. They are the very tentative meanings, as of April 1952, which my experience has had for me, and some of the bothersome questions which their absurdity raises. I will put each idea or meaning in a separate lettered paragraph, not because they are in any particular logical order, but because each meaning is separately important to me.

    a. I may as well start with this one in view of the purposes of this conference. *My experience has been that I cannot teach another person how to teach.* To attempt it is for me, in the long run, futile.

b. *It seems to me that anything that can be taught to another is relatively inconsequential, and has little or no significant influence on behavior.* That sounds so ridiculous I can't help but question it at the same time that I present it.

c. *I realize increasingly that I am only interested in learnings which significantly influence behavior.* Quite possibly this is simply a personal idiosyncrasy.

d. *I have come to feel that the only learning which significantly influences behavior is self-discovered, self-appropriated learning.*

e. *Such self-discovered learning, truth that has been personally appropriated and assimilated in experience, cannot be directly communicated to another.* As soon as an individual tries to communicate such experience directly, often with a quite natural enthusiasm, it becomes teaching, and its results are inconsequential. It was some relief recently to discover that Søren Kierkegaard, the Danish philosopher, had found this too, in his own experience, and stated it very clearly a century ago. It made it seem less absurd.

f. As a consequence of the above, *I realize that I have lost interest in being a teacher.*

g. When I try to teach, as I do sometimes, I am appalled by the results, which seem a little more than inconsequential, because sometimes the teaching appears to succeed. When this happens I find that the results are damaging. It seems to cause the individual to distrust his own experience, and to stifle significant learning. *Hence I have come to feel that the outcomes of teaching are either unimportant or hurtful.*

h. When I look back at the results of my past teaching, the real results seem the same—either damage was done, or nothing significant occurred. This is frankly troubling.

i. As a consequence, *I realize that I am only interested in being a learner, preferably learning things that matter, that have some significant influence on my own behavior.*

j. *I find it very rewarding to learn,* in groups, in relationship with one person as in therapy, or by myself.

k. *I find that one of the best, but most difficult ways for me to learn is to drop my own defensiveness,* at least temporarily, and try to understand the way in which his experience seems and feels to the other person.

l. *I find that another way of learning for me is to state my own uncertainties, to try to clarify my puzzlements, and thus get closer to the meaning that my experience actually seems to have.*

m. This whole train of experiencing, and the meanings that I have thus far discovered in it, seem to have launched me on a process which is both fascinating and at times a little frightening. *It seems to mean letting my experience carry me on, in a direction which appears to be forward, toward goals that I can but dimly define, as I try to understand at least the current meaning of that experience.* The sensation is that of floating with a complex stream of experience, with the fascinating possibility of trying to comprehend its ever changing complexity.

I am almost afraid I may seem to have gotten away from any discussion of learning, as well as teaching. Let me again introduce a practical note by saying that by themselves these interpretations of my own experience may sound queer and aberrant, but not particularly shocking. It is when I realize the *implications* that I shudder a bit at the distance I have come from the commonsense world that everyone knows is right. I can best illustrate that by saying that if the experiences of others had been the same as mine, and if they had discovered similar meanings in it, many consequences would be implied.

a. Such experience would imply that we would do away with teaching. People would get together if they wished to learn.

b. We would do away with examinations. They measure only the inconsequential type of learning.

c. The implication would be that we would do away with grades and credits for the same reason.

d. We would do away with degrees as a measure of competence partly for the same reason.

Another reason is that a degree marks an end or a conclusion of something, and a learner is only interested in the continuing process of learning.

e. It would imply doing away with the exposition of conclusions, for we would realize that no one learns significantly from conclusions.

I think I had better stop there. I do not want to become too fantastic. I want to know primarily whether anything in my inward thinking as I have tried to describe it, speaks to anything in your experience of the classroom as you have lived it, and if so, what the meanings are that exist for you in *your* experience.

POSTNOTE

This article is a classic because it had a significant influence on educational practice during the 1960s and 1970s, and some of its effects are still with us. Rogers's personal philosophy of teaching and learning, so well expressed in this selection, is of course quite controversial. Give it a little test for yourself. Think of a couple of the most significant things you have learned as a human being. Now think of how you learned them. Did someone teach them to you, or did you discover them yourself through experience? Try a different approach and ask yourself what of significance you have ever been taught. Make your own evaluation. Be specific. What do you think about Rogers's statements now?

DISCUSSION QUESTIONS

1. Do you agree or disagree with Rogers's ideas on teaching and learning? Why?
2. Do Rogers's statements have any implications for you as a teacher? Explain your answer.
3. Identify three points in the article with which you agree and three with which you disagree.

RELATED WEBSITE RESOURCES

WEB RESOURCES:

Carl Rogers and Humanistic Education. Available at:

http://www.sageofasheville.com/pub_downloads/ CARL_ROGERS_AND_HUMANISTIC_EDUCATION. pdf.

This site provides a clear explanation of Rogers's views on how education should be reformed.

Nondirective Teaching. Available at:

http://al038.k12.sd.us/Nondirective% 20Teaching.ppt.

This PowerPoint presentation provides a clear outline of the key concepts underlying Rogers's educational ideas.

The Educated Person

Ernest L. Boyer

Ernest L. Boyer (1928–1995) was one of the key figures in American education during the last half of the twentieth century. He held numerous positions in education from classroom teacher to president of the Carnegie Foundation for the Advancement of Teaching. Throughout his career he was widely respected for his sound, balanced views. A deeply religious man, he brought what he called his "people-centered" principles to all

his work. This essay, published the year of his death, lays out with great clarity his major convictions on what should be taught in our schools.

"The Educated Person" (pp. 16–26), by Ernest L. Boyer, from *1995 ASCD Yearbook: Toward a Coherent Curriculum* by James A. Beane (Ed.), Alexandria, VA: ASCD. © 1995 by ASCD. Reprinted with permission. Learn more about ASCD at www.ascd.org.

As we anticipate a new century, I am drawn back to questions that have, for generations, perplexed educators and philosophers and parents. What *is* an educated person? What *should* schools be teaching to students?

In searching for answers to these questions, we must consider first not the curriculum, but the human condition. And we must reflect especially on two essential realities of life. First, each person is unique. In defining goals, it is crucial for educators to affirm the special characteristics of each student. We must create in schools a climate in which students are empowered, and we must find ways in the nation's classrooms to celebrate the potential of each child. But beyond the diversity of individuals, educators also must acknowledge a second reality: the deeply rooted characteristics that bind together the human community. We must show students that people around the world share a great many experiences. Attention to both these aspects of our existence is critical to any discussion of what all children should learn.

What, then, does it mean to be an educated person? It means developing one's own aptitudes and interests and discovering the diversity that makes us each unique. And it means becoming permanently empowered with language proficiency, general knowledge, social confidence, and moral awareness in order to be economically and civically successful. But becoming well educated also means discovering the connectedness of things. Educators must help students see relationships across the ·disciplines and learn that education is a communal act, one that affirms not only individualism, but community. And for these goals to be accomplished, we need a new curriculum framework that is both comprehensive and coherent, one that can encompass existing subjects and integrate fragmented content while relating the curriculum to the realities of life. This curriculum must address the uniqueness of students' histories and

FOCUS QUESTION

There is no more important question than the one answered here: "What is most worth knowing?"

KEY TERMS

- Carnegie unit
- Educated person

experiences, but it also must guide them to understand the many ways that humans are connected.

Some schools and teachers are aiming to fully educate students, but most of us have a very long way to go in reaching this goal. Today, almost all students in U.S. schools still complete Carnegie units in exchange for a diploma. The time has come to bury the old Carnegie unit; since the Foundation I now head created this unit of academic measure nearly a century ago, I feel authorized to declare it obsolete. Why? Because it has helped turn schooling into an exercise in trivial pursuit. Students get academic "credit," but they fail to gain a coherent view of what they study. Education is measured by seat time, not time for learning. While curious young children still ask why things are, many older children ask only, "Will this be on the test?" All students should be encouraged to ask "Why?" because "Why?" is the question that leads students to connections.

In abandoning the Carnegie unit, I do not endorse the immediate adoption of national assessment programs; indeed, I think we must postpone such programs until we are much clearer about what students should be learning. The goal, again, is not only to help students become well informed and prepared for lifelong learning, but also to help them put learning into the larger context of discovering the connectedness of things. Barbara McClintock, the 1983 winner of the Nobel Prize for Physiology–Medicine, asserts: "Everything is one. There is no way to draw a line between things." Contrary to McClintock's vision, the average school or college catalog dramatizes the separate academic boxes.

Frank Press, president of the National Academy of Sciences, compares scientists to artists, evoking the magnificent double helix, which broke the genetic code. He said the double helix is not only rational, but beautiful. Similarly, when scientists and technicians watch the countdown to a space launch, they don't say, "Our formulas worked again." They respond, "Beautiful!" instinctively reaching for the aesthetic term to praise a technological achievement. When physicist Victor Weisskopf was asked, "What gives you hope in troubled times?" he replied, "Mozart and quantum mechanics." Most schools, however, separate science and art, discouraging students from seeing the connections between them.

How, then, can we help students see relationships and patterns and gain understanding beyond the separate academic subjects? How can we rethink the curriculum and use the disciplines to illuminate larger, more integrated ends?

Human Commonalities

In the 1981 book *A Quest for Common Learning*, I suggested that we might organize the curriculum not on the basis of disciplines or departments, but on the basis of "core commonalities." By core commonalities, I mean universal experiences that make us human, experiences shared by all cultures on the planet. During the past decade and a half, my thinking about this thematic structure has continued to evolve. I now envision eight commonalities that bind us to one another:

I. The Life Cycle

As life's most fundamental truth, we share, first, the experience that connects birth, growth, and death. This life cycle binds each of us to others, and I find it sad that so many students go through life without reflecting on the mystery of their own existence. Many complete twelve or sixteen years of formal schooling not considering the sacredness of their own bodies, not learning to sustain wellness, not pondering the imperative of death.

In reshaping the curriculum to help students see connections, I would position study of "The Life Cycle" at the core of common learning. Attention would go to nutrition, health, and all aspects of wellness. For a project, each student would undertake the care of some life form.

My wife is a certified nurse-midwife who delivers babies, including seven grandchildren of our own. Kay feels special pain when delivering the baby of a teenage girl because she knows that she is delivering one child into the arms of another, and that both have all too often lived for nine months on soda and potato chips. Some young mothers first learn about the birth process between the sharp pains of labor.

Too many young women and young men pass through our process of education without learning about their own bodies. Out of ignorance, they suffer poor nutrition, addiction, and violence. "Maintaining children's good health is a shared responsibility of parents, schools, and the community at large," according to former Secretary of Education William Bennett (1986, p. 37). He urges elementary schools "to provide children with the knowledge, habits, and attitudes that will equip them for a fit and healthy life."

Study of the Life Cycle would encourage students to reflect sensitively on the mystery of birth and growth and death, to learn about body functions and thus understand the role of choice in wellness, to carry some of their emotional and intellectual learning into their relations with others, and to observe, understand, and respect a variety of life forms.

II. Language

Each life on the planet turns to symbols to express feelings and ideas. After a first breath, we make sounds as a way of reaching out to others, connecting with them. We develop a variety of languages: the language of words (written and spoken), the language of symbols (mathematics, codes, sign systems), and the language of the arts (aesthetic expressions in language, music, painting, sculpture, dance, theater, craft, and so on). A quality education develops proficiency in the written and the spoken word, as well as a useful knowledge of mathematical symbol systems and an understanding that the arts provide countless ways to express ourselves.

Our sophisticated use of language sets human beings apart from all other forms of life. Through the created words and symbols and arts, we connect to one another. Consider the miracle of any moment. One person vibrates his or her vocal cords. Molecules shoot in the direction of listeners. They hit the tympanic membrane; signals go scurrying up the eighth cranial nerve. From that series

of events, the listener feels a response deep in the cerebrum that approximates the images in the mind of the speaker. Because of its power and scope, language is the means by which all other subjects are pursued.

The responsible use of language demands both *accuracy* and *honesty*, so students studying "Language" must also learn to consider the ethics of communication. Students live in a world where obscenities abound. They live in a world where politicians use sixty-second sound bites to destroy integrity. They live in a world where clichés substitute for reason. To make their way in this world, students must learn to distinguish between deceit and authenticity in language.

Writers and mathematicians have left a long and distinguished legacy for students to learn from. Through words, each child can express something personal. Through symbols, each child can increase the capacity to calculate and reason. Through the arts, each child can express a thought or a feeling. People need to write with clarity, read with comprehension, speak effectively, listen with understanding, compute accurately, and understand the communicative capabilities of the arts. Education for the next century means helping students understand that language in all its forms is a powerful and sacred trust.

III. The Arts

All people on the planet respond to the aesthetic. Dance, music, painting, sculpture, and architecture are languages understood around the world. "Art represents a social necessity that no nation can neglect without endangering its intellectual existence," said John Ruskin (Rand 1993). We all know how art can affect us. Salvador Dali's painting *The Persistence of Memory* communicates its meaning to anyone ever haunted by time passing. The gospel song "Amazing Grace" stirs people from both Appalachia and Manhattan. "We Shall Overcome," sung in slow and solemn cadence, invokes powerful feelings regardless of the race or economic status of singer or audience.

Archaeologists examine the artifacts of ancient civilization—pottery, cave paintings, and musical instruments—to determine the attainments and quality of a culture. As J. Carter Brown (1983) observes, "The texts of man's achievements are not written exclusively in words. They are written, as well, in architecture, paintings, sculpture, drawing, photography, and in urban, graphic, landscape, and industrial design."

Young children understand that the arts are language. Before they learn to speak, they respond intuitively to dance, music, and color. The arts also help children who are disabled. I once taught deaf children, who couldn't speak because they couldn't hear. But through painting, sculpture, and rhythm, they found new ways to communicate.

Every child has the urge and capacity to be expressive. It is tragic that for most children the universal language of the arts is suppressed, then destroyed, in the early years of learning, because traditional teaching does not favor self-expression and school boards consider art a frill. This is an ironic deprivation when the role of art in developing critical thinking is becoming more widely recognized.

Jacques d'Amboise, former principal dancer with the New York City Ballet, movie star, and founder of the National Dance Institute, offers his view on how art fits into education: "I would take the arts, science and sports, or play, and make all education involve all of them. It would be similar to what kindergarten does, only more sophisticated, right through life. All of the disciplines would be interrelated. You dance to a poem: poetry is meter, meter is time, time is science" (Ames and Peyser 1990).

For our most moving experiences, we turn to the arts to express feelings and ideas that words cannot convey. The arts are, as one poet has put it, "the language of the angels." To be truly educated means being sensitively responsive to the universal language of art.

IV. Time and Space

While we are all nonuniform and often seem dramatically different from one another, all of us have the capacity to place ourselves in time and space. We explore our place through geography and astronomy. We explore our sense of time through history.

And yet, how often we squander this truly awesome capacity for exploration, neglecting even our personal roots. Looking back in my own life, my most important mentor was Grandpa Boyer, who lived to be one hundred. Sixty years before that, Grandpa moved his little family into the slums of Dayton, Ohio. He then spent the next forty years running a city mission, working for the poor, teaching me more by deed than by word that to be truly human, one must serve. For far too many children, the influence of such intergenerational models has diminished or totally disappeared.

Margaret Mead said that the health of any culture is sustained when three generations are vitally interacting with one another—a "vertical culture" in which the different age groups are connected. Yet in America today we've created a "horizontal culture," with each generation living alone. Infants are in nurseries, toddlers are in day care, older children are in schools organized by age. College students are isolated on campuses. Adults are in the workplace. And older citizens are in retirement villages, living and dying all alone.

For several years, my own parents chose to live in a retirement village where the average age was eighty. But this village had a day-care center, too, and all the three- and four-year-olds had adopted grandparents to meet with every day. The two generations quickly became friends. When I called my father, he didn't talk about his aches and pains, he talked about his little friend. And when I visited, I saw that my father, like any proud grandparent, had the child's drawings taped to the wall. As I watched the two of them together, I was struck by the idea that there is something really special about a four-year-old seeing the difficulty and courage of growing old. And I was struck, too, by watching an eighty-year-old being informed and inspired by the energy and innocence of a child. Exposure to such an age difference surely increases the understanding of time and personal history.

The time has come to break up the age ghettos. It is time to build intergenerational institutions that bring together the old and young. I'm impressed by the "grandteacher" programs in the schools, for example. In the new core curriculum, with a strand called "Time and Space," students should discover their own roots and complete an oral history. But beyond their own extended family, all students should also become well informed about the influence of the culture that surrounds them and learn about the traditions of other cultures.

A truly educated person will see connections by placing his or her life in time and space. In the days ahead, students should study *Western* civilization to understand our past, but they should study *non-Western* cultures to understand our present and our future.

V. Groups and Institutions

All people on the planet belong to groups and institutions that shape their lives. Nearly 150 years ago, Ralph Waldo Emerson observed, "We do not make a world of our own, but rather fall into institutions already made and have to accommodate ourselves to them." Every society organizes itself and carries on its work through social interaction that varies from one culture to another.

Students must be asked to think about the groups of which they are members, how they are shaped by those groups, and how they help to shape them. Students need to learn about the social web of our existence, about family life, about how governments function, about the informal social structures that surround us. They also must discover how life in groups varies from one culture to another.

Civic responsibility also must be taught. The school itself can be the starting point for this education, serving as a "working model" of a healthy society in microcosm that bears witness to the ideals of community. Within the school, students should feel "enfranchised." Teachers, administrators, and staff should meet often to find their *own* relationship to the institution of the school. And students should study groups in their own community, finding out about local government.

One of my sons lives in a Mayan village in the jungle of Belize. When my wife and I visit Craig

each year, I'm impressed that Mayans and Americans live and work in very similar ways. The jungle of Manhattan and the one of Belize are separated by a thousand miles and a thousand years, and yet the Mayans, just like us, have their family units. They have elected leaders, village councils, law enforcement officers, jails, schools, and places to worship. Life there is both different and very much the same. Students in the United States should be introduced to institutions in our own culture and in other cultures, so they might study, for example, both Santa Cruz, California, and Santa Cruz, Belize.

We all belong to many groups. Exploring their history and functions helps students understand the privileges and the responsibilities that belong to each of us.

VI. Work

We all participate, for much of our lives, in the commonality of work. As Thoreau reminds us, we both "live" and "get a living." Regardless of differences, all people on the planet produce and consume. A quality education will help students understand and prepare for the world of work. Unfortunately, our own culture has become too preoccupied with *consuming*, too little with the tools for *producing*. Children may see their parents leave the house carrying briefcases or lunch pails in the morning and see them come home again in the evening, but do they know what parents actually do during the day?

Jerome Bruner (1971) asks: "Could it be that in our stratified and segmented society, our students simply do not know about local grocers and their styles, local doctors and their styles, local taxi drivers and theirs, local political activists and theirs? ... I would urge that we find some way of connecting the diversity of the society to the phenomenon of school" (p. 7). A new, integrative curriculum for the schools needs to give attention to "Producing and Consuming," with each student studying simple economics, different money systems, vocational studies, career planning, how work varies from one culture to another, and with each completing a work project to gain a respect for craftsmanship.

Several years ago when Kay and I were in China, we were told about a student who had defaced the surface of his desk. As punishment, he spent three days in the factory where desks were made, helping the woodworkers, observing the effort involved. Not surprisingly, the student never defaced another desk.

When I was Chancellor of the State University of New York, I took my youngest son, then eight, to a cabin in the Berkshires for the weekend. My goal: to build a dock. All day, instead of playing, Stephen sat by the lake, watching me work. As we drove home, he looked pensive. After several miles, he said, "Daddy, I wish you'd grown up to be a carpenter—instead of you-know-what!"

VII. Natural World

Though all people are different, we are all connected to the earth in many ways. David, my grandson in Belize, lives these connections as he chases birds, bathes in the river, and watches corn being picked, pounded into tortillas, and heated outdoors. But David's cousins in Boston and Princeton spend more time with appliances, asphalt roadways, and precooked food. For them, discovering connectedness to nature does not come so naturally.

When I was United States Commissioner of Education, Joan Cooney, the brilliant creator of *Sesame Street*, told me that she and her colleagues at Children's Television Workshop wanted to start a new program on science and technology for junior high school kids. They wanted young people to learn a little more about their world and what they must understand as part of living. Funds were raised, and *3–2–1 Contact* went on the air. To prepare scripts, staff surveyed junior high school kids in New York City, asking questions such as "Where does water come from?"— which brought from some students the disturbing reply, "The faucet." They asked, "Where does light come from?" and heard, "The switch." And they asked, "Where does garbage go?" "Down the chute." These students' sense of connectedness stopped at the VCR or refrigerator door.

Canadian geneticist David Suzuki, host of *The Nature of Things*, says: "We ought to be greening the school yard, breaking up the asphalt and concrete.... We have to give children hand-held lenses, classroom aquariums and terrariums, lots of field trips, organic garden plots on the school grounds, butterfly gardens, trees. Then insects, squirrels— maybe even raccoons and rabbits—will show up, even in the city. We've got to reconnect those kids, and we've got to do it very early.... Our challenge is to reconnect children to their natural curiosity" (Baron Estes 1993).

With all our differences, each of us is inextricably connected to the natural world. During their days of formal learning, students should explore this commonality by studying the principles of science, by discovering the shaping power of technology, and, above all, by learning that survival on this planet means respecting and preserving the earth we share.

VIII. Search for Meaning

Regardless of heritage or tradition, each person searches for some larger purpose. We all seek to give special meaning to our lives. Reinhold Niebuhr said, "Man cannot be whole unless he be committed, he cannot find himself, unless he find a purpose beyond himself." We all need to examine values and beliefs, and develop convictions.

During my study of the American high school, I became convinced ours is less a school problem and more a youth problem. Far too many teenagers feel unwanted, unneeded, and unconnected. Without guidance and direction, they soon lose their sense of purpose—even their sense of wanting purpose.

Great teachers allow their lives to express their values. They are matchless guides as they give the gift of opening truths about themselves to their students. I often think of three or four teachers, out of the many I have worked with, who changed my life. What made them truly great? They were well informed. They could relate their knowledge to students. They created an active, not passive, climate for learning. More than that, they were authentic human beings who taught their subjects and were open enough to teach about themselves.

Service projects instill values. All students should complete a community service project, working in day-care centers and retirement villages or tutoring other students at school. The North Carolina School of Science and Math develops an ethos of responsible citizenship. To be admitted, a child must commit to sixty hours of community service per summer and three hours per week during the school year (Beach 1992, p. 56).

Martin Luther King, Jr., preached: "Everyone can be great because everyone can serve." I'm convinced the young people of this country want inspiration from this kind of larger vision, whether they come across it in a book or in person, or whether they find it inside themselves.

Values, Beliefs, and Connections

What, then, does it mean to be an educated person? It means respecting the miracle of life, being empowered in the use of language, and responding sensitively to the aesthetic. Being truly educated means putting learning in historical perspective, understanding groups and institutions, having reverence for the natural world, and affirming the dignity of work. And, above all, being an educated person means being guided by values and beliefs and connecting the lessons of the classroom to the realities of life. These are the core competencies that I believe replace the old Carnegie units.

And all of this can be accomplished as schools focus not on seat time, but on students involved in true communities of learning. I realize that remarkable changes must occur for this shift in goals to take place, but I hope deeply that in the century ahead students will be judged not by their performance on a single test but by the quality of their lives. It is my hope that students in the classrooms of tomorrow will be encouraged to create more than conform, and to cooperate more than

compete. Each student deserves to see the world clearly and in its entirety and to be inspired by both the beauty and the challenges that surround us all.

Above all, I pray that Julie and David, my granddaughter in Princeton and my grandson in Belize, along with all other children on the planet, will grow to understand that they belong to the same human family, the family that connects us all.

Fifty years ago, Mark Van Doren wrote, "The connectedness of things is what the educator contemplates to the limit of his capacity." The student, he says, who can begin early in life to see things as connected has begun the life of learning. This, it seems to me, is what it means to be an educated person.

References

Ames, Katrine, and Marc Peyser. (Fall/Winter 1990). "Why Jane Can't Draw (or Sing, or Dance …)." *Newsweek* Special Edition: 40–49.

Baron Estes, Yvonne. (May 1993). "Environmental Education: Bringing Children and Nature Together." *Phi Delta Kappan* 74, 9: K2.

Beach, Waldo. (1992). *Ethical Education in American Public Schools*. Washington, D.C.: National Education Association.

Bennett, William J. (1986). *First Lessons*. Washington, D.C.: U.S. Department of Education.

Boyer, Ernest L. (1981). *A Quest for Common Learning: The Aims of General Education*. Washington, D.C.: Carnegie Foundation for the Advancement of Teaching.

Brown, J. Carter. (November/December 1983). "Excellence and the Problem of Visual Literacy." *Design for Arts in Education* 84, 3.

Bruner, Jerome. (November 1971). "Process of Education Reconsidered." An address presented before the 16th Annual Conference of the Association for Supervision and Curriculum Development.

Rand, Paul. (May 2, 1993). "Failure by Design," *The New York Times*, p. E19.

POSTNOTE

The late Ernest Boyer was widely acknowledged during the last two decades of the twentieth century as America's leading practitioner of education. In this classic article, Boyer demonstrates his considerable power as a profound educational thinker. There is no more important or fundamental question in education than "What is most worth knowing?" Schools have a mission, derived from the society at large, to prepare children to become fully developed people, to prepare them for the demands of adult life in an unknown future. As educators, our mission is to identify what our students need today and will need in the future. But the universe of knowledge, which once inched along at a snail's pace, is currently racing ahead like a sprinter. The child's future, which once we could say would be much like his or her parents' life, now is impossible to predict.

In this essay, Ernest Boyer lays out his answer to the question of what an educated person most needs to know. Though there is great merit in his educational vision, questions arise: What from civilization's heritage of knowledge and wisdom should be presented to students? And how many of us as teachers have a clear sense of goals; that is, goals which are guided by a similar vision of what a person really is and what a person ought to become?

DISCUSSION QUESTIONS

1. What feature of Boyer's "educated person" do you believe currently receives the greatest attention in our schools?
2. What feature of his vision do you believe receives the least attention today? Why?
3. Why do you think there is so little discussion of the question, "What is most worth knowing?"

RELATED WEBSITE RESOURCES AND VIDEO CASE

WEB RESOURCES:

The Ernest Boyer International Award for Innovative Excellence in Teaching, Learning, and Technology. Available at:

http://www.teachlearn.org/boyer.html.

This site is attempting to continue the educational legacy of Ernest Boyer through promoting an annual conference and awards program for outstanding teachers.

The Ernest Boyer Center at Messiah College. Available at:

http://www.messiah.edu/boyer_center/about_boyer/.

This center is dedicated to promoting and continuing the influence of one of Messiah College's most distinguished alums.

▶❚❚ TEACHSOURCE VIDEO CASE

EDUCATION REFORM: TEACHERS TALK ABOUT NO CHILD LEFT BEHIND

No Child Left Behind (NCLB), the legislative act currently guiding reform in the United States, can be seen as an attempt to help our schools reach Boyer's ideal of an "educated person." Key to NCLB is state-level tests to determine student progress and a new set of guidelines for the determination of what constitutes a "highly qualified teacher." Go to the website for the Education Media Library at CengageBrain.com to watch the video clips, study the artifacts in the case, and reflect on the following questions.

1. The educators in this video speak of the importance of understanding individual student data. Why, according to the video, is this so important?

2. The educators on this video offer their opinions as to the advantages and disadvantages of NCLB. List two advantages and two disadvantages.

FOR ANOTHER PERSPECTIVE:

Mary Anne Raywid, Accountability: What's Worth Measuring? **www.cengage.com/login**

38

The Kind of Schools We Need

Elliot W. Eisner

Elliot W. Eisner is Lee Jacks Emeritus Professor of Education and Art at Stanford University. A trained artist, Eisner has been for several decades the preeminent spokesperson for the arts in education. In addition, he has brought a fresh voice to the core curricular question, "What should we teach our children?" His latest book is *Re-Imagining Schools: The Selected Works of Elliot Eisner* (World Library of Educationalists Series).

"The Kind of Schools We Need," by Elliot Eisner. Reprinted by permission of the author.

FOCUS QUESTION

What kind of schools do we want ... really?

InTASC

Standards: 2, 3, 4, 5, 7, and 10

KEY TERMS

- Accountability
- Intrinsic motivation
- Standards
- Transfer of learning
- Vouchers

As everyone knows, there is both great interest in and great concern about the quality of education in American schools. Solutions to our perceived educational ills are often not very deep. They include mandating uniforms for students to improve their behavior; using vouchers to create a competitive climate to motivate educators to try harder; testing students each year for purposes of accountability; retaining students whose test scores have not reached specified levels; paying teachers and school administrators bonuses in relation to the measured performance of their students; and defining standards for aims, for content, for evaluation practices, and, most important, for student and teacher performance.

Ironically, what seldom gets addressed in our efforts to reform schools is the vision of education that serves as the ideal for both the practice of schooling and its outcomes. We are not clear about what we are after. Aside from literacy and numeracy, what do we want to achieve? What are our aims? What is important? What kind of educational culture do we want our children to experience? In short, what kind of schools do we need?

What we do seem to care a great deal about are standards and monitoring procedures. We want a collection of so-called best methods that will guarantee success. We want a testing program that will display the results of our efforts, often in rank-ordered league standings. We want an assessment program that allows little space for personal judgment, at least when it comes to evaluation. Personal judgment is equated with subjectivity, and we want none of that. We want to boil down teaching and evaluation practices to a scientifically grounded technology.

Whether we can ever have a scientific technology of teaching practice, given the diversity of the students we teach, is problematic. Artistry and professional judgment will, in my opinion, always be required to teach well, to make intelligent education policy, to establish personal relationships with our students, and to appraise their growth. Those of us who work in the field of education are neither bank tellers who have little discretion nor assembly line workers whose actions are largely repetitive. Each child we teach is wonderfully unique, and each requires us to use in our work that most exquisite of human capacities, the ability to make judgments in the absence of rules. Although good teaching uses routines, it is seldom routine. Good teaching depends on sensibility and imagination. It courts surprise. It profits from caring. In short, good teaching is an artistic affair.

But even artistry can profit from a vision of the kind of education we want to provide. The reason I believe it is important to have a vision of education is because without one we have no compass, no way of knowing which way we are headed. As a result, we succumb to the pet ideas that capture the attention of policy makers and those with pseudo-solutions to supposed problems. Is it really the case that more testing will improve teaching and learning or that uniforms will improve student behavior and build character? I have my doubts. We need a conception of what good schools provide and what students and teachers do in them. So let me share with you one man's vision of the kind of schools we need.

The kind of schools we need would provide time during the school day at least once a week for teachers to meet to discuss and share their work, their hopes, and their problems with their colleagues. It is the school, not the university, that is the real center of teacher education.

The idea that the school is the center of teacher education is built on the realization that whatever teachers become professionally, the process is not finished when they complete their teacher education program at age 21. Learning to teach well is a lifetime endeavor. The growth of understanding and skill in teaching terminates only when we do.

This fact means that we need to rethink whom the school serves. The school serves the teachers who work there as well as the students who learn there. The school needs to be designed in a way that affords opportunities to teachers to learn from one another. Such learning is so important that it should not be an addendum, relegated to an after-school time slot. Teachers, like others who do arduous work, are tired at the end of the day.

Learning from our colleagues certainly deserves space and attention, and, even more important, it requires a reconceptualization of the sources of teacher development. One thing we can be sure of is that the school will be no better for the students who attend than it is for the teachers who teach there. What we do typically to improve teaching is to send teachers somewhere else to be "inserviced"—every 6,000 miles or so—usually by someone who has never seen them teach. The expectation is that what teachers are exposed to will somehow translate more or less automatically into their classrooms. Again, I have my doubts.

Teaching from a cognitive perspective requires a change in paradigm, what Thomas Kuhn once described as a "paradigm shift." Such shifts are changes in conception. From a behavioral perspective, change requires the development of those sensibilities and pedagogical techniques that make it possible to realize the conceptions and values that one defines for oneself educationally. Of course, the cognitive and the behavioral cannot truly be separated; I make the distinction here for purposes of clarity. What one conceptualizes as appropriate gives direction and guidance to what one does. And what one is able to do culminates in what one achieves. Schools ought to be places in which teachers have access to other teachers so that they have an opportunity to create the kind of supportive and educative community that culminates in higher-quality education than is currently provided.

The kind of schools we need would make teaching a professionally public process. By "professionally public" I mean that teachers would have opportunities to observe other teachers and provide feedback. No longer would isolated teachers be left to themselves to figure out what went on when they were teaching; secondary ignorance is too prevalent and too consequential to depend on one's personal reflection alone. I used the term "secondary ignorance," and I used it intentionally. I like to make a distinction between what I refer to as *primary* ignorance and *secondary* ignorance.

Primary ignorance refers to a condition in which an individual recognizes that he does not know something but also recognizes that, if he wanted to know it, he could find out. He could inquire of others, he could use the library, he could go to school. Primary ignorance is a condition that in some sense is correctable and often easily correctable.

Secondary ignorance, however, is another matter. When an individual suffers from secondary ignorance, not only does she not know something, but she does not know that she does not know. In such a situation, correcting the problem may not be possible. Secondary ignorance is as consequential for the process of parenting and for the sustenance of friendships as it is for the conduct of teaching. The way in which one remedies secondary ignorance is not through self-reflection, but through the assistance of others. Really good friends can help you understand aspects of your behavior that you might not have noticed. These observations need not be negative. It is as important to appreciate one's virtues as to become cognizant of one's weaknesses.

For this process to occur professionally, teachers need access to other teachers' classrooms. Teaching needs to be made a professionally public endeavor. The image of the teacher isolated in a classroom from 8 a.m. to 3 p.m. for five days a week, 44 weeks per year, is not the model of professional teaching practice that we need. If even world-class artists and athletes profit from feedback on their performance from those who know, so too do the rest of us. We need a conception of schooling that makes possible teachers' access to one another in helpful and constructive ways. This will require redefining what the job of teaching entails.

For most individuals who select teaching as a career, the expectation is that they will be with children exclusively, virtually all day long. But teachers also need to interact with other adults so that the secondary ignorance that I described can be ameliorated.

The model of professional life that I am suggesting will not be easy to attain. We are often quite sensitive about what we do in our own classrooms, and many of us value our privacy. Yet privacy ought not to be our highest priority. We ought to hold as our highest priority our students' well-being. And their well-being, in turn, depends on the quality of our pedagogical work. This work, I am arguing, can be enhanced with the assistance of other caring adults.

The kind of schools we need would provide opportunities for members of subject-matter departments to meet to share their work. It would recognize that different fields have different needs and that sharing within fields is a way to promote coherence for students.

Departmentalization in our schools has been a long-standing way of life. It usually begins at the middle school level and proceeds through secondary school. Teachers of mathematics have a field and a body of content that they want to help students understand; so too do teachers of the arts. These commonalties within subject-matter fields can promote a wonderful sense of esprit, a sense built on a common language to describe shared work. The strength of the educational programs in these fields can be promoted when teachers in departmentalized systems have opportunities to meet and share their work, to describe the problems they have encountered, and to discuss the achievements they have made. In short, different fields often have different needs, and these different needs can be met within the school through the colleagueship that teachers within a discipline share. The department in the middle school and in the high school provides a substantial structure for promoting the sense of community I have described.

The kind of schools we need would have principals who spend about a third of their time in classrooms, so that they know firsthand what is going on. We often conceive of the role of the school principal not only as that of a skilled administrator but also as that of an educational leader. At least one of the meanings of educational leadership is to work with a staff in a way that will make leadership unnecessary. The aim of leadership in an educational institution is to work itself out of a job.

What this approach requires, at a minimum, is an understanding of the conditions of the school and the characteristics of the classrooms in which teachers work. To understand the school and the classroom requires that school administrators leave their offices and spend at least a third of their time in teachers' classrooms. In the business community this is called "supervision by walking around."

The term supervision is a bit too supervisory for my taste. I am not sure that school administrators have "super" vision. But they should have a grasp of what happens in their schools—substantively, as well as administratively. Administrators can be in a position to recognize different kinds of talents among faculty members; they can help initiate activities and support the initiatives of teachers. They can develop an intimacy that will enable them to promote and develop the leadership potential of teachers. Thus, paradoxically, the principal as leader is most successful when he or she no longer leads but promotes the initiative and leadership of others.

The kind of schools we need would use videotaped teaching episodes to refine teachers' ability to take the practice of teaching apart—not in the negative sense, but as a way of enlarging our understanding of a complex and subtle process. No one denies that teaching is a subtle and complex art. At least it is an art when it is done well. To teach really well, it is necessary to reflect on the processes of one's own teaching and on the teaching practices of others. Our ability to perform is related, as I suggested above, to our understanding of the relationship between teaching and learning. This relationship can be illuminated through the analysis of videotaped episodes of teaching practices. Just what is a teacher up to when he or she teaches? What are the consequences? What are the compromises and trade-offs that exist in virtually any context? What institutional or organizational pressures in a school must teachers contend with? How does a teacher insert herself into her teaching? What does his body language express?

Questions such as these can be profitably addressed through the analysis of videotapes. Indeed, the collaborative analysis of a teaching episode can provide a very rich resource that can illuminate differences in perspective, in educational values,

and in the meanings being conveyed. This is all to the good. Teaching is not reducible to a single frame. From my perspective, the use of such tapes not only can make our understanding of teaching more appropriately complex, but it can also refine our ability to see and interpret the process of teaching. And the more subtle perspective on teaching that such analysis creates can only enhance the quality of what we have to say to one another about the kind of work we do.

The kind of schools we need would be staffed by teachers who are interested in the questions students ask after a unit of study as they are in the answers students give. On the whole, schools are highly answer-oriented. Teachers have the questions, and students are to have the answers. Even with a problem-solving approach, the focus of attention is on the student's ability to solve a problem that someone else has posed. Yet the most intellectually demanding tasks lie not so much in solving problems as in posing questions. The framing of what we might oxymoronically call the "telling question" is what we ought to care much more about.

Once students come to deal with real situations in life, they will find that few of them provide defined problems. On the contrary, the primary task is often to define a problem so that one can get on with its solution. And to define a problem, one needs to be able to raise a question.

What would it mean to students if they were asked to raise questions coming out of a unit of study? What kinds of questions would they raise? How incisive and imaginative would these questions be? Would the students who do well in formulating questions be the same ones who do well when asked to converge upon a correct answer?

What I am getting at is the importance of developing an intellectual context designed to promote student growth. That context must surely give students an opportunity to pose questions and to entertain alternative perspectives on what they study. The last thing we want in an intellectually liberating environment is a closed set of attitudes and fealty to a single set of correct answers.

The kind of schools we need would not hold as an ideal that all students get to the same destinations at the same time. They would embrace the idea that good schools increase the variance in student performance and at the same time escalate the mean.

To talk about the idea that schools should increase individual differences rather than reduce them may at first seem counterintuitive and perhaps even antidemocratic. Don't we want all students to do the same? If we have a set of goals, don't we want all students to achieve them? To both of those questions I would give a qualified yes and no.

Individuals come into the world with different aptitudes, and, over the course of their lives, they develop different interests and proclivities. In an ideal approach to educational practice—say, one in which teaching practices were ideally designed to suit each youngster—each youngster would learn at an ideal rate. Students whose aptitudes were in math would travel farther and faster in that subject than students who had neither interest nor aptitude in math but who, for example, might have greater aptitude in language or in the visual arts. In those two fields, students would travel faster and farther than those with math aptitudes but with low interests or proclivities in language or the arts. Over time, the cumulative gap between students would grow. Students would travel at their own optimal rates, and some would go faster than others in different areas of work.

What one would have at the end of the school year is wide differences in students' performance. At the same time, since each program is ideally suited to each youngster, the mean for all students in all of the areas in which they worked would be higher than it would be in a more typical program of instruction.

Such a conception of the aims of education would actually be instrumental to the creation of a rich culture. It is through our realized aptitudes that we can contribute to the lives of others and realize our own potential. It is in the symbiotic relationships among us that we come to nurture one another, to provide for others what they cannot provide—at least, not as well—for themselves, and to secure from others the gifts they

have to offer that we cannot create—at least, not as well—for ourselves.

The idea that getting everyone to the same place is a virtue really represents a limitation on our aspirations. It does not serve democratic purposes to treat everybody identically or to expect everyone to arrive at the same destination at the same time. Some students need to go farther in one direction and others need to go farther in a different direction because that's where their aptitudes lie, that's where their interests are, and that's where their proclivities lead them.

The British philosopher and humanist Sir Herbert Read once said that there were two principles to guide education.[1] One was to help children become who they are not; the other was to help children become who they are. The former dominates in fascist countries, he believed, where the image defined by the state becomes the model to which children must adapt. The fascist view is to help children become who they are not. Read believed that education was a process of self-actualization and that in a truly educational environment children would come to realize their latent potentials. In this age of high technology and highly monitored systems and standards, I believe that Read's views bear reflection.

The kind of schools we need would take seriously the idea that a child's personal signature, his or her distinctive way of learning and creating, is something to be preserved and developed. We are not in the shoe manufacturing business. By saying that we are not in the shoe manufacturing business, I mean that we are not in the business of producing identical products. On an assembly line, one seeks predictability, even certainty, in the outcomes. What one wants on both assembly lines and airline flights are uneventful events. No surprises.

In education, surprise ought to be seen not as a limitation but as the mark of creative work. Surprise breeds freshness and discovery. We ought to be creating conditions in school that enable students to pursue what is distinctive about themselves; we ought to want them to retain their personal signatures, their particular ways of seeing things.

Of course, their ways of seeing things need to be enhanced and enriched, and the task of teaching is, in part, to transmit the culture while simultaneously cultivating those forms of seeing, thinking, and feeling that make it possible for personal idiosyncrasies to be developed. In the process, we will discover both who children are and what their capabilities are.

The kind of schools we need would recognize that different forms of representation develop different forms of thinking, convey different kinds of meaning, and make possible different qualities of life. Literacy should not be restricted to decoding text and number.

Normally the term literacy refers to the ability to read, and numeracy, the ability to compute. However, I want to recast the meaning of literacy so that it refers to the process of encoding or decoding meaning in whatever forms are used in the culture to express or convey meaning. With this conception in mind and with the realization that humans throughout history have employed a variety of forms to express meaning, literacy becomes a process through which meanings are made. Meanings, of course, are made in the visual arts, in music, in dance, in poetry, in literature, as well as in physics, in mathematics, and in history. The best way to ensure that we will graduate semiliterate students from our schools is to make sure that they have few (or ineffective) opportunities to acquire the multiple forms of literacy that make multiple forms of meaning possible.

That meanings vary with the forms in which they are cast is apparent in the fact that, when we bury and when we marry, we appeal to poetry and music to express what we often cannot express literally. Humans have invented an array of means through which meaning is construed. I use the word *construe* because meaning making is a construal, both with respect to the perception of forms made by others and with respect to the forms that we make ourselves.

We tend to think that the act of reading a story or reading a poem is a process of decoding. And it is. But it is also a process of encoding. The individual reading a story must *make* sense of the story; he or she must produce meanings from the marks on the page. The mind must be constructive, it must be active, and the task of teaching is to facilitate effective mental action so that the work encountered becomes meaningful.

The kind of schools we need would recognize that the most important forms of learning are those that students know how to use outside of school, not just inside school. And the teachers in such schools would consistently try to help students see the connections between the two. The transfer of learning cannot be assumed; it needs to be taught.

The idea that transfer needs to be taught is not a new one. I reiterate an old idea here because it is absolutely fundamental to effective education. If all that students get out of what they learn in history or math or science are ideas they rapidly forget and cannot employ outside of the context of a classroom, then education is a casualty. The point of learning anything in school is not primarily to enable one to do well in school—although most parents and students believe this to be the case—it is to enable one to do well in life. The point of learning something in school is to enrich life outside of school and to acquire the skills and ideas that will enable one to produce the questions and perform the activities that one's outside life will require.

In the field of education, we have yet to begin to conceive of educational evaluation in these terms. But these are precisely the terms that we need to employ if what we do in school is to be more than mere jumping through hoops.

The kind of schools we need would take seriously the idea that, with regard to learning, the joy is in the journey. Intrinsic motivation counts the most because what students do when they can do what they want to do is what really matters. It is here that the educational process most closely exemplifies the lived experience found in the arts. We ought to stop reinforcing our students' lust for "point accumulation."

Point accumulation is *not* an educational aim. Educational aims have to do with matters of enlightenment, matters of developing abilities, matters of aesthetic experience. What we ought to be focusing our attention on is the creation of conditions in our classrooms and in our schools that make the process of education a process that students wish to pursue. The joy must be in the journey. It is the quality of the chase that matters most.

Alfred North Whitehead once commented that most people believe that a scientist inquires in order to know. Just the opposite is true, he said. Scientists know in order to inquire. What Whitehead was getting at was the idea that the vitality, challenge, and engagement that scientists find in their work is what matters most to them. At its best, this kind of satisfaction is an aesthetic experience.

We don't talk much about the aesthetic satisfactions of teaching and learning, but those of us who have taught for more than a few years know full well the feeling we experience when things go really well in our teaching. When things go really well for students, they experience similar feelings.

We ought not to marginalize the aesthetic in our understanding of what learning is about because, in the end, it is the only form of satisfaction that is likely to predict the uses of the knowledge, skills, and perspectives that students acquire in school. There is a huge difference between what a child *can* do and what a child *will* do. A child who learns to read but has no appetite for reading is not really succeeding in school. We want to promote that appetite for learning, and it ought to be built on the satisfactions that students receive in our classrooms. It is the aesthetic that represents the highest forms of intellectual achievement, and it is the aesthetic that provides the natural high and contributes the energy we need to want to pursue an activity again and again and again.

The kind of schools we need would encourage deep conversation in classrooms. They would help students learn how to participate in that complex and subtle art, an art that requires learning how to listen as well as how to speak. Good conversation is an activity for which our voyeuristic interest in talk shows offers no substitute.

It may seem odd recommending that deep conversation be promoted in our classrooms. Conversation has a kind of shallow ring, as if it were something you do when you don't have anything really important to do. Yet conversation, when it goes well, when the participants really listen to each other, is like an acquired taste, an acquired skill. It does not take much in the way of resources, but, ironically, it is among the rarest features of classroom life. It is also, I believe, among the rare features of our personal life, and that is why we often tune in to Oprah Winfrey, Larry King, and other talk show hosts to participate vicariously in conversation. Even when the conversations are not all that deep, they remain interesting.

How do we help students learn to become listeners? How do we enable them to understand that comments and questions need to flow from what preceded and not simply express whatever happens to be on one's mind at the time? How do we enable students to become more like the members of a jazz quartet, whose interplay good conversation sometimes seems to emulate? Conversation is akin to deliberation, a process that searches for possible answers and explores blind alleys as well as open freeways. How do we create in our classrooms a practice that, when done well, can be a model of intellectual activity?

Of course, all of us need to learn to engage in deep conversation. In many ways, we need to model what we expect our students to learn. But I am convinced that conversation about ideas that matter to students and teachers and that occupy a central place in our curriculum can be a powerful means of converting the academic institutions we call schools into intellectual institutions. Such a transformation would represent a paradigmatic shift in the culture of schooling.

The kind of schools we need would help students gradually assume increased responsibility for framing their own goals and learning how to achieve them. We want students eventually to become the architects of their own education. The long-term aim of teaching is to make itself unnecessary.

Saying that the long-term aim of teaching is to render itself unnecessary is simply to make explicit what I hope readers have gleaned from my arguments here. Helping students learn how to formulate their own goals is a way to enable them to secure their freedom. Helping them learn how to plan and execute their lives in relation to those goals is a way of developing their autonomy. Plato once defined a slave as someone who executes the purposes of another. Over the grade levels, we have conceived of teaching as setting problems that students solve. Only rarely have we created the conditions through which students set the problems that they wish to pursue. Yet this is precisely what they will need to be able to do once they leave the protected sphere of the school.

It is interesting to me that, in discourse about school reform and the relation of goals and standards to curriculum reform, the teacher is given the freedom to formulate means but not to decide upon ends. The prevailing view is that professional judgment pertains to matters of technique, rather than to matters of goals.

I believe this conception of school reform is shortsighted. If our students were simply inert entities, something like copper or plastic, it would be possible in principle to formulate methods of acting on them that would yield uniform responses. A thousand pounds of pressure by a punch press on a steel plate has a given effect. But our students are not uniform, they are not steel, and they do not respond in the same way to pressures of various kinds. Thus teachers will always need the discretionary space to determine not only matters of means but also matters of ends. And we want students, gradually to be sure, to have the opportunity to formulate ends as well. Withholding such opportunities is a form of de-skilling for both teachers and students.

The kind of schools we need would make it possible for students who have particular interests to pursue those interests in depth and, at the same time, to work on public service projects that contribute to something larger than their own immediate interests. This twofold aim—the ability to serve the self through intensive study and the desire and ability to provide a public service—is like the head and tail of a coin. Both elements need to be a part of our educational agenda.

The long-term aim of education may be said to be to learn how to engage in personally satisfying activities that are at the same time socially constructive. Students need to learn that there are people who need services and that they, the students themselves, can contribute to meeting these people's needs. Service learning is a move in the right direction. It affords adolescents an opportunity to do something whose scope is beyond themselves. The result, at least potentially, is the development of an attitude that schools would do well to foster. That, too, should be a part of our curricular agenda.

The kind of schools we need would treat the idea of "public education" as meaning not only the education of the public inside schools, but also the education of the public outside schools. The school's faculty will find it difficult to proceed farther or faster than the community will allow. Our task, in part, is to nurture public conversation in order to create a collective vision of education.

Realistically speaking, our responsibilities as educators extend beyond the confines of our classrooms and even beyond the walls of our schools. We also have responsibilities to our communities. We need desperately to create educational forums for members of the community in which the purposes and processes of education can be discussed, debated, and deliberated and from which consensus can be arrived at with regard to our broad mission as an educational institution. Parents need to know why, for example, inquiry-oriented methods matter, why rote learning may not be in the best long-term interest of their children, why problem-centered activities are important, and why the ability to frame telling questions is crucial.

Most parents and even many teachers have a yellow-school-bus image when it comes to conceiving what teaching, learning, and schooling should look like. The yellow school bus is a metaphor for the model of education that they encountered and that, all too often, they wish to replicate in the 21st century. Our schools, as they are now designed, often tacitly encourage the re-creation of such a model. Yet we know there is a better way. That better way ought to be a part of the agenda the community discusses with teachers and school administrators. Principals and school superintendents ought to perform a leadership role in deepening that community conversation. Without having such a conversation, it will be very difficult to create the kind of schools we need.

I acknowledge that the features of schooling that I have described will not be easy to attain, but they are important. We get so caught up in debating whether or not we should extend the school year that we seem to forget to consider what should go into that year. We seem to forget about our vision of education and the kind of educational practices that will move the school in the direction we value. Too often we find ourselves implementing policies that we do not value. Those of us in education need to take a stand and

to serve as public advocates for our students. Who speaks for our students? We need to.

Some of the features I have described—perhaps all of them—may not be ones that you yourself cherish. Fine. That makes conversation possible. And so I invite you to begin that conversation in your school, so that out of the collective wisdom of each of our communities can come a vision of education that our children deserve and, through that vision, the creation of the kind of schools that our children need.

Note

1. Herbert Read, *Education Through Art* (New York: Pantheon Books, 1944).

POSTNOTE

Elliot Eisner's contributions to education span many areas, including art education, curriculum development, qualitative research, and educational connoisseurship. His renaissance qualities earn him a place among our classic authors.

As young graduate students, both editors of *Kaleidoscope* were privileged to have Elliot Eisner (at the time, himself a rather young professor) as a teacher. It was at the height of interest in B. F. Skinner's behaviorism and during the applications of programmed instruction and behavioral objectives to American classrooms. There was a heady belief throughout the educational community that this new movement would soon transform our schools. Professor Eisner would have little of it. His was one of the few voices at that time to raise questions and urge caution.

Today we are in the midst of a new national movement that many believe will revolutionize our

schools and lead to much higher levels of academic achievement among our students. As he has throughout his career, Eisner is again asking the hard questions, this time about standards and the effects of the tests we use to gauge our successes and failures to reach those standards. Here, he asks us to step back and think hard about what we really desire. "What kind of schools do we *really* need?"

DISCUSSION QUESTIONS

1. In what specific ways has Eisner's article challenged you? Or do you agree with everything he seems to suggest?
2. What are the challenges and hurdles to overcome to achieve the kind of schools that Eisner suggests?
3. What are the most positive suggestions for school improvement that the author makes?

RELATED WEBSITE RESOURCES

WEB RESOURCES:

Association for Supervision and Curriculum Development. Available at:

http://www.ascd.org.

This extensive website, maintained by the leading curriculum organization in the country, has extensive materials and resources for educators.

Curriculum and Instruction, Thomas B. Fordham Institute. Available at:

http://www.edexcellence.net.

This website, sponsored by the reform-minded Fordham Institute, is a leading source of criticism of what is currently taught in our schools.

39

The Moral North Star

William Damon

William Damon is Professor of Education at Stanford University and Director of the Stanford Center on Adolescence, Stanford, California; 650-725-8205; wdamon@stanford.edu.

"The Moral North Star," by William Damon, 2008 *Educational Leadership* 66(2), pp. 8–13. © 2008 by ASCD. Reprinted with permission. Learn more about ASCD at www.ascd.org.

FOCUS QUESTION

What is the role of "purpose" in the life of a student?

InTASC

Standards 2, 3, and 9

KEY TERMS

- Moral North Star
- Purpose

When I entered high school, achieving excellence was about the farthest thing from my mind. I had no reason to believe I could excel in coursework, and I saw no particular reason to try. I did care about not getting in trouble, but that required only a modicum of effort. Like many students, I quickly learned the lesson that Theodore Sizer (1984) formulated in *Horace's Compromise*: As long as I did well enough not to humiliate myself or the school, most teachers would leave me alone.

But two things happened during 9th grade that changed my attitude toward academic pursuits forever. Neither experience seemed dramatic or strange, nor did their significance dawn on me immediately. Yet they remain memorable because they ignited sparks of motivation that still endure. What's more, in my recent research I have found that the academic awakenings of students who find their own "paths to purpose" (Damon, 2008) often occur in ways that are strikingly similar to the initial stirrings of interest that I felt so long ago.

Two Turning Points

Early in that first year of high school, for one of my weekly assignments in English class, I handed in my usual half-finished and thoroughly mediocre piece of work. But this time I made the mistake of muttering a feeble excuse as I passed the essay to my teacher, along the lines of "I didn't spend much time on this, but I know these weekly assignments don't count for much." My teacher, a crusty old gentleman who had undoubtedly seen thousands of similarly lackadaisical efforts in his time, nevertheless took the time to pull me aside for a word of advice. He peered over his glasses, fixed me in a stern gaze, and said, "Mr. Damon, *everything* you do in this world counts." Perhaps because of the earnest way he said it, or perhaps because the idea was so foreign to my careless way of thinking at the time, the message left an impression that kept ringing in my ears from that day forward.

My other memorable experience came later that year when I worked on the school newspaper. I joined the newspaper to cover sports: I wasn't a good enough athlete to make the teams, but I enjoyed watching the games and hanging out with the players. My first assignment was to cover a game that was of little interest to anyone. A group of Eastern European immigrants had formed an amateur soccer team and had requested a practice match with our varsity team. It was a pretty good game, with the visiting team more than holding its own, but that was not the story that captured my imagination. I stayed to talk with the immigrants after the game, and they spoke passionately about coming to America, the hard lives they had left behind, what political freedom meant to them, and their hopes for themselves and their families in this new land. This conversation opened a world of cultural and historical understanding that went far beyond what I had been learning in social studies. What's more, when I wrote a story for the newspaper about these immigrants' lives, my friends read it and commented that they were fascinated.

I had found an enthralling purpose. In my 14-year-old mind, the act of discovering previously unknown information and then communicating it to others seemed incredibly worthwhile and powerful. After that, I had no trouble devoting attention to my school writing assignments. I was determined to learn the skills that I would need to successfully pursue the mission I had found so captivating. My eventual choice of a career as a scholar and researcher began with the personal passion I discovered that day.

These two 9th grade experiences had a number of things in common. First, they increased my motivation to learn and gave me a reason to strive for excellence. Second, they made me think about what kind of person I was and what I could accomplish with the knowledge my school offered. Third, they imparted to me the idea that my efforts could serve a useful purpose if I made good choices about how to spend my time.

In the first incident, I became aware that my actions matter. In the second, I found a way to contribute something of value through an engaging activity that drew on academic skills. The notion of accomplishing a worthy purpose captured my imagination, guided my choices, and spurred my energies toward the pursuit of excellence.

My 9th grade experiences had one other commonality that I note with regret: Despite the invaluable educational benefits that they imparted, both experiences are marginal to the main concerns being expressed about U.S. schools today. Across the education landscape, policymakers, experts, and practitioners are engaging in great debates about the need for testing and accountability, the content of the curriculum, and the proper uses of instructional methods such as computer technology. I do not mean to diminish these essential concerns. But largely missing from the debates is a central question: How can we get students to see the knowledge and skills we expect them to learn in school as important to their own lives and aspirations?

This is not simply a matter of academic motivation in the conventional sense—motivation to study hard enough to get good grades and fulfill course requirements. Rather, it is a question of the *purpose* behind the requirements. Why is schooling useful in the first place? On a personal level, why should a particular student bother to learn the knowledge offered in school and strive to use it in a masterful and ethical way—that is, aim for intellectual and moral excellence?

Students with Purpose— and Without

Some educators may worry that introducing the big "why" questions that help students find purpose may distract attention away from the subject matter that schools are expected to convey. The opposite is true: Only when students discover personal meaning in their work do they apply their efforts with focus and imagination.

The question of purpose is what psychologists call an *ultimate concern* (Emmons, 1999) because it gives meaning to short-term goals (such as passing tests and getting good grades) by asking where these short-term goals will lead. Purpose acts as a moral north star on the route to excellence: It offers a steady beacon for inspiring and directing students' best efforts over the long haul, within the classroom and beyond.

Unfortunately, highly purposeful students are the exception rather than the rule in our classrooms. In research for the Stanford Youth Purpose Project (Damon, 2008), we found that about 20 percent of students in our diverse national sample were approaching their studies with a clear sense of purpose. These youngsters stood out from their peers because they knew why they were in school: They had found a meaningful direction for their lives, and they wanted to prepare themselves for it. They appeared to be thriving in the classroom and beyond.

Some of these highly purposeful students are truly amazing. These are a few such students:

- Ryan, a boy who became concerned about families in Africa without enough clean water to drink. By age 12, Ryan had raised millions of dollars to build drinking wells in developing countries and had started a foundation to further these efforts.
- Nina, who after witnessing the ravages of lung cancer in her West Virginia town, spent years of her adolescence leading a youth chapter of the American Cancer Society to support cancer research and social policy and is now pursuing a medical career.
- Pascal, an aspiring jazz musician who combines a creative flair with serious study, intense practice, and a good grasp of the pragmatic realities of succeeding in a music career.
- Barbara, who by age 16 had joined with a friend to lead an organization called "Don't Be Crude!" which promotes environmentally cleaner ways for Texas farmers to dispose of used oil from their tractors than simply dumping it on the fields.

At the other extreme, approximately a quarter of our sample had little interest in long-term goals of any kind. It was difficult to talk with them about purpose because they were not looking for much beyond their day-to-day existence. Some were

content with their purposelessness, seeming to enjoy the hedonistic opportunities that this state of mind offered. Others felt dejected, anxious, apathetic, or some combination thereof. Not many of these students were making good use of their school years, let alone seeking excellence.

In the mid-range of our sample, between the purposeful and purposeless students, we found a large group (55 percent) who had experienced moments of purpose but who had not yet sustained a commitment to any particular aspiration. Some among this group were dabblers who were skipping from one interest to another without quite knowing why; some were dreamers who had visions of what they would like to become but no realistic sense of how to get there. With the right kind of guidance, all of these students could find the unique purpose that would give meaning to their work in school—and in life. But to make this happen, teachers must address the question of why academic knowledge is important.

Addressing the "Why" Question

Teachers can address this "why" question across the curriculum. Why do people need to learn history or math? Why is it useful to read and write well or to spell words correctly? Why do we expect you and your fellow students to excel in the work that we assign you?

In my work with high schools, I have found that instruction in the sciences offers a vivid context for raising "why" (and "why not") questions. Such questions can spur students' interest in what many of them see as an obscure and difficult subject. Some years ago, I tried out this approach during a summer school program for gifted high school students. We discussed research in microbiology in the context of ethical questions such as the desirability of human genetic engineering and cloning. Students applied themselves vigorously to the difficult scientific readings, motivated at least in part by their enhanced appreciation for the contested moral issues at stake.

Beyond the curriculum, teachers and school counselors can raise questions of purpose in the context of vocational choices. "Why have I [the teacher] chosen teaching as my occupation?" Addressing this question with students, which teachers too rarely do, exposes students to a respected adult's own quest for purpose. The idea that teaching is a calling for a dedicated individual would provide inspiring insights into vocational possibilities for our students.

In a broader sense, students could benefit from more discussion in school about the vocational implications of the coursework that they are doing. Not only, What kind of jobs can people who excel in algebra do? but also, What does this kind of work accomplish? Why is it important? How can I find out more about where my math talents could take me and how I could use them to establish a fulfilling career?

To foster the pursuit of moral excellence, teachers can introduce students to figures from recent history who have acted with integrity and courage in the face of pressure and personal risk, such as Nelson Mandela, Václav Havel, Katharine Graham, and Boris Yeltsin. In addition, teachers and other school staff can address ethical problems that arise in schools not simply as rule breaking but also as violations of deeper moral purposes, helping students reflect on the question, Why do we have rules against cheating in the first place? If students realize that the moral purpose behind such rules is to preserve standards of fairness, honesty, trust, and integrity, they will endorse and uphold the rules with far more determination than if they merely see the rules as another set of demands from school authorities.

We can build a culture of purpose for students in thousands of ways throughout the school day. Some of these ways require nothing more than a well-directed remark or question from an attentive teacher. Others open up new possibilities for enlivening the curriculum materials at the core of the school's academic mission. A working paper that Stanford graduate student Matt Andrews prepared for me documented a number of ways in which teachers can foster reflection about purpose in the classroom. These strategies—which include many that teachers have used throughout their careers—gain greater power when teachers use them in combination as part of an intentional effort to put purpose at the center of schooling. For example, teachers can

- Engage in regular conversations with students about their hopes, dreams, and aspirations in life.
- Recognize student accomplishments that indicate beyond-the-self concerns.
- Link present school activities with the future life plans of students.
- Probe for deeper thinking by frequently asking, Why? when students give cryptic answers to questions.
- Connect school lessons to larger world issues.
- Provide students with the pedagogical reasons behind a particular activity or lesson.
- Develop lessons that make visible how students' actions contribute to wider systems (for example, a science unit that links student behavior to ecological impact).
- Introduce students to purpose in discussion of vocations.
- Create biographical units about purposeful people that include both famous people and locals who have direct contact with students.
- Nurture civic purpose by encouraging responsible citizenship within the school and beyond.

Building Purposeful Citizens

This last item, nurturing civic purpose, is crucial today. Among all the causes that inspired the purposeful youth in our study, civic leadership came in dead last. Few young people today aspire to positions of civic responsibility (mayor, council member, senator, president, and so on).

There are many possible explanations for this finding, such as the paucity of admirable political leaders as portrayed by current media accounts. Whatever the reason, the lack of civic purpose is a grave concern for the future of democracy, which relies on constant renewal by new cadres of committed young people. A democratic society will wither if it does not benefit from the talents and energies of each generation as it comes of age.

Schools must live up to their responsibilities to prepare students for full citizenship, and they must do so with the same standards of excellence that they hold for more narrowly defined academic pursuits. As in all areas of learning, the surest way to encourage dedication to informed citizenship among students is to help them understand why their participation is important—why it matters, how they can make a difference, and where they can find their personal sense of purpose.

References

Damon, W. (2008). *The path to purpose: Helping our children find their calling in life*. New York: The Free Press.

Emmons, R. (1999). *The psychology of ultimate concerns*. New York: Guilford.

Sizer, T. (1984). *Horace's compromise: The dilemma of the American high school*. Boston: Houghton Mifflin.

Author's Note: The John Templeton Foundation and the Thrive Foundation for Youth provided support for the Stanford Youth Purpose Project. Arthur Schwartz introduced me to the phrase "moral north star."

POSTNOTE

One of the most damaging legacies of the social turmoil of the 1960s and 1970s has been the belief that all morality was relative and private and, in particular, that the schools had no business trying to "indoctrinate" children with moral principles and ideas. Fueled by disagreements over the Vietnam War, recreational drugs, and the then-new sexual and feminist revolutions, many teachers and school districts withdrew from conscious attempts to engage students in the larger moral questions of life, questions such as, "What are you planning to do with your life?" When these and similar questions go unasked, students will think they are either unimportant or their teachers aren't interested in the larger context of their lives.

DISCUSSION QUESTIONS

1. In your school experience, have you had teachers who inquired about your sense of purpose, your "moral north star"?
2. What do you see as the dangers of engaging students in questions of "purpose?"

RELATED WEBSITE RESOURCES AND VIDEO CASE

WEB RESOURCES:

Character Education Partnership. Available at:

http://www.character.org.

The Character Education Partnership (CEP) is an umbrella organization that has pioneered the revival of character education in schools. Its website offers an array of information and resources for educators.

Practical Guidance Resources Educators Can Trust. Available at:

http://charactered.net/.

This website has many useful lessons for those interested in teaching core values, such as honesty and perseverance.

▶❙❙ TEACHSOURCE VIDEO CASE

SCHOOLS USE EFFECTIVE SCHOOLS CORRELATES

This video shows teachers and students in KIPP (Knowledge Is Power Program) schools in a variety of teaching and learning situations. While much of the video deals with teaching techniques, the video also shows how the KIPP school has established an impressive moral environment. Go to the website for the Education Media Library at CengageBrain.com to watch the video clips, study the artifacts in the case, and reflect on the following questions.

1. What are the specific attributes of this school that contribute to an ethical environment?

2. What specific qualities of this school reinforce the ideas in William Damon's article?

3. Which of the rules and approaches used to create a moral environment mentioned in this video could not be employed in all public schools? Why and why not?

40

The Ethics of Teaching

Kenneth A. Strike

Kenneth Strike is Professor of Cultural Foundations of Education at Syracuse University and a member of the National Academy of Education.

"The Ethics of Teaching," by Kenneth A. Strike, *Phi Delta Kappan,* October 1988. Reprinted with permission of Phi Delta Kappa International, www.pdkintl.org. All rights reserved.

FOCUS QUESTION

What are the ethical principles that underlie teaching?

KEY TERMS

- Benefit maximization
- Equal respect
- Ethics
- Values

Mrs. Porter and Mr. Kennedy have divided their third-grade classes into reading groups. In her class, Mrs. Porter tends to spend the most time with students in the slowest reading group because they need the most help. Mr. Kennedy claims that such behavior is unethical. He maintains that each reading group should receive equal time.

Miss Andrews has had several thefts of lunch money in her class. She has been unable to catch the thief, although she is certain that some students in the class know who the culprit is. She decides to keep the entire class inside for recess, until someone tells her who stole the money. Is it unethical to punish the entire class for the acts of a few?

Ms. Phillips grades her fifth-grade students largely on the basis of effort. As a result, less able students who try hard often get better grades than students who are abler but less industrious. Several parents have accused Ms. Phillips of unethical behavior, claiming that their children are not getting what they deserve. These parents also fear that teachers in the middle school won't understand Ms. Phillips' grading practices and will place their children in inappropriate tracks.

The Nature of Ethical Issues

The cases described above are typical of the ethical issues that teachers face. What makes these issues ethical?

First, ethical issues concern questions of right and wrong—our duties and obligations, our rights and responsibilities. Ethical discourse is characterized by a unique vocabulary that commonly includes such words as *ought* and *should, fair* and *unfair.*

Second, ethical questions cannot be settled by an appeal to facts alone. In each of the preceding cases, knowing the consequences of our actions is not sufficient for determining the right thing to do. Perhaps, because Mrs. Porter spends more time with the slow reading group, the reading scores in her class will be more evenly distributed than the scores in Mr. Kennedy's class. But even knowing this does not tell us if it is fair to spend a disproportionate amount of time with the slow readers. Likewise, if Miss Andrews punishes her entire class, she may catch the thief, but this does not tell us whether punishing the entire group was the right thing to do. In ethical reasoning, facts are relevant in deciding what to do. But by themselves they are not enough. We also require ethical principles by which to judge the facts.

Third, ethical questions should be distinguished from values. Our values concern what we like or what we believe to be good. If one enjoys Bach or likes skiing, that says something about one's values. Often there is nothing right or wrong about values, and our values are a matter of our free choice. For example, it would be difficult to argue that someone who preferred canoeing to skiing had done something wrong or had made a mistake. Even if we believe that Bach is better than rock, that is not a reason to make people who prefer rock listen to Bach. Generally, questions of values turn on our choices: what we like, what we deem worth liking. But there is nothing obligatory about values.

On the other hand, because ethics concern what we ought to do, our ethical obligations are often independent of what we want or choose. The fact that we want something that belongs to someone else does not entitle us to take it. Nor does a choice to steal make stealing right or even "right for us." Our ethical obligations continue to be obligations, regardless of what we want or choose.

Ethical Reasoning

The cases sketched above involve ethical dilemmas: situations in which it seems possible to give a reasonable argument for more than one course of action. We must think about our choices, and we must engage in moral reasoning. Teaching is full of such dilemmas. Thus teachers need to know something about ethical reasoning.

Ethical reasoning involves two stages: applying principles to cases and judging the adequacy or applicability of the principles. In the first stage, we are usually called upon to determine the relevant ethical principle or principles that apply to a case,

to ascertain the relevant facts of the case, and to judge the facts by the principles.

Consider, for example, the case of Miss Andrews and the stolen lunch money. Some ethical principles concerning punishment seem to apply directly to the case. Generally, we believe that we should punish the guilty, not the innocent; that people should be presumed innocent until proven guilty; and that the punishment should fit the crime. If Miss Andrews punishes her entire class for the behavior of an unknown few, she will violate these common ethical principles about punishment.

Ethical principles are also involved in the other two cases. The first case involves principles of equity and fairness. We need to know what counts as fair or equal treatment for students of different abilities. The third case requires some principles of due process. We need to know what are fair procedures for assigning grades to students.

However, merely identifying applicable principles isn't enough. Since the cases described above involve ethical dilemmas, it should be possible to argue plausibly for more than one course of action.

For example, suppose Miss Andrews decides to punish the entire class. It could be argued that she had behaved unethically because she has punished innocent people. She might defend herself, however, by holding that she had reasons for violating ethical principles that we normally apply to punishment. She might argue that it was important to catch the thief or that it was even more important to impress on her entire class that stealing is wrong. She could not make these points by ignoring the matter. By keeping the entire class inside for recess, Miss Andrews could maintain, she was able to catch the thief and to teach her class a lesson about the importance of honesty. Even if she had to punish some innocent people, everyone was better off as a result. Can't she justify her action by the fact that everyone benefits?

Two General Principles

When we confront genuine ethical dilemmas such as this, we need some general ethical concepts in order to think our way through them. I suggest two: the principle of benefit maximization and the principle of equal respect for persons.

The principle of benefit maximization holds that we should take that course of actions which will maximize the benefit sought. More generally, it requires us to do that which will make everyone, on the average, as well off as possible. One of the traditional formulations of this principle is the social philosophy known as utilitarianism, which holds that our most general moral obligation is to act in a manner that produces the greatest happiness for the greatest number.

We might use the principle of benefit maximization to think about each of these cases. The principle requires that in each case we ask which of the possible courses of action makes people generally better off. Miss Andrews has appealed to the principle of benefit maximization in justifying her punishment of the entire class. Ms. Phillips might likewise appeal to it in justifying her grading system. Perhaps by using grades to reward effort rather than successful performance, the overall achievement of the class will be enhanced. Is that not what is important?

It is particularly interesting to see how the principle of benefit maximization might be applied to the question of apportioning teacher time between groups with different levels of ability. Assuming for the moment that we wish to maximize the overall achievement of the class, the principle of benefit maximization dictates that we allocate time in a manner that will produce the greatest overall learning.

Suppose, however, we discover that the way to produce the greatest overall learning in a given class is for a teacher to spend the most time with the *brightest* children. These are the children who provide the greatest return on our investment of time. Even though the least able children learn less than they would with an equal division of time, the overall learning that takes place in the class is maximized when we concentrate on the ablest.

Here the principle of benefit maximization seems to lead to an undesirable result. Perhaps we should consider other principles as well.

The principle of equal respect requires that our actions respect the equal worth of moral agents. We

must regard human beings as intrinsically worthwhile and treat them accordingly. The essence of this idea is perhaps best expressed in the Golden Rule. We have a duty to accord others the same kind of treatment that we expect them to accord us.

The principle of equal respect can be seen as involving three subsidiary ideas. First, it requires us to treat people as ends in themselves, rather than as means to further our own goals. We must respect their goals as well.

Second, when we are considering what it means to treat people as ends rather than as means, we must regard as central the fact that people are free and rational moral agents. This means that, above all, we must respect their freedom of choice. And we must respect the choices that people make even when we do not agree.

Third, no matter how people differ, they are of equal value as moral agents. This does not mean that we must see people as equal in abilities or capacities. Nor does it mean that we cannot take relevant differences between people into account when deciding how to treat them. It is not, for example, a violation of equal respect to give one student a higher grade than another because that student works harder and does better.

That people are of equal value as moral agents does mean, however, that they are entitled to the same basic rights and that their interests are of equal value. Everyone, regardless of native ability, is entitled to equal opportunity. No one is entitled to act as though his or her happiness counted for more than the happiness of others. As persons, everyone has equal worth.

Notice three things about these two moral principles. First, both principles (in some form) are part of the moral concepts of almost everyone who is reading this article. These are the sorts of moral principles that everyone cites in making moral arguments. Even if my formulation is new, the ideas themselves should be familiar. They are part of our common ethical understandings.

Second, both principles seem necessary for moral reflection. Neither is sufficient by itself. For example, the principle of equal respect requires us to value the well-being of others as we value our own well-being.

But to value the welfare of ourselves *and* others is to be concerned with maximizing benefits; we want all people to be as well-off as possible.

Conversely, the principle of benefit maximization seems to presuppose the principle of equal respect. Why, after all, must we value the welfare of others? Why not insist that only our own happiness counts or that our happiness is more important than the happiness of others? Answering these questions will quickly lead us to affirm that people are of equal worth and that, as a consequence, everyone's happiness is to be valued equally. Thus our two principles are intertwined.

Third, the principles may nevertheless conflict with one another. One difference between the principle of benefit maximization and the principle of equal respect is their regard for consequences. For the principle of benefit maximization, only consequences matter. The sole relevant factor in choosing between courses of action is which action has the best overall results. But consequences are not decisive in the principle of equal respect; our actions must respect the dignity and worth of the individuals involved, even if we choose a course of action that produces less benefit than some other possible action.

The crucial question that characterizes a conflict between the principle of benefit maximization and the principle of equal respect is this:

When is it permissible to violate a person's rights in order to produce a better outcome? For example, this seems the best way to describe the issue that arises when a teacher decides to punish an entire class for the acts of a few. Students' rights are violated when they are punished for something they haven't done, but the overall consequence of

the teacher's action may be desirable. Is it morally permissible, then, to punish everyone?

We can think about the issue of fair allocation of teacher time in the same way. Spending more time with the brightest students may enhance the average learning of the class. But we have, in effect, traded the welfare of the least able students for the welfare of the ablest. Is that not failing to respect the equal worth of the least able students? Is that not treating them as though they were means, not ends?

The principle of equal respect suggests that we should give the least able students at least an equal share of time, even if the average achievement of the class declines. Indeed, we might use the principle of equal respect to argue that we should allocate our time in a manner that produces more equal results—or a more equal share of the benefits of education.

I cannot take the discussion of these issues any further in this short space. But I do want to suggest some conclusions about ethics and teaching.

First, teaching is full of ethical issues. It is the responsibility of teachers, individually and collectively, to consider these issues and to have informed and intelligent opinions about them.

Second, despite the fact that ethical issues are sometimes thorny, they can be thought about. Ethical reflection can help us to understand what is at stake in our choices, to make more responsible choices, and sometimes to make the right choices.

Finally, to a surprising extent, many ethical dilemmas, including those that are common to teaching, can be illuminated by the principles of benefit maximization and equal respect for persons. Understanding these general ethical principles and their implications is crucial for thinking about ethical issues.

POSTNOTE

Ethics seems to be making a comeback. We may not be behaving better, but we are talking about it more. Street crime and white-collar crime, drugs and violence, our inability to keep promises in our personal and professional lives—all these suggest a renewed need for ethics.

Kenneth Strike points out that teaching is full of ethical issues. It is true that teachers make promises to perform certain duties and that they have real power over the lives of children. This article, however, speaks to only one end of the spectrum of ethical issues faced by the teacher: what we call "hard-case" ethics, complex problems, often daunting dilemmas. Certainly, these are important, but there are also everyday teaching ethics—the issues that fill a teacher's day: Should I correct this stack of papers or watch *Glee?* Should I "hear" that student's vulgar comment or keeping strolling right by? Should I reread this story again this year before I teach it tomorrow or spend some time chatting with my colleagues in the teachers' lounge? Should I bend down and pick up yet another piece of paper in the hall or figure I've done my share for the day?

Like hard-case ethical issues, these questions, in essence, ask, "What's the right thing to do?" Our answers to these everyday questions often become our habits, good and bad. These, in turn, define much of our ethical behavior as teachers. Finally, it is our habitual behavior that may be our most powerful teacher.

DISCUSSION QUESTIONS

1. What three factors or qualities make an issue an ethical one?
2. What two ethical principles are mentioned in the article? Give your own examples of classroom situations that reflect these principles.
3. Do you believe that all one needs to be a moral teacher is to make ethical decisions? Why or why not?

RELATED WEBSITE RESOURCES AND VIDEO CASE

WEB RESOURCES:

Professional Ethics Issues and Topics. Available at:

http://www.ethicsweb.ca/resources/professional/issues.html.

This is part of the Applied Ethics Resources on the World Wide Web which, while dealing with ethics in many fields, has some resources on the teaching profession.

Character Education Partnership. Available at:

http://www.character.org.

The Character Education Partnership (CEP) is an umbrella organization that has pioneered the revival of character education in schools. Its website offers an array of information and resources for educators.

▶❚❚ TEACHSOURCE VIDEO CASE

ETHICAL DILEMMAS FOR TEACHERS AND ADMINISTRATORS

In this video, Vincent Ferandino, former Executive Director of the National Association for Elementary Principals, discusses the pressures on principals to raise students' achievement test scores and identifies some misuses of these scores. Stacey Moskowitz, an elementary teacher, says parents should be involved with their children's education so they know what is happening with their children in the classroom. Go to the website for the Education Media Library at CengageBrain.com to watch the video clips, study the artifacts in the case, and reflect on the following questions.

1. What are the primary ethical dilemmas identified by Ferandino and what other ethical issues to you believe principals regularly confront?
2. In what way could mandated high-stakes tests have an ethical impact on a principal or a teacher?

The Teacher's Ten Commandments: School Law in the Classroom

Thomas R. McDaniel

Thomas R. McDaniel is senior vice president and professor of education at Converse College in Spartanburg, South Carolina.

"The Teacher's Ten Commandments: School Law in the Classroom," by Thomas R. McDaniel, Revised and updated from *Phi Delta Kappan*, June 1979. Reprinted with permission of Phi Delta Kappa International, www.pdkintl.org. All rights reserved.

In recent years public school teachers have been made painfully aware that the law defines, limits, and prescribes many aspects of a teacher's daily life. Schools are no longer protected domains where teachers rule with impunity; ours is an age of litigation. Not only are parents and students ready to use the courts for all manner of grievances against school and teacher, the growing legislation itself regulates more and more of school life. In addition to an unprecedented number of laws at all levels of government, the mind-boggling array of complex case law principles (often vague and contradictory) adds to the confusion for the educator.

The Ten Commandments of School Law described below are designed to provide the concerned and bewildered teacher with some significant general guidelines in the classroom. While statutes and case law principles may vary from state to state or judicial circuit to judicial circuit, these school law principles have wide applicability in the United States today.

Commandment I: Thou Shalt Not Worship in the Classroom

This may seem something of a parody of the Biblical First Commandment—and many teachers hold that indeed their religious freedom and that of the majority of students has been limited by the court cases prohibiting prayer and Bible reading—but the case law principles here have been designed to keep public schools *neutral* in religious matters. The First Amendment to the Constitution, made applicable by the Fourteenth Amendment to state government (and hence to public schools, which are agencies of state government), requires that there be no law "respecting the establishment of religion or prohibiting the free exercise thereof." As the Supreme Court declared in the *Everson* decision of 1947, "Neither [a state nor the federal government] can

FOCUS QUESTION

What are the overarching legal principles that can guide the work of a teacher?

KEY TERMS

- Academic freedom
- Due process

pass laws that aid one religion, aid all religions, or prefer one religion over another." Such rules, said the Court, would violate the separation of church and state principle of the First Amendment.

In 1971 the Supreme Court ruled in *Lemon* v. *Kurtzman* that separation of church and state required that government action or legislation in education must clear a three-pronged test. It must: 1) not have a religious purpose, 2) not have the primary effect of either enhancing or inhibiting religion, and 3) not create "excessive entanglement" between church and state. This Lemon Test has been attacked by Justice Anton Scalia and others in recent years but continues to be used (at least as a guideline) in court rulings. In a 1992 case, *Lee* v. *Wiseman*, the Supreme Court ruled that an invocation and benediction at commencement by a clergyman was unconstitutional—perhaps because the school principal chose the clergyman and gave him directions for the content of the prayer. In another 1992 case a circuit court of appeals upheld a policy that permitted high school seniors to choose student volunteers to deliver nonsectarian, nonproselytizing invocations at graduation ceremonies. Courts continue to wrestle with questions about "establishment" and "freedom" of religion. However, acts of worship in public schools usually violate the neutrality principle—especially when they appear to be planned and promoted by school officials.

On the other hand, public schools may offer courses in comparative religion, history of religion, or the Bible as literature, because these would be academic experiences rather than religious ones. "Released-time" programs during school hours for outside-of-school religious instruction have been held to be constitutional by the Supreme Court (*Zorach* v. *Clauson*, 1952). Two states, Georgia and South Carolina, had state laws in place by 2008 that permitted the granting of academic credit for such off-campus released time Bible courses, and several other states are considering requiring Biblical or other religious literacy courses as part of the regular curriculum.

Other religious practices that have been struck down by the Supreme Court include a Kentucky statute requiring that the Ten Commandments be posted in every public school classroom, a Michigan high school's 30-year practice of displaying a 2-foot by 3-foot portrait of Jesus in the hallways, laws in Arkansas and Louisiana requiring that "scientific creationism" (based on Genesis) be taught in science classes to "balance" the teaching of evolution, and the Gideons' distribution of Bibles in the public schools of Indiana.

The Supreme Court has questioned (or struck down) certain practices such as invocations at football games (*Santa Fe Independent School District* v. *Doe*, a 2000 ruling), nativity scenes and other religious displays, and laws requiring a "moment of silence" when the purpose is to promote prayer. On the other hand, most "moment of silence" laws have been found to be legal under the First Amendment. Finding the line that separates church and state has not been easy: The "wall of separation" has often seemed more like a semi-permeable membrane.

In 1984, Congress passed the Equal Access Act. This statute made it unlawful for any public secondary school receiving federal funds to discriminate against any students who wanted to conduct a meeting on school premises during "non-instructional time" (before and after regular school hours) if other student groups (such as clubs) were allowed to use school facilities during these times. Religious groups that are voluntary and student initiated (not officially sponsored or led by school personnel) may, under the EAA, meet on school premises. Such meetings may not be conducted or controlled by others not associated with the school nor may they interfere with educational activities of the school. In a 1990 case (*Westside Community Schools* v. *Mergens*) the Supreme Court upheld the constitutionality of the EAA and declared this federal statute did not violate the First Amendment or any of the three prongs of the Lemon Test. However, a 1993 case (*Sease* v. *School District of Philadelphia*) in Pennsylvania disallowed a gospel choir that advertised itself as sponsored by the school district, was directed by the school secretary, had another school employee attending all practices, and had non-school persons regularly attending meetings of the choir. There were several violations of the EAA in this case.

The application of the neutrality principle to education has resulted in some of the following guidelines for public schools:

1. Students may not be required to salute the flag nor to stand for the flag salute, if this conflicts with their religious beliefs.
2. Bible reading, even without comment, may not be practiced in a public school when the intent is to promote worship.
3. Prayer is an act of worship and as such cannot be a regular part of opening exercises or other aspects of the regular school day (including grace at lunch).
4. Worship services (e.g., prayer and Bible reading) are not constitutional even if voluntary rather than compulsory. Not consensus, not majority vote, nor excusing objectors from class or participation makes these practices legal.
5. Prayer and other acts of worship (benedictions, hymns, invocations, etc.) at school-related or school-sponsored events are increasingly under scrutiny by courts and may be disallowed when found to be initiated or controlled by school officials.

Commandment II: Thou Shalt Not Abuse Academic Freedom

Under First Amendment protection, teachers are given the necessary freedom and security to use the classroom as a forum for the examination and discussion of ideas. Freedom of expression is a prerequisite for education in a democracy—and the schools, among other responsibilities, are agents of democracy. Students are citizens too, and they are also entitled to freedom of speech. As Justice Abe Fortas, who delivered the Supreme Court's majority opinion in the famous *Tinker* decision (1969), put it:

> It can hardly be argued that either students or teachers shed their constitutional rights at the schoolhouse gate.... In our system state-operated schools may not be enclaves

of totalitarianism … [and] students may not be regarded as closed-circuit recipients of only that which the state chooses to communicate.

Case law has developed over the years to define the parameters of free expression for both teachers and students.

In one decision, the U.S. Supreme Court upheld a school district that suspended a student for violating the school's no disruption rule prohibiting "obscene, profane language" after the student had delivered a nominating speech on behalf of another student during a student assembly. The speech included several sexual references, and the Supreme Court held that the student's speech may be disciplined when it is proved to be "vulgar, lewd, and plainly offensive" (*Bethel School District # 403* v. *Fraser,* 1986). In a more recent case, the U.S. Supreme Court sided with school principal Morse when she disciplined and suspended high school student Frederick for displaying a banner with the words "Bong Hits 4 Jesus" at a school-sanctioned parade during school hours and supervised by teachers and administrators. Frederick was off school grounds, across the street from the school, and caused no disruption. Nonetheless, because of the presumed drug message, the Court said restricting such student speech served an important state interest and it was, therefore, proper (*Morse* v. *Frederick,* 2007).

Consider these guidelines regarding First Amendment freedom of expression in the classroom:

1. Teachers may discuss controversial issues in the classroom if they are relevant to the curriculum, although good judgment is required. Issues that disrupt the educational process, are demonstrably inappropriate to the legitimate objectives of the curriculum, or are unreasonable for the age and maturity of the students may be prohibited by school officials. The routine use of profanity by teachers is not a protected First Amendment right (*Martin* v. *Parrish*, 1986, Fifth Circuit Court).
2. Teachers may discuss current events, political issues, and candidates so long as neutrality and balanced consideration prevail. When teachers

become advocates and partisans, supporters of a single position rather than examiners of all positions, they run the risk of censure.

3. A teacher may use controversial literature containing "rough" language but must "take care not to transcend his legitimate professional purpose" (*Mailoux* v. *Kiley*, 1971, U.S. District Court, Massachusetts). Again, courts will attempt to determine curriculum relevance, disruption of the educational process, and appropriateness to the age and maturity of the students.

4. Teachers and students are increasingly (but not yet universally) guaranteed symbolic free speech, including hair length and beards, armbands, and buttons. Courts generally determine such issues in terms of the "substantial disruption" that occurs or is clearly threatened. Dress codes for students are generally allowable when they are intended to provide for health, safety, and "decency." When they exist merely to promote the "tastes" of the teacher or administration, they have usually been struck down by the courts.

5. Teachers have some control over school-sponsored publications and plays. In *Hazelwood School District* v. *Kuhlmeier* (1988) the Supreme Court held that "educators do not offend the First Amendment by exercising editorial control over the style and content of student speech in school-sponsored expressive activities so long as their actions are reasonably related to legitimate pedagogical concerns." This authority, however, does not extend to censorship of student expression. It also does not appear to extend to a school board's banning and regulating textbooks and other "learning materials" (*Virgil* v. *School Board of Columbia County*, 1989, Eleventh Circuit).

6. Teachers do not have a constitutional right to use any teaching method they want. School district officials and boards may establish course content and teaching methods as matters of policy. Courts will support such policies but will examine the reasonableness of sanctions against teachers. For example, a California

court ruled that firing a teacher for unwittingly permitting students to read obscene poetry was too severe (*De Groat* v. *Newark*, 1976), while a nine-month suspension of a West Virginia teacher for showing cartoons of "Fritz the Cat" undressing was judged appropriate (*DeVito* v. *Board of Education*, 1984).

Teachers, in short, are free to deal with controversial issues (including politics and sex) and to use controversial methods and materials if these are educationally defensible, appropriate to the students, and not "materially and substantially" disruptive. But school boards also have authority to maintain curricular policies governing what (and even how) teachers should teach. Courts use a balancing test to determine when students' and teachers' rights to academic freedom must give way to the competing need of society to have reasonable school discipline—free of "material and substantial disruption" (*Tinker*, 1969).

Commandment III: Thou Shalt Not Engage in Private Activities That Impair Teaching Effectiveness

Of all the principles of school law, this commandment is probably the most difficult to delineate with precision. The private and professional areas of a teacher's life have been, for the most part, separated by recent court decisions. A mere 75 years ago teachers signed contracts with provisions prohibiting marriage, falling in love, leaving town without permission of the school board, smoking cigarettes, loitering in ice-cream stores, and wearing lipstick. But now a teacher's private life is considered his or her own business. Thus, for example, many court cases have established that teachers have the same citizenship rights outside the classroom that any other person has.

Teachers, however, have always been expected by society to abide by high standards of personal conduct. Whenever a teacher's private life undermines effective instruction in the class, there is a possibility that the courts will uphold his or her dismissal. To guard against this possibility, the teacher should consider some of the following principles:

1. Teachers may belong to any organization or association—but if they participate in illegal activities of that organization they may be dismissed from their job.

2. A teacher may write letters to newspapers criticizing school policies—unless it can be shown that such criticism impairs morale or working relationships. In the landmark *Pickering* decision (1968), the Supreme Court upheld a teacher who had written such a letter but pointed out that there was in this case "no question of maintaining either discipline by immediate supervisors or harmony among co-workers...."

3. Teachers do not have a right to air private grievances or personnel judgments publicly. Free speech on public issues should not lead teachers to criticize superiors or other school employees in public settings. In a 1983 case, *Connick* v. *Myers*, the Supreme Court ruled against a discharged public employee, saying that he spoke out "not as a citizen upon matters of public concern but instead as an employee on matters of personal interest." A judge in Florida, applying *Connick* to a history teacher discharged for outspoken criticism of his administrators, ruled that the teacher's speech was "nothing more than a set of grievances with school administrators over internal school policies" (*Ferrara* v. *Mills*, 1984). Teachers should distinguish between *public* citizenship issues and *private* personnel issues before making controversial and critical public comments about their schools.

4. A teacher's private affairs do not normally disqualify him or her from teaching except to the extent that it can be shown that such affairs undermine teaching effectiveness. Teachers who are immoral in public, or who voluntarily (or through indiscretion) make known in public private acts of immorality, may indeed be dismissed. Courts are still debating the rights of homosexual teachers, with decisions falling on both sides of this issue.

5. Laws which say that teachers may be dismissed for "unprofessional conduct" or "moral turpitude" are interpreted narrowly, with the burden of proof on the employer to show that the particular circumstances in a case constitute "unfitness to teach." Dismissal must be based on fact, not mere rumor.

6. Whenever a teacher's private affairs include sexual involvement with students, it may be presumed that courts will declare that such conduct constitutes immorality indicating unfitness to teach. Teachers may even be disciplined or dismissed for relationships with students who have already graduated. That was the ruling in a 2004 Michigan case when Laura Flaskamp was denied tenure because she was found to have had a sexual relationship with a student within nine months after the student's graduation.

Commandment IV: Thou Shalt Not Deny Students Due Process

The Fourteenth Amendment guarantees citizens "due process of law" whenever the loss of a right is at stake. Because education has come to be considered such a right (a "property" right), and because students are considered to be citizens, case law in recent years has defined certain procedures to be necessary in providing due process in particular situations:

1. A rule that is patently or demonstrably unfair or a punishment that is excessive may be found by a court to violate the "substantive" due process of a student (see, for example, the Supreme Court's 1969 *Tinker* decision). At the heart of due process is the concept of fair play, and teachers should examine the substance of their rules and the procedures for enforcing them to see if both are reasonable, nonarbitrary, and equitable.

2. The extent to which due process rights should be observed depends on the gravity of the

offense and the severity of punishment that follows. The Supreme Court's *Goss* v. *Lopez* decision (1975) established minimal due process for suspensions of 10 days or less, including oral or written notice of charges and an opportunity for the student to present his or her side of the story.

3. When students are expelled from school, they should be given a statement of the specific charges and the grounds for expulsion, a formal hearing, names of witnesses, and a report of the facts to which each witness testifies (see the leading case, *Dixon* v. *Alabama State Board of Education*, 1961). Furthermore, it is probable that procedural due process for expelled students gives them the right to challenge the evidence, cross-examine witnesses, and be represented by counsel. (See, for example, the New York Supreme Court's 1967 *Goldwyn* v. *Allen* decision.) Finally, such students may appeal the decision to an impartial body for review.

4. Special education students have an added measure of due process protection. In 1990 Congress consolidated earlier special education federal statutes—including the 1975 Education of All Handicapped Children Act (Public Law 94-142)—into the Individuals with Disabilities Education Act (IDEA). These laws stipulate extensive due process rights for *all* children with disabilities (whether or not they have "the ability to benefit") to ensure a free, "appropriate" education. These provisions include prior written notice before any proposed change in a child's educational program; testing that is non-discriminatory in language, race, or culture; parental access to records; fair and impartial hearing by the State Education Agency or local district; and a student's right to remain in a current placement until due process proceedings are completed. These due process guarantees supersede district-level policies relating to placement, suspension, or expulsion of students. As the Supreme Court ruled in *Honig* v. *Doe* (1988), the IDEA does not allow even for a "dangerous exception" to

the "stay put" provision. The IDEA was revised in 2004 and—along with the No Child Left Behind Act of 2001 and the Americans with Disabilities Act (ADA), passed by Congress in 1990—provides strong federal protection for the educational rights of disabled students.

It is advisable for schools to develop written regulations governing procedures for such areas as suspension, expulsion, discipline, publications, and placement of the disabled. The teacher should be aware of these regulations and should provide his or her administration with specific, factual evidence whenever a student faces a serious disciplinary decision. The teacher is also advised to be guided by the spirit of due process—fairness and evenhanded justice—when dealing with less serious incidents in the classroom.

Commandment V: Thou Shalt Not Punish Behavior Through Academic Penalties

It is easy for teachers to lose sight of the distinction between punishing and rewarding academic performance, on the one hand, and disciplinary conduct on the other. Grades, for example, are frequently employed as motivation for both study behavior and paying-attention behavior. There is a great temptation for teachers to use one of the few weapons still in their arsenal (i.e., grades) as an instrument of justice for social infractions in the classroom. While it may indeed be the case that students who misbehave will not perform well academically because of their conduct, courts are requiring schools and teachers to keep those two domains separate.

In particular, teachers are advised to heed the following general applications of this principle:

1. Denial of a diploma to a student who has met all the academic requirements for it but who has broken a rule of discipline is not permitted. Several cases (going back at least as far as the 1921 Iowa *Valentine* case) are on record to

support this guideline. It is also probable that exclusion from a graduation ceremony as a punishment for behavior will not be allowed by the courts.

2. Grades should not be reduced to serve disciplinary purposes. In the *Wermuth* case (1965) in New Jersey, the ruling against such practice included this observation by the state's commissioner of education: "Whatever system of marks and grades a school may devise will have serious inherent limitations at best, and it must not be further handicapped by attempting to serve disciplinary purposes too." In a 1984 case in Pennsylvania (*Katzman* v. *Cumberland Valley School District*), the court struck down a policy requiring a reduction in grades by two percentage points for each day of suspension.

3. Lowering grades—or awarding zeros—for absences is a questionable legal practice. In the Kentucky case of *Dorsey* v. *Bale* (1975), a student had his grades reduced for unexcused absences, and under the school's regulation, was not allowed to make up the work; five points were deducted from his nine-weeks' grade for each unexcused absence. A state circuit court and the Kentucky Court of Appeals declared the regulation to be invalid. The courts are particularly likely to invalidate regulations that constitute "double jeopardy"—e.g., suspending students for disciplinary reasons and giving them zeros while suspended.

In general, teachers who base academic evaluation on academic performance have little to fear in this area. Courts do not presume to challenge a teacher's grades *per se* when the consideration rests only on the teacher's right or ability to make valid academic judgments.

Commandment VI: Thou Shalt Not Misuse Corporal Punishment

Corporal punishment is a controversial method of establishing discipline. The Supreme Court refused to disqualify the practice under a suit (*Ingraham* v. *Wright*, 1977) in which it was argued that corporal punishment was "cruel and unusual punishment" and thus a violation of the Constitution's Eighth Amendment. An increasing number of states—up from only two in 1979 to 27 in 2001—ban corporal punishment in public schools.

In those states not prohibiting corporal punishment, teachers may—as an extension of their *in loco parentis* authority—use "moderate" corporal punishment to establish discipline. There are, however, many potential legal dangers in the practice. *In loco parentis* is a limited, perhaps even a vanishing, concept, and teachers must be careful to avoid these misuses of corporal punishment if they want to stay out of the courtroom:

1. The punishment must never lead to permanent injury. No court will support as "reasonable" or "moderate" that physical punishment which permanently disables or disfigures a student. Many an assault and battery judgment has been handed down in such cases. Unfortunately for teachers, "accidents" that occur during corporal punishment and ignorance of a child's health problems (brittle bones, hemophilia, etc.) do not always excuse a teacher from liability.

2. The punishment must not be unreasonable in terms of the offense, nor may it be used to enforce an unreasonable rule. The court examines all the circumstances in a given case to determine what was or was not "reasonable" or "excessive." In 1980 the Fourth Circuit Court of Appeals ruled that "excessive" corporal punishment might well violate Fourteenth Amendment rights. In 1987 the Tenth Circuit Court of Appeals reached a similar conclusion.

3. The punishment must not be motivated by spite, malice, or revenge. Whenever teachers administer corporal punishment in a state of anger, they run a high risk of losing an assault and battery suit in court. Since corporal punishment is practiced as a method of correcting student behavior, any evidence that physical force resulted from a teacher's bad temper or quest for revenge is damning. On the other hand, in an explosive situation (e.g., a fight)

teachers may protect themselves and use that force necessary to restrain a student from harming the teacher, others, or himself.

4. The punishment must not ignore such variables as the student's age, sex, size, and physical condition.

5. The punishment must not be administered with inappropriate instruments or to parts of the body where risk of injury is great. For example, a Texas case ruled that it is not reasonable for a teacher to use his fists in administering punishment. Another teacher lost a suit when he struck a child on the ear, breaking an eardrum. The judge noted, "Nature has provided a part of the anatomy for chastisement, and tradition holds that such chastisement should there be applied." It should be noted that creating mental anguish and emotional stress by demeaning, harassing, or humiliating a child may be construed as illegal punishment too.

6. Teachers must not only take care not to harm children by way of corporal punishment; they also have a responsibility to report suspected child abuse by parents or others. Congress passed the National Child Abuse Prevention and Treatment Act in 1974 and followed with stronger laws in 1988 and 1992. Child abuse is a state (not federal) crime with many variations in definition and reporting procedure. But *all* states require reporting if the neglect or abuse results in physical injury. Teachers need not be absolutely certain of abuse but must act "in good faith" if they have "reason to believe" a child is being subjected to abuse or neglect. Every state also provides legal protection from suit for such reporting. In most states, failure to report is a misdemeanor.

Courts must exercise a good deal of judgment in corporal punishment cases to determine what is "moderate," "excessive," "reasonable," "cruel," "unusual," "malicious," or "capricious." Suffice it to say that educators should exercise great care in the use of corporal punishment.

Commandment VII: Thou Shalt Not Neglect Students' Safety

One of the major responsibilities of teachers is to keep their students safe from unreasonable risk of harm or danger. The major cases involving teachers grow out of negligence charges relating to the teacher's failure to supervise properly in accordance with *in loco parentis* obligations (to act "in place of the parents"), contractual obligations, and professional responsibility. While the courts do not expect teachers to protect children from "unforeseeable accidents" and "acts of God," they do require teachers to act as a reasonably prudent teacher should in protecting students from possible harm or injury.

Negligence is a tort ("wrong") that exists only when the elements of *duty, violation, cause,* and *injury* are present. Teachers are generally responsible for using good judgment in determining what steps are necessary to provide for adequate supervision of the particular students in their charge, and the given circumstances dictate what is reasonably prudent in each case. A teacher who has a duty to his or her students but who fails to fulfill this duty because of carelessness, lack of discretion, or lack of diligence may violate this duty with a resultant injury to a student. In this instance the teacher may be held liable for negligence as the cause of the injury to the student. The Paul D. Coverdell Teacher Protection Act of 2002, part of the federal No Child Left Behind Act, immunizes teachers from liability if they are "acting within the scope of the teacher's employment or responsibilities."

Several guidelines can help teachers avoid this all-too-common and serious lawsuit:

1. Establish and enforce rules of safety in school activities. This is particularly important for the elementary teacher, since many injuries to elementary students occur on playgrounds, in hallways, and in classroom activity sessions. The prudent teacher anticipates such problems and establishes rules to protect students from such injuries. Generally, rules should be written, posted, and taught.

2. Be aware of school, district, and state rules and regulations as they pertain to student safety. One teacher was held negligent when a child was injured because the teacher did not know that there was a state law requiring safety glasses in a shop activity. It is also important that a teacher's own rules not conflict with regulations at higher levels. *Warn* students of any hazard in a room or in an instructional activity.

3. Enforce safety rules when violations are observed. In countless cases teachers have been found negligent when students repeatedly broke important safety rules, eventually injuring themselves or others, or when a teacher should have foreseen danger but did not act as a "reasonably prudent" teacher would have in the same situation to correct the behavior. One teacher observing a mumblety-peg game at recess was held negligent for not stopping it before the knife bounced up and put out an eye of one of the players.

4. Provide a higher standard of supervision when students are younger, disabled, and/or in a potentially dangerous activity. Playgrounds, physical education classes, science labs, and shop classes require particular care and supervision. Instruction must be provided to ensure safety in accordance with the children's maturity, competence, and skill.

5. Learn first aid, because teachers may be liable for negligence if they do not get or give prompt, appropriate medical assistance when necessary. While teachers should not give children medicine, even aspirin, they should, of course, allow any legitimate prescriptions to be taken as prescribed. There should be school policy governing such procedures.

6. Advise substitute teachers (and student teachers) about any unusual medical, psychological, handicapping, or behavioral problem in your class. If there are physical hazards in your class—bare light cords, sharp edges, loose boards, insecure window frames, etc.—warn everyone about these too. Be sure to report such hazards to your administration and janitorial staff—as a "prudent" teacher would do.

7. Be where you are assigned to be. If you have playground, hall, cafeteria, or bus duty, be there. An accident that occurs when you are someplace other than your assigned station may be blamed on your negligence, whereas if you had been there it would not be so charged. Your responsibility for safety is the same for extracurricular activities you are monitoring as it is for classes.

8. If you have to leave a classroom (particularly a rowdy one), stipulate the kind of conduct you expect and make appropriate arrangements—such as asking another teacher to check in. Even this may not be adequate precaution in terms of your duty to supervise if the students are known to be troublemakers, are quite immature, or are mentally retarded or emotionally disabled. You run a greater risk leaving a science class or a gym class than you do a social studies class.

9. Plan field trips with great care and provide for adequate supervision. Many teachers fail to realize that permission notes from home—no matter how much they disclaim teacher liability for injury—do not excuse a teacher from providing proper supervision. A parent cannot sign away this right of his or her child. Warn children of dangers on the trip and instruct them in rules of conduct and safety.

10. Do not send students on errands off school grounds, because they then become your agents. If they are injured or if they injure someone else, you may well be held liable. Again, the younger and less responsible the child, the greater the danger of a teacher negligence charge. To state the obvious, some children require more supervision than others.

Much of the advice is common sense, but the "reasonably prudent" teacher needs to be alert to the many requirements of "due care" and "proper supervision." The teacher who anticipates potentially dangerous conditions and actions and takes reasonable precautions—through rules, instruction, warnings, communications to superiors, and presence in assigned stations—will do a great deal in minimizing the chances of pupil injury and teacher negligence.

Commandment VIII: Thou Shalt Not Slander or Libel Your Students

This tort is much less common than negligence, but it is an area of school law that can be troublesome. One of the primary reasons for the Family Educational Rights and Privacy Act (1974) was that school records contain so much misinformation and hearsay and so many untrue (or, at least, questionable) statements about children's character, conduct, and morality that access to these records by students or their parents, in order to correct false information, seemed warranted. A teacher's right to write anything about a student under the protection of confidential files no longer exists. Defamation of character through written communication is "libel" while such defamation in oral communication is "slander." There are ample opportunities for teachers to commit both offenses.

Teachers are advised to be careful about what they say about students (let alone other teachers!) to employers, colleges, parents, and other personnel at the school. Adhere to the following guidelines:

1. Avoid vague, derogatory terms on permanent records and recommendations. Even if you do not intend to be derogatory, value judgments about a student's character, life-style, or home life may be found defamatory in court. In one case, a North Carolina teacher was found guilty of libel when she said on a permanent record card that a student was "ruined by tobacco and whiskey." Avoid characterizing students as "crazy," "immoral," or "delinquent."

2. Say or write only what you know to be true about a student. It is safer to be an objective describer of what you have observed than to draw possibly unwarranted and untrue conclusions and judgments. The truth of a statement is strong evidence that character has not been defamed, but in some cases where the intent has been to malign and destroy the person, truth is not an adequate defense.

3. Communicate judgments of character only to those who have a right to the information. Teachers have "qualified privileged communication," which means that so long as they communicate in good faith information that they believe to be true to a person who has reason to have this information, they are protected. However, the slandering of pupils in a teachers' lounge bull session is another thing altogether.

4. If a student confides a problem to you in confidence, keep that communication confidential. A student who is on drugs, let us say, may bring you to court for defamation of character and/or invasion of privacy if you spread such information about indiscriminately. On the other hand, if a student confides that he or she has participated in a felonious crime or gives you information that makes you aware of a "clear and present" danger, you are obligated to bring such information to the appropriate authorities. Find out the proper limits of communication and the authorized channels in your school and state.

5. As a related issue, be careful about "search and seizure" procedures too. Generally, school lockers are school property and may be searched by school officials if they have reasonable grounds to suspect that the locker has something dangerous or illegal in it. In its landmark 1985 decision in *New Jersey* v. *T.L.O.*, the Supreme Court rejected the notion that school officials had to have the police standard of "probable cause" before conducting a search; the court approved the lower standard of "reasonable suspicion." So long as both the grounds (i.e., reason) and scope are reasonable, school personnel can search student suspects. The growing concern in society about drugs and weapons in school has led courts to support school officials conducting searches for dangerous or illegal items. For example, the U.S. Supreme Court

approved drug testing—requiring the "seizure" of urine samples—for high school athletes (*Vernonia*, 1995) and later for all students involved in extracurricular activities (*Earls*, 2002). Strip searches, however, are often deemed to be too intrusive (*Safford, 2008*), and some states prohibit this practice by way of state statutes.

Teachers need to remember that students are citizens and as such enjoy at least a limited degree of the constitutional rights that adult citizens enjoy. Not only "due process," "equal protection," and "freedom of religion" but also protection from teacher torts such as "negligence" and "defamation of character" is provided to students through our system of law. These concepts apply to all students, including those in elementary grades.

Commandment IX: Thou Shalt Not Photocopy in Violation of Copyright Law

In January, 1978, the revised copyright law went into effect and with it strict limitations on what may be photocopied by teachers for their own or classroom use under the broad concept of "fair use." The "fair use" of copyrighted material means that the use should not impair the value of the owner's copyright by diminishing the demand for that work, thereby reducing potential income for the owner.

In general, educators are given greater latitude than most other users. "Spontaneous" copying is more permissible than "systematic" copying. Students have greater latitude than teachers in copying materials.

Teachers may:

1. Make a single copy for their own research or class preparation of a chapter from a book; an article from a periodical or newspaper; a short story, poem, or essay; a chart, graph, diagram, cartoon, or picture from a book, periodical, or newspaper.
2. Make multiple copies for classroom use only (but not to exceed one copy per student) of a complete poem, if it is fewer than 250 words and printed on not more than two pages; an excerpt from a longer poem, if it is fewer than 250 words; a complete article, story, or essay, if it is fewer than 2,500 words; an excerpt from a prose work, if it is fewer than 1,000 words or 10% of the work, whichever is less; one chart, graph, diagram, drawing, cartoon, or picture per book or periodical.

However, teachers may not:

1. Make multiple copies of work for classroom use if another teacher has already copied the work for use in another class in the same school.
2. Make copies of a short poem, article, story, or essay from the same author more than once in the same term.
3. Make multiple copies from the same collective work or periodical issue more than three times a term. (The limitations in Items 1–3 do not apply to current news periodicals or newspapers.)
4. Make a copy of works to take the place of anthologies.
5. Make copies of "consumable" materials such as workbooks, exercises, answer sheets to standardized tests, and the like.

More recent technologies have led to extended applications of the "fair use" doctrine:

1. The "fair use" doctrine does not apply to copyrighted computer software programs; however, teachers may load a copyrighted program onto a classroom terminal or make a "backup" copy for archival purposes. Teachers may not make copies of such programs for student use. In 1991 the Department of Justice and Department of Education called on schools to teach the ethical use of computers to counteract illegal copying of software.
2. Schools may videotape copyrighted television programs but may keep the tape no longer than 45 days without a license. Teachers may use the tapes for instruction during the first 10 consecutive days after taping but may repeat such use only once. Commercial videotapes

may not be rented to be played for instruction (or entertainment) in classrooms.

3. Scanning copyrighted material into a computer and distributing it via the Internet is a violation of copyright law. The Internet should be viewed as a giant photocopying machine. Bills are now in Congress to restrict and punish those who misuse the Internet. We may expect to see other legal complications from this emerging technology: defamation, obscenity, threats of violence, disruption of the academic environment, and sexual harassment—to list but a few.

When teachers make brief, spontaneous, and limited copies of copyrighted materials other than consumables, they are likely to be operating within the bounds of fair use. Whenever multiple copies of copyrighted materials are made (within the guidelines above), each copy should include a notice of the copyright. Teachers should consult media specialists and others in their school about questions relating to "fair use"—whether for print, videotape, or computer materials.

Commandment X: Thou Shalt Not Be Ignorant of the Law

The axiom, "Ignorance of the law is no excuse," holds as true for teachers as anyone else. Indeed, courts are increasingly holding teachers to higher standards of competence and knowledge commensurate with their higher status as professionals. Since education is now considered a right—guaranteed to black and white, rich and poor, "normal" and disabled—the legal parameters have become ever more important to teachers in this litigious era.

How, then, can the teacher become aware of the law and its implications for the classroom? Consider the following possibilities:

1. Sign up for a course in school law. If the local college or university does not offer such a course, attempt to have one developed.

2. Ask your school system administration to focus on this topic in inservice programs.

3. Tap the resources of the local, state, and national professional organizations for pertinent speakers, programs, and materials.

4. Explore state department of education sources, since most states will have personnel and publications that deal with educational statutes and case law in your particular state.

5. Establish school (if not personal) subscriptions to professional journals. *Phi Delta Kappan, Journal of Law and Education*, and *Mental Disability Law Reporter* are only a few of the journals that regularly have columns and/or articles to keep the teacher aware of new developments in school law.

6. Make sure that your school or personal library includes such books as *Teachers and the Law* (Louis Fischer et al., 7th edition, Longman, 2007); *The Law of Schools, Students, and Teachers* (Kern and David Alexander, 7th edition, West, 2007); *Special Education Law* (Peter Latham et al., Pearson Education, Inc., 2008); and *Deskbook Encyclopedia of American School Law* (Data Research, Rosemount, Minnesota, 1996). Monthly newsletters can keep schools up-to-date in the school law area. Consider a subscription to *School Law Bulletin* (Quinlan Publishing Company, Boston) or *Legal Notes for Educators* (Data Research, Rosemount, Minnesota).

The better informed teachers are about their legal rights and responsibilities, the more likely they are to avoid the courtroom—and there are many ways to keep informed.

My Teacher's Ten Commandments are not exhaustive, nor are they etched in stone. School law, like all other law, is constantly evolving and changing so as to reflect the thinking of the times; and decisions by courts are made in the context of particular events and circumstances that are never exactly the same. But prudent professionals will be well served by these commandments if they internalize the spirit of the law as a guide to actions as teachers—in the classroom, the school, and the community.

POSTNOTE

The United States is an increasingly litigious society. Rather than settle disagreements and disputes face to face, we quickly turn over our problems to lawyers. In recent years, business owners and managers, doctors, and even lawyers have been held liable for various consequences of their work. Such situations were almost unknown to their colleagues in an earlier age.

Although relatively few teachers have been prosecuted successfully in the courts, the number of cases has dramatically increased. Therefore, it is important for teachers both in training and in service—to be aware of areas of legal vulnerability. McDaniel, himself a former teacher, has presented an outstanding summary of the law as it affects teachers.

DISCUSSION QUESTIONS

1. Before reading this article, were you aware that school law governed teachers' behavior as much as it does? In which of the areas described by McDaniel do you, personally, feel most vulnerable? Why?
2. As a teacher, what steps can you take to protect yourself from legal liability?
3. Which of these "commandments" has the most negative impact on the effectiveness of the average teacher? Why?

RELATED WEBSITE RESOURCES AND VIDEO CASE

WEB RESOURCES:

Acceptable Use Policies: A Handbook. Available at:

http://www.pen.k12.va.us/go/VDOE/Technology/AUP/home.shtml.

This handbook, available on the Internet, is produced by the Virginia Department of Education. It is a rich source of information on using the Internet in schools and developing acceptable use policies.

The Legal Information Institute's Supreme Court Collection. Available at:

http://supct.law.cornell.edu/supct/index.html

This website gives you access to the most important Supreme Court school-related decisions.

 TEACHSOURCE VIDEO CASE

LEGAL AND ETHICAL DIMENSIONS OF TEACHING: REFLECTIONS FROM TODAY'S EDUCATORS

In this video case, you will witness a discussion among a group of teachers, an administrator, and a lawyer about legal and ethical issues in schools. You will also hear the real concerns of practitioners seeking to do the correct thing. Go to the website for the Education Media Library at CengageBrain.com to watch the video clips, study the artifacts in the case, and reflect on the following questions.

1. What is your response to teacher Kate Malinowski's discussion of how she tries to model ethical behavior for both students and fellow teachers?
2. What legal questions are discussed about what students can and cannot legally say in school?

 The companion website for this text includes useful study tools and resources. Go to CengageBrain.com to access links to relevant websites, glossaries, flashcards, an article review form, and more.

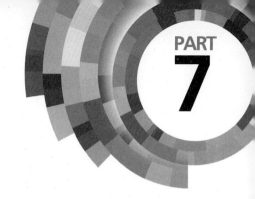

Educational Reform

Since the 1983 publication of *A Nation at Risk,* a report of President Reagan's National Commission on Excellence in Education, American schools have been in what is referred to as an "era of school reform." Both educators and private citizens are worried about our schools' ability to supply an adequately educated workforce. New jobs in the Information Age require workers to solve problems, often as team members; write and speak proficiently; and carry out higher levels of mathematical computations. Dismal research reports on the academic achievement of American students—particularly when compared with students from other countries—have sent a clear message: Something must be done.

In recent years, the primary response has been at the state level, where governors and legislatures across the country have passed laws requiring higher standards for students and teachers alike. Recently their efforts have been reinforced and financially supported by the federal No Child Left Behind Act. In addition, ways of more effectively and efficiently organizing schools have surfaced—some borrowed from industry, some from schools in other nations. Increasingly, parents, politicians, and policymakers are also examining and experimenting with ways to offer students greater educational choice. This section presents a number of ways to consider educational reform and offers an overview of some of the most important developments in reforming education.

42

Putting Money Where It Matters

Karen Hawley Miles

Karen Hawley Miles is executive director and founder of Education Resource Strategies, a nonprofit organization in Boston, Massachusetts, that specializes in strategic planning, organization, and resource allocation in urban public school districts.

FOCUS QUESTION

There are only so many dollars to spend on education. How should they be spent?

KEY TERMS

- Accountability
- Professional development
- Standards-based education
- Title I

The focus in the United States on creating accountable, standards-based education is pushing districts and schools to more clearly define their goals and priorities for student learning. Districts and states make headlines with bold proclamations about the importance of academic achievement for all students. But the gap between rhetoric and reality threatens hopes for improvement. While teachers scramble to help students meet more ambitious academic targets, school and district spending patterns and organization structures have changed little in the past three decades (Miles, 1997a). No matter what school leaders and communities say is important, the way schools and districts use their dollars, organize their staff, and structure their time dictates the results.

As public institutions, schools and districts try to do everything for everyone—and do it all without making enemies. New dollars come to schools in small increments over time, usually tied to specific purposes. We add new priorities and programs on top of the old. Instead of restructuring and integrating school and district organizations, we create specialties and departments to meet newly defined needs. Schools and districts now spend significantly more to educate each pupil than ever before (Snyder & Hoffman, 1999). Taking advantage of these resources to meet higher academic standards requires a political will and singleness of purpose that is difficult to sustain in public schools. Such action also demands an attention to organizational and budget details that does not come naturally to many educators and policymakers.

If we hope to meet our seemingly unreachable goals, districts and schools must define priorities for student performance, make choices about how to organize to meet them, and then move the dollars and people to match those commitments. If school leaders give priority to improving academic achievement, for example, then the district staff and budget should shift to support that goal. If the district declares that all students will read by 3rd grade, then staff, dollars, and time should support more effective literacy teaching. Districts and schools should expect to give up some long-standing and useful programs to support these choices.

Matching Dollars to Priorities

For the past 10 years, I have helped districts and schools rethink their use of resources to support their reform efforts. In partnership with New American Schools and with support from Pew Charitable Trusts, I have worked with four large urban districts to analyze their district and school spending and then consider ways to reallocate dollars. My colleagues and I have discovered that, in many cases, the dollars needed for reform efforts are there, but they are tied up in existing staff, programs, and practices. We have found that schools need help shifting their use of resources to take advantage of what they already have and that districts often lag behind schools in changing their own spending and organization structures. To support schools in raising student performance, most districts need to realign spending and staffing in at least five ways.

Restructure Salaries to Attract and Retain High-Quality Teachers

It is no secret that U.S. teaching salaries lag behind those of other professions. The discrepancy is especially great for two types of teachers needed in schools: high-performing students from top colleges who have many other career options and teachers trained in math and science (Mohrman, Mohrman, & Odden, 1995). The earnings gap grows wider over a teaching career (Conley & Odden, 1995). Maximum teaching salaries fall well below those in other professions, meaning that the most talented individuals sacrifice much higher potential earnings if they remain in teaching. Districts need to reconsider their practice of paying all teachers the same regardless of subject area. In addition, they must find ways to restructure teacher salaries and responsibilities to provide the most talented, productive teachers with the opportunity to earn more competitive salaries during their careers.

Increasing salaries significantly without bankrupting districts means taking a hard look at the way salary dollars are spent. Since the 1920s, virtually all districts have used a salary structure that applies to every teacher regardless of grade or subject. Teachers can move up the salary ladder either by logging more years of teaching or accumulating education credits. Most districts increase salaries far more for experience than they do for education (Miles, 1997b). Boston Public Schools, for example, spent 36 percent of its 1998–99 salary budget to buy years of experience (29 percent) and education credits (7 percent).

For this investment to make sense for students, both teaching experience and accumulated credits would have to be clearly linked to student achievement. But research shows that after the first five years, the quality of teaching does not automatically improve with either course credits or years of teaching (Hanushek, 1994; Murnane, 1996). Experience and course-work have value, but neither is a fail-safe investment without coaching, hard work, and systems that reward and encourage good teaching. Many districts are currently experimenting with increasing teacher salaries on the basis of more direct measures of teaching quality. Most of these plans give bonuses to teachers who meet certain criteria or student performance targets. These extra dollars are nice symbols, but the plans that have the most promise for significantly raising teacher salary levels redirect existing salary dollars even as they seek to add more.

Redirect District Staff and Spending from Compliance Efforts to Provide Schools with Integrated Support and Accountability

Using standards to measure school performance changes the role of the district office. If schools do not have to report student performance, schools and districts are only held accountable for whether they do as they are told and keep children safe. As a result, curriculum offices issue guidebooks and sometimes check whether they are used, and districts create departments to monitor whether dollars from each funding source are spent as stipulated.

When schools become accountable for student learning, the district role must shift to helping schools measure student learning and supporting the changes in teaching and organization that best support improvement. Most districts need to focus more on four purposes: defining standards and targets, supporting schools and teachers, creating accountability, and restructuring school organizations.

Supporting these four goals is often possible by reallocating existing resources. In many large districts, the traditional compliance focus has resulted in a structure that spreads resources thinly across many schools and priorities. For example, one district was surprised to find that it devoted nine experts to supervising services across 30 schools. Each expert was responsible for making sure that schools met program requirements in one specific area, such as special education, Title I, bilingual education, literacy, or technology. Because these nine individuals focused on only one issue in multiple schools, they could conduct only superficial reviews of effectiveness, and they certainly couldn't provide support to underperforming schools. Even though the district devoted $24,000 in salaries and benefits to each school, the schools barely felt an impact. Instead, the schools needed deeper, integrated school support in specific areas where improvement was most needed.

Shift More Resources to Teaching Literacy in Grades K–3

Research consistently shows that smaller group sizes matter most in early grades when students learn to read (Wenglinsky, 2001). It also shows that when students don't learn to read by 3rd grade, they continue to fall farther behind in school and are more likely to be assigned to costly special education programs and to drop out of school. Research suggests concrete ways to improve reading achievement:

- Class size reduction in grades pre-K–2 can make an important, lasting difference in student achievement.
- Small reductions in class size make little difference; only when class sizes get down to 15–17 students does achievement increase predictably.

- Even smaller group sizes, including one-on-one instruction, are critical for developing readers, especially those from disadvantaged homes.
- If teachers don't change their classroom practice to take advantage of class size reductions, they can't expect improved student performance.

To incorporate these lessons, both districts and schools need to shift their use of existing resources. U.S. school districts average one teacher for every 17 students—with the ratio much higher in many urban districts—and one adult for every nine students. Yet, elementary school class size averages in the mid-20s (Miles, 1997a; Snyder & Hoffman, 1999). Most districts allocate more staff and dollars per pupil to high schools than to elementary schools.

To focus resources where they matter most, districts need to look first at how much they spend at the elementary school level compared to the high school level. Next, they need to invest to ensure that teachers have access to powerful professional development in teaching literacy. Third, they must actively support school-level changes that shift resources toward literacy instruction.

This active support of school-level changes in the use of resources creates special challenges for districts. For example, many schools have found ways to create small reading groups for part of the day by making group sizes larger at other times of the day. Others have reconsidered the role of each teacher, support person, and instructional aide to ensure that they support the focus on literacy. In some schools, this may mean changing the role of physical education, art, and music teachers or making these class sizes larger. It may mean hiring a highly trained literacy specialist instead of a traditional librarian. And redirecting resources toward literacy will mean integrating bilingual, Title I, and special education teachers more fully into a school-wide literacy strategy. Schools need help making these shifts, which require changes in district policy, contract language, and staff allocation practices. Districts also need to be prepared to defend school leaders who abandon popular, but outmoded or less important, programs and staff positions to support literacy efforts.

Invest Strategically in Professional Development for Teachers

To take advantage of smaller class sizes and to improve literacy instruction, districts need to offer teachers high-quality professional development. The assertion that districts invest only a small percentage of their budgets in professional development has become a cliché among education reformers. Although some districts may need to invest more money, the priority, for many, will be to refocus existing efforts to create more effective professional development and more useful teacher time. Research shows that professional development that responds to school-level student performance priorities, focuses on instruction, and provides coaching for individual teachers and teams over time can have a powerful impact on teacher practice. But professional development doesn't follow this model in most districts. And providing teachers with more professional time and intensive coaching support can seem expensive to districts that use a few traditional workshops as their "training."

In a detailed analysis of four large urban district budgets, we found that districts spend more than they think on professional development (Miles & Hornbeck, 2000). In these four districts, spending on professional development from all sources ranged 2–4 percent of the district budget. These figures are much larger than those districts traditionally report and manage. For example, one district reported $460,000 spent on strategic professional development, but the district actually spent nearly 20 times this amount when professional development efforts by all departments and sources were included. Worse, our analysis showed that professional development spending is often divided among many fragmented, sometimes conflicting, programs managed by different departments. Spending to support improved academic instruction represented only a fraction of total dollars in these districts, and the amount aimed at literacy instruction was even smaller. Harnessing these dollars requires district and school leaders to challenge the status quo and to abandon worthwhile initiatives in order to support more integrated models of professional development.

Reduce Spending on Nonacademic Teaching Staff in Secondary Schools

The traditional comprehensive high school often employs more teaching staff in nonacademic subjects than it does in English, math, science, and history. Traditional high schools devote only about half of each student's school day to courses covering academic skills, resulting in more than half the high school resources being aimed at goals that are not measured by the state and district standards. This allocation of resources also means that class sizes for the core subjects are usually 30 students or more, with teachers responsible for a total of more than 125 students.

But changing the balance of staff to make a meaningful difference in student loads and academic time would require some high schools to double the number of academic staff. And shifting more resources toward academic subjects means reducing staff in other areas and challenging the structure—or even the existence—of such cherished programs as band and athletics. Given the number of the changes and their sometimes painful nature, it is unreasonable and impractical to expect principals or school-based decision-making groups to make them on their own. Until districts take steps to change the mix of staff, many high schools will make marginal improvements at best.

Making Choices

Organizing resources to act on urgent priorities, such as teaching all students to read in urban schools, requires leaders to take politically difficult stands. Union, district, and school board leaders need courage and strong community support to say:

- Even though all subjects are important, literacy is most important.
- Even though all teachers are important, those who bring deep subject knowledge and can integrate across disciplines or programs are worth more.
- Even though band, sports, and other electives can be a crucial part of a balanced education,

the community must find new ways to pay for and provide them.

- Even though student readiness and social health provide a base for student learning, schools cannot be held accountable for providing all services to students, and they aren't staffed to do so.
- Even though investments in teacher professional development and technology may mean an extra student in your class, we can't build and sustain excellent schools without more of such investments.

Ensuring Adequate Funding

Regardless of overall spending levels, district and community leaders need to articulate priorities and direct spending to support them. But they must also ensure that schools have enough money to begin these tasks. There is no one way to define how much money is enough, but a few test questions can help put district spending in perspective: How does spending per pupil in your district compare to spending in other districts with similar student populations? How do teacher salary levels compare? How does the community's tax rate compare to the tax rates in similar districts?

If the community is underinvesting in education, leaders need to make the case for increased spending. But a community may be more likely to support increases in spending if citizens see that leaders have clear priorities and are willing to make difficult choices to ensure that new dollars get to the heart of improving student achievement.

References

Conley, S., & Odden, A. (1995). Linking teacher compensation to teacher career development: A strategic examination. *Educational Evaluation and Policy Analysis, 17,* 253–269.

Hanushek, E. A. (1994). *Making schools work: Improving performance and controlling costs.* Washington, DC: Brookings Institute.

Miles, K. H. (1997a). Finding the dollars to pay for 21st century schools: Taking advantage of the times. *School Business Affairs, 63*(6), 38–42.

Miles, K. H. (1997b). *Spending more on the edges: Public school spending from 1967 to 1991.* Ann Arbor, MI: UMI Press.

Miles, K. H., & Hornbeck, M. J. (2000). *Reinvesting in teaching: District spending on professional development.* Arlington, VA: New American Schools.

Mohrman, A., Mohrman, S. A., & Odden, A. (1995). Aligning teacher compensation with systemic school reform: Skill-based pay and group-based performance rewards. *Educational Evaluation and Policy Analysis, 18,* 51–71.

Murnane, R. J. (1996). Staffing the nation's schools with skilled teachers. In E. A. Hanushek & D. W. Jorgenson (Eds.), *Improving America's schools: The role of incentives* (pp. 243–260). Washington, DC: National Academy Press.

Snyder, T. D., & Hoffman, C. M. (1999). *Digest of education statistics 1999.* Washington, DC: National Center for Education Statistics, Office of Educational Research and Improvement, U.S. Department of Education.

Wenglinsky, H. (2001, June). The effect of class size on achievement [Memorandum]. Available: www.ets.org/search97cgi/s97_cgi

POSTNOTE

Advocates of school choice, including school vouchers and charter schools, often point fingers at the educational bureaucracies in large school districts as major culprits for student academic failures. These critics argue that these bureaucracies waste money, respond to problems too slowly, and lack accountability.

Rather than just criticizing large school districts, the author works actively with large school systems on how to get "more bang for the buck." The thrust of her recommendations is to invest money in good teachers and their continued professional development. More and more policymakers are coming to the conclusion that high-quality teachers are essential to successful educational reform, and school systems must be redesigned to provide the conditions and support that allow teachers to succeed. If school districts make student learning their top priority, then they must surely conclude that teachers need and deserve good working conditions to bring about student academic achievement. Only by investing in good teachers will we achieve the results with students that we seek.

DISCUSSION QUESTIONS

1. The author argues that school districts need to reconsider the practice of paying all teachers the same regardless of subject matter. Do you agree with her argument that because highly qualified teachers in certain subject fields (mathematics or special education, for example) are in short supply, their salaries need to be increased in order to attract people to the positions? Why or why not?

2. Do you agree with the author's suggestion that school districts might have to reduce staff—or even abandon programs such as band and athletics—to focus more on academics? Why or why not?

3. What additional recommendations would you make to ensure that educational dollars are spent wisely by school districts on the most important programs?

RELATED WEBSITE RESOURCES

WEB RESOURCES:

Education Resource Strategies. Available at: http://www.educationresourcestrategies.org/. This is the site for Ms. Miles's organization.

Center for Educational Reform. Available at: http://www.edreform.com/Home/. This center, led by educational reformer Jeanne Allen, has been a major force in promoting charter schools across the nation.

43

Teacher Pay for Performance: Context, Status, and Direction

Matthew G. Springer and Catherine D. Gardner

Matthew G. Springer is director of the federally funded National Center on Performance Incentives and research assistant professor of public policy and education, Vanderbilt University, Nashville, Tenn. **Catherine D. Gardner** is a policy and outreach analyst at the National Center on Performance Initiatives.

Matthew G. springer and Catherine D. Gardner, "Teacher Pay for Performance," *Phi Delta Kappan*, v.91, no. 8, May 2010, pp. 8–15. Reprinted with permission of Phi Delta Kappa International, www.pdkintl.org. All rights reserved.

FOCUS QUESTION

Can a fair system of rewarding superior teaching be developed and actually used in American public schools?

InTASC
Standard 10

KEY TERMS

- Compensation systems
- Incentives

It's hard to miss the news about pay for performance in the American K–12 public education system. For the past decade, Google News reports an average of 4,558 news stories per year on teacher pay for performance. This doesn't even begin to tally the countless blogs, tweets, and other popular information tools.

Financial investments in pay for performance programs and policies have also grown substantially. Florida, Minnesota, and Texas have allocated over $550 million to incentive pay programs that reward teacher performance. Funding for the federally sponsored Teacher Incentive Fund (TIF) quadrupled in 2010, and the Obama Administration's 2011 budget request designated an additional $950 million for a new Teacher and Leader Innovation Fund that would support the development and implementation of performance-oriented approaches to recruiting, retaining, and rewarding highly effective educators.

Perhaps more important than the direct allocation of dollars, current education reform efforts, including the Race to the Top program, put performance pay center stage. In some states, in order to get a piece of the coveted $4.35 billion Race to the Top pie, state legislators met in special sessions to remove institutional barriers to judging teacher performance, retaining and rewarding their most effective practitioners, and counseling out the lowest performers. The largest portion of the 500-point Race to the Top rubric for grading state applications is pay for performance (U.S. Department of Education 2009).

Although policy makers and the media are paying more attention to performance pay, the concept itself isn't new. Discussions about pay for performance for teachers go back as early as 1867 and were part of almost every decade of the last century. Understanding some of the history of pay for performance helps put the current discussion in context.

A Brief History

In its earliest forms, teaching in the United States was a community affair. Schools in the 1800s were small, one-room buildings where students focused on the 3R's: reading, writing, and arithmetic. More than 77% of Americans lived in rural communities (Protsik 1995: 2).

In the classroom, the requirements for teachers focused more on moral character and less on education. Many teachers, most of whom were women, were quite young and had only an elementary education themselves. Teaching was considered a temporary post until a woman married, when she was expected to dedicate herself to motherhood and housekeeping. Indeed, some schools mandated that female teachers retire upon marriage (Protsik 1995: 4).

Compensation systems reflected these early priorities. Many teachers were remunerated through a system called the *boarding round* or *room and board* compensation model, which meant that teachers moved into the home of a student for a week at a time, rotating among student homes throughout the school year. Families covered room and board and supervised the comings and goings of the teacher to ensure that she had the proper moral character to be a good role model for their children.

As the nation's economic foundation shifted from agriculture to industry, the purpose and role of schooling also shifted. Multi-room buildings where students were separated by age and ability slowly replaced one-room schoolhouses. As academic requirements and rigor intensified, so did standards for teachers and administrators. And, with new standards came a new approach to teacher pay known as the *grade-based* compensation model. Grade-based compensation was intended to reflect the level of skill needed to educate a child at his or her grade level, such as elementary or high school. High school teachers typically earned more than elementary teachers because it was believed that elementary students were easier to educate. Though a dramatic improvement from the boarding rounds model, the graded compensation model was still far from fair.

Most grade-based compensation policies, particularly those in large urban school systems, fostered gender inequities. Women were typically relegated to grammar schools, where they earned around one-half to one-quarter that of male teachers at the same school. Even if a female teacher managed to secure a high school post, high school principals frequently used a subjective performance evaluation of teachers, which further intensified the pay gap between men and women.

As the 20th century turned, however, pay practices began to reflect new modalities, including equalizing pay for women and reducing nepotism, which invariably favored white males. In 1921, Denver, Colo., and Des Moines, Iowa, successfully negotiated and introduced the *position-automatic* or *single salary* schedule for teachers. In this system, a teacher's salary was based on two criteria deemed most important: degree held and years of teaching experience. Endorsed by the National Education Association (NEA) in 1944, 97% of all schools had adopted the single salary schedule by 1950. By the 1999–00 school year, nearly 100% of teachers were paid according to the single salary schedule (Podgursky 2009).

A Perfect Storm

In spite of its near universal adoption, the single salary schedule has not been without detractors. Efforts to reform teacher compensation, including various attempts at implementing more performance- and market-oriented pay policies, have been nearly constant in the education policy cycle (see Table 1 for a summary of some of the more prominent types of teacher compensation reform). However, efforts at reforming teacher pay practices, like many reforms in the U.S. education system, failed to take root.

While stakeholders may be skeptical and ask, "Why now?" or think to themselves, "Here we go again," dismissing current reform efforts carte blanche misses an important point: Things are different now. Several of the key differences follow.

TABLE 1   Examples of Teacher Compensation Reform

Career Ladders	Popular in the 1980s and early 1990s, career ladders create different categories, or levels, that reward teachers with higher salaries. Each level is associated with increased mastery or competence. In most instances, career ladders require teachers to pass either formal or informal credentialing or to assume additional responsibilities in order to advance. Career ladders provide new roles with additional pay and responsibilities as teachers increase their knowledge and skills.
Knowledge- and Skills-Based Pay	Knowledge- and skills-based pay rewards teachers for acquiring additional knowledge and skills thought to improve a teacher's overall effectiveness. For instance, teachers may be rewarded above and beyond the traditional salary schedule increase for pursuing an advanced degree. Examples may include taking additional professional development coursework, pursuing dual certification, completing a teaching portfolio, or completing National Board for Professional Teaching Standards certification.
Pay for Performance	Pay for performance, or merit pay, offers financial incentives to individual teachers, groups of teachers, or whole schools based on predetermined tasks related to measurable student achievement outcomes. Awards can be given for a multitude of reasons, including student performance, increased student attendance rates, graduation rates, dropout rates, classroom observations, and portfolio completion. Unlike knowledge- and skills-based pay, which rewards teachers for activities thought to correlate with increased effectiveness, pay for performance plans reward teachers for measurable outcomes of their effectiveness.
Hard-to-Staff Bonuses	Hard-to-staff bonuses, or market-oriented compensation, reward teachers based on market factors, including teaching location and subject, and are characteristically a response to broader supply-and-demand considerations in a particular school, district, or state. The most prevalent forms are hard-to-staff school or subject and so-called combat pay. Hard-to-staff schools are commonly those that serve a high proportion of economically disadvantaged, minority, or low-achieving students and are generally in urban or remote rural areas. Hard-to-staff subjects are typically mathematics, science, and special education. They are identified as hard-to-staff by a relative dearth of qualified applicants. Hard-to-staff subjects can be based on individual school or district needs.
	A common mechanism for awarding hard-to-staff bonuses is through recruitment and retention bonuses. Recruitment stipends are awarded to new teachers at a school and are used as a tool for influencing the teacher to accept a teaching position in the school. In some locations, recruitment stipends are awards for multiple years after a teacher accepts the new position (see, for instance, AISD REACH in Austin, Texas). Retention stipends are distributed to teachers who continue working in their position or school following the summer vacation. Retention stipends are generally thought to improve student achievement in hard-to-staff schools by decreasing the continual turnover and overabundance of novice teachers emblematic of these schools.

Data Systems and Measures of Effective Teaching

One of the most influential critiques of teacher pay for performance came in 1986, when Richard Murnane and David Cohen documented the experiences of six districts where performance pay had been in place for more than five years. According to the authors, performance monitoring—or measuring the output of teachers—was one reason why pay for performance failed.

Compared with other professionals, teacher performance is more difficult to measure in valid, reliable, and fair ways. For instance, a salesman can be measured by his total sales, and a doctor can bill according to her hours. But how do we measure student learning and attribute this learning to an individual teacher?

Today, the relevance of this argument may be waning. Many states and districts have developed sophisticated longitudinal data systems that permit matching administrative records on individual students and their teachers. With this have come more exact techniques that allow estimation of the contribution of a teacher to a student's learning. In addition, research that seeks to develop and validate promising measures of effective teaching is gaining momentum.

As data systems and tools for collecting this information continue to be upgraded and the evaluative measures to assess teacher performance are advanced even further, the ability for education systems to measure the output of teachers could potentially rival those found in other sectors.

Teachers Matter

In addition to advances in data systems, several studies have quantified the importance of effective teaching on student learning, thereby focusing attention more squarely on developing strategies for improving the quality of the teacher workforce.

Using data collected as part of the Income Maintenance Experiment, a welfare reform experiment in the early 1970s in Gary, Ind., economist Eric Hanushek was among the first scholars to undertake a value-added analysis of teacher effectiveness. He found the most effective teachers in Gary produced 1.5 grade-level equivalents of annual achievement growth in their students while the least-effective teachers produced only .5 grade levels worth of growth (Hanushek 1992).

Similar conclusions have been reported in a number of other empirical studies. For example, a 1996 study authored by value-added pioneer William Sanders reported a difference of 50 percentile points in student achievement between students who encountered three consecutive years of teachers at or above the 80th percentile of performance and those students who encountered three consecutive years of teachers in the bottom 20th percentile of performance (Sanders and Rivers 1996).

Finally, based on data from several Texas school districts, Hanushek and Steven Rivkin (2004) further highlighted the importance of effective teaching by concluding that if a student encounters an above-average teacher for five years in a row, that could overcome the achievement gap typically found between students qualifying for free or reduced-price lunches and those from higher-income backgrounds. Combined, these research findings have helped focus both education stakeholders and policy makers on the singular importance of teachers.

Inefficiencies and Rigidities in Pay Practices

Another reason pay for performance systems stand a better chance this time around is a matter of dollars. Simply put, the single salary pay schedule is riddled by inefficiencies. Most teachers in the United States' 15,000 public school districts are paid based on years of experience and level of education (that is, the single salary schedule), both of which have been found to be only weakly correlated with student achievement (Goldhaber 2002; Hanushek, Kain, and Rivkin 1999). In other words, teachers are now paid according to criteria that researchers suggest have little connection to actual performance of teachers in the classroom.

What's more, teacher compensation accounts for most of a school district's operating budget. According to the U.S. Department of Education, school districts spent $179 billion on salaries and $50 billion on benefits for instructional personnel during the 2004-05 school year, accounting for around 60% of K–12 current expenditures and 90% of current instructional expenditures. This has led some to characterize the current pay practices as an extremely costly and inefficient use of resources.

Furthermore, in a 2009 report, Marguerite Roza and Raegen Miller addressed the importance of decoupling teacher salary from master's degrees. The sheer amount of money spent on the master's degree pay bump is staggering, particularly given the fact that about 90% of teachers' master's degrees are not subject specific and bear no relation to student achievement. While an education-specific master's degree appears to be irrelevant in terms of teacher effectiveness, the financial incentives for earning a master's degree are strong. Indeed, between 1997 and 2007, the education-specific master's had the highest growth rate of all master's degrees (Roza and Miller 2009).

In addition to simple dollars, research from the personnel economics literature adds an important perspective. More specifically, evidence suggests that pay for performance programs will tend to attract and retain individuals who are particularly good at the activities to which incentives are attached, and they will repel those who are not. That is, while incentives can raise the productivity of the typical employed worker, pay for performance systems can also raise the overall quality of the workforce simply by attracting more effective workers into the profession (Lazear 2003; Podgursky and Springer 2007).

View this table:

TABLE 2 **Experimental and Quasi-Experimental Evaluations of Teacher Pay for Performance Programs**

PROGRAM	STUDY PERIOD	SAMPLE	RESULTS
UNITED STATES			
Project on Incentives in Teaching Nashville, Tenn.	2007–2009	147 treatment and 152 control teachers (grades 5-8).	In progress
Project on Team-Level Incentives in Teaching Round Rock, Texas	2009–2010	41 treatment and 41 control group teams (grades 6-8).	In progress
Recognizing Excellence in Academic Leadership Program Chicago, Ill.	2008–2011	32 Teacher Advancement Program (TAP) schools.	In progress
School-Wide Performance Bonus Program New York, N.Y.	2008–2009	191 treatment and 131 control group schools (elementary, middle, and K–8). More than 100,000 students in grades 3-8.	In progress
Texas Educator Excellence Grant Program	2007–2009	2,150 schools were eligible for treatment.	No effect

INTERNATIONAL			
International Christelijk Steuenlonds Incentive Program Kenya	1998–1999	100 primary schools, 1,000+ teachers, 50,342 students.	Modest, positive effect for high-stakes assessment. No effect on low-stakes assessment.
Randomized Evaluation Project Andra Pradesh, India	2006–2008	300 schools and 68,000+ student observations.	Modest, positive effect on high-stakes assessment (about 0.12 to 0.19 standard deviations after year one and 0.16 to 0.19 standard deviations after year two).
Ministry of Education's School Performance Program Israel	1994–1997	62 schools (37 nonreligious, 18 religious, and 7 Arab schools).	Modest, positive effect for average credit hours earned, average science credits earned, average test score, and proportion of students taking Israel's matriculation exam.
Teacher-Incentive Experiment Israel	2001	4,109 students and 27 schools.	Modest, positive effect for number of exit exam credits earned in mathematics (increased 18%) and in reading (increased 17%).
Carrera Magisterial Mexico	1998–2003	850,000+ classroom-year observations, 810 primary school teachers, 209 secondary school teachers.	No effect for primary school teachers; modest, positive effect for secondary school teachers (about 3% to 15% of standard deviation).
	2000–2002	76,567 teachers and 27,123 schools.	Small, positive effects (<10% of standard deviation).

© Cengage Learning, 2013.

Shifting Attitudes

Another reason pay for performance programs are poised to be more than a passing fad involves a shift in stakeholder attitudes. In many ways, pay for performance programs have been their own worst enemy. Poorly designed and ill-conceived first-generation attempts at implementation left teachers and their unions with decidedly negative views. These experiences left many reluctant to participate in newer programs and, more generally, stigmatized the performance pay movement as something teachers unwaveringly oppose.

In recent years, however, a growing number of studies on teacher attitudes toward compensation reform suggest teachers aren't necessarily as opposed to pay for performance systems as once thought.

In Austin, Texas, for example, 74% of teachers thought their district's pay for performance program was a positive change in teacher pay practices (Burns, Gardner, and Meeuwsen 2009).

Moreover, many current programs have responded to critiques of earlier experiences. For instance, in many of the early programs, teachers competed against one another for bonus awards. As such, early studies, including the critique by Murnane and Cohen, cautioned that this competitive structure potentially reduced teacher collaboration and, as a consequence, may decrease the overall productivity of schools. While this may have been the case, as the education sector learns more about designing performance pay plans, several locations are experimenting with systems that don't place teachers or schools in direct competition for bonus awards. Performance pay programs may also reward teams of teachers or all personnel in a school, further reducing the risk of competition and decreased collegiality.

In addition to changes in educator attitudes, support of teacher pay for performance policies now transcends political boundaries (Goldhaber 2009; Hannaway and Rotherham 2008). Historically, Republicans led the charge for teacher pay reforms. In the 2008 presidential election, however, the three leading Democratic presidential candidates advocated for performance pay policies in education. Furthermore, other leaders, such as Rep. George Miller (D-Calif.), chairman of the House Education and Labor Committee, have been on the front lines in support of performance pay. Indeed, Miller recently noted that, "If we want our students to succeed, we have to begin giving our teachers the respect and resources they deserve.... This will require a seismic shift in the way we talk about and treat teachers, and it starts with [an] important investment in programs that reward teacher excellence" (Anderson 2009).

Finally, the nation's two leading teacher associations—the NEA and American Federation of Teachers (AFT)—have also augmented their position on teacher compensation reform in recent years. Traditionally adamantly opposed to market- and performance-oriented pay reforms, both unions, the AFT in particular, have participated in the design and implementation of several high-profile programs, including Denver's ProComp, Austin's REACH, and Nashville's Project on Incentives in Teaching. In fact, following the successful negotiation of New York City's School-Wide Performance Bonus Program in 2007, AFT president Randi Weingarten (then president of the New York City United Federation of Teachers) stated, "Rather than being pilloried as an obstacle ... we created a program that may promote the collaboration and respect that are necessary for great schools.... We have taken a negative—individual merit pay—and come up with a positive alternative that makes it a plus for educators and kids" (Weingarten 2007).

What's Next?

Taken as a whole, pay for performance is now poised to become more reality than simple rhetoric. That said, moving forward deliberately and purposefully will be important. In particular, research must play a critical role. To date, the little research surrounding pay for performance paints a mixed picture (see Table 2), with many of the most rigorous studies still under way or having been conducted abroad.

Policy makers and education stakeholders at all levels would benefit from more unbiased assessments of teacher compensation reform programs and policies, as well as the effect of their various design components. For instance, should individual teachers or teams of teachers be rewarded, or perhaps a combination of both? Should the measure be based on student growth or attainment? What criteria should be included? Should it be based strictly on student test scores, or should other measures, like principal evaluations, be included? If other measures are included, what should be the weight of each element? Since the design of an incentive program can lead to dramatic effects on students, teachers, and administrators, we must take the lessons learned from these evaluations and continue to both evaluate and refine programs to maximize their effectiveness.

In addition to ongoing research and evaluation, data systems need continued development. Even though these systems at the state- and district-level have helped drive policy innovations around teacher compensation, they haven't been designed to inform high-stakes personnel decisions. Among the weaknesses are seemingly mundane errors, such as inaccurate course codes, to more significant errors, such as assigning the same unique identifier to multiple students. Many structural errors can also be found, including systems that don't account for student mobility (both within and between schools) and too few data snapshots to accurately capture what's happening in schools and classrooms. When these systems are used to reward teachers, it's imperative they accurately capture what's happening in classrooms.

Related to the development of data systems, there needs to be a continued push for more accurate and reliable tools for assessing individual and team performance. As many teachers will attest, far more happens in a classroom than can be measured on a standardized assessment. And roughly 70% of educators don't instruct a course or a grade covered by a standardized assessment. Research is ongoing in this area and must be included in the design of pay for performance systems.

Balancing the interests of all stakeholders is crucial when designing and developing pay for performance systems. While stakeholder engagement and buy-in is critically important, the interests and preferences of individual actors may water down the power of the incentive. For example, a study of a pilot incentive pay program in Texas, in which multiple stakeholders were engaged in plan development, found that many schools chose to distribute relatively small awards across all school personnel, regardless of individual performance. The relatively weak incentive system didn't appear to induce any significant changes in teacher productivity (Taylor and Springer 2009).

Finally, we must stay focused on the bigger picture of schooling. Even if pay for performance programs and policies ultimately play an important role in reforming K–12 public schools, these reforms can't be implemented in a vacuum. Teacher pay alone will not improve the quality of teaching and, by extension, improve levels of student learning. Compensation reform is just one element to be implemented alongside reforms that retool resource allocation and deployment norms; teacher hiring, tenure, and dismissal practices; and the standards and assessments systems, among other areas.

References

Anderson Nick. "Performance Pay for Teachers Would Quadruple Under Bill Approved by Hill." *The Washington Post*, Dec. 13, 2009. www.washingtonpost.com/wp-dyn/content/article/2009/12/12/AR2009121202691.html.

Burns Susan, Gardner Catherine D., Meeuwsen Joyce. *An Interim Evaluation of Teacher and Principal Experiences During the Pilot Phase of AISD REACH.* Nashville, Tenn.: National Center on Performance Incentives Working Paper Series, 2009.

Goldhaber Dan. "The Mystery of Good Teaching." *Education Next* 2, no. 1 (Spring 2002): 1–17.

Springer Matthew G., Goldhaber Dan. "The Politics of Teacher Pay Reform." In *Performance Incentives: Their Growing Impact on American K–12 Education*, ed. Springer Matthew G. Washington, D.C.: Brookings Institution Press, 2009.

Hannaway Jane, Rotherham Andrew J. "Collective Bargaining in Education and Pay for Performance." *Working Paper no. 2008–11.* Nashville, Tenn.: National Center on Performance Incentives, 2008.

Hanushek Eric A. "The Trade-off Between Child Quantity and Quality." *Journal of Political Economy* 100, no. 1 (1992): 84–117.

Hanushek Eric A., Rivkin Steven G. "How to Improve the Supply of High-Quality Teachers." *Brookings Papers on Education Policy* (2004): 7–25.

Hanushek Eric A., Kain John F., Rivkin Steven G. "Do Higher Salaries Buy Better Teachers?" *NBER Working Paper* no. 7082. Cambridge, Mass.: National Bureau of Economic Research, 1999.

Lazear Edward P. "Teacher Incentives." *Swedish Economic Policy Review* 10 (2003): 179–214.

Murnane Richard J., Cohen David. "Merit Pay and the Evaluation Problem: Why Most Merit Pay Plans Fail and Few Survive." *Harvard Education Review* 56, no. 1 (1986): 1–17.

Springer Matthew G. Podgursky Michael. "A Market-Based Perspective on Teacher Compensation Reform." In *Performance Incentives: Their Growing Impact on American K–12 Education,* ed. Springer Matthew G. Washington, D.C.: Brookings Institution Press, 2009.

Podgursky Michael, Springer Matthew G. "Teacher Performance Pay: A Review." *Journal of Policy Analysis and Management* 26, no. 4 (2007): 909–949.

Protsik Jean. *History of Teacher Pay and Incentive Reform.* Washington, D.C.: Educational Resources Information Center, 1995.

Roza Marguerite, Miller Raegen. *Separation of Degrees: State-By-State Analysis of Teacher Compensation for*

Master's Degrees. Seattle, Wash.: Center on Reinventing Public Education Rapid Response Brief, 2009.

Sanders William L., Rivers June C. *Cumulative and Residual Effects of Teachers on Future Student Academic Achievement.* Knoxville, Tenn.: Value-Added Research and Assessment Center, University of Tennessee, 1996.

Taylor Lori, Springer Matthew G. "Optimal Incentives for Public Sector Workers: The Case of Teacher-Designed Incentive Pay in Texas." *Working Paper* no. 2009–05. Nashville, Tenn.: National Center on Performance Incentives, 2009.

U.S. Department of Education. "Race to the Top Application for Initial Funding." *CFDA Number: 84.395A.* Washington, D.C.: U.S. Department of Education, 2009.

Weingarten Randi. "Turning Negative to Positive." *New York Teacher,* Oct. 18, 2007.

POSTNOTE

It is a truism that few people go into teaching for the money. The occupation's chief rewards are intrinsic, such as always knowing one is doing crucial work. Nevertheless, many teachers and many in the public have been concerned in recent years that superior teachers are subjected to the same pay scale as inferior teachers. A belief exists, too, that this condition keeps many talented potential teachers from entering the profession. These concerns are providing political energy to the pay for performance movement discussed in this article. Many teachers, however, are concerned that pay for performance will weaken colleagueship and interject an element of destructive competition. Organizers fear that the union solidarity and the spirit of all-in-the-same-boat will weaken their capacity to bargain for all teachers. One of the stronger counterclaims supporting pay for performance asserts that the United States has thrived under a free market concept and now it is time to apply it to our public schools. We will surely see more debate, controversy, and experimentation around this issue in the coming months and years.

DISCUSSION QUESTIONS

1. Do you believe that adopting pay for performance will increase the attractiveness of teaching as a career?
2. If pay for performance becomes the dominant way teachers are rewarded, do you believe it will necessarily improve the education of children?

RELATED WEBSITE RESOURCES

WEB RESOURCES:

National Center on Performance Incentives at Vanderbilt University's Peabody College of Education and Human Development. Available at:

http://www.performanceincentives.org/.

This research center is a leading resource on current studies and activities around the issues of pay for performance and teacher incentive plans.

Center for Educational Reform. Available at:

http://www.edreform.com/Home/.

This educational policy center is a leader in innovative and sometimes controversial plans to improve teaching and learning.

44

The Seven Deadly Sins of No Child Left Behind

Paul D. Houston

Paul D. Houston is the former executive director of the American Association of School Administrators, Arlington, VA and author of *Giving Wings to Children's Dreams: Making Our Schools Worthy of Our Children* [Corwin].

Paul D. Houston, "The Seven Deadly Sins of No Child Left Behind" *Phi Delta Kappan,* June 2007, pp. 744–748. Reprinted with permission of Phi Delta Kappa International, www.pdkintl.org. All rights reserved.

HAVE YOU ever considered that the remedy for being lost is not to drive faster? You have to stop and change direction. For five years the major school reform agenda in America has been the No Child Left Behind (NCLB) Act, which was part of the most recent reauthorization of the Elementary and Secondary Education Act (ESEA). Now ESEA is up for another reauthorization by Congress, and everyone is wondering what is going to happen next. It has been suggested that NCLB be expanded to high schools or that more interventions or national standards be required. But more is not the solution. It is time to change direction.

It is now universally accepted, even by those who authored the bill, that NCLB is flawed and needs fixing. In fact, describing the law as flawed might be charitable. If you take the definition of "sin" as a "shameful offense," then it could be argued that NCLB is full of sin because it has proved itself to be an offense against good education. For that reason, merely adding a growth model to the accountability provisions or creating some additional flexibility for English-language learners will not fix the underlying structural weaknesses of the law. Neither will adding more money. You can't get something designed for one purpose to be effective at fulfilling a very different purpose, no matter how many resources you apply to it. While there are aspects of the law that could be fixed, there are flaws in it that are so fundamental that there is not enough paint and spackle in the world to make them presentable.

Many will dismiss any criticism of NCLB now just as they have dismissed previous criticism. In the past, critics have been accused of exhibiting "the soft bigotry of low expectations" and have been labeled "apologists for a failed system." The generic response to critics has been that educators don't want to be held accountable. Now the contention is that America is failing to

FOCUS QUESTION

In spite of such good intentions, what has gone wrong with No Child Left Behind?

KEY TERMS

- Average Yearly Progress (AYP)
- Elementary and Secondary Education Act (ESEA)

remain competitive in the global economy and that if we don't put more rigor into the education system our children will not be able to compete.

None of these retorts are accurate or particularly useful.

The Need for a Systemic Solution

One could argue that there is much in the U.S. education system that is not effective and needs to change and that NCLB's focus on accountability has helped to illuminate this need. Some educators may have held inappropriately low expectations for their students, so requiring schools to disaggregate test-score data by race, disability, socioeconomic status, and English proficiency helps make certain that schools do not paper over the lack of success of some of their students. But the most fundamental problem facing education is that the current system is perfectly designed to yield the current results. If we are not happy with the current results, a systemic solution is called for. NCLB, which adopts assessment as its key strategy, does not begin to deal with education in a systemic way.

The deadly sins of NCLB are largely the result of a set of wrong assumptions about the problems facing schools and children. If we continue to fix things that are not really broken, we will simply break those things that work while the real problems go unattended.

Sin Number 1: Assuming that Schools are Broken

Most education reform is driven by a belief that the system is badly broken and must be fixed. In fact, the system is quite successful in fulfilling its historical mission of preparing children for an agricultural and industrial economy. It is not broken. It is a well-oiled machine doing the wrong thing. The problem is that the world now requires a different set of skills. Indeed, the jobs that the education system was designed to fill are in short supply. What is required is a hard look at what schools need to produce and then a total retooling aimed at achieving that end. Schools haven't failed at their

mission. The mission has changed. Some might argue that NCLB will lead to the retooling needed in education. But that is true only if you believe that the road to the future is paved with low-level tests that measure discrete bits of knowledge. The reality is that anyone in business will tell you that successful workers in the new global economy must have skills of collaboration, ingenuity, problem solving, comfort with ambiguity, and a dozen other things—none of which are tested for and subsequently taught as a result of NCLB. Schools that focus on 21st-century skills are doing so in spite of NCLB, not because of it.

The truth is that many schools and school systems in the United States work remarkably well for most students. Furthermore, the system is made up of over 50 million children, over 95,000 schools, and over 14,000 districts. Most of these children, schools, and districts are pretty successful, even under the restrictive expectations of NCLB. Even using average yearly progress (AYP) under NCLB as a measure, most kids meet most of the standards. Were it not for the "all or nothing" aspect of the scoring system, only a small fraction of the schools in America would be having difficulty making AYP.

And even the harshest critic of public education must admit that the majority of students are not failing. Nevertheless, we have constructed a federally mandated system that treats all school districts, schools, and children pretty much the same—whether they are failing or succeeding dramatically. Would a business that has a high failure rate in one factory and a low one in another subject both to the same treatment? Would a doctor treat a patient with a head cold the same way she would treat one with lung cancer? Any rational response to our educational challenges would examine the range of school performance and act accordingly.

Sin Number 2: Conflating Testing with Education

Testing is an important part of the educational process. Teachers need to know what kids know and how they are progressing, and the public has a right to have a snapshot of how well benchmarks are being met. But testing must be kept in perspective. A number of states were making significant progress on their statewide plans before NCLB was implemented, and they had to step back from more sophisticated uses of assessments to meet the lower standards set by NCLB.

When student achievement is discussed, it has now come to mean test results. Yet the least sophisticated citizen among us understands that there is much more to education than what can be tested. When our sole emphasis is squarely on a single aspect of education, the entire process gets distorted. One of the greatest dangers posed by NCLB is that we will reach a point where most kids meet an acceptable standard set by the tests but do so at the expense of a broader and deeper learning experience. Setting standards can be useful, but only if the standards do not lead to standardization. A wise man once pointed out to me that training makes people alike and education makes them different. If we put too much emphasis on a lower, common denominator, we will be sacrificing higher possibilities for our children.

Sin Number 3: Harming Poor Children and Ignoring the Realities of Poverty

ESEA was originally created to address the needs of poor and minority children. While great strides have been made, much remains to be done. Those who wrote and voted for NCLB ostensibly did so out of a belief that we should not leave some children behind. However, broadening the law's requirements well beyond those most in need to include all schools and all children has caused educators to take their eyes off the ball. A recent study showed that the children closest to making AYP, not those most in need of assistance, are the ones receiving the bulk of the attention. Drilling poor students on basic skills while their middle-class counterparts partake of a richer curriculum will not close the real learning gap between students. It simply further limits the possibilities for poor children.

While Washington has created a system that ostensibly helps poor children, it doesn't want to talk about the impact of poverty on school success. Those who see poverty as an intervening variable have been accused of having lowered expectations for disadvantaged children. This has meant there has been no real discussion about what might be needed to really leave no child behind. While history is replete with stories of heroic exceptions (e.g., Lincoln was born in a log cabin and became President), there is no evidence that whole groups of people have been elevated by ignoring the chains that bind them.

Everyone in America knew which children were being left behind long before NCLB became law. A massive system of testing was not required. When you are born without adequate prenatal care, when you do not have sufficient health care as a toddler, when your parents do not know how to provide cognitive stimulation and cannot afford high-quality preschool programs, chances are you will come to school with a working vocabulary that is just a fraction of the vocabularies of middle-class children. You have already been left behind.

Still, most educators put their shoulders to the wheel and try to push it uphill anyway. Sometimes they succeed. But when they fail, as they often do, they know that any law that fails to acknowledge the broader systemic issues that cause some children to be hobbled by circumstances is a law that will not work. The sad fact is that schools can and should help disadvantaged children—but schools can't do it all. Leaving no child behind also requires us to leave no family and no community behind. The inequities that exist between school districts and between states further complicate the issue. For example, the children in Cuyahoga Heights, Ohio, receive twice as much financial support for their schools as do the children in nearby East Cleveland. Yet the taxpayers in Cuyahoga Heights have to tax themselves only about one-third as much as those in East Cleveland in order to create this unequal result. At the same time, children in California are not getting nearly the same level of school support that the children of Connecticut get.

How can we pretend to have a national law that holds educators accountable for outcomes when the resources are so uneven? Put most simply, some children get left behind because our society, through a series of policy decisions, has chosen to leave them behind. Testing and sanctions on schools will not change that reality.

Sin Number 4: Relying on Fear and Coercion

Motivation has always been the key to good education. Unfortunately, NCLB relies for motivation on the blunt force of threats and punishments. It starts by assuming that those at the top know better than those farther down the line, even though those nearest the bottom are charged with actually doing what is needed to educate children. By using fear and coercion as a change strategy, NCLB ensures compliance but blocks the pursuit of excellence for teachers and children. While you can beat people into submission, you can't beat them into greatness.

You can't inspire children by means that either turn them off or traumatize them. Children are subjected to days of examinations annually, with the time taken away from instruction. Indeed, we have actually reduced the time we spend on instruction so that we can increase the time we spend on measuring the results of instruction. To offset this, many schools have chosen to neglect subjects not covered by the tests, so that the curriculum has narrowed. Many children have chosen to turn off and not try. Others have felt traumatized by the pressure. Cognitive scientists are clear that the emotion of fear blocks clear thinking by impeding neural processing. Any educational model that relies on fear undercuts its own aims.

Collaboration, not coercion, is what is needed. While most educators believe accountability is an important part of the public education experience, supporters of NCLB fail to see that other options for accountability exist. Accountability systems will work only where there is collaboration and trust between the federal government and the schools. Good accountability systems would be broader in nature and would actually allow us to examine the broader needs of a child's learning.

Sin Number 5: Lacking Clarity

Any accountability system should be clear and understandable to those it is accountable to: parents and other citizens. Most parents find the AYP model to be confusing and, when explanations are given, counterintuitive. Why would you measure completely different groups in the same way and compare the results? Why would a school that fails to make progress in one cell be treated the same as one that fails to make progress in all cells? Why would you hold special education children, who have individual education plans because of their needs, to the same standard as children who do not have the same needs? Why would you test children in English when they do not yet speak English? Any accountability system needs to have a sense of authenticity if it is to be useful.

Sin Number 6: Leaving Out the Experts

Those at the federal level do not—and cannot—know better how to educate a child than those working at the child's level. In other professions, while guidelines are created for public safety, bureaucrats don't try to second-guess the work of professionals who deliver services. For example, pilots, while subject to rules and regulations, are still presumed to know better how to fly the plane than their passengers. No federal law that takes the professionals out of the decision-making process will ever work. Professional judgment must be taken into account if we have any hope that NCLB will work. Jamming a comprehensive set of mandates down the throats of those who must carry out the mandates is doomed—not just because of the insurgency it creates, but because many ideas that look so good in Washington just don't work in Weehawken.

Sin Number 7: Undermining our International Competitiveness

Finally, the greatest sin committed by NCLB is a sin of omission. NCLB fails to address the core question for America: How do we sustain our place in a global environment? NCLB's answer is that drilling our children will allow them to compete with the Chinese. Yet the real winners in the coming competition between East and West will not be the nations that focus on basic skills but those that cultivate high-level skills and ingenuity. In that regard, America has had an edge for some time. Our society seems to produce unusually creative and entrepreneurial people. Most of those people went to our public schools. In fact, much of America's creativity emanated from those in our society who had been left behind.

Whether in music, sports, or technology, innovation comes from the edge, where many of those children who are left behind congregate. These individuals have enormous capacity to lift our society to new levels through their creativity. Harvard psychologist Ellen Langer has pointed out that fear of evaluation, an acceptance of absolutes, and mindless ideas about our mistakes can stop us from being creative and responsive to the world.

She has said that such mental paralysis comes from "anything hierarchical [that] suggests that there is a single metric—a 'right' way of understanding the world." If America is to continue to lead the world, we must begin to undo the damage created by a system that is built upon the notion that there is a single right way to do education.

How can we sustain our creativity while paring down our education to a stimulus-response system of learning that reduces knowledge to a series of test bubbles and communicates to children that what is on the test is the only thing worth learning? The great danger we face is that, in our rush to build skills, we undermine our wisdom. Then we will all be left behind. For that reason NCLB needs to be deposited in the dustbin of history, and Congress, with the assistance of educators and other citizens, needs to think more broadly and deeply about how to build on and make use of the talents of our poorest citizens.

POSTNOTE

Some ten years ago, with much fanfare and rare political cooperation, President Bush and the U.S. Congress passed the No Child Left Behind Act [NCLB]. Federal funding for education increased dramatically and hopes were high for a substantial improvement in the quality of education offered to American children. Along with additional monies, a new spirit of accountability was launched and schools across the nation embraced higher standards and more robust assessment of results. While clearly positive results have come from NCLB, the dreams of the reformers have fallen well short of their expectation. The author of this article has been a key player on the national education scene for several decades. His indictment of our schools as well-oiled machines doing the wrong thing flows from long experience and observation. His claims that our schools are failing the children of the poor are vivid and calls for strong action. As we prepare this volume for publication, Congress is getting ready to reauthorize and to reform many aspects of No Child Left Behind, and we hope his "seven sins" are attended to.

RELATED WEBSITE RESOURCES AND VIDEO CASE

WEB RESOURCES:

Education Week. Available at:

http://www.edweek.org/ew/issues/no-child-left-behind/.

EdWeek, as it is known, is a key publication in the field and is an excellent resource to use to follow developments in No Child Left Behind and other policy issues.

Center for Educational Policy. Available at:

http://www.cep-dc.org/.

This Washington, D.C.–based center has been a major source of ideas and research in education since 1995. It is both an advocate for public schools, and a source of ideas for improvement.

▶❚❚ TEACHSOURCE VIDEO CASE

ED REFORM: TEACHERS TALK ABOUT NO CHILD LEFT BEHIND

This video finds teachers and administrators discussing the issues and problems surrounding the implementation of the NCLB legislation. Go to the website for the Education Media Library at CengageBrain.com to watch the video clips, study the artifacts in the case, and reflect on the following questions.

1. What are the parallels between their views and those of Paul Houston on NCLB?

2. What additional concerns does Houston add to your understanding?

America's Commitment to Equity Will Determine Our Future

Linda Darling-Hammond

Linda Darling-Hammond is the Charles E. Ducommon Professor of Education at Stanford University and served as chief educational advisor to President Barack Obama during his 2008 campaign for the presidency.

Creating schools that enable all children to learn requires the development of systems that enable all educators and schools to learn. At heart, this is a capacity-building enterprise leveraged by clear, meaningful learning goals and intelligent, reciprocal accountability systems that guarantee skillful teaching in well-designed, adequately resourced schools for all learners. It is not only possible but imperative that America close the achievement gap among its children by addressing the yawning opportunity gap that denies these fundamental rights. Given the critical importance of education for individual and societal success in the flat world we now inhabit, inequality in the provision of education is an antiquated tradition the United States can no longer afford. If No Child Left Behind is to be anything more than empty rhetoric, we will need policy strategy that creates a 21st-century curriculum for all students and supports it with thoughtful assessments; access to knowledgeable, well-supported teachers; and equal access to school resources.

For the United States to make progress on its longstanding inequalities, we will need to make the case to each other that none of us benefits by keeping any of us ignorant, and, as a society, all of us profit from the full development of one another's abilities.

As the fate of individuals and nations is increasingly interdependent, the quest for access to an equitable, empowering education for all people has become a critical issue for the American nation as a whole. As a country, we can and must enter a new era. No society can thrive in a technological, knowledge-based economy by depriving large segments of its population of learning. The path to our mutual well-being is built on educational opportunity. Central to our collective future is the recognition that our capacity to survive and thrive ultimately depends on ensuring to all of our people what should be an unquestioned entitlement—a rich and inalienable right to learn.

FOCUS QUESTION

How and why should the original No Child Left Behind Act be changed and improved?

KEY TERMS

- Assessment
- Intelligent accountability
- No Child Left Behind Act
- Reciprocity
- Standards for schools
- Standards for systems
- Standards of practice

Reciprocal, Intelligent Accountability

Standards for student learning are meaningless unless they are accompanied by the means to ensure that they can indeed be met by students in all schools. Thus, policies that ensure students' opportunities to learn are as important a part of an accountable education system as are standards for student performance.

In the currently prevailing paradigm in the United States, accountability has been defined primarily as the administration of tests and the attachment of sanctions to low test scores. Yet, from a child and parent perspective, this approach does not ensure high-quality teaching each year; nor does it ensure that students have the courses, books, materials, support services, and other resources they need to learn. In this paradigm, two-way accountability does not exist: Although the child and the school are accountable to the state for test performance, the state is not accountable to the child or his school for providing adequate educational resources.

Furthermore, as we have seen, test-based accountability schemes have sometimes undermined education for the most vulnerable students by narrowing curriculum and by creating incentives to exclude low-achieving students in order to boost scores. Indeed, while tests can provide some of the information needed for an accountability system; they are not the system itself. Genuine accountability should heighten the probability of good practices occurring for all students, reduce the probability of harmful practice, and ensure that there are self-corrective mechanisms in the system—feedback, assessments, and incentives—that support continual improvement.

If education is actually to improve and the system is to be accountable to students, accountability should be focused on ensuring the competence of teachers and leaders, the quality of instruction, and the adequacy of resources, as well as the capacity of the system to trigger improvements. In addition to *standards of learning* for students, which focus the system's efforts on meaningful goals, this will require *standards of prac-*

tice that can guide professional training, development, teaching, and management at the classroom, school, and system levels, and *opportunity to learn standards* that ensure appropriate resources to achieve the desired outcomes.

In addition to relevant, valid, and useful information about how individual students are doing and how schools are serving them, accountability should encompass how a school system hires, evaluates, and supports its staff, how it makes decisions, how it ensures that the best available knowledge will be acquired and used, how it evaluates its own functioning, and how it provides safeguards for student welfare.

This more complete conception is similar to what has been described as Finland's strategy of "reciprocal, intelligent accountability," in which:

> schools are increasingly accountable for learning outcomes and education authorities are held accountable to schools for making expected outcomes possible. Intelligent accountability in the Finnish education context preserves and enhances trust among teachers, students, school leaders and education authorities in the accountability processes and involves them in the process, offering them a strong sense of professional responsibility and initiative. This has had a major positive impact on teaching and, hence, on student learning. (Sahlberg 2007)

If new standards are to result in greater student learning, rather than greater levels of failure, accountability policies will need to ensure that teachers and other educators have the knowledge and skills they need to teach effectively to the new standards, help schools evaluate and reshape their practices, and put safeguards in place for students who attend failing schools.

Standards of Practice: Ensuring Professional Accountability

If students are to be expected to achieve higher standards, it stands to reason that educators must meet higher standards as well. They must know how to teach in ways that enable students to master challenging content and that address the special needs of different learners. High and rigorous standards for teaching are a cornerstone of a professional accountability system focused on student learning. Professional accountability acknowledges that the only way we can ensure that students will be well taught is by ensuring that they have knowledgeable and committed teachers. As Lee Shulman has stated:

> The teacher remains the key. The literature on effective schools is meaningless, debates over educational policy are moot, if the primary agents of instruction are incapable of performing their functions well. No microcomputer will replace them, no television system will clone and distribute them, no scripted lessons will direct and control them, no voucher system will bypass them. (Shulman 1983: 504)

Professional accountability aims to ensure educators' competence through rigorous preparation, certification, selection, and evaluation of practitioners, as well as continuous professional learning and peer review of practice. It requires that educators make decisions on the basis of the best available professional knowledge; it also requires that they pledge their first commitment to the welfare of the client. Thus, rather than encouraging teaching that is procedure-oriented and rule-based, professional accountability seeks to create practices that are *client-oriented* and *knowledge-based*. Professional accountability seeks to ensure that all educators will have had access to profession-wide knowledge concerning best practices, not just what they picked up by themselves on the job; that they will have made a moral commitment to use this knowledge in the best interests of their students; and that they will continually seek to discover new knowledge and increasingly effective practices for themselves and their colleagues.

To achieve this, current ad hoc approaches to teacher and principal recruitment, preparation, licensing, hiring, and ongoing professional development must be reshaped so that all students will have access to teachers and school leaders who can be

professionally accountable. This will require a serious overhaul of preparation and licensing standards so that they reflect the critical knowledge and skills for teaching, evaluated through high-quality performance assessments demonstrating that prospective teachers can actually teach effectively. It will require major investments in and greater accountability from teacher and leadership education programs, evaluated by the performance of their graduates on these assessments and other measures. And it will require more effective evaluation and professional learning systems in schools, so that tenure is earned based on demonstrated competence and ongoing assessment of practice, and outcomes guide expectations and supports for professional development.

Standards for Schools: Developing Organizational Accountability

Quality teaching depends not just on teachers' knowledge and skill but on the environments in which they work. Schools need to offer a coherent curriculum focused on higher-order thinking and performance across subject areas and grades; time for teachers to work intensively with students to accomplish challenging goals; opportunities for teachers to plan with and learn from one another; and regular occasions to evaluate the outcomes of their practices.

If schools are to become more responsible and responsive, they must, like other professional organizations, make evaluation and assessment part of their everyday lives. Just as hospitals have standing committees of staff that meet regularly to look at assessment data and discuss the effectiveness of each aspect of their work—a practice reinforced by their accreditation requirements—so schools must have regular occasions to examine their practices and effectiveness.

As Richard Rothstein and colleagues describe in *Grading Education: Getting Accountability Right* (2008), school-level accountability can be supported by school inspections, like those common in many other nations, in which trained experts, usually highly respected former practitioners, evaluate schools by spending several days visiting classrooms, examining random samples of student work, and interviewing students about their understanding and their experiences, as well as looking at objective data such as test scores, graduation rates, and the like. In some cases, principals accompany inspectors into classrooms and are asked for their own evaluations of the lessons. In this way, inspectors are able to make judgments about the instructional and supervisory competence of principals. As described earlier, inspectors may also play a role in ensuring the quality and comparability of school-based assessments (as in England and Australia), as well as schools' internal assessment and evaluation processes (as in Hong Kong).

In most countries' inspection systems, schools are rated on the quality of instruction and other services and supports, as well as students' performance and progress on a wide range of dimensions including and going beyond academic subject areas, such as extracurriculars, personal and social responsibility, the acquisition of workplace skills, and the extent to which students are encouraged to adopt safe practices and a healthy lifestyle. Schools are rated as to whether they pass inspection, need modest improvements, or require serious intervention, and receive extensive feedback on what the inspectors both saw and recommend. Reports are publicly posted. Schools requiring intervention are then given more expert attention and support, and placed on a more frequent schedule of visits. Those that persistently fail to pass may be placed under local government control and could be closed if they are not improved.

An Americanized version of the inspectorate system, designed by former members of the British inspectorate with U.S educators, has been piloted in several states and cities, including New York, Rhode Island, and Chicago (Ancess 1996; Wilson 1995). The process has proved an extremely effective strategy for enabling schools to get an objective look at their practices, creating an evidence base that honors the broader goals of education and complements test information, and providing diagnostics and recommendations that are essential for

any serious improvement ultimately to occur. When practicing educators are among the members of the teams, they also learn directly about colleagues' practices and how to evaluate education in ways that travel back with them to their own schools, creating a learning system across the state. This approach could be developed by building on these efforts or by reconceptualizing current school accreditation to focus more directly on teaching and learning, with leadership from full-time trained experts who guide the work of the volunteer participants on teams that can, thus, be more consistent and effective.

Standards for the System: Creating Safeguards for Students

An effective intervention system for diagnosing and remedying the sources of school failure is an essential component of an accountability system that works for students. If teaching and learning are to improve, federal and state accountability efforts must be structured to enhance opportunities for school learning and professional development. They should also ensure that necessary resources—ranging from qualified teachers to curriculum materials—are put in place where schools are failing.

It is critical that state and federal efforts to recognize success and remedy failure be based on thoughtful, educationally sound means for identifying schools that are succeeding or failing. When incentives are triggered by simplistic measurements such as average school test scores, perverse incentives can be created that harm students. Measures need to be based on the growth and success of all students in the school and on educationally sound evaluations of school practices. The incentive structure must provide incentives for schools that provide high-quality education to be rewarded for opening their doors to the students who are in the greatest educational need and for supporting the spread of successful practices to other schools.

A genuinely accountable system recognizes that school problems can be caused as much by district and state policies—including unequal funding, hiring and assignment of unqualified personnel, and counterproductive curriculum policies—as they are by conditions within the school. Thus, the responsibility for correcting school failings must be shared. When there are serious shortcomings in schools' practices and outcomes, states should involve expert teams in evaluating the root causes of school failure—including the qualifications of personnel, the nature of curriculum resources, student access to high-quality teaching, administrative strategies, organizational structures, and other essential aspects of students' experiences in school—and, with the district and school, develop a plan to correct them.

If policy changes are needed to implement a remedy or to ensure that the problems experienced by the school do not recur on a regular basis (in that school or in other schools), then the state and local district should also assume responsibility for developing new policies that are more supportive of school success and that ensure the protection of students' entitlement to high-quality education. Schools should have expert technical assistance to support their efforts to change. If they cannot do so successfully, however, with infusions of resources and help, they should be redesigned or closed, and their buildings used to house new school models created by educators who can design them for greater success.

In a system of shared accountability, *states* would be responsible for providing sufficient resources, for ensuring well-qualified personnel, and for adopting standards for student learning. *School districts* would be responsible for distributing school resources equitably, hiring and supporting well-qualified teachers and administrators (and removing those who are not competent), and encouraging practices that support high-quality teaching and learning. *Schools* would be accountable for creating a productive environment for learning, assessing the effectiveness of their practices, and helping staff and parents communicate with and learn from one another. *Teachers and other staff* would be accountable for identifying and meeting the needs of individual students as well as meeting professional standards of practice. Together with colleagues, they would continually assess and revise their strategies to better meet the needs of students.

Revamping No Child Left Behind

No Child Left Behind (NCLB) will be considered for reauthorization in 2010 and will have much to do with the accountability strategies adopted by states across the country. While problematic in its implementation, NCLB is a historic piece of legislation that has succeeded in drawing attention to the need for higher learning standards and greater equity in educational outcomes. By flagging differences in student performance by race and class, it shines a spotlight on long-standing inequalities that can trigger attention to the needs of students neglected in many schools. And by insisting that all students are entitled to qualified teachers, the law has stimulated important recruitment and retention efforts in states where low-income and "minority" students have experienced a revolving door of inexperienced, untrained teachers.

The goals of NCLB are the right ones; however, we have seen that the law's design and implementation have narrowed the curriculum, caused schools to abandon some successful programs, and created incentives for keeping and pushing low-achievers out of schools. In addition, its complex rules for showing "Adequate NYearly Progress"—which require schools to meet more than 30 separate testing targets annually—have labeled many successful and improving schools as failing, while preventing adequate attention to the truly failing schools that states should focus on. Because of a number of Catch 22s in the accountability formula, more than 80% of the nation's schools will have failed 10 "make AYP" by 2014 even if they are high-achieving or rapidly improving.

Hundreds of proposals for tweaking NCLB have been made, but a substantial paradigm shift is required if the nation's education system is to support powerful learning for all students. The Forum on Education and Accountability, a group of over 100 education and civil rights organizations, has argued that "the law's emphasis needs to shift from applying sanctions for failing to raise test scores to holding states and localities accountable for making the systemic changes that improve student achievement" (2004).

This should include encouraging thoughtful measures of student performance that can support the kind of learning we need in schools and developing a better method for charting school progress. Although the current law calls for multiple measures and for assessing higher-order thinking skills, it lacks incentives to encourage better assessments. To address these problems, Congress should:

• **Fund an intensive development effort** that enables federal labs, centers, and universities in collaboration with states to develop, validate, and test high-quality performance assessments, and to train the field of practitioners—ranging from a new generation of state and local curriculum and assessment specialists to teachers and leaders—who can be involved in the development, administration, and scoring of these assessments in valid and reliable ways. The federal government should also fund high-quality research on the validity, reliability, instructional consequences, and equity consequences of these assessments.

• **Encourage improvements in state and local assessment practice.** To model high-quality test items and better measure the standards, the federal government should move the National Assessment of Educational Progress toward a more performance-oriented assessment, as it was when it was launched in the 1950s, with tasks that evaluate students' abilities to solve problems, explain, and defend their ideas. The new Elementary and Secondary Education Act should provide incentives and funding for states to refine their state assessments and introduce related, high-quality, locally administered performance assessments than evaluate critical thinking and applied skills. It should also support states in making such assessments reliable, valid, and practically feasible through teacher professional development and scorer training and moderation systems.

• **Ensure more appropriate assessment for special education students and English language learners** by underwriting efforts to develop, validate, and disseminate more appropriate assessments in the content areas for these students, and by ensuring that the law and regulations encourage assessments based on professional testing standards for these groups. This would include helping develop and requiring the use of tests that are language-accessible for English language learners and appropriate for special education students, and evaluating their gains at all points along the achievement continuum.

A new set of measures is also essential for evaluating school progress. Currently, NCLB requires states to show 100% of students reaching "proficiency" by 2014, setting separate targets every year for subgroups defined by race, ethnicity, socioeconomic status, language background, and special education status and labeling schools that meet any single target as failing to make AYP. It is impossible with the current metrics to distinguish, for example, between a school that shows little gain for its students on any of the tests and one that shows substantial gains for all groups but had a 94% testing participation rate on one test in one subject area, rather than the required 95%.

Furthermore, under current rules, all schools that serve English language learners will eventually be declared failing, because a Catch-22 provision in the law requires reaching 100% proficiency for this group but removes students from the subgroup after they become proficient, making the target impossible to meet. Schools that serve a steady stream of new immigrants who are non-native English speakers are, by definition, unable to make AYP under the law, no matter how successful they are in helping their students learn English over time. In addition, as we have noted, the focus on increasing test outcomes alone has created incentives for schools to boost scores by keeping or pushing out low-scoring students, especially those with special needs and English language learners. School incentives should recognize the value of keeping students in school as well as improving learning.

To address these problems, Congress should replace the current "status model" for measuring school progress with a Continuous Progress Index that evaluates school progress on an index of measures that includes a range of assessments of student learning along with school progression and graduation rates. Such an index would evaluate students' growth over time, across the entire achievement continuum, thus focusing attention on progress in all students' learning, not just on those who fall at the so-called "proficiency bubble." This would recognize schools' gains with students who score well below and above a single cut score and encourage more appropriate inclusion of special education students and English language learners. The index could accommodate state and local assessments of student learning that capture more complex inquiry and problem-solving skills. It could also include assessments of subject areas beyond reading and mathematics—such as writing, science, and history—which are important in their own right and essential to develop students' knowledge and literacy skills as they are applied in the content areas.

A Continuous Progress Index would give schools a single challenging but realistic growth target to aim for each year for each student group (rather than 30 or 40 separate targets)—one that increases more steeply for groups that are farther behind, so that incentives focus both on raising the bar and closing the achievement gap. It would encourage schools' attention to all students' learning and allow for several kinds of important evidence about progress to be considered in evaluating schools. It would also more clearly identify those that are truly failing, so that states can focus their resources for improvement where they are most needed, using a school quality review process, as described above, to diagnose school needs and to support more productive interventions.

Rather than placing all the onus of reform on the individual school, a revamped Elementary and Secondary Education Act would recognize that many of the sources of problems in failing schools are structural and systemic, rather than idiosyncratic, and that failing public schools in many states are seriously underfunded and grossly understaffed. In some cases, a majority of teachers are untrained and inexperienced, due to short-sighted and unaccountable licensing and hiring practices at the state and district levels. These schools are dumping grounds for the failures of the system. They are allowed to function in this way because they serve powerless minorities and constituencies without clout, and because the system must rob some Peter in order to pay some other Paul. The solution to their problems does not lie within the schools themselves, but with major structural changes within the system as a whole. Such changes will require honesty and courage in facing the educational dirty laundry that has been allowed to accumulate across the country, as well as foresight in adopting policies that seriously address the issues of educational equity, professional accountability, and systemwide restructuring.

References

Ancess, Jacqueline. *Outside/Inside, Inside/Outside: Developing and Implementing the School Quality Review.* New York: National Center for Restructuring Education, Schools, and Teaching, Teachers College, Columbia University, 1996.

Forum on Education and Accountability. "Joint Organizational Statement on 'No Child Left Behind' Act." Submitted to U.S. Congress on Oct. 21, 2004. www.edaccountability.org/Joint_Statement.html.

Rothstein, Richard, Rebecca Jacobsen, and Tamara Wilder. *Grading Education: Getting Accountability Right.* New York: Teachers College Press, 2008.

Sahlberg, Pasi. "Education Policies for Raising Student Learning: The Finnish Approach." *Journal of Education Policy* 22, no. 2 (March 2007): 147–171.

Shulman, Lee S. "Autonomy and Obligation: The Remote Control of Teaching." In *Handbook of Teaching and Policy,* ed. Lee S. Shulman and Gary Sykes. New York: Longman, 1983.

Wilson, Thomas A. *Reaching for a Better Standard: English School Inspection and the Dilemma of Accountability for American Schools.* New York: Teachers College Press, 1995.

POSTNOTE

The author of this essay, Linda Darling-Hammond, is one of the nation's leading educational policy wonks and a key advisor in the power centers of public education. She, like many other reformers, has been disappointed by the implementation of the 2002 No Children Left Behind legislation which was launched with good intentions and high hopes. Like many well-intended reforms, NCLB has had several unintended consequences. The schools were required to regularly test students in math and reading and, therefore, teachers were strongly urged to give special attention to these subjects. Since the NCLB legislation has real teeth enabling financial punishment to schools which failed to achieve adequate test results in these subjects, teachers focused heavily on increasing students' test scores. While some desired changes have occurred, some "undesired" changes have also occurred. One is that many teachers over-focused on raising test scores and took a "drill, baby, drill" instructional approach which dulled students' enthusiasm for learning. Another is that it became common to short-change certain subject matter, such as music, art and history, in order to devote more class time to preparation for the so-called "high stakes tests."

As our book goes to press, the U.S. Congress is debating and redrafting the NCLB legislation. Professor Darling-Hammond's analysis of the inconsistency of NCLB's attention to evaluating students and schools but failing to do the same for the performance of school districts and state systems will undoubtedly influence these deliberations. It is unfair to punish many students and some teachers for poor results, but ignore the actions, performance, and responsibilities of school districts and state departments of education. It is like inspecting the soundness of the lower rungs of a ladder and ignoring the safety of the higher rungs.

Her suggested remedies, while admirable in the ingenuity of their conception and fairness, do raise questions. First, even if the educational research community were able to come up with the extensive evaluative systems called for in her proposals, would we be able to afford the huge expense required? Currently, the country is straining to support the educational *status quo*, and there are many worthy reform proposal waiting in the wings for implementation. Would this proposal be the most "dollar-wise" investment? Second, would the new targets for evaluation and assessment, that is, the school district central administrators and state-level bureaucrats, support and cooperate with these proposals? Would they embrace these new and job-threatening evaluative measures? And when was the last time you heard about a general being court-martialed?

DISCUSSION QUESTIONS

1. What are these standards of practice that the author is advocating?
2. What are the standards for systems and organizational accountability?
3. In what ways could the author's changes in the NCLB legislation improve our schools?

RELATED WEBSITE RESOURCES AND VIDEO CASE

WEB RESOURCES:

Center for Educational Reform. Available at:

http://www.edreform.com/Home/.

This think-tank has been a leader in the school reform effort and regularly addresses the NCLB legislation.

Education Week. Available at:

http://www.edweek.org/ew/index.html.

This newspaper is an outstanding source of information and commentary on school issues, including developments surrounding NCLB.

▶II TEACHSOURCE VIDEO CASE

NO CHILD LEFT BEHIND (NCLB): GOOD INTENTIONS, REAL PROBLEMS

Arne Duncan, U.S. Secretary of Education, Jonathan Kozol, education activist, and a number of others discuss No Child Left Behind. This 2002 landmark education law requires all public schools receiving federal funds to meet certain standards for student achievement and teacher quality. NCLB's criticism includes the lack of funds to support it adequately, lack of national standards (each state determines its own level of "proficiency"), and schools have two years to show improvement of each student subgroup achievement or else the school is labeled "failing." Go to the website for the Education Media Library at CengageBrain.com to watch the video clips, study the artifacts in the case, and reflect on the following questions.

1. What ideas or criticism does this video add to those reported by Professor Darling-Hammond in her article above?

2. Many in this video claim that lack of funds is the cause of NCLB's limited success in improving public schools. Do you agree or disagree? Why?

3. Can we have educational accountability without having unpleasant consequences for poor performance?

46

How to Get the Teachers We Want

Frederick Hess

Frederick M. Hess is director of education policy studies at the American Enterprise Institute and an executive editor of *Education Next*.

"How to Get the Teacher's We Want," *Education Next*, Summer 2009, Vol. 9, No. 3. Reprinted by permission.

FOCUS QUESTION

Are we deploying America's teachers wisely and can we do it better?

KEY TERMS

- 68 percent problem
- Human capital
- Instructional aides
- Modal recruit
- Specialization

"Human capital" is quickly becoming the new site-based management. While few are sure what it means, everyone craves it, has a model to deliver it, and is quick to tout its restorative powers. It's trendy and impressive sounding, but too often settles for recycling familiar nostrums or half-baked ideas in the guise of new jargon.

Our schools are in a constant, unending race to recruit and then retain some 200,000 teachers annually. Given that U.S. colleges issue perhaps 1.4 million four-year diplomas a year, schools are seeking to bring nearly one of seven new graduates into the teaching profession. No wonder shortages are endemic and quality a persistent concern.

It does not have to be this hard. Our massive, three-decade national experiment in class-size reduction has exacerbated the challenge of finding enough effective teachers. There are other options. Researchers Martin West and Ludger Woessmann have pointed out that several nations that perform impressively on international assessments, including South Korea, Hong Kong, and Japan, boast average middle-school class sizes of more than 35 students per teacher.

To improve schooling, the U.S. has adopted the peculiar policy of hiring ever more teachers and asking them each to do the same job in roughly the same way. This dilutes the talent pool while spreading training and salaries over ever more bodies. As Chester Finn wryly observed in *Troublemaker*, the U.S. has opted to "invest in many more teachers rather than abler ones.... No wonder teaching salaries have barely kept pace with inflation, despite escalating education budgets." Since the early 1970s, growth in the teaching force has outstripped growth in student enrollment by 50 percent. In this decade, as states overextended their commitments during the real estate boom, the ranks of teachers grew at nearly twice the rate of student enrollment. If policymakers had maintained the same overall teacher-to-student ratio since the 1970s, we would need 1 million fewer teachers, training could be focused on a smaller and more able population, and average teacher pay would be close to $75,000 per year.

Even without the constraint of limits on class size, trying to retrofit an outdated model of teaching is a fool's errand. Today's teaching profession is the product of a mid-20th-century labor model that relied on a captive pool of female workers, assumed educators were largely interchangeable, and counted on male principals and superintendents to micromanage a female teaching workforce. Preparation programs were geared to train generalists who operated with little recourse to data or technology. Teaching has clung to these industrial rhythms while professional norms and the larger labor market have changed. By the 1970s, however, schools could no longer depend on an influx of talented young women, as those who once would have entered teaching began to take jobs in engineering and law. The likelihood that a new teacher was a woman who ranked in the top 10 percent of her high school cohort fell by 50 percent between 1964 and 2000. Meanwhile, policymakers and educators were slow to tap new pools of talent; it was not until the late 1980s that they started tinkering with alternative licensure and midcareer recruitment. Even then, they did little to reconfigure professional development, compensation, or career opportunities accordingly.

Even "cutting-edge" proposals typically do not challenge established routines, but instead focus on filling that 200,000-a-year quota with talented 22-year-olds who want to teach into the 2040s. Perhaps the most widely discussed critique of teacher preparation of the past decade, the hotly debated 2006 study by the National Center for Policy Analysis, *Educating School Teachers*, simply presumed that teacher recruitment ought to be geared toward new college graduates who would complete beefed-up versions of familiar training programs before being cleared to enter the same old jobs. Absent was any reconsideration of who should be teaching or any inclination to question the design of the enterprise.

There are smarter, better ways to approach the challenge at hand: expand the hiring pool beyond recent college graduates; staff schools in ways that squeeze more value out of talented teachers; and use technology to make it easier for teachers to be highly effective. A 21st-century human-capital strategy for education should step back from the status quo and revisit existing assumptions.

Who Should Teach?

Recruiting new college graduates for teaching positions made sense 40 years ago, when the typical graduate could expect to hold just five jobs in an entire career. Today, graduates may have held four jobs by age 30. This early career transience, coupled with the increasing prevalence of midcareer transitions, makes it impractical at best to try to identify future teachers at age 20, fully train them before they enter the profession, and then expect them to remain in teaching jobs for decades. That is a sure-fire recipe for repelling today's most talented entrants. The composition of the teaching force is changing of its own accord—even in the absence of coherent new strategies to support this shift. In the 1990–91 federal Schools and Staffing Survey, among teachers of grades 9–12, 70 percent had entered the profession by age 25 and just 6 percent had entered after age 35. In the 2003–04 survey, the most recent data available, the number who had entered by age 25 had declined to just over half (56 percent), while 16 percent had started after age 35. Thus, those who entered the teaching profession after the age of 25 made up just one-tenth of 1 percent of all teachers in 1990–91 but 4.1 percent of all teachers in 2003–04.

Highly effective teaching entails not only the application of research-based methods, but also leadership, content knowledge, life experience, organization, commitment, wisdom, enthusiasm, and applied knowledge (including a practical sense of how schooling can be put to use). The median working adult who transfers laterally into teaching has likely enjoyed more opportunities to develop these qualities and skills than has the average new college graduate.

The population of college-educated workers already well into their first or second career, made comfortable by early success and now open to more rewarding, meaningful, and engaging work, appears to be substantial. One can safely estimate this population to be in the millions. A 2008 survey by the Woodrow Wilson National Fellowship Foundation reported that 42 percent of college-educated Americans aged 24 to 60 would consider becoming a teacher, and would be more likely to do so if they could count on quality training and support and expect to start at salaries of $50,000 or more. Those who expressed an interest in teaching as a second career were more academically accomplished than those who were not interested. Given current life spans and career trajectories, it is reasonable to imagine that many 35- or 45-year-old entrants might teach for 20 years or more.

It is entirely plausible that a recruitment strategy that seeks to attract a larger percentage of mature entrants could reduce rates of attrition. In 2002, Anthony Morris, now a Mississippi superintendent, studied 1,895 Mississippi teachers and found that older, second-career teachers were more likely to stay in teaching than younger entrants. The National Center for Education Information has concluded, "Individuals who have entered teaching through alternate routes at older ages are more inclined to stay in teaching for longer than people entering teaching in their early-to-late 20s and 30s."

The evidence at hand recommends abandoning the presumption that new college graduates be the backbone of new teacher recruitment. We should not discourage young entrants or discount the notion that some 22-year-olds are ready to play a valuable role in schools, either for a limited period of time (e.g., the private school or Teach For America model) or by committing to a career of classroom teaching. Such recruits, when promising, should be courted and welcomed. But there are good reasons not to presume that the just-out-of-college-teacher should be the *modal* recruit.

The 68 Percent Problem

Currently, there are approximately 3.3 million K–12 teachers in the United States, representing nearly 10 percent of the college-educated workforce. It should be no great surprise that

some educators are far more skilled than others at teaching reading or mentoring at-risk youth. Yet schools and school systems casually waste scarce talent by operating on the implicit assumption that most teachers will be similarly adept at everything. In a routine day, a terrific 4th-grade reading teacher might give lessons in reading for just one hour, while spending another five hours teaching other subjects in which she is less effective, filling out paperwork, and so on. This is an extravagant waste of talent, especially when there is widespread agreement that reading is an area of high-impact instruction that deserves special emphasis. In fact, general enthusiasm for mainstreaming children with special needs, untracked classrooms, and "differentiated instruction" have increased the breadth of demands placed on a typical teacher. Although about 60 percent of today's K–12 teachers have a master's or specialist's degree, these credentials generally have little impact on work routines or the scope of an individual's responsibilities.

Schools require all teachers to devote time and energy to bureaucratic duties, patrolling hallways and cafeterias, taking attendance, and compiling report cards. The problem here is that school and district officials are conscious of expenses related to salary and materials but fail to account for the opportunity costs of not leveraging the talent already in the schools. Even schools that tout their commitment to professional development and data-driven instruction press teachers to operate as generalists rather than leveraging their particular skills.

Two decades of surveys by the National Center for Education Statistics (NCES) suggest that the typical teacher spends only about 68 percent of classroom time on instruction related to core academic subjects, with the remainder consumed by administrative tasks, fund-raising, assemblies, socialization, and so forth. Provisions for substantial numbers of sick days as well as collective bargaining agreements and management practices that result in the universal imposition of noninstructional responsibilities have all conspired to ensure that schools do not maximize the contributions from the talent they do have.

Rewriting the Job Description

The challenge, in short, is to find ways to "squeeze more juice from the orange" by using support staff, instructional specialization, and technology to ensure that effective educators are devoting more of their time to educating students. There are a number of possible approaches to the problem.

One course of action would entail hiring support staff who have not undergone as much training as teachers and are relatively inexpensive. Assigning administrative and other noninstructional tasks to the support staff would free up teachers to perform the work for which they are best suited. Teachers would be deployed according to their particular talents and focused preparation. Elementary reading instruction, for example, might be recognized as a role distinct from other tasks, with research-based preparation for diagnosing, instructing, and supporting early readers taught in highly specialized training programs. Teaching in remedial math at the secondary level might be another area suited to taking advantage of specific skills and training. Alternatively, rather than continuing to accept the notion that one either is a teacher or is not, schools might embrace hybrid positions to allow talented educators to grow by leveraging their skills in new ways, even as they continue teaching. A district might downsize its central office and invest those dollars in freeing up talented veterans to take on half-time teaching loads, with the other 50 percent of their time devoted to such responsibilities as professional development, curriculum development, or parent outreach. Rather than walling off instruction from these kinds of positions, teachers might be given the chance to grow in the course of their professional life without having to abandon the classroom.

K–12 schooling already employs a large number of school-based personnel who are not teachers; support staff (including aides, librarians, guidance counselors, and so forth) account for about 30 percent of school employees. NCES reports that there are more than 600,000 "instructional aides" in K–12 schools, but the scant evidence available leaves one skeptical that these employees are utilized in a fashion that maximizes teacher effectiveness or alleviates teacher responsibilities. Indeed, the two populations have grown in tandem in recent decades.

Other professions arrange work patterns much differently. In medicine, a century's worth of gains has been reaped by increasing specialization: the American Medical Association now recognizes 199 specialties. Today there are 5 million medical professionals in the U.S., but just 500,000 physicians. The rest are trained practitioners with complementary talents. In a well-run medical practice, surgeons do not spend time filling out patient charts or negotiating with insurance companies; these responsibilities are left to nurses or support staff. Similarly, not even junior attorneys are expected to file their own paperwork, compile their billing reports, or type letters to clients. These tasks are performed by paralegals and secretaries.

Such efforts to fully utilize talent and expertise have been largely absent in schooling, apart from some small-scale initiatives. One innovation worth exploring employs community resources to augment school staff. Boston-based Citizen Schools, for example, provides highly regarded after-school instruction and career-based learning by arranging for local volunteers to work with students on a regular basis. Rather than simply mentoring or tutoring students, participants teach weekly modules that tackle complex projects with interested students. Citizen Schools leverages the expertise of local professionals on a part-time (and cost-free) basis and points to the promise of approaches that do not wholly depend on full-time, career-long staffing. The key is to stop thinking of teaching as an "all-or-nothing" job and to create models that include the support and opportunity for steady part-timers who also have other obligations or complementary jobs. This "consultant" approach could reflect the way other kinds of organizations tap into particular expertise or retain the service of talented professionals despite changing life circumstances.

Another approach would utilize technology for tasks where teachers are able to add limited value. For instance, monitoring student achievement via technology might alleviate the need for teachers to devote substantial time to administering, grading, and entering data generated by formative assessments. One such example is provided by Wireless Generation software, which enables elementary school teachers to use Palm Pilots as tools in assessing and tracking early reading performance. This saves teachers substantial time in the assessment and data-entry process, and makes immediately available a wealth of easily manipulated information on student performance.

Technology can also be used to change the way some education services are delivered. Today's model requires schools with many classrooms, each featuring a teacher working face-to-face with a particular group of students. This "people-everywhere" strategy is expensive and limits the available talent pool, as some potentially effective educators may be unwilling to relocate to the communities where they are needed. Thus far this has not been a challenge for the premier school districts, like those in Westchester (New York), Montgomery (Maryland), or Fairfax (Virginia) counties, or for charter school operators like KIPP (Knowledge Is Power Program) or Uncommon Schools, but it does impose a ceiling on the number of schools and districts that can rely on the people and strategies that drive success in these organizations. In accepting the assumption that each classroom should include a generic "teacher" and as few children as possible, these schools are entirely dependent on their ability to attract talented, high-energy staff, dramatically limiting the likelihood that these admired programs will be able to achieve the hoped-for scale.

Perhaps the most significant impact of education technology is its potential to eliminate obstacles posed by geography. Web-based delivery systems can take advantage of the wealth of highly educated, English-speaking people in nations like India willing to tutor children at relatively inexpensive rates. Washington, D.C.–based SMARTHINKING, Inc., uses American and international tutors to provide intensive instruction to students. Students can log on to the company's web site 24 hours a day, seven days a week, and work in real time with experts in various academic subjects.

When technology is used to deliver instruction or tutoring from a distance, it offers opportunities to create "classrooms" with large numbers of children (as in South Korea or Singapore) and to streamline the "teacher's" role. In either case, the challenge of finding enough high-quality local personnel becomes more manageable. Technology also makes it easier for schools in different locations to communicate or share staff and enables central administrators to deliver support to campuses hundreds of miles away.

Some skeptics have suggested that technology cannot be substituted for and very likely cannot meaningfully augment the work that teachers do. This argument underlies the dismal failure in education to use new technologies, from the television to the PC to the Internet, as labor-saving devices (see "How Do We Transform Our Schools?" *features*, Summer 2008). Schools similarly have foundered under a "supplement, not supplant" mind-set in which there has been fierce resistance to fully utilizing cutting-edge innovations. Too often, discussions about the use of computers, web-based delivery, and instructional software fail to consider what needs to be done in policy, school organization, or within the teaching profession to take full advantage of those tools.

Different Pay for Different Work

Rethinking recruitment assumptions and job descriptions requires new models for salaries and benefits. If the ideal new teacher is a recent college graduate who intends to remain in the profession for decades, there is a logic to relying on seniority to allocate salary and positional perks. If, however, the ideal entrant is someone aged 30 to 55 who has worked for several years in another field and accumulated experience and skills, this paradigm is needlessly constraining. Benefit systems that penalize shorter terms of service are a stumbling block for second-career teachers; comparable salaries and a defined-contribution 401(k)-type retirement plan make a lateral move more attractive.

While the aim should be to create a profession with various roles and specializations, it should not be presumed that differential compensation requires finely graded hierarchies. Even seemingly sophisticated proponents of compensation reform have too often advocated variations on the blunt Pavlovian approach of paying more for higher student test scores while neglecting the broader design of the profession. After all, every teacher under a Denver Public Schools ProComp-style system still enters teaching at roughly the same salary and with roughly the same job description. Every teacher pursues the same bonuses and seeks to climb the same career ladder. This would be akin to a law firm requiring every new J.D. to start as a paralegal and then eventually become a lawyer, or hospitals requiring every new M.D. to begin as a nurse, then become a general practitioner, and eventually a specialist.

Law and medicine have weakened or even severed the link between an employee's formal place in an organizational hierarchy and expected compensation. By allowing pay to reflect perceived value, these fields have fostered norms whereby accomplished attorneys or doctors spend their careers making use of their skills and earn outsized compensation without ever moving into management or administration. That kind of a model in education would permit truly revolutionary approaches to recruiting and retaining quality educators.

In moving away from the familiar pay scale, it's not enough to simply add bonuses atop the existing arrangement. If teachers are tutoring over the web or providing support services, their compensation needs to be reshaped accordingly. Payment might be by the hour, for each student successfully served, or in some other fashion—but it requires systemic redesign that even radical reformers have yet to undertake.

Ultimately, the goal is to rethink the teacher challenges of the 21st century. We are feeling our way toward a new and hopefully more fruitful era of teaching and learning. We have been slowed by habits of mind, culture, and institutional inertia that imagine a future for schools and school districts that embodies today's familiar assumptions. While we should recognize that institutions change slowly and celebrate incremental advances, we should not allow that to obscure the goal: to recruit the most promising talent and then foster a more flexible, rewarding, and performance-focused profession.

POSTNOTE

Teachers are the vital core of our educational system. They are, also, by far the most costly aspect of schooling. Frederick Hess's analysis strongly suggests that we, as a nation, are trapped in narrow ways of thinking about the work of teaching and are using this precious resource foolishly. One of Hess's major points is that, while other professions have made major improvements through specialization, education has kept to a one-fits-all model of the teacher. Most vividly seen in elementary classrooms, the classroom teacher has to be a master of teaching mathematics, language arts, science, and an variety of other subjects. He or she must also be able to teach an array of student abilities from the gifted to the intellectually limited. This, plus maintaining discipline and myriad records, monitoring lunchrooms and playgrounds, keeping close communications with parents and serving on various school-related committees.

As this entire section on school reform demonstrates, there is no end of suggestions for improving American education. The reforms suggested in this article, however, may have a greater possibility of seeing fruition because of one fact: the condition of our economy. All but a handful of our nation's 15,000 school districts are not confronted with huge budget problems. The economic imperatives faced by these school districts may be the catalyst to bring about the wiser use of the talents of America's teaching force.

DISCUSSION QUESTIONS

1. What are the author's key criticisms of the way American schools use our "teaching resources?" Do you agree or disagree?
2. What is the author's point about younger teacher and older teacher candidates?
3. Would you be more comfortable as a classroom "generalist" or "specialist?"

RELATED WEBSITE RESOURCES

WEB RESOURCES:

Center for Teaching Quality. Available at:

http://www.teachingquality.org/.

The CTQ is an advocacy group to improve teaching through research and advocating improved practices.

American Enterprise Institute for Public Policy Research. Available at:

http://www.aei.org/ra/29.

AEI is a leading policy think tank and has long had a concern for educational reform. This site will take you to other articles by Frederick Hess and by AEI scholars dealing with educational policy.

47

Reflections on the Charter School Movement

Thomas Toch

Thomas Toch is executive director of the Association of Independent Schools of Greater Washington and a former guest scholar at the Brookings Institution.

Thomas Toch, "Reflections on the Charter School Movement," *Phi Delta Kappan*, vol. 91, no. 8, May 2010, pp. 70–71 Reprinted with permission of Phi Delta Kappa International, www.pdkintl.org.

Two decades ago, I learned about charter schools while strolling through a Minneapolis suburb with Ted Kolderie, a civic gadfly who was helping local legislators craft a bill that would make Minnesota the first state to permit the hybrid public schools. He wanted to combat the bureaucracy of traditional public school systems, he told me, and to encourage educators to become entrepreneurs. Today, about 4,600 charter schools spread across 39 states and the District of Columbia, educating about 1.5 million students. They've become a permanent part of the education landscape. And now the Obama Administration is making charters a cornerstone of its multi-billion-dollar federal education reform agenda. I've visited maybe 100 charter schools since my walk with Kolderie. Here's some of what I've learned:

Charter schools have brought many talented people to the cause of public school improvement. This new generation of social entrepreneurs includes Ivy League graduates and Rhodes scholars committed to helping the disadvantaged and drawn to public schooling by the independence offered by charter schools.

The charter movement has also attracted bad actors more interested in enriching themselves than students. There are stories of educational failure and financial malfeasance in charter schools just as unscrupulous trade schools fed off the federal financial aid system for many years.

Some contend that the nearly 500 charter school closures between 2004-05 and 2008-09 (about 2,000 charters opened during the same period) are a sign of an effective marketplace, one that rewards winners and punishes losers to a much greater degree than traditional public school systems. But, given the demand in urban centers for alternatives to traditional public schools, the closure of 500 charter schools (which, of course, is a good thing) reflects as much as anything a lack of scrutiny of charter school applications. For much of the past two decades, quantity has been a higher priority than quality in the charter school movement.

FOCUS QUESTION

How effective have charter schools been in reforming public education?

KEY TERMS

- Charter Management Organizations (CMOs)
- Charter school
- Race to the Top

Only recently has the charter community begun to make good on its original pledge of more accountability in return for more autonomy, thanks to the work of people like Greg Richmond, president of the National Association of Charter School Authorizers, who have argued, correctly, that a few bad charter schools are likely to have a much greater influence on the prospects of the charter movement than a lot of good charters. But accountability remains weak in a number of key states, and the charter world remains deeply divided over whether the locus of accountability should rest with consumers or regulators.

Charter schools collectively have hardly been the salvation that many reformers had hoped. Researchers continue to debate the right traditional public school comparison groups. But it's clear there are at least as many bad charters as good ones and that, while a relative handful have produced truly outstanding results, many aren't any better than traditional public schools, and some are worse.

Charter Management Organizations

With over a half billion dollars in foundation funding and the financial expertise of venture-capital-like enterprises such as the San Francisco-based New-Schools Venture Fund, some four dozen nonprofit charter management organizations (CMOs) have set out to build networks of top charter schools. A decade into the experiment, they've managed to open about 350 schools with some 100,000 seats, a far cry from the 5,000 failing public schools that Secretary of Education Arne Duncan hopes to fix or replace. And many of the organizations are struggling financially and academically.

It would be much less difficult for CMOs to open more high-quality and financially sound schools if they received as much public funding as traditional public schools and didn't have to find and pay for their facilities. And it would be easier for them to make their budgets work if they weren't trying to expand.

But the high cost of the typically small schools (they average 300 students), intensive support for schools and students, and other features that have produced the best results have left a number of the organizations financially strapped. The 17 CMOs supported by the NewSchools Venture Fund reported spending an average of 18% of their revenue on their central offices in 2007-08 to make sure their schools got the help they needed to be successful—three times the level of central office spending allowed under the business plans of several of the organizations.

Attracting the talented teachers and principals willing to work the long hours needed to launch new schools in difficult environments has also proven challenging. The 17 CMOs in the New-Schools orbit reported that, in 2007-08, an average of 40% of their teachers had been in teaching two years or less. It's been hard to expand charter schooling outside major urban centers where entrepreneurial young educators want to live and where foundation funding is concentrated. The Charter School Research Project reports that 41% of California's charters are in Los Angeles and 90% of Illinois' charters are in Chicago.

For-Profit Charters

The for-profit wing of the charter school movement hasn't fared significantly better in trying to achieve the reform trifecta of scale, quality, and sustainability. Touted two decades ago as an engine of revolutionary reform, in 2008-09 for-profit management companies that ran more than three schools ran 650 traditional public schools and charter schools enrolling 301,000 out of the nation's 55 million students, the Education Public Interest Center at the University of Colorado-Boulder reports. Two of the companies—K–12 and Connections Academy—educated 50,000 of those students over the Internet.

Charters haven't influenced traditional public schools as much as school reformers had hoped. A few charter schools have demonstrated that disadvantaged students can be taught to sharply higher standards. But charters haven't produced enough competitive pressure on traditional public schools to cause them to embrace ambitious reforms the way the rise of FedEx led the U.S. Postal Service to launch Express Mail and other innovations. In many cities, charter schools have put more competitive pressure on urban Catholic schools than on public school systems, as significant numbers of parochial-school families migrate to tuition-free charter schools.

Some charter advocates have lost faith in the reform strategy. Much has been made of historian Diane Ravitch's break with charters and other market-based reforms in her new book, *The Death and Life of the Great American School System: How Testing and Choice Are Undermining Education* (Basic Books, 2010). But no less significant is the conclusion by prominent conservative policy analyst Chester Finn that "charter schools are uneven at best."

Still, the original insight shared by Kolderie and other originators of the charter school concept is sound: The entrepreneurial ethic created by the independence that charter schools have over staffing, budgets, and instruction can be a powerful catalyst of school improvement. Successful schools as different as Deborah Meier's Central Park East Secondary School and those in the KIPP network have demonstrated the potential of such independence. We can't build the high-performing education system our economy demands on the bureaucratic foundations of traditional public schooling.

But the many troubles in the charter school movement also suggest that we cannot leave charter school quality to the market. Libertarian-leaning charter school advocates are wrong when they say that parents voting with their feet are sufficient to ensure that charter schools do right by students and taxpayers. And it's not enough to argue, as some advocates do, that charter schools need only be as good as the public schools they replace. How does that help students?

In the long run, the goal should be to introduce into traditional school systems the autonomy that charter schools enjoy today, a step that New York City is taking. But in the short term, opening fewer but stronger charter schools would be the best way to convince policy makers and the public of the potential of charter schools to help improve public schooling. Secretary of Education Arne Duncan has pressed states during the evolution of the federal Race to the Top school reform competition to lift caps on the number of new charter schools they permit. Perhaps, given the charter school movement's performance over the years, that shouldn't be his highest priority.

POSTNOTE

Since it first came into being in the 1990s, the charter school movement has exploded in terms of growth. It has become one of the primary tools in educational reform. While some advocates tout charter schools as the best answer to reform public education in the United States, Thomas Toch states that charter schools have not been the salvation that many reformers had hoped. They often suffer from being under resourced, having poor accountability, and producing academic achievement not much different than traditional public schools. There are a number of highly successful charter schools, such as the KIPP academies and Chicago's Urban Prep Academy, which garner great publicity, but most charter schools don't outperform their traditional school counterparts. In spite of this fact, many charter school are fully subscribed and attract long waiting lists of students who want to attend.

A powerful factor that favors charter schools is parents' right to choose the school their children attend. Getting to choose one's school usually produces an allegiance and commitment to the school that neighborhood schools often lack. The charter schools can also lay down conditions that parents and students must meet to continue being enrolled, which traditional schools cannot enforce. So, in spite of so-so overall results, expect charter schools to continue to grow in demand and in numbers.

DISCUSSION QUESTIONS

1. Do you generally support the charter school movement? Why or why not?

2. Should teachers in charter schools be required to meet the same licensure requirements as teachers in traditional public schools? Support your position.

3. What conditions should state departments of education place upon charter schools to ensure quality control and accountability?

RELATED WEBSITE RESOURCE

WEB RESOURCE:

US Charter Schools. Available at:

http://www.uscharterschools.org/pub/uscs_docs/o/index.htm.

This web site promotes the charter school movement, and provides information about charter schools.

 The companion website for this text includes useful study tools and resources. Go to CengageBrain.com to access links to relevant websites, glossaries, flashcards, an article review form, and more.

Diversity and Social Issues

The United States is a nation of great diversity—in races, cultures, religions, languages, and lifestyles. Although these forms of diversity are part of what makes the United States strong, they nevertheless create challenges. The major challenge is how to recognize and respect these forms of diversity while still maintaining a common culture to which each subgroup can feel welcomed and valued. Early in the twentieth century, American schools tried to create a "melting pot," where group differences were boiled away so that only "Americans" survived. Today, the notion of cultural pluralism has replaced the assimilationist perspective, with the metaphor of a "mosaic" or "quilt" replacing that of the melting pot.

The readings in this section of the book address diversity issues such as multicultural education, immigration and languages, gender issues, and inclusion of children with disabilities. Some of these topics are controversial. The viewpoints of both strong proponents and opponents of the various positions are articulated in the articles. As you read the selections, try to sort out your own positions on the issues.

48

Whose Problem Is Poverty?

Richard Rothstein

Richard Rothstein is research associate at the Economic Policy Institute. From 1999 to 2002 he was the national education columnist of the *New York Times*. He is the author of *Grading Education: Getting Accountability Right*, and *Class and Schools: Using Social, Economic* and *Educational Reform to Close the Black-White Achievement Gap*.

Richard Rothstein, "Whose Problem Is Poverty?" *Educational Leadership*, v. 65, no. 7, April 2008, pp. 8–13. Reprinted by permission of the author.

FOCUS QUESTION

What effect does poverty have on school achievement?

InTASC
Standards 1, 9, and 10

KEY TERM

- National Assessment of Educational Progress

In my work, I've repeatedly stressed this logical claim: If you send two groups of students to equally high-quality schools, the group with greater socioeconomic disadvantage will necessarily have lower *average* achievement than the more fortunate group.[1]

Why is this so? Because low-income children often have no health insurance and therefore no routine preventive medical and dental care, leading to more school absences as a result of illness. Children in low-income families are more prone to asthma, resulting in more sleeplessness, irritability, and lack of exercise. They experience lower birth weight as well as more lead poisoning and iron-deficiency anemia, each of which leads to diminished cognitive ability and more behavior problems. Their families frequently fall behind in rent and move, so children switch schools more often, losing continuity of instruction.

Poor children are, in general, not read to aloud as often or exposed to complex language and large vocabularies. Their parents have low-wage jobs and are more frequently laid off, causing family stress and more arbitrary discipline. The neighborhoods through which these children walk to school and in which they play have more crime and drugs and fewer adult role models with professional careers. Such children are more often in single-parent families and so get less adult attention. They have fewer cross-country trips, visits to museums and zoos, music or dance lessons, and organized sports leagues to develop their ambition, cultural awareness, and self-confidence.

Each of these disadvantages makes only a small contribution to the achievement gap, but cumulatively, they explain a lot.

I've also noted that no matter how serious their problems, all disadvantaged students can expect to have higher achievement in better schools than in worse ones. And even in the same schools, natural human variability ensures a distribution of achievement in every group. Some high-achieving disadvantaged students always outperform typical middle class students, and some low-achieving middle class students fall behind typical disadvantaged students.

The achievement gap is a difference in the *average* achievement of students from disadvantaged and middle class families.

I've drawn a policy conclusion from these observations: Closing or substantially narrowing achievement gaps requires combining school improvement with reforms that narrow the vast socioeconomic inequalities in the United States. Without such a combination, demands (like those of No Child Left Behind) that schools fully close achievement gaps not only will remain unfulfilled, but also will cause us to foolishly and unfairly condemn our schools and teachers.

Distorting Disadvantage

Most educators understand how socioeconomic disadvantage lowers average achievement. However, some have resisted this logic, throwing up a variety of defenses. Some find in my explanations the implication that disadvantaged children have a genetic disability, that poor and minority children can't learn. They say that a perspective that highlights the socioeconomic causes of low achievement "blames the victim" and legitimizes racism. Some find my analysis dangerous because it "makes excuses" for poor instruction or because demands for social and economic reform "let schools off the hook" for raising student achievement. And others say it's too difficult to address nonschool problems like inadequate incomes, health, or housing, so we should only work on school reform. The way some of these critics see it, those of us who call attention to such nonschool issues must want to wait until utopian economic change (or "socialism") becomes a reality before we begin to improve schools.

Some critics cite schools that enroll disadvantaged students but still get high standardized test scores as proof that greater socioeconomic equality is not essential for closing achievement gaps— because good schools have shown they can do it on their own. And some critics are so single-mindedly committed to a schools-only approach that they can't believe anyone could seriously

advocate pursuing *both* school and socioeconomic improvement simultaneously.

Seeing Through "No Excuses"

The commonplace "no excuses" ideology implies that educators—were they to realize that their efforts alone were insufficient to raise student achievement— would be too simple-minded then to bring themselves to exert their full effort. The ideology presumes that policymakers with an Olympian perspective can trick teachers into performing at a higher level by making them believe that unrealistically high degrees of success are within reach.

There's a lack of moral, political, and intellectual integrity in this suppression of awareness of how social and economic disadvantage lowers achievement. Our first obligation should be to analyze social problems accurately; only then can we design effective solutions. Presenting a deliberately flawed version of reality, fearing that the truth will lead to excuses, is not only corrupt but also self-defeating.

Mythology cannot, in the long run, inspire better instruction. Teachers see for themselves how poor health or family economic stress impedes students' learning. Teachers may nowadays be intimidated from acknowledging these realities aloud and may, in groupthink obedience, repeat the mantra that "all children can learn." But nobody is fooled. Teachers still know that although all children can learn, some learn less well because of poorer health or less-secure homes. Suppressing such truths leads only to teacher cynicism and disillusion. Talented teachers abandon the profession, willing to shoulder responsibility for their own instructional competence but not for failures beyond their control.

Mythology also prevents educators from properly diagnosing educational failure where it exists. If we expect all disadvantaged students to succeed at levels typical of affluent students, then even the best inner-city teachers seem like failures. If we pretend that achievement gaps are entirely within teachers' control, with claims to the contrary only "excuses," how can we distinguish better from worse classroom practice?

Who's Getting Off the Hook?

Promoters of the myth that schools alone can overcome social and economic causes of low achievement assert that claims to the contrary let schools "off the hook." But their myth itself lets political and corporate officials off a hook. We absolve these leaders from responsibility for narrowing the pervasive inequalities of American society by asserting that good schools alone can overcome these inequalities. Forget about health care gaps, racial segregation, inadequate housing, or income insecurity. If, after successful school reform, all adolescents regardless of background could leave high school fully prepared to earn middle class incomes, there would, indeed, be little reason for concern about contemporary inequality. Opportunities of children from all races and ethnic groups, and of rich and poor, would equalize in the next generation solely as a result of improved schooling. This absurd conclusion follows from the "no excuses" approach.

Some critics urge that educators should not acknowledge socioeconomic disadvantage because their unique responsibility is to improve classroom practices, which they *can* control. According to such reasoning, we should leave to health, housing, and labor experts the challenge of worrying about inequalities in their respective fields. Yet we are all citizens in this democracy, and educators have a special and unique insight into the damage that deprivation does to children's learning potential.

If educators who face this unfortunate state of affairs daily don't speak up about it, who will? Educators and their professional organizations should insist to every politician who will listen (and to those who will not) that social and economic reforms are needed to create an environment in which the most effective teaching can take place.

And yes, we should also call on housing, health, and antipoverty advocates to take a broader view that integrates school improvement into their advocacy of greater economic and social equality. Instead, however, critical voices for reform have been silenced, told they should stick to their knitting, fearing an accusation that denouncing inequality is tantamount to "making excuses."

What We Can Do

It's a canard that educators advocating socioeconomic reforms wish to postpone school improvement until we have created an impractical economic utopia. Another canard is the idea that it's impractical to narrow socioeconomic inequalities, so school reform is the only reasonable lever. Modest social and economic reforms, well within our political reach, could have a palpable effect on student achievement. For example, we could

- Ensure good pediatric and dental care for all students, in school-based clinics.
- Expand existing low-income housing subsidy programs to reduce families' involuntary mobility.
- Provide higher-quality early childhood care so that low-income children are not parked before televisions while their parents are working.
- Increase the earned income tax credit, the minimum wage, and collective bargaining rights so that families of low-wage workers are less stressed.
- Promote mixed-income housing development in suburbs and in gentrifying cities to give more low-income students the benefits of integrated educations in neighborhood schools.
- Fund after-school programs so that inner-city children spend fewer nonschool hours in dangerous environments and, instead, develop their cultural, artistic, organizational, and athletic potential.

None of this is utopian. All is worth doing in itself, with the added benefit of sending children to school more ready to learn. Educators who are unafraid to advocate such policies will finally call the hand of those politicians and business leaders who claim that universal health care is too expensive but simultaneously demand school reform so they can posture as defenders of minority children.

In some schools, disadvantaged students are effectively tracked by race, denied the most qualified teachers and the best curriculum. Failure is both expected and accepted. Unfortunately, some educators do use socioeconomic disadvantage as an excuse for failing to teach well under adverse conditions. But we exaggerate the frequency of this excuse. Some teachers excuse poor practice, but others work terribly hard to develop disadvantaged students' talents. Where incompetence does exist, we should insist that school administrators root it out.

But consider this: The National Assessment of Educational Progress (NAEP), administered to a national student sample by the federal government, is generally considered the most reliable measure of U.S. students' achievement. Since 1990, the achievement gap between minority and white students has barely changed, feeding accusations that educators simply ignore the needs of minority youth. Yet average math scores of black 4th graders in 2007 were higher than those of white 4th graders in 1990 (National Center for Education Statistics, 2007, p. 10). If white achievement had been stagnant, the gap would have fully closed. There were also big math gains for black 8th graders (National Center for Education Statistics, 2007, p. 26). The gap stagnated only because white students also gained.

In reading, scores have remained flat. Perhaps this is because math achievement is a more direct result of school instruction, whereas reading ability also reflects students' home literacy environment. Nonetheless, the dramatic gains in math do not suggest that most teachers of disadvantaged students are sitting around making excuses for failing to teach. Quite the contrary.

Reticent About Race

It is puzzling that some find racism implied in explanations of why disadvantaged students typically achieve at lower levels. But to understand that children who've been up at night, wheezing from untreated asthma, will be less attentive in

school is not to blame those children for their lower scores. It is to explain that we can enhance those students' capacity to learn with policies that reduce the epidemic incidence of asthma in low-income communities—by enforcing prohibitions on the use of high-sulfur heating oil, for example, or requiring urban buses to substitute natural gas for diesel fuel—or provide pediatric care, including treatment for asthma symptoms. Denying the impact of poor health on learning leads to blaming teachers for circumstances completely beyond their control.

The fact that such conditions affect blacks more than whites reflects racism in the United States. Calling attention to such conditions is not racist. But ignoring them, insisting that they have no effect if teaching is competent, may be.

Some critics lump my analyses of social and economic obstacles with others' claims that "black culture" explains low achievement. Like other overly simplistic explanations of academic failure, cultural explanations can easily be exaggerated. There is, indeed, an apparent black-white test-score gap, even when allegedly poor black and white students are compared with one another or even when middle class black and white students are compared with one another. But these deceptively large gaps mostly stem from too-broad definitions of "poor" and "middle class." Typically, low-income white students are compared with blacks who are much poorer, and middle class black students are compared with whites who are much more affluent. If we restricted comparisons to socioeconomically similar students, the residual test-score gap would mostly disappear (see Phillips, Crouse, & Ralph, 1998).

But probably not all of it. Responsible reformers are seeking to help low-income black parents improve childrearing practices. Others attempt to reduce the influence of gang role models on black adolescents or to raise the status of academic success in black communities. Generally, these reformers are black; white experts avoid such discussions, fearing accusations of racism.

This is too bad. If we're afraid to discuss openly the small contribution that cultural factors make to achievement gaps, we suggest, falsely, that we're hiding something much bigger.

Dancing Around the Issue

I am often asked to respond to claims that some schools with disadvantaged students have higher achievement, allegedly proving that schools alone *can* close achievement gaps. Certainly, some schools are superior and should be imitated. But no schools serving disadvantaged students have demonstrated consistent and sustained improvement that closes— not just narrows—achievement gaps. Claims to the contrary are often fraudulent, sometimes based on low-income schools whose parents are unusually well educated; whose admissions policies accept only the most talented disadvantaged students; or whose students, although eligible for subsidized lunches, come from stable working-class and not poor communities.

Some claims are based on schools that concentrate on passing standardized basic skills tests to the exclusion of teaching critical thinking, reasoning, the arts, social studies, or science, or of teaching the "whole child," as middle class schools are more wont to do. Increasingly, such claims are based on high proportions of students scoring above state proficiency standards, defined at a low level. Certainly, if we define proficiency down, we can more easily reduce achievement gaps without addressing social or economic inequality. But responsible analysts have always defined closing the achievement gap as achieving similar score distributions and average scale scores among subgroups. Even No Child Left Behind proclaims a goal of proficiency at "challenging" levels for each subgroup. Only achieving such goals will lead to more equal opportunity for all students in the United States.

Beyond Either/Or

Nobody should be forced to choose between advocating for better schools or speaking out for greater social and economic equality. Both are essential. Each depends on the other. Educators cannot be effective if they make excuses for poor student performance. But they will have little chance for success unless they also join with advocates of social and economic reform to improve the conditions from which children come to school.

References

National Center for Education Statistics. (2007). *The nation's report card: Mathematics 2007*. Washington, DC: Author. Available: http://nces.ed.gov/nationsreportcard/pdf/main2007/2007494.pdf

Phillips, M., Crouse, J., & Ralph, J. (1998). Does the black-white test score gap widen after children enter school? In C. Jencks & M. Phillips (Eds.), *The black-white test score gap* (pp. 229–272). Washington, DC: Brookings Institution Press.

Note

1. For further discussion of this issue, see my book *Class and Schools: Using Social, Economic, and Educational Reform to Close the Black-White Achievement Gap* (Economic Policy Institute, 2004) and "The Achievement Gap: A Broader Picture" (*Educational Leadership*, November 2004).

   Author's note: For documentation of the specific critiques referenced in this article, readers can contact me at riroth@epi.org.

POSTNOTE

In 1966 the U.S. government published a controversial study, *Equality of Educational Opportunity*, usually referred to as the Coleman Report, in honor of the lead researcher and author, James Coleman. One of the main findings of the report was that the family background of a student (socioeconomic status) was a stronger predictor of a student's educational achievement than what went on in schools. Children from more privileged families achieved at higher rates than children from less privileged homes.

Richard Rothstein reminds us in this article that if we as a nation want to increase academic achievement among our K–12 students, we must find a way to address the issues of poverty that so strongly affect academic achievement among the poor. We cannot just focus on improving education—standards, assessment, and financing—without also addressing the negative effects of poverty—poor health care, crime, low birth rate, and parental education levels. Unless we attack these poverty issues, we are not going to achieve the educational outcomes that we seek.

DISCUSSION QUESTIONS

1. Restate in your own words the relationship between the social and economic disadvantages of poor children and the achievement gap.
2. What do you believe are the key reasons that we have been unable to achieve greater social and economic equality?
3. In your opinion, what ought to be done to promote greater social and economic equality?

RELATED WEBSITE RESOURCES AND VIDEO CASE

WEB RESOURCES:

The Children's Defense Fund. Available at:

http://www.childrensdefense.org.

The Children's Defense Fund champions policies and programs that lift children out of poverty; protect them from abuse and neglect; and ensure their access to health care, quality education, and a moral and spiritual foundation.

The Annie E. Casey Foundation. Available at:

http://www.aecf.org.

The primary mission of the Foundation is to foster public policies, human-service reforms, and community supports that more effectively meet the needs of today's vulnerable children and families.

▶️ TEACHSOURCE VIDEO CASE

PARENTAL INVOLVEMENT IN SCHOOL CULTURE

In this video case you will see how literacy specialist Linda Schwertz engages parents in a book-publishing venture. Go to the website for the Education Media Library at CengageBrain.com to watch the video clips, study the artifacts in the case, and reflect on the following questions.

1. What ways can you think of to engage parents in their children's school? What ways are demonstrated in this video case?
2. What are the major obstacles that prevent parents from being involved in their children's school, and how can those obstacles be overcome?

A Considered Opinion: Diversity, Tragedy, and the Schools

Diane Ravitch

Diane Ravitch is a historian of education, an educational policy analyst, and former United States Assistant Secretary of Education. She is a nonresident senior fellow in the Brookings Governmental Studies program and a research professor at New York University's Steinhardt School of Education.

A Considered Opinion: Diversity, Tragedy, and the Schools, by Diane Ravitch. Reprinted by permission of author.

FOCUS QUESTION

What is the appropriate balance between teaching an American culture, on the one hand, and teaching about the contributions of various ethnic and racial minorities, on the other hand? Is it an either-or situation?

InTASC
Standards 2 and 5

KEY TERMS

- Assimilation
- Melting pot
- Multicultural education

As U.S. immigration has surged over the past quarter-century, educators have been developing a new response to demographic diversity in the classroom. The public schools have turned away from their traditional emphasis on assimilating newcomers into the national "melting pot." Instead, they have put a new emphasis on multicultural education, deemphasizing the common American culture and teaching children to take pride in their racial, ethnic, and national origins. In the wake of the terrorist attacks on New York City and Washington last September 11, however, the tide may be turning away from multiculturalism. Americans' remarkable display of national unity in the aftermath of the attacks could change the climate in the nation's schools as much as it has the political climate in Washington.

Immigration is central to the American experience. Though it is on the rise today, immigration is proportionately smaller now than it was in the first three decades of the 20th century. The census of 2000 found that about 10 percent of the population was foreign-born. In the censuses of 1900, 1910, and 1920, that share was some 14 percent. (Then as now, the nation's black population was about 12 percent.) In those early years of the last century, American society was not certain of its ability to absorb millions of newcomers. The public schools took on the job of educating and preparing them for social, civic, and economic participation in the life of the nation.

What did the public schools in those early years do about their new clientele? First, they taught them to speak, read, and write English—a vital necessity for a successful transition into American society. Because many children served as translators for their parents, these skills were valuable to the entire family in negotiating with employers, shops, and government agencies. The schools also taught habits of good hygiene (a matter of public health), as well as appropriate self-discipline and behavior. More than the three "Rs," schools taught children how to speak correctly, how to behave in a group, how to meet deadlines, and how to dress for different situations (skills needed as much by native-born rural youth as by immigrant children). Certainly, the schools taught foreign-born children about American history (especially about national holidays, the Constitution, the Revolutionary War, and the Civil War), with a strong emphasis on the positive aspects of the American drama.

They also taught children about the "American way of life," the habits, ideals, values, and attitudes (such as the American spirit of individualism) that made their new country special. If one could sum up this education policy, it was one that celebrated America and invited newcomers to become full members of American society.

During the late 1960s and early 1970s, assimilation came to be viewed as an illegitimate, coercive imposition of American ways on unwitting children, both foreign-born and nonwhite. With the rise of the black separatist movement in 1966, black nationalists such as Stokely Carmichael began inveighing against racial integration and advocating community control of public schools in black neighborhoods. In response, many black educators demanded African-American history, African-American heroes, African-American literature, and African-American celebrations in the public schools. In the 1970s, the white ethnic revival followed the black model, and soon government was funding celebrations of ethnic heritage in the schools. By the mid-1970s, just as immigration was beginning to increase rapidly, the public schools no longer focused on acculturating the children of newcomers to American society. Instead, they encouraged children to appreciate and retain their ethnic and racial origins.

The expectation that the public schools will teach children about their racial and ethnic heritage has created enormous practical problems. First, it has promoted the belief that what is taught in school will vary in response to the particular ethnic makeup of the school. Thus, a predominantly African-American school will learn one set of lessons, while a predominantly Hispanic school will learn yet another, and an ethnically mixed school will learn—what? Second,

schools have begun to lose a sense of a distinctive American culture, a culture forged by people from many different backgrounds that is nonetheless a coherent national culture. No state in the nation requires students to read any particular book, poem, or play. Today schools are uncertain about how to teach American history, what to teach as "American" literature, and how to teach world history without omitting any corner of the world (many children learn no world history). Third, the teaching of racial and ethnic pride is itself problematic, as it appears to be a continuation in a new guise of one of the worst aspects of American history.

From our public schools' experiences over the past century, we have learned much about the relative advantages and disadvantages of assimilationism and multiculturalism in the public schools.

Assimilation surely has its strengths. A democratic society must seek to give every young person, whether native-born or newcomer, the knowledge and skills to succeed as an adult. In a political system that relies on the participation of informed citizens, everyone should, at a minimum, learn to speak, read, and write a common language. Those who would sustain our democratic life must understand its history. To maximize their ability to succeed in the future, young people must also learn mathematics and science. Tailoring children's education to the color of their skin, their national origins, or their presumed ethnicity is in some fundamental sense contrary to our nation's founding ideals of democracy, equality, and opportunity.

And yet we know that assimilationism by itself is an inadequate strategy for American public education, for two reasons. First, it ignores the strengths that immigrants have to offer; and second, it presumes that American culture is static, which is surely not true. When immigrants arrive in America, they tend to bring with them, often after an emotionally costly journey, a sense of optimism, a strong family and religious tradition, and a willingness to work hard—values and attitudes that our society respects, but that affluence and media cynicism have eroded among many of our own citizens.

But neither is "celebrating diversity" an adequate strategy for a multiracial, multi-ethnic society like ours. The public schools exist to build an American community, to help both newcomers and native-born children prepare for adulthood as fellow citizens. Strategies that divide children along racial and ethnic lines encourage resentment and alienation rather than mutual respect. The ultimate democratic lesson is human equality, and the schools must teach our children that we are all in the same boat, all members of one society, regardless of race, ethnicity, or place of origin.

We learned that lesson the hardest way possible on September 11, when thousands of people from many countries died together in a single tragedy.

How will America's schools respond in the days ahead? It seems clear that they must make a pact with the children in their care. They must honor the strong and positive values that the children's families bring to America, and in return

they must be prepared to give the children access to the best of America's heritage.

America's newcomers did not come to our shores merely to become consumers. They came to share in our democratic heritage and to become possessors of the grand ideas that created and sustained the democratic experiment in this country for more than two centuries. They too have a contribution to make to the evolving story of our nation. Whether they do so will depend in large part on whether our educational system respects them enough to help them become Americans.

The terrible events of this past fall have shown that Americans of all races and ethnic groups share a tremendous sense of national spirit and civic unity. They recognize that, whatever their origins, they share a common destiny as Americans. America's schools should honor that reality.

POSTNOTE

Diane Ravitch is one of the leading educational thinkers in the United States. Her training as a historian makes her a keen observer of educational trends and an advocate of strengthening student learning in core content subjects. As such, her article is one of our Classic picks.

The tensions Ravitch discusses, between multiculturalism and monoculturalism, between diversity and acculturation, are old and deep in the American schools. Emphasis has shifted back and forth toward one or the other extreme over the years, depending on historical events and, often, the energies of advocates. Currently, because of a huge influx of immigrants into the United States during the 1990s, and fueled by the 9/11 attacks on our country, the emphasis is shifting toward acculturation and a rebirth of patriotism. Nevertheless, this strikes us as

an unnecessary distinction. Our national motto is "E pluribus unum," from the many comes the one. A good school can honor the varied backgrounds of its students and at the same time teach all the requirements and expectations of good citizens. To do less is to miseducate.

DISCUSSION QUESTIONS

1. How was multiculturalism taught or exhibited in your schooling, and how did students respond to the school's efforts?

2. Have you seen a change in emphasis on either multiculturalism or national acculturation since 9/11?

3. What ideas do you have for dealing with these issues in your classroom?

50

Diversity Within Unity: Essential Principles for Teaching and Learning in a Multicultural Society

James A. Banks, Peter Cookson, Geneva Gay, Willis D. Hawley, Jacqueline Jordan Irvine, Sonia Nieto, Janet Ward Schofield, and Walter G. Stephan

James A. Banks is the Kerry and Linda Killinger Endowed Chair in Diversity Studies and director of the Center for Multicultural Education, University of Washington. **Peter Cookson** is an instructor at Teachers College, Columbia University. **Geneva Gay** is a professor of education and faculty associate at the Center for Multicultural Education, University of Washington. **Willis D. Hawley** is a professor of education and public affairs, University of Maryland. **Jacqueline Jordan Irvine** is the Charles Howard Candler Professor of Urban Education, Emory University. **Sonia Nieto** is a professor of language, literacy, and culture, University of Massachusetts, Amherst. **Janet Ward Schofield** is a professor of psychology and a senior scientist at the Learning Research and Development Center, University of Pittsburgh. **Walter G. Stephan** is professor emeritus of psychology, New Mexico State University.

"Diversity Within Unity: Essential Principles for Teaching and Learning in a Multicultural Society," by James A. Banks, Peter Cookson, Geneva Gay, Willis D. Hawley, Jacqueline Jordan Irvine, Sonia Nieto, Janet Ward Schofield, and Walter G. Stephan, *Phi Delta Kappan 83*, no. 3 (November 2001), pp. 196–203. Reprinted with permission of Phi Delta Kappa International, www.pdkintl.org. All rights reserved.

What do we know about education and diversity, and how do we know it? This two-part question guided the work of the Multicultural Education Consensus Panel, sponsored by the Center for Multicultural Education at the University of Washington and the Common Destiny Alliance at the University of Maryland. This article is the product of a four-year project during which the panel, with support from the Carnegie Corporation of New York, reviewed and synthesized the research related to diversity.

The panel members are an interdisciplinary group consisting of two psychologists, a political scientist, a sociologist, and four specialists in multicultural education. The panel was modeled after the consensus panels that develop and write reports for the National Academy of Sciences. In such panels, an expert group studies research and practice and arrives at a conclusion about what is known about a particular problem and the most effective actions that can be taken to solve it.

The findings of the Multicultural Education Consensus Panel, which we call *essential principles* in this article, describe ways in which education policy and practice related to diversity can be improved. These principles are derived from both research and practice. They are designed to help practitioners in all types of schools increase student academic achievement and improve intergroup skills. Another aim is to help schools successfully meet the challenges of and benefit from the diversity that characterizes the United States.

FOCUS QUESTION

What do we know about education and diversity, and how do we know it?

InTASC

Standards 1, 2, 3, 5, 6, 7, 8, 9, and 10

KEY TERMS

- Achievement gap
- Conflict resolution
- Culturally responsive teaching
- Formative assessment
- Multicultural education
- Summative assessment

Schools can make a significant difference in the lives of students, and they are a key to maintaining a free and democratic society. Democratic societies are fragile and are works in progress. Their existence depends on a thoughtful citizenry that believes in democratic ideals and is willing and able to participate in the civic life of the nation. We realize that the public schools are experiencing a great deal of criticism. However, we believe that they are essential to ensuring the survival of our democracy.

We have organized the 12 essential principles into five categories: 1) teacher learning; 2) student learning; 3) intergroup relations; 4) school governance, organization, and equity; and 5) assessment. Although these categories overlap to some extent, we think readers will find this organization helpful.

Teacher Learning

Principle 1. Professional development programs should help teachers understand the complex characteristics of ethnic groups within U.S. society and the ways in which race, ethnicity, language, and social class interact to influence student behavior. Continuing education about diversity is especially important for teachers because of the increasing cultural and ethnic gap that exists between the nation's teachers and students. Effective professional development programs should help educators to 1) uncover and identify their personal attitudes toward racial, ethnic, language, and cultural groups; 2) acquire knowledge about the histories and cultures of the diverse racial, ethnic, cultural, and language groups within the nation and within their schools; 3) become acquainted with the diverse perspectives that exist within different ethnic and cultural communities; 4) understand the ways in which institutionalized knowledge within schools, universities, and the popular culture can perpetuate stereotypes about racial and ethnic groups; and 5) acquire the knowledge and skills needed to develop and implement an equity pedagogy, defined by James Banks as instruction that provides all students with an equal opportunity to attain academic and social success in school.[1]

Professional development programs should help teachers understand the complex characteristics of ethnic groups and how such variables as social class, religion, region, generation, extent of urbanization, and gender strongly influence ethnic and cultural behavior. These variables influence the behavior of groups both singly and interactively. Indeed, social class is one of the most important variables that mediate and influence behavior. In his widely discussed book, *The Declining Significance of Race,* William Julius Wilson argues that class is becoming increasingly important in the lives of African Americans.[2] The increasing significance of class rather than the declining significance of race might be a more accurate description of the phenomenon that Wilson describes. Racism continues to affect African Americans of every social class, but it does so in complex ways that to some extent—though by no means always—reflect social-class status.

If teachers are to increase learning opportunities for all students, they must be knowledgeable about the social and cultural contexts of teaching and learning. Although students are not solely products of their cultures and vary in the degree to which they identify with them, there are some distinctive cultural behaviors that are associated with ethnic groups.[3] Thus teachers should become knowledgeable about the cultural backgrounds of their students. They should also acquire the skills needed to translate that knowledge into effective instruction and an enriched curriculum.[4] Teaching should be culturally responsive to students from diverse racial, ethnic, cultural, and language groups.

Making teaching culturally responsive involves strategies such as constructing and designing relevant cultural metaphors and multicultural representations to help bridge the gap between what students already know and appreciate and what they are to be taught. Culturally responsive instructional strategies transform information about the home and community into effective classroom practice. Rather than rely on generalized notions of ethnic groups that can be misleading, effective teachers use knowledge of their students' culture and ethnicity as a framework for inquiry. They also use culturally responsive activities, resources, and strategies to organize and implement instruction.

Student Learning

Principle 2. Schools should ensure that all students have equitable opportunities to learn and to meet high standards. Schools can be thought of as collections of opportunities to learn.[5] A good school maximizes the learning experiences of its students. One might judge the fairness of educational opportunity by comparing the learning opportunities students have within and across schools. The most important of these opportunities to learn are 1) teacher quality (indicators include experience, preparation to teach the content, participation in high-quality professional development, verbal ability, and opportunity to receive teacher rewards and incentives); 2) a safe and orderly learning environment; 3) time actively engaged in learning; 4) low student/teacher ratio; 5) rigor of the curriculum; 6) grouping practices that avoid tracking and rigid forms of student assignment based on past performance; 7) sophistication and currency of learning resources and information technology used by students; and 8) access to extracurricular activities.

Although the consequences of these different characteristics of schools vary with particular conditions, the available research suggests that, when two or more cohorts of students differ significantly in their access to opportunities to learn, differences in the quality of education also exist.[6] Such differences affect student achievement and can undermine the prospects for positive intergroup relations.

The content that makes up the lessons students are taught influences the level of student achievement. This is hardly surprising, but the curriculum students experience and the expectations of teachers and others about how much of the material they will learn vary from school to school. In general, students who are taught curricula that are more rigorous learn more than their peers with similar prior knowledge and backgrounds who are taught less-demanding curricula. For example, earlier access to algebra leads to greater participation in higher-level math courses and to increased academic achievement.

Principle 3. The curriculum should help students understand that knowledge is socially constructed and reflects researchers' personal experiences as well as the social, political, and economic contexts in which they live and work. In curriculum and teaching units and in textbooks, students often study historical events, concepts, and issues only or primarily from the points of view of the victors.[7] The perspectives of the vanquished are frequently silenced, ignored, or marginalized. This kind of teaching privileges mainstream students—those who most often identify with the victors or dominant groups—and causes many students of color to feel left out of the American story.

Concepts such as the "discovery" of America, the westward movement, and the role of the pioneers are often taught primarily from the points of view of the European Americans who constructed them. The curriculum should help students to understand how these concepts reflect the values and perspectives of European Americans and describe their experiences in the United States. Teachers should help students learn how these concepts have very different meanings for groups indigenous to America and for those who were brought to America in chains.

Teaching students the different—and often conflicting—meanings of concepts and issues for the diverse groups that make up the U.S. population will help them to better understand the complex factors that contributed to the birth, growth, and development of the nation. Such teaching will also help students develop empathy for the points of view and perspectives of various groups and will increase their ability to think critically.

Principle 4. Schools should provide all students with opportunities to participate in extracurricular and cocurricular activities that develop knowledge, skills, and attitudes that increase academic achievement and foster positive interracial relationships. Research evidence that links student achievement to participation in extracurricular and cocurricular activities is increasing in quantity and consistency.[8] There is significant research that supports the proposition that participation in after-school programs, sports activities, academic clubs, and school-sponsored social activities contributes to academic performance, reduces dropout rates and discipline problems, and enhances interpersonal skills among students from different ethnic backgrounds. Kris Gutiérrez and her colleagues, for example, found that "nonformal learning contexts," such as after-school programs, are useful in bridging home and school cultures for students from diverse groups.[9] Jomills Braddock concluded that involvement in sports activities was particularly beneficial for male African American high school students.[10] When designing extracurricular activities, educators should give special attention to recruitment, selection of leaders and teams, the cost of participating, allocation of school resources, and opportunities for cooperative intergroup contact.

Intergroup Relations

Principle 5. Schools should create or make salient superordinate or cross-cutting groups in order to improve intergroup relations. Creating supcrordinate groups—groups with which members of other groups in a given situation identify—improves intergroup relations.[11] When membership in superordinate groups is salient, other group differences become less important. Creating superordinate groups stimulates fellowship and cohesion and so can mitigate preexisting animosities.

In school settings many superordinate groups can be created or made salient. For example, it is possible to create superordinate groups through extracurricular activities. And many existing superordinate groups can be made more salient: the classroom, the grade level, the school, the community, the state, and even the nation. The most immediate superordinate groups (e.g., the school chorus rather than the state of California) are likely to be the most influential, but identification with any superordinate group can reduce prejudice.

Principle 6. Students should learn about stereotyping and other related biases that have negative effects on racial and ethnic relations. We use categories in perceiving our environment because categorization is a natural part of human information processing. But the mere act of categorizing people as members of an "in group" and an "out group" can result in stereotyping, prejudice, and discrimination.[12] Specifically, making distinctions between groups can lead to the perception that the "other group" is more homogeneous than one's own group, and this, in turn, can lead to an exaggeration of the extent of the group differences. Thus categorizing leads to stereotyping and to behaviors influenced by those stereotypes.

Intergroup contact can counteract stereotypes if the situation allows members of each group to behave in a variety of ways across different contexts, so that their full humanity and diversity are displayed. Negative stereotypes can also be modified in noncontact situations by providing members of the "in group" with information about members of the "out group" who disconfirm a stereotype across a variety of situations.[13]

Principle 7. Students should learn about the values shared by virtually all cultural groups (e.g., justice, equality, freedom, peace, compassion, and charity). Teaching students about the values that virtually all groups share, such as those described in the UN Universal Bill of Rights, can provide a basis for perceived similarity that can promote favorable intergroup relations.[14] In addition, the values themselves serve to undercut negative intergroup relations by discouraging injustice, inequality, unfairness, conflict, and a lack of compassion. The value of egalitarianism deserves special emphasis since a number of theories suggest that it can help to undermine stereotyping and prejudiced thinking and can help restrict the direct expression of racism.[15]

Principle 8. Teachers should help students acquire the social skills needed to interact effectively with students from other racial, ethnic, cultural, and language groups. One of the most effective techniques for improving intercultural relations is to teach members of the cultural groups the social skills necessary to interact effectively with members of another culture.[16] Students need to learn how to perceive, understand, and respond to group differences. They need to learn not to give offense and not to take offense. They also need to be helped to realize that, when members of other groups behave in ways that are inconsistent with the norms of the students' own group, these individuals are not necessarily behaving antagonistically.

One intergroup relations trainer asks members of the minority and majority groups to discuss what it feels like to be the target of stereotyping, prejudice, and discrimination.[17] Sharing such information informs the majority group of the pain and suffering their intentional or thoughtless acts of discrimination cause. It also allows the members of minority groups to share their experiences with one another. Other techniques that involve sharing experiences through carefully managed dialogue have also been found to improve intergroup relations.[18]

One skill that can be taught in schools in order to improve intergroup relations is conflict resolution.[19] A number of school districts throughout the U.S. are teaching students to act as mediators in disputes between other students.

Principle 9. Schools should provide opportunities for students from different racial, ethnic, cultural, and language groups to interact socially under conditions designed to reduce fear and anxiety. One of the primary causes of prejudice is fear.[20] Fear leads members of social groups to avoid interacting with members of other groups and causes them discomfort when they do. Fears about members of other groups often stem from concern about threats—both realistic and symbolic—to the "in group." Many such fears have little basis in reality or are greatly exaggerated.

To reduce uncertainty and anxiety concerning interaction with members of other groups, the contexts in which interactions between groups take place should be relatively structured, the balance of members of the different groups should be as equal as possible, the likelihood of failure should be low, and opportunities for hostility and aggression should be minimized. Providing factual information that contradicts misperceptions can also counteract prejudice that is based on a false sense of threat. Stressing the similarities in the values of the groups should also reduce the degree of symbolic threat posed by "out groups" and thus reduce fear and prejudice.

School Governance, Organization, and Equity

Principle 10. A school's organizational strategies should ensure that decision making is widely shared and that members of the school community learn collaborative skills and dispositions in order to create a caring learning environment for students. School policies and practices are the living embodiment of a society's underlying values and educational philosophy. They also reflect the values of those who work within schools. Whether in the form of curriculum, teaching strategies, assessment procedures, disciplinary policies, or grouping practices, school policies embody a school's beliefs, attitudes, and expectations of its students.[21] This is true whether the school is one with extensive or limited financial resources, whether its student body is relatively monocultural or richly diverse, or whether it is located in a crowded central city or an isolated rural county.

School organization and leadership can either enhance or detract from the development of learning communities that prepare students for a multicultural and democratic society. Schools that are administered from the top down are unlikely to create collaborative, caring cultures. Too often schools talk about democracy but fail to practice shared decision making. Powerful multicultural schools are organizational hubs that include a wide variety of stakeholders, ranging from students, teachers, and administrators to parents and members of the community. Indeed, there is convincing research evidence that parent involvement, in particular, is critical in enhancing student learning.[22] And a just multicultural school is receptive to working with all members of the students' communities.

Principle 11. Leaders should ensure that all public schools, regardless of their locations, are funded equitably. Equity in school funding is a critical condition for creating just multicultural schools. The current inequities in the funding of public education are startling.[23] Two communities that are adjacent to one another can provide wholly different support to their public schools, based on property values and tax rates. Students who live in poor communities are punished because they must attend schools that are underfunded by comparison to the schools in more affluent communities.

The relationship between increased school expenditures and school improvement is complex.[24] But when investments are made in ways that significantly improve students' opportunities to learn—such as increasing teacher quality, reducing class size in targeted ways, and engaging parents in their children's education—the result is likely to be improved student knowledge and skills.

The failure of schools and school systems to provide all students with equitable resources for learning will, of course, work to the disadvantage of those receiving inadequate resources and will usually widen the achievement gap between schools. Since achievement correlates highly with students' family income and since people of color are disproportionately represented in the low-income sector, inequity in opportunities to learn contributes to the achievement gap between students of color and white students.

Assessment

Principle 12. Teachers should use multiple culturally sensitive techniques to assess complex cognitive and social skills. Evaluating the progress of students from diverse racial and ethnic groups and social classes is complicated by differences in language, learning styles, and cultures. Hence the use of a single method of assessment will probably further disadvantage students from particular social classes and ethnic groups.

Teachers should adopt a range of formative and summative assessment strategies that give students an opportunity to demonstrate mastery. These strategies should include observations, oral examinations, performances, and teacher-made as well as standardized assessments. Students learn and demonstrate their competencies in different ways. The preferred mode of demonstrating task mastery for some is writing, while others do better speaking, visualizing, or performing; some are stimulated by competition and others by cooperation; some prefer to work alone, while others would rather work

in groups. Consequently, a variety of assessment procedures and outcomes that are compatible with different learning, performance, work, and presentation styles should be used to determine whether students are mastering the skills they need to function effectively in a multicultural society.

Assessment should go beyond traditional measures of subject-matter knowledge and include consideration of complex cognitive and social skills. Effective citizenship in a multicultural society requires individuals who have the values and abilities to promote equality and justice among culturally diverse groups.

Conclusion

Powerful multicultural schools help students from diverse racial, cultural, ethnic, and language groups to experience academic success. Academic knowledge and skills are essential in today's global society. However, they are not sufficient to guarantee full and active participation in that society. Students must also develop the knowledge, attitudes, and skills needed to interact positively with people from diverse groups and to participate in the civic life of the nation. Students must be competent in intergroup and civic skills if they are to function effectively in today's complex and ethnically polarized nation and world.

Diversity in the nation's schools is both an opportunity and a challenge. The nation is enriched by the ethnic, cultural, and language diversity of its citizens. However, whenever diverse groups interact, intergroup tension, stereotypes, and institutionalized discrimination develop. Schools must find ways to respect the diversity of their students and to help create a unified nation to which all citizens have allegiance. Structural inclusion in the public life of the nation together with power sharing will engender feelings of allegiance among diverse groups. Diversity within unity is the delicate goal toward which our nation and its schools should strive. We offer these design principles in the hope that they will help education policy makers and practitioners realize the elusive but essential goals of a democratic and pluralistic society.

Notes

1. James A. Banks, "Multicultural Education: Historical Development, Dimensions, and Practice," in James A. Banks and Cherry A. McGee Banks, eds., *Handbook of Research on Multicultural Education* (San Francisco: Jossey-Bass, 2001), pp. 1–24.

2. William Julius Wilson, *The Declining Significance of Race: Blacks and Changing American Institutions* (Chicago: University of Chicago Press, 1978).

3. A. Wade Boykin, "The Triple Quandary and the Schooling of Afro-American Children," in Ulric Neisser, ed., *The School Achievement of Minority Children: New Perspectives* (Hillsdale, N.J.: Erlbaum, 1986), pp. 57–92.

4. Geneva Gay, *Culturally Responsive Teaching: Theory, Research, and Practice* (New York: Teachers College Press, 2000).

5. Linda Darling-Hammond, *The Right to Learn* (San Francisco: Jossey-Bass, 1997).

6. Robert Dreeben and Adam Gamoran, "Race, Instruction, and Learning," *American Sociological Review*, vol. 51, 1986, pp. 660–69.

7. James A. Banks, *Cultural Diversity and Education: Foundations, Curriculum, and Teaching,* 4th ed. (Boston: Allyn and Bacon, 2001).

8. Jomills Braddock, "Bouncing Back: Sports and Academic Resilience Among African-American Males," *Education and Urban Society*, vol. 24, 1991, pp. 113–31; Jacquelynne S. Eccles and Bonnie L. Barber, "Student Council, Volunteering, Basketball, or Marching Band: What Kind of Extracurricular Involvement Matters?," *Journal of Adolescence Research*, January 1999, pp. 10–43; and Jennifer A. Goorman, ed., *After-School Programs to Promote Child and Adolescent Development: Summary of a Workshop* (Washington, D.C.: National Academy Press, 2000).

9. Kris D. Gutiérrez et al., "Building a Culture of Collaboration Through Hybrid Language Practices," *Theory into Practice,* vol. 38, 1999, pp. 87–93.

10. Braddock, op. cit.

11. Samuel Gaertner et al., "The Contact Hypothesis: The Role of a Common Ingroup Identity on Reducing Intergroup Bias," *Small Group Research,* vol. 25, 1994, pp. 224–49.

12. Henri Tajfel and John C. Turner, "The Social Identity Theory of Intergroup Behavior," in Stephen Worchel and William G. Austin, eds., *Psychology of Intergroup Relations,* 2nd ed. (Chicago: Nelson-Hall, 1986), pp. 7–24.

13. Lucy Johnston and Miles Hewstone, "Cognitive Models of Stereotype Change," *Journal of Experimental Social Psychology,* vol. 28, 1992, pp. 360–86.

14. Lawrence Kohlberg, *Essays on Moral Development* (New York: Harper & Row, 1981).

15. Samuel L. Gaertner and John F. Dovidio, "The Aversive Form of Racism," in John F. Dovidio and Samuel L. Gaertner, eds., *Prejudice, Discrimination, and Racism* (Orlando, Fla.: Academic Press, 1986), pp. 61–90; and Irwin Katz, David C. Glass, and Joyce Wackenhut, "An Ambivalence-Amplification Theory of Behavior Toward the Stigmatized," in Worchel and Austin, pp. 103–17.

16. Stephen Bochner, "Culture Shock," in Walter Lonner and Roy Malpass, eds., *Psychology and Culture* (Boston: Allyn and Bacon, 1994), pp. 245–52.

17. Louis Kamfer and David J. L. Venter, "First Evaluation of a Stereotype Reduction Workshop," *South African Journal of Psychology,* vol. 24, 1994, pp. 13–20.

18. Ximena Zúñiga and Biren Nagda, "Dialogue Groups: An Innovative Approach to Multicultural Learning," in David Schoem et al., eds., *Multicultural Teaching in the University* (Westport, Conn.: Praeger, 1993), pp. 233–48.

19. Morton Deutsch, "Cooperative Learning and Conflict Resolution in an Alternative High School," *Cooperative Learning,* vol. 13, 1993, pp. 2–5.

20. Gaertner and Dovidio, op. cit.; and Walter G. Stephan, *Reducing Prejudice and Stereotyping in Schools* (New York: Teachers College Press, 1999).

21. Sonia Nieto, *The Light in Their Eyes: Creating Multicultural Learning Communities* (New York: Teachers College Press, 1999).

22. Joyce L. Epstein, "School and Family Partnerships," in Marvin C. Alkin, ed., *Encyclopedia of Educational Research,* 6th ed. (New York: Macmillan, 1992), pp. 1139–51.

23. Jonathan Kozol, *Savage Inequalities: Children in America's Schools* (New York: Crown Publishers, 1991).

24. Eric A. Hanushek, "School Resources and Student Performance," in Gary Burtless, ed., *Does Money Matter? The Effect of School Resources on Student Achievement and Adult Success* (Washington, D.C.: Brookings Institution Press, 1996), pp. 43–73.

POSTNOTE

Multicultural education is a controversial issue, partly because there is no generally accepted definition. Some people see multicultural education as being divisive, creating separate pockets of different cultures, rather than helping to create a common culture. Others see multicultural education as valuing cultural pluralism, and recognizing that cultural diversity is a valuable resource that should be preserved and extended. The committee that wrote this article rejects both assimilation and separatism as ultimate goals. They recognize that each subculture exists as part of an interrelated whole. Multicultural education reaches beyond awareness and understanding of cultural differences to recognize the right of these different cultures to exist and to value that existence.

In addition to valuing cultural diversity, multicultural education is also based on the concept of *social justice*, which seeks to do away with social and economic inequalities for those in our society who have been denied these benefits in a democratic society. African Americans, Native Americans, Asian Americans, Hispanic Americans, women, disabled individuals, people with limited English proficiency, persons with low incomes, members of particular religious groups, and homosexuals are among those groups that have at one time or another been denied social justice. Educators who support multicultural education see establishing social justice for all groups of people who have experienced discrimination as a moral and ethical responsibility. Extending the concept of multicultural education to include a broader population has also contributed to its controversy.

DISCUSSION QUESTIONS

1. In your own words, what does multicultural education mean?
2. In your opinion, should cultural pluralism be a goal of our society and its schools? Why or why not?
3. What examples of multicultural education can you describe from your own education?

RELATED WEBSITE RESOURCE AND VIDEO CASE

WEB RESOURCES:

Multicultural Pavilion. Available at:

http://www.edchange.org/multicultural/index.html/.

This site also provides excellent resources for teachers, research, and articles on multicultural education.

 TEACHSOURCE VIDEO CASE

CULTURALLY RESPONSIVE TEACHING: A MULTICULTURAL LESSON FOR ELEMENTARY STUDENTS

In this video, you'll see how a literacy specialist weaves a lesson on multiculturalism into a traditional lesson on the five-paragraph essay. Go to the website for the Education Media Library at CengageBrain.com to watch the video clips, study the artifacts in the case, and reflect on the following questions.

1. How does this project reflect the principles of culturally responsive teaching?
2. How can you go about acquiring more knowledge of the world and its people?

51

Caring Closes the Language-Learning Gap

Mary Borba

Mary Borba is an associate professor in teacher education at California State University, Stanislaus.

Mary Borba, "Caring Closes the Language-Learning Gap," *Phi Delta Kappan*, v. 90, no. 9, May 2009, pp. 681–685.

It was a hectic August morning, the first day of work for teachers after the summer break. The secretary was helping an immigrant family register two children; an older sibling had come along to translate. The secretary seemed harried and showed little patience with this added task. She had difficulty pronouncing the child's first name and asked that it be spelled as she wrote it on the registration form. E-s-c-o-l-a-s-t-i-c-a. Once she got the name down, the secretary suggested shortening the name to Tica to facilitate pronunciation for teachers and to make it easier for the child to learn to write it. The look on those parents' faces has remained with me to this day. It was evident they were appalled that anyone would even consider the thought of changing their child's sacred name.

As a new teacher, that experience taught me the importance of a family's first contact with school and how a positive and accepting environment communicates that all are accepted, important, and welcome at school. This lesson continues to be critical today.

Although we've learned a great deal about literacy learning and instruction, the gap in academic achievement between English speakers and English learners continues to concern educators, parents, and legislators.

The rising expectations for literacy and the increasing number of students from diverse backgrounds contribute to this achievement gap. But educators can employ a variety of strategies for reaching out to families of English learners. Many of these activities were initiated in response to the changing demographics at the school where I was principal. The numbers of English learners increased significantly within two years, and the staff had to quickly adjust and respond to this shift.

Family Involvement

Educators sometimes misjudge immigrant families' ability to contribute to their children's school success, especially those of English learners (August and Shanahan 2006). However, families powerfully influence the academic achievement

FOCUS QUESTION

What can schools do to assist English language learners to succeed in schools?

InTASC
Standards 1, 2, 3, 7, and 10

of their children, and most take a strong interest in what happens in schools (Au 2002).

Cummins (1986, 2003) found that parents' involvement in their child's school has a positive effect on academic success. However, immigrant families often don't know how to assist their children at home, especially if they speak little English. Cummins found that teachers who involve families see positive results. In addition, communicating with immigrant families demonstrates that they are important and that their language and culture are valued and essential to their child's success.

Home-School Communication

As a former teacher and principal, I found many ways to involve limited-English-speaking parents in school life. When any family walks into the office, clerical staff should greet them warmly and patiently offer assistance. Because our office staff was not bilingual, we arranged to have bilingual personnel available on days when we expected many immigrant families to visit the school, such as during parent-teacher conferences and back-to-school nights. We translated school newsletters, calendars, and reminders into Spanish. Our phone system had a weekly automated phone call to homes in English and Spanish, and each call ended by reminding parents of the family's positive effect on their children and the school. These small efforts helped build rapport and communicate our desire to include all families in the life of the school.

As principal, I made it a priority to be in front of the school at the beginning and end of each day to greet families. The care and respect I communicated was well received and contributed to parents' feeling that I was approachable, friendly, and helpful. Families felt that they could share concerns, ask questions, give feedback, and ask for assistance, which helped build trust and confidence in the school.

Schools Supporting Families

Igoa (1995) reported that when a family leaves all that is familiar to them and is transported to a new country, they may experience distress or shock. In addition to long work days and a feeling of despair that may accompany people who live in unfamiliar surroundings, this stress takes tremendous energy.

I had many conversations with immigrant parents about their struggles, especially how to parent when faced with foreign situations. Fathers often worked at jobs in other towns, and mothers were the sole parent during the week. These mothers sometimes felt helpless trying to structure family life in order to increase school success or to change children's negative behaviors. As a result of these issues, we began a parent education program in which families could learn how the school system functioned, increase their parenting skills, and learn strategies to support school achievement. Parents and grandparents became more visible on campus and more comfortable coming to me, the principal, for assistance and support.

When I was a classroom teacher, I solicited parent assistance to prepare audiotapes in our Portuguese families' primary language. Many parents had a limited education, and asking them to read extensively was a challenge. But, they could listen to tapes to increase their understanding of how children learn and grow. We read and taped articles and chapters from Portuguese books related to parenting, education, and psychology. Each tape included only one article or chapter and came with a journal in which parents could write reflections and give feedback.

Igoa (1995) discussed the importance of the school recognizing the home culture and helping bolster family relationships. She stressed that honoring the child's home language contributed to the child's confidence. Loving, secure relationships with parents are important for children, and these are strengthened when the school values what families have to offer their children and the school community. If children believe their family's values are inferior to those of the school, it affects how they view themselves and their ability to integrate who they are with the expectations of the school. When families are insecure, struggle to survive, and speak little or no English, school principals and teachers need to make it a priority to communicate and encourage participation in their children's life at school.

Most immigrant families at our school spoke little English. To help them, we supported English classes two evenings a week in our school library. Childcare and snacks were provided for the children. We encouraged anyone in the community to attend, not just families with children in school. Our goal was not only for families to learn English, but also for their children to see how their parents valued education.

Family Involvement in Learning Activities

Immigrant children feel tremendous pressure to assimilate into American culture and often believe they must give up their family's ways of doing things. Teachers contribute to this view when they suggest that the child leave behind his or her old life. The consequences of such messages may divide a family. Igoa (1995) argued that when educators help children embrace both languages and cultures, it strengthens the bridge between the home and school.

Some schools don't have the resources to provide instruction in each child's home language. However, instruction in the primary language helps children build a cognitive foundation for subsequent instruction in English. At our school, we bought library books in the primary language and bilingual texts for parents to share with their children. Home conversations and interactions around these texts brought families together, and the information children learned in their primary language became background knowledge for lessons in English.

When teachers ask parents who are limited in English to speak only English at home, they interrupt children's cognitive development, which hinders their progress in school (Diaz-Rico and Weed 1995). In addition, these parents aren't good role models in English and can contribute to poor language skills. It is better to encourage parents to continue speaking their primary language at home. Many research studies have found that cognitive and academic development in the first language has

an extremely important and positive effect on second language learning at school (Collier 1995). Skills developed in the first language are easily transferred to the second language and are crucial for academic success. And when parents and children speak the language they know best, they are working at a higher cognitive level.

Instructional videos in English, DVDs, and audiobooks also stimulate rich talk in the primary language for families. Although the media are in English, the vivid images encourage discussion. Conversations related to nature, famous people, and places enrich learning for students.

Learning About the Family

Increasing language competence and sharing cultural backgrounds were part of the after-school program for English learners at our school. During my tenure as principal, our computer lab increased opportunities for learning English. The after-school Language Club permitted English learners to work in the computer lab with an individualized ESL software program. In addition, we focused on helping the children learn about their homeland and family histories. Students interviewed family members to collect information for their writing during Language Club. They proudly shared their written efforts, and we found many commonalities across families and cultures. Other computer programs used images, videos, digital video-on-demand, and an online teaching service that led to rich talk and shared writing, which supported students' independent writing. High school students worked with individual students, encouraging them to extend their writing and helping them edit and publish their stories and prepare a final oral presentation. Many of these high school students were also from immigrant families, which affirmed the younger students' efforts.

Families Supporting Schools

Involving parents in a child's education is a primary goal of schools. However, despite evidence of the positive effects of family involvement, teachers sometimes fail to systematically encourage family involvement.

There is a myth among educators that it is difficult to involve immigrant families if teachers don't speak their language (Samway and McKeon 1999). However, teachers in the schools where I worked found numerous ways to bring parents into the school. Even when parents didn't speak English proficiently, they assisted with art projects, listened to children read, supervised math games, checked home-work, prepared instructional materials, and learned how to work with their own children simply by observing the teacher. Immigrant parents assisted on field trips, supervised the cafeteria, monitored restrooms, played soccer or jumped rope, and performed a variety of tasks in the school. This motivated many volunteers to learn English so that they could talk with more children while at school.

Professional Development

All educators must know about learning a second language in order to provide effective instruction. For example, students need to be encouraged to understand messages in English and to use the language for real purposes (Collier 1995; Gibbons 2002). They need opportunities for social interaction that require the use of the language, even if imperfectly. Language development is gained over many years and is accelerated by knowledgeable teachers (Cummins 2003).

When teachers understand these processes, their expectations are more realistic, they are better able to scaffold learning appropriately, and they are prepared to keep parents informed as students become more proficient in English.

Teachers who use group work increase the language that English learners hear, and the interaction with other speakers requires them to speak more. Group work that focuses on learning a subject allows English learners to continue to develop academically. We can't place the English learner on hold while they learn English. However, teachers need to teach students how to work in groups.

Gibbons argues that "productive talk does not just happen—it needs to be deliberately and systematically planned, just as we plan literacy events" (2002, p. 38). Explaining to families how classrooms are structured to promote language learning provides them with a window to how schools and classrooms promote student success.

My school prepared our most limited English learners by recruiting community volunteers. The volunteers came to the school once or twice a week to give students a jump start on upcoming topics in classroom lessons. They met individually with students to skim a textbook chapter and discuss the photos and graphics or to read and discuss a text to provide the background knowledge to understand the upcoming topic.

In this way, English learners who most needed support could preview the topic and be exposed to vocabulary and concepts that would be introduced later in the classroom. Primary students had community members who read aloud to expand the children's language and deepen their comprehension. As a result, children were prepared to actively participate in class.

Shared reading and writing strategies allow English learners to read and write more difficult texts than they would otherwise be able to do independently (Crawford 2003). Massive amounts of independent reading for older students and multiple interactive read-alouds for younger students contribute to language growth (Krashen 2004). In addition, an emphasis on developing vocabulary with rich, contextualized experiences in all areas of the curriculum contributes to increased language learning opportunities.

Classroom teachers used these and other strategies to scaffold learning for English learners. As teachers became more sensitive to and skillful in meeting the needs of English learners, their connections with immigrant families increased. As students' success improved in the mainstream classroom, so did their sense of appreciation for themselves as bilingual and bicultural individuals.

Increasing knowledge about family backgrounds and lifestyles is essential to improving teacher attitudes and skills for building home-school partnerships.

Although I encouraged teachers to make learning and celebrating students' cultures a regular activity throughout the year, we ended the year with a schoolwide multicultural celebration. Dancers, displays, guest presenters, and special classroom activities brought families to school to share the rich diversity of our community. Families developed displays about their countries, and a cultural museum was constructed in the cafeteria for students, families, and community members to visit. This year-end event confirmed for me that children and their families will not care about learning unless they sense we care about who they are and where they come from.

Conclusion

Educators must take the first step toward entering the world of the immigrant family in a caring and respectful manner. School leadership and adequately prepared teachers are necessary to promote expertise in instructing English learners, knowledge about immigrant family backgrounds, positive home-school communication, and opportunities for family involvement in learning activities at school and at home. A sensitivity to the needs of immigrant families contributes to building a strong bridge between languages and cultures. When children and their families are proud of who they are, children are more likely to do well in schools.

References

Au, Kathryn. "Multicultural Factors and the Effective Instruction of Students of Diverse Backgrounds." In *What Research Has to Say About Reading Instruction*, ed. Alan E. Farstrup and S. Jay Samuels, pp. 392–412. Newark, Del.: International Reading Association, 2002.

August, Diane, and Timothy Shanahan, eds. *Developing Literacy in Second-Language Learners: Report of the National Literacy Panel on Language-Minority Children and Youth*. Mahway, N.J.: Lawrence Erlbaum Associates and the Center for Applied Linguistics, 2006.

Collier, Virginia. *Promoting Academic Success for ESL Students*. Woodside, N.Y.: Bastos Educational Books, 1995.

Crawford, Alan N. "Communicative Approaches to Second-Language Acquisition: The Bridge to Second-Language Literacy." In *English Learners: Reaching the Highest Level of English Literacy*, ed. Gilbert G. Garcia. Newark, Del.: International Reading Association, 2003.

Cummins, Jim. "Empowering Minority Students: A Framework for Intervention." *Harvard Educational Review 56*, no. 1 (1986): 18–36.

Cummins, Jim. "Reading and the Bilingual Student: Fact and Fiction." In *English Learners: Reaching the Highest Level of English Literacy*, ed. Gilbert G. Garcia. Newark, Del.: International Reading Association, 2003.

Diaz-Rico, Lynne T., and Katherine Weed. *The Crosscultural, Language, and Academic Development Handbook*. Boston, Mass.: Allyn & Bacon, 1995.

Gibbons, Pauline. *Scaffolding Language, Scaffolding Learning: Teaching Second Language Learners in the Mainstream Classroom*. Portsmouth, N.H.: Heinemann, 2002.

Igoa, Cristina. *The Inner World of the Immigrant Child*. New York: St. Martin's Press, 1995.

Krashen, Stephen. *The Power of Reading*. Portsmouth, N.H.: Heinemann, 2004.

Samway, Katherine, and Denise McKeon. *Myths and Realities: Best Practices for Language Minority Students*. Portsmouth, N.H.: Heinemann, 1999.

POSTNOTE

More than 5.3 million English language learners (ELLs) are enrolled in public elementary and secondary schools (almost 11 percent of the total enrollment), and this number has increased every year for the last decade. The large majority of ELL students are concentrated in the states of California, Texas, New York, Florida, and Illinois. Across the United States, ELL students speak more than 400 different languages, with Spanish being the predominant foreign language. Twenty-one percent of all U.S. five-to-seventeen-year-olds speak a language other than English at home, and 5 percent speak English with difficulty.

The suggestions made by the author, based on both research findings and her own experiences, provide helpful guidance on how schools can reach and teach these students. Her main suggestion to involve parents in a variety of ways in their children's education is the key to helping these children succeed in school.

DISCUSSION QUESTIONS

1. Do you believe ELLs should receive instruction in both their first language and English, or just in English? Why?
2. What other reasons, in addition to language issues, do you think contribute to the poor academic performance of so many immigrant and minority students?
3. What experiences have you had in working with non-native English-speaking children? If you haven't had any, what might you do to be a better teacher for them?

RELATED WEBSITE RESOURCE AND VIDEO CASE

WEB RESOURCE:

National Clearinghouse for English Language Acquisition. Available at:

http://www.ncela.gwu.edu.

Funded by the U.S. Department of Education, this site contains hundreds of articles, links, databases, and online assistance in the area of English language acquisition.

▶❙❙ TEACHSOURCE VIDEO CASE

BILINGUAL EDUCATION: AN ELEMENTARY TWO-WAY IMMERSION PROGRAM

This video case introduces two teachers and their students who are involved in a two-way bilingual program. That is, all students learn to read, write, and communicate in *both* English and Spanish in all subject areas. Go to the website for the Education Media Library at CengageBrain.com to watch the video clips, study the artifacts in the case, and reflect on the following questions.

1. Which of the models described here does this classroom most resemble? Why?
2. How are these teachers demonstrating the teaching tips listed here?
3. Do you agree with the teacher's assessment of the pros and cons of her program? Why or why not? What would you add?

52

The Latino Education Crisis

Patricia Gándara

Patricia Gándara is professor of education at the University of California, Los Angeles, and Co-director of the Civil Rights Project. She is the co-author, with Frances Contreras, of *The Latino Education Crisis: The Consequences of Failed Social Policies* (Harvard University Press, 2009).

"The Latino Education Crisis," by Pedro Gandara, 2010 *Educational Leadership* 67(5), pp. 24–30. © 2010 by ASCD. Reprinted with permission. Learn more about ASCD at www.ascd.org.

From their first day of kindergarten to their last day of school, Latinos, on average, perform far below most of their peers. They now constitute the largest minority group in the United States and the fastest growing segment of its school-age population. As such, they are inextricably bound up with the nation's future.

The Latino public school population nearly doubled between 1987 and 2007, increasing from 11 to 21 percent of all U.S. students (National Center for Education Statistics [NCES], 2009b). The U.S. Census Bureau predicts that by 2021, one of four U.S. students will be Latino. In key states in the U.S. Southwest, such as Texas and California, the Latino school-age population is already approaching one-half of all students. In these states, the future is already here.

But it's a troubling picture. Latinos are the least educated of all major ethnic groups (see Figure 1). Although a large gap exists between the college completion rates of whites and blacks, both groups show steady growth. However, the growth in college degrees for Latinos is almost flat. The failure over more than three decades to make any progress in moving more Latino students successfully through college suggests that what we have been doing to close achievement gaps is not working. This fact has enormous consequences for the United States, as the job market continues to demand more education and Latinos continue to make up a larger and larger portion of the workforce.

Behind at the Start

Can schools close these gaps? It is instructive to look back to the first days of schooling to see the differences that exist at that point. Data from the 1998 Early Childhood Longitudinal Study show that only one-half as many Latino children as white children fall into the highest quartile of math and reading skills at the *beginning* of kindergarten, and more than twice as many fall into the lowest quartile. The gap is even wider between Latino and Asian students (see Figure 2).

FOCUS QUESTION

What can schools do to narrow the education gap between Latino students and their nonminority peers?

InTASC

Standards 1, 2, 3, 7, and 10

KEY TERMS

- Dual language program
- Head Start
- Magnet schools
- Two-way immersion programs

FIGURE 1   Bachelor's Degree Completion by Ethnicity

ETHNICITY	YEAR				
	1975	1985	1995	2005	2008
White	24	24	29	34	37
Black	11	12	15	18	21
Latino	9	11	9	11	12

The figures represent the percentage of 25- to 29-year-olds in the United States who completed a bachelor's degree or higher.

Source: *Current Population Survey (CPS), Annual Social and Economic Study Supplement*, 1971–2005, previously unpublished tabulation, November 2005, and *American Community Survey 2008*, by U.S. Census Bureau, Washington, DC: U.S. Department of Commerce.

FIGURE 2   Percentage of Kindergartners Scoring at Highest and Lowest Quartiles, on the 1998 Early Childhood Longitudinal Study

ETHNIC GROUP	READING		MATH	
	HIGHEST QUARTILE	LOWEST QUARTILE	HIGHEST QUARTILE	LOWEST QUARTILE
White	30	18	32	18
Asian	39	13	38	13
Black	15	34	10	39
Latino	15	42	14	40
Native American	9	57	9	50

Source: *America's Kindergartners: Findings from the Early Childhood Longitudinal Study*, by J. West, K. Denton, and E. Germino-Hausken, 2000, Washington, DC: National Center for Education Statistics.

Access to preschool education, of which Latino children have less than any other major group (NCES, 2009a), contributes to some of this early gap, but it cannot account for all of it. The evidence shows that poverty is the culprit. Young Latino children are more than twice as likely to be poor as white children and are even more likely to be among the poorest of the poor. At least one-third of Latino families lack health insurance; many Latino children rarely see a doctor, dentist, or optometrist, and so they often go to school with toothaches, uncorrected vision problems, and untreated chronic health problems (Berliner, 2009). Many also go to school hungry. These all constitute serious impediments to learning that schools are often poorly equipped to address.

Latino students are many more times as likely as students from other ethnic groups to come from homes where parents do not speak English well—or at all—and where parental education is low. More than 40 percent of Latina mothers lack even a high school diploma, compared with only 6 percent of white mothers; and only about 10 percent of Latina mothers have a college degree or higher, compared with almost one-third of white mothers (see Figure 3). Although Latino students may come from loving homes, limited education and resources do affect their education outcomes. There is no

FIGURE 3 Mother's Education Level by Ethnicity

ETHNICITY	LESS THAN HIGH SCHOOL	HIGH SCHOOL	BACHELOR'S DEGREE OR HIGHER
Latino	41.3%	28.6%	9.9%
White	5.9%	29.0%	31.7%
Black	18.2%	34.4%	15.3%
Asian	16%	22.2%	44.7%

Asian percentages were based on a small sample, so they may not be entirely representative.

Source: *Current Population Survey (CPS), Annual Social and Economic Study Supplement, 1971–2005*, previously unpublished tabulation, by U.S. Census Bureau, 2005, Washington, DC: U.S. Department of Commerce. Available: http://nces.ed.gov/pubs2007/minoritytrends/tables/table_5.asp

better predictor of how well children will fare in school than parents' education attainment (Murnane, Maynard, & Ohls, 1981).

It is difficult for parents to impart to their children experiences and knowledge that they do not have. Many studies have shown that school benefits poor children more than middle-class children (Alexander, Entwisle, & Olsen, 1997; Coleman, 1966); in the case of poor children, schools offer what parents cannot, whereas for middle-class children, school supplements what the home and community routinely offer. Under the right conditions, schools could conceivably close the gaps for Latino children, but the schools that serve most Latino students today have not met those conditions.

Segregated from the Mainstream

In the United States as a whole, Latinos are slightly more likely than black students (39.5 percent vs. 38.3 percent) to attend hypersegregated schools—those that are 90 to 100 percent nonwhite. In the large central cities in the west, more than 60 percent of Latinos attend hypersegregated schools (Orfield & Frankenberg, 2008).

This means that many Latino students lack access to peers from the mainstream U.S. culture, which inhibits their understanding of the norms, standards, and expectations of the broader society. For example, these students may rarely come into contact with anyone who has gone to college or who intends to go, so the aspirations and knowledge about getting to college never develop. It also means that Latino students are likely to attend underresourced schools with poorer facilities and less-qualified teachers than mainstream students experience.

The Need for Comprehensive Support

Factors like health care; intense neighborhood segregation (which results in school segregation); and the language and resources of the family may seem beyond the scope of what most schools can reasonably address. But other factors—such as teacher quality, school facilities and resources, and a rich curriculum—are very much within the purview of schools.

One key to successfully meeting Latino students' needs is to conceptualize our efforts as a *continuum* of interventions rather than discrete interventions; according to the literature, the effect of a single intervention tends to fade in the absence of sustained supportive environments. Preschool won't, on its own, permanently narrow or close achievement gaps, just as the effects of an intervention in elementary school will probably not last through high school.

The evidence suggests that a continuing net of support for disadvantaged students is likely to significantly improve their academic outcomes and reduce the wide gaps in achievement that now exist. It follows that under these conditions, students will be more likely to graduate from high school and successfully prepare for college.

A Focus on Early Childhood

If Latino children are going to catch up with their more-advantaged peers, they must have access to high-quality preschool. We have never been successful in closing these achievement gaps after students are in elementary school.

A number of studies have demonstrated the effectiveness of high-quality Head Start–type programs that provide comprehensive services to students and their families. The research on Head Start has demonstrated "moderate effects on pre-academic skills, greater parental awareness of the needs of their children and increased skills in meeting those needs, and provision of health and nutrition services and information" (Gándara & Contreras, 2009, p. 259). Of course, once children leave Head Start, they also lose the health and family support services that are so important for many low-income Latino students.

In his study of Oklahoma's universal preschool program, Gormley (2008) documented that Latino students benefited more than any other category of student from attending preschool. In both reading and math readiness, the Latinos in the program performed approximately one year above those Latino students who did not attend preschool. Students in full-day kindergarten also outperformed those who attended a half-day program. The researchers attributed the score gains to the policy of hiring fully credentialed teachers and paying them at the same salary level as other teachers. The teachers not only were competent, but also were likely to stay and build strong programs at the center over time. Other researchers have found similar gains for low-income preschool students in high-quality programs (Karoly et al., 1998).

The single biggest argument against providing universal preschool—apart from its cost—is that research has shown that the positive effects are not sustained for many students; students show an initial rise in test scores that seems to disappear after one or two years of school (Currie & Thomas, 1995). However, researchers have argued that this is probably because the schools these students attend are too weak to sustain the positive effects of preschool.

Research has also shown that students' environments outside school probably contribute more to schooling outcomes than in-school factors do. Compared with all other developed nations of the world, the United States provides the weakest safety net for its low-income students and their families (Rainwater & Smeeding, 2005). This surely contributes to the erosion of positive effects of schooling interventions.

A Focus on K–12 Supports

To sustain the effects of early interventions, it is crucial to strengthen the capacity of K–12 schools to monitor and support students once they arrive at school. Some programs, such as Project GRAD (www.projectgrad.org), have attempted to bundle research-based interventions that follow students as a cohort through their K–12 years. These include well-established programs, such as the University of Chicago School Mathematics Project (http://ucsmp.uchicago.edu) and Success for All (www.successforall.net). In fact, consistent with other studies, the Success for All researchers found good outcomes for Spanish-speaking students in their regular English curriculum but superior outcomes using their bilingual curriculum (Slavin & Cheung, 2005).

Although Project GRAD takes a whole-school reform approach, it also monitors students and their progress. Recent findings indicate that students who stay in the program longer appear to benefit the most and that careful monitoring of individual students is central to the effectiveness of education interventions (Gándara & Bial, 2001).

Dual-Language and Two-Way Immersion Programs

Programs promoting bilingualism have been found to produce superior academic outcomes for both Latino students whose first language is Spanish and for non-Spanish speakers, while also developing a strong competence in a second language (see Genesee, Lindholm-Leary, Saunders, & Christian,

2006). Such programs, whose goal is to transform monolingual speakers of either English or Spanish into fully bilingual and biliterate students, have mushroomed in recent years. Because the programs give equal status to both languages and typically enroll Latino students alongside non–Latino students, they have the additional advantage of fostering positive intergroup relations and increasing Latino students' social capital, as the Latino students are fully integrated with their middle-class peers (Morales & Aldana, 2010). These programs usually have long waiting lists.

Magnet Schools

Magnet schools often specialize in a specific field, such as medicine, the arts, or science. A number of studies have shown that in addition to benefitting from a more desegregated schooling experience, magnet school students tend to outperform students in regular public and private schools in both reading and math scores on standardized tests (Frankenberg & Seigel-Hawley, 2008).

Dropout Prevention and College-Going Programs

High school programs that focus on immediate issues such as dropout prevention and college-going tend to be more successful for Latino youth than those with less focused goals. Effective programs tend to share five components (Gándara & Bial, 2001). They (1) provide at least one key person whose job it is to know, connect with, and monitor the progress of each student; (2) structure a supportive peer group that reinforces program goals; (3) provide access to strong curriculum that leads to college preparation; (4) attend to students' cultural backgrounds; and (5) show students how they can finance their education, providing scholarships when possible.

One high school program that focuses specifically on preparing Latino students for college is the Puente Project, which is active in 36 California high schools. Through a school support team,

the program provides a net of services: two years of intensive college-preparatory English, focusing on writing skills and incorporating Latino literature; intensive college counseling; and a mentor from the community who acts as a guide and role model. The program has doubled the college-going of participating students and has motivated them to attend more selective schools. This is important because Latino students tend to enroll in less selective colleges than they qualify for (Fry, 2004), and students who attend more selective schools tend to have higher graduation rates (Sigal & Tienda, 2005). Key to the success of the program is its strong adult-student connections and the availability of a counselor to advocate for the students.

School Attachment and Belonging

Latino students' extraordinarily high dropout rate is related, in part, to their lack of attachment to school and a sense of not belonging. A crucial means by which students attach to school and form supportive friendship groups is through extracurricular activities—sports, band, newspaper, and other clubs. Unfortunately, Latino students are less likely to participate in these activities, either because they perceive the club to be exclusive or because of logistical problems, like needing to work or help out at home after school or not having transportation or the money required for the activity. Latino students' absence from these activities is also related to their lack of access to the same social circles as their middle-class peers, reducing their chances of being invited into these activities.

Schools that effectively address this issue find ways to incorporate clubs, sports, and other activities into school routines and bring the benefits of these activities into the classroom. For example, some schools mix students in heterogeneous classes and create conditions for students from different groups to interact in conditions in which they are more equal in status (see Gibson, Gándara, & Koyama, 2004).

How School-Community Partnerships Can Help

Schools alone cannot close the yawning gaps in achievement. But schools can partner with other institutions to help narrow those gaps. Collaboration in the following three areas can make a significant difference for many Latino students.

- *Create magnet schools that appeal to middle-class parents.* Some interventions are not costly in terms of dollars but require spending political capital. For example, in gentrifying areas of the inner cities, we could attack the problem of neighborhood and school segregation through thoughtful and progressive planning. The apartments that have sprung up in formerly downtrodden areas typically market to professional single people and young couples without children—the assumption being that young families do not want to live in the city center. We need to create attractive options by offering desegregated, high-quality schools adjacent to open spaces that could serve both the families of young professionals and inner-city residents. Because dual-language programs often appeal to middle-class parents, it would make sense to include such programs as features of new inner-city magnet schools.
- *Work with health and social service agencies.* Because access to health care and social services is an acute problem for Latino families, schools should be the primary contact for these kinds of services for youth. The Center for Health and Health Care in Schools (n.d.) reports that in 2006, there were more than 1,800 school-based health centers around the United States, providing care for children who might otherwise not have been able to access it. Although this is an encouraging number, it represents a small fraction of U.S. schools that serve low-income students and Latinos.

  An evaluation of California's Healthy Start Program, which provides integrated services primarily to Latino children and families, showed that it reduced needs for food, clothing, transportation, and medical and dental care; improved clients' emotional health and family functioning; reduced teen risk behaviors; modestly improved grade point averages; and reduced student mobility (Wagner & Golan, 1996). Nevertheless, the program has progressively lost funding.

  One study found that such programs are difficult to operate because of the need to integrate many services that compete with one another for dollars (Romualdi, 2000). However, if we can stabilize funding, these programs can make a big difference in the lives of Latino children. Placing medical, dental, and social services in an accessible, safe place makes sense if the goal is to help schools do their job of teaching these students.

  Critics have argued against the "effectiveness" of these centers, in part because research has failed to show that they significantly raise standardized test scores. But children who arrive at school with basic health, emotional, and nutritional needs unmet are not ready to learn. It only makes sense to evaluate the centers on their primary mission—healthier developmental outcomes for children that ultimately lead to better opportunities to learn. Moreover, if such programs can create family attachments to a school, thereby reducing student mobility, this could result in long-term benefits for Latino students.
- *Reach out to parents in culturally appropriate ways.* Many studies have shown that a primary reason that Latino students do not complete college degrees is because they don't understand how to prepare for college or even why they should attend. Their parents, who have often not completed high school in the United States, are even less familiar with these issues.

However, given the opportunity, most parents are eager to help their children succeed in school. One example of an effective program designed specifically for Latino immigrant parents is the Parent Institute for Quality Education (PIQE). Founded in San Diego, California, in 1987 but now operating in both Washington, D.C., and Texas, PIQE teaches parents, in nine weekly evening sessions, how to monitor their children's progress, advocate on their behalf, and prepare them for college. Many of the staff members who run the program were once parent participants. One evaluation of the program found that participating parents read more with their children and understood more about how they could support their children's education (Chrispeels, Wang, & Rivero, 2000).

Doing Whatever It Takes

No silver bullet or single program can close the enormous gap between Latino students and their peers with respect to academic achievement and attainment. But it's in all of our interests to find ways to begin the process of narrowing those gaps. This will require the collaborative efforts of both schools and social service agencies. It will also take the political courage to acknowledge that schools cannot do this alone—and that the rest of society will need to step up to the challenge.

References

Alexander, K., Entwisle, D., & Olsen, L. (1997). *Children, schools, and inequality*. Boulder, CO: Westview Press.

Berliner, D. (2009). *Poverty and potential: Out-of-school factors and school success*. Boulder, CO, and Tempe, AZ: Education and the Public Interest Center.

Center for Health and Health Care in Schools. (n.d.). *Health services*. Available: www.healthinschools.org/Health-in-Schools/Health-Services.aspx

Chrispeels, J., Wang, J., & Rivero, E. (2000). *Evaluation summary of the impact of the Parent Institute for Quality Education on parent's engagement with their children's schooling*. Available: www.piqe.org/Assets/Home/ChrispeelEvaluation.htm

Coleman, J. (1966). *Equality of educational opportunity*. Washington, DC: U.S. Government Printing Office.

Currie, J., & Thomas, D. (1995). Does Head Start make a difference? *American Economic Review, 85*, 341–364.

Frankenberg, E., & Seigel-Hawley, G. (2008). *Rethinking magnet schools in a changing landscape.*

Los Angeles: Civil Rights Project/Proyecto Derechos Civiles.

Fry, R. (2004). *Latino youth finishing college: The role of selective pathways*. Washington, DC: Pew Hispanic Center. Available: http://pewhispanic.org/reports/report.php?ReportID=30

Gándara, P., & Bial, D. (2001). *Paving the way to postsecondary education*. Washington DC: National Center for Education Statistics.

Gándara P., & Contreras, F. (2009). *The Latino education crisis: The consequences of failed social policies*. Cambridge, MA: Harvard University Press.

Genesee, F., Lindholm-Leary, K., Saunders, W., & Christian, D. (2006). *Educating English language learners: A synthesis of research evidence*. New York: Cambridge University Press.

Gibson, M., Gándara, P., & Koyama, J. (Eds.). (2004). *School connections: U.S. Mexican youth, peers, and school achievement*. New York: Teachers College Press.

Gormley, W. (2008). The effects of Oklahoma's pre-K program on Hispanic children. *Social Science Quarterly, 89*, 916–936.

Karoly, L. A., Greenwood, P. W., Everingham, S. S., Hoube, J., Kilburn, M. R., Rydell, C. P., Sanders, M., et al. (1998). *Investing in our children: What we know and don't know about the costs and benefits of early childhood interventions*. Santa Monica, CA: RAND.

Morales, P. Z., & Aldana, U. (2010). Learning in two languages: Programs with political promise. In P. Gándara & M. Hopkins (Eds.), *Forbidden language: English learners and restrictive language policies*. New York: Teachers College Press.

Murnane, R., Maynard, R., & Ohls, J. (1981). Home resources and children's achievement. *The Review of Economics and Statistics, 63*(3), 369–377.

National Center for Education Statistics. (2009a). *The condition of education*. Washington, DC: U.S. Department of Education.

National Center for Education Statistics. (2009b). Racial/ethnic enrollment in public schools. Indicator 7. In *The condition of education*. Washington, DC: U.S. Department of Education.

Orfield, G., & Frankenberg, E. (2008). *The last have become first: Rural and small town America lead the way of desegregation*. Los Angeles: UCLA Civil Rights Project/Proyecto Derechos Civiles.

Rainwater, L., & Smeeding, T. (2005). *Poor kids in a rich country: America's children in comparative perspective.* New York: Russell Sage.

Romualdi, E. V. (2000). Shared dream: A case study of the implementation of Healthy Start (California). (Doctoral dissertation, University of California, Davis). *Dissertation Abstracts International, 61*(09). (UMI No. 9315947).

Sigal, A., & Tienda, M. (2005). Assessing the mismatch hypothesis: Differentials in college graduation rates by institutional selectivity. *Sociology of Education, 78*(4), 294–315.

Slavin, R., & Cheung, A. (2005). A synthesis of research on language of reading instruction for English language learners. *Review of Educational Research, 75*, 247–284.

Wagner, M., & Golan, S. (1996). *California's Healthy Start school-linked services initiative: Summary of evaluation findings.* Menlo Park, CA: SRI International.

POSTNOTE

Latinos are the fastest growing segment of the American population, and the U.S. Census predicts that by 2021, one of four U.S. students will be Latino. Unfortunately, Latino children consistently lag behind their white counterparts in terms of academic achievement, and drop out of school in alarming proportions. What are the problems and what can be done about them? As the author of this article points out, Latino children enter kindergarten already behind white and Asian-American students in both math and reading skills. The author acknowledges that lack of access to pre-school education is part of the explanation, but that poverty is the main culprit. Latino children are more than twice as likely to be poor as are white children, which limits their access to health care and good nutrition, both being requisites for good school performance. Furthermore, many Latino parents are poorly educated and do not speak English well—or at all.

While schools can try to address the educational deficits that Latino children bring to the classroom, there is a limit as to how much they can succeed without addressing the root cause of their problems—poverty.

DISCUSSION QUESTIONS

1. Do you agree with the author's position that poverty is the root cause of Latino children's poor academic performances? Why or why not?

2. What initiatives would you recommend to address the achievement gap between Latino and African American students on the one hand, and white and Asian American students on the other hand?

3. How can you prepare yourself for the ethnic diversity you are likely to encounter in the classroom?

RELATED WEBSITE RESOURCE

WEB RESOURCE:

New York State Library: Selected Hispanic and Latino Web Sites. Available at:

http://www.nysl.nysed.gov/reference/hisref.htm.

A list of websites that address various Hispanic/Latino issues and concerns, such as education, entertainment, business, cultural and advocacy groups, and general resources.

53

Enabling or Disabling? Observations on Changes in Special Education

James M. Kauffman, Kathleen McGee, and Michele Brigham

James M. Kauffman is professor emeritus, Curry School of Education, University of Virginia. **Kathleen McGee** is a special education teacher at the high school level. **Michele Brigham** is a high school special education teacher in Loudoun County, Virginia.

"Enabling or Disabling? Observing on Changes in Special Education," by James M. Kaufmann, Kathleen McGee, and Michele Brigham, *Phi Delta Kappan*, April 2004, pp. 613–620. Reprinted with permission of Phi Delta Kappa International, www.pdkintl.org. All rights reserved.

Schools need demanding and distinctive special education that is clearly focused on instruction and habilitation.[1] Abandoning such a conception of special education is a prescription for disaster. But special education has increasingly been losing its way in the single-minded pursuit of full inclusion.

Once, special education's purpose was to bring the performance of students with disabilities closer to that of their nondisabled peers in regular classrooms, to move as many students as possible into the mainstream with appropriate support.[2] For students not in regular education, the goal was to move them toward a more typical setting in a cascade of placement options.[3] But as any good thing can be overdone and ruined by the pursuit of extremes, we see special education suffering from the extremes of inclusion and accommodation.

Aiming for as much normalization as possible gave special education a clear purpose. Some disabilities were seen as easier to remediate than others. Most speech and language disorders, for example, were considered eminently remediable. Other disabilities, such as mental retardation and many physical disabilities, were assumed to be permanent or long-term and so less remediable, but movement *toward* the mainstream and increasing independence from special educators were clear goals.

The emphasis in special education has shifted away from normalization, independence, and competence. The result has been students' dependence on whatever special programs, modifications, and accommodations are possible, particularly in general education settings. The goal seems to have become the *appearance* of normalization without the *expectation* of competence.

Many parents and students seem to want more services as they learn what is available. Some have lost sight of the goal of limiting accommodations in order to challenge students to achieve more independence. At the same

FOCUS QUESTION

As you read this article, are you persuaded that the pendulum toward full inclusion has swung too far, thus reducing special education services for youngsters who might need them?

InTASC

Standards 1, 2, 3, 6, 7, 8, and 10

KEY TERMS

- Inclusion
- Individualized education program (IEP)
- Mainstreaming

time, many special education advocates want all services to be available in mainstream settings, with little or no acknowledgment that the services are atypical. Although teachers, administrators, and guidance counselors are often willing and able to make accommodations, doing so is not always in students' best long-term interests. It gives students with disabilities what anthropologist Robert Edgerton called a cloak—a pretense, a cover, which actually fools no one—rather than actual competence.[4]

In this article, we discuss how changes in attitudes toward disability and special education, placement, and accommodations can perpetuate disability. We also explore the problems of ignoring or perpetuating disability rather than helping students lead fuller, more independent lives. Two examples illustrate how we believe good intentions can go awry—how attempts to accommodate students with disabilities can undermine achievement.

"*But he needs resource….*" Thomas, a high school sophomore identified as emotionally disturbed, was assigned to a resource class created to help students who had problems with organization or needed extra help with academic skills. One of the requirements in the class was for students to keep a daily planner in which they entered all assignments; they shared their planner with the resource teacher at the beginning of class and discussed what academic subjects would be worked on during that period.

Thomas consistently refused to keep a planner or do any work in resource (he slept instead). So a meeting was set up with the assistant principal, the guidance counselor, Thomas, and the resource teacher. As the meeting was about to begin, the principal announced that he would not stay because Thomas felt intimidated by so many adults. After listening to Thomas' complaints, the guidance counselor decided that Thomas would not have to keep a planner or show it to the resource teacher and that the resource teacher should not talk to him unless Thomas addressed her first. In short, Thomas would not be required to do any work in the class! When the resource teacher suggested that under those circumstances, Thomas should perhaps be placed in a study hall, because telling the parents

that he was in a resource class would be a misrepresentation, the counselor replied, "But he *needs* the resource class."

"*He's too bright….*" Bob, a high school freshman with Asperger's Syndrome, was scheduled for three honors classes and two Advanced Placement classes. Bob's IEP (individualized education program) included a two-page list of accommodations. In spite of his having achieved A's and B's, with just a single C in math, his mother did not feel that his teachers were accommodating him appropriately. Almost every evening, she e-mailed his teachers and his case manager to request more information or more help for Bob, and she angrily phoned his guidance counselor if she didn't receive a reply by the end of the first hour of the next school day.

A meeting was scheduled with the IEP team, including five of Bob's seven teachers, the county special education supervisor, the guidance counselor, the case manager, the principal, and the county autism specialist. When the accommodations were reviewed, Bob's mother agreed that all of them were being made. However, she explained that Bob had been removed from all outside social activities because he spent all night, every night, working on homework. The accommodation she demanded was that Bob have *no* homework assignments. The autism specialist agreed that this was a reasonable accommodation for a child with Asperger's Syndrome.

The teachers of the honors classes explained that the homework in their classes, which involved elaboration and extension of concepts, was even more essential than the homework assigned in AP classes. In AP classes, by contrast, homework consisted primarily of practice of concepts learned in class. The honors teachers explained that they had carefully broken their long assignments into segments, each having a separate due date before the final project, and they gave illustrations of their expectations. The director of special education explained the legal definition of accommodations (the mother said she'd never before heard that accommodations could not change the nature of the curriculum). The director also suggested that, instead of Bob's sacrificing his social life, perhaps it would be more appropriate for him to take standard classes. What Bob's mother was asking, he concluded, was not legal. She grew angry, but she did agree to give the team a "little more time" to serve Bob appropriately. She said she would "be back with her claws and broomstick" if anyone ever suggested that he be moved from honors classes without being given the no-homework accommodation. "He's too bright to take anything less than honors classes, and if you people would provide this simple accommodation, he would do just fine," she argued. In the end, she got her way.

Attitudes Toward Disability and Special Education

Not that many decades ago, a disability was considered a misfortune—not something to be ashamed of but a generally undesirable, unwelcome condition to be overcome to the greatest extent possible. Ability was considered more desirable than disability, and anything—whether a device or a service—that helped people with disabilities to do what those without disabilities could do was considered generally valuable, desirable, and worth the effort, cost, and possible stigma associated with using it.

The disability rights movement arose in response to the widespread negative attitudes toward disabilities, and it had a number of desirable outcomes. It helped overcome some of the discrimination against people with disabilities. And overcoming such bias and unfairness in everyday life is a great accomplishment. But the movement has also had some unintended negative consequences. One of these is the outright denial of disability in some cases, illustrated by the contention that disability exists only in attitudes or as a function of the social power to coerce.[5] The argument that disability is merely a "social construction" is particularly vicious in its effects on social justice. Even if we assume that disabilities are socially constructed, what should that mean? Should we assume that socially constructed phenomena are not "real," are not important, or should be discredited? If so, then consider that dignity, civil rights, childhood, social justice, and nearly every other phenomenon that we hold dear are social constructions. Many

social constructions are not merely near and dear to us, they are real and useful in benevolent societies. The important question is whether the idea of disability is useful in helping people attain dignity or whether it is more useful to assume that disabilities are not real (i.e., that, like social justice, civil rights, and other social constructions, they are fabrications that can be ignored when convenient). The denial of disability is sometimes expressed as an aversion to labels, so that we are cautioned not to communicate openly and clearly about disabilities but to rely on euphemisms. But this approach is counterproductive. When we are able only to whisper or mime the undesirable difference called disability, then we inadvertently increase its stigma and thwart prevention efforts.[6]

The specious argument that "normal" does not exist—because abilities of every kind are varied and because the point at which normal becomes abnormal is arbitrary—leads to the conclusion that no one actually has a disability or, alternatively, that everyone has a disability. Then, some argue, either no one or everyone is due an accommodation so that no one or everyone is identified as disabled. This unwillingness to draw a line defining something (such as disability, poverty, or childhood) is based either on ignorance regarding the nature of continuous distributions or on a rejection of the unavoidably arbitrary decisions necessary to provide special services to those who need them and, in so doing, to foster social justice.[7]

Another unintended negative consequence of the disability rights movement is that, for some people, disability has become either something that does not matter or something to love, to take pride in, to flaunt, to adopt as a positive aspect of one's identity, or to cherish as something desirable or as a badge of honor. When disability makes no difference to us one way or the other, then we are not going to work to attenuate it, much less prevent it. At best, we will try to accommodate it. When we view disability as a desirable difference, then we are very likely to try to make it more pronounced, not to ameliorate it.

Several decades ago, special education was seen as a good thing—a helpful way of responding to disability, not something everyone needed or should have, but a useful and necessary response to the atypical needs of students with disabilities. This is why the Education for All Handicapped Children Act (now the Individuals with Disabilities Education Act) was written. But in the minds of many people, special education has been transformed from something helpful to something awful.[8]

The full-inclusion movement did have some desirable outcomes. It helped overcome some of the unnecessary removal of students with disabilities from general education. However, the movement also has had some unintended negative consequences. One of these is that special education has come to be viewed in very negative terms, to be seen as a second-class and discriminatory system that does more harm than good. Rather than being seen as helpful, as a way of creating opportunity, special education is often portrayed as a means of shunting students into dead-end programs and killing opportunity.[9]

Another unintended negative consequence of full inclusion is that general education is now seen by many as the *only* place where fair and equitable treatment is possible and where the opportunity to learn is extended to all equally.[10] The argument has become that special education is good only as long as it is invisible (or nearly so), an indistinguishable part of a general education system that accommodates all students, regardless of their abilities or disabilities. Usually, this is described as a "unified" (as opposed to "separate") system of education.[11] Special education is thus something to be avoided altogether or attenuated to the greatest extent possible, regardless of a student's inability to perform in a general setting. When special education is seen as discriminatory, unfair, an opportunity-killing system, or, as one writer put it, "the gold-plated garbage can of American schooling,"[12] then it is understandable that people will loathe it. But this way of looking at special education is like seeing the recognition and treatment of cancer as the cause of the problem.

The reversal in attitudes toward disability and special education—disability from undesirable to inconsequential, special education from desirable to awful—has clouded the picture of what special education is and what it should do for students with disabilities. Little wonder that special education stands accused of failure, that calls for its demise have become vociferous, and that contemporary practices are often more disabling than enabling. An unfortunate outcome of the changing attitudes toward disability and special education is that the benefit of special education is now sometimes seen as freedom from expectations of performance. It is as if we believed that, if a student has to endure the stigma of special education, then the compensation should include an exemption from work.

Placement Issues

Placing all students, regardless of their abilities, in regular classes has exacerbated the tendency to see disability as something existing only in people's minds. It fosters the impression that students are fitting in when they are not able to perform at anywhere near the normal level. It perpetuates disabilities; it does not compensate for them.

Administrators and guidance counselors sometimes place students in programs for which they do not qualify, even as graduation requirements are increasing and tests are mandated. Often, these students' *testing* is modified although their *curriculum* is not. The students may then feel that they have beaten the system. They are taught that the system is unfair and that the only way to win is by gaming it. Hard work and individual responsibility for one's education are often overlooked—or at least undervalued.

Students who consistently fail in a particular curriculum must be given the opportunity to deal with the natural consequences of that fact as a means of learning individual responsibility. For example, social promotion in elementary and middle school teaches students that they really don't have to be able to do the work to pass. Students who have been conditioned to rely on social promotion do not believe that the cycle will end until it does so—usually very abruptly in high school. Suddenly, no one passes them on, and no one gives them undeserved credit. Many of these students do not graduate in four years. Some never recover, while others find themselves forced to deal with a very distasteful situation.

No one wants to see a student fail, but to alter any standard without good reason is to set that same student up for failure later in life. Passing along a student with disabilities in regular classes, pretending that he or she is performing at the same level as most of the class or that it doesn't really matter (arguing that the student has a legal "right" to be in the class) is another prescription for disappointment and failure in later life. Indeed, this failure often comes in college or on the job.

Some people with disabilities do need assistance. Others do not. Consider Deborah Groeber, who struggled through degenerative deafness and blindness. The Office of Affirmative Action at the University of Pennsylvania offered to intercede at the Wharton School, but Groeber knew that she had more influence if she spoke for herself. Today, she is a lawyer with three Ivy League degrees.[13] But not every student with disabilities can do or should be expected to do what Groeber did. Our concern is that too many students with disabilities are given encouragement based on pretense when they could do much more with appropriate special education.

Types of Accommodations

Two popular modifications in IEPs are allowing for the use of calculators and granting extended time on tests and assignments. Calculators can be a great asset, but they should be used when calculating complex problems or when doing word problems. Indiscriminate use of a calculator renders many math tests invalid, as they become a contest to see if buttons can be pushed successfully and in the correct order, rather than an evaluation of ability to do arithmetic or use mathematical knowledge.

Extended time on assignments and tests can also be a useful modification, but it can easily be misused or abused. Extended time on tests should mean *continuous* time so that a test is not studied for first and taken later. Sometimes a test must be broken into smaller segments that can be completed independently. However, this could put students with disabilities at a disadvantage, as one part of a test might help with remembering another part. Extensions on assignments need to be evaluated each time they are given, not simply handed out automatically because they are written into an IEP. If a student is clearly working hard, then extensions may be appropriate. If a student has not even been attempting assignments, then more time might be an avoidance tactic. Sometimes extended time means that assignments pile up and the student gets further and further behind. The result can then be overwhelming stress and the inability to comprehend discussions because many concepts must be acquired in sequence (e.g., in math, science, history, and foreign languages).

Reading tests and quizzes aloud to students can be beneficial for many, but great caution is required. Some students and teachers want to do more than simply read a test. Reading a test aloud means simply reading the printed words on the page *without* inflections that can reveal correct answers and without explaining vocabulary. Changing a test to open-notes or open-book, without the knowledge and consent of the classroom teacher, breaches good-faith test proctoring. It also teaches students dependence rather than independence and accomplishment. Similarly, scribing for a student can be beneficial for those who truly need it, but the teacher must be careful not to add details and to write only what the student dictates, including any run-on sentences or fragments. After scribing, if the assignment is not a test, the teacher should edit and correct the paper with the student, as she might do with any written work. But this must take place *after* the scribing.

How Misguided Accommodations Can Be Disabling

"Saving" a child from his or her own negative behavior reinforces that behavior and makes it a self-fulfilling prophecy. Well-intentioned guidance counselors often feel more responsibility for their students' success or failure than the students themselves feel. Sometimes students are not held accountable for their effort or work. They seem not to understand that true independence comes from *what* you know, not *whom* you know. Students who are consistently enabled and not challenged are never given the opportunity to become independent. Ann Bancroft, the polar explorer and dyslexic, claims that, although school was a torment, it was disability that forged her iron will.[14] Stephen Cannell's fear for other dyslexics is that they will quit trying rather than struggle and learn to compensate for their disability.[15]

Most parents want to help their children. However, some parents confuse making life *easier* with making life *better* for their children. Too often, parents feel that protecting their child from the rigors of academic demands is in his or her best interest. They may protect their child by insisting on curricular modifications and accommodations in assignments, time, and testing. But children learn by doing, and not allowing them to do something because they might fail is denying them the opportunity to succeed. These students eventually believe that they are not capable of doing what typical students can do, even if they are. Sometimes it is difficult for teachers to discern what a student actually can do and what a parent has done until an in-class assignment is given or a test is taken. At that point, it is often too late for the teacher to do much remediation. The teacher may erroneously conclude that the student is simply a poor test-taker.

In reality, the student may have been "protected" from learning, which will eventually catch up with him or her. Unfortunately, students may not face reality until they take a college entrance exam, go away to college, or apply for a job. Students who "get through" high school in programs of this type often go on to flunk out of college. Unfortunately, the parents of these students frequently blame the college for the student's failure, criticizing the post-secondary institution for not doing enough to help. Instead, they should be upset both with the secondary institution for not preparing the child adequately for the tasks to come and with themselves for their own overprotection.

The Benefits of Demands

Many successful adults with disabilities sound common themes when asked about their ability to succeed in the face of a disability. Tom Gray, a Rhodes Scholar who has a severe learning disability, claims that having to deal with the hardest experiences gave him the greatest strength.[16] Stephen Cannell believes that, if he had known there was a reason beyond his control to explain his low achievement, he might not have worked as hard as he did. Today, he knows he has a learning disability, but he is also an Emmy Award–winning television writer and producer.[17] Paul Orlalea, the dyslexic founder of Kinko's, believes God gave him an advantage in the challenge presented by his disability and that others should work with their strengths. Charles Schwab, the learning-disabled founder of Charles Schwab, Inc., cites his ability to think differently and to make creative leaps that more sequential thinkers don't make as chief reasons for his success. Fannie Flagg, the learning-disabled author, concurs and insists that learning disabilities become a blessing *only if you can overcome them*.[18] Not every student with a disability can be a star performer, of course, but all should be expected to achieve all that they can.

Two decades ago, special educators thought it was their job to assess a student's achievement, to understand what the student wanted to do and what an average peer could do, and then to develop plans to bridge the gap, if possible. Most special educators wanted to see that each student had the tools and knowledge to succeed as independently as possible. Helping students enter the typical world was the mark of success for special educators.

The full-inclusion movement now insists that *every* student will benefit from placement in the mainstream. However, some of the modifications and accommodations now being demanded are so radical that we are doing an injustice to the entire education system.[19] Special education must not be associated in any way with "dumbing down" the curriculum for students presumed to be at a given grade level, whether disabled or not.

Counselors and administrators who want to enable students must focus the discussion on realistic goals and plans for each student. An objective, in-depth discussion and evaluation must take place to determine how far along the continuum of successfully completing these goals the student has moved. If the student is making adequate progress independently, or with minimal help, special education services might not be necessary. If assistance is required to make adequate progress on realistic goals, then special education may be needed. Every modification and every accommodation should be held to the same standard: whether it will help the student attain these goals—*not* whether it will make life easier for the student. Knowing where a student is aiming can help a team guide that student toward success.

And the student must be part of this planning. A student who claims to want to be a brain surgeon but refuses to take science courses needs a reality check. If a student is unwilling to attempt to reach intermediate goals or does not succeed in meeting them, then special education cannot "save" that student. At that point, the team must help the student revisit his or her goals. Goals should be explained in terms of the amount of work required to complete them, not whether or not the teacher or parent feels they are attainable. When goals are presented in this way, students can often make informed decisions regarding their attainability and desirability. Troy Brown, a university dean and politician who has both a doctorate and a learning disability, studied at home with his mother. He estimates that it took him more than twice as long as the average person to complete assignments. Every night, he would go to bed with stacks of books and read until he fell asleep, because he had a dream of attending college.[20]

General educators and special educators need to encourage all students to be responsible and independent and to set realistic expectations for themselves. Then teachers must help students to meet these expectations in a more and more independent manner. Special educators do not serve students well when they enable students with disabilities to become increasingly dependent on their parents, counselors, administrators, or teachers—or even when they fail to increase students' independence and competence.

Where We Stand

We want to make it clear that we think disabilities are real and that they make doing certain things either impossible or very difficult for the people who have them. We cannot expect people with disabilities to be "just like everyone else" in what they can do. The views of other writers differ:

> The human service practices that cause providers to believe that clients [students] have inadequacies, shortcomings, failures, or faults that must be corrected or controlled by specially trained professionals must be replaced by conceptions that people with disabilities are capable of setting their own goals and achieving or not. Watered-down curricula, alternative grading practices, special competency standards, and other "treat them differently" practices used with "special" students must be replaced with school experiences exactly like those used with "regular" students.[21]

We disagree. In our view, students with disabilities *do* have specific shortcomings and *do* need the services of specially trained professionals to achieve their potential. They *do* sometimes need altered curricula or adaptations to make their learning possible. If students with disabilities were just like "regular" students, then there would be no need whatever for special education. But the school experiences of students with disabilities obviously will not be—*cannot* be—just like those of students without disabilities. We sell students with disabilities short when we pretend that they are no different from typical students. We make the same error when we pretend that they must *not* be expected to put forth extra effort if they are to learn to do some things—or learn to do something in a different way. We sell them short when we pretend that they have competencies that they do not have or pretend that the competencies we expect of most students are not important for them.

Like general education, special education must push students to become all they can be. Special education must countenance neither the pretense of learning nor the avoidance of reasonable demands.

Notes

1. James M. Kauffman and Daniel P. Hallahan, *Special Education: What It Is and Why We Need It* (Boston: Allyn & Bacon, forthcoming).

2. Doug Fuchs et al., "Toward a Responsible Reintegration of Behaviorally Disordered Students," *Behavioral Disorders,* February 1991, pp. 133–47.

3. Evelyn Deno, "Special Education as Development Capital," *Exceptional Children,* November 1970, pp. 229–37; and Dixie Snow Huefner, "The Mainstreaming Cases: Tensions and Trends for School Administrators," *Educational Administration Quarterly,* February 1994, pp. 27–55.

4. Robert B. Edgerton, *The Cloak of Competence: Stigma in the Lives of the Mentally Retarded* (Berkeley, Calif.: University of California Press, 1967); idem, *The Cloak of Competence,* rev. ed. (Berkeley, Calif.: University of California Press, 1993); and James M. Kauffman, "Appearances, Stigma, and Prevention," *Remedial and Special Education,* vol. 24, 2003, pp. 195–98.

5. See, for example, Scot Danforth and William C. Rhodes, "Deconstructing Disability: A Philosophy for Education," *Remedial and Special Education,* November/December 1997, pp. 357–66; and Phil Smith, "Drawing New Maps: A Radical Cartography of Developmental Disabilities," *Review of Educational Research,* Summer 1999, pp. 117–44.

6. James M. Kauffman, *Education Deform: Bright People Sometimes Say Stupid Things About Education* (Lanham, Md.: Scarecrow Education, 2002).

7. Ibid.

8. James M. Kauffman, "Reflections on the Field," *Behavioral Disorders,* vol. 28, 2003, pp. 205–8.

9. See, for example, Clint Bolick, "A Bad IDEA Is Disabling Public Schools," *Education Week,* 5 September 2001, pp. 56, 63; and Michelle Cottle, "Jeffords Kills Special Ed. Reform School," *New Republic,* 18 June 2001, pp. 14–15.

10. See, for example, Dorothy K. Lipsky and Alan Gartner, "Equity Requires Inclusion: The Future for All Students with Disabilities," in Carol Christensen and Fazal Rizvi, eds., *Disability and the Dilemmas of Education and Justice* (Philadelphia: Open University Press, 1996), pp. 144–55; and William Stainback and Susan Stainback, "A Rationale for Integration and Restructuring: A Synopsis," in John W. Lloyd, Nirbhay N. Singh, and Alan C. Repp, eds., *The Regular Education Initiative: Alternative Perspectives on Concepts, Issues, and Models* (Sycamore, Ill.: Sycamore, 1991), pp. 225–39.

11. See, for example, Alan Gartner and Dorothy K. Lipsky, *The Yoke of Special Education: How to Break It* (Rochester, N.Y.: National Center on Education and the Economy, 1989). For an alternative view, see James M. Kauffman and Daniel P. Hallahan, "Toward a Comprehensive Delivery System for Special Education," in John I. Goodlad and Thomas C. Lovitt, eds., *Integrating General and Special Education* (Columbus, Ohio: Merrill, 1993), pp. 73–102.

12. Marc Fisher, "Students Still Taking the Fall for D.C. Schools," *Washington Post,* 13 December 2001, p. B-1.

13. Elizabeth Tener, "Blind, Deaf, and Very Successful," *McCall's,* December 1995, pp. 42–46.

14. Christina Cheakalos et al., "Heavy Mettle: They May Have Trouble Reading and Spelling, but Those with the Grit to Overcome Learning Disabilities Like Dyslexia Emerge Fortified for Life," *People,* 30 October 2001, pp. 18, 58.

15. Ibid.

16. Ibid.

17. Stephen Cannell, "How to Spell Success," *Reader's Digest,* August 2000, pp. 63–66.

18. Cheakalos et al., op cit.

19. Anne Proffit Dupre, "Disability, Deference, and the Integrity of the Academic Enterprise," *Georgia Law Review,* Winter 1998, pp. 393–473.

20. Cheakalos et al., op cit.

21. James E. Ysseldyke, Bob Algozzine, and Martha L. Thurlow, *Critical Issues in Special Education,* 3rd ed. (Boston: Houghton-Mifflin, 2000), p. 67.

POSTNOTE

The movement toward full inclusion of children with disabilities into the regular education classroom has gained considerable support and momentum in the last fifteen years. Many supporters of full inclusion contend that disabled youngsters have a civil right to be educated with their nondisabled peers. The authors of this article, while supportive of inclusion, believe the movement has gone too far by not always serving the students' long-term interests. The authors believe that many parents, by insisting on the full inclusion of their child in the regular classroom, are denying the child the full range of services that are available in special education settings, particularly for those students whose disabilities are more severe.

DISCUSSION QUESTIONS

1. What aspects of inclusion seem to cause controversy, and why is this so?
2. Have you had any experiences working with children with disabilities? If so, describe the circumstances and your successes or failures. If you haven't worked with children with disabilities, are you planning to get this experience? If so, how?
3. What do you think are the strongest arguments made by the authors of this article? If you could ask them a question, what would it be?

RELATED WEBSITE RESOURCE AND VIDEO CASE

WEB RESOURCE:

University of Virginia: A Web Resource for Special Education. Available at:

http://special.edschool.virginia.edu.

This website contains much information about special education.

▶❚❚ TEACHSOURCE VIDEO CASE

INCLUDING STUDENTS WITH HIGH INCIDENCE DISABILITIES: STRATEGIES FOR SUCCESS

In this video, you'll see how a veteran teacher accommodates the learning needs of all her students in her elementary inclusion classroom. Go to the website for the Education Media Library at CengageBrain.com to watch the video clips, study the artifacts in the case, and reflect on the following questions.

1. This teacher uses several strategies to help all of her students develop as writers. What are the strengths of each of these strategies and which ones might you want to include in your own teaching repertoire?
2. What technologies can be used to help address various learning challenges experienced by these and similar students?

54

Making Inclusive Education Work

Richard A. Villa and Jacqueline S. Thousand

Richard A. Villa is president of Bayridge Consortium, San Diego, California. **Jacqueline S. Thousand** is professor in the College of Education at California State University– San Marcos.

"Making Inclusive Education work," by Richard A. Villa and Jacqueline S. Thousand, 2003, *Educational Leadership 61*(2), pp. 19–23. © 2003 by ASCD. Reprinted with permission. Learn more about ASCD at www.ascd.org.

FOCUS QUESTION

As you read this article, think of the various benefits and challenges that inclusion presents to both the classroom teacher and the disabled child.

InTASC

Standards 1, 2, 3, 6, 7, 8, and 10

KEY TERMS

- Complementary teaching
- Consultation
- Coteaching
- Differentiated instruction
- Inclusion
- Least restrictive environment (LRE)
- Parallel teaching
- Supportive teaching

As an educator, you are philosophically committed to student diversity. You appreciate that learning differences are natural and positive. You focus on identifying and capitalizing on individual students' interests and strengths. But making inclusive education work requires something more: It takes both systems-level support and classroom-level strategies.

Since the 1975 implementation of the Individuals with Disabilities Education Act (IDEA), federal law has stated that children with disabilities have the right to an education in the least restrictive environment (LRE). According to the act, removal from general education environments should occur only when a student has failed to achieve satisfactorily despite documented use of supplemental supports, aids, and services.

During the past 28 years, the interpretation of what constitutes the least restrictive environment has evolved, along with schools' and educators' abilities to provide effective supports. As a result, increased numbers of students with disabilities are now served in both regular schools and general education classes within those schools.

When IDEA was first promulgated in 1975, schools generally interpreted the law to mean that they should mainstream students with mild disabilities— for example, those with learning disabilities and those eligible for speech and language services—into classes where these students could keep up with other learners, supposedly with minimal support and few or no modifications to either curriculum or instruction. In the early 1980s, however, the interpretation of least restrictive environment evolved to include the concept of integrating students with more intensive needs—those with moderate and severe disabilities—into regular classrooms. By the late 1980s and early 1990s, the interpretation evolved into the approach now known as *inclusion:* the principle and practice of considering general education as the placement of first choice for all learners. This approach encourages educators to bring necessary supplemental supports, aids, and services into the classroom instead of removing students from the classroom for those services.

As the interpretation of least restrictive environment has changed, the proportion of students with disabilities included in general education has increased dramatically. By 1999, 47.4 percent of students with disabilities spent 80 percent or more of their day in general education classrooms, compared with 25 percent of students with disabilities in 1985 (U.S. Department of Education, 2003).

Although the 1997 reauthorization of IDEA did not actually use the term *inclusion,* it effectively codified the principle and practice of inclusion by requiring that students' Individualized Education Programs (IEPs) ensure access to the general education curriculum. This landmark re-authorization broadened the concept of inclusion to include academic as well as physical and social access to general education instruction and experiences (Kluth, Villa, & Thousand, 2002).

Despite the continued evolution toward inclusive education, however, tremendous disparities exist among schools, districts, and states. For example, the U.S. Department of Education (2003) found that the percentage of students with disabilities ages 6–21 who were taught for 80 percent or more of the school day in general education classrooms ranged from a low of 18 percent in Hawaii to a high of 82 percent in Vermont. Further, the nature of inclusion varies. In some schools, inclusion means the mere physical presence or social inclusion of students with disabilities in regular classrooms; in other schools, it means active modification of content, instruction, and assessment practices so that students can successfully engage in core academic experiences and learning.

Why can some schools and districts implement inclusion smoothly and effectively, whereas others cannot? Three sources give guidance in providing high-quality inclusive practice. First, research findings of the past decade have documented effective inclusive schooling practices (McGregor & Vogelsberg, 1998; National Center on Educational Restructuring and Inclusion, 1995; Villa, Thousand, Meyers, & Nevin, 1996). Second, our own experiences as educators suggest several variables. Third, we interviewed 20 nationally recognized leaders in the field of inclusive education who, like ourselves, provide regular consultation and training throughout the United States regarding inclusive practice.

A Systems Approach

Successful promotion and implementation of inclusive education require the five following systems-level practices: connection with other organizational best practices; visionary leadership and administrative support; redefined roles and relationships among adults and students; collaboration; and additional adult support when needed.

Connection with Best Practices

Inclusive education is most easily introduced in school communities that have already restructured to meet the needs of their increasingly diverse student populations in regular education. Initiatives and organizational best practices to accomplish this aim include trans-disciplinary teaming, block scheduling, multi-age student grouping and looping, schoolwide positive behavior support and discipline approaches, detracking, and school-within-a-school family configurations of students and teachers. These initiatives facilitate the inclusion and development of students with disabilities within general education.

School leaders should clearly communicate to educators and families that best practices to facilitate inclusion are identical to best practices for educating all students. This message will help members of the school community understand that inclusion is not an add-on, but a natural extension of promising research-based education practices that positively affect the teaching and learning of all students.

Visionary Leadership

A national study on the implementation of IDEA's least restrictive environment requirement emphasized the importance of leadership—in both vision and practice—to the installation of inclusive education. The researchers concluded,

How leadership at each school site chose to look at LRE was critical to how, or even whether, much would be accomplished beyond the status quo. (Hasazi, Johnston, Liggett, & Schattman, 1994, p. 506)

In addition, a study of 32 inclusive school sites in five states and one Canadian province found that the degree of administrative support and vision was the most powerful predictor of general educators' attitudes toward inclusion (Villa et al., 1996).

For inclusive education to succeed, administrators must take action to publicly articulate the new vision, build consensus for the vision, and lead all stakeholders to active involvement. Administrators can provide four types of support identified as important by frontline general and special educators: personal and emotional (for example, being willing to listen to concerns); informational (for example, providing training and technical assistance); instrumental (for example, creating time for teachers to meet); and appraisal (for example, giving constructive feedback related to implementation of new practices) (Littrell, Billingsley, & Cross, 1994).

Visionary leaders recognize that changing any organization, including a school, is a complex act. They know that organizational transformation requires ongoing attention to consensus building for the inclusive vision. It also requires skill development on the part of educators and everyone involved in the change; the provision of extra common planning time and fiscal, human, technological, and organizational resources to motivate experimentation with new practices; and the collaborative development and communication of a well-formulated plan of action for transforming the culture and practice of a school (Ambrose, 1987; Villa & Thousand, in press).

Redefined Roles

For school personnel to meet diverse student needs, they must stop thinking and acting in isolated ways: "These are my students, and those are your students." They must relinquish traditional roles, drop distinct professional labels, and redistribute their job functions across the system. To facilitate this role redefinition, some schools have developed a single job description for all professional educators that clearly articulates as expected job functions collaboration and shared responsibility for educating all of a community's children and youth.

To help school personnel make this shift, schools must clarify the new roles—for example, by making general education personnel aware of their legal responsibilities for meeting the needs of learners with disabilities in the least restrictive environment. In addition, schools must provide necessary training through a variety of vehicles, including in-service opportunities, coursework, co-teaching, professional support groups, and other coaching and mentoring activities. After clarifying teachers' new responsibilities and providing training, schools should encourage staff members to reflect on how they will differentiate instruction and design accommodations and modifications to meet the needs of all students. School administrators should monitor the degree of collaboration between general and special educators. They should also include implementation of IEP-mandated activities as part of ongoing district evaluation procedures.

Collaboration

Reports from school districts throughout the United States identify collaboration as a key variable in the successful implementation of inclusive education. Creating planning teams, scheduling time for teachers to work and teach together, recognizing teachers as problem solvers, conceptualizing teachers as frontline researchers, and effectively collaborating with parents are all dimensions reported as crucial to successful collaboration (National Center on Educational Restructuring and Inclusion, 1995).

Achievement of inclusive education presumes that no one person could have all the expertise required to meet the needs of all the students in a classroom. For inclusive education to work, educators must become effective and efficient collaborative team members. They must develop skills in creativity, collaborative teaming processes, co-teaching, and interpersonal communication that will enable them to work together to craft diversified learning opportunities for learners who have a wide range of interests, learning styles, and intelligences (Thousand & Villa, 2000; Villa, 2000a; Villa, Thousand, & Nevin, in preparation). In a study of more than 600 educators, collaboration emerged as the only variable that predicted positive attitudes toward inclusion among general and special educators as well as administrators (Villa et al., 1996).

Adult Support

An "only as much as needed" principle dictates best practices in providing adult support to students. This approach avoids inflicting help on those who do not necessarily need or want it. Thus, when paraprofessionals are assigned to classrooms, they should be presented to students as members of a teaching team rather than as people "velcroed" to individual students.

Teaching models in which general and specialized personnel work together as a team are effective and efficient ways of arranging adult support to meet diverse student needs (National Center on Educational Restructuring and Inclusion, 1995; Villa, 2002b). Such models include

- *Consultation.* Support personnel provide assistance to the general educator, enabling him or her to teach all the students in the inclusive class.
- *Parallel teaching.* Support personnel—for example, a special educator, a Title I teacher, a psychologist, or a speech language therapist—and the classroom teacher rotate among heterogeneous groups of students in different sections of the general education classroom.
- *Supportive teaching.* The classroom teacher takes the lead role, and support personnel rotate among the students.
- *Complementary teaching.* The support person does something to complement the instruction provided by the classroom teacher (for example, takes notes on a transparency or paraphrases the teacher's statements).
- *Coteaching.* Support personnel coteach alongside the general education teacher.

Promoting Inclusion in the Classroom

Several curricular, instructional, and assessment practices benefit all the students in the classroom and help ensure successful inclusion. For instance, in a study conducted by the National Center on Educational Restructuring and Inclusion (1995), the majority of the districts implementing inclusive education reported cooperative learning as the most important instructional strategy supporting inclusive education. Some other general education theories and practices that also effectively support inclusion are

- Current theories of learning (such as multiple intelligences and constructivist learning).
- Teaching practices that make subject matter more relevant and meaningful (for example, partner learning, project- and activity-based learning, and service learning).
- Authentic alternatives to paper-and-pencil assessment (such as portfolio artifact collection, role playing, and demonstrations).
- A balanced approach to literacy development that combines whole-language and phonics instruction.
- Thematic/interdisciplinary curriculum approaches.
- Use of technology for communication ·and access to the general education curriculum.
- Differentiated instruction.

Responding to Diversity

Building on the notion of differentiated instruction (Tomlinson, 1999), universal design provides a contemporary approach to facilitate successful inclusion (Udvari-Solner, Villa, & Thousand, 2002).

In the traditional retrofit model, educators determine both content and instructional and assessment strategies without taking into consideration the special characteristics of the actual learners in the classroom. Then, if a mismatch exists between what students can do and what they are asked to do, educators make adjustments. In contrast, educators using the universal design framework consider the students and their various learning styles first. Then they differentiate curriculum *content, processes,* and *products* before delivering instruction.

For example, in a unit on the history of relations between the United States and Cuba, students might access *content* about the Cuban Missile Crisis by listening to a lecture, interviewing people who were alive at that time, conducting Internet research, reading the history text and other books written at a variety of reading levels, or viewing films or videos. The teacher can differentiate the *process* by allowing students to work independently, in pairs, or in cooperative groups. Additional processes that allow learners of differing abilities and learning styles to master standards include a combination of whole-class instruction, learning centers, reflective journal writing, technology, and field trips. Finally, students may demonstrate their learning through various *products,* including written reports, debates, role-plays, PowerPoint presentations, and songs.

Thus, students can use a variety of approaches to gain access to the curriculum, make sense of their learning, and show what they have learned. A universal design approach benefits every student, not just those identified as having disabilities.

Differentiating to enable a student with disabilities to access the general education curriculum requires creative thinking. Four options suggest varying degrees of student participation (Giangreco, Cloninger, & Iverson, 1998).

- First, a student can simply join in with the rest of the class.
- Second, multilevel curriculum and instruction can occur when all students involved in a lesson in the same curriculum area pursue varying levels of complexity.
- Curriculum overlapping is a third option, in which students working on the same lesson pursue objectives from different curricular areas. A student with severe disabilities, for example, could practice using a new communication

device during a hands-on science lesson while others focus primarily on science objectives.

- The fourth option, and the last resort, involves arranging alternative activities when a general education activity is inappropriate. For example, a student may need to participate in an activity within his Individualized Education Program, such as employment training in the community, that falls outside the scope of the general education curriculum.

Bridging the Gap

Systems-level and classroom-level variables such as these facilitate the creation and maintenance of inclusive education. Systemic support, collaboration, effective classroom practices, and a universal design approach can make inclusive education work so that students with disabilities have the same access to the general education curriculum and to classmates as any other student and the same opportunity for academic, social, and emotional success.

Inclusive education is a general education initiative, not another add-on school reform unrelated to other general education initiatives. It incorporates demonstrated general education best practices, and it redefines educators' and students' roles and responsibilities as creative and collaborative partners. The strategies described here can bridge the gap between what schools are doing well and what they can do better to make inclusion part and parcel of a general education program.

References

Ambrose, D. (1987). *Managing complex change.* Pittsburgh, PA: The Enterprise Group.

Giangreco, M. F., Cloninger, C. J., & Iverson, V. S. (1998). *Choosing outcomes and accommodations for children (COACH): A guide to educational planning for students with disabilities* (2nd ed.). Baltimore: Paul H. Brookes.

Hasazi, S., Johnston, A. P., Liggett, A. M., & Schattman, R. A. (1994). A qualitative policy study of the least restrictive environment provision of the Individuals with Disabilities Education Act. *Exceptional Children, 60,* 491–507.

Kluth, P., Villa, R. A., & Thousand, J. S. (2002). "Our school doesn't offer inclusion" and other legal blunders. *Educational Leadership, 59*(4), 24–27.

Littrell, P. C., Billingsley, B. S., & Cross, L. H. (1994). The effects of principal support on special and general educators' stress, job satisfaction, school commitment, health, and intent to stay in teaching. *Remedial and Special Education, 15*, 297–310.

McGregor, G., & Vogelsberg, T. (1998). *Inclusive schooling practices: Pedagogical and research foundations.* Baltimore: Paul H. Brookes.

National Center on Educational Restructuring and Inclusion. (1995). *National study on inclusive education.* New York: City University of New York.

Thousand, J. S., & Villa, R. A. (2000). Collaborative teaming: A powerful tool in school restructuring. In R. A. Villa & J. S. Thousand (Eds.), *Restructuring for caring and effective education: Piecing the puzzle together* (2nd ed., pp. 254–291). Baltimore: Paul H. Brookes.

Tomlinson, C. A. (1999). *The differentiated classroom.* Alexandria, VA: ASCD.

Udvari-Solner, A., Villa, R. A., & Thousand, J. S. (2002). Access to the general education curriculum for all: The universal design process. In J. S. Thousand, R. A. Villa, & A. I. Nevin (Eds.), *Creativity and collaborative learning* (2nd ed., pp. 85–103). Baltimore: Paul H. Brookes.

U.S. Department of Education. (2003). *Twenty-third annual report to Congress on the implementation of the Individuals with Disabilities Education Act.* Washington, DC: Author.

Villa, R. A. (2002a). *Collaborative planning: Transforming theory into practice* [Videotape]. Port Chester, NY: National Professional Resources.

Villa, R. A. (2002b). *Collaborative teaching: The coteaching model* [Videotape]. Port Chester, NY: National Professional Resources.

Villa, R. A., & Thousand, J. S. (in press). *Creating an inclusive school* (2nd ed.). Alexandria, VA: ASCD.

Villa, R. A., Thousand, J. S., Meyers, H., & Nevin, A. (1996). Teacher and administrator perceptions of heterogeneous education. *Exceptional Children, 63*, 29–45.

Villa, R. A., Thousand, J. S., & Nevin, A. (in preparation). *The many faces of co-teaching.* Thousand Oaks, CA: Corwin Press.

POSTNOTE

Working successfully with children with disabilities is one of the most challenging tasks facing beginning teachers. Over 6 million students, 12 percent of the total school population, receive federal aid for their disabilities, so it is likely that you will have students with disabilities in your classroom. It is important that you approach instruction for these children as you would for other students: expect diversity, expect a range of abilities, and look for the particular strengths and learning profiles of each student. If you are a regular education teacher, work with the special education teachers in your school to coordinate instruction and services for your students with disabilities. If you are a special education teacher, you will be expected to work closely with regular education teachers to provide the least restrictive environment and best instruction possible for these children. Only by working closely together can regular and special education teachers ensure that "no child is left behind."

DISCUSSION QUESTIONS

1. What concerns, if any, do you have about teaching children with disabilities? What can you do to address those concerns?
2. Is full inclusion a good idea? What limitations, if any, do you see in its implementation?
3. How would you go about ensuring that your regular education students are accepting of and helpful to any students with disabilities who might be in your class?

RELATED WEBSITE RESOURCE AND VIDEO CASES

WEB RESOURCE:

Council for Exceptional Children. Available at:

http://www.cec.sped.org.

This website of the national professional organization for special education contains many helpful resources.

▶❚❚ TEACHSOURCE VIDEO CASE

INCLUSION: GROUPING STRATEGIES FOR INCLUSIVE CLASSROOMS

In this video case, you'll see how a classroom teacher works with an inclusive specialist and additional support staff to ensure that each child in her fourth- and fifth-grade inclusion classroom succeeds in a unit on the Caribbean. Go to the website for the Education Media Library at CengageBrain.com to watch the video clips, study the artifacts in the case, and reflect on the following questions.

1. What did you notice about the collaborations that took place between the students with individual needs and typical learners? How would you characterize these interactions?
2. In structuring the groups of students for this unit, what aspects do the teacher and the inclusion specialist consider?

▶❚❚ TEACHSOURCE VIDEO CASE

MANAGING AN INCLUSIVE CLASSROOM: HIGH SCHOOL MATH INSTRUCTION

In this video case, you will see how a general education math teacher and a special education teacher who specializes in math-related learning problems work together to secure the best mathematics education for all of their students. Go to the website for the Education Media Library at CengageBrain.com to watch the video clips, study the artifacts in the case, and reflect on the following questions.

1. Have you observed an inclusive classroom? If so, compare and contrast your classroom with the classroom in the video case.
2. The teachers in the video speak of the importance of setting behavioral norms at the beginning of the year. What might a teacher do to encourage student discussion which would lead to a similar code of classroom conduct?
3. What, in your opinion, might be the benefits and challenges of the model shown in the video case?

55

With Boys and Girls in Mind

Michael Gurian and Kathy Stevens

Michael Gurian is cofounder of the Gurian Institute, and **Kathy Stevens** is director of the Gurian Institute, located in Colorado Springs, Colorado.

"With Boys and girls in Mind," by Michael Gurian and Kathy Stevens, 2004, *Educational Leadership* 62(3), pp. 40–44. © 2004 by ASCD. Reprinted with permission. Learn more about ASCD at www.ascd.org.

Something is awry in the way our culture handles the education needs of boys and girls. A smart 11-year-old boy gets low grades in school, fidgets and drifts off in class, and doesn't do his homework. A girl in middle school only uses the computer to instant-message her friends; when it comes to mastering more essential computer skills, she defers to the boys in the class.

Is contemporary education maliciously set against either males or females? We don't think so. But structurally and functionally, our schools fail to recognize and fulfill gender-specific needs. As one teacher wrote,

> For years I sensed that the girls and boys in my classrooms learn in gender-specific ways, but I didn't know enough to help each student reach full potential. I was trained in the idea that each student is an individual. But when I saw the PET scans of boys' and girls' brains, I saw how differently those brains are set up to learn. This gave me the missing component. I trained in male/female brain differences and was able to teach each individual child. Now, looking back, I'm amazed that teachers were never taught the differences between how girls and boys learn.

New positron emission tomography (PET) and MRI technologies enable us to look inside the brains of boys and girls, where we find structural and functional differences that profoundly affect human learning. These gender differences in the brain are corroborated in males and females throughout the world and do not differ significantly across cultures.

It's true that culture affects gender role, gender costume, and gender nuances—in Italy, for example, men cry more than they do in England—but role, costume, and nuance only affect some aspects of the learning brain of a child. New brain imaging technologies confirm that genetically templated brain patterning by gender plays a far larger role than we realized. Research into gender and education reveals a mismatch between many of our boys' and girls' learning brains and the institutions empowered to teach our children. We will briefly explore some of the differences, because recognizing these

FOCUS QUESTION

In what ways will schools and teaching practices need to change to address the differences in how boys and girls learn?

InTASC

Standards 1, 2, 3, 5, 7, and 8

KEY TERM

• Nature-based approach

differences can help us find solutions to many of the challenges that we experience in the classroom. Of course, generalized gender differences may not apply in every case.

The Minds of Girls

The following are some of the characteristics of girls' brains:

- A girl's corpus callosum (the connecting bundle of tissues between hemispheres) is, on average, larger than a boy's—up to 25 percent larger by adolescence. This enables more "cross talk" between hemispheres in the female brain.
- Girls have, in general, stronger neural connectors in their temporal lobes than boys have. These connectors lead to more sensually detailed memory storage, better listening skills, and better discrimination among the various tones of voice. This leads, among other things, to greater use of detail in writing assignments.
- The hippocampus (another memory storage area in the brain) is larger in girls than in boys, increasing girls' learning advantage, especially in the language arts.
- Girls' prefrontal cortex is generally more active than boys' and develops at earlier ages. For this reason, girls tend to make fewer impulsive decisions than boys do. Further, girls have more serotonin in the bloodstream and the brain, which makes them biochemically less impulsive.
- Girls generally use more cortical areas of their brains for verbal and emotive functioning. Boys tend to use more cortical areas of the brain for spatial and mechanical functioning (Moir & Jessel, 1989; Rich, 2000).

These "girl" brain qualities are the tip of the iceberg, yet they can immediately help teachers and parents understand why girls generally outperform boys in reading and writing from early childhood throughout life (Conlin, 2003). With more cortical areas devoted to verbal functioning, sensual memory, sitting still, listening, tonality, and mental cross talk, the complexities of reading and writing come easier, on the whole, to the female brain. In addition, the female brain experiences approximately 15 percent more blood flow, with this flow located in more centers of the brain at any given time (Marano, 2003). The female brain tends to drive itself toward stimulants—like reading and writing—that involve complex texture, tonality, and mental activity.

On the other hand, because so many cortical areas are used for verbal-emotive functioning, the female brain does not activate as many cortical areas as the male's does for abstract and physical-spatial functions, such as watching and manipulating objects that move through physical space and understanding abstract mechanical concepts (Moir & Jessel, 1989; Rich, 2000). This is one reason for many girls' discomfort with deep computer design language. Although some girls excel in these areas, more males than females gravitate toward physics, industrial engineering, and architecture. Children naturally gravitate toward activities that their brains experience as pleasurable—"pleasure" meaning in neural terms the richest personal stimulation. Girls and boys, within each neural web, tend to experience the richest personal stimulation somewhat differently.

The biological tendency toward female verbal-emotive functioning does not mean that girls or women should be left out of classes or careers that use spatial-mechanical skills. On the contrary: We raise these issues to call on our civilization to realize the differing natures of girls and boys and to teach each subject according to how the child's brain needs to learn it. On average, educators will need to provide girls with extra encouragement and gender-specific strategies to successfully engage them in spatial abstracts, including computer design.

The Minds of Boys

What, then, are some of the qualities that are generally more characteristic of boys' brains?

- Because boys' brains have more cortical areas dedicated to spatial-mechanical functioning, males use, on average, half the brain space that females use for verbal-emotive functioning. The cortical trend toward spatial-mechanical functioning makes many boys want to move objects through space, like balls, model airplanes, or just their arms and legs. Most boys, although not all of them, will experience words and feelings differently than girls do (Blum, 1997; Moir & Jessel, 1989).

- Boys not only have less serotonin than girls have, but they also have less oxytocin, the primary human bonding chemical. This makes it more likely that they will be physically impulsive and less likely that they will neurally combat their natural impulsiveness to sit still and emphatically chat with a friend (Moir & Jessel, 1989; Taylor, 2002).

- Boys lateralize brain activity. Their brains not only operate with less blood flow than girls' brains, but they are also structured to compartmentalize learning. Thus, girls tend to multitask better than boys do, with fewer attention span problems and greater ability to make quick transitions between lessons (Havers, 1995).

- The male brain is set to renew, recharge, and reorient itself by entering what neurologists call a *rest state*. The boy in the back of the classroom whose eyes are drifting toward sleep has entered a neural rest state. It is predominantly boys who drift off without completing assignments, who stop taking notes and fall asleep during a lecture, or who tap pencils or otherwise fidget in hopes of keeping themselves awake and learning. Females tend to recharge and reorient neural focus without rest states. Thus, a girl can be bored with a lesson, but she will nonetheless keep her eyes open, take notes, and perform relatively well. This is especially true when the teacher uses more words to teach a lesson instead of being spatial and diagrammatic. The more words a teacher uses, the more likely boys are to "zone out," or go into rest state. The male brain is better suited for symbols, abstractions, diagrams, pictures, and objects moving through space than for the monotony of words (Gurian, 2001).

These typical "boy" qualities in the brain help illustrate why boys generally learn higher math and physics more easily than most girls do when those subjects are taught abstractly on the chalkboard; why more boys than girls play video games that involve physical movement and even physical destruction; and why more boys than girls tend to get in trouble for impulsiveness, shows of boredom, and fidgeting as well as for their more generalized inability to listen, fulfill assignments, and learn in the verbal-emotive world of the contemporary classroom.

Who's Failing?

For a number of decades, most of our cultural sensitivity to issues of gender and learning came from advocacy groups that pointed out ways in which girls struggled in school. When David and Myra Sadker teamed with the American Association of University Women in the early 1990s, they found that girls were not called on as much as boys were, especially in middle school; that girls generally lagged in math/science testing; that boys dominated athletics; and that girls suffered drops in self-esteem as they entered middle and high school (AAUW, 1992). In large part because of this advocacy, our culture is attending to the issues that girls face in education.

At the same time, most teachers, parents, and other professionals involved in education know that it is mainly our boys who underperform in school. Since 1981, when the U.S. Department of Education began keeping complete statistics, we have seen that boys lag behind girls in most categories. The 2000 National Assessment of Educational Progress finds boys one and one-half years behind girls in reading/writing (National Center for Education Statistics, 2000). Girls are now only negligibly behind boys in math and science, areas in which boys have historically outperformed girls (Conlin, 2003). Our boys are now losing frightening ground in school, and we must come to terms with it—not in a way that robs girls, but in a way that sustains our civilization and is as powerful as the lobby we have created to help girls. The following statistics for the United States illustrate these concerns:

- Boys earn 70 percent of Ds and Fs and fewer than half of the As.
- Boys account for two-thirds of learning disability diagnoses.
- Boys represent 90 percent of discipline referrals.
- Boys dominate such brain-related learning disorders as ADD/ADHD, with millions now medicated in schools.
- 80 percent of high school dropouts are male.
- Males make up fewer than 40 percent of college students (Gurian, 2001).

These statistics hold true around the world. The Organisation for Economic Co-operation and Development (OECD) recently released its three-year study of knowledge and skills of males and females in 35 industrialized countries (including the United States, Canada, the European countries, Australia, and Japan). Girls outperformed boys in every country. The statistics that brought the male scores down most significantly were their reading/writing scores.

We have nearly closed the math/science gender gap in education for girls by using more verbal functioning—reading and written analysis—to teach such spatial-mechanical subjects as math, science, and computer science (Rubin, 2004; Sommers, 2000). We now need a new movement to alter classrooms to better suit boys' learning patterns if we are to deal with the gaps in grades, discipline, and reading/writing that threaten to close many boys out of college and out of success in life.

The Nature-Based Approach

In 1996, the Gurian Institute, an organization that administers training in child development, education, and male/female brain differences, coined the phrase *nature-based approach* to call attention to the importance of basing human attachment and education strategies on research-driven biological understanding of human learning. We argued that to broadly base education and other social processes

on anything other than human nature was to set up both girls and boys for unnecessary failure. The institute became especially interested in nature-based approaches to education when PET scans and MRIs of boys and girls revealed brains that were trying to learn similar lessons but in widely different ways and with varying success depending on the teaching method used. It became apparent that if teachers were trained in the differences in learning styles between boys and girls, they could profoundly improve education for all students. Between 1998 and 2000, a pilot program at the University of Missouri–Kansas City involving gender training in six school districts elicited significant results. One school involved in the training, Edison Elementary, had previously tested at the bottom of 18 district elementary schools. Following gender training, it tested in the top five slots, sometimes coming in first or second. Statewide, Edison outscored schools in every subject area, sometimes doubling and tripling the number of students in top achievement levels. Instead of the usual large number of students at the bottom end of achievement testing, Edison now had only two students requiring state-mandated retesting. The school also experienced a drastic reduction in discipline problems.

Statewide training in Alabama has resulted in improved performance for boys in both academic and behavioral areas. Beaumont Middle School in Lexington, Kentucky, trains its teachers in male/female brain differences and teaches reading/writing, math, and science in separate-sex classrooms. After one year of this gender-specific experiment, girls' math and science scores and boys' Scholastic Reading Inventory (SRI) scores rose significantly.

The Nature-Based Classroom

Ultimately, teacher training in how the brain learns and how boys and girls tend to learn differently creates the will and intuition in teachers and schools to create nature-based classrooms (see "Teaching Boys, Teaching Girls" for specific strategies). In an elementary classroom designed to help boys learn, tables and chairs are arranged to provide ample space for each child to spread out and claim learning space. Boys tend to need more physical learning space than girls do. At a table, a boy's materials will be less organized and more widely dispersed. Best practice would suggest having a variety of seating options—some desks, some tables, an easy chair, and a rug area for sitting or lying on the floor. Such a classroom would allow for more movement and noise than a traditional classroom would. Even small amounts of movement can help some boys stay focused.

The teacher can use the blocks area to help boys expand their verbal skills. As the boys are building, a teacher might ask them to describe their buildings. Because of greater blood flow in the cerebellum—the "doing" center of the human brain—boys more easily verbalize what they are doing than what they are feeling. Their language will be richer in vocabulary and more expansive when they are engaged in a task.

An elementary classroom designed to help girls learn will provide lots of opportunities for girls to manipulate objects, build, design, and calculate, thus preparing them for the more rigorous spatial challenges that they will face in higher-level math and science courses. These classrooms will set up spatial lessons in groups that encourage discussion among learners.

Boys and Feelings

An assistant principal at a Tampa, Florida, elementary school shared a story of a boy she called "the bolter." The little boy would regularly blow up in class, then bolt out of the room and out of the school. The assistant principal would chase him and get him back into the building. The boy lacked the verbal-emotive abilities to help him cope with his feelings.

After attending male/female brain difference training, the assistant principal decided to try a new tactic. The next time the boy bolted, she took a ball with her when she went after him. When she found the boy outside, she asked him to bounce the ball back and forth with her. Reluctant at first, the boy started bouncing the

ball. Before long, he was talking, then sharing the anger and frustration that he was experiencing at school and at home. He calmed down and went back to class. Within a week, the boy was able to self-regulate his behavior enough to tell his teacher that he needed to go to the office, where he and the assistant principal would do their "ball routine"

Teaching Boys, Teaching Girls

For Elementary Boys

- Use beadwork and other manipulatives to promote fine motor development. Boys are behind girls in this area when they start school.
- Place books on shelves all around the room so boys get used to their omnipresence.
- Make lessons experiential and kinesthetic.
- Keep verbal instructions to no more than one minute.
- Personalize the student's desk, coat rack, and cubby to increase his sense of attachment.
- Use male mentors and role models, such as fathers, grandfathers, or other male volunteers.
- Let boys nurture one another through healthy aggression and direct empathy.

For Elementary Girls

- Play physical games to promote gross motor skills. Girls are behind boys in this area when they start school.
- Have portable/digital cameras around and take pictures of girls being successful at tasks.
- Use water and sand tables to promote science in a spatial venue.
- Use lots of puzzles to foster perceptual learning.
- Form working groups and teams to promote leadership roles and negotiation skills.
- Use manipulatives to teach math.
- Verbally encourage the hidden high energy of the quieter girls.

and talk. Because he was doing something spatial-mechanical, the boy was more able to access hidden feelings.

Girls and Computers

The InterCept program in Colorado Springs, Colorado, is a female-specific teen mentor-training program that works with girls in grades 8–12 who have been identified as at risk for school failure, juvenile delinquency, and teen pregnancy. Inter-Cept staff members use their knowledge of female brain functioning to implement program curriculum. Brittany, 17, came to the InterCept program with a multitude of issues, many of them involving at-risk behavior and school failure.

One of the key components of InterCept is showing teenage girls the importance of becoming "tech-savvy." Girls use a computer-based program to consider future occupations: They can choose a career, determine a salary, decide how much education or training their chosen career will require, and even use income projections to design their future lifestyles. Brittany quite literally found a future: She is entering a career in computer technology.

The Task Ahead

As educators, we've been somewhat intimidated in recent years by the complex nature of gender. Fortunately, we now have the PET and MRI technologies to view the brains of boys and girls. We now have the science to prove our intuition that tells us that boys and girls do indeed learn differently. And, even more powerful, we have a number of years of successful data that can help us effectively teach both boys and girls.

The task before us is to more deeply understand the gendered brains of our children. Then comes the practical application, with its sense of purpose and productivity, as we help each child learn from within his or her own mind.

References

American Association of University Women. (1992). *AAUW Report: How schools shortchange girls.* American Association of University Women Foundation.

Baron-Cohen, S. (2003). *The essential difference: The truth about the male and female brain.* New York: Basic Books.

Blum, D. (1997). *Sex on the brain: The biological differences between men and women.* New York: Viking.

Conlin, M. (2003, May 26). The new gender gap. *Business Week Online.* Available: www. businessweek. com/magazine/content/03_21/b3834001_mz001. htm

Gurian, M., Henley, P., & Trueman, T. (2001). *Boys and girls learn differently! A guide for teachers and parents.* San Francisco: Jossey-Bass/John Wiley.

Havers, F. (1995). Rhyming tasks male and female brains differently. *The Yale Herald, Inc.* New Haven, CT: Yale University.

Marano, H. E. (2003, July/August). The new sex scorecard. *Psychology Today,* 38–50.

Moir, A., & Jessel, D. (1989). *Brain sex: The real difference between men and women.* New York: Dell Publishing.

National Center for Education Statistics. (2000). *National Assessment of Educational Progress: The nation's report card.* Washington, DC: U.S. Department of Education.

Organisation for Economic Co-operation and Development. (2003). *The PISA 2003 assessment framework.* Author.

Rich, B. (Ed.). (2000). *The Dana brain daybook.* New York: The Charles A. Dana Foundation.

Rubin, R. (2004, Aug. 23). How to survive the new SAT. *Newsweek,* p. 52.

Sommers, C. (2000). *The war against boys.* Simon and Schuster.

Taylor, S. (2002). *The tending instinct.* Times Books.

POSTNOTE

The authors of this article argue that for true gender equity to occur in our schools, teaching practices need to address the different needs of male and female brains. They also argue that these brain differences help to explain why girls generally outperform boys in reading and writing, while boys generally learn higher mathematics and physics more easily than most girls when those subjects are taught abstractly. This is a highly controversial position, as Lawrence Summers, the president of Harvard University, discovered in 2005. Addressing a group of faculty members, he made comments suggesting that women don't perform as well as men in higher mathematics and that the reason is at least partly because of innate differences in men and women. His remarks provoked a maelstrom of protests from many faculty members.

The position taken by the authors of this article raises another interesting question. Will both girls and boys perform better academically in a single-sex setting? Can teachers better address the particular needs of boys and girls when only one gender is present in class? Research on single-sex schools by Anthony Bryk and his colleagues demonstrates rather conclusively that girls are more likely to flourish academically in a girls-only setting. Anecdotal evidence suggests that many young boys also do better when taught by male teachers in a single-sex setting.

DISCUSSION QUESTIONS

1. Which group, girls or boys, do you believe is shortchanged the most in schools today? Why do you think so?
2. What are your views on the value of single-sex education?
3. What problems or obstacles can you identify in trying to implement teaching practices that address the differences in boys' and girls' brains?

RELATED WEBSITE RESOURCE AND VIDEO CASE

WEB RESOURCE:

The Gurian Institute. Available at:

http://www.gurianinstitute.com.

This institute contains educational materials and provides workshops on how boys and girls learn differently.

▶❚❚ TEACHSOURCE VIDEO CASE

GENDER EQUITY IN THE CLASSROOM: GIRLS AND SCIENCE

In this video case, you'll see how a middle school science teacher promotes science learning for all his students: boys and girls. Go to the website for the Education Media Library at CengageBrain.com to watch the video clips, study the artifacts in the case, and reflect on the following questions.

1. Do you agree that it is important for students to have gender or ethnic-minority role models in different academic and career areas, as the teachers in the video case suggest? Why or why not?
2. This video focuses on girls and science. How can a teacher ensure equity in mixed-gender classrooms?

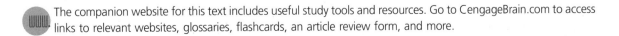 The companion website for this text includes useful study tools and resources. Go to CengageBrain.com to access links to relevant websites, glossaries, flashcards, an article review form, and more.

Tips for Teaching: Educator's Resource Guide

Classroom Observation

This appendix is designed to help you develop skills in observing classrooms and schools. You will probably benefit most by reading the rest of this section rather quickly now and rereading it carefully before you observe schools and classrooms. Since the material on the following pages is somewhat technical, you can probably assimilate it best when you know that you will be making use of it soon.

Issues Related to Observation

Virtually all teacher education programs provide opportunities for the prospective teacher to observe experienced teachers. Observation may take place "live," or it may involve viewing digital recordings of classroom sessions. Either alternative can be extremely valuable if it offers an opportunity for insight into how a classroom is organized, how the teacher relates to different students, or how different forms of instruction can be used. However, observation of a classroom can be boring, tedious, and educationally irrelevant. What is it that makes observation valuable or worthless? The difference is a matter of knowing specifically what you are attempting to observe and why, being able to gather information accurately, and interpreting your information in order to learn from it. Thus, to really benefit from observing an actual classroom, you must have some training in observational techniques.

It is physically and mechanically impossible to record *everything* that occurs in a classroom, let alone in an entire school. Thus, any technique used to gather data about the classroom environment must of necessity be selective. This is a built-in and unavoidable limitation of all recording instruments and techniques of observation.

Furthermore, the observer's background and training influence the classroom phenomena he or she chooses to focus on and the ways in which he or she interprets them. If the variable in question is aggressive behavior among students, for example, an educational psychologist may interpret a classroom outbreak as a result of the teacher's inconsistent reward pattern. An anthropologist might view it as a normal event within the youth subculture. A student teacher, because of personal needs and anxieties, might assume that the students are misbehaving because they do not really like him or her. For this reason, objective interpretation is as impossible as comprehensive observation. However, knowing the limitations of observational techniques will help observers interpret the data better, and being aware of their own particular perceptual habits will help them exert caution in interpretation.

Another problem is that anytime someone or something new and different enters a classroom, that person or thing affects the dynamics of the group in some way. Your presence may cause the teacher to be somewhat more nervous, thus affecting his or her behavior. The students, aware of your presence, may turn their heads to see what you are doing. If you are collecting data using some mechanical equipment, such as a camcorder, the teacher's and students' behavior will be affected. Therefore, you can never observe or collect information completely free from the effects of your presence. What you can do, however, is to become a frequent enough visitor to the classroom that your presence will not produce unusual or severe reactions from the regular classroom participants. You can also locate yourself physically in the room to reduce your obtrusiveness and to stay out of the students' direct line of sight.

As an observer in someone else's classroom, you are a guest and, as such, need to behave accordingly. This means that you should:

- Make your dress and appearance consistent with what the school expects its teachers to wear. If you are uncertain about this, ask your college instructor.
- Refrain from judging the school or teachers too quickly if you see things happening with which you disagree. Remember, you probably do not have all the information you need to make such judgments, and you need to accord the teachers some respect for their judgments and decisions. As the old Native American proverb states, "Don't judge another until you've walked a mile in his moccasins."
- Not assume that what you see one day is typical of what occurs often. That may or may not be the case. Frequent observations are necessary before one can speak with confidence about patterns or typical behavior.
- Maintain confidentiality. Although you may need to report your observations in some format to your college instructor, it is unprofessional to tattle or gossip to your peers about a particular teacher or classroom. If you feel the need to discuss some incident or events that occurred in a particular school or classroom, try to maintain confidentiality regarding the identities of the particular persons involved. The classroom participants should not suffer embarrassment or harm as a result of your field experience.

Data-Gathering Techniques

The observational methods used in education were developed by the behavioral and social sciences to gather data about and interpret complex environments; they were later found to be appropriate for use in schools as well. This section will introduce you to some of these tools and approaches, as well as the kinds of preliminary decisions and subsequent interpretation that give meaning to observation. The scrupulous observer must ask certain questions: What specifically will be observed? Which method of gathering data will be most effective? What do these data mean? To learn from observation, then, the observer needs (1) objectives, (2) a way to record observations, and (3) a way to interpret observations with respect to objectives.

Observation should not be aimless. If you are to find out what life in the classroom is like, you must decide which aspects you wish to focus on. Your objective may be very broad, such as: "What does the teacher do and say during a class period?" Or it may be as narrow as: "How many times does a particular student speak to another student?"

From the data that you collect you can form a hypothesis about why certain things occur, and you can test this hypothesis by making predictions about what should happen if it is correct. If your prediction is not validated, you can reexamine your data and try to develop another explanation. If your prediction is validated repeatedly, you will know that you are moving in the direction of understanding what is happening in the classroom and, possibly, why. For example, suppose your objective is to examine the teacher's verbal interaction with each individual student. After performing frequency counts—recording how many times the teacher calls on each student, or how many times each student volunteers information or asks the teacher a question—over a period of a week, you might hypothesize about the frequency distribution for the following week. If your predictions are validated, you should then try to interpret your findings. Was the teacher displaying a bias against certain students? Did the teacher systematically ignore the students seated in a particular part of the room? Were certain groups of students—for example, girls or certain socioeconomic groups—treated in particular ways? Caution must be exercised in drawing conclusions, however, because rival hypotheses may explain the same phenomena.

The point to be emphasized is that to understand the happenings in a classroom, you must select objectives that provide you with a focus. Since you cannot see, hear, and interpret everything, you must be selective. To be selective, you must establish the purpose of your observation.

You may find one of the following techniques of data gathering particularly appropriate, given your objectives, the equipment available, and the degree of access you have to a school. All have been used profitably by classroom observers.

Techniques of Data Gathering

- Note taking
- Observation systems
- Seating charts
- Analysis of artifacts
- Interviews
- Video and digital recordings

Note Taking

Probably the most common means of gathering data in the school is note taking. The method is borrowed from cultural anthropologists, who take copious notes of their observations while living with the natives of an unfamiliar culture. You can use the same approach to accumulate information about the interpersonal relationships, values, or social status of individuals in a class.

If you choose the note-taking approach, certain preliminary decisions will have to be made. First, how comprehensive should your notes be? You will be attempting to record everything you see that relates to your objective. Thus, the broader your objective, the more you will have to record. In many instances it will be difficult for you to decide quickly on the relevance of a specific event. A handy rule of thumb: When in doubt, write it down. Too much information is better than not enough, for insufficient data can lead to frustration and to erroneous conclusions.

Second, you must decide whether to write a description of what you see and hear, or simply record what is said verbatim. Should you write down your impressions of incidents, or should you be as objective as possible? We recommend that, whenever possible, data be recorded verbatim. In trying to summarize or describe what takes place, you are likely to substitute your own perceptions for what was actually happening. If you wish also to record your impressions, insights, inferences, and comments, keep them in the margin or draw brackets around them to distinguish them from the raw data. This distinction is crucial because of the tendency to make inferences based on selected perceptions or personal biases. If we are happy, we tend to see happy people; if tired, we see the teacher's and students' behavior through the filter of fatigue and interpret it accordingly. We may see relationships that do not actually exist and miss ones that do. Therefore, recognizing that complete objectivity is impossible, we should still aim to achieve it rather than rely on our own interpretations of events.

You will find that recording nonverbal behavior tends to be much more impressionistic than recording verbal behavior. If we observe a student fidgeting in her seat, picking her nose, and looking out the window, it is tempting to assert that she is bored; yet that is an inference. Keep checking on yourself to make sure you are distinguishing between actual behavior and inferences drawn from behavior.

It is much easier to be comprehensive in your note taking if you establish a standard format and abbreviations. For example, indenting student comments will help you distinguish them from teacher comments and will save you from repeatedly having to indicate who is talking. Abbreviating words by omitting vowels, employing homonyms, and using phonetic representations will also allow you to record more efficiently and quickly. If you have experience at text messaging, those skills should come in handy!

Note taking has a number of advantages as a means of gathering data about classroom actions. It is relatively simple and very economical. You can flip back and forth in your notes easily when you begin to interpret the data. The notes can be cut up and juxtaposed in whatever fashion you want to help you discern patterns or repeated themes. You can assimilate ideas and events rapidly by scanning written notes. And notes constitute a permanent record, which you can keep to compare with other observations and to develop, support, or reject hypotheses.

A major disadvantage of note taking is the difficulty of recording everything you can see and hear. Even though you have selected limited objectives to guide your observations, action often develops so fast that you fall behind and miss some of what is said or done. Taking notes forces you to keep your eyes on the paper in front of you and prevents you from observing the class without interruption. In other words, your observation system tends to become overloaded with stimuli. Nevertheless, note taking is probably the most frequently used method of gathering data in the classroom.

Systematic Observation Systems

Observation systems make use of lists of categories—as minuscule as sneezes or smiles or as broad as teacher-student rapport—to record verbal or nonverbal interaction in the classroom according to predefined rules and definitions. Prior to the observation, decisions are made concerning what is to be observed, the method of observation and recording data, and how the data will be analyzed and used.

Although many observation systems have been developed, only a few are in general use. Probably the best-known category system for observing teachers and pupils is Flanders's Interaction Analysis (see Figure A-1). Flanders identified ten different categories of verbal behavior; the first seven apply to teacher talk, the next two to student talk, and the final category records silence or confusion. The categories are: (1) accepting student feelings; (2) giving praise; (3) accepting, clarifying, or making use of a student's ideas; (4) asking a question; (5) lecturing, giving facts or opinions; (6) giving directions; (7) giving criticism; (8) student response; (9) student initiation; and (10) confusion or silence. Categories 1–4 represent indirect teacher influence, and categories 5–7 represent direct teacher influence. An observer using Flanders's system will record, every three seconds, the category of verbal behavior occurring at that instant; then an analysis is made of verbal interaction during the entire class period. Thus, a profile of the teacher's direct or indirect influence can be obtained.

Flanders's system has limitations, but it can be a helpful and informative tool in analyzing a certain kind of verbal behavior in the classroom. It has been used extensively, and considerable research data have been collected. Instructional booklets and audiotapes are available to students interested in learning to use the system and to interpret data. Many universities and colleges, as well as public schools, have used Interaction Analysis to help teachers analyze their teaching.

Seating Charts

Using seating charts as an observational tool provides a familiar way of looking at classrooms. Seating charts are useful for collecting important aspects of classroom behavior, such as pupil attentiveness, and they are easy to use.

FIGURE A-1   Categories for Interaction Analysis

TEACHER TALK

Indirect Influence

1. ACCEPTS FEELING: accepts and clarifies the tone of feeling of the students in an unthreatening manner. Feelings may be positive or negative. Predicting or recalling feelings are included.

2. PRAISES or ENCOURAGES: praises or encourages student action or behavior. Jokes that release tension, but not at the expense of another individual; nodding head; or saying "um hm" or "go on" are included.

3. ACCEPTS or USES IDEAS of STUDENT: clarifying, building, or developing ideas suggested by a student. As teacher brings more of his own ideas into play, shift to category 5.

4. ASKS QUESTIONS: asking a question about content or procedure with the intent that a student provides an answer.

Direct Influence

5. LECTURING: giving facts or opinions about content or procedure; expressing his own ideas, asking rhetorical questions.

6. GIVING DIRECTIONS: giving directions, commands, or orders which students are expected to comply with.

7. CRITICIZING or JUSTIFYING AUTHORITY: statements intended to change student behavior from unacceptable to acceptable pattern; bawling out someone; stating why the teacher is doing what he is doing; extreme self-reference.

STUDENT TALK

8. STUDENT TALK—RESPONSE: talk by students in response to teacher. Teacher initiates the contact or solicits student statement.

9. STUDENT TALK—INITIATION: talk initiated by student. If "calling on" student is only to indicate who may talk next, observer must decide whether student wanted to talk.

SILENCE

10. SILENCE or CONFUSION: pauses, short periods of silence, and periods of confusion in which communication cannot be understood by the observer.

---

*There is NO scale implied by these numbers. Each number is for classification, designating a particular kind of communication event. To write these numbers down during observation is merely to identify and enumerate.

Figure A-2 illustrates how a seating chart can be used to collect data on student on-task and off-task behavior. Each box represents a student, and the boxes are located on the paper to reflect each student's physical location in the classroom. Within each box is a sequence of numbers, each representing one observation of the student. Depending on the length of the observation time period, there may be fewer or more than the eleven observations represented in this instrument. A list of categories with their code symbols, a legend, is also given. The on-task and off-task behaviors are symbolized by letters that represent shorthand reminders of the behavior categories. (Figure A-2 has the coded observations already recorded.) This instrument and others like it are flexible and can be adapted to fit the observer's and the teacher's needs. Many of the on-task and off-task behaviors can be anticipated in advance of the actual observation. However, if one occurs that was not anticipated, just add it to the legend.

When you are ready to begin the observation, identify the time you begin and then observe the first student. What is he or she doing? Code the behavior appropriately and place the code in the box next to the number 1. Then move quickly to the next student and repeat the process, again placing the code next to the number 1. Continue until you have observed all the students (or at least the ones that you are planning to observe), and then start your second round of observations with the first student and repeat the sequence. Each time you get ready to begin a new observation cycle, record the time you start. The times that you see listed on the instrument in Figure A-2 are not placed there in advance of the actual observation. They are there simply to remind you to record the time so you will know how much time was required for each observation cycle.

With some practice and familiarity with the instrument, you will soon be able to move quickly from student to student while coding the student's behavior. Remember, you are sampling the student's behavior. The more observations you make, the greater the confidence you can have that your sample validly and reliably represents the full set of behaviors the students demonstrated.

Whereas you can analyze each student's pattern of behavior by looking at each box, it is much more difficult to grasp the broader picture of the total class's on-task and off-task behavior. However, you can do this by developing a matrix with the types of behavior listed along one dimension and the time intervals along the other dimension; in this way you can obtain an overall view of the class (Figure A-3). To interpret these data with some accuracy, it is necessary to know what activities are supposed to be occurring throughout the lesson. Do not try to interpret too much from data unless you know what happened in the class.

There are several things worth noting about the data presented in Figure A-3. First, note the percentage of pupils on task throughout the lesson. At the beginning of the lesson the figure is 50 percent, and it climbs to 85 percent after ten minutes. Is there some explanation for why it took ten minutes to reach an 85 percent on-task rate? Similarly, why was there a sharp decline in the on-task percentage rate during the last six minutes?

FIGURE A-2   Pupil On-Task/Off-Task Behavior

Purpose: To determine which students are on or off task during a lesson, and what specific behaviors they are engaged in.

Lesson Type: Teacher-led discussion in eighth-grade social studies.

Note:

On Task
L = listening
TN = taking notes
H = hand raised
T+ = talking (discussion related)

Off Task
R− = reading (non-class related)
T− = talking (non-class related)
WS = working on another subject
OS = out of seat
O = other

	1	2	3	4	5	6	7	8	9	10	11
Time	9:15	9:17	9:20	9:22	9:25	9:27	9:29	9:32	9:34	9:37	9:40
Corrine	L	L	TN	TN	H	T+	L	L	TN	TN	OS
Mike	T−	T−	WS	WS	WS	WS	OS	T−	H	OS	OS
Jim	T−	T−	L	L	L	TN	H	TN	T+	T+	O
Nancy	R−	R−	R−	L	L	L	TN	T+	OS	OS	OS
Jo	WS	WS	L	L	TN	TN	L	L	H	T+	T+
Mary Kay	L	L	TN	TN	TN	T+	T−	L	L	H	H
Will	OS	O	O	O	T−	R−	R−	R−	R−	H	OS
Mildred	L	L	L	TN	T+	T+	H	L	L	L	H
Carlos	L	L	L	L	L	TN	TN	TN	TN	TN	TN
James	OS	T−	T−	T−	L	L	L	TN	TN	TN	L
Frank	H	H	TN	TN	TN	L	L	L	L	L	T+
Betty	L	L	L	L	L	TN	L	L	L	L	L
Marilyn	R−	R−	R−	WS	WS	WS	WS	WS	WS	H	H
Fran	H	L	L	T+	T+	L	H	TN	TN	TN	TN
Howie	OS	L	L	TN	TN	T+	T−	T−	T−	OS	OS
Jack	T+	TN	TN	TN	L	L	L	WS	WS	WS	WS
Bob	T+	TN	L	L	L	TN	H	H	O	O	O
Maria	L	L	L	L	H	L	L	L	L	L	L
Vince	T−	T−	T−	L	L	L	H	T+	OS	OS	OS
Chet	R−	R−	R−	R−	L	TN	TN	TN	TN	R−	R−

Source: Adapted from James M. Cooper, "Observation Skills," in *Developing Skills for Instructional Supervision,* ed. James M. Cooper (New York: Longman, 1984), p. 96.

FIGURE A-3 On-Task/Off-Task Matrix

	BEHAVIOR CATEGORIES										
	1	2	3	4	5	6	7	8	9	10	11
	9:15	9:17	9:20	9:22	9:25	9:27	9:29	9:32	9:34	9:37	9:40
On Task											
Listening	6	8	9	8	9	7	7	7	5	4	3
Taking notes	0	2	4	6	4	6	3	5	5	4	2
Hand raised	2	1	0	0	2	0	5	1	2	3	3
Talking (discussion related)	2	0	0	0	2	4	0	2		2	2
Off Task											
Reading (non-class related)	3	3	3		0						
Talking (non-class related)	3	4	2	1		0	2	2		0	0
Working on another subject	1	1	1	2	2	2	1	2	2	1	1
Out of seat	3	0	0	0	0	0	1	0	2	4	6
Other	0	1	1	1	0	0	0	0	1	1	2
Percentage of students on task	50	55	65	70	85	85	75	75	65	65	50

Second, during the beginning of the lesson there were as many as four students engaged in non–class-related talking. Why?

Third, why were so many students out of their seats during the last six minutes of the class? Was the teacher aware of them? The data do not provide us with answers to these questions, but they do provoke us to ask the questions.

If you are interested in learning more about other observation systems, the following books and articles will be helpful:

- Acheson, Keith A., and Meredith Damien Gall. *Techniques in the Clinical Supervision of Teachers,* 4th ed. New York: Longman, 1997.
- Borich, Gary D. *Observation Skills for Effective Teaching,* 5th ed. Columbus, OH: Allyn & Bacon, 2011.
- Good, Thomas L., and Jere E. Brophy. *Looking in Classrooms.* 10th ed. Columbus, OH: Allyn & Bacon/Merrill Education, 2007.

Analysis of Artifacts

Much can be learned about life in the classroom without directly observing teachers and students. The textbooks and supplementary materials in use can reveal a *lot* to the careful observer. Similarly, the tests given, the placement of chairs and desks, the materials displayed on the bulletin board, and the audio-visual equipment used (or neglected) are clues about what activities take place and what kind of learning is valued.

Tests Given   What kinds of questions are on the examinations? Do they emphasize the acquisition of facts to the exclusion of solving problems, analyzing or synthesizing ideas, making evaluations, comparing or contrasting different points of view, drawing inferences from limited data, or forming generalizations?

Placement of Chairs and Desks   Do the chairs and desks always face the teacher, the dominant person in the classroom? Or are they frequently grouped in small circles, indicating opportunities for pupil–pupil interaction?

Materials Displayed on the Bulletin Board   Is the bulletin board primarily a construct of the teacher, or does it display student work? What student works are displayed?

Audiovisual Equipment   Is a multimedia approach used so that students may learn from a variety of sources?

You probably have the idea by now: clues about what a teacher thinks is important, whether students are involved in instruction as well as learning, and how the teacher views his or her role can be garnered by a careful analysis of materials used and produced in the classroom. Valuable inferences may be made from data available to the naked eye, but it is crucial to remember that such inferences are only hypotheses and that additional data must be gathered to confirm or invalidate them.

Interviews

Interviewing teachers, students, administrators, counselors, librarians, and other school personnel is an excellent way to gather data about life in school. People who play different roles in the school, and thus see it from different vantage points, often have highly disparate views of it. The cook in the school kitchen may have a very different opinion of the food's quality than the students or the teachers, and the administrator's view of detention hall is probably very unlike the students'. Questioning the students about what occupies most of their time in the classroom, what they think the school's purpose is, why they go to school or, in general, how their good teachers differ from the poor ones can produce fascinating and highly valuable data. Some sample questions follow. The answers to them should help you better understand life in a particular school.

1. Where is the school located in the community?
2. How old is the school?
3. Is it a parent-, teacher-, administration-, or student-centered school? What evidence leads you to your conclusion?
4. Is there a school media center or library? Where is it? How does a student gain access to it? What are the library procedures?
5. Where is the nurse's office? What are the major concerns of the health administrator in this school? What are the major complaints (types of illnesses)? What are the procedures for being sent home or remaining in the health office?
6. Where does physical education take place? What are the usual activities? Who participates? What do students do if they are not participating?
7. What is the procedure for tardy students?
8. Who administers this procedure?
9. Do students move from one classroom to another during the school day? How is this accomplished?
10. Is there a formal dress code? Or an informal one? How would you describe the school's dress code?
11. What are some frequent causes of disciplinary action against students?
12. Is there a teachers' lounge? How is it used?
13. Is there a student council and does it have any real power to promote change in the school? If the answer is "yes," ask for some examples. Does the student council represent the entire student body, or is it a select group?
14. Do parents come to the school? If so, when and for what reasons?
15. Do students congregate in identifiable patterns in the lunch room?
16. Are there extracurricular activities, such as music, sports, clubs, and meetings?
17. Does the school empty quickly at the end of the day?
18. If you are investigating a secondary school, does it have a newspaper? Ask the editor or a staffer what its function is and how much freedom students have to print what they wish.
19. Are students bused to school? If you can, ride a school bus one day to see what it is like. Is it different in the morning than in the afternoon?
20. Listen to the students' language, in class and out. Is there any difference?
21. Ask an administrator, secretary, custodian, teacher, librarian, and nurse to describe the student population.
22. Are students trusted? What evidence can you find one way or the other?
23. What is unusual about this school?
24. What do the school's administrators do? What are their major areas of responsibility? What are the major pressures on them?[*]

---

[*]The authors are indebted to Professor Emma Cappelluzzo of the University of Massachusetts for many of these questions. Used by permission.

Answers to these questions will help you to gain an understanding of the culture of the school, the "hidden curriculum" of the school, and what life in the school is like for students.

Video and Digital Recordings

Public schools and colleges are making increasing use of mechanical recording devices as analytical and training tools. Both audio and video recorders have been available for quite a while, and now DVDs and digital video clips are also available. All these devices have enabled teachers and researchers to analyze what happens in the classroom more completely and objectively. Recording devices can register both the image and the sound of classroom interaction, and the resulting record is more accurate and comprehensive than either notes or an observation schedule. Such devices have many other advantages: The recordings can be replayed without limit, the available features make it possible to locate or repeat a particular passage quickly, and the data can be stored almost indefinitely.

The same criteria or objectives may be applied to recorded data as to live observation. The advantage, of course, is that something that is missed in the first viewing can be repeated until the viewer has absorbed it, a luxury unavailable in live observation. You might wish to analyze verbal interactions using Flanders's Interaction Analysis, or to watch the behavior of a particular child, or to count the number of encouraging gestures the teacher makes toward students. The possibilities are endless.

Many teacher education programs are collecting digital recordings to demonstrate particular classroom phenomena to prospective teachers; some show only a single "critical incident." The video can be stopped to allow speculation about how the teacher will or should respond, started again to view the teacher's actual actions, and stopped for further discussion. The TeachSource video cases produced by Cengage Learning that have been cited at the end of many of the articles, along with many support articles noted throughout this book, are excellent examples of the power of video recordings to reveal classroom interactions.

We have not attempted to train you in the techniques, methods, and tools of classroom observation, believing that to be better and more appropriately accomplished as part of your teacher education program. Instead, we have tried to acquaint you with methods that have been—and are currently being—used by educators to better understand school environments.

Study Tips

Teachers play many roles, from communicator to character educator. One of a teacher's most central tasks is to be a learning specialist, someone skilled at helping others gain new information, organize it, and make it available for recall later.

Sample of the Tools for Learning

Here is a list of some of the skills, which we call *tools for learning,* that we believe ought to be taught to all students:

- *Various methods for remembering important information.* This largely involves teaching people how not to forget: how to move information from the fleeting short-term memory to the more enduring long-term memory.

- *Two or three methods of taking notes and saving important information.* Definite skills are associated with capturing what another person is saying, and students should systematically learn these skills.

- *Study reading.* A person practices "study reading" when the material is complex and contains information he or she wants to remember later. This technique is quite different from reading a novel or reading a telephone book. This set of skills lies at the heart of academic success, as well as success in many jobs.

- *Preparing for different kinds of tests.* Schools should show students how to study for different types of tests, such as objective and essay tests, and how to deal with test anxiety in various situations. Because examinations and tests do not end with graduation, schools should teach students how to cope with and master these challenges.

- *Doing research.* Students need to learn how to get answers to questions by using libraries, the Internet, expert sources, and data-gathering resources of all kinds. In essence, these skills focus on finding and accessing different data sources and using the information to solve a problem.

- *Thinking through a problem in a systematic way.* Instead of jumping to conclusions or relying on how they feel about an issue, students should learn how to think critically.

- *Generating creative ideas.* Much of life in and out of school requires new solutions or imaginative resolutions. Students need to learn techniques for generating novel and creative ideas individually, as well as group-oriented techniques such as brainstorming.

- *Getting the academic job done.* Students need to know how to set goals, develop a work plan, monitor their own behavior, bring a task to successful closure, and gradually become more successful at academic learning. This is important not simply to succeed in school, but because the modern workplace demands these same skills.

Many college students (pre-service teachers included) come to higher education well equipped to handle the new and more demanding study requirements. They can study effectively. However, they do not know how they do it nor are they able to pass on their skills to others. Many more college students falter under the new academic demands they encounter on campus. The methods that worked for them in high school are not adequate in college. Frequently, these students become frustrated and discouraged. They drop out or fatalistically settle for being a "C student" or worse. They convince themselves that they "just don't have it."

What they fail to realize (or were never told) is that the "it" that they do not have is quite learnable. The "it" is a group of acquirable skills and techniques. The "it" can make the difference between a successful and happy college educated person and a failure.

The Internet is filled with excellent study skill websites which address problems such as time management, test taking, writing research papers for particular subjects, note taking, and many other specific skills. Two sites, in particular, are:

http://www.stthomas.edu/academicsupport/handouts/default.
html and
http://www.how-to-study.com/

We urge you to make a small investment in sharpening your study skills for two reasons: first, to get the very highest return on your substantial investment of time and money; and second, to equip yourself to be the learning specialist expected of every teacher.

How to Participate in Discussions

An important part of one's education is learning how to speak in a group setting and participate in organized discussion. While some students acquire these skills in high school, many do not. Whether through shyness, reticence, or just a lack of skill, these students are cut off from one of the major benefits of a college education: the ability to participate in the give-and-take exchange so necessary in a democratic society and so many occupations and professions.

Being able to speak in a group setting, listening, and responding to others is crucial in the teaching profession. Whether in your own classroom, faculty meetings, or as a member of a professional association, educators must be able to actively engage in deliberations. They must be able to debate positions, engage in the formulation of plans, and perform a variety of other activities which require discussion skills.

Your college years are the ideal setting to overcome your reticence and gain the skills to actively engage in group discussions. The following are a few valuable websites which can guide you toward becoming comfortable and proficient in discussions.

http://www.lc.unsw.edu.au/onlib/pdf/disc.pdf
http://www.yorku.ca/srowley/critdiscuss.htm
http://www.swccd.edu/~asc/lrnglinks/oldiscbd.html
http://www.abacon.com/commstudies/groups/roles.html

Web Resources for Teachers

The following are the primary educational organizations of interest to educators and their websites.

National Education Association (**http://www.nea.org**)
American Federation of Teachers (**http://www.aft.org**)
United States Department of Education (**http://ed.gov**)
Council for Exceptional Children (**http://www.cec.sped.org**)
National Science Teachers Association (**http://www.nsta.org**)
National Council of Teachers of English (**http://www.ncte.org**)
National Council for the Social Studies (**http://www.ncss.org**)
National Association for Music Education (**http://www.menc.org**)
National Association for the Education of Young Children (**http://www.naeyc.org**)
Association of Career and Technical Education (**http://www.acteonline.org**)
International Reading Association (**http://www.reading.org**)
National Council of Teachers of Mathematics (**http://www.nctm.org**)
American Council on the Teaching of Foreign Language (**http://www.actfl.org**)
National Art Education Association (**http://www.arteducators.org**)
American Alliance for Health, Physical Education, Recreation and Dance (**http://www.aahperd.org**)
Association for Education Communications and Technology (**http://www.aect.org**)

Nationwide Special-Interest Groups in Education

National School Boards Association (**http://www.nsba.org**)
American Association of School Administrators (**http://www.aasa.org**)
ASCD (**http://www.ascd.org**)
American Educational Research Association (**http://www.aera.net**)
Council of Chief State School Officers (**http://www.ccsso.org**)
Association of Teacher Educators (**http://www.ate1.org/pubs/home.cfm**)
American Association of Colleges for Teacher Education (**http://www.aacte.org**)

GLOSSARY

Note: Boldfaced terms that appear within definitions can be found elsewhere in the glossary.

Academic freedom The ability of teachers to teach about an issue or to use a source without fear of penalty, reprisal, or harassment.

Academic learning time Time spent by students performing academic tasks with a high success rate.

Acceptable use policy (AUP) A statement of rules governing student use of school computers, especially regarding access to the Internet.

Accountability The effort to hold a party responsible for the results of an activity.

Achievement gap Differences in educational achievement between students of different socioeconomic or racial and ethnic groups.

Aesthetic Appreciative of or responsive to that which is beautiful.

American Federation of Teachers (AFT) The nation's second-largest teacher's association/union. Founded in 1916, it is affiliated with the AFL-CIO, the nation's largest union.

Assertive behavior The ability to stand up for one's legitimate rights in ways that make it less likely that others will ignore or circumvent them.

Assessment The process of determining students' learning progress.

Assimilation The absorption of an individual or a group into the cultural tradition of a population or another group.

Assistive technology The array of devices and services that help people with special needs to perform better in their daily lives. Such devices include motorized chairs, remote control units that turn appliances on and off, computers, and speech synthesizers.

At-homeness A sense of awareness of and equanimity with the world in which one lives.

At risk A term used to describe conditions—for example, poverty, poor health, or learning disabilities—that put children in danger of not succeeding in school.

Average Yearly Progress (AYP) Students must show demonstrable improvement toward meeting state standards. Under NCLB, schools with students who do not make adequate yearly progress are subject to a variety of corrective measures.

Behavioral indicators of child abuse Changes or signals in a child's behavior that suggest the child is being abused or neglected.

Benchmarks Standards by which something can be measured or judged.

Benefit maximization An ethical principle suggesting that individuals should choose the course of action that will make people generally better off.

Bilingual education A variety of approaches to educating students who speak a primary language other than English.

Bloom's Taxonomy A classification of learning objectives within education proposed in 1956 by a committee of educators chaired by Benjamin Bloom who also edited the first volume of the standard text, *Taxonomy of educational objectives: The classification of educational goals.*

Carnegie unit A measure of clock time used to award high school credits toward graduation.

Charter Management Organizations (CMOs) Non-profit organizations that run public charter schools.

Charter school School in which the educators, often joined by members of the local community, have made a special contract, or charter, with the school district. Usually the charter allows the school a great deal of independence in its operation.

Child abuse Physical, emotional, or sexual maltreatment or neglect of a child.

Coalesced content standard A modest repacking or reworking of a state's existing curricular standards.

Coalition of Essential Schools (CES) A coalition of hundreds of schools exemplified by small, personalized learning communities.

Common Core Curriculum *See* **Core Knowledge Curriculum**.

Common school Public elementary schools that are open to children of all races, nationalities, and classes. During the 19th century, the common school became the embodiment of universal education.

Compensation In teaching, refers to annual salary and benefits.

Complementary teaching A term used in special education when a support person does something to complement the instruction provided by the classroom teacher, such as taking notes or paraphrasing the teacher's statements.

Comprehensive high school The predominant form of secondary education in the United States in the 20th century. It provides both a preparation for college and a vocational education for students not going to college.

Conflict resolution A process for resolving a dispute or disagreement.

Constructivism A theory, based on research from cognitive psychology, that people learn by constructing their own knowledge through an active learning process, rather than by simply absorbing knowledge directly from another source.

Consultation When support personnel in special education provide assistance to general educators, enabling them to teach all the students in an inclusive class.

Content standards Statements outlining the knowledge and skills that students are expected to learn.

Continuous reconstruction of experience A curricular principle in which the student's daily experience serves as the focus of learning.

Cooperative learning An educational strategy, composed of a set of instructional methods, in which students work in small, mixed-ability groups to master the material and to ensure that all group members reach the learning goals.

Core Knowledge Curriculum A curriculum developed by the Core Knowledge Foundation based on a strong, specific elementary core of studies, including literature, history, mathematics, science, art, and music.

Coteaching A situation in which two teachers, often a special education teacher and a general education teacher, teach the same class together.

Council for Exceptional Children A national organization of individuals concerned about the education of children with special needs or gifts. The organization promotes research, public policies, and programs that champion the rights of exceptional individuals.

Culturally responsive teaching A method of embracing students' cultural backgrounds by modifying classroom conditions or activities to include elements that relate to the students' culture.

Curriculum All the organized and intended experiences of the student for which the school accepts responsibility.

Cyberbullying Bullying through information and communication technologies, such as mobile phone text messages, e-mail messages, Internet chatrooms, and social networking websites such as MySpace, Facebook, and Bebo.

Developmentally responsive Being alert and sensitive to the mental, emotional, and physical changes of students and being respectful of their needs and interests.

Dewey, John American philosopher, educator, and author (1859–1952) who taught that learning by doing should form the basis of educational practice.

Diagnostic assessment Assessments given to students prior to instruction to determine what they already know and do not know.

Didactic instruction A lecture approach to teaching that emphasizes compliant behavior on the part of the student while the teacher dispenses information.

Differentiation (differentiated instruction) A variety of techniques used to adapt instruction to the individual ability levels and learning styles of each student in the classroom.

Discipline problems Violations of, or students who violate, classroom rules.

Dominance The teacher's ability to provide clear purpose and strong guidance regarding both academics and student behavior.

Dual language program A bilingual education program whose goal is to transform monolingual speakers of either English or Spanish (or another language) into fully bilingual and biliterate students.

Due process The deliberative process that protects a person's constitutional right to receive fair and equal protection under the law.

Early childhood education Programs that concentrate on educating young children (usually up to age eight). Early childhood education has become an important priority in helping children from disadvantaged backgrounds achieve educational parity with other children.

Educated person An individual who is able to see the connectedness of all things.

Education Testing Service A nonprofit organization, ETS conducts assessment and policy research and develops assessments and related services, including such assessments as the Graduate Record Examination.

Emotional literacy The ability to precisely identify and communicate our feelings.

Empathetic listening Attending to another by participating in his or her feelings or ideas.

Equal educational opportunity The legal principle that all children should have equal chances to develop their abilities and aptitudes to the fullest extent regardless of family background, social class, or individual differences.

Elementary and Secondary Education Act (ESEA) The federal government's single largest investment in elementary and secondary education, including Title I. Originally passed in 1965 and periodically reauthorized by Congress, most recently in 2001 as the No Child Left Behind Act.

Equal respect An ethical principle suggesting that our actions acknowledge the equal worth of humans (i.e., the Golden Rule).

Ethics A branch of philosophy that emphasizes values that relate to "good" and "bad" behavior; examining morality; and rules of conduct. Proponents believe that an educated person must have these values and that all children should be taught them.

Feedback The return of information about the result of a process or activity.

Fight-or-flight response A psychological term referring to a behavioral pattern of either immediate conflict or fleeing when difficulties are encountered.

Fixed mind-set An attitude whereby students care whether they are judged smart or not smart.

Formative assessment *See* **Formative evaluation**.

Formative evaluation Evaluation used as a means of identifying a particular point of difficulty and prescribing areas in need of further work or development. It is applied in developmental or implementation stages.

"Good" school A favorable judgment made about a school based on variable criteria, such as student achievement, test scores, low delinquency, and/or school climate.

Growth mind-set An attitude whereby students care about learning and believe intellectual ability can be developed through effort and education.

Head Start A federally funded compensatory education program, in existence since the mid-1960s, that provides additional educational services to young children suffering from the effects of poverty.

High-performing school A place where adults and children live, grow, and learn well.

High-stakes accountability *See* **High-stakes tests**.

High-stakes tests The use of standardized test scores as a major determinant of significant educational outcomes, such as graduation, admission, or promotion.

Home schooling A movement that allows parents to keep their children out of regular public or private school and to educate them in the home.

Human capital An economic term for the stock of competences, knowledge and personality attributes embodied in the ability to perform labor so as to produce economic value.

Human perfectibility The view that the human species is capable of reaching heights of achievement.

Inclusion The commitment to educate each child, to the maximum extent appropriate, in the regular school and classroom, rather than moving children with disabilities to separate classes or institutions.

Inconsequential learning Information taught by another, rather than self-discovered, which has little or no importance to the learner.

Individualized education program/plan (IEP) A management tool required for every student covered by the provisions of the **Individuals with Disabilities Education Act**. It must indicate a student's current level of performance, short- and long-term instructional objectives, services to be provided, and criteria and schedules for evaluation of progress.

Individuals with Disabilities Education Act (IDEA) Federal law passed in 1990, extending and expanding the provisions of the Education for All Handicapped Children Act of 1975.

Inservice training Training provided by a school or school district to improve the skills and competencies of its professional staff, particularly teachers.

Institutional perspective The point of view or policy position of a social entity such as a school.

Instructional scaffolding Refers to supports that teachers provide to the learner during problem solving—in the form of reminders, hints, and encouragement—to ensure successful completion of a task.

International Baccalaureate (IB) A high quality international curriculum offered in three programs (elementary, middle, and high school levels).

Interstate Teacher Assessment and Support Consortium (InTASC) A project sponsored by the Council of Chief State School Officers that has identified standards for what teachers should know and be able to do.

Intrinsic motivation Motivation that comes from the satisfaction of doing something, in contrast to **extrinsic motivation**, which comes from the reward received for doing something.

Least restrictive environment (LRE) A requirement of the **Individuals with Disabilities Education Act** that students with special needs should participate in regular education programs to the extent appropriate.

Long-term memory Memory in which associations among items are stored, as part of the theory of a dual-store memory model.

Magnet schools An alternative school that provides instruction in specified areas such as the arts, medicine, or science. In many cases, they are established as a method of promoting voluntary desegregation in schools.

Mainstreaming The practice of placing special education students in general education classes for at least part of the school day, while also providing additional services, programs, or classes as needed.

Melting pot A metaphor and historical theory that suggests that although America takes in a wide variety of peoples (races, creeds, nationalities, and classes), the process of living in this country and being an American melts away differences so that all peoples blend together.

Merit pay The system of paying teachers according to the quality of their performance, usually by means of a bonus given for meeting specific goals.

Mobile learning Learning that occurs via mobile devices, e.g., phones, laptops, iPods,and MP3 players, that connect to the Internet.

Moral ecology The ethical balance or pattern needed to maintain a society.

Multicultural education An approach to education intended to recognize cultural diversity and foster the cultural enrichment of all children and youth.

Multiple intelligences theory A theory of human intelligence advanced by Howard Gardner, which suggests that humans have the psychobiological potential to solve problems or to fashion products that are valued in at least one cultural context. Gardner's research indicates at least eight and maybe nine separate faculties.

A Nation at Risk: The Imperative for Educational Reform A highly influential 1983 national commission report calling for extensive education reform, including more academic course requirements, more stringent college entrance requirements, upgraded and updated textbooks, and longer school days and years.

National Assessment of Educational Progress (NAEP) The National Assessment of Educational Progress (NAEP) is the largest nationally representative and continuing assessment of what America's students know and can do in various subject areas. Assessments are conducted periodically in mathematics, reading, science, writing, the arts, civics, economics, geography, and U.S. history.

National Board for Professional Teaching Standards (NBPTS) A professional agency that is setting voluntary standards for what experienced teachers should know and be able to do in more than thirty different teaching areas.

National Council for Accreditation of Teacher Education (NCATE) Nationally recognized organization awarding voluntary accreditation to college-level teacher education programs. Approximately 600 colleges and universities in the United States are accredited through NCATE.

National Education Association (NEA) The nation's largest teachers' association, founded in 1857 and having a membership of over 3.2 million educators.

Nature-based approach Basing education strategies upon a research-driven, biological understanding of human learning.

No Child Left Behind Act The most recent reauthorization, in 2001, of the Elementary and Secondary Education Act, the federal government's single largest investment in elementary and secondary education, including Title I.

Parallel teaching A situation in which support personnel (such as a special educator or Title I teacher) and the classroom teacher rotate among heterogeneous groups of students in different sections of the general education classroom.

Paraprofessional A trained aide who assists a professional, such as a teacher's aide.

Pedagogy The art or profession of teaching.

Pedagogic caring Instruction with a strong component of consideration for the total world of the learner.

Performance assessment A form of assessment that requires students to actually perform, such as writing or drawing, to demonstrate the knowledge or skill being measured.

Performance-based assessment See **Performance assessment**.

Physical indicators of child abuse Physical symptoms that suggest a child is being abused.

Professional development Continuous advances in teacher's knowledge and skills; lifelong learning.

Progressive school A school that focuses on students' personal and social development. See **Progressivism.**

Race to the Top A $4.35 billion United States Department of Education program designed to spur reforms in state and local district K–12 education. It is a part of the American Reinvestment and Recovery Act of 2009.

Reflective practitioner An individual who has established the habit of reviewing his or her performance in order to continually improve practice.

Rubric A set of rules for scoring student products or student performance. Typically takes the form of a checklist or a rating scale.

School choice Allowing parents to select alternative educational programs for their children, either within a given school or among different schools.

Self-discovered learning Private truths that each individual has personally uncovered and assimilated into his or her consciousness.

Social justice The concept of doing away with social and economic inequalities for those in our society who have been denied these benefits of a democratic society.

Social reconstruction Desired goal of progressive education's focus on teaching the child to function in the community.

Socially equitable An environment which is democratic and fair, and which provides every student with high-quality teachers, resources, and learning opportunities.

Standard Exemplary performance that serves as a benchmark.

Standards-based education See **Standard** and **Standards movement**.

Standards-based reform See **Standards movement**.

Standards movement Efforts at the local, state, and federal level to make clear exactly what students need to know and be able to do and, therefore, what schools need to teach. Implicit in the standards movement is an attempt to increase the academic achievement of students.

Summative assessment See **Summative evaluation**.

Summative evaluation Evaluation used to assess the adequacy or outcome of a program after the program has been fully developed and implemented.

Supportive teaching A situation in an inclusive classroom in which the classroom teacher takes the lead role, and support personnel rotate among the students.

Teacher competencies The characteristics that make a teacher qualified to do the job, including various areas of subject-matter expertise and a wide range of personality variables. Some school reform proposals urge that teachers undergo periodic assessment of their competencies to maintain licensure or earn incentives.

Teacher expectations A teacher's preconceptions about how a given student will behave or perform.

Teaching portfolio Collection of such items as research papers, pupil evaluations, teaching units, and videocassettes of lessons to reflect the quality of a teacher's teaching. Portfolios can be used to illustrate to employers the teacher's expertise or to obtain national board certification.

Title I (Chapter 1) Part of the 1965 Elementary and Secondary Education Act that delivers federal funds to local school districts and schools for the education of students from low-income families. It also supplements the educational services provided to low-achieving students in those districts.

Traditional school A school that seeks to transmit to its students the best knowledge, skills, and values in society.

Transfer of learning Connection or application of learned material to future knowledge or skill acquisition.

Two-way immersion programs See the definition for dual-language programs.

Values Principles or qualities we like or believe to be good or desirable. Certain concepts, such as responsibility, justice, fairness, and caring, are frequently mentioned as values that form the basis of civil life and morality.

Voucher programs A type of **school choice** plan that gives parents a receipt or written statement that they can exchange for the schooling they feel is most desirable for their child. The school, in turn, can cash in its received vouchers for the money to pay teachers and buy resources.

Working memory The ability to actively hold information in the mind needed to do complex tasks such as reasoning, comprehension and learning.

Zero-tolerance policies School policies calling for automatic suspension or expulsion of students who bring forbidden items, such as drugs or weapons, to school, or who engage in forbidden behavior while at school.

Zone of proximal development A range of tasks that a person cannot do alone yet but can accomplish when assisted by a more skilled partner. This zone is the point at which instruction can succeed and real learning is possible.

INDEX

Note: Page numbers followed by *f* refer to figure. Page numbers followed by *t* refer to tables. Page numbers beginning with A refer to Appendix.